D1082089

The Growth of a City

Power and Politics in
Portland, Oregon
1915 to 1950

E. Kimbark MacColl

The Georgian Press
1979

Published by The Georgian Press Company
2620 S. W. Georgian Place
Portland, Oregon 97201

Cover and Title Page designed by Corinna Campbell Cioeta

Sketches for the front cover and frontispiece by Elizabeth Rocchia

Library of Congress Cataloging in Publication Data

MacColl, E. Kimbark, 1925-
  The growth of a city

  Bibliography: p.
  Includes index.
  1. Business and politics — Oregon — Portland — History.
  2. Portland, Or. — Economic conditions. 3. Portland,
  Or. — Politics and government. I. Title.
  HC108.P87M29   320.9'795'49   79-22316

ISBN 0-9603408-1-5

Manufactured in the United States of America

Typography and Layout by Publications Specialists, Portland, Oregon

Printed by Artline Printing, Inc., Portland, Oregon

Published November, 1979

To Leeanne,
my enthusiastic and supportive partner,
my children,
who have happily endured an exhausting ordeal,
and Sam,
my everpresent companion and watchdog

Contents

PART II — FROM ONE WAR THROUGH ANOTHER: 1917-1950

Preface

In many respects, *The Growth of a City* is a sequel to my earlier work, *The Shaping of a City, Business and Politics in Portland, Oregon, 1885-1915*. This volume has a slightly different format. It is more topical in organization. It incorporates additional types of comparative data and provides lengthier coverage of banking, business and utility history. In attempting to examine how a city like Portland grew into a large decentralized metropolitan region during the first half of the 20th century, the primary focus is still upon business and political relationships and the interaction of various elite groups. The second major concern is with the use of land and people's perceptions of private property.

Neither in my previous work nor in this volume have I attempted to write an all-inclusive urban history, at least by current definition. I have tried, however, to analyze and depict some important facets of one city's history. The work might more aptly be described as a case study of how business and politics functioned at the decision making level, beginning 65 years ago in a western American city, in which the political process served the traditional 19th century free enterprise economic model. In addition to private investment, attention is given to the vast amounts and variety of public funds, both federal and local, that have been expended in the Portland area since 1900, and to their impact on the region's economic, social and political development.

My examination of the decisions that have affected the physical growth of the Portland metropolitan area includes an analysis of the personal interests, attitudes and values that have supported and shaped those decisions. In making such an inquiry, I have explored the question of perceptions: How citizens have perceived their urban and suburban environments and their public and private roles in the broader community.

While not discounting the importance of quantitative data and analysis, I wish to re-emphasize the essentiality of the human or personal dimension in the historical decision making process. As one who has not only researched thoroughly Portland's business and political history, but has been closely involved with the city's business and political life over the past 25 years, I have concluded even more strongly than I did three years ago that the personal element is often **the** essential factor in the decisions that are reached, especially in the political or governmental arena.

My emphasis on the personal dimension, coupled with a felt need to make value-weighted interpretations, provoked some of the more critical reviews of my earlier work. The implication of such comments was that my approach was unsophisticated, too presentist and really not serious urban history. The critiques, as such, may well have been deserved, but they may also have been self-incriminating to those who made them. The historical profession, along with the social sciences generally, has in recent years allowed itself to become overly neutralized by its data. It has taken shelter under an umbrella of self-defined objectivity. This phenomenon may be one reason why much recent historical writing has made so little apparent impact on the general public, apart from the fact that it tends to be dull reading.

While I am in general agreement with Henry Steele Commager's dictum, as stated in *The Search for a Usable Past*, that "the historian's task is not to judge but to understand. . . . He is not God," as an historian who is concerned with human values and ethics, and with the human consequences of previously approved decisions, I feel compelled to make an occasional moral judgment despite inherent risks. The historian who merely provides understanding may be abjuring one of the primary humanistic purposes of his profession. Moral neutralism, bordering on complacency, is often the unintended result. As both historians and citizens, we may find ourselves unwittingly accepting the consequences of past decisions regardless of their merit and the reasons for which they were made. Were Americans more inclined to give human concerns their rightful primacy over property rights, some valuable public insights might be gained from the commitment and some costly human and fiscal errors of the past might not be so readily repeated.

In the research and writing of this book I received the indispensible aid and understanding of several members of my family: My wife Leeanne, my youngest daughter Alexandra and my oldest son Kim, Jr., who provided me with the benefit of his legal acumen. I also owe a great debt of gratitude to my editor and layout director Kerry Hoover and to his two skillful assistants, Dan Carter and Teresa Jesionowska. I want to thank Jane Vogland, the Port of Portland Librarian, and retired Professor Dorothy O. Johansen of Reed College for their time and valuable aid. My deepest appreciation is extended to the staffs of the Portland City Club, the University of Oregon Special Collections Library, the

Oregon Historical Society, the Oregon Jewish Oral History and Archives Project and the Portland Bureau of Planning for their gracious hospitality and assistance. I am particularly indebted to Ivan Bloch for his wise counsel in matters pertaining to the historical development of hydroelectric power in the Pacific Northwest. To other venerable Oregonians, too numerous to mention here but whose names are listed in the Notes, I express my sincere thanks for giving me their valuable time for personal interviews.

— E. Kimbark MacColl

September 1979

*Downtown Portland, from King's
Heights, with Mt. Hood in
the background — 1912*

Introduction

The Past in the Present

Forty-seven years ago, Portland's most prominent realtor, Chester A. Moores, asked his audience: "In the entire history of Portland, do you know any individual who has ever made a fortune in the stock market — and kept it! No," said Moores.

> "The great personal fortunes of Portland originated into full stature through profits in real estate. . . . New fortunes will be made in the immediate future by those smart enough and courageous enough to step forth and take advantage of present real estate development investment opportunities."[1]

Many of Portland's pioneer first families, like the Corbetts, Failings and Ladds, were thoroughly tutored in the principles of making money through real estate, but it was to be California oilman Ralph B. Lloyd who was to reap the greatest rewards from the most ambitious program of urban land acquisition by one person in Portland's history, beginning in the early 1920s. Over the past 60 years, the most extensive and profitable real estate developments have been financed by "outside" money — by Californians, Canadians and Easterners.

* * * * *

The early proprietors were frugal men. As former University of Oregon President Charles H. Chapman noted in 1923, "They pinched the city up along streets too narrow for anything but camel traffic."[2] They contracted with an itinerant surveyor to lay out approximately 50 square blocks with 200 foot dimensions. This arrangement provided eight lots to the block and more corner lots within each tract, resulting in a higher realization of land sale profits — more money to the proprietors.

* * * * *

Portland achieved its rank as one of the country's wealthiest cities by saving rather than spending. For years, not only did the city rank low in educational expenditures, but in expenditures for most other public services as well. Even in the general category of private expenditures, the ostentatious display of wealth

1

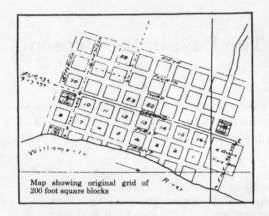

Map showing original grid of 200 foot square blocks

S.W. Oak Street — 60 foot width

Central S.W. Dock District — 1915

"The city . . . was treated not as a public institution, but a private commercial venture to be carved up in any fashion that might increase the turnover and further the rise in land values."[3]

(Lewis Mumford, 1961)

2

was frowned upon by the upper classes, as it still is. Old Portland money was made,

" . . . without competition, . . . without real enterprise,"

declared banker and civic leader E. B. MacNaughton in 1960.[4]

*　　*　　*　　*　　*

Throughout much of the city's history, or until recently at least, Portland's business and banking leadership has been dominated by white, largely Anglo-Saxon males, centered — but not exclusively so — in the Arlington Club. Organized as a "Social Club" in 1867, the members over the years have considered themselves,

" . . . a company of men, . . . [who] cherish the opportunity to fraternize for mutual enjoyment and relaxation, and to discuss destiny pertinent to them and the city."[5]

Like the Arlington Club membership, the corporate and bank boards of directors have been closely knit, with few Jews and practically no women — mostly all sociably compatible. As Senior Federal Judge Gus J. Solomon noted,

"Portland won't have Jewish presidents of banks and utilities until they are socially acceptable. . . . The big deals in town are not conducted in offices, but are conducted over the lunch tables at the Arlington Club and the University Club."

Shortly after his arrival in Portland 50 years ago, Solomon asked a gentile lawyer why he had not hired any Jews. The reply:

"In 75 years our firm has never found a Jewish fellow that fit."[6]

*　　*　　*　　*　　*

Little wonder, then, that the business leadership and the city government that carefully served it, showed so little interest in the social problems that were rapidly engulfing Portland after World War II, especially those related to minority housing and employment. As the major metropolis of a supposedly enlightened and progressive state, Portland was considered by the Urban League to be " . . . the worst city north of the Mason-Dixon line."

"No city outside the deep south had the suppression or the compression that Portland had in housing and employment. It was not pleasant to be a Negro in this town," said former Portland Urban League Director Bill Berry.[7]

3

S.W. Park Blocks leading to the Arlington Club

"Portland has one wide and beautiful street downtown. It runs about halfway through the city, from south to north, and all of a sudden it stops. The Arlington clubhouse has been built squarely across it and bars its course to the logical terminus. . . . That rich men's cluhouse, standing where it does, is the concrete embodiment of Oregon's inferiority complex which sooner or later has blocked every move toward beauty and greatness."[8]

(Charles H. Chapman, 1923)

4

*　　*　　*　　*　　*

In company with most American cities during the first half of this century, Portland experienced a number of notable business successes and failures. Excluding from consideration the lumber, paper and grain enterprises, one can cite the accomplishments of institutions like Jantzen, Pendleton, Iron Fireman, Hyster, ESCO, Oregon Portland Cement, the First National and U. S. National Banks, Equitable Savings and Loan, and Meier & Frank Company. The failures on the other hand were few but traumatic, the most obvious being those of the Ladd & Tilton and Northwestern National Banks. The utilities managed to survive numerous near financial disasters, successfully resisting efforts to municipalize their operations. Forty years ago, the Portland General Electric Company and its traction properties could have been publicly acquired for less than $50 million.

*　　*　　*　　*　　*

As with most of America's urban development, Portland's growth was — and still is — dominated by the concept of the sanctity of private property ownership, divorced from public or social constraints. The "right to make a profit" has often been a euphemism for avarice. No institution could exceed the Portland Realty Board in its zeal to protect and enhance the unrestrained speculative proclivities of private property owners. And no clearer example of greed — tempered by stupidity — could be found than the exploitation of the Ladd & Tilton Bank assets by the Wilcox Investment Company.

*　　*　　*　　*　　*

Portland's recorded history is replete with examples of businessmen, bankers and lawyers who used elective public office for private ends. The most exploited publicly elected body was the Multnomah County Board of Commissioners. Until recent years, the board was controlled by the real estate interests.

In 1924, the entire board was recalled for improperly awarding three Willamette River bridge contracts.

In 1931, two of the three commissioners were officers of the young Benjamin Franklin Savings & Loan Association.

*　　*　　*　　*　　*

Conflicts of interest have also been frequent within the appointed "citizen" agencies, with the dock commission, the port commission, and the planning commission leading the pack. Inevitably, the very interests whose activities were subject to regulation dominated the regulatory agencies. Below are a few of the numerous examples:

5

James O. Elrod helped to organize the Ross Island Sand and Gravel Company while he sat on the permit granting dock commission.

James H. Polhemus founded the Portland Dredging Company, the forerunner of the Willamette Western Corporation, while he was general manager of the Port.

John Burgard, 20 year chairman of the dock commission, sold insurance policies through his agency to cover dock commission properties.

Architect Ellis Lawrence was a member of the planning commission that approved the construction of the Public Market-Journal Building which he subsequently designed.

Architect Glenn Stanton designed the much contested Nabisco plant in 1948 while serving as chairman of the city planning commission.

*   *   *   *   *

Although Portland's location at the confluence of two major rivers — in the heart of a region rich in natural resources — preordained its future prosperity, the city's development throughout its first 60 years was primarily an extension of processes attempted and refined in the East and Middle West. A recent comparative study of the urban west draws a conclusion aptly characterizing Portland's growth, at least until the time of World War I. Notes Kansas historian Lawrence H. Larsen:

"Uncontrolled capitalism led to disorderly development that reflected the abilities of individual entrepreneurs rather than most other factors. The result was the establishment of a society that mirrored and made the same mistakes as those made earlier in the rest of the country."[9]

During the first half of the 20th century, Portland managed to escape many of the severe urban problems resulting from the industrial and technological revolutions — conditions common to the older Eastern cities. But it was still exposed to private exploitation, especially by the railroads, the utilities and the real estate interests.

Sixty years ago the railroads and the public utilities ruled the roost, with strong support from the banks. Recent times have witnessed the expanded activities of the real estate developers, with even stronger underwriting by banks, savings and loan associations, pension funds and life insurance companies. There are exceptions to be sure, but the dominant patterns are well established.

6

A City of Paradoxes

Portland's paradoxes reflected Oregon's paradoxes which continually baffled outside observers, especially during the decades between the two world wars. As the *New York Times* commented in 1937, following the U. S. Supreme Court's reversal (*De Jonge v. Oregon*) of a Portland conviction under Oregon's criminal syndicalist law: "Oregon is supposed to be one of the most progressive and liberal minded of all States. Yet its courts had approved of a heavy blow at a fundamental liberty."[10] In 1921, Oregon had enacted one of the harshest anti-radical statutes in the United States.

Oregon's supposed liberal reputation stemmed from the Theodore Roosevelt era when the state led the country in the passage of legislation, enacting such progressive reforms as the Initiative, Referendum and Recall. Within a generation, however, the political climate reversed itself, and the Initiative became the key governmental instrument effecting the reactionary about-face. In November, 1922, the voters, with a large plurality in Multnomah County, succumbed to the enticements of the Ku Klux Klan and approved an anti-Catholic, anti-private school initiative measure that was to be declared unconstitutional by the U. S. Supreme Court in 1925. The Klan, with strong lower middle class and blue collar appeal, pledged itself to do battle against "Koons, Kikes and Katholics."

*   *   *   *   *

Less than a decade later, an Independent Republican Jew, department store executive Julius Meier, was overwhelmingly elected governor on a public power platform in a state dominated by the private utilities that subsequently emasculated almost every effort to organize people's utility districts.

During the strife-ridden 1930s when Portland was faced with a series of devastating strikes along the waterfront and within the timber industry, Oregonians retreated under cover of their traditional conservatism, assuming anti-union, anti-radical, and even anti-Communist stances to defend their perceived sacred property rights. General Charles H. Martin was elected governor in 1934 on a "law and order" platform that was equally dedicated to preserving the privileges enjoyed by the private utilities. Ten years later, however, liberal Republican law school dean Wayne Morse was elected to the U. S. Senate. Much to the horror of his supporters, Morse transformed himself into one of the two or three most vigorously outspoken liberals within Congress. He subsequently changed his registration to Democrat and managed to survive in office for a total of 24 years.

*   *   *   *   *

7

Apart from politics, Portlanders have exhibited an equal amount of contradictory behavior in almost every other facet of their urban existence. They professed love for their downtown center and yet they let it become dirty and shabby, or as one of the state's leading architects, Jamieson Parker, exclaimed in 1935, just plain "ugly." The process of deterioration peaked in the 1950s with the destruction of many fine old landmarks to clear the way for some new Willamette River bridge ramps and adjacent parking lots. Twenty years later, however, the city in company with private interests totally reversed direction and invested huge sums in belated restoration efforts aimed at preserving the few remaining structures that had escaped the bulldozer. If nothing else, the energy crisis along with inflation made restoration of old buildings profitable. Suddenly, ancient structures had charm, human scale and great historic value.

*   *   *   *   *

As a sedate, maidenly and respectable city whose first families liked to trace their roots back to the Puritan villages of New England, Portland had long boasted of having the world's longest bar, Erickson's, just two blocks from the waterfront. The liquor trade was so profitable that before state prohibition took effect in January 1916, about 25 percent of the city's general operating funds were derived from liquor license fees. And yet when the teetotalling lumber baron, Simon Benson, donated 20 beautifully crafted bronze drinking fountains to the city so that his loggers and other citizens would not have to resort to bars in order to quench their thirsts, he was proclaimed a local hero.

*   *   *   *   *

Although Oregon ranked first in 1915 with the largest number of students per thousand of the state's total population enrolled in higher education, of the 30 largest American cities in 1918 Portland ranked 20th in per capita expenditures on education generally.[11] And whereas Portland ranked first in the country for the largest per capita number of library books in circulation — indicating a high literacy rate that would presume an equally high level of civic knowledge and interest — less than 50 percent of the city's eligible electors were registered to vote in the 1915 municipal elections. Historically, Portlanders have been apathetic voters. The 1913 reform city charter received the support of only 12 percent of the eligible electorate. Barely 22 percent of the eligible electorate had even bothered to vote.

*   *   *   *   *

In 1911, an ultra-conservative Portland establishment proudly hailed the founding of a distinctly liberal institution of higher learning, Reed College. But when its first president, William Trufant Foster, turned out to be a "wide-eyed"

8

Benson's fountains across from the Portland Hotel on S.W. Broadway.

Erickson's Saloon, West Burnside St. between 1st and 2nd. The site of the world's longest bar.

pacifist in the super-heated war year of 1917, most of the local support evaporated. As members of his first faculty, Foster attracted a remarkable group of young professors who would subsequently rise to national leadership in their respective fields: People like Karl T. Compton, the physicist who later became president of MIT; William F. Ogburn, a sociologist at the University of Chicago; and Paul Douglas, the University of Chicago political scientist who served in the U. S. Senate for many years as a colleague of Wayne Morse. Portland was the loser when a discouraged William T. Foster left Reed in 1919 with the establishment sighing "good riddance."

*   *   *   *   *

Citing some paradoxes that he encountered on his first visit to the state, Englishman John Leader noted that Oregonians were insensible to the drudgery of their women. Yet nowhere did he find women placed idealistically on a higher plane. "Women," he wrote, "are probably slaves all over the world, but it seems worse in Oregon."[12] Oregon women had received their voting rights in 1912, seven years in advance of the United States constitutional amendment, but the reform had produced no apparent changes in the socio-economic structure. As John Gunther was to comment in 1947, Oregon seemed to make little use of its liberal reforms. "The promise was superb, and the performance relatively indifferent."[13]

As a knowledgeable observer, Leader should have mentioned the abominable employment conditions for Oregon's working class women. Even with new minimum wage regulations in effect during and after the war years, a weekly wage of approximately $9 was well below the average minimum wage received by the male working force. Prior to the passage of the 1913 Oregon minimum wage law, the first in the nation to stand the test of the U. S. Supreme Court (*Stettler v. O'Hara* — 1916), Oregon's working class women were slaves to a system that treated them almost like animals — in some cases worse. As Louis Brandeis argued in his brief before the Supreme Court:

> "Regarding cows we know that even proper feeding is not enough, or proper material living conditions. . . . Experience has taught us that harsh language addressed to a cow impairs her usefulness. Are women less sensitive than beasts in these respects?"[14]

Under the leadership of Father Edwin Vincent O'Hara, the Oregon Consumers' League had discovered in 1912 that many Portland women working in canneries and box factories were earning less than $3.00 a week and that $6.00 was considered a good wage. The League figured that $8.00 a week was an acceptable minimum on which a woman could be expected to support herself, excluding dependents.[15]

*   *   *   *   *

10

As a final paradox, Leader noted that he knew of no more law abiding people than Portlanders, and yet he found more hold-ups in Portland during the winter of his visit than "among the five hundred millions of the British Empire."[16] In 1915, Portland ranked 27th out of America's 30 largest cities in per capita police expenditures.[17] Its citizens had long accepted such anomalies because they did not like to face reality. As Leader declared: "Portland's biggest vice is her exaggerated virtue."[18]

Doc Lane and Colonel Wood

The Portland "paradox" was perhaps best exemplified in the lives of two of the city's most distinguished citizens: Dr. Harry Lane and Col. Charles Erskine Scott Wood. In 1915, Lane, the former mayor of Portland — the fearless independent physician who loved children and nature, the defender of the people's rights against corporate abuse — was in the third year of his first term as the junior Democratic U. S. Senator from Oregon. Colonel Wood (the Colonel was a militia title), called C. E. S. by friend and foe alike, was prospering at the height of his legal practice at the age of 63. As one of Portland's most colorful figures with respect to his varied interests, talents and wit, Wood had already achieved a noteworthy career as a soldier, lawyer, painter and poet. For over ten years, Lane and Wood had been close political friends, and when Lane went to Washington they maintained a continuous and lengthy correspondence.

Writing to Lane in July 1913, Wood revealed little bashfulness in describing his legal talents:

> "There is one rather peculiar characteristic, it seems to me, about my own career, and that is that I am attorney for the Banks and Power and Light Companies and the big corporations, and have their confidence, and I am also attorney (gratis) for the labor unions, the Socialists and all the labor people who get into trouble or want advice, and have their confidence. . . . My influence, I would say, with labor people is as great in California as it is North, and at the same time I am also attorney for some of the largest California capitalists, such as the Fleishhackers."[19]

Engaging in a bit of rationalization, Wood explained that it was not his purpose to brag of influence, but to show "that a man may help both sides, labor and capital, to see the good there is in the other side, and the errors in their own, and maintain the respect of each."

Over the next eight months, Wood and Lane revealed some basic differences of opinion, or possibly differences of interpretation, as to what constituted true party loyalty and what justified a position of independence on matters of party policy. On March 31, 1914, Wood informed Lane that he would not support George Chamberlain in his bid for renomination as the senior U. S. Senator from Oregon. Chamberlain had been a generally consistent supporter of President Woodrow Wilson's administration, but he was opposed to Wilson's desire to have Congress restore the Panama Canal tolls which had been repealed for American ships by the Taft administration.

To Wilson and Wood, the repeal of tolls discriminated against foreign shipping and was a breach of the Hay-Pauncefote Treaty. The action was also viewed as a form of public subsidy to private shipping companies. Wood considered Chamberlain "lacking in strong basic principles." He accused the senior senator of refusing to support the President "because the Portland Journal and the business interests of Portland were howling . . . upon no higher ground than the dirty dollar."[20] Four years later, Portland business and shipping interests expressed their appreciation to Senator Chamberlain by contributing to a fund for the purchase and maintenance of an automobile for the senator's use.[21]

To Wood, fundamental principles could not be compromised. And one of his most strongly held principles was opposition to the granting of special privileges to any person, group or corporation. In this instance, at least, his principles were in complete accord with President Wilson's policy. Wood drew a distinction between "fundamental" principles and their application. Policy questions which involved the application of principles were by their very nature political — open to debate. Wood could justify opposition to established party policy if it conflicted with his fundamental principles — not an unusual occurrence in Wood's political career. As an unreconstructed individualist, Wood often found himself at odds with the Oregon Democratic Party hierarchy. Understandably, he was never elected to public office although he was once nominated for the U. S. Senate.

Early in June, the senate voted 50 to 35 to repeal the canal toll exemption law, and Lane joined Chamberlain on the losing side. Just prior to the vote, Lane received a long written lecture from Wood on the essence of party loyalty. Referring to Lane's campaign in 1912, C. E. S. declared that "it was not a question of personality" that elected him (Lane) to office, but "one of sending a man back there who would support the President. . . . It was just as necessary to have a senate supporting the President in democratic principles as to have a Democratic president."[22] C. E. S. felt that Lane was obligated to support the President. He had built his campaign on just such a pledge. This was not a matter of fundamental principle which might justify independence. "On questions of administrative policy the administration senators ought to back up the President, yielding their own personal beliefs. . . . Personal independence of legislators if carried far enough is going, in the future as in the past, to lead to such lack of cohesion as will produce party failure."[23]

In later years Wood's dire prediction became a reality. Incohesiveness did indeed become a dominant characteristic of Oregon politics — especially Democratic Party politics — that became increasingly subjected to personal squabbles. As was to be the case with Senator Wayne Morse in the 1950s, the "fundamental principles," however defined, tended to get mixed up with personal idiosyncracies. Of course, Harry Lane had never been a party man,

12

Harry Lane   *"C. E. S." Wood*

Hotel Benson Newspaper Men's Reception honoring former President William Howard Taft, August 22, 1915. Seated on Taft's left were Governor James Withycombe, Senator George Chamberlain and Senator Harry Lane. The Oregonian *publisher Henry L. Pittock was seated on his far right.*

strictly speaking. He had won elections to office, often in defiance of the party hierarchy. As mayor of Portland he had accomplished little of lasting value because he had no leverage over the leaders of either party. But he was popular with voters in a heavily Republican city. His independent spirit was a symbol — albeit a somewhat unrealistic one — around which the "common people" could rally in defiance of the established business-political leadership.

Lane certainly did not conform to the modern stereotype of the free-spending liberal. In 1914, he was called "the human question mark" by his senatorial colleagues. He was reported as being "the most inquisitive man in Congress" when it came to federal appropriations. He was opposed to deficits and to what he called the "pure waste of public funds." Declared Lane: "If the State of Oregon had been treated as liberally, proportionately, as one or two Western states I might name, we would have not less than 150 public buildings today, where actually we have not more than a dozen." Lane cited cases of $50,000 and $75,000 public buildings erected in towns "that have not 1000 souls within their limits."[24] Concerns of this sort were matters of fundamental principle to Senator Harry Lane 60 years ago. They are still considered matters of fundamental principle to most Oregon voters today.

C. E. S. Wood "never cared a damn for party" except when "party represented principle," as he wrote to Lane,[25] but Wood had never been elected to office. "I want to be frank," he told Lane. "I do not believe a man can always be consistent or always hold to his pledges any more than he can hold to the famous pledge to 'love and honor until death do us part.' Circumstances may arise which render it inevitable that a pledge be broken; but it should be exceedingly rare."[26] Wood's open extra-marital relationship with Mrs. Sarah Bard Field fell into this category, much to the horror of proper Portland society. (Wood later married Mrs. Field.) And when Senator Lane in April 1917 voted against America's declaration of war on Germany, an act that led to Lane's vilification in Portland, friend Wood respected his decision as one based on fundamental principle even though Wood himself supported the Wilson administration's war policy.

The Paradox of Local Government

Portland city politics, being non-partisan after 1913, at least in theory, reflected the same spirit of independence that marked both Lane's and Wood's private and public lives. As a consequence, personalities tended to dominate the issues, even though the issues were often wrapped in a covering of principles. Lack of cohesion — called confusion by some — became the norm rather than the exception. In the years following 1913, Portland's commission form of government, the city's only major Progressive Era reform, came under increasingly heavy critical fire. It was not efficient enough to please many leaders of the business community who also yearned for more effective political control, and it lacked the necessary discipline of party organization that was deemed essential to the likes of Colonel Wood.

14

Municipal reform in the pre-World War I years involved a paradox: "The ideology of an extension of political control and the practice of its concentration."[27] The expansion of popular involvement represented a noble ideal that did not always work out to the satisfaction of those who had originally supported it. It was primarily a political tactic, with more negative than positive consequences when applied to the decision making process. The initiative, referendum and recall became overused and abused, and the direct primary failed to produce more than a handful of strong, disinterested political leaders. But "the rule of the people" that elected independent spirits like Harry Lane, Rufus Holman and Wayne Morse to the senate, Julius Meier to the governorship and Dorothy Lee to the mayor's office following World War II, such actions did embody an ideal, however nebulous or paradoxical.

You Can't Tell How Far a Frog Will Jump

PART I

PRE-WAR DECISIONS AND POST-WAR CONSEQUENCES

1914 downtown aerial survey.

The County Courthouse is at the bottom center. To the west and north can be seen the Failing and Corbett residential blocks, further to the west and north can be seen the YMCA and the Portland Hotel. Directly to the north of the Portland Hotel is the Northwest National Bank Building that replaced the Marquam Building, currently known as the American Bank Building. The Broadway Bridge can be seen in the upper right.

Chapter 1

Portland the Spinster Goes Dry

A month after the United States entered "The Great War," *Collier's Weekly* published a lengthy article on Portland that shocked the local establishment. Written by Californian Wilbur Hall, "Portland the Spinster" presented an image of the city strongly at variance with the one that the Portland Chamber of Commerce had been carefully fashioning since the Lewis and Clark Exposition of 1905. "You see Portland first at her worst," Hall declared, "the way that most American cities are seen." Hall described his drive from the Union Station through the city's "sorriest and shabby streets" to the "sedate and orderly" buildings of the business district which he complimented for their white and yellow tones. Hall warned his readers to beware of "Portland's maniac pavement washing machines,"[1] thus giving the city public recognition for attempting to keep its streets clean, an effort that few of its West Coast neighbors could match.

Wilbur Hall's Visit in 1916

When Hall had made his visit in late 1916, he encountered a subdued Portland. Statewide prohibition had been in effect for almost a year. Lower West Burnside Street, the major east-west arterial that divided the northern and southern portions of the old city, was no longer that "wicked" place where "rovers drank, gambled and caroused with robust, open-handed prodigality and profane whole-heartedness." The "lurid atmosphere" had begun to fade when the "gin palaces closed their doors."[2] But the North Burnside district, through which reporter Hall had driven after his arrival, still bore the scars of its boisterous past. Prostitution and gambling were far from dead and alcohol was being dispensed on the sly. Called "coon town" by the local police, veteran Chief Lee V. Jenkins recalled 20 years later: "I had a beat from Fifth to Twelfth Street and from Burnside to Glisan Street. That was one of the toughest districts in the city at that time. There were more than one thousand colored [Negroes] people living within the boundaries of those streets."[3]

No doubt this statement revealed far more about the police department than it did about North Burnside. Jenkins was not noted for his human sensitivities. In truth, the members of Portland's stable and hard working Negro community epitomized the good old fashioned virtues. They happened to reside in the "tough" district because most Negro adult males worked nearby for either the railroads, the Union Station or the hotels. North Burnside housing was older and cheaper, and its ethnic and social diversity was traditional in contrast to the

17

Portland Hotel

more homogeneous residential sections of upper Northwest and Southwest Portland where the first families lived. These were naive times, when *The Oregonian* artist Murphy "could still sketch a Pullman porter as a thick-lipped 'darky' who called Mr. Tourist 'boss' in a quaint dialect."[4]

Reporter Hall might have taken his taxi to the new Imperial Hotel where he could book a room with a bath for $2 and meet its proprietor Phil Metschan, Jr., a local power in Republican party politics. He could have gone to the new and larger Multnomah and Benson Hotels or to the prestigious old Portland Hotel with its grandiose appointments. For dinner he would have enjoyed the recently opened Il Rigoletto Cafe where he would be offered either an Italian or French dinner prepared with "the highest standards of cuisine" for less than one dollar. But such personal details were not recounted. Wilbur Hall did wander through the downtown streets after dinner where he found that the first families had "retired to their castles." They had turned the city over to "their tenants and dependents, . . . the common people,"[5] whom he observed to be "very middle class, hospitable, pleasant, democratic," and usually in company with their children.

"A Backwoods Town"

Most visitors to Portland in the pre-war era mentioned at least three phenomena that they observed: The narrow, congested streets of the downtown, the roses growing everywhere and the stacks of cordwood that dotted the sidewalks adjacent to the residences. Wilbur Hall noticed something else that surprised him: A "$60,000 cow pasture" right in the middle of the city. Having travelled widely, he knew that the spirit of every city was usually expressed in one unique landmark. In New York, it was the Woolworth Building; in Chicago, Michigan Avenue; in Philadelphia, Independence Square; but in Portland, could it be Corbett's "cow corral?" Was this the "concrete embodiment of the spirit of Miss Portland, spinster?" he asked. For years, pioneer banker Henry W. Corbett's widow had permitted her cow to graze on the north half of her residential block, the site of the present Pacific Building. The animal's reputation had spread far beyond the region, and many a tourist would not leave the city without a first-hand glimpse of this unusual spectacle. Reporter Hall wondered whether the Corbett cow pasture was a symbol of the kind of mind that dominated Portland, one that "scorns to consider change."[6]

Native son Jack Reed would have said, "Yes." Returning home briefly in July 1914 after a well publicized assignment as a war correspondent covering Pancho

Residence of Mrs. H. W. Corbett, Fifth and Yamhill Streets

Villa's exploits in Mexico, the son of the socially prominent Charles Jerome Reeds found Portland "dull as ever." Although wined and dined in the homes of his family's friends, Reed felt obliged to escape "the stuffy atmosphere" of Portland's cold and decorous society by seeking out a local International Workers of the World (IWW) meeting hall or by attending a lecture by the famous anarcho-socialist Emma Goldman, in company with his old mentor, C. E. S. Wood. When invited to address the University Club, instead of presenting a travel talk on life in foreign lands, he "delivered an impassioned speech about exploitation and class war" that annoyed his staid audience beyond memory.[7] To old Portland society, Jack Reed was considered "a radical of the worst sort."[8]

When Reed returned to New York to resume his old life among the Greenwich Village set, he renewed his friendship with some former acquaintances, including Margaret Sanger, the founder of the American birth control movement. Mrs. Sanger's incipient organization, publisher of the monthly magazine *The Woman Rebel*, grew out of the national women's suffrage movement that was gaining gradual acceptance throughout the country as it had in Oregon in 1912. But the birth control issue was much more divisive than that of women's suffrage. It tended to split the old time Populists and Progressives from the younger radicals who saw the issue as a personal and social one. Whereas the Roosevelt Progressives and even many of the Wilsonian Democrats favored large families in the old American tradition, the John Reeds and Margaret Sangers saw "poor workers burdened by immense families. . . . Rich women already knew how to prevent conception while the poor were forced by moral and religious sanctions to keep on bearing children."[9]

In the winter of 1916, following the opening of the first United States birth control clinic, Mrs. Sanger was convicted and briefly jailed in New York City for sending "obscene matter" through the mails. Undaunted, she set out across the country the following spring to spread the gospel to the more progressive states like Oregon. While speaking at Portland's Heilig Theater on June 19th, she and six of her associates (three males and three females) were arrested for selling the booklet "Family Limitation." Protests arrived from everywhere, addressed to liberal Democratic Mayor H. R. Albee who proceeded to answer as many as he could. In one response, Albee told a protestor that the booklet contained pages that "had no bearing on the subject" and which his administration "adjudged obscene." Entire pages were devoted "to the explanation and the joy of cohabitation."[10]

For the trial that began on June 30th, Jack Reed's old friend Col. C. E. S. Wood, acted as defense attorney. Wood tore the city ordinances to shreds — a second, tighter ordinance had in fact been passed by the council after Mrs. Sanger's arrest. The subject of birth control, asserted Wood, along with the related matters against which the city council ordinances were supposedly directed, "have been approved by the world's greatest lay minds and the highest courts. . . . Portland is a backwoods town. It is the only city on the map to oppose this movement of instruction." The second ordinance passed just the previous week was *ex post facto* and clearly unconstitutional, charged Wood. And then, in a moment of great emotion, Wood reached the peak of his eloquent defense with the ringing declaration: "If Portland's statute is legal then the Holy Bible is obscene." Calling this occasion "one of the most important trials of the age," Wood concluded: "Rabelais would be indicted and tried under the laws of Oregon, yet his books are for sale in every well-regulated bookstore."[11]

Six days later, the court ruled "Family Limitation" obscene. The subject of birth control itself was not on trial, the judge said. For almost two years, the city had been officially censoring movies — a policy that had enjoyed wide public support. The city had every right, continued the judge, to censor obscene literature that would be deemed objectionable to the majority of Portland's citizens. Having upheld the city's public policy, the judge meted out no punishment, only $10 fines that were then suspended.[12]

The Sanger decision most likely found some strong support among Portland's recently enfranchised women if a study published in 1919 was accurate. Reed sociologist William F. Ogburn examined the women's vote in the 1914 elections and found it to be generally conservative especially in social matters. Ogburn gave particular note to the large majority of women voters who had supported prohibition.[13] Perhaps a clue to their feelings on this issue was revealed by Wilbur Hall when he reported the substance of a conversation that he had with a Portland lady a few months after Margaret Sanger's conviction.

> "I said: 'What is the most noticeable effect of prohibition in Oregon, as you observe it?'
>
> Her answer was prompt. 'The most noticeable?' she echoed. 'It is that now our husbands come home to lunch.' "[14]

Under the initial Oregon law, each individual was permitted to import a definite amount of spirits and beer each month, provided the importation was made for personal use. The supply was to be kept at home and drunk there. In the November 1916 Oregon election the "bone dry amendment" was passed, though by only 3000 votes statewide while Multnomah County electors opposed it by a healthy 9500 votes. When Oregon joined the war effort five months later, it was a totally dry state — legally, but not in practice. There was no question that even with the earlier exceptions in effect, prohibition was largely responsible for the reduction in the total number of criminal offenses from 1916 until the war's end.[15] On balance, however, prohibition proved costly to the city. The treasury lost $375,000 annually in liquor license fees and about half that amount in municipal court fines. A special tax levy was enacted but the proceeds did not match the losses. Probably the most disastrous consequence of prohibition, however, both locally and nationally, was the creation of the bootlegging industry and the resultant corruption of police and other public officials. Portland was not immune to this development.

As might be suspected, neither prohibition nor women's suffrage had much effect on the reduction of prostitution. The number of vice arrests remained fairly constant until 1917, approximately 600 a year. The influx of wartime shipyard workers was to increase the trade. District Attorney Walter Evans was still hard at work trying to enforce the 1913 anti-vice legislation, but he received only lukewarm cooperation from the city police department, especially after the election of Mayor George L. Baker in the spring of 1917. Only the most obvious violations were noticed by Capt. Jenkins and the vice squad. According to the Portland *Telegram* in November 1917, the "javelins" that had been "hurled at citadels of sin" were not flying quite so fast and furiously. "Following the Vice Commission's report [in 1912] there was some stirring about cleaning up Portland. But five years have elapsed since then and it is fair to assume that the old conditions have returned."[16]

Some Concerned Citizens

The apathy that seemed to follow in the wake of most reform movements in American society — and Portland's 1912 anti-vice crusade was no exception — mystified Portland lawyer Joseph N. Teal, one of a handful of rare citizens who gave time well beyond the call of duty in the service of city and country. In his autobiographical notes, composed in the mid-twenties, Teal commented:

> "It is of no particular moment to point out why movements for civic betterment so often fail. In a word, it is man's failures, man's weaknesses, his unwillingness or inability to stand the gaff and not infrequently personal interest that are the reefs on which the ship strikes. . . . The experience I gained . . . convinced me that we have the government we want to have and that good government is based on the interest the citizen takes therein. I have always said and still believe that in time, dependent on its size and conditions, 50 determined, intelligent, loyal and honest citizens having an eye solely to the public welfare, can, if they really want to and will give the time, clean up any city in America. . . . What, however, is interesting is that for years . . . substantially the same ones did the work. I have never been able to account for this. Whether it was a new charter for the city, municipal reform, transportation or conservation, the same names always appeared."[17]

Teal had led an energetic civic life ever since his marriage to the daughter of David P. Thompson, former Mayor of Portland and American Minister to Turkey. Active in the Oregon Bar,[18] Teal was a director of numerous local corporations, a member of the Finance Committee of the Democratic National Committee and a director of the San Francisco Federal Reserve Bank. His deepest involvement, however, was with transportation matters, especially those related to waterborne commerce.

Heralded as "the father of the public dock ideal in Portland," Teal had long been critical of the way in which the railroads had dominated Portland commerce, especially the Port of Portland Commission. It was Teal who first charged publicly that the railroad corporations owned most of the private docks

22

Joseph N. Teal

and available waterfront land, giving them effective control over the transportation of goods both into and out of the port of Portland. Believing that Portland's future rested "upon the water," Teal led the local effort to create the Commission of Public Docks in 1910, an action that resulted in the opening of the first municipal dock in 1914.

After World War I, in the last decade of his life, Teal briefly served on the United States Shipping Board in Washington while at the same time spearheading an investigation by the Interstate Commerce Commission into the discriminatory railroad rate structure that gave priority treatment to the Puget Sound ports. A victorious 1921 ICC decision in favor of Portland was one of the happiest moments of Teal's life. It merely confirmed his long held conviction that if one worked "in the public interest," took the time and did not hurry, "the war" could be won — in this case, the war against the railroads.[19] In April of 1920, Teal also lent his support to a bill in Congress to provide for through bills of lading and through rates to include motor transport lines as well as railroads, giving motor trucks the same role as the old short line railroads. Teal foresaw the day when motor trucks would become an integral part of the national rail network.[20]

Matters related to transportation were also of consuming interest to another unusual Portlander, Norwegian born Simon Benson. What started as a fight with the lumber shippers ended up in a love affair with the automobile. After a number of years as an impoverished farmer and logger, Benson began to accumulate timberlands in the St. Helens, Oregon area that would expand in size to over 45,000 acres. He built some donkey engines, small locomotives used in switching, from discarded parts and constructed a logging rail line, all of which saved him considerable harvesting time and labor costs. As his production grew, he decided to ship to the prosperous Southern California market, but he found the railroad and coastal freight rates to be exorbitant. So he hit upon the scheme of building gigantic 835 foot rafts, each carrying about 4.5 million feet of logs. Described as looking like capsized battleships, the rafts were towed 1100 miles to San Diego where he had a sawmill waiting to cut them up. By such resourcefulness, Benson saved over $150,000 a year.[21]

In late 1910, Benson sold his timber holdings for approximately $4.5 million and set about investing his time and money in a variety of ways. Besides donating 20 bronze drinking fountains to the city, he gave $100,000 to construct the first unit of a new public polytechnic high school. From his own experience, he knew the importance of trade skills that were rarely included in the conventional high school curriculum. In 1913, he opened the $1 million replica of Chicago's Blackstone Hotel that currently bears his name on property leased from his close friend, lumberman John Yeon. The Benson Hotel lost so much money initially that he assumed the active management himself and within three years it was showing a handsome profit. In 1921, after he had moved his residence to Beverly Hills, California, Benson deeded the city a nine acre plat overlooking the Willamette River, between North Greeley and Going Streets, later dedicated as Madrona Park.

From the experience of his mechanized logging operations, Benson came to believe that the automobile would supplant the horse just as his donkey engines had supplanted his oxen. Automobiles would require better roads and paved highways so he became, in his own words, "a good roads crank." In an interview with local historian Fred Lockley, Benson reminisced:

"Do you know why I kept up such an agitation for better roads? It was because we kept talking about getting back to the land, and what it really meant was 'getting back to the mud.' How could we expect to get more producers upon the land and imprison men each winter on their farms with impassable roads? No wonder the children didn't want to stay on the farms."[22]

Benson traveled all over the West and in his own words, spent "about $200,000 on good roads and playgrounds." He took an interest in building a highway along the Columbia River and purchased the adjacent Multnomah and Wahkeena Falls for public park and recreational purposes, to prevent the intrusion of "hot dog stands and mammy's chicken shacks." He was accused of being a visionary, a spendthrift and a "kook" as he campaigned in 1917 for a $6

24

J. B. Yeon

Simon Benson

Benson Hotel

million public bond issue for good roads. A year earlier, Congress had passed the first federal highway legislation that appropriated matching funds on a dollar for dollar basis. The bond issue was designed to provide Oregon's share.

Due to his efforts, along with friends John Yeon, Rufus Holman, *Oregon Journal* publisher C. S. Jackson, Jay Bowerman, and James J. Hill's son-in-law, Sam Hill, of the state of Washington, the scenic Columbia River Highway was built, the state bond measure passed, and in 1919 Oregon became the first state in the nation to impose a gasoline tax for highway construction and improvement. In recognition of his untiring efforts, Benson was named the first chairman of the Oregon State Highway Commission after it was reconstituted as a citizen agency in 1917.[23]

By July of 1915 when the Columbia River Highway was officially opened[24] — complete except for its hard surfacing — over 23,000 automobiles were registered in Oregon, about one third of which operated in Multnomah County. Benson's good friend, John B. Yeon, had been supervising the highway's construction in his capacity as the unsalaried Roadmaster of Multnomah County. Like Benson, Yeon was a successful lumberman and real estate owner who devoted himself and much of his money to the public interest. A Canadian by birth, Yeon started out as a penniless and inexperienced logger at the age of twenty. By the time he was 41, he had amassed a considerable fortune. The secret to his success, he told a *Journal* reporter,

> " . . . lay in the fact that during dull seasons I did not close down my camp like most of the loggers did, but kept at work, keeping my equipment in shape and assembling my logs so that when good times came again, I was ready to put my logs on the market and get the top price."[25]

In 1906, Yeon sold his timber holdings and bought his first major downtown property for $125,000, the quarter block on the southeast corner of Broadway and Stark, the future site of the Imperial Hotel. Within a year, he invested another $275,000 for the sites of the future Benson Hotel and his own Yeon Building, which, when it opened in 1910, was the tallest structure in Portland. It is still one of the finest commercial buildings in the city. John Yeon went first class in all that he did, and when he left office in 1918, Multnomah County had one of the outstanding county road systems in the West. As Wilbur Hall commented, referring to the Columbia River project:

> "The result is a highway unique in America for its scenic wonder, its permanence, its safety, and its resemblance to the old Roman roads of Europe."[26]

Under John Yeon's critical eye and close supervision, the highway work was done for $25,000 less than it would have cost had a private contractor performed the job. Such a record was unheard of, at least in Oregon's most recent past. When Simon Benson resigned from the State Highway Commission in 1920,

America's Premier Scenic Asset.

Portland to Astoria

Governor Withycombe persuaded the reluctant Yeon to accept the chairmanship. For these and other public services, including his determination to invest his own Oregon-made money in Oregon, John B. Yeon received as high public praise as had ever been accorded any Oregonian.[27]

A third member of the public spirited group of citizens who were prime movers of the Columbia River Highway project was Portland-born Rufus C. Holman. A colorful and outspoken public figure, Holman began his illustrious and often controversial political career with his election to the Board of Multnomah County Commissioners in 1913. In contrast to Benson, Teal and Yeon, Holman dedicated 32 years to professional politics after a ten year spell in the paper box business.

For the ten years that he was on the county commission, Rufus Holman made transportation his major responsibility. Not only did he provide the first official governmental backing for the Columbia River Highway project, but along with John Yeon he initiated and supervised the paving of the county road system to accommodate the waves of new residents flooding into the eastern reaches of the city and county. As the scenic highway was nearing completion, Holman revealed a trait that was to mark his subsequent political career — hard-headed independence. He fired John Yeon as the county roadmaster because Yeon had personally approved the construction of Vista House on Crown Point, the most spectacular viewpoint along the entire Columbia River. Holman claimed that he had only approved a $12,000 expenditure for a small covered structure. Whether through a misunderstanding or not, Yeon had gone ahead on his own initiative, hired architect Edgar Lazarus of Baltimore, and built a much larger stone facility projected to cost $100,000. This controversy was to touch off a long-standing feud that would adversely affect Holman's future political career as he set his sights on higher offices.

Another major road project drawing Holman's attention was the construction of an automobile-streetcar bridge to connect Portland with Vancouver, Washington. The span across the Columbia River was officially opened on Valentine's Day, 1917. Thousands of people from both states gathered for the celebration that Holman had helped to organize in his capacity as Chairman of the Interstate Bridge Committee. Preceded by two streetcars, the Oregon delegation formed a line of automobiles more than a mile long. For hours, a steady stream of traffic and pedestrians flowed both ways across the new bridge. As one commentator noted, after the ceremonies at Vancouver, Mayor Albee and the county and city commissioners returned to Portland by automobile, quietly eating cheese and crackers on the way.[28] The spirits that traditionally accompanied such public christenings were absent.

Local Government on Trial

Portland's new commission form of government[29] over which Mayor Albee presided — although not approved by the voters with much enthusiasm in 1913

28

— did get off to a successful start, primarily because the first commissioners elected were a "group of able men, devoted to the public welfare, and determined to do whatever was necessary to make the plan a success."[30] This was the judgment of a Portland City Club report published in the 1930s. The City Club itself was born just three years after the reform charter went into effect. Patterned upon similar organizations in the East, city clubs like Portland's "were spawned during the Golden Age of community reform movements." Dedicated to "guarding the public trust and ferreting out the flaws and evils in public laws and institutions,"[31] the Portland organization soon came to be known as "The Conscience of the City."[32]

Following the unsuccessful attempt in 1914 to recall Mayor Albee and two commissioners,[33] a number of civic-minded young men had begun to meet weekly at the First Presbyterian Church to discuss public matters. Not members of "the city's entrenched 'old families,' . . . these upstarts"[34] decided that they would like to do more than just gripe about the state of municipal government. With the strong support of some students and faculty of Reed College, the group formed a weekly men's luncheon club that grew to over 100 members within a year.

In retrospect, it was unfortunate that the now prestigious City Club selected as its first annual dinner speaker a man who was the antithesis of everything the club represented: Joseph R. Bowles, president of the Northwest Steel Company. Bowles headed the largest and most productive shipyard on the West Coast during the War, but four years after his City Club speech he was to be indicted for bribing a government official and convicted of contempt of court.[35] He was a greedy, domineering and difficult person, with no sense of civic responsibility.[36]

Bowles represented a type of private entrepreneur, all too common in Portland history, who squeezed the maximum private windfall profits from public decisions. He had the "foresight" to buy properties that would some day be needed for public purposes. When the dock commission was assembling the package of land that would serve as the site for its first municipal dock, Bowles surfaced as the owner of a tiny but key strip that was worth no more than $10,000. He demanded $77,000 and after lengthy negotiation was awarded $35,000.[37]

Problems of this sort plague all city governments and Mayor Albee's young administration was no exception. The first two municipal docks and the new civic auditorium were the only major public projects approved by the Portland voters until Albee left office in the spring of 1917. The adverse impact of the European War on Portland's export trade triggered a three year recession that produced a $30 million decline in Portland's assessed property values. The period 1915-1917 brought strict economy to city government and it was not until George L. Baker was elected mayor in June 1917 that the voters showed any inclination to commit the city to some long range projects — in this instance, park acquisition and development.

The success of the park levy election was the first of many victories that would be achieved by the city's new superintendent of Parks, Charles Paul Keyser who was to dedicate 32 years to the job. Keyser had political skills not possessed by his predecessor, the gifted landscape architect E. T. Mische. On numerous occasions after his retirement, Keyser would describe himself as "a combination of engineer, politician, real estate speculator and sociologist." Quick to understand what was going on politically, Keyser took the public pulse and found a growing awareness of the need for small neighborhood parks and playgrounds. He drafted a measure for a park levy of .4 mils, to yield $100,000 annually, and he personally promoted the plan all over the city, especially among community groups. His astounding success represented a personal triumph because the 1917 city budget had cut normal park operational expenditures by over 25 percent. After the measure passed, it became known as the "Green Line" millage, and the first park acquired was Duniway, on the land filled site of the old garbage dump at the foot of Marquam Ravine in Southwest Portland. Today it provides track and field facilities for the public, Portland State University and the YMCA.[38]

In the two year period leading up to America's involvement in the war, the city council gave attention to a number of controversial matters including riverfront improvement, city planning, water meters, municipal garbage collection, vice, public transit rates and slum housing conditions, but little was accomplished of long range significance. The major physical development — an increase of Portland's city limits by over 25 percent — resulted from the annexation of St. Johns and Linnton in 1915 after both cities voted to merge with their large neighbor. The Linnton addition included a huge tract of nearly 4000 acres out of which Portland was to create Forest Park 30 years later.

The residents of St. Johns soon became increasingly irritated with their new city fathers when it took almost a year to attach the North Portland residents to the city's Bull Run water system. The desire for an ample, clean and cheaper municipal water supply had provided the major support for annexation, but Portland and the private St. Johns Water Works, that drew most of its resource from wells along the Willamette River, could not agree on a fair purchase price. Thus for the better part of a year, the St. Johns users continued to pay their high water charges in addition to their new Portland city taxes.

By the end of the Albee administration, Portland city government had obviously experienced severe retrenchment in expenditures financed from the city's general fund. While the population had grown by five percent since 1915, the general fund had been reduced by over 20 percent, from $3.22 million to $2.5 million. The city's civil service work force had been cut by 16 percent.[39] And it was during this very time, paradoxically, that the commission form of government came under serious attack for its alleged waste and inefficiency.

Rising to its defense, City Attorney W. P. LaRoche reported in April 1917 that the commission form was costing much less than the old councilmanic government did. In fact, the cost of city government had decreased by over eight percent in four years.[40] But this evidence did not deter two unsuccessful efforts to

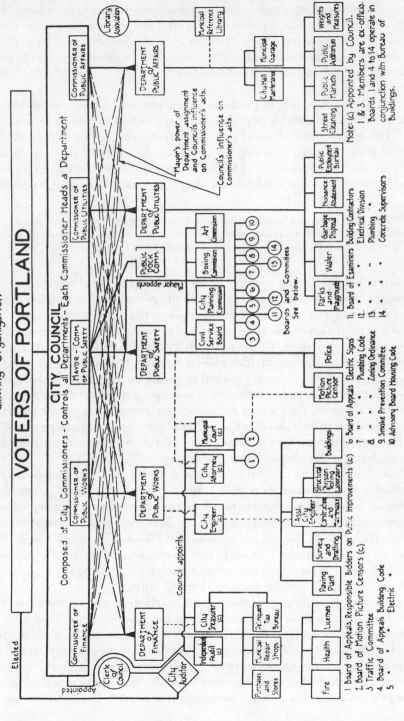

Portland's Commission Government
Existing Organization

VOTERS OF PORTLAND

Elected

CITY COUNCIL
Composed of City Commissioners - Controls all Departments - Each Commissioner Heads a Department

| Commissioner of Finance | Commissioner of Public Works | Mayor - Comm. of Public Safety | Commissioner of Public Utilities | Commissioner of Public Affairs |

Appointed

Clerk of Council

City Auditor

Council appoints

Mayor appoints

Library Association

Municipal Reference Library

DEPARTMENT OF FINANCE
- Purchases and Stores
- Municipal Repair Shops
- Independent Audit (c)
- City Treasurer (c)
- Delinquent Tax Bureau
- Fire
- Health
- Licenses

DEPARTMENT OF PUBLIC WORKS
- Paving Plant
- Survey and Drafting
- City Engineer (c)
- Asst. City Engineer
- Construction and Maintenance
- Structural Division Testing Laboratory
- City Attorney (c)
- Municipal Court
- Buildings

DEPARTMENT OF PUBLIC SAFETY
- Motion Picture Censor
- Police
- Civil Service Board
- City Planning Commission
- Boxing Commission
- Art Commission

Public Dock Comm.

DEPARTMENT OF PUBLIC UTILITIES
- Parks and Playgrounds
- Water
- Garbage Disposal
- Nuisance Abatement
- Public Employment Bureau

DEPARTMENT OF PUBLIC AFFAIRS
- Street Cleaning
- Public Markets
- Public Auditorium
- City Hall Maintenance
- Municipal Garage
- Weights and Measures

"Mayor's power of Department assignment and Council's influence on Commissioner's acts.

Council's influence on Commissioner's acts.

Boards and Committees See below.

3 4 5 6 11 12
7 8 13 14
9 10

1. Board of Appeals, Responsible Bidders on Public Improvements (c)
2. Board of Motion Picture Censors (c)
3. Traffic Committee
4. Board of Appeals Building Code
5.   "   "   Electric   "
6. Board of Appeals Electric Signs
7.   "   "   Plumbing Code
8.   "   "   Zoning Ordinance
9. Smoke Prevention Committee
10. Advisory Board Housing Code
11. Board of Examiners Building Contractors
12.   "   "   Electrical Division
13.   "   "   Plumbing   "
14.   "   "   Concrete Supervisors

Note: (c) Appointed by Council.
1 & 3 Members are ex-officio.
Boards 1 and 4 to 14 operate in conjunction with Bureau of Buildings.

1933

abolish it. One attempt, not surprisingly, came from a group of prominent North Portland, Peninsula and St. Johns property owners led by realtor Coe A. McKenna. They were backed by William M. Killingsworth, a veteran Albina resident who had extensive real estate interests throughout the city. They even prepared a new 200 page city charter that would restore the old council of eleven part-time members.

Six months earlier, two of Portland's most successful business leaders had publicly announced similar criticisms but neither had favored a return to the past. "The model of the efficient business enterprise, . . . rather than the New England town meeting, provided the positive inspiration"[41] for B. S. Josselyn and Simon Benson. Josselyn, the former president of Portland's giant corporate property owner, The Portland Railway Light & Power Company, declared:

> "Safe, economic and businesslike government of municipal affairs should follow the lines of what has been considered best in large business affairs, which, if good for the investor, should also be good for the taxpayer."[42]

Josselyn favored the city manager form, the Dayton Plan. Simon Benson also favored the city manager model. He told the city council that he could save $1000 a day for the city if he could be allowed to operate the city's business as he would handle a private enterprise. His most recent experience with the Benson Hotel supported this contention. To Benson, the city commission form of government was not only wasteful but inefficient — it was like having "five mayors." He suggested a small volunteer city council receiving no pay that would determine policy and that would hire a professional manager who might be worth as much as $25,000 a year.[43] This would have been an exceptionally high municipal salary anywhere in 1916, let alone in Portland where the mayor was paid $6000 and the commissioners were receiving $5000. But Benson wanted efficiency and believed that the city should be willing to pay for it.

Although not delving into salary details, Josselyn went one step further. He suggested a five member, part-time, unpaid, "self-perpetuating" commission that would, however, be subject to recall. As candidates for such an august body, he recommended the top command of the business establishment: Wealthy grain merchant T. B. Wilcox, lumberman, Art Museum benefactor W. B. Ayer, druggist and civic activist William F. Woodward, banker and public benefactor William M. Ladd, department store owner Adolphe Wolfe, and the city's leading financier, the First National Bank's Abbot L. Mills.[44]

It is unclear whether any of these distinguished gentlemen were consulted before their names were publicized, but is not unclear what kind of a city government they would have run. It might have been honest, in a strictly legal sense, but whether it could have been any more efficient would have depended to a large degree on how the city's problems and needs were perceived. These men came from a tight little group, the same ones who had pretty much dominated Portland's life before Harry Lane became mayor in 1905. They had lost control,

Henry E. Reed

and they wanted it back. They were decent men of obviously good civic intentions. Benson, Ladd, Mills, Ayer and Woodward had devoted endless hours of personal time to civic betterment as they understood such efforts. But they had a limited view of the city's changing urban landscape and its increasingly serious social problems such as unemployment and slum housing. Furthermore, Ladd and Wilcox were living outside the city on sumptuous estates in the suburban countryside.

When given the opportunity, the voters did not take such criticisms too seriously. At the election of June 4, 1917, they decisively defeated two initiative measures to abolish the commission form of government.

The reformers would have been wiser to investigate Multnomah County government which had traditionally been downrated by Portland's leaders, except for those like Yeon and Holman. Apart from eliminating inefficiency and waste, if the reformers also wanted to ferret out corruption, the county should have been their target. Not until 1924, when the three commissioners were recalled, did Portlanders become aware of the mess that they had in their own backyard. When Holman tried to do something about it in 1923, he was defeated. The example set by Henry Reed in his successful effort to reform the County Assessor's office in 1913 should have opened a few eyes.

Henry E. Reed, a relentless compiler of statistical data and a Portland history buff, was a highly regarded property appraiser when he decided to run for Multnomah County Assessor in 1913. For some years he had heard rumors about corruption in veteran assessor B. D. Sigler's office and after a little research into the records, he became convinced of it. What he found makes an interesting tale.

Chief Deputy Assessor L. H. Maxwell had bought 7.4 acres of land in the Woodlawn district for $6000. He also assumed the bonded assessment for street improvements amounting to $1932. For less than a total of $8000, Maxwell had

33

acquired property that was assessed in 1908 at $10,000, with a market value of twice that amount. Early in 1909 he had apparently brought pressure on the property's owner, the Portland Railway Light & Power Company, to sell the property to him. Maxwell's assistant had informed the company that his boss wanted the land and would pay only $6000 plus improvement costs. The company objected but gave in for obvious reasons: It needed Mr. Maxwell's friendship. The utility was the largest property owner in the city, with holdings worth twice those of the major railroads combined.

The deed was signed by no other than the same B. S. Josselyn who was to attack the "waste and inefficiency" of the city commission eight years later. Assessor Sigler personally approved the deal. The tract was subsequently platted into 56 lots and assessed at $12,300 in 1913, with a market value of approximately $24,000. Maxwell's major partner was A. Y. Beach, brother of S. C. Beach, a long time Republican Party minor boss, and in 1913 a deputy assessor under Sigler.[45]

This type of "honest graft," to use a phrase coined by Boss George Washington Plunkitt of New York City, was common practice in Portland public life for many years. It was more prevalent on the county level, however, particularly in the 1920s and early thirties when the realtors were in control. It was an example of a kind of interest conflict that has long plagued most cities, including Portland. While such behavior may not have been illegal, strictly speaking, much of it was clearly unethical. Like municipal government generally, it was a game in which all participants scored some points at public expense.

34

Chapter 2

"Hard Times Made Harder"

Prior to the launching of the European War in 1914, President Woodrow Wilson's "New Freedom" — the political and economic philosophy underlying his first administration — began to exert some impact on the thinking of even the most conservative elements of traditional Portland Republicanism. The influence of Wilson's plea for a more humanitarian spirit in government and business manifested itself in at least two ways: (1) An expanded social awareness, and (2), a willingness, albeit reluctant in most cases, to accept a greater degree of economic regulation as one means of trying to preserve order in an increasingly complex society. But even for those few who willingly accepted such changes, the potential consequences were viewed with some trepidation.

As former Portlander James G. Woodworth, vice president of the Northern Pacific Railroad, wrote to his close friend, U. S. National Bank president John C. Ainsworth with whom he shared similar thoughts:

> "The money which is used for business purposes in this country is controlled by a comparatively small number of persons. . . . It seems reasonable to say that if the minority in this country who have the money and own the property have not been fair with the majority who own little or nothing, we can have peace and general satisfaction only as the minority may yield something or satisfy the majority that wrongful accusations have been made. . . . But it must be admitted that . . . there is a very marked socialistic tendency, not only in our new legislation, but also in the administration of existing laws.
> It is one thing to urge the rights of property and another to say that money is the only power. The older men of this generation not only believe in property rights, but they are too strong in the belief that money is the only real power."[1]

Both Ainsworth and Woodworth were aware of some of the obvious inequities afflicting American society. Woodworth favored the improvement of living conditions for the lower classes (e.g., housing), but, he warned:

> " . . . improvement is not going to come from the enactment and enforcement of laws, but rather from the changed attitude of the individual toward his fellow man. . . . If our population can be to a greater extent christianized we will have peace and plenty, but if we instead become more heathenized we will have . . . hard times."[2]

Woodworth's diagnosis of society's ills may have been partially accurate, but his prescribed medication was doomed to failure, especially as the United States geared up for a wartime economy. The city soon faced some severe economic and

35

Calm prevails at the downtown Lownsdale Park.

social conditions that it was not prepared to handle. The new shipyards and machine shops attracted a large inflow of population. Changed land use patterns resulted from the creation of new industrial zones and hastily devised working class residential arrangements. "Hard times" became harder as wartime housing became intertwined with established slum housing and poverty conditions.

The traditionally cautious power structure, composed of Portland's leading business executives and bankers like John C. Ainsworth and Abbot L. Mills, was not growth-oriented. As the war came to an end, the established leadership was to find itself challenged by a younger group, heavily representative of the real estate and construction trades — interests that proved to be even more motivated by money and power than the older generation cited by Woodworth. Overlooked in the rush to expand general economic development was the need to furnish basic social services to meet basic human requirements — services that the profit-oriented private enterprise system and the government that attended it were not in business to provide.

Economic Trends During the War

The period spanning the First World War was marked by uneven economic growth in Portland. The city did not experience the wartime boom enjoyed by Seattle to the north. Part of the reason lay in Portland's dependence on world wide trade that was curtailed by wartime restrictions. Another reason was the favored treatment accorded Seattle by the transcontinental railroads. A third, and perhaps more significant factor, was Portland's traditional caution, except perhaps in real estate ventures. Banker E. B. MacNaughton referred to this syndrome when he said that in Seattle, people went into debt to promote growth. In Portland, debt was a cardinal sin.[3]

Wilbur Hall encountered the same attitudes during his visit:

> "Portland thinks Seattle forward, pert, and radical. She thinks San Francisco quite impossible. If pressed, she would probably confess to a sort of approval of Philadelphia and a warm affection for Boston.[4] . . . One optimist whom I met advances the notion that Portland's 'solid men' — meaning the Ladds and the Hoyts and the Corbetts, and so on, I suppose — have it in their power to prevent another boom in Portland, and that they will exert that power successfully."[5]

In the decade up to 1914, Portland had experienced the most substantial growth in its young history.[6] It became one of the nation's leading exporters of

The Battleship Oregon, *flagship of the Pacific Fleet during the early years of World War I, at anchor in the Willamette River.*

lumber and wheat, but it was essentially a trading, not a manufacturing, center. Manufacturing for the most part was confined to utilizing the raw materials produced locally. The local output, with the exception of war shipbuilding, was not large enough to enable Portland's manufacturers to compete with the much larger Eastern concerns. Portland was therefore often at the mercy of outside forces that it could not control. Its economy was subjected to sharp fluctuations.

The European war produced a recession in Portland. Total foreign exports from the port dropped 77 percent from 1915 to 1916. Foreign grain exports dropped 82 percent and foreign lumber exports 63 percent during the same period.

The recession was characterized by several contradictory trends. While the unemployment rate doubled for the unskilled and seasonal workers, with annual relief payments soaring to $306,000,[7] demand for the skilled craft trades rose sharply. From 1915 to 1925, Portland's skilled craftsmen enjoyed a 59% increase in wages — the highest rate in the nation among the 30 largest cities. In 1918, the average wage for skilled trades was 88 cents per hour.[8] Portland was essentially a non-union shop town and it was noted for the lowest strike record on the West Coast.

The real estate and housing market showed similar contradictions. New low-priced housing starts dropped 50 percent. There were no large scale corporate housing contractors in Portland. The construction of higher priced city and suburban residences leveled off initially but began to rise in late 1916, especially in East Multnomah County and in the farther reaches of East Portland. In the decade from 1910 to 1920, the number of East Side residents increased from 58 to 71 percent of the city's total population and most of the increase was housed in single family residences. The appeal of the single family, owner-occupied home was characteristic of Portland from its earliest days. In 1916, 75 percent of Portland's population lived in residences, 50 percent of which were owner-occupied. The remainder of the population resided as follows: 10 percent in duplexes, 8 percent in apartments, and 6 percent in lodging and light housekeeping units.[9]

The prospective home buyer needed accumulated savings to purchase even a low-priced home because the ever cautious local banks limited first mortgages to 50 percent of purchase price. The banks apparently had sufficient funds to underwrite the construction and sale of new lower-cost single or multi-family units but such practices were considered risky and not in accord with traditional bank policy. Local bank resources doubled in the decade from 1910 to 1920, but most of the loan and mortgage money went to developers and land speculators for higher-cost residential, farm and industrial properties, or to more expensive single family homes. The major savings and loan associations, e.g., Equitable, tended to invest in similar types of properties. By 1918, when local war industry was in full swing, a serious low-cost housing shortage developed. Dense slum conditions were created, particularly on the more compact West Side of the Willamette River where the average family size was larger and where the bulk of the run-down hotels and residences existed, adjacent to commercial and industrial enterprises such as the shipyards.

The Portland business-political establishment — at least that portion of it that was reflected in the readership of the *Oregon Voter* — was proud of the fact that Portland experienced one of the lowest general increases in living costs of any major city in the country during the decade following 1915. Portland's home water rates were two-thirds of those in Seattle and one-fifth of those in San Francisco. The per capita tax rate was equally low — $27.97 in 1918 — in comparison with its West Coast neighbors: San Francisco, $46.72; Seattle, $47.30; and Los Angeles, $57.30.[10] As might be expected, a low tax rate produced an equally low level of public services. Of the 30 largest cities in 1918, Portland ranked 27th in police, 15th in fire and 20th in school expenditures per capita.[11] Apparently unbothered by such ratings, Portland voters in June 1919 defeated a two mil tax increase that not only would have increased salaries for police and firemen, but would have provided for an East Side police station and some essential City Hall repairs.

Social Consequences

In the category of city planning, Portland spent no money whatsoever until 1919, and the social consequences of such inaction proved to be costly.

As James J. Sawyer of the Oregon Conference of City Planning Commissioners reported:

"Portland's industrial, commercial and residential development in the main has been along the lines of least resistance. This is due to the topographical fact that the city is surrounded by hills and bisected by a river. The waterways and natural ravines offered the only available avenues of entrance into Portland. These things determined the lines of her principal streets and the center of her commercial activities. . . . The temptation is to seek the cheapest sites [for industries], notwithstanding the fact that this is not the best principle to follow in most instances."[12]

Sawyer noted that the lesser industries and commercial enterprises that followed the population growth began to seek new locations. Coal yards, oil tank storage sites, garages, neighborhood stores and laundries were forcing back existing residences. A 1916 survey listed a large number of unoccupied and abandoned residences in the close-in district of the West Side, from the Union Depot to the South Auditorium district.[13] And while 50 percent of the city's business firms were situated within this same area with a higher than average number located in office buildings, by 1919 the centers were beginning to shift to the East Side, spurred on by the paving of the major East Side arterials and the completion of the viaducts over the Union Pacific rail line. Fears were expressed by Sawyer and others that the East Side would follow the same pattern of development as had occurred across the river in the older sections of the city.

The ill effects of unguided city growth were most noticeable along the southwest river front and much less obvious along some of the older commercial-residential slum strips hidden from the river — districts not normally visited by the leaders of Portland society. Wilbur Hall commented that the river was "dirty and prosaic." Moreover, he said, "the private docks are inadequate, old fashioned and poorly equipped."[14] Joseph Teal had leveled such charges for years, putting much of the blame on the railroads and old family estates that owned most of the private dock land. Portland dock commission member, the respected C. B. Moores, agreed. Portland's business leaders had been "pennywise and pound foolish."[15] But it was one thing for the city's business leaders to react positively to Moores' charge and generate local support for waterfront improvement which they did and which was partially carried out during the decade of the twenties. It was quite another matter to become exercised over slum housing conditions for the poor and to do something about them beyond some pious exclamations of shock.

The First National Bank's president, Abbot L. Mills, probably the city's most prominent private citizen in 1918, was astounded by what he observed as he undertook a personally conducted tour of the city's most depressed housing sites.

The West Side Dock and Warehousing Area

40

"Frequently, when showing friends about Portland, the question has been asked as to where the poor element was located — the tenement section, and I have always answered proudly with the statement that we had nothing of this sort. . . . I found conditions that I did not know existed. . . . It would astonish lots of citizens of Portland to see the squalor in which some of our citizens live, the utter lack of sanitation and ventilation, and the utter disregard of health in which people who inhabit such sections live. Why some of the places were veritable rat holes, filthy beyond description, without light, as dark as the black hole of Calcutta, of which we have read. . . . There is no use for any false modesty about it."[16]

This was a revealing statement from a man who had been intimately involved in Portland business and politics for 30 years, one of B. S. Josselyn's candidates for the distinguished volunteer commission with which Josselyn hoped to replace the existing full-time city commission. Portland's leaders apparently did not realize that serious slum conditions existed, nor could they perceive what had caused them. Little local publicity had been given to a nationally circulated article in *The Survey* of April 10, 1915. The report revealed that Portland was little different from other cities; that it had severe pockets of poverty resulting from unemployment but "aggravated by the presence of a vast number of casual laborers."[17]

Mills and his business and social friends, at least in their public statements, failed to comprehend the changes that had overtaken American society by 1918. They perceived no banking or business responsibility for the creation of such humanly degrading conditions. They lived in a world apart. Portland to them was a city of fine homes, gardens and exclusive clubs, populated by successful, sophisticated and cultured people.

The immediate housing crisis of 1918 resulted from the influx of war workers to the shipyards. Less than 2000 new homes had been constructed in Portland since 1914, but most of these were sold to upper and middle income purchasers. With a population growth of approximately 25,000 in that same period of time, there was practically no low cost housing available for the new arrivals except abandoned structures that were hastily and crudely renovated in the areas of the city that already contained the pockets of severe poverty.

Old hotels were changed into lodging and tenement houses without proper alterations. Old houses were moved into South Portland, near the shipyards and placed on lots regardless of light and air. In some instances as many as three houses were placed on one lot. Old single family residences, long past their prime, were converted into multiple dwellings housing from 3 to 15 families without the installation of additional plumbing.

Reed College Professor Jesse Short made the following notes after visiting some of the worst sites:

"Apartment house, 111 S. W. Sheridan, vacant business places below; 13 two-room apartments — 2 baths, very unsanitary; 2 toilets used by both sexes, in

41

bad condition; no water in any apartment; stove heat; entire house in bad repair — some parts unsafe — fire hazard.

"Gem Hotel, S. W. First and Sheridan, ground floor shoe repair and vacant spaces; second floor houses 100 people, one faucet (dirty) is sole source of water for occupants, only a few rooms receive light and air from the outside, one toilet per 14 units, windowless and ventilates into windowless hall.

"Apartment house, 710 S. E. Union; 28 one-room apartments — stove heat — pipes through walls — 12 apartments without a window — only source of air is hall into which the one toilet on each floor ventilates over dwarf partitions. One bath for 14 apartments — broken plaster — filth — bed bugs — fire hazard. *Leased by a well known realty company that is taking a leading part in opposing Housing Committee.*"[18]

Conditions of this sort had been intensifying for some time, but it was not until the federal government in 1918 threatened to send their shipbuilding orders elsewhere unless Portland improved its housing stock that the local business-political leadership took notice. Even the conservative, business-oriented *Oregon Voter* was impelled to editorialize:

"No friends, we are not talking about Patterson, New Jersey, but our own Rose City of Portland, Oregon. . . . The editor went . . . and saw for himself. . . . The conditions are serious. . . . Portland must give the problem intelligent and humane attention or it will have something more serious on its civic conscience than it has had for many a year."[19]

Portland's businessmen and bankers, however, did not perceive any private or public role in the eradication of slum housing as such. Apart from the passage of housing and building codes, they drew a line when it came to governmental actions that threatened to assume functions traditionally reserved for private enterprise, except in particular instances where private investment could obviously not be expected to reap a profit. Housing for the shipyard workers, as distinct from that for the chronically poor, was a legitimate federal responsibility, according to Abbot Mills.

"Portland cannot furnish such funds. It is just as essentially a part of the duty of the government to provide money for building houses for workers to live in as it is to finance shipbuilding yards to build ships.[20]

Mills was fearful that with the war's end such houses would be abandoned after the shipyards closed. The federal government could move or tear them down with ease but private owners could not afford to do so.

Impact of Streetcar Lines

The unguided city growth that helped to create the slum districts and exacerbate the housing problems was integrally tied to the expansion of the

Housing for wartime workers was the object of criticism from both local and national sources. On the right is an example of tenement housing; shown below is a workingman's hotel.

Goose Hollow District — 1915

electric streetcar lines and interurban railroads. In addition to the visual pollution of poles and wires, the heavy electric cars were noisy. As a result, residential property immediately along the streetcar routes became less desirable. Those householders who could afford to moved away and their "abandoned" property became attractive to commercial development. The property could be purchased for a reasonable price and the houses converted into stores and shops.[21]

Most of the working class districts, with the exceptions of St. Johns and Goose Hollow, harbored a heavy concentration of streetcar and railroad tracks, e.g., Slabtown, Buckman, Sunnyside, Albina. South Portland, with the highest concentration of tracks, also contained the most severe slum conditions. In the case of Goose Hollow, the heavily used Jefferson Street car line had a noticeably deteriorating effect on adjacent properties.

Albina's history[22] provides a first rate example of what can happen to an urbanized community that grows without long term public planning and historical perspective, or of what can befall a human settlement that is controlled by private economic interests concerned mostly with immediate profits. Through much of its early existence, Albina was essentially a company town, controlled by the Oregon Railway and Navigation Company and its successor, the Union Pacific Railroad. Following a common pattern in American history, the gradual expansion of non-residential uses of land produced mixtures of use, often to the detriment of each, and every new non-residential use decreased the residential population. This development tended to drive out the more affluent white and in turn attract the poor white and the black.

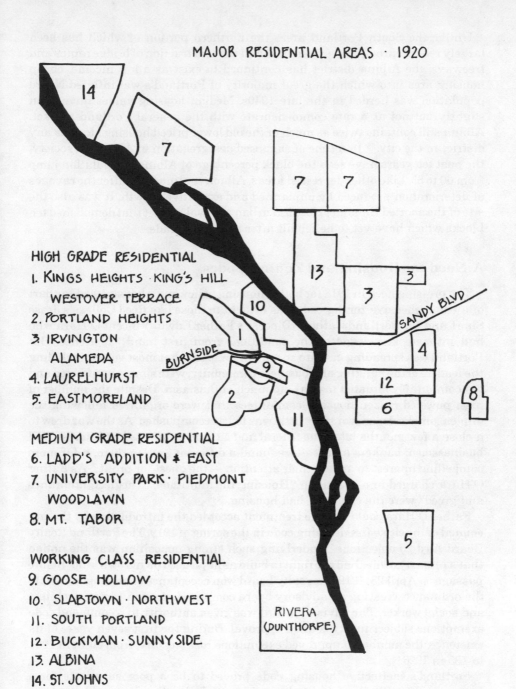

14

7

7 7

13

3 3

SANDY BLVD

10

1

4

BURNSIDE

9

12

8

2

6

11

5

RIVERA
(DUNTHORPE)

HIGH GRADE RESIDENTIAL
1. KINGS HEIGHTS · KING'S HILL
    WESTOVER TERRACE
2. PORTLAND HEIGHTS
3. IRVINGTON
    ALAMEDA
4. LAURELHURST
5. EASTMORELAND

MEDIUM GRADE RESIDENTIAL
6. LADD'S ADDITION & EAST
7. UNIVERSITY PARK · PIEDMONT
    WOODLAWN
8. MT. TABOR

WORKING CLASS RESIDENTIAL
9. GOOSE HOLLOW
10. SLABTOWN · NORTHWEST
11. SOUTH PORTLAND
12. BUCKMAN · SUNNYSIDE
13. ALBINA
14. ST. JOHNS

45

Unlike the South Portland area, the northern portion of which has been largely rebuilt through urban renewal and the construction of bridge ramps and freeways, the Albina district has continued to exist as a low income, cheap housing area into which the great majority of Portland's war-inflated Negro population was herded in the late 1940s. Median housing values have risen slightly but not at a rate commensurate with the general Portland market. Albina still contains twice as much of the old lower priced housing stock as any district in the city.[23] In a time of supposed desegregation in American society, the past ten years have seen the black percentage of Albina's population jump from 60 to 85. Like other depressed areas, Albina continues to suffer the ravages of deterioration produced by unplanned and exploitive growth. It was also the site of the aborted Emanuel Hospital urban renewal project that demolished ten blocks which have yet to be rebuilt after nearly a decade.

A Need for Housing and Zoning Codes

The pressing need in 1918 for both a housing policy and a housing code as part of a comprehensive zoning code was evident to those like Reed College's Jesse Short and the Portland Catholic Diocese's Father Edwin Vincent O'Hara who had intimate knowledge of the conditions from first hand experience. But Portland was spreading out into so many new areas that most voters, including the leaders of the banking and business community, were simply unaffected and too comfortably situated to work up much enthusiasm. Despite the number of high powered citizen housing committees that were organized following the unpleasant disclosures of 1918, little was to be accomplished. As the war drew to a close a few months later, the federal and city governments lost interest, and businessmen, bankers and realtors found a different and, to them, a far more compelling interest to attract their attention — the quest for profits. As Father O'Hara charged in a speech on "Housing the Multitude," "neglect, ignorance and greed" were the causes of bad housing."[24]

Father O'Hara could cite the treatment accorded the introduction by the city council of the city's first housing code in the spring of 1919. The Portland Realty Board filed 26 objections. Underlying such strong opposition was the notion that a property owner had the right to build as he pleased on his own land. Before passage on April 23, 1919, the realty board won acceptance of an amendment to the ordinance, creating an advisory board comprised of a contractor, architect and social worker. The advisory board was given authority to recommend code exemptions subject to city council approval. During the first seven years of its existence, the number of approved exemptions rose steadily, from eight in 1921 to 135 in 1926.[25]

Portland's ineffective housing code proved to be a poor substitute for a housing policy. But it would be almost 60 years before the city would develop a positive housing policy that was more than a limited housing code.

Chapter 3

The Early Jewish Communities

In the minds of many Portlanders, the early Jewish community is usually associated with South Portland, the area west of the Willamette River that contained some of the city's worst slum settlements prior to the first world war. A Jewish community did develop in South Portland, but not until the late 1890s, and it was populated largely by immigrants from Eastern Europe and Russia.

The South Germans

Most of Portland's earliest Jewish immigrant families came from rural Bavarian and Bohemian towns in Southern Germany and they tended to settle in the downtown area, often living above their stores or places of employment in the early years. A number of Portland's most prominent families in the decade before the war came from this early immigrant group: Meier, Goldsmith, Fleischner, Mayer, Hirsch, Jacobs and Simon, just to mention of few of them. The first Jewish congregation was organized in 1858 and the first synagogue, Temple Beth Israel, was built in 1861 in the heart of the downtown, at S. W. Fifth Avenue and Oak Street.

Following a pattern of commercial activity that was similar to that pursued by early Jewish immigrants in other parts of the United States, many of the men became peddlers. After accumulating sufficient resources they opened small stores near the river along Front and Yamhill Streets. As to the pattern of settlement, however, Portland's early Jewish families experienced conditions that proved to be fairly unique in American society. With apparent ease they quickly became integrated into the city's community life. They established reputations for integrity and civic responsibility while at the same time building prosperous enterprises in wool manufacturing and the merchandising of dry goods, clothing, furniture, jewelry and groceries. Some years ago, Portland Rabbi Julius Nodel commented upon the unique experience of the early Jewish merchants and their families:

> "Before the mass of Eastern European immigration hit Portland, there was no trace of a specific Jewish neighborhood. A ghetto in Portland was non-existent. Physically and socially Jews lived and worked next to Christians; they had a firm sense of belonging; they were Northwesterners body and soul."[1]

Although no particular residential pattern emerged, as the city moved into its third decade many of the more prosperous Jewish families located close to the

47

north Park Blocks, from Salmon to Clay Streets and from the Park Blocks west to Twelfth Avenue. Temple Beth Israel moved to Twelfth and Main in 1889. Seven years earlier, the Calvary Presbyterian Church, currently called The Old Church, had been built four blocks south on Clay Street to minister to the needs of William S. Ladd and other prominent gentiles who lived in the area. In subsequent years, the residential mix became even more heterogeneous with the Henry Ladd Corbetts, Simon Bensons, Abraham Meiers, Ben Sellings, Sigmund Franks, Ralph Jacobs, C. A. Dolphs and Isaac Gevurtzes all residing nearby, with their children attending either the Portland Academy or the Ladd (formerly Park) School. The fact that the Ladd School, on the site of the present Portland Art Museum, had the largest enrollment of any elementary school in Portland in 1914 (1176 pupils) indicates the size and variety of the urban neighborhood that once thrived on the edge of the downtown core. Today, neither the north Park Blocks nor the Portland State University district that includes the southern portion of the Park Blocks supports any elementary school.

Success in Business and Public Life

From their earliest years in Portland, the more successful Jews exhibited a strong sense of public responsiblity and an appetite for public life. Two of Portland's earliest mayors came from this group: Bernard Goldsmith (1869-71)

The Florentine styled houses of the Isaac and Ralph Jacobs families on the north side of Montgomery Street, present site of the Ione Plaza, in the South Park Blocks — Portland State University district

Temple Beth Israel, S. W. Main Street and 12th Avenue. Erected in 1889 by the German Jews. Destroyed by fire in 1923. Over the years, Beth Israel was identified with the German ethnic element inclined towrd reform Judaism, with a congregation that represented the upper crust of Jewish society in Portland.

Ladd School

and Philip Wasserman (1871-73), a pioneer banker and co-founder of the First National Bank. Austrian born Louis Fleischner served as State Treasurer (1870-74) and Bavarian native Joseph Simon reigned as the state's Republican boss for almost 40 years until he retired from active politics in 1911. Simon was a partner in Portland's most prestigious law firm (Dolph, Mallory, Simon & Gearin) that represented the legal and corporate interests of the early Corbetts, Failings and Ladds among others. He served in the state senate for 14 years, the United States Senate for five years and was the mayor of Portland from 1909 to 1911. Merchant Solomon Hirsch, partner in the dry goods firm of Fleischner & Mayer — the largest such enterprise west of the Mississippi River — and also a native of Bavaria, made an equally significant, if not more honorable, contribution to Oregon's public life with 11 years in the state senate and three years as U. S. Minister to Turkey. Staunchly conservative, Hirsch should be remembered as one of Oregon's most ethical Republicans — an intriguing accomplishment in the light of his party's reputation at the time.[2] As a candidate for the United States Senate in 1885, he missed by one vote — his own — of being elected by the legislature in a tumultuous session that was marked by the worst kind of political chicanery.

For a quarter of a century until his death in 1931, the outstanding Jewish leader in Portland was merchant Ben Selling. So well regarded was he by Jew and gentile alike that he was chosen as the first recipient of the First Citizen Award in 1928, much to the credit of the Portland Realty Board. There was irony in this selection because Ben Selling possessed none of the acquisitive instincts so often associated with the realty trade. As Rabbi Nodel admiringly noted:

"The man who most vigorously translated the 'Love thy neighbor . . . ' commandment into daily action was Ben Selling, self-appointed champion not only of Russian Jews, but of suffering humanity anywhere."[3]

Born in San Francisco in 1852, Selling was brought to Portland in his tenth year by his family after his father had opened a general merchandise store. As a young man, Selling launched a wholesale boot and shoe business and then opened a clothing store, both of which seemed to thrive. Although he was to die a millionaire, Selling viewed money as a means, not as an end. Making a living was of secondary importance to him. As his son Dr. Lawrence Selling told Rabbi Nodel, his real purpose in life was to help his fellow man. "Giving was his hobby and his passion."[4] And he gave profusely. Through his efforts and his own contributions, Portland raised $100,000 for Armenian Relief work, more per capita than any other city in America. During the depressions of 1893 and 1907 he established kitchens for the unemployed that served over 450,000 meals for 5 cents each. For this effort he was named the founder of "The Workingman's Club." He was a major supporter of the Waverly Baby Home and the Jewish Neighborhood House in South Portland. He established the scholarship loan fund at the University of Oregon Medical School and funded the Oriental Jewish

Ben Selling

manuscript collection of the Hebrew Union College Library in Cincinnati. The list could be extended for pages. Suffice it to say, Ben Selling probably gave away more money in proportion to his income than any Oregon citizen since the state was founded.

In contrast to many of his Jewish and gentile friends, Selling did not try to prove his worth to anyone. He lived simply and unostentatiously. He did not aspire to move to higher ground, although he and his wife did move to the upper floors of the Hotel Benson the last decade of his life. During the World War, he bought $400,000 worth of Liberty Bonds and wore the same business suit for three years. His reply to a reporter's query as to how one could conserve clothing during the war was in true character: "There is no sense in people buying so many suits; they should wear their old ones."[5] A lack of pretentiousness marked his office activity as well as his personal attire.

> "A steady stream of indigent students, bankrupt businessmen, itinerant beggars, traveling institutional solicitors, campaign directors, Old World rabbis . . . found their way into his cluttered little office, which consisted of only a desk and an extra chair tucked away in a tiny corner. . . . The extra chair was usually occupied by some supplicant."[6]

Ben Selling was a man of strong beliefs despite his tolerance of others and their differences. According to his daughter-in-law he had "a very austere reputation. . . . He was a very opinionated man with marvelous opinions."[7] He practiced what he preached, not only in philanthropy but in public life as well. After a short spell on the Port of Portland Commission, he accepted appointment as a charter member to the Portland Dock Commission — a tour of duty that lasted for ten years. He was elected to the state senate in 1910 and was the clear

51

choice for senate president during the 1911 session. Defeated by Harry Lane for the United States Senate in 1912, he remained in the state senate until he ran for the assembly in 1914. As could be expected he was chosen house speaker. He is only the third person in Oregon's history to have held both legislative leadership posts. In the tradition of Solomon Hirsch, whose family endowed a wing of the Portland Art Museum, Ben Selling was an honorable, public spirited and generous Republican — a true conservative in the best sense of the term.

The year following Ben Selling's death, four of the more than 40 employees who had worked for him in various of his stores filed suit in district court, claiming that Selling had told them on different occasions that he planned to will his business to his employees. Roscoe C. Nelson, the attorney for Selling's estate, asserted during the trial that such claims were indeed ridiculous. He described Selling as a man of unimpeachable integrity who wrote everything down. Such a momentous decision would never have been left out of his will. Nelson related how Selling had kept the stores functioning during the depression in order to benefit the employees, although he had every reason to retire due to his advanced age of 80. He always paid high salaries and year-end bonuses to those who deserved them. Losing the lower court decision, the employees carried their case to the state supreme court which in turn affirmed the previous action.[8]

Two neighbors of Ben Selling's who were later arrivals but of German stock were Sigmund Frank and Isaac Gevurtz — two men of the same age whose families were to have a significant impact on the future shaping of Portland. Although Gevurtz was of Silesian extraction, his wife was German and the family identified with the Temple Beth Israel ethnic element. I. Gevurtz and Sons that opened in 1881 on S. W. Front Street developed over the years into one of Portland's leading furniture enterprises. Starting as a second hand furniture credit store — $1 down and $1 a week — the business grew into a full-fledged wholesale and retail operation that generated considerable equity.

In the decade before the war, oldest son Philip, who was running the business for Isaac, launched the company on a program of extensive real estate and construction activity that furnished Portland some of its finest hotels and apartment houses. Unfortunately for the family, Philip was a "wheeler-dealer" type who overextended his credit lines, and with the recession of 1914 the company went into bankruptcy. The Multnomah, Mallory, Philip and Carlton Hotels were taken over and sold by the First National Bank as were the Highland Court, American, Cecelia, Lois and Lilian Apartments. The Foster Hotel, designed for the working class and built on the site of a famous 19th century house of ill-fame in the North Burnside district, suffered the same fate. Had Isaac Gevurtz been physically well enough to resume the company's direction, the bank had informed him that not only would it not foreclose on the properties but that it would loan the company any amount needed, so well regarded was he for his integrity and financial acumen. But such was not to be case. After a lingering illness, Isaac died in March of 1917.[9]

The Gevurtz family reorganized the business and under the able direction of three younger sons the furniture company never again fell on hard times.

Sigmund Frank, a native of Bechtheim, Germany, arrived in Portland in 1872 to take a job clerking for Aaron Meier who ran a small general merchandise store on S. W. Front Street. Trained as a professional musician, Frank had met Meier in San Francisco and the elder merchant had taken a liking to the young man. Frank more than proved his worth and was made a partner in 1874, thus giving birth to the firm of Meier & Frank. In 1885, Sigmund married Aaron's daughter, Fanny, whom, legend has it, he had been instructing in piano and violin.

When Aaron Meier died in 1889 at age 58, Sigmund took over the store and in 21 years at the helm "made the name Meier & Frank known throughout the Pacific Coast country." He never sought public office but he gave of his time and means freely, although not on a par with Ben Selling. Because of his interest in music he is credited with having "established the early professional music life of Portland which later developed into the Portland Symphony Orchestra."[10]

The Multnomah Hotel

Opened by Philip Gevurtz with great fanfare in 1912. Portland's largest, it was acquired by Eric Hauser and thrived for many years. Today it is a federal government office building.

Sigmund Frank did, in fact, perform as the principal violinist with the symphony for several years before his death.

In subsequent years, Meier & Frank became Oregon's leading department store. It made a lot of money for both families prior to its acquisition by the May Company in the period 1965-1967. It also propelled a member of each family into Oregon's public limelight. Aaron's youngest son, Julius, was to become governor in 1931 and Sigmund's youngest son, Aaron, was to become Portland's most influential business leader in the 1940s and '50s, with a close tie to city politics. Upon Sigmund Frank's death in 1910, the store's presidency went to Aaron Meier's oldest son and Sigmund's nephew, Abraham Meier, who was a close friend and neighbor of Ben Selling and Simon Benson.

By the beginning of the war, Portland's Jewish community numbered approximately 8000, the great majority of whom had arrived during the previous two decades. The total has varied little over the past 65 years although in the mid-twenties it rose to 11,000. The bulk of the new immigrants came from Slavic lands and this factor was to cause a number of problems for the older more established German ethnic elements. Temple Beth Israel attempted to keep its membership lists "pure from Eastern-European infiltration."[11] Even Ben Selling had to draw the line. Giving generous financial help was one thing, but close personal and social contact was an entirely different matter. Most of the new arrivals from "the Russian pale" were directed to settle in the lower income property section of South Portland. The district became known as "Little Russia." By 1914, one-fourth of the pupils enrolled in the Failing Grammar School, located in the heart of the district, were of Russian extraction.

South Portland: A Jewish Ghetto?[12]

The so-called "Jewish ghetto" of South Portland dates back to the end of the 19th century, a period that witnessed the movement of over two million Jews from Eastern Europe to this country. The Jews fled not only to escape conscription into the Czar's anti-Semitic army but also to remove themselves and their families from the imminent threat of the pogrom. Although many thousands of the new immigrants remained implanted on the East Coast, a number of enterprising and adventurous Jews pioneered their way to the West.

Initially, the Jews chose to settle where they were welcome, where they sensed a comfortable rapport with their neighbors. The language was alien to them, and they possessed little money and few skills or connections with which to facilitate their entrance into American society. The fraternal warmth which the Jews exuded toward one another was, therefore, a saving grace. Upon entering a strange, cold city, they could always contact a relative or a friend. The existence of relatives who had previously arrived in America played a significant role in determining where these immigrants finally settled.

Indeed, one might even view the perpetuation of the "Jewish ghetto" in the United States as being a result of an immigrant's fundamental concern for

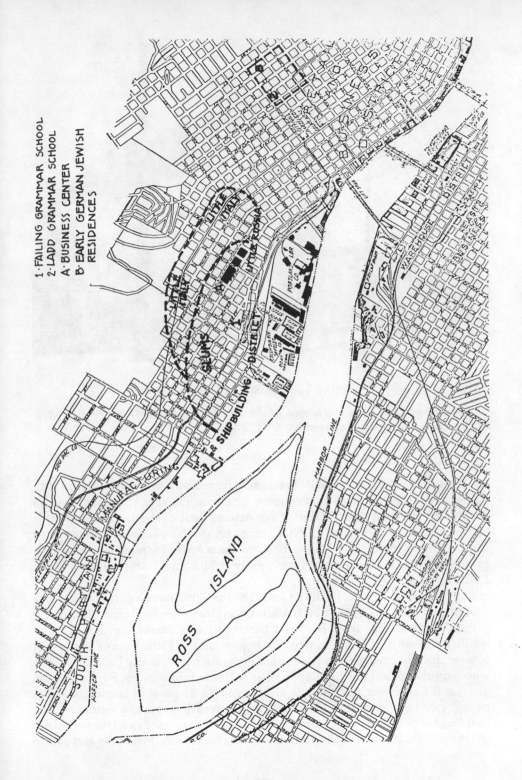

1. FAILING GRAMMAR SCHOOL
2. LADD GRAMMAR SCHOOL
A. BUSINESS CENTER
B. EARLY GERMAN JEWISH RESIDENCES

Congregation Shaarie Torah

Erected in 1905 as an offshoot of Neveh Zedek that was experiencing internal dissension. Located on S. W. First.

relatives, religion, basic life style and ease of fraternization when mingling with fellow Jews. Coupled with this concern for commodious environment was an even more important trait — that of self-determination. The Jews brought this trait with them from Europe and it became very much a part of their lives when they settled in the United States. The two traits were of utmost importance in establishing the strong sense of "community" which was characteristic of South Portland until after World War I.

The "Jewish ghetto" in Portland from 1890 until 1920 was located on property now largely occupied by the South Auditorium Urban Renewal area. Geographically, the ghetto ran from Harrison Street to Curry Street, going north and south, and from the Willamette River to approximately Fifth Avenue, going east to west. Interspersed among the Jewish population were many Italian families who moved to South Portland upon their entrance into the city. For both these groups, the area was amenable to all their needs. The cost of housing was not excessively high since, by the end of the nineteenth century, a number of the buildings were already beginning to exhibit tell-tale signs of age. Due to the lack of transportation, most of the Jewish peddlers had to rely on a horse and cart to haul their wares; close proximity to the city's core area made the junk business more convenient. For the first two decades of the twentieth century, the main artery to the downtown area was the streetcar that ran along First Avenue from Fulton to Grant; it then went up Grant Street to Third Avenue, turned on Third and proceeded back to the center of town. Thus, South Portland was an area that furnished the residents with both convenient accessibility to the city and affordable housing.

The "hub" of the neighborhood, the business center, was located on First Avenue and Front Street, between Arthur and Sherman. There one found the kosher markets, the drugstores, the "deli's" and the bakeries: Mr. Cottell's drugstore, Mr. Harper's deli, Mosler's bakery, Korsun's market and Colistro & Halprin's grocery, one of Portland's unique institutions. Colistro was a southern Italian and Halprin a Russian Jew.

Until the Depression, community life in South Portland was extremely active.

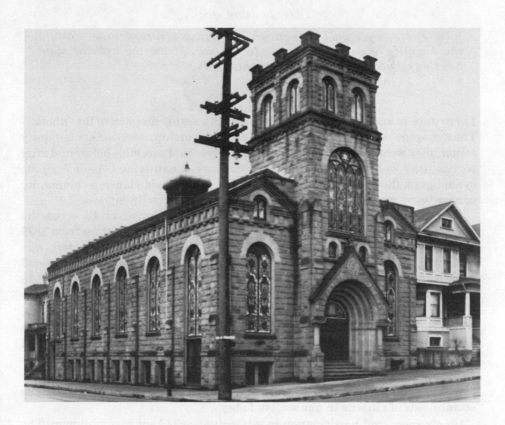

Congregation Neveh Zedek

Erected in 1904 to serve the Russian immigrants. Located at S. W. 6th Avenue and Hall Street, it was destroyed in 1964.

57

Older housing stock

S. W. First Avenue and Sherman Street. This was a fringe area, separating the majority of Jewish residents to the north from the extreme slum housing adjacent to the world war shipyards.

There were, at one time, six synagogues within walking distance of the "ghetto." The synagogues provided people with a place of worship as well as a community center; they were meeting places where the Jews could assemble before and after service; they were places for family fun and social gatherings. Aside from the synagogues, the immigrants also had the Neighborhood House, a community service agency run by the wealthier, first generation German Jews.

The Neighborhood House was originally located on First and Hall, across the street from Shaarie Torah synagogue. It remained at that location from 1899 until 1910, when a new building, on Second Avenue and Woods Street, was dedicated. The real importance of the Neighborhood House was that it offered Americanization and sewing classes for all the immigrants who desired to attend. The B'nai B'rith for men, the Hassadh for women, the South Parkway club for couples, and the synagogues, the Neighborhood House and the B'nai B'rith Building for everyone, supplied the necessary social interaction for the Jewish and Italian communities. The Italians, though, were much less inclined towards involvement in groups than were the Jews. In effect, the synagogues and community centers fulfilled a role for their participants not entirely dissimilar to men's organizations and country clubs that fulfill the various social needs of citizens in our society today.

Involvement and participation in city politics was kept to a minimum. The men were concerned about national politics, voting and obtaining their citizenship papers, but, aside from those aims, their attention was focused primarily upon the inner community of South Portland. The women, as such,

S. W. Caruthers and First Street

were never involved in politics or city affairs. They remained at home, cared for the children, and attempted to retain some of the warmer, happier memories and traditions of the Old Country.

For the great majority of Jews, education was the paramount concern; without it, one simply could not progress in life. The yearning for an education was further stimulated by the Jews' sense of self-determination and eagerness to get ahead. Dropping out of school rarely occurred. The residents of South Portland were so inwardly oriented that they not only had their own newspaper, but they nominally denoted an acknowledged leader as "mayor."

South Portland could thus be characterized as a tightly interwoven complex of forces — as a self-contained entity. Life was focused upon the inner community and not the external world, upon the peer group and not involvement in city-wide politics.

One of the crucial elements of life in South Portland, from 1890 until 1920, was the weekend informal street activity. The visiting which transpired was perhaps the most important form of entertainment for the Jews. Every Saturday evening, after the Sabbath had been observed, the residents would stroll up and down the streets chatting with their friends and relatives as they went. The busiest area was along First Avenue from Caruthers to Sherman. Neighbors would visit one another and refreshments would always be served. Meanwhile, the stores were opened for a few hours while the strollers passed by. The streets were alive and teeming with activity as the Jews meandered through the community eating their sunflower seeds, buying ice-cream, or stopping at the

Gem Theatre to view the weekly serial.

With time, the area felt the pressures of change. Increasingly, more and more people began to move away. When the Jews went so did the Italians, many of whom moved to the southeast section of the city around Clinton Street and even into Ladd's Addition. In fact, many of the early residents of Ladd's Addition were Italian truck farmers. Prosperity for some and "The American Way" for most, spurred many families to purchase residences in the "nicer" sections of Portland. Whereas the wealthiest of the German Jews moved to Portland Heights and even to Dunthorpe. Others, including the more successful Russian and Polish Jews, moved to Irvington, Laurelhurst and the Westover Terraces.

The most successful of the Russian Jews, and probably the most successful of all Jewish immigrants to Portland, was Sam Schnitzer. In 1935, he told his story to *The Oregon Journal*. It is a unique account and merits repeating in full.

"I was born in Russia on July 12, 1880. My father and my three brothers all live in Portland. I came to the United States when I was 24 years old. I was drafted into the Russian army in 1903, when I was 23 years old. Right then Russia was preparing to fight Japan, but I didn't feel that I wanted to kill any Japanese or have any Japanese people kill me, so I watched my chance and without consulting the captain of my company I resigned one night and escaped into Austria. I had no money. I tried very hard to get a job at a dollar a week but nobody seemed to need my services. So I wrote to my uncle who had gone to the United States to send me $110 to pay for my ticket to New York City. He sent me the money, but the letter was addressed wrong and it was returned to the dead letter office and finally sent back to him. He wrote me again, enclosing the money, but this was four months after I had deserted from the Russian army, and most of that time I went on very short rations.

When I got to New York I got a job at $4 a week. Four other young men and myself rented a room at $7.50 a month. That meant it cost me $1.50 a month for a place to sleep. No, we didn't have beds; we slept on the floor. I allowed myself 5 cents for breakfast and 10 cents for dinner. Out of my salary of $208 for the year I managed to save $85. I bought a second-class ticket to Portland, arriving here in 1905.

I found there were lots of junkmen in Portland, so I went to work for Sam Nudelman, working in his tobacco store at $6 a week, working 16 hours a day. When I had saved $45 I went down to Astoria and started in business for myself. I had no money to buy a horse or wagon, so I started in the junk business, and I was my own horse and wagon. I bought old sacks, brass and copper, old iron and bottles, and carried them on my back till I got as much as I could carry. Then I would take them to a yard where I stored them. If I bought an old kitchen range or some heavy article I would wait till I had bought enough to make a load, and then would hire an express wagon to go around with me and collect them and haul them to the dock. I shipped them to Portland.

After three years I came to Portland and started in the junk business here. One day I went to the basement of the Portland Hotel to bid on some junk. There I met another junkman, named Henry Wolf. We talked the matter over and decided to go into business. We took in a third man, each of us agreeing to put up $1000. When it came time to put up the money, Henry said he had a large horse and a wagon, which he would put in at $250. He had some old junk in his basement which he would put in at $300. I had a lot of pipes that I had bought from the Union Oil company after its big fire. I put these in at $500. When it came to putting up the cash, Henry and my partner and I found that all of us had figured on the others putting up the cash, as we were all short of cash. After a few months Henry Wolf and I bought out our partner, and Wolf and I went in together, agreeing to put the cash into the partnership when we had made it out of the business.

We decided to call our firm the Alaska Junk Company. We started in a little building with 25-foot frontage at 227 Front Street. The man we had bought out prospered, and eight years later came to us and wanted to buy back his third interest, but Henry and I decided not to take any partners.

I was married in the fall of 1906 to Rosa Finkelstein. Like myself, my wife was born in Russia. We have seven children — five boys and two girls."[13]

In the 70 years since Sam Schnitzer and Henry Wolf formed their partnership — it later dissolved with some bitterness — the Schnitzer family has created a veritable empire of diverse enterprises that are world-wide in scope. Although one of the five sons operates independently, together the total assets of the Schnitzer family holdings exceed $200 million. None of them has yet approached Ben Selling in generosity, but each has made his way into the upper echelons of Portland's residential or cultural life. As a family, the Schnitzers have come a long distance from S. W. Arthur Street, in South Portland between First and Second Avenues, where Sam lived until 1920.

The Dispersal of the Jewish Community

Perhaps the most important single factor in the dispersal of the South Portland Jewish population was the growing use of the automobile. The advent of the "auto" changed the entire concept of "city." The people of South Portland were no longer required to walk to a friend's home, stroll to the corner store, or take a streetcar downtown. People's social lives were drastically altered. The area deteriorated badly and with the introduction of the shipyards before the war, a commercial-industrial invasion took over. The first city zoning code of 1924 divided the district between general manufacturing-commercial and unrestricted manufacturing.

Since 1970, through the combined efforts of the city government and various neighborhood groups, plans have been approved to downzone further the area between Barbur Boulevard and the interstate freeway, to make it possible to retain the community as a predominately residential district. Historical conservation restrictions are going into effect and many of the older homes are being restored. South Portland, below the urban renewal area, is still a low income district. Although the median family income rose slightly from 1960 to 1970, the median housing value actually doubled, a statistic that reflects a less intense but still a substantial amount of home improvement before the policy changes of the 1970s. The ratio of owner-occupied to renter-occupied units was as low as any in the city in 1970 (1-1),[14] but this condition has improved in the past

The American Way

Sigmund Frank's eldest son, Lloyd, built this grandiose estate on Palatine Hill in Dunthorpe in the early 1920s. Currently the site of Lewis and Clark College, "Fir Acres" surpassed all others with the possible exception of Theodore B. Wilcox's estate on the West Slope.

Max Hirsch built his Portland Heights mansion in the early 1920s on S. W. Prospect Drive. No relation to Solomon, Max was a cousin of Mrs. Aaron Meier and a native of Bavaria. He worked for Meier & Frank before starting the Hirsch-Weiss and White Stag Companies.

The Max Hirsch Mansion on Portland Heights

few years. Present trends would indicate that the South Portland-Lair Hill district will continue to attract older and younger adults but fewer families with children. The nearly inaccessible Failing Elementary School has been closed for years. With the rerouting of some traffic patterns, the area may regain some of its former human activity — minus the children playing in the streets.

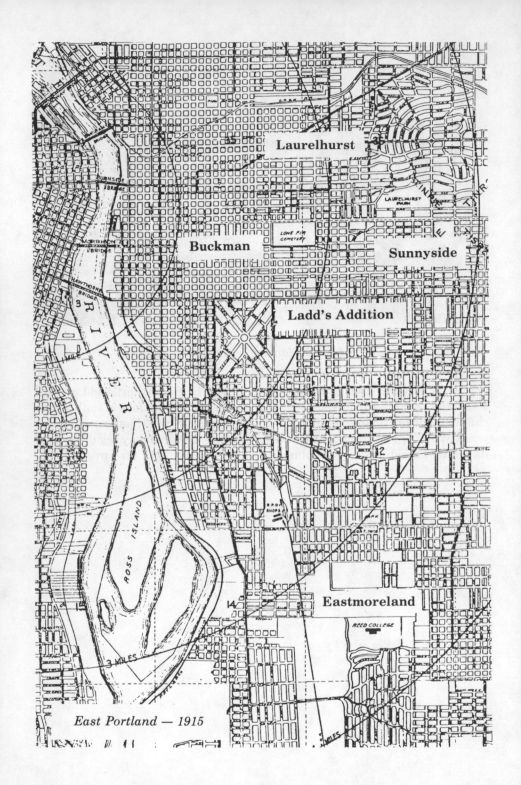

Laurelhurst

Buckman

Sunnyside

Ladd's Addition

Eastmoreland

East Portland — 1915

64

Chapter 4

Money and Mobility:
Some Real Estate Trends

Money was the name of the game. "One way to make money — one sure way," declared Portland Realty Board president Frank L. McGuire, "is to invest in Portland real estate and to become foremost in the maelstrom of activity which is inevitable."[1]

This ever-optimistic real estate promoter was anticipating a glorious post-war development three months before America even declared war. Early in 1917, Portland was beginning to hit its stride again after a lull of almost three years. "Real estate will soon be real estate once more," McGuire proclaimed. "The chances for the investor to make money are similar to those offered at the time of the Lewis and Clark fair."[2]

For almost a decade after the exposition opened in June of 1905, Portland had experienced its most explosive population and construction boom,[3] and the realtors had not forgotten it. In fact, the Portland Realty Board was organized in 1906 for the express purpose of promoting "the fulfillment of the city's destiny."[4] Growth! Included in its top command were individuals who played a predominate role in the physical shaping of the city — at least until after World War II. Many of the 1917 group, entrepreneurs like Frank McGuire, were young and relative newcomers, but they were aggressive and dedicated to their cause. The interests of the old families were also well represented, particularly by four civic activists: Seattle native Paul C. Murphy, Bostonite E. B. MacNaughton and the Strong brothers, Frederick H. and Robert H., members of a prominent pioneer family and administrators of the old Corbett and Ladd estates. In 1928, the Realty Board was to become so imbued with its own advancement that it arrogated to itself the honor of annually selecting Portland's First Citizen, an award that has been faithfully and often deservedly bestowed with great seriousness for 51 years.

The Realty Board was primarily interested in new property investment and secondarily in the profitable improvement and sale of older properties. In 1915, at the low ebb of the market, some of is members even declared a willingness to donate large factory sites free to "commendable factory enterprises" that would utilize local raw materials.[5] As a group, the realtors were not interested in social problems stemming from the kind of slum housing conditions that shocked banker Abbot Mills. Furthermore, as Jesse Short revealed, it was not uncommon to find the worst slum residences leased to prominent realtors because, historically, slum housing has always produced a high rate of return for investors. Not surprisingly, the Realty Board leaders generally opposed all attempts to increase property taxes and to establish housing and zoning codes. In their almost total concern for the unrestricted pursuit of private profits, they disregarded with equal fervor the city's need for basic public services. In a letter to Joseph Teal, prominent merchant Leo Friede deplored the inability of the realtors and their friends to perceive a relationship between realty values and public services. Friede cited "the absolute indifference of our citizens to show any zeal or activity in what promotes the welfare of cities, namely public necessities."[6]

In the mid-twenties, the *Pacific Northwest Real Estate Bulletin*, under a column headed "Advice to Realtors," published an article entitled "How to Make Money." Four general principles were emphasized:

1. Always buy a corner lot of no less than 100 square feet.

2. Always buy on a thoroughfare, never on a side street. Two thoroughfares and transfer points are the best.

3. Always buy in front of progress, not behind it. Buy between the old business part of town and the best residential section.

4. Do not be afraid to buy too far out; growth will catch up.

The article concluded aphoristically: "Owning a piece of the earth is permanent! It cannot be taken away from you."[7]

The historical record would indicate that Portland's first families were thoroughly tutored in the principles of making money through real estate; however, their initial fortunes were derived from other ventures, especially river transportation, banking and merchandising — often interrelated. William S. Ladd, Henry W. Corbett, Cicero H. Lewis and Henry Failing, for example, not only founded banks but were early investors in numerous other enterprises, including transportation, utilities, insurance, manufacturing and of course real estate.

Ladd's private bank, Ladd & Tilton, built its assets on investments in business enterprises over which Ladd himself often gained control: The Portland Flouring Mills, headed by protege Theodore B. Wilcox, and The Oregon Iron & Steel Company, headed by son William M. Ladd, to name just two. An initial $50,000 bank investment grew to $15 million in 50 years. Ladd's vast real estate holdings in and around Portland were largely created, certainly in the early years, out of forfeited mortgages and defaulted bank loans. The properties had been wisely selected, and their value grew through careful management and patience. By 1909, sixteen years after Ladd's death, the Ladd estate property holdings were worth in excess of $5 million.

Residence Parks

Apart from a few choice downtown properties, most of William S. Ladd's real estate was acquired for either industrial or agricultural purposes. There is no evidence to indicate that Ladd envisioned planned urban or suburban developments on any of his properties with the sole exception of a 126 acre tract on the East Side that became known as Ladd's Addition. Ladd had secured ownership of the property in the early 1880s as part of a larger farm tract of 367 acres. It cost him about $10,000. Eleven years later, it was worth approximately $1 million.

There is no evidence to indicate who or what directly influenced Ladd to have his addition designed in a form so radically different from the traditional grid plan that afflicted most of Portland. He undoubtedly had read about the accomplishments of landscape architects like Frederick Law Olmsted. He, or one of his sons, may even have visited and viewed some of Olmsted's handiwork, especially his treatment of the grounds surrounding the nation's capitol building and the Washington Monument. But regardless, there can be no question that the Ladds had a unique concept of an urban garden village.

Ladd's Addition, along with some other "far out" properties to be developed by the Ladd estate, was a natural outgrowth of an eastern suburban movement that began to take form in the 1850s and which, in turn, was a product of a general rural cemetery and public parks movement. To be financially successful, developments like Ladd's Addition needed access to an efficient

Ladd's Addition, circa 1918

public transportation system and an ample supply of drinking water. It had both. In fact, William S. Ladd was to be accused of abusing his position as chairman of the Board of Water Commissioners when he directed that the main Bull Run water conduit be built under Division Street, the southern boundary of the addition.

The Oregonian Souvenir, 1892, published the earliest description of Ladd's addition. The account was most likely based on a personal interview. It is worth quoting in full.

> "Mr. Ladd has had the addition all platted and laid out and it is perhaps not going too far to assert that this is the most attractive addition ever put on the Portland market. The property is reached by three different lines of electric cars and is in every sense strictly inside city property.
>
> In no addition ever before put on the Portland market has such attention been paid to beautifying the property as Mr. Ladd is able to guarantee in the new Ladd's Addition. He has not only made every preparation to pave all the streets of the addition with asphaltum, at his own expense, but he has provided for supplying the residents of this tract with gas and electric lights, he has arranged for a splendid system of sewerage and drainage, a system perfected in the most modern lines of scientific research; he will lay sidewalks fronting on every block and he will have a perfect water system that will insure residents an ample supply of the purest water for domestic purposes. Mr. Ladd's well known aversion to the liquor traffic has led him to make provisions for excluding saloons from this tract for all time. He will allow no liquor to be sold on the property, a reservation which insures residents here the freedom from a great annoyance which has baffled the efforts of many of the residents of Portland to remedy, more especially where the saloon was located within the immediate vicinity of their homes."[8]

Riverview Cemetery — S. W. Portland — Developed by the Ladds

Ladd's Addition was developed slowly, over a span of some ten years before and after the first world war. By 1959, the neighborhood was to be zoned for duplex apartment density, with commercial and manufacturing along its borders. As one recent study has reported, "the effect of this unfortunate zoning is beginning to be evident in the general poorer condition of the residences" located close to the main arterials. And yet the fact that the basic integrity of the neighborhood has withstood the "assaults" of the last 25 years would indicate that Ladd's original scheme was sound even though it might be judged "antique by present standards."[9]

The Ladd Estate Company was incorporated in 1908 for one specific reason: The 1907 Oregon Banking Act required private banks to incorporate, thus opening their books to public scrutiny. Prior to 1908, all of the varied Ladd family investments had been managed through the Ladd & Tilton Bank, second in total assets to the Corbett's and Failing's First National Bank. In 1907, president William M. Ladd had lost $2.5 million through the failure of the Title Guarantee & Trust Company. To protect the Ladd & Tilton Bank, he accepted the financial backing of his brother-in-law, Standard Oil heir Frederick B. Pratt of Brooklyn, New York. By an exchange of stock, the Ladds relinquished control of Ladd & Tilton to Pratt. Although the Ladds and their associates continued to manage the bank, part of the agreement with Pratt was to spin off some of the real estate properties into a separate corporation, divest the other properties from bank control and gradually liquidate them.

In 1909, the Ladd Estate Company sold its 462 acre Hazelfern Farm to the Laurelhurst Company for roughly $2 million. Acquired in the early 1870s for an average of $20 an acre, these "far out" grazing lands for William Ladd's prize Guernsey and Jersey dairy herds returned a profit of over 2000 percent.[10] The purchasers, drawing on the experience of their general sales agent and co-investor, Paul C. Murphy, proceeded to plat a residential development of 444 acres that exceeded Ladd's Addition as an imaginative break from the older square grid pattern. Murphy had developed a similar Laurelhurst park in Seattle with the assistance of the Olmsted brothers, the sons of the late Frederick Law Olmsted of Brookline, Massachusetts. John Olmsted had helped to design the layout for the 1905 Lewis and Clark Exposition. He had also drafted a master plan for Portland's public park system in 1904. Portland's Laurelhurst appeared to reflect a distinct Olmsted influence.

The city had already developed eastward well beyond the Laurelhurst tract. The Rose City Park development was platted in 1907. Both districts were being served by the Sandy Boulevard streetcar line of the Portland Railway Light & Power system, but the Laurelhurst developers wanted a second line to bisect the tract along East Glisan Street. By the time the first homes were opened in early 1910, a Laurelhurst resident could make it to downtown in 15 minutes.

Laurelhurst's original plat contained a park approximately 30 acres in size. As the first houses were being built, the city purchased 31 acres for $92,000. Under the direction of E. T. Mische and Paul Keyser, the city park department created a natural wonderland: Swamps were drained; an artificial lake was constructed that was connected to an artificial stream with some simulated waterfalls; and nature trails and paved walks were installed within tree stands and garden settings. Ten years later the park was named the most beautiful in the West by the Pacific Coast Parks Convention.[11]

Here indeed was a "High Class Residence Park" as the Laurelhurst Company advertised its urban village. Prestige was related to restrictions that in turn were related to money and social class. Not only was the selling of alcoholic beverages prohibited, as per Ladd's Addition, but no apartments, hotels, flats, stables or commercial buildings of any sort were to be allowed. Adding a restriction that became common with prestige properties, there were to be no sales to Chinese, Japanese or Negroes. The Alameda Park development to the north of Laurelhurst wrote an even broader exclusion into its printed brochure: "No people of undesirable colors and kinds." Standard sized lots sold for approximately $2500 including improvement assessments, and houses had to cost at least $3000. The Laurelhurst Club was an added attraction, offering tennis and a center for neighborhood activities.

Legally, the Laurelhurst Company was divorced from the Ladd & Tilton Bank and the Ladd estate, but in reality the same people were running it. Edward Cookingham was president. He was also the vice president and chief executive officer of both the bank and the Ladd estate. Frederick H. Strong was secretary while continuing as manager of the estate. His brother Robert H. Strong was a director while serving as manager of the Corbett estate. The Corbetts and Ladds were intermarried and Henry Ladd Corbett served on the board of the Ladd & Tilton Bank while also an officer and director of the First National Bank. Seattle native Paul C. Murphy was the only outsider; he served as vice president and general sales agent. In 1918, Murphy was to be elected president of the Portland Realty Board.

Because of these kinds of relationship, it is unclear how much was actually paid to whom and by whom for the purchase of the Laurelhurst properties. Although $2 million was the published sale price, the Ladd estate, also called the Ladd Investment Company, assumed a mortgage of over $1 million. But regardless of whose interest lay where, the development proved successful. After one year in business, the Laurelhurst Company had sold 2300 lots for a total of $1,250,000.[12]

Over the years, Laurelhurst managed to maintain the identity and character that its original developers envisaged. In a sense, it has been a defended neighborhood, protected from the deterioration that has afflicted the mixed-use areas of the city, like Sunnyside to the south and Buckman to the west.[13] It has developed a community pride and has always been attractive to families in the middle income bracket. In the ever-mobile world of the prestige oriented it has maintained a high degree of stability in its resident population.[14] It has remained in its own eyes the "Addition with Character,"[15] even though the original racial exclusions were officially removed years ago. Prior to the mid-

Home of Paul C. Murphy
Laurelhurst

The Laurelhurst Club

71

Eastmoreland — 1953

Eliot Hall — Reed College (1913)

1950s, the Realty Board did not approve sales to Negroes in Portland's exclusive residence parks. In the 1970s, with property cost as the major discriminating factor, approximately one-half of one percent of Laurelhurst's population is black.

The Ladd estate's second residence park was located in the southeast corner of Portland in an area that came to be known as Eastmoreland. In this instance, the estate did not create a fictional development corporation as it had done for Laurelhurst. One reason may have been that William M. Ladd, president of both the Ladd & Tilton Bank and the Ladd Estate Company, took a personal interest in the establishment of Reed College.

Early in 1910, a few months after the Ladd Estate Company had decided to develop W. S. Ladd's Crystal Springs Farm property, William M. Ladd arranged for the donation of some 40 acres as the campus site on which to locate Reed College, which opened in the fall of 1911 in a leased building on S. W. Jefferson Street. He also contracted with the city's most prestigious architectural firm of Doyle, Patterson and Beach to design a master plan for both the college and an adjacent residential development that he hoped would emulate the Laurelhurst project. Two hundred and seventy-five acres containing 1270 home sites were platted. For Reed College, architect Albert E. Doyle conceived a grandiose scheme that was patterned upon one of the Oxford University college campuses. In subsequent years, the college received additional donations of land so that by 1926 the campus contained roughly 100 acres. The master plan was to undergo radical alteration over the years, with only three of the originally conceived "English collegiate gothic" structures actually being built.

The adjacent Eastmoreland residential development moved at a slow pace. The recession that began in 1914 had reduced real estate sales to a trickle. By 1916, three years after the college had moved into its new quarters, only 460 lots had been sold. Young realtor F. N. Clark devised some promotional literature that was loaded with snob appeal, giving particular attention to the Reed College connection. But the major drawback to Eastmoreland's progress, apart from the recession, was the lack of adequate streetcar service to the downtown. This condition was to afflict Eastmoreland residents for many years. In fact, by 1926, when the residents organized their own company and purchased for approximately $1 million all the undeveloped real estate, 428 home sites were still unsold.

One Eastmoreland attraction that was unique to Portland was the construction in 1917 of the first nine holes of the Eastmoreland Municipal Golf Course. Until the course opened for play on July 4, 1918, at a fee of 25 cents per round, Portland had only three golf clubs — all private: Waverley, Portland and Tualatin. In 1916, William Ladd had been persuaded to give the city park department the free use of 150 acres for six years. Former U. S. amateur champion H. Chandler Egan, a recently arrived resident of Medford, designed the course which proved immensely popular. In 1922, when the lease expired, Paul Keyser failed to persuade the city council to purchase the property for

$95,000 through a special tax levy, but he did succeed in having the course declared a public utility. This arrangement permitted the city to float utility certificates of indebtedness and to finance the purchase by subsequent fee revenues. In later years the city purchased additional acreage from the Ladd estate and Egan designed the second nine holes. During the early years of the Great Depression of the 1930s, the course was nearly closed due to indebtedness. It was saved by the issuance of life memberships for $100 each.[16]

Over the years Eastmoreland has followed a pattern of social development similar to that of Laurelhurst. In 1970, the median family income was the same, with the median housing value slightly higher. Eastmoreland's housing stock has greater variety at both ends of the scale. The most unique characteristic of the neighborhood, however, is the low ratio of rental housing, the lowest in Portland.[17] Eastmorelanders have tended to stay put. Their isolation and their ample recreational facilities in addition to their proximity to Reed College life have made the community unusually stable. The majority of the faculty, in the early years at least, lived near the college. The community was to fight several successful battles in defense of its territorial rights, mostly against the Southern Pacific Railroad. In the process, it established one of the strongest neighborhood associations in Portland.

The "Flats" and the Hills

Realtor F. N. Clark, into whose hands the Ladd estate had entrusted the sale of its Eastmoreland properties, was also deeply involved in the sale of Guild's Lake Industrial Center properties and adjacent homesites on the upper Westover Terraces addition in Northwest Portland. This unique land use project involved a double development: The creation of the terraces and the filling of Guild's Lake by dirt and gravel transferred from the terraces to the lake by giant hydraulic sluices. The Ladd estate owned a small portion of the flat property near the lake and Henry Ladd Corbett was an investor in the development of the terraces. Beginning in 1910, the developers built a 12 million gallon pumping station at the lake side. They then proceeded to transform the rough and steeply graded hillside of the Goldsmith tract into potentially appealing but bare residential sites, while at the same time conveying enough fill material over the distance of a mile to convert much of Portland's largest lake into 50 acres of dry land.

Guild's Lake had been the naturally beautiful site of the Lewis and Clark Exposition in 1905, but nothing remained in later years to commemorate either the explorers or the event that had honored them. By 1915, F. N. Clark had sold over $600,000 of Guild's Lake Industrial Center property. In March of that supposedly depressed year, Clark sold 56 lots for $161,000.

Hill property, like the riverfront industrial flats, was in high demand in the post-exposition era. As Howard Evarts Weed, a noted landscape architect, told the Portland Realty Board in 1911: "Nearly all American cities have their finest

Henry L. Pittock and his mansion

residences on the hills which command views of the surrounding city and country."[18] And Portland was no exception. Beginning in 1909, *The Oregonian* publisher Henry L. Pittock spent five years and an undetermined amount of money building Portland's finest mansion on Imperial Heights, the highest large residential site that could be reached by automobile and still command an eastward view stretching 180 degrees from Milwaukie to Sauvie Island. Pittock spared little in landscaping his 46 acre woodland that 50 years later would become the property of the Portland Park Bureau.

The move to the 22 room mansion from the six room cottage that Pittock had occupied for over 50 years on S. W. 10th was probably the most dramatic example of upward social mobility in Portland's history. When Pittock died five years later at the age of 83 he was to leave an estate worth millions, much of it acquired during the last 20 years of his life in collaboration with his son-in-law Frederick W. Leadbetter, who bought the Loewenberg mansion on King's Hill adjacent to City Park.

Portlanders of lesser resources than Henry Pittock, but with similar ambitions, had started building homes on Portland Heights in the late 1880s. Unfortunately, many of these early houses were literally stuck on property that "was laid out utterly disregarding the "topography."[19] Howard Weed's criticism of the engineering and basic planning for much of the early Portland Heights development was a rephrasing of some comments that Mayor Harry Lane had addressed to the city council in 1906. Lane had recommended a plan to terrace

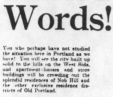

the hills by employing a system of contour approaches in place of the frightfully ugly and costly method now pursued of cutting them into square blocks and deep cuts, called streets, which are not only expensive but leave the land in many instances almost unapproachable."[20]

By 1909, due perhaps to the influence of people like John Olmstead, Mayor Lane and architect Ellis Lawrence, the majority of homes being constructed seemed to adapt more to the natural topography. Since most of the upper Portland Heights lots followed no set pattern or size limitation, a wide variety of building styles and shapes became possible.[21] Except for one four block section of the Heights, no multi-family residences have been permitted to date. Commercial activities have been limited to one grocery store, a couple of decorator antique shops and one gas station. The area is also served by two grade schools, two churches and one fire station. From its earliest development phase, Portland Heights benefited from efficient and accessible streetcar service, an advantage not fully shared by the later hillside developments of Kings and Arlington Heights and Westover Terraces.

The Kings and Arlington Heights Additions began development almost simultaneously with the organization of the Laurelhurst Company. In September 1909, the Amos King Estate sold 90 undeveloped acres to a local syndicate for $500,000, one of the largest real estate transactions recorded to that date. A year later the Arlington Heights Addition immediately to the south was platted for development. Both projects ran into construction and financial difficulties that were compounded by the recession of 1914. In December of that year, architect Ellis Lawrence, the first dean of the University of Oregon School of Architecture, wrote his former partner:

"About Kings Heights, it's a pretty nasty mess. Everything is gone as far as the stockholders are concerned unless some of the big men come thru and they will not until pressure is brought to bear on them which no one dares to do apparently. Kcasey has dumped some $15,000 into the project and has by some arrangement . . . taken over the whole thing. His gamble is on saving his investment. You might get some lots up there by assuming but we were up yesterday and there is absolutely nothing doing, houses unsold and but two or three living on the tract, the engineering is rotten, in grades, lines and lots."[22]

The Westover Terraces project experienced similar problems although it was more thoroughly engineered and planned than its neighbors to the south. All three of these hillside developments would not prove profitable until the 1920s. They provided a good example of the inherent risks of real estate investment, the importance of timing and the need for patience. Solid financial underwriting was essential. Within a generation their value as prestige properties would become apparent to the upwardly mobile affluent families who would move from the nearby "flats" in search of status and the highest levels that afforded the best views. Immediately following World War I, the hillside homes were to sell briskly for prices of as much as $5000, up 40 percent in two years.[23]

This 1918 view from Westover Terraces catches the northern portion of Northwest Portland's "Flats" — the Slabtown district — and takes in the southern portion of Guild's Lake. The Industrial Center fill is to the left of the Thurman Street baseball stadium. Swan Island, covered with tree growth is visible at the upper left; the Portland Flouring Mills plant is across the river, in the center; and the Balfour-Guthrie Oceanic Dock across the river at the far right.

The Northwest district was perhaps Portland's most diverse and densely populated region. The housing mix included low cost, workers' homes and apartments, directly to the right of the stadium, and some of Portland's finest old mansions along 19th Avenue to the Nob Hill neighborhood (not shown). Middle income row houses were popular just east of Nob Hill. Portland's two largest hospitals — Good Samaritan and St. Vincent — were just under the crest of Westover Terraces. The city's most socially prestigious church, Trinity Episcopal, moved in 1907 to N. W. 19th Avenue where it remains to this day.

The lumber mills, warehouses and docks along the waterfront provided employment to many of the local residents. Beginning in the late 1960s,

Northwest Portland was rediscovered. Through tighter zoning restrictions that have kept commercial and industrial encroachment limited, many old homes have been restored and traffic patterns re-directed. With a density of approximately 25,000 per square mile, Northwest Portland is the most densely populated area in Oregon. It is also one of the liveliest, with all varieties of human and commercial activity and the strongest neighborhood organization in Portland. To quote a recent study, Northwest Portland is a "diversity of old and young, families and singles, rich and poor, liberal and conservative. Multi-family and apartment buildings are intermixed with older single-family housing."[24]

The Northwest "Flats" area is unique in Portland. In contrast to Buckman and Sunnyside which were low rent workers' districts from their earliest years and which have continued to deteriorate, the Northwest has experienced a radical shift upward in home values and social cohesiveness. The containment of industrial and commercial intrusion has been a positive factor in this development. In the decade to 1970, the median housing value increased 250 percent. Included were the hillside homes, occupied mainly by higher income single families at a much lower density.

Suburban Estates

"To withdraw like a hermit and live like a prince — this was the purpose of the original creators of the suburb."[25] As the writings of Lewis Mumford have shown, the suburb became visible almost as early in history as the city itself. The suburb provided an escape from the density, noise and drabness of city life. For the wealthy, a life of privacy and princedom seemed appropriate, almost necessary as a visible embodiment of their high status in society. For those less affluent who followed in their wake, suburban living might restore dreams of Jeffersonian democracy as well as provide a small, intimate community of identifiable people.

As recent history has shown, however, the suburb "has lost the conditions that preserved the landscape around it." Most suburban developments have, ironically, produced "a low-grade uniform environment from which escape is impossible. . . . What the suburb retains today is largely its original weaknesses: Snobbery, segregation, status-seeking, political irresponsibility."[26] Portland's upper income suburban development offers numerous illustrations of Mumford's thesis, but two areas are particularly noteworthy for providing examples of different types of suburban growth: The Tualatin Valley (Raleigh Hills) and the Rivera (Dunthorpe) sections.

The Pacific Telephone & Telegraph Company Survey of 1916 published a map to show the areas of expected metropolitan growth over the next 20 years. The survey predicted that the upper Tualatin Valley to the southwest would be opened up and that it would provide "a counter-balance" to the "extension of built-up territory in the east of the city limits."[27] Until the Portland Heights streetcar line was extended to the Council Crest Amusement Park in 1907, "people were not well acquainted with the region beyond the hills," noted a farmstead resident of the valley in 1912. "Persons, born and raised in Portland, admitted when they took their first ride to the Crest that they 'just supposed there was nothing but hills all the way to the ocean.' "[28] Access through the valley from Portland was limited until the opening of a rock quarry near Council Crest improved the existing primary roads. To be sure, the Southern Pacific Red Electric ran along the southern edge of the upper valley, but many of the development possibilities were hidden behind heavy timber growth and small hills.

One Portland entrpreneur was well aware of the richness that lay in the upper Tualatin Valley soil but he did not envisage a suburban development beyond planning for his own needs. Theodore Burney Wilcox bought approximately 160 acres of the old 320 acre Peter Smith donation land claim. It was lush and fertile farm land, with at least one stream winding its way through the property. Starting construction in 1915, Wilcox was prepared to spend over $125,000 on one of the most elaborate suburban estates ever built in Oregon. Two years later he moved from his medium size city home in the King's Hill district of Portland to his new 14 bedroom mansion that was patterned after a colonial southern manor. The grounds included spacious sunken gardens to the west, and a

T. B. Wilcox

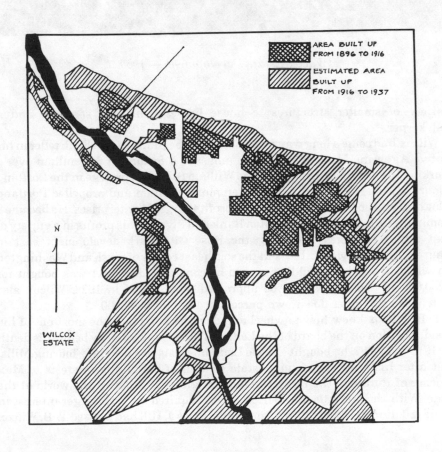

Wilcox Estate Development — 1960

variety of smaller structures to house horses, chickens, servants and a gatekeeper.[29]

Wilcox had come a long way from his modest beginnings as a bank teller in his native Agawam, Massachusetts. He amassed a fortune of $10 million over a working life of 40 years. Employed as William S. Ladd's protege in the Portland Flouring Mills, he soon rose to the command position and propelled Portland Flouring into one of the nation's most profitable grain enterprises. He became a dominant force in the Ladd & Tilton Bank and invested his profits in a variety of real estate packages, including the Rose City Park development east of Laurelhurst. The quarter block at the southeast corner of Sixth and Washington on which the Wilcox Building was to be constructed in 1911 was bought for $250,000 in 1908; it was to be appraised at $675,000 in 1928. Wilcox also purchased two other downtown parcels in 1908 for $300,000.

T. B. Wilcox knew how to wheel and deal; he had made the most out of his inside position on the board of the Ladd & Tilton Bank. Shortly before his death in 1918 at age 62, he bought out the Ladd interests in Portland Flouring Mills. But after his death, his family estate sold all of its milling interests to Max Houser of Portland, the largest individual grain exporter in the world at the time. With the proceeds, the Wilcox estate acquired an even larger interest in Ladd & Tilton. In 1909, railroad magnate James J. Hill had praised T. B. Wilcox as the one who had "done more than any other man in Portland . . . to develop the commerce of the Columbia River and gain recognition for the Northwest throughout the world."[30] He provided a similar stimulus to the future growth of the Tualatin Valley.

Country roads like Shattuck and Patton that bordered his estate were expanded into arterials and Scholls Ferry Road to the west became a major thoroughfare. The Bertha-Beaverton state highway was built adjacent to the Southern Pacific Red Electric, providing even more direct access to the valley from downtown Portland. But it was to be almost 30 years before the big explosion occurred. In 1948, the Wilcox family sold the property to the Columbia Preparatory School which operated the plant for six years. In June of 1955, the estate was finally sold for residential subdivision development. Today, close to 2000 people live on the former Wilcox grounds. Much of the landscaping has disappeared but the old house is still standing, providing rental units for the elderly.

If T. B. Wilcox had not been interested in the stately farm life, he most likely would have settled in the Rivera-Dunthorpe[31] section of Southwest Portland where one of his daughters was to build a large home several years later. In the early 1880s, the Ladds purchased considerable real estate in the wooded areas along the Willamette River, about four miles south of what was to become the shipyard slum district of 1917. Along with the Corbetts and Failings, they developed an extensive cemetery on a beautiful hillside overlooking the river. For 90 years, Riverview Cemetery has been the final resting place for Portland's prominent families. The first electric streetcar line terminated at the north side of the cemetery.

Some 15 years previously, William S. Ladd and his business partner Simeon Reed had purchased hundreds of acres south and to the west of the Riverview site, believing them to contain valuable deposits of iron ore for their Oregon Iron & Steel Company which had a plant in what is now the city of Lake Oswego. These two major land acquisitions, in addition to the opening of the Southern Pacific commuter rail line along the river, provided the stimulus for the future development of an exclusive residential district where many of the city's wealthiest families were to build "imposing homes."

One of the first to develop land along the river in the Rivera (Abernethy Heights) district was Scotsman Peter Kerr who had arrived in Portland in 1888. Within ten years he was to accumulate a considerable fortune in the grain business, become president of the Arlington Club and assume a prominent place in Portland society generally. His brother Thomas Kerr, who was later to reside nearby, joined Peter in the family grain business and married the daughter of Donald Macleay, founder of the U. S. National Bank. Late in 1909, four years after their marriage, Mr. and Mrs. Peter Kerr decided to move out of the old cottage which had been his bachelor quarters before marriage and build a formal estate. Peter Kerr contracted with John Olmsted of Brookline, Massachusetts, to redesign the entire landscape. He also hired Dean Ellis

Lawrence of the University of Oregon School of Architecture to design him a Scottish Baronial style manor.

Peter Kerr and John Olmsted carried on a lengthy and detailed correspondence. Kerr was concerned about where the house should be located and about the trails, formal gardens, pasture land and fruit grove. In this regard, one letter from Olmsted was particularly interesting and revealing:

"With respect to the new house site, my feeling was that in spite of the manifest advantages of a site close to the bluff, the distant view would be more agreeable from a house site further back from the bluff, because in that case you could provide a picturesque foreground on your own place and could so manage the plantations as to conceal the sordid little houses of the town of Milwaukee [sic] across the river, while still retaining in full view the wooded hills beyond the magnificent view of Mount Hood."[32]

John and his brother Frederick had inherited the reputation and business of their renowned father, Frederick Law Olmsted. Two of the elder Olmsted's principles of environmental planning were: (1) That it must include "social analysis," and (2), that it should be "directed toward the development of greater equality among all of the citizens of a community, particularly those who are disadvantaged."[33] Frederick Olmsted applied these principles to the planning of his early city parks. Toward the end of his life, however, he and his sons spent increasingly more time planning for the rich — in such projects as George Vanderbilt's Biltmore estate in North Carolina. Social analysis hardened into a form of social snobbery, with the early environmental movement tending to become an elitist attempt to preserve the princely privacy of the wealthy. To this day, the environmental-preservationist movement still carries some strong elitist overtones that are rightly viewed with suspicion by the disadvantaged.

John Olmsted's perceptions may well have been shared by the Kerr brothers and their neighbor C. H. Lewis. They could hardly be expected to spend money on formal gardens and exotic plantings and then have to gaze down upon "the sordid little houses . . . of Milwaukee." (Olmsted misspelled the name of Oregon's Milwaukie, believing it the same as Milwaukee, Wisconsin.) As a matter of fact, Peter Kerr did not relish spending anything that was not essential. The following August, he complained to Olmsted that the "plans were unnecessarily detailed and expensive." A few months later, Olmsted submitted "a cheaper method," but he advised Kerr against selling any of the land.[34] In his methodical way, Kerr supervised every detail of the landscaping and house construction. He even imported an interior decorator from Princeton, New Jersey. In the end, he spent approximately $26,000 on the house and at least an equal amount on the grounds. But these expenditures were substantially less than those recorded by his friend T. B. Wilcox on his Tualatin Valley estate.

In contrast to the future development of the Wilcox estate, however, the Rivera properties, e.g., Kerr's, were not subdivided. Many of them have remained in the hands of the original families and their descendents. Where subdivision has

Peter Kerr

The Kerr Estate

William M. Ladd

William M. Ladd's home in Dunthorpe, built in 1920 on 16 acres, Ellis Lawrence, architect.

occurred, the plots have normally been of at least three-quarters of an acre. Peter Kerr lived on at Elk Rock until he died in 1957 at the age of 95. After his death, the family gave the estate to the Episcopal Diocese for use as its administrative headquarters. The famous Elk Rock gardens were to be preserved. In fact, several years before his death, Kerr had presented Elk Island across the river — on which Elk Rock itself actually stood — to the city of Portland for use as a public park. He bought the land, he said, "to prevent its being sold for logging, to preserve it as a pretty place for all to enjoy."[35]

West and slightly south of Elk Rock, in a large wooded area long owned by the Oregon Iron & Steel Company, William M. Ladd filed a 125 acre plat for the upper Dunthorpe residential development in January of 1916. Ladd's Oregon Iron & Steel Company, in the final stages of its dissolution, drafted a property deed that conveyed all of its Dunthorpe real estate — approximately 215 acres including lower Dunthorpe — to the Ladd Estate Company for $1. To insure its exclusive character, the deed for upper Dunthorpe contained a variety of specific provisions or "agreements" as they were called:

1. Only residential dwellings could be built, except for outbuildings to house domestic animals. Swine and goats were expressly prohibited.

2. The minimum cost of a main house was $3000; for detached outbuildings, $1000.

3. No advertising sign could be displayed on the property.

4. No residence or any part thereof could be used or occupied by "persons of African or Mongolian descent,"[36] except that persons of "said races" could be employed as servants.

5. No selling or disposal of intoxicating liquor.

6. Each property owner would receive one share in the Dunthorpe Maintenance Corporation for each unit of 2500 square feet of property. The annual maintenance charge to each property owner was 5¢ per 100 square feet, up to 1/20th the value of the property. Provision was made to increase this fee as needs arose, but by nor more than 10¢ square feet per year.[37]

As described, this was the most restrictive deed in the greater Portland area. It was written at the behest of William M. Ladd, the ranking leader of Portland's native aristocracy, a person who dedicated his life to the better causes: YMCA, Portland Art Museum and Reed College. Ladd was a prototype of the well educated man of inherited wealth who enjoyed his station in life. He fulfilled community responsibilities thrust upon him by virtue of his position in society and he tried to function successfully in the world of competitive business that required talents which he did not possess. He once told E. B. MacNaughton that he would have preferred the life of a farmer to that of a banker and businessman. He might well have achieved a degree of success in farming that was denied him in business.

In fairness to Ladd, however, he should be credited for his overall contribution to Reed College and for his promotion of the "residence park" scheme of city planning which has had a lasting impact on Portland's growth. He valued quality and obviously had a keen aesthetic sense. Like his relatives and close friends in the Kerr, Corbett, Failing and Lewis clans, he was a person of good intentions who devoted much time to worthy public causes. But he was a prisoner of his class and his social perceptions were limited. He lived in a world remote from the slum conditions of South Portland even though he would skirt them each day as he travelled to and from his Dunthorpe estate.

Like most real estate developers — especially those of quality — the maintenance of property values was important to him. The Dunthorpe project held promise of substantial future profits. Restrictions were deemed essential to safeguard property rights. In attracting the status seekers — from the old as well as the new families — Dunthorpe proved to be an immediate success. As a defended neighborhood like Portland Heights, but with perhaps a touch more class, Dunthorpe was to maintain a high degree of stability among its residents. Over the years, it has not been uncommon for an estate, or even a plain residence, to pass from one generation to another.

Sullivan's Gulch to the Northeast

The Ladds and the Wilcoxes played an important role in opening up the "far out" sections of Northeast Portland. Two years before the Laurelhurst Company

Sullivan's Gulch

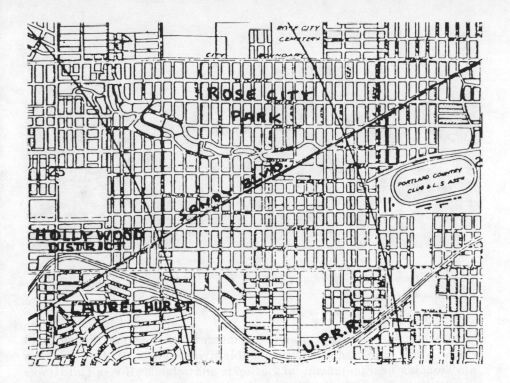

was organized, Wilcox and three of his downtown investor friends[38] incorporated the Rose City Park Association to purchase and develop roughly 1000 acres of former farm lands, some of which had already been platted and subdivided. Over the years, there has been wide disagreement as to the exact boundaries of Rose City Park. But since the formation of the Rose City Park Neighborhood Association, it has been generally accepted that Rose City runs from N. E. 37th to 72nd, and from the Union Pacific Railroad tracks to Fremont Street. To be included in the area were the Hollywood district that developed in the 1920s and the Beaumont district to the north.[39]

The developers clearly envisaged a residential type of village in a park but, in contrast to the later and adjacent Laurelhurst development, it was to be geared to the working class. The first deeds carried a number of familiar restrictions: No commercial activities or saloons and no sales or rentals to Chinese; and buildings could not be closer than 15 feet from the street and could cost no less than $1500.

Rose City's growth as a remunerative real estate development — Wilcox and his partners were to realize an 800 percent profit from the venture — was assured by various actions that had been taken many years before the association was incorporated. As early as 1855, Sandy Road had been surveyed as a route to transport farm products to the small town on the banks of the Willamette. It soon became the major eastern entrance into Portland for horses, carts and then

89

Intersection of Sandy Boulevard, U. P. R. R. and S. E. 37th Avenue looking west.

automobiles. At its eastern terminus, it merged into Columbia Slough Road which in turn connected with the Columbia River Highway that wound down into Troutdale near the juncture of the Sandy and Columbia Rivers. Until it was paved in 1912, Sandy Road was almost impassable during the rainy season. As one observer described it, there was "a sea of almost bottomless mud"[40] that had to be crossed on wooden boards. Sandy Road, later upgraded to boulevard status, cut a diagonal swath through farm land, including that of W. S. Ladd's Hazel Fern property, on its way to S. E. 12th Avenue. At S. E. 37th, it crossed the Union Pacific Railroad tracks that had been put down in 1881 by the Oregon Railway and Navigation Company.

Early in 1906, after the Rose City area was annexed to Portland, a streetcar line was constructed down the middle of Sandy Road. Eventually it was to extend beyond S. E. 82nd Avenue. Rose City residents, along with the real estate developers who "convinced" the Portland Railway Light & Power Company to build the line, were to have direct access to downtown Portland.

Over the long span of Portland's history, the OR&N rail line, i.e., the Union Pacific, that skirted the southern boundary of Rose City Park was to have an even greater impact than Sandy Boulevard on the growth of Portland's eastern metropolitan region. Not only did it attract unplanned industrial growth, such as the Doernbecher Furniture factory and the Pacific Car Foundry plant, but it led to the construction of Portland's first post-World War II freeway, the Banfield, that became the western terminus of Interstate 80N.

Back in September 1881, Henry Villard, along with his local investment partners, William S. Ladd and Henry Failing, received a perpetual franchise from the city of East Portland and Multnomah County that enabled the OR&N

to lay a one track rail line down Sullivan's Gulch into East Portland. The gulch was a natural depression, or ravine, that extended from an inlet in the Willamette River up to S. E. 33rd Avenue. In Portland's early years, it was not uncommon for the gulch to flood with water up to as far as 16th Avenue. After the railroad acquired its franchise, the lower end of the gulch was filled and as the city grew northeastward, the major north-south avenues were bridged over the gulch and its railroad tracks. When the Union Pacific acquired the OR&N properties in 1887, it used the Sullivan's Gulch route for its transcontinental passenger and much of its freight service.

Four years after Wilcox and his associates opened up the Rose City property, Judge John Twohy of Spokane purchased roughly 11 platted blocks of the Jenne tract on which to construct a railcar manufacturing plant. The site was reasonably cheap and it had ready access to rail service. Furthermore, Twohy Brothers Inc. already had orders to fill for both the Union Pacific and Southern Pacific Railroads which were controlled by E. H. Harriman, a friend of Judge Twohy. In June of 1917, William Piggott of Seattle's Pacific Car Foundry Company purchased the Twohy Brothers operation and proceeded to fill a wartime order from the Russian government for 1000 freight cars. Thus, in less than a decade, a major industrial site was launched in Portland devoid of any

Columbia Steel Casting Company

Circa 1950 — Site of Pacific Car Foundry Company. Rose City Park on the left.

planning whatsoever. It was sandwiched between two planned residential districts, Laurelhurst and Rose City, and would someday be bordered on the north by Normandale Park. In subsequent years, other steel fabricating plants[41] would be built nearby, merely adding to the dichotomous land uses of the area. Considering the impact of these industrial incongruities and the commercial growth that would afflict Sandy Boulevard it was remarkable that Laurelhurst and Rose City were able to survive as residential districts, although Rose City did lose some of its early residential properties to commercial activity.

At the time that the first Laurelhurst homes were being built, the city began to give attention to the matter of grade separation at the Sandy Boulevard and 37th Avenue crossing of the Union Pacific rail line. Sullivan's Gulch flattened out about 1000 yards west of the intersection so that the north-south streets crossed the tracks at grade. When the idea of building a viaduct over the tracks was first considered by the city council a storm of protest arose. Over 50 written remonstrances were filed with the council from property owners adjacent to the intersection. They cited the "great damage to the property" that would result; it would "mar the landscape" and "impose inconveniences on the neighborhood."[42]

The nearby residents of Laurelhurst and Rose City believed themselves to be living in a kind of suburb to Portland. Even 20 years later, when Fred G. Meyer built the first of his 23 shopping centers at 41st and Sandy, he announced the event as the first suburban shopping center for Portland. The residents had no power to block industrial or commercial invasion of their neighborhoods, but they could and did block the viaduct for five years.

Only extreme danger to human life forced official action. By charter, the city had to pass an ordinance declaring a grade crossing to be dangerous and directing the city engineer to prepare plans for its elimination. The Oregon Railroad Commission had already cited the Union Pacific for its failure to provide adequate crossing protection. The city engineer was also required to consult with the railroad's engineers. And finally, the cost of raising or lowering the tracks not within street lines was to be borne by the railroad. All other costs, including damage to abutting property, were to be borne, 60 percent by the railroad, 20 percent by the city from general funds, and 20 percent by an assessment district.[43]

In October 1915, the city council formally declared nine crossings between East 33rd Avenue and the city boundary at 82nd Avenue to be dangerous. Plans were filed in 1916 for depressing the tracks over the entire distance, with steel reinforced concrete viaducts to cover four lines of tracks. The plans called for the lowering of the tracks by 12 feet throughout the distance, with the excavation to be made in three cuts. The estimated city's cost was $550,000 and that of lowering the tracks was projected to be $500,000.

Beginning in late 1916 with the 37th Avenue crossing, the most complicated of the viaducts, the work took three years to complete. Seven of the viaducts served the Rose City area so that once they were completed, Rose City experienced

N. E. Sandy Boulevard as it was in 1916. Below is city engineer Olaf Laurgaard's drawing of the viaduct.

Same view — 1978

tremendous growth. Rose City Park became a city within a city, with all of the public services and community and commercial activities that urban life required. One particular activity center was unique to Portland: The Portland Country Club and Livestock Association. For years before its demise in the 1920s, "this fashionable club was the scene of horse races, automobile contests and motorcycle derrings-do that drew wide-eyed fans from far points, most conveyed to the scene by streetcar."[44]

One particular club event that drew wide attention to Rose City long before the viaducts were built was the first airmail flight in the Pacific Northwest. It took off from the track on August 10, 1912, with 1500 letters destined for the Vancouver Barracks, 13 minutes away on the Washington side of the Columbia River. The Rose City residents thrived on this kind of excitement. After the country club was disbanded, the city acquired the property and Paul Keyser built Portland's second municipal golf course which became the pride and joy of the local residents.

Like most lower middle income residential areas, Rose City was to change markedly over the years. Whereas in 1923 the ratio of owner to renter occupancy was 9-1, in 1970 it was only 3-1.[45] In terms of median family income and housing values, it has steadily lost ground to Laurelhurst. Commercial activity has grown along both Sandy Boulevard and the extended Sullivan's Gulch corridor. Laurelhurst has been immune to much of this development while Rose City has been almost overrun by it.

Growth and Planning: In Retrospect

"The growth of the city must no longer be left either to chance or to the judgment of the individual property owner. There must be no struggle between groups of property owners who may find it to their immediate pecuniary interest to compete with each other in establishing new centers of values. No longer may chance be the controlling factor in city growth."[46]

These words were not uttered in 1978. They were spoken by city planner James J. Sawyer in 1919. Unfortunately for Portland's future they went unheeded. Money was too powerful a motive to contain individual freedom of action. Neither the realtors, the bankers nor City Hall listened to Lewis Mumford when he addressed the City Club in 1938. Mumford was particularly critical of the mixture of residential and industrial uses. He suggested the acquisition of lands, neither immediately on the river nor adjacent to existing residential neighborhoods, to be developed as model industrial parks or industrial towns within the city limits. Had Portland's business-political leadership followed the advice of Mumford and the Pacific Northwest Regional Planning Committee 40 years ago, Portland might not be faced today with the dilemma of trying to accommodate both the expansion requirements of local industry and the residential needs and restoration efforts of local neighborhood associations like Rose City Park.

N. E. 47th Street

These photos illustrate the development of the East Side. Above, in a photo taken in 1916, the landscape is rural, with a dirt country road running between farmers' fields. Below, the 1978 photo shows the Providence Hospital complex, with its addition under construction in the foreground and the Child Care Center in the background, on the east side of N. E. 47th. Medical-dental offices are seen on the west side of 47th.

Chapter 5

The Impact of
Land Transportation on
Metropolitan Growth

Of all the economic forces that affected the physical shaping of Portland and its metropolitan region, the land transportation industry has had the greatest single impact. Beginning with the railroads, then the street railways and the electric streetcars, both urban and interurban, and, finally, the automobile and trucks, all have exercised a dominant force within particular historical periods.

Most of the companies that were formed to develop the railroads and street railways were mixed, in the sense that they contained elements of private investment together with extensive public underwriting. Such subsidies included federal land grants, franchises and land rights-of-way, and public funds to construct terminals and bridges. As with all utilities that have purported to serve the public, the transportation industry has required heavy capitalization — enormous amounts of invested capital in the form of issued stocks and bonds. This economic fact of life proved initially to be a blessing, but as America approached the years of the first world war, the excessive capitalization of the land transportation industry was one of the major causes of its decline. Along with increasing labor and maintenance costs, the heavy interest payments that were required to service the long-term bonded debt created the need to raise rates. And this condition in turn provoked serious public policy questions.

Some Crucial Issues: Finance and Control

The major issue in land transportation that began to emerge during the period from 1915 to 1920, when passenger service and revenues achieved their historical peak, related to public ownership of facilities. The question was being asked, not only in Portland but throughout North America: Could a public transportation system survive through private ownership if it was to meet fully the needs of an expanding population, keep its rates stable in the face of inflated costs, pay the interest due on its bonded indebtedness, and distribute a respectable dividend to its stockholders?

Following the war, serious consideration was given in Washington, D. C. by the Wilson Administration to the Plumb Plan — a proposal to grant the United States government permanent control over the American rail network with the same powers that it had exercised during the war. (In December 1917, President

Wilson, using his war powers, took possession of all the United States railroads, valued at $20 billion.) The plan died for lack of support. President Wilson's illness, the League of Nations controversy and the conservative tide of the 1918 elections produced the Esch-Cummins Act of 1920 that returned the railroads to private control, thus leading to the gradual demise of their passenger service over the next half century.

At the local level, beginning in 1916, numerous proposals were to be made for the city to acquire the properties of the Portland Railway Light and Power Company's urban transit network. The experiences of the French and German streetcar utilities were examined. They were in private hands initially, regulated by strict governmental controls, but in most cases when their franchises expired the municipalities assumed ownership. In Portland, the franchise was not due to expire until 1933. Banker Abbot Mills had taken care of that problem in 1903 before the local utilities were merged and sold to the Clark interests of Philadelphia.[1] The legal complexities of gaining public control and of determining fair compensation for condemnation always seemed to overwhelm sporadic efforts in support of municipal ownership. Even apart from outright public control, there were other matters that involved public authority — or at least should have. Could the city exercise any decision over where the PRL&P ran its lines? Historically, there had been little city-wide coordination of transportation services with projected industrial or residential developments.

Like most western towns and cities, Portland had always been subjected to railroad and street railway exploitation, despite whatever benefits such developments brought to the region. Easy access and cheap land were the primary determinants of where the track was laid. From Portland's railroad experience, examples are numerous. To cite three: The OR&N track down Sullivan's Gulch, later acquired by the Union Pacific; the Southern Pacific tracks on both sides of the Willamette River; and the Great Northern railroad cut that bisected North Portland.

Portland had a similar experience with its urban traction lines, except for the early street railway network that served the older, established neighborhoods. The advent of electricity drastically changed the old routings. Greater efficiency and speed increased the opportunities to expand service for both urban and suburban growth. But there was no planning for such growth; no attempt was made to determine the public need for a particular real estate development and there was no appraisal of the governmental or transportation costs required to service it.

Before 1900, realtors and transit companies had often worked together in an informal arrangement that assured a reasonably high level of ridership between the scattered population centers. By 1910, however, many of the new real estate and commercial developments were being placed piecemeal on vacant lands that had been bypassed as the city had expanded outward. These properties were inaccessible to existing rail lines and, as auto and truck use accelerated, government was compelled to construct costly road connections. Government

98

was therefore at the mercy of the private developer whose basic concern was profit volume. The rule of chance was to result in an enormous waste of both public and private resources. Many of the critical land use and environmental problems that have afflicted the mid-twentieth century Portland metropolitan area have their roots in the free-wheeling, *laissez faire* conditions that shaped land transportation routes in the period immediately before and after 1915.

The Railroads

The historian who examines the history of the railroads, or the history of any utility for that matter, is struck by a tone of arrogant defensiveness that seems to pervade the public statements of their corporate executives and lawyers. In a speech that was written for delivery in 1915, Portland railroad attorney James B. Kerr bemoaned that:

" . . . the attitude of the public toward the great aggregations of capital which have made possible the cheapest and most efficient transportation known to the civilized world has seemed to be one of unalterable hostility."[2]

Kerr along with his partner, Judge Charles H. Carey, provided Portland counsel for the Great Northern and Northern Pacific Railroads. Although he believed that "the development of the transportation facilities of the Pacific Northwest" had just begun, he was fearful of the railroad taxes that had "increased by leaps and bounds. . . . It would be impossible," declared Kerr, "to point to any other business which maintains itself and still pays a tax of 12 cents on every dollar of revenue."[3]

The theme that all of the utility lawyers seemed to emphasize was the necessity to protect the investment of private capital; it had to be "secure against confiscation." But Kerr added an interesting twist: "The investment of private capital . . . must also give promise of sufficient ultimate returns to compensate for the lean years of pioneering."[4]

In examining the personal fortunes of the great railroad builders like Hill, Harriman, Stanford, Huntington and Crocker one could easily be amused by Kerr's reference to the lean years of pioneering. Certainly through the first decade of the century, both the Harriman and Hill systems were earning a comfortable return that averaged over nine percent. The second decade was another story. Inflated costs, increased capital requirements and restrictive rate regulation began to squeeze the profits. The Esch-Cummins Act actually stipulated that five and one-half percent was a fair rate of profit for railroads and one-half of all profits above six percent were to be returned to the Treasury of the United States, in repayment for government improvements made during the war.

The public had little need to feel sorry for the railroads. By 1870 they had already received over a half-billion dollars from just the states, counties and cities of the country. By 1900 they had been given over 184 million acres of public lands. In 1921 they were to receive a $500 million loan from the federal government, an action that prompted U. S. Supreme Court Justice Louis Brandeis to comment: "Ultimately the government will have to take over the railroads and it is just as well to do it piecemeal in that way."[5]

Brandeis assumed that they would probably never be able to repay the borrowed funds and that the governmemt would automatically end up a big investor and part owner.

The railroads had only themselves to blame for their public image. Kerr even admitted this when he said that:

"The railroad wrecking president of 30 years ago who assailed his competitor by bearing his stock on Wall Street has given way to the executive who so drives his machine as to secure the maximum of efficiency . . . "[6]

One wonders, however, if the new executive of 1915 and thereafter was really any different. Fifty years later when the railroads were on shaky ground, corporate shareholders received $502 million in cash dividends, the highest in the industry's history.

In the spring of 1913, following the federal court decree that split up the Harriman System, the Union Pacific and Southern Pacific spent large sums of money to defeat two initiative ordinances that would have annulled their franchises to continue to operate separate tracks on S. E. First and Second Avenues. The ordinances were designed to force the railroads to comply with the new 1913 city charter provision that required common track use when the public interest was involved. The city wanted to open up the streets for development as municipal shipping districts. The railroads should have supported this action. In the long run it would have been in their best interests to acquiesce. Sixty five years later, the near East Side still suffers from this gross abuse of public rights.

One of the major arguments successfully employed by the railroads was as follows:

"How will it be possible to procure money for great enterprises if the companies must report to the financial institutions furnishing capital that franchises under which the railroads operate are repudiated at the polls!"[7]

This same question was to be posed time and again over the succeeding half-century, on numerous occasions when the city developed plans that threatened to impede the free operation of the railroad franchises. The most recent example was during the construction of the East Bank freeway in the 1960s when the state was required to install the most dangerous freeway curve in Oregon in order to accommodate the Southern Pacific and bypass the very same tracks.

Historically, the Southern Pacific had been the least popular of the major rail networks serving Portland. The Hill system should have been equally unpopular. For years both the Great Northern and Northern Pacific Railroads had discriminated against Portland in freight rates charged to most grain shippers. Because James J. Hill had close personal and economic ties with Tacoma and Seattle business interests, these two cities had received preferred treatment for over 30 years. In 1921, the Interstate Commerce Commission was to invalidate the long-standing rate structure and grant Portland the lower rates that it deserved.

Hill was a master of the art of public relations. He made periodic visits to Portland and delivered eloquent speeches advertising his corporate contributions to the state's transportation needs. He was a colorful man and an articulate writer. He was also a shrewd if not unethical businessman. He kept grain merchant T. B. Wilcox happy for years by granting the Portland Flouring Mills secret rebates on all flour and grain shipments.

In contrast to Hill, Edward H. Harriman, who had died in 1909, was a withdrawn and colorless figure who abhorred publicity. His predecessors in the Southern Pacific, Messrs. Huntington, Stanford and Crocker — viewed locally

A 1918 view of the intersection of the Southern Pacific Railroad tracks and S. W. Second Avenue. The tracks were removed in the 1930s and Barbur Boulevard was built on the right-of-way. Further north, the boulevard becomes S. W. 4th Avenue.

101

as greedy robber barons — had never come to Portland. Harriman, in fact, proved to be just as shrewd and a far more efficient manager than Hill. Simon Benson discovered this quality while attempting to negotiate the rail shipment of his lumber to San Diego. Without any competition, the Southern Pacific had long been charging a higher proportionate rate to ship from Portland to California than to ship from anywhere else in Oregon to the California market.

Portland's most prolonged and bitter controversy with the Southern Pacific involved the use of steam locomotives on S. W. Fourth Avenue (the current Barbur Boulevard) that ran along the western boundary of the Lair Hill-Corbett district of South Portland. Mayor Harry Lane had fought hard to rewrite this franchise in 1906, but the council, feeling heavy corporate pressure, refused to support his efforts. Seven months later, in the spring of 1907, the public outcry had grown so loud that the council voted 6-5 to require the railroad to terminate use of freight cars and steam locomotives on Fourth Avenue within 18 months.

When the deadline arrived, however, the S. P. refused to discontinue the use of Fourth Avenue for steam locomotives. The city brought suit in federal court and won. The railroad then appealed the ruling to the higher courts. Five years later, in November 1912, the U. S. Supreme Court upheld the city's inherent right of police powers. When the matter was returned to the council in December 1912, lawyer Charles H. Carey, who normally represented the Hill interests, but whose reputation for influencing city councils was unequalled, pleaded in behalf of his client. True to form, the council wilted, gave into corporate pressure and granted the continuance of steam locomotive use for $500 a year compensation. *The Portland Daily News* said it was worth at least $1000 a month. Within two years, however, the S. P. electrified the Fourth Avenue line for its Red Electrics and the steam locomotives were finally removed.

The Oregon and California Lands

The Southern Pacific found itself before the U. S. Supreme Court again in 1913 when it contested a 1908 congressional act that returned to the U. S. government 2,075,616 acres of unsold Oregon and California land grants. Back in the days of Ben Holladay, the Oregon & California Railroad, later acquired by the Southern Pacific, received a federal land grant of 20 square miles for every mile of track laid on the route from Portland to California. The railroad had to agree to sell the land to actual settlers, in tracts no larger than 160 acres and for no more than $2.50 per acre. As the years passed, the company encountered difficulty abiding by the terms of the agreement. For one thing, most of the land it had chosen was heavily timbered and not suitable for farming use. For another, the railroad was pressured by eastern and midwestern lumber interests which coveted the virgin timber stands and which were willing to pay more than $2.50 per acre. Although just how much more was paid is not clear, by 1908 the company apparently had sold almost 700,000 acres illegally in addition to the legal sales which totalled 130,000. In 1909, the U. S. Attorney's office was to charge that prominent

Portland lumberman Everett S. Collins had illegally purchased 29,247 acres of O&C land in Clackamas County[8] — the basis of the family's profitable Ostrander Timber Company of Mollala.

Possibly as a result of the 1905 timber fraud trials[9] that publicized the deception perpetrated on the Oregon public by the large timber operators, the Southern Pacific halted further land grant sales and held the remaining lands as a timber reserve. This action provoked the State of Oregon to seek federal redress and resulted in the congressional act of 1908. The Supreme Court held that the lands should be returned to the government but ordered the government to reimburse the Southern Pacific for the unsold lands at $2.50 per acre. Subsequent federal enactments in 1916 and 1937 established a formula for remitting to the Oregon counties, in which the O&C lands were located, 50 percent of timber sale receipts — a handsome bounty over the past 60 years that, unfortunately for Portland, failed to provide much revenue to Multnomah County.[10]

The Electric Interurbans[11]

The period from 1900 to 1915 was the golden era of the interurban electric railways, the transit network that provided transportation for commuters and leisure seekers between Portland and the suburbs, and through the Willamette Valley as far south as Eugene. It was during this same period that Portland underwent its most explosive urban growth and the interurbans played an important role in this development.

Over a span of almost 25 years, electrically operated transit had mushroomed to the point that by 1915 the Portland area had the third most extensive electric railway system in America. After a stage of rapid construction and cutthroat competition, followed by the inevitable consolidation that awaited most utilities, three companies dominated the field. The largest, most profitable and longest lived was the Portland Railway Light and Power Company's interurban division that operated on the east side of the river after leaving downtown. The second in size was the Oregon Electric-United Railways network that was owned by the Hill interests and operated by the Spokane, Portland and Seattle Railroad (SP&S). The third and latest to become involved was the Southern Pacific Red Electric system that arrived belatedly in 1912, almost too late to insure a financial success. The latter two systems operated solely on the west side of the Willamette and were compatible with the standard gauge tracks and performance requirements of their parent railroads.

The Portland Railway Light and Power interurban division grew out of the various intracity networks that were consolidated in the period 1902 to 1907. Before 1900, the longer intracity lines were considered suburban. As early as 1895, *The Oregonian* had noted that the construction of these "suburban" railways led to the rapid settlement of all east side districts for three miles or more back from the river. Of course in 1895, four years after consolidation and

103

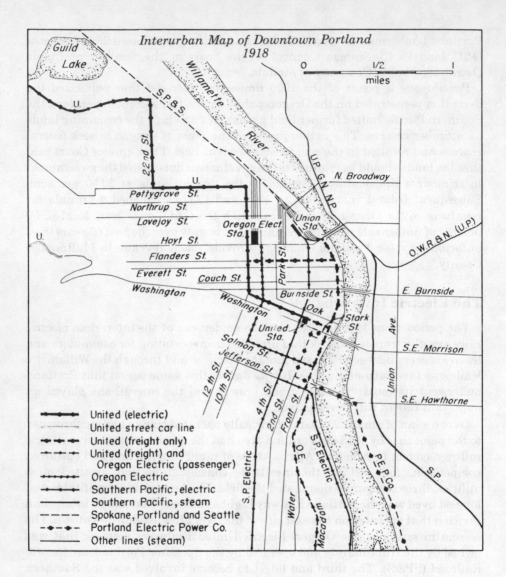

Interurban Map of Downtown Portland
1918

0   1/2   1
miles

Guild Lake

Willamette River

S.P.&B.S.

U.P. G.N. N.P.

N. Broadway

22nd St.

Pettygrove St.
Northrup St.
Lovejoy St.
Hoyt St.
Flanders St.
Everett St.
Washington

Oregon Elect. Sta.

Union Sta.

O.W.R.&N. (U.P.)

Park St.

Couch St.

Washington

Burnside St.

E. Burnside

Oak

Stark St.

United Sta.

S.E. Morrison

Salmon St.
Jefferson St.

12th St.
10th St.
4th St.
2nd St.
Front St.

S.E. Hawthorne

S.P. Electric

Water

Macadam

O.E.

S.P. Electric

Union Ave.

P.E.P. Co.

S.P.

Legend:
- ●━●━● United (electric)
- ‑‑‑‑‑ United street car line
- ●--●--● United (freight only)
- ●-‑●-‑● United (freight) and Oregon Electric (passenger)
- ●●●●●● Oregon Electric
- ●‑‑●‑‑● Southern Pacific, electric
- ─────── Southern Pacific, steam
- ‑ ‑ ‑ ‑ Spokane, Portland and Seattle
- ●‑●‑●‑● Portland Electric Power Co.
- ━━━━━ Other lines (steam)

two years after the advent of the electrics, any region more than one and one-half miles from downtown was considered suburbia.

> "Mount Tabor, three miles east of the line of the river, is easily reached by any of the three lines of railway centering in that vicinity as points a few blocks distant from the river were a few years since. The entire peninsula separating Portland from the Columbia river is dotted with pleasant suburban homes as the direct result of a steam motor line connecting this city and Vancouver, a line afterward electrified and over which now run modern electric cars. Fulton Park, 3½ miles south of Portland, and all that stretch of country lying between this city and Milwaukie, six miles distant, afford attractive sites for suburban

104

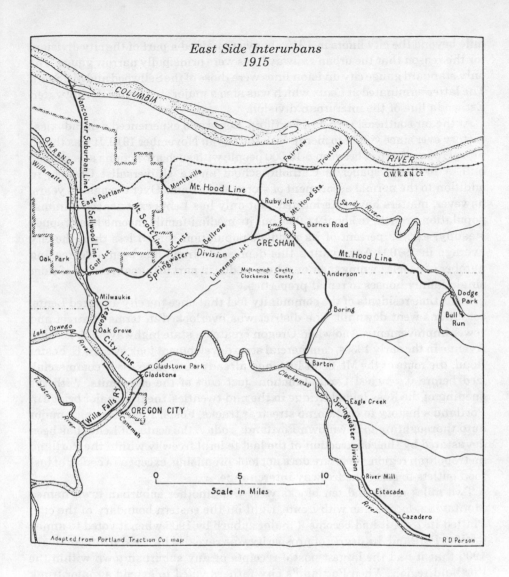

East Side Interurbans
1915

COLUMBIA

Vancouver Suburban Line

O.W.R & N C?

Willamette

East Portland

RIVER

Fairview

Troutdale

O.W.R.& N.C?

Montavilla

Mt. Hood Line

Ruby Jct.

Mt. Hood Sta.

Sandy River

Mt. Scott Line

Sellwood Line

Lents

Bellrose

Barnes Road

GRESHAM

Mt. Hood Line

Oak Park

Golf Jct.

Springwater Division

Linnemann Jct.

Multnomah County
Clackamas County

Anderson

Dodge Park

Milwaukie

Boring

Bull Run

Lake Oswego

Oak Grove

Oregon City Line

Tualatin River

Willamette River

Gladstone Park

Gladstone

Barton

Clackamas

River Mill

Eagle Creek

Willa Falls RY

OREGON CITY

Canemah

Springwater Division

Estacada

Cazadero

0   5   10

Scale in Miles

Adapted from Portland Traction Co. map

R.D.Person

homes which are within a few minutes ride of the business center of Portland. The electric car has been the direct promoter of the extension of Portland's boundary lines, and it has been the medium through which the people of the suburbs have been placed in close touch with city life as it exists in the brilliantly lighted streets of the metropolis after nightfall."[12]

By 1915, both the Fulton Park (Corbett) and Vancouver (Union) lines were transferred to the city division, an example of how the early interurbans were gradually incorporated into the urban system as the city expanded. On the other hand, the Sandy line that ran through Rose City Park and extended more than a mile beyond the city limits in 1915 always remained a part of the city division, for the reason that the urban railway lines were principally narrow gauge. The only standard gauge city division lines were those of the Sellwood and Mt. Scott. The latter terminated at Lents which was also a major stop for the Springwater-Estacada line of the interurban division.

At the far southeast corner of Portland, Lents had experienced a paradoxical history ever since voting to merge with the city in November 1912. It was then a prosperous suburb of between 8-10,000 people with such attractions as a grange hall, a local newspaper, a Catholic school and a Universalist Church, in addition to the normal assortment of stores and a bank. Over the past 65 years, however, matters have deteriorated. Not only has Lents experienced minimal population growth, to about 11,000, but its median family income has dropped steadily, e.g., 62 percent of its resident population earned less than the city average in 1970.[13] Aggravating this depressing trend has been a decreasing number of people owning their own homes, due in part to the conversion of older single family houses to rental properties.

Long time residents of the community feel that once the city annexed Lents, conditions went downhill. The district was overlooked in terms of street and sewer improvements. And when Oregon created a state highway on S. E. 82nd Avenue in the early 1930s, commercial strip development took over. S. E. Foster Road, the route of the Mt. Scott line, had already been excessively commercialized before it reached Lents Junction, just east of the city limits. With the opening of the Ross Island Bridge in the mid-twenties, the first major bridge in Portland's history to contain no streetcar tracks, Foster Road became a major auto thoroughfare to downtown Portland. Today, the center of Lents has been devastated by the construction of the last federal freeway within the Portland metropolitan region. Its future does not look promising, except as a center of fast food outlets to serve the freeway interchange.

Two miles north and ten blocks west was another suburban town named Montavilla, located, as with Lents, right on the eastern boundary of the city. Platted in 1889, it had become a major suburb by 1906 when it voted to annex itself to Portland. Its degree of prosperity was revealed by the startling notice in 1906 that it had the largest postal receipts of any suburban town within the Portland region. When Portland's city fathers voted to extend a major trunk sewer line through the center of the community, the local residents quickly raised their one-third share of the million dollar cost and paid the city in cash — a record that has probably never been equalled in Portland's history.[14]

Concurrent with Montavilla's joining Portland, the Mt. Hood Railway and Power Company was incorporated to operate a steam line from the Union Pacific tracks at S. E. 90th Avenue to the hydro plant at Bull Run. This was Montavilla's first interurban rail connection. It was purchased and electrified by the PRL&P in 1912-1913. Montavilla had enjoyed urban streetcar service ever since the Mt. Tabor line was extended along its southern boundary. Then, at the behest of the Laurelhurst Company in 1910, the Glisan Street line was built to

S. E. 92nd Avenue. The 10,000 residents of the former suburban community enjoyed fast, efficient service, as long as they wanted to go in the direction of downtown.

In contrast to Lents, Montavilla was to maintain a reasonable degree of social cohesiveness and some community vitality, or as one oldtimer has described it with some embellishment, "a happy mix of business houses, social places and dwellings pleasantly situated on the shoulder of Mt. Tabor."[15] Over the past half century, the median family income has nearly matched that of the city generally, but housing trends have not been healthy. The S. E. 82nd Avenue corridor has brought aesthetic and social deterioration to the area, to the point that most of the pleasantness of community life referred to above has been squeezed into a ten block wide strip between Mt. Tabor and 82nd Avenue. Residential ownership has been nearly wiped out along 82nd so that the community as a whole has a low (1-1) ratio of owner to renter occupied units.[16]

Whereas the electric interurban had brought efficient and fast transit service to a community that possessed a high degree of liveability 60 years ago, as the traffic arterials were built and the undeveloped sections filled in, the automobile brought ruin to at least one-third of the area's residential neighborhoods. Throughout the decade of the 1920s, and for a long time after the first zoning code went into effect in 1924, the city planning commission approved practically every request for commercial conditional use permits along S. E. 82nd. The final

Union Pacific Crossing — S. E. 82nd and Halsey — Looking south
September 1916

First Gas Station — S. E. 82nd and Stark

blow came in August 1937 when both the planning commission and the city council approved the rezoning of the state highway from multi-family to commercial-industrial use. Because of heavy automobile traffic, S. E. 82nd "was no longer desirable as a residential street."

There is an obscure but interesting story[17] about the early Mt. Hood interurban that stopped at Montavilla on its way to Bull Run. The company was reported to have drafted a plan that would have extended the electric rail line from its juncture with the Union Pacific down through Sullivan's Gulch, running parallel to the U. P.'s tracks, over the Steel Bridge and thence into downtown Portland. Had such a plan materialized, it would have provided direct, high speed rapid transit service between a downtown terminal and the thickly populated sections of Portland's greater East Side, including Gresham. In view of the State Highway Department's current plans to construct a similarly located light rail line from Gresham to Portland at a cost of over $160 million, one can sadly contemplate the public savings to future generations had the original plan been implemented. There is no record of the reasons for not undertaking it, and there is no guarantee that even had it been built it could have survived the demise of the Bull Run line in the late 1920s and the freeway construction of the 1950s.

The life span of the Portland interurbans was relatively short considering the amount of investment involved. The East Side Interurbans of the PRL&P proved to be an exception to national trends. When they finally abandoned the passenger business in 1958, they had amassed one of the longest periods of

108

The Bull Run Interurban at Dodge Park, 1925

service of any interurban system in the United States. Their impact upon population growth and settlement patterns was largely over by 1915.[18] But they continued to make money from passenger service for another decade in contrast to their competitors on the West Side.

The Recreation Areas

One of the reasons for their prosperity was the development of amusement and scenic parks that were owned by the PRL&P system itself. Located at the far ends of the lines and removed from easy road access, the parks acted as magnets, attracting thousands of passengers on weekends and holidays when the business commuter level was low. Canemah Park above Willamette Falls was opened in the summer of 1902 and the price of a 30 mile roundtrip ticket was 25 cents. The 70 acre Estacada Recreational Park on the Clackamas River was opened in 1904 and included a new dance pavilion and a 30 room hotel. Fishing was one of the main attractions. On weekends and holidays as many as 20 trainloads were filled with eager passengers who were willing to make the 70 mile roundtrip for 50 cents. Dodge Park near the Bull Run power plant offered similar water related recreational activities but on a smaller scale. It was a favorite family picnic spot.

Within easy reach of downtown Portland was The Oaks Amusement Park, probably the most popular amusement center in Portland's history. Opened in

1907, it remained in operation until the second world war forced its closure in 1943.[19] It was a boon to the interurban system which normally could not expect to capture much short-haul traffic. The park offered attractions to meet every taste: Classical and popular concerts, comic operas and vaudeville acts. Even the famed bandmaster John Philip Sousa conducted several performances inside the large covered "Airdome." Roller coasters, merry-go-rounds, a roller skating rink and dance pavilion helped to attract a Sunday or holiday crowd of as many as 30,000 people. For those who wanted a formal meal, a large restaurant with an elaborate roof garden and wide porch was available for use. On special occasions, hot air balloon rides, high wire performers and firework displays were offered the patrons. During the first season alone, from May 1 to October 1, 1907, over 350,000 Portlanders went through the turnstiles.[20]

In the summer of 1915, the Portland Railway Light and Power Company decided to develop a mile of Columbia River beach front property of which it was part owner. The Vancouver line of the PRL&P, terminating on Hayden Island, passed within a few hundred yards of the beach that was located on Sand Island, an eastward extension of Hayden Island. For years local residents had used the spot for picnicking, camping and swimming. Desiring to make some revenue off the property, as well as to increase weekend and holiday interurban passenger revenues, the Columbia Beach owners leased the land to concessionaires who built and operated all the necessary facilities. Portland's first accessible large-scale bathing beach proved an immediate success, so much so that weekend passenger revenues increased by 550 percent during the first full summer of operation in 1916. Unfortunately for the PRL&P, the construction of a 700 foot automobile causeway in 1916 threatened the railway's access control. Before long, thousands of cars would be entering the beach grounds.

After the interstate bridge opened in 1917, the cars won out. In subsequent years, Hayden Island became the site of the lively and prosperous Jantzen Beach Amusement Park. Over the past 15 years, the park has been replaced by the expansive Hayden Island-Jantzen Beach Center, combining a shopping center and residential units with the largest convention facility north of San Francisco. The property was purchased in 1977 for $40 million by the Hillman interests of Pittsburgh, Pennsylvania.

The West Side Lines

The first electric interurban to serve the West Side of Portland was the Oregon Electric that began operation in 1908. Organized and promoted by a group of Oregon and New York investors led by the First National Bank's Abbot L. Mills and Henry L. Corbett, the Oregon Electric was purchased by the James J. Hill interests in 1910 in an attempt to outflank, and compete with, the Harriman System's Southern Pacific. The S. P. had neglected passenger service on the hillier and more inaccessible West Side except for its Willamette Valley steam line that went through the Rivera and Lake Oswego districts on its way south. It

West Side Interurbans

also had a steam freight line that carried some passengers to Beaverton, Forest Grove and Corvallis. But compared to the East Side, the West Side remained relatively undeveloped and unserved by interurban transit.

During the first three years of operation, the Oregon Electric ran 38 trains per day to and from Portland to the Salem and Forest Grove terminals. After the line was completed to Eugene in 1912, over 50 trains were operated daily. The Hill interests integrated the electric service into their entire network of steam railroads and ocean shipping: Two six deck, steel hulled steamships provided continuous service between the Columbia River and San Francisco. By 1915 when passenger traffic reached its peak, the Oregon Electric ran over 100 trains daily on its lines between Portland and Eugene. One of the more famous trains, and certainly the most elegant one in the Northwest, was the "Owl" which left

111

Portland and Eugene at midnight and took a leisurely trip through the Willamette Valley, arriving at its destination in time for breakfast. As described by *The Electric Railway Journal*:

> "The sleeping cars for the Oregon Electric Railway are finished inside in handsomely figured mahogany with inlaid lines and marquetry figures in neat design. Floor covering in the main compartment is Wilton carpet, the seats are upholstered in figured frieze plush and the trimmings throughout the cars are statuary bronze. The ceilings are decorated in green and gold."[21]

The Oregon Electric also ran two special trains to Salem: The Supreme Court Special, intended primarily for lawyers when the court was in session, and the "Capitol City Flyer" that left Portland at 9:15 a.m. and arrived in Salem at 10:50 a.m., travelling the 50 miles in 95 minutes including time for two stops. Railroad economics, together with the growth of automobile use, forced the termination of these special services in 1928. For the next five years the line lost a total of $6.5 million and service was reduced accordingly. Finally in 1933, an average of only 16 passengers per trip rode the remaining trains. Branding such conditions as farcical, the company quit the passenger business for good.

Like the Oregon Electric, the Southern Pacific Red Electrics arrived on the scene too late to have any real impact on population growth in the southwest suburban regions of Portland. In fact, their appearance in 1914 coincided with the onset of the European war which created a recession in the Oregon economy and a slowdown in the new housing construction. The S. P. had concluded belatedly that it was offered no choice but to compete with the Oregon Electric. Its west side steam lines had been losing money, except on the Oswego run, and it was under fire from the city council to electrify its Fourth Avenue entrance into downtown Portland. In 1920, at the peak of its passenger traffic, it ran 64 trains daily to and from Portland. Although its service was not as elegant as that of the Oregon Electric, its newer equipment was faster.[22]

Having invested too much capital too quickly and at the wrong time, and having tried to service areas that were already being served (districts not dense enough to support mass transit), the Southern Pacific Red Electric system began to curtail operations in 1924 and went out of the passenger business altogether in 1929. It was never able to capture more than a small portion of the post-world war population growth in the Beaverton valley. The expanded use of the auto, truck and bus, the resurfacing of Canyon and Scholls Ferry Roads and the construction of the new Bertha Beaverton highway adjacent to its tracks all combined to hasten the arrival of the final day.

Two other conditions had a negative impact on the West Side lines. Operating on standard gauge tracks with regular railroad equipment and facilities, the electric interurbans found themselves subject to the same three man crew regulation that was applied to all of the long-haul railroads. A further restriction that affected operating revenues was the flat rate that the Oregon State Railroad Commission, later renamed the Public Service Commission, decreed for all

*An Oregon Electric Local on S. W. 10th at Stark
1912*

railroad passenger service. With sharply inflated post-war costs, a rigid rate schedule, competition from the internal combustion engine and a diminishing ridership, the electric interurbans were doomed as private passenger carriers.

It was actually the carriage of freight that saved the Oregon Electric and its affiliate, United Railways, until they dropped their passenger service completely. The Red Electric lines never did carry more than minimal freight. Initially, freight carriage had been an afterthought. But by the first world war it was bringing in more than half of the revenue on the Hill lines. With the PRL&P East Side interurbans, freight carriage was not much of a factor until the time of the second world war. During World War I, however, all of the interurbans took on freight service as part of the war effort. Forty years later, all of the surviving interurban tracks would be carrying freight and many of the abandoned roadbeds would be paved over for highway and freeway use.

The fourth interurban, United Railways, merits historical attention primarily for its freight hauling rather than its passenger carrying operation which was limited from the beginning. Its electric service to the suburban town of Linnton only lasted from 1909 to April of 1915 when the company closed down operations into Portland after being denied a fare increase. The company's significance lay in its profitable real estate and freight operations, particularly after it was acquired by the James J. Hill interests in September 1909. Of all the street railway franchises issued, however, United Railways caused the city the most problems. This lasted from 1906 until 1940 when the city finally removed its Front Avenue tracks to clear the way for Harbor Drive.[23]

Apart from an extensive commuter service to Linnton for six years, United operated primarily as a freight line on S. W. Macadam Avenue to South Portland, where it serviced shipyards and lumber mills, and on Front Avenue, where it provided the Oregon Electric a connection to the SP&S passenger terminal and freight yards in Northwest Portland. It did, however, construct a passenger streetcar line up West Burnside and Barnes Road to the Mt. Calvary Cemetery, a branch that was later absorbed by the PRL&P. After the termination of its Linnton service, United continued to run a combined passenger-freight service from Linnton through the Cornelius Tunnel to Wilkesboro and Keasey until it replaced electricity with steam in 1923. Until 1943, when most of its properties were formally absorbed by the SP&S, it continued to run freight from the upper Tualatin Valley to Portland. When its Front Avenue tracks were pulled up in 1940, United provided a needed belt railway connection to the Portland terminals for all of SP&S's Tualatin and Willamette Valley freight operations.

But perhaps United's most significant impact on the city of Portland was its early investment in Guild's Lake real estate. Beginning with an initial purchase of 250 acres for $250,000 in March 1906, United was to spend millions in behalf of its owners, the SP&S and the Hill interests, to create an extensive industrial park, much of it on landfill dredged from the Willamette River by the Port of

Linnton

114

Portland. Ever since that date, the Northern Pacific, now the Burlington Northern, has been the major property owner along the northwest side of the Willamette River.

Surrounded by James J. Hill's rail lines, Linnton was a small town resting on a narrow shelf along the river, nestled under the Tualatin Mountains. It had a variable population of less than 2000, comprising permanent residents and transients, with many of its workers living in Portland. Incorporated in 1910 as a company town, Linnton was developed to serve as the site for two large lumber mills, the Clark-Wilson and West Oregon Companies, and a major shipyard, the Columbia Engineering Works. In 1913, the Portland Gas & Coke Company moved its manufacturing plant to within Linnton's southern boundary and the large oil refiners began to purchase sites for their extensive shipping and storage needs. Three months after United dropped its passenger service, Linnton voted to be annexed to Portland. By this action, Linnton made a significant contribution to Portland's history. It brought with it much of what has come to be known since 1945 as the Forest Park Reserve, the largest semi-wilderness park within a city's limits in the continental United States. With either luck or foresight, Linnton had annexed most of the property in December 1912.

Linnton's history was tied closely to the fortunes of the lumber industry.

Linnton Transit Company buses (1920) that replaced the United Railways passenger service

During a recession, its economy would suffer and its population would decline. In the pre-prohibition era, according to one oldtimer:

> "The town was wild. There were seven saloons in it; men from the mills would come in and would end up fighting. . . . We had our own jail, police and curfew."[24]

The record indicates that conditions did not change appreciably after 1916, for another long-time resident has declared that prohibition never did exist in Linnton:

> "There was nothing but bootleggin' from here to St. Helens. . . . People had to try and keep from selling it to each other."[25]

Implications for Future Growth

Whereas the West Side interurbans did not have much immediate effect on population settlement *per se*, they did exercise an important long-range influence on the physical shaping of the metropolitan countryside and its urban centers: Beaverton, Tigard and Hillsboro. The improved highways, with their inevitable strip developments, tended to follow the tracks into the cities which were to be faced with increasingly severe traffic congestion since the tracks were not bridged over. The center of Beaverton provides the best example, with the convergence of two major highways and two rail lines, the Southern Pacific and the Burlington Northern (the old Oregon Electric roadbed). The Fred Meyer Company, operator of 25 major shopping centers in the metropolitan area, is currently constructing its largest center adjacent to the eastern juncture of all four routes.

The interurban freight lines were to have an important impact on the growth of suburban commercial and industrial activity which uses the accessible rail services. The open land between Beaverton, Tigard, Tualatin and Oswego in 1926 — much of it in farm use — has become a major warehouse distribution center for the Portland metropolitan region. Expansive residential and shopping center growth has accompanied this development, to the point that the area has become the fastest growing section of metropolitan Portland. Development has been so widely spread, with minimum land use planning control, that there is insufficient density to allow for effective mass transit service. Oregon's largest employer, Tektronix, built its main industrial campus northwest of Beaverton. The thousands who work there commute largely by private automobile. The lack of coordination and planning between private development and needed public services is proving to be increasingly costly.

The Population Research Center at Portland State University projects the greatest growth to occur in the Tualatin district, between Interstate 5 and the Burlington Northern (the old Oregon Electric) Railroad tracks. Experiencing a 25 percent growth in 1978, Tualatin is expected to increase its size from 5900 to 28,000 by the year 2000.

116

Aerial view of the center of Beaverton — 1964

The Demise of Electric Rail Service

In the last analysis, it was to be the unregulated use of automobiles, buses and trucks, subsidized by state and federal highways, that brought the land transportation industry to the brink of bankruptcy. In the early 1920s, Paul Shoup, president of the Pacific Electric Railway Company of Los Angeles, a Southern Pacific subsidiary, wrote an eloquent defense of electric railways that he declared to be "essential to the public of the United States."[26] They needed protection from unregulated competition or they would be destroyed. The future president of the parent Southern Pacific Company cited "the situation in Oregon," where the S. P. maintained an extensive "Red Electric" network in addition to its traditional railroad operation. The Oregon Public Service Commission, said Shoup, did not have the regulatory authority enjoyed by California's Railroad Commission, with adequate power to "stop economic wastes resulting from unbridled competition. . . . The electric lines operating in the suburban districts out of Portland have had their revenue so cut down by wholly unregulated motor bus competition as to make it probable that the electric railway service will . . . become a thing of the past."[27]

Shoup's prediction was to prove accurate, but he could not foresee in 1920 one other set of factors that were to exercise a determining influence on the future decline of electric rail service: The aggressive marketing and lobbying tactics of the General Motors Corporation and its allies in the oil and tire industries. The weapons they employed produced the fatal blows.

118

Chapter 6

The Battle Over The Six-Cent Fare

The Portland Railway Light & Power Company (PRL&P) was Portland's largest property owner in 1915. It comprised three divisions: Electric power, interurban and railway. In electric power generation it received some competition from San Francisco investor Herbert Fleishhacker's Northwestern Electric Power Company which had its city plant in the basement of the Pittock Block. But its two transportation divisions enjoyed a monopoly of all East Side interurban and city streetcar service.

The company grew out of a series of mergers that culminated in 1906 under the local leadership of Portland's two leading bankers: The First National Bank's Abbot L. Mills and the U. S. National Bank's John C. Ainsworth. Ownership then passed from local control to a family investment company in Philadelphia by the name of E. W. Clark & Co. All previously issued franchises to each of the earlier component companies were transferred to the new incorporation. In subsequent years when the company experienced further ownership changes, the franchises were transferred again. To this day, the surviving Portland General Electric Company operates under the authority of five basic franchises, one of which was awarded 96 years ago. All were granted with no time limitations. As with every private utility, franchise integrity has always been sacred. It has proven to be one of the magnets to attract investors.

Franklin T. Griffith and the PRL&P

In 1913, the year that Franklin T. Griffith took over the presidency from B. S. Josselyn, the company achieved its maximum profitability. The railway division carried 89.5 million passengers over its 34 lines and 195 miles of tracks. Energy costs and wages were stable and the standard five-cent fare proved more than adequate to provide a handsome return to stockholders. In the two year period (1913-1914) the company invested over $2 million in capital improvements. It owned a fleet of 570 streetcars of which 400 were in regular service. Total company profits were further enhanced by increasing interurban receipts from its own lines and by the power that the company was supplying to the Oregon Electric and Southern Pacific interurban operations.

Upon assuming office, lawyer Griffith was optimistic about his company's future. In his first official act, he granted a one percent per hour increase in pay to the entire labor force of over 4000. Operational efficiency was to be his major long-range goal. His immediate concern was the company's attitude toward the public. "The public must know all the facts," he declared. "We need an open air policy" and "a new era of understanding between corporations and the public."

In a statement that must have shaken a few of the old guard from Portland's business establishment, Griffith exclaimed: "Public service corporations are no longer private enterprises."[1]

Griffith's commitment to "an open air policy" was to undergo severe strain in subsequent years when costs increased, ridership dropped off and public opposition to a fare increase hardened. But the initial challenge to his new policy came from the city charter of 1913 that required all franchised utilities to file annual statements of earnings with the city auditor. In March of 1915, Griffith sent the city council a bitter letter in which he claimed that the charter provision was "unconstitutional. . . . It impaired the company's franchise" that had been granted in 1903.[2] Griffith was not alone in filing such a complaint. The Portland Gas & Coke Company, also owned by eastern investors, charged that its perpetual franchise, granted by the territorial legislature in 1859 just prior to statehood, exempted it from complying with the charter requirement. Under protest, however, both companies filed their statements annually and eventually became reconciled to the procedure. It was one thing for Griffith and his good friend over at the gas company, Guy Talbot, to provide the public with information which they chose to release; it was quite another matter to be forced to publicize information that the law required to be accurate.

In the spring of 1916, Portland Railway Light & Power noticed an ominous trend. Earnings had been decreasing for three years, ridership was off by 15 million, and April's cash surplus was only $2531. President Griffith decided that the company had to seek a one-cent fare raise. He blamed the increasing use of commuter automobiles and jitney buses for the decrease in passengers carried. There was nothing that could be done about the growth of the daily east and westbound vehicular bridge traffic that had doubled since 1913, from 15,000 to 30,000 vehicles, but Griffith could and did attack the jitneys. They were private motor cars that ran adjacent to the tracks, picking up carloads of passengers for five cents each. They were not regulated and would not be franchised until the winter of 1918. Their official life would be short, however, as the council was to outlaw their use in June 1918. Griffith was not happy about the prospect of granting franchises to the jitneys, but barring their exclusion, route and schedule regulation might at least diminish direct competition with the streetcars. Apart from his own company's experience, Griffith could cite that of the Los Angeles Railway Company which had seen its total annual ridership drop by 17.7 million — all due to unregulated jitneys, it was claimed.

By seeking a fare increase, PRL&P invited the scrutiny of the Oregon State Public Service Commission. The city council's role was uncertain. The city commissioners assumed that they had the final approval, but in fact a little noticed provision in a 1901 state law gave ultimate jurisdiction to the legislature. The legislature, in turn, had granted this power first to the railroad commission and then to the public service commission. Neither agency, however, had had any opportunity to exercise its authority over streetcar fares because there had been no requested increase in 15 years.

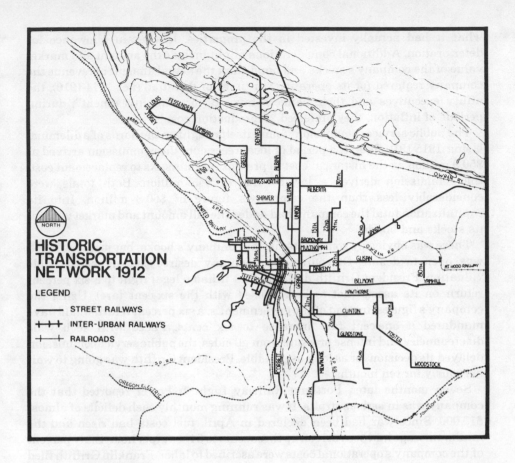

HISTORIC
TRANSPORTATION
NETWORK 1912

LEGEND

▬▬▬▬ STREET RAILWAYS

+++++ INTER-URBAN RAILWAYS

+—+—+ RAILROADS

Evaluating the Rate Base

In examining the records, the commission faced a number of problems. It was almost impossible to separate the railway division properties and operational costs from those of the electric power and interurban divisions. It decided, in December 1916, to treat the whole company as a single unit in establishing a rate base. The major question facing the commission was that of determining an accurate valuation of company assets. The U. S. Supreme Court had ruled in 1898 (*Smyth v. Ames*) that the rates set must yield a "fair return" to the carrier on the "value" of its property, "the theory being that since this property is being used in the service of the public, to compel its public use without just compensation would amount to confiscation."[3]

But just how was such a "value" to be ascertained? There were two accepted formulas. One, "reproduction less depreciation," took into account the cost of reproducing the properties at current prices, less an allowance for the properties' depreciation. The other, the "historical cost" or "original prudent investment" formula, suggested that the company was entitled to receive a fair return on what it had actually invested in the properties, less again allowance for deterioration. Additional considerations might include the amount and market value of the company's stocks and bonds and the actual amount of revenue the company required for its operation. In times of deflation (i.e., 1914-1916), the utility executives and their bankers favored "prudent investment"; during periods of inflation, they preferred "reproduction cost."

The public service commission[4] found itself caught on the horns of a dilemma. Using 1915-1916 figures, a period of local recession, the commission arrived at $50.9 million as the historical cost to present investors. As to replacement cost, the commission derived a lower value of $45 million. Both totals were considerably less than the company's figure of $60.8 million. Into its capitalization total the company had added the full amount and market value of its stocks and bonds.

There was obviously some water in the company's books, but just how much was open to debate. Of course, the company desired the highest possible valuation. President Griffith declared that it had a legal right to a six percent return on its assets (not to be confused with the six-cent fare). Using the company's figures, instead of the government's, a six percent return would have mandated a one-cent fare increase to six cents. Faced with such wide discrepancies and intense pressure from all sides, the public service commission delayed its decision for as long as possible. President Griffith was going to wait nervously for ten months.

Seven months later, Portland Railway Light & Power reported that the company was in serious straits. It was running monthly cash deficits of almost $13,000. Since war had been declared in April, fuel costs had risen and the minimum wage had been driven up three cents to 34 cents per hour. Sixty percent of the company's operational costs were ascribed to labor. Franklin Griffith filed formal requests with both the city council and the public service commission for immediate redress. But he encountered some strong opposition at city hall.

Recently appointed city commissioner Dan Kellaher charged that "the company was trying to put something over on the city." And City Attorney George LaRoche declared that "85 percent of the public cannot afford six cents."[5] Early in September, Griffith warned that if the company did not receive the six-cent fare soon, service would be curtailed and fewer cars would be on line. But at a meeting on September 7th, City Attorney LaRoche told Griffith that expenses could be reduced in other ways. He went on to charge that there was "water in the PRL&P stock," and the the company was "more profitable" than its officers would admit. Ten days later, the U. S. Supreme Court upheld the six-cent fare in a case not involving Portland. Griffith felt that his appeal had been strengthened, but he was in for a surprise.

October 5, 1917 was a fateful day for the utility president. Not only did the public service commission deny the fare increase by a 2-1 vote, but it approved an increase in the maximum wage to 45 cents per hour. The commission majority felt that a shorter basic workday and a reasonable wage increase were both justified. The company was told in no uncertain terms just where it could reduce and consolidate some of its service. The largest operational losses were produced by the streetcar lines that served certain upper income areas: Kings Heights, Arlington Heights, Alameda, Westover Terraces and Eastmoreland. Declared the commission: "City patrons should not be expected to bear the losses on these lines," because the company did not own them. They had been constructed by the real estate developers for promoting their "wildcat real estate tracts." Portland Railway Light & Power had entered into contracts with the owners to service the lines for which the owners had agreed to pay equipment depreciation and track maintenance costs. Since 1914, when the real estate market collapsed, the payments had been in default.

The commission further recommended that the city consider reducing bridge tolls and franchise payments and assume the street paving costs that resulted from track laying and maintenance, a sum that amounted to $66,000 in 1916.[6] The commission apparently did not realize that to effect these reductions, the city charter would have to be amended by popular vote and that the public climate was not favorable in 1917.

For two months Franklin Griffith kept his composure, at least in public. But on December 11, 1917, he let out a blast. "Ruin faces us," he charged. "We can't borrow and we've got no credit."[7] Griffith made a personal appeal to the public service commission in Salem. He carried with him the facts and figures to show how the wartime inflation was killing the company. Wage increases were bad enough but fuel costs had risen astronomically: 325 percent in 1916 and 180 percent through nine months of 1917. The commission took the appeal under advisement, and on January 5, 1918, it voted unanimously to approve the six-cent fare, effective January 15th. Commissioner Frank J. Miller wrote attorney Joseph N. Teal that the action was justified to prevent the company from going into receivership.[8]

In a lengthy statement, the commission examined all facets of the company's operation, including the possibility of municipal ownership. It concluded that "the cost of service would not be less if the city should take over the streetcar system and operate it." It was felt that the operating expenses "would be the same as at present, while power instead of being furnished as now at cost would have to be paid for at commercial rates."

Using the "historic" or "prudent investment" formula, the commission appraised the railway division properties at $30.8 million and the electric power division at $20.1 million.

"Under condemnation, it is not likely that the property could be bought for any less than the Commission's valuation, and if the courts took account of the present scale of prices, of materials and labor, the costs would be increased at least 25%. Money for such purposes could not be obtained [by the city] for less than 6%, so that the interest charge would be at least as large as now. . . . Under city management service could be maintained only by a resort to one or more of the following expedients: Reducing services, cutting wages, raising fares, or making up the deficit by taxation."[9]

The first day of the six-cent fare.

The commission might also have pointed out that the PRL&P was paying annual taxes of over $700,000 in 1916. Municipal ownership would remove that income source from the public treasury. It would also eliminate from the city coffers the $66,000 received from bridge tolls and franchise payments.

"Six-cent fare now rules the city," reported the headlines of *The Oregonian* on January 16, 1918. Apparently, the change went into effect with a minimum of confusion and discomfort as passengers had to reach for the extra penny and the conductors had to break change for a dime. Hundreds of patrons seized the first opportunity to buy tickets, either in strips of five or in books of 50 for $2.75 (5.5¢ each). But three days later, at the regular meeting of the city council, the reaction was far from calm. On the motion of Commissioner Kellaher, the council voted to request that the PSC rescind its approval of the six-cent fare. But before taking the vote, the council received and read a blistering letter from Circuit Judge Henry McGinn, a long-time foe of the Portland Railway Light & Power Company and of its president, Franklin T. Griffith.

Replying negatively to Mayor Baker's invitation to attend the meeting and tell the council what they should do about the six-cent fare case, McGinn said: "I do not intend to play Mr. Baker's game of camouflage." McGinn charged that "Baker and the council are elected and hired to protect the public interests in this and all matters. . . . They are in the position to get the facts. . . . If they don't, it's their fault. . . . Their invitation is bunk. . . . I know their game and I won't play it for them."[10] McGinn wanted the jitneys franchised. The next day, the council took the initial step. In a first reading, it voted to approve a franchise for the largest of the jitney operators, the Portland Trackless Car Company. But final approval was to be delayed.

The Protagonists: Kellaher, McGinn and Griffith

Commissioner Dan Kellaher and Judge Henry McGinn were a colorful pair. They were formidable opponents of all utilities. Democrat Dan Kellaher, a staunch friend of labor, had represented Multnomah County in the state senate from 1909 to 1915. He had also been a member of the dock commission from 1912 to 1916. Preaching a "fair deal" for Portland's citizens, he had long advocated strict control of all public utilities. Failing in this effort, the city should assume public ownership. In the tradition of Harry Lane, Kellaher also urged free garbage collection and an adequate disposal system. He was obviously not popular with *The Oregonian*, which once described him as "an exploded bomb, a fired sky-rocket, a sagging balloon."[11]

Such epithets had long been bestowed upon Judge Henry McGinn. Often cited as one of the most picturesque figures in Oregon, McGinn had as varied a career as anyone in the state's history. Starting out as a political lieutenant of Henry W. Corbett and Joseph Simon, he was involved in all of the dirty political dealings that afflicted the Republican Party at the turn of the century. Vice and gambling operations drew his public support. For years he had been a consort of the notorious Madame P. Shong. He loved booze and women and was not afraid to admit it. Despite his personal reputation, he was such an able lawyer, and such an eloquent speaker, when sober, that his services were eagerly sought. His voice carried authority in a community that ostensibly disdained his type of pleasures. McGinn was an emotional eccentric, a robust and witty Portland-born Irishman who always considered himself a friend of the common people. True to form, one month after the state had voted its "bone dry" amendment in

THE RIGHTS
OF MAN WEIGH
MORE THAN
THE RIGHTS
OF MONEY.

THE
BENCH

COMMON
PEOPLE

HARRY
MURPHY

Judge Henry E. McGinn

126

November 1916, Judge McGinn upheld the right of Oregonians to manufacture their own wine for their own use. Quoting freely from the Bible, the judge declared that man had an inherent right to make and drink his own wine.[12]

Before his second election to the court in 1911, McGinn had experienced a metamorphosis — he became a thorough-going reformer and publicly confessed his past sins.[13] His personal habits did not change, only the targets of his wrath. He had never cared for Mayor George L. Baker whom he considered a "wheeler-dealer" promoter who had sold his soul to the Republican Party establishment, the very group that had launched and supported McGinn's early career. Cited by Walter Pierce at the time of his death in 1922 as "one of the most striking characters I have ever known," McGinn was to die in his favorite brothel and be mourned by Portland's elite. For a populist type of reformer who loved to attack the business establishment, McGinn proved to be an astute investor. He was to leave an estate worth $836,000. In all of Portland's history, Henry McGinn came closest to being the "town character," and he thrived on it.

A week after his first blast at the council, Judge McGinn accused the city fathers of "going back into partnership with the Portland Railway Light & Power Company." He recounted some past history which he knew from first-hand experience — the days when the original Portland General Electric Company and the early street railway companies controlled local politics through bribery and other forms of pressure. He cited Mayor Baker's opposition to the jitneys and accused him of buckling under to Franklin T. Griffith. Quoting his favorite source, the Holy Bible, McGinn asserted: "The ox knoweth his owner and the ass his master's crib."[14]

Undoubtedly, McGinn, Kellaher and others of similar feelings were successful in generating public pressure. On February 1, 1918, the council voted $30,000 to undertake a formal examination of the Portland Railway Light & Power Company books. It also expressed a double interest in evaluating the current service of the company and in re-examining the company's existing franchises.

A whole month passed with nary a public utterance from Judge McGinn. Then on March 4th, *The Oregon Journal* headlined an article, "McGinn back on the job." Addressing a local fraternal group, McGinn declared: "My friends, I have failed you lately . . . I have not attended these meetings. . . . You know, my friends, I have my faults. Would God that I had not, but I have them."[15] This was a polite way to inform his patrons that he had been on a bender for the better part of three weeks, but that he was now dried out and back on the attack. Taking aim at the public service commission, McGinn said: "Franklin T. Griffith took snuff on Saturday and the . . . commission sneezed on Sunday."[16]

Two days later, the fiery judge ridiculed Griffith.

"Franklin T. Griffith is a fine bookkeeper, one of the best in the country. And when he started to value the property of the Portland Railway Light & Power Company, he put down every rusty screw and bolt and battered rail and horse car in the scrapheap of the company until the valuation got so high the Public

Service Commission could still lop off $11 million and yet leave several million more than it ought to be. . . . The Portland Railway Light & Power Company and the Public Service Commission are robbing the people."[17]

Franklin T. Griffith was the antithesis of Henry McGinn. He **was** trained as a bookkeeper and held his first two jobs in California and Oregon City in that capacity. While employed as a cashier for the Willamette Pulp & Paper Co., he studied law at night. Early in his 21st year he passed the Oregon Bar examination and established a practice in Oregon City where he became a legal adviser to the paper mills and to the old Portland General Electric Company which had a generating plant at Willamette Falls. One thing led to another: He moved his practice to Portland and became involved with Portland Railway Light & Power Company legal matters. He soon became so intimately acquainted with the financial and legal intricacies of the fast growing utility empire that he was the natural choice to succeed B. S. Josselyn in 1913 at the age of 43.

The Minnesota native was obviously bright, energetic and ambitious. But in contrast to Henry McGinn, he was quiet and cautious. As one article depicted him:

" 'Safety First' is the slogan of Franklin T. Griffith. It permeates the Portland Railway Light & Power Company . . . and everything else with which he has anything to do. . . . Mr. Griffith takes great pleasure in touring in his Cadillac Eight and there isn't a more careful automobile enthusiast anywhere when it comes to considering the 'other fellow.' "[18]

Griffith had bought his first automobile in 1910, the year that he had moved his residency to Ladd's Addition.

Few people in Portland's history were to make as much of an impact on the city's growth as Franklin T. Griffith. He was to maintain active business involvement for almost 40 years. In addition to his dominant leadership of the major local private utility, he was to engage in an active law practice and be associated with over ten local corporations as either an officer or director.[19] His primary accomplishment, to be recounted in Chapter 14 was his successful effort to restore local control of both the Portland General Electric Company and the Portland Traction Company, the two major survivors of the old Portland Railway Light & Power Company. In the process, he saved the company, almost single handedly, from bankruptcy during the decade of the 1930s. Unlike Henry McGinn, Franklin T. Griffith never actively engaged in politics, although he strongly supported the Republican Party and opposed with equal vigor all attempts to municipalize the private power companies. He became the leading spokesman for the private ownership of electric utilities. Some might question his judgment, social values or corporate affiliations, but few could doubt his courage and ability. Upon his death in 1952 at the age of 82,

Frank T. Griffith

former governor Oswald West praised Griffith as an "honest man; a gentleman and a square shooter."

The Aftermath of the Six-Cent Fare

The six-cent fare was only a temporary solution to meet an immediate crisis, according to lawyer James B. Kerr. It merely covered the wage increase of October 1917. Kerr and Griffith realized that in itself it "was not sufficient to provide a return to the stockholders over and above the fixed charges of operation, depreciation, taxes and interest."[20] Furthermore, both men recognized the fact that additional wage increases would be demanded in the future. City council, however, appeared to be unconcerned about the company's future requirements including its ability to satisfy stockholders. After the courts had validated the fare increase in March 1918, the council was pressured by Henry McGinn and others to consider some measures to return the fare to five cents.

Alluding to the recommendation of the public service commission, council member A. L. Barbur introduced a controversial ordinance that would be referred to the people in the May election. It passed by a 3-2 vote with C. A. Bigelow and Dan Kellaher voting no. The measure proposed that public service utilities no longer be required to pay their share of street improvements and sewer construction; that they be exempted from paying bridge tolls, franchise charges and license fees; and that they no longer be required to furnish free transportation to police and firemen. The measure also provided for the levying of a city tax to cover the loss of revenue.[21]

The May referendum vote was negative despite the quarter page ads that the PRL&P ran almost daily for ten days before the election. The company was not anxious to restore the five-cent fare, but it figured that it would probably gain in the long run by not having to pay the tolls and other extra charges which could only increase if the wartime inflation continued. Furthermore, there was no guarantee that the public service commission would agree to a fare reduction if the company could prove it still needed the six-cent fare despite the elimination of the extra charges. Kellaher, McGinn and their followers, who were substantial in number, wanted the fare reduction but were unwilling to release the company from obligations that they felt all utilities should be expected to pay. Furthermore, the mere suggestion of a tax levy to bail out a private utility was anathema to the opponents.

Having lost this round, Franklin Griffith's next challenge came from the federal government. During the winter and spring of 1918 a number of complaints were filed with the U. S. Emergency Fleet Corporation over the infrequency of streetcar service to the wartime shipyards and industrial plants. Additional complaints referred to the distances travelled and to the poor quality of the housing that was available to the wartime workers, particularly in South Portland. President Griffith should have been aware of this latter problem because he was a major owner of the Heath Shipbuilding Company that was constructing wooden hulls under government contract at its plant in the heart of the South Portland waterfront district.

After a thorough investigation, the federal inspector recommended that the government loan the Portland Railway Light & Power Company sufficient funds to purchase 25 additional streetcars. There was too much congestion during rush hours and there was need to expand service along the South Portland waterfront. Tied to this recommendation, however, was a commitment from the city of Portland and its business leadership to improve the condition of wartime housing.

Although the company received the streetcars, the "improved housing" never advanced beyond the talking stage. City planner Charles H. Cheney, an advisor to the council on planning matters, strongly recommended that the council establish definite industrial and residential zones before any new streetcar service was contemplated or planned. The city's first zoning code of 1919 was to embody just such a recommendation but the voters defeated it after an

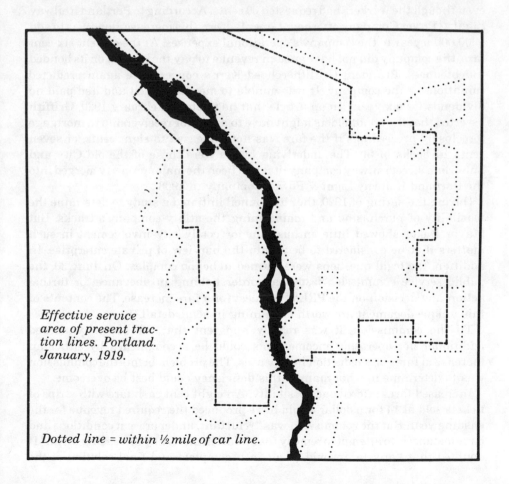

Effective service area of present traction lines. Portland. January, 1919.

Dotted line = within ½ mile of car line.

exhaustive and well financed campaign of opposition, led by the Portland Realty Board.

In October 1918, one month before the Armistice was declared, the public service commission awarded the city transit workers a five cent an hour raise. Franklin Griffith was worried. He could see future wage demands developing and realized that the company would have to request a further fare increase, to perhaps as high as eight cents. He did not relish having to repeat the agonies of 1917. It was of little solace to be informed by the federal government that "Portland's streetcar service now is superior to that of any other city in the country."[22] The problem was, who would pay for it?

The Public Ownership Question

In July 1919 the public service commission awarded the city transit workers another five cent per hour raise. The maximum wage was now 50 cents an hour even though the workers had requested 60 cents. According to Portland Railway Light & Power Company attorney, James B. Kerr, this increase alone was to add $300,000 a year to the company's operational expenses. At the current six-cent fare, the company did not have enough revenue to pay the interest on its bonded indebtedness. President Griffith echoed Kerr's concern. He again predicted ruination for the company. It was unable to meet its deficit and had paid no dividends for six years. In an article that he wrote in February 1920, Griffith asserted that the bondholders might have to apply for receivership in mortgage foreclosure proceedings if the fare was not increased to eight cents, or seven cents in books of 50. The underlying bonds were those of the old City and Suburban street railway company that had been the major property merged into the Portland Railway Light & Power Company in 1906.

During the spring of 1920, the city council initiated a study to determine the feasibility of purchasing and maintaining the utility company's tracks. But Mayor Baker showed little enthusiasm for costly city involvement in such matters that he considered to be within the purview of private enterprise. In addition, the legal questions were deemed to be too complex. On June 20, the public service commission issued an order holding in abeyance for further action any decision on the PRL&P request for a fare increase. The contents of this unique document are worth examining in some detail.[23]

To the commission, it was readily apparent that the company needed additional net operating income. This could be accomplished by either an increase in fares or a reduction in expenses. The problem before the commission was to determine in what manner this deficiency could best be overcome.

Increased fares offered one possibility. An eight cent cash fare with strips of tickets sold at 14 for a dollar would have produced the required revenue for the ensuing year. But the commission was "reluctant, under present conditions and circumstances, to attempt to remedy the situation merely by increasing fares." It doubted that "any fare would result in a complete and final solution of the difficulties of the Portland street railway system" at the time. This was essentially a political decision. The initiative was being tossed back to the city.

According to the commission, the city had the authority to relieve the company of a number of costs that should be borne by all of Portland's citizens and not by just the transit ridership. Assuming that public transit performed an important city service, why should not the city maintain the streets and bridges for streetcars in the same manner that it did for private automobiles, buses and trucks? The company was being forced to carry the entire burden of its service and the costs were paid by the car riders in the form of fares. "The injustice" was "apparent." The company would save $200,000 in 1920 were the city to assume the extra costs, including $22,000 of free rides to city employees. In Seattle, which went municipal in 1918, one division of the city government actually reimbursed another division $30,000 for the transportation of policemen and firemen.

The commission carried its case for city financial responsibility one step further by advocating that Portland acquire the street railway tracks and treat them as the streets and bridges were treated — thoroughfares for public use, to be enjoyed equally by all citizens.

> "Inasmuch as provision is made for the vehicular, motor and pedestrian traffic by the city, is it not consistent that it should also provide and maintain a highway of steel in the form of street railway tracks for the use of the greater portion of its citizens who are dependent, by force of circumstances, upon the street railway for rapid transit?"[24]

The state authority rejected the argument that the electric street railway had become partially obsolete as a means of rapid transit, despite the increased use of autos, buses and trucks.

> "While it is impossible to predict what the future will develop in the way of improvements and economies, certainly, until a more efficient, more economical and more practicable means of rapid transit is found, the electric railway cannot be said to be obsolete."[25]

The commission concluded its order with two statements: (1) It strongly recommended that streetcar service be eliminated for the leased lines not owned by the company (i.e., Westover Terraces etc.), and (2), it adjudged the service on the other lines to be "reasonably satisfactory and as good as the car riders [desired] to pay for."

The fare increase question was to remain unresolved for several months (see Chapter 14) and during the interim Frank Griffith became increasingly disturbed. He knew that 91 streetcar companies (representing 11 percent of the total mileage in the United States) were currently either in the hands of receivers, or already foreclosed and abandoned. It appeared to him that Portland might follow suit.

The experiences of cities like San Francisco, Seattle, Detroit, New York and Toronto which either had already assumed or were in the process of assuming municipal ownership of their public transit systems could offer neither a model nor much encouragement to people such as Dan Kellaher of Portland. The traditional requirements that usually had to be met in some measure in order to ensure a successful municipal take-over were lacking in Portland's case. They were:

1. A widespread dissatisfaction with the existing service.

2. A leadership in city hall committed to the change.

3. Ineffective administration of the private utility.

4. The imminent expiration of the franchise to allay costly and time consuming litigation.

5. The endorsement of the local press.

6. A reasonable cost that appears bearable by the city without too much strain on the city's financial resources.

Toronto, which today is considered to have the finest municipal public transit system in North America, qualified on all counts when its citizens voted approval in 1918 by an overwhelming margin of 11-1.[26] The takeover was consummated in 1921 upon expiration of the franchise. The record would seem to indicate that the City of Los Angeles would have assumed ownership of the Los Angeles Railway system in 1927 had not its owner, Henry E. Huntington, died in the middle of negotiations which were subsequently cancelled by the executors of his estate.[27]

From the experiences of Toronto and other cities, however, it seems only fair to conclude that municipal ownership in itself did not necessarily lead to a more viable or cost efficient transit system. Seattle and Detroit were to suffer for years from a decreasing ridership and heavy indebtedness. Toronto, on the other hand, was blessed with fortuitous circumstances that gave it certain unique advantages: (1) The conservative legacy of the private company which had not overextended its lines; (2) the city's geography and its high level of population density; (3) the low level of automobile ownership in Canadian as compared with American cities. Portland, for example, not only possessed the fourth highest rate of automobile ownership among major North American cities (223 per 1000 of population), almost twice that of Toronto's, but it was proportionately more spread out than Toronto, with a lower than average population density. Toronto, furthermore, was fortunate to enjoy 30 years of extraordinarily efficient management, from 1924 to 1954.[28]

In comparison with that of Toronto's, Portland's experience, at least until the mid-1920s, offers certain lessons: (1) The dangers inherent in granting long-term franchises which were to the advantage of the private company and its investors; (2) the risks of overextending trackage and service into areas of low

134

density without being able to effect coordination of future residential and commercial development with the existing transit network; (3) the failure of government to perceive that its extensive road building programs would encourage expanded automobile use at the expense of the private transit company. Few could fault the quality of management enjoyed by the Portland Railway Light & Power Company; but the company had no control over real estate developments and automobile use.

If Portland had assumed ownership of the private transit company in the 1920s, a sound case could be made that the municipal system would have suffered the same fate as the Portland Railway Light & Power Company which was to change its name to the Portland Electric Power Company (PEPCO) in 1924. Knowing the calibre of Portland city governments and the reluctance of Portland voters to assume additional financial burdens, a municipally-owned system would probably not have received the requisite public support to ensure its survival. On the other hand, under municipal ownership the consequences could not have been any worse and the public's resources might have been better protected, and any profits that might have accrued from the operation would have gone into the municipal treasury and not back to Philadelphia. Local control might well have provided certain benefits but only if the local populace and its government were willing to assume the responsibilities necessary to maximize such advantages.

As it was, Portland struggled along with its private transit system. By 1926, PEPCO's annual ridership would decrease to less than 90 million — still a large number of passengers being served daily. But the decline would continue and the profits would gradually disappear, forcing service cuts that would become self-defeating.

PART II

FROM ONE WAR THROUGH ANOTHER, 1917-1950

"Socialists as well as Democrats and Republicans must enjoy their political rights even though one disbelieves in Socialism. ... [This] proceeding is virtually an attempt to indict a political party and to deny it representation in the Legislature. This is not, in my judgment, American government."

Charles Evans Hughes,
statement prepared for the
New York Legislature, January 1920

"If there is any principle of the Constitution that more imperatively calls for attachment than any other it is the principle of free thought — not free thought for those who agree with us but freedom for the thought that we hate."

Oliver Wendell Holmes, Jr.
(*U. S. v. Schwimmer*, 1928)

"The greater the importance of safeguarding the community from incitements to the overthrow of our institutions by force and violence, the more imperative is the need to preserve inviolate the constitutional rights of free speech, free press and free assembly in order to maintain the opportunity for free political discussion, to the end that government may be responsive to the will of the people and that changes, if desired, may be obtained by peaceful means. Therein lies the security of the Republic, the very foundation of constitutional government."

Charles Evans Hughes
(*DeJonge v. Oregon*, 1937)

Chapter 7

Patriotism and Fear, 1917-1923

During the first week of March 1917, the United States Senate was debating a bill to arm American merchant ships carrying materiel that was destined for Allied use in the war against Germany. The German government had reinstituted unlimited submarine warfare on February 1st and President Woodrow Wilson strongly believed that the United States had no recourse but to defend America's neutral rights: To arm its merchant ships whose cargoes were vital to the Allied cause. Fourteen senators were opposed to this action, including Oregon's Harry Lane.

Lane Opposes War

Senator Lane was accused in the Portland press of joining in a filibuster, even though he never uttered a word on the senate floor. He had publicized his opposition, however, with a subsequent declaration that he would have voted for the bill if the armed ships had been prevented from carrying munitions. After the senate adjourned on March 4th without taking final action on the measure, Lane received word from home that "the newspapers have been harpooning you something awful." One friend wrote that a decided majority of the people to whom he had spoken "insist that you did exactly right. . . . It is the newspapers that are doing most of the kicking."[1]

One month later, the local press was to crucify Harry Lane when he voted along with five other senators to oppose the American declaration of war on Germany. As *The Oregonian* editorialized: "Next to being ashamed of Harry Lane for what he has done . . . the people of Oregon are ashamed of themselves for having sent Harry Lane to the United States Senate."[2]

Future United States Senator Richard L. Neuberger was to note in 1938 that "the hatred fomented in Oregon against Lane was without parallel in the history of the far west."[3] The bankers and utility company presidents voiced bitter denunciation of Oregon's junior senator. The most outspoken critic was Emery Olmstead, president of the Northwestern National Bank and one of the most ambitious of Portland's new breed of younger executives who were taking over from the old families. Olmstead took the leadership within Portland's business community to organize a recall campaign against Lane. But the senator's death on May 23, 1917, aborted the effort. Seven weeks after he had cast his fateful vote, Harry Lane died. On his way home to Portland with his family, he had stopped off in San Francisco where he suffered a fatal stroke. As *The Oregon Journal* commented coolly: "He paid for his choice with his life."[4]

137

The traumatic events of the ensuing sixty years of world history have led many diplomatic historians to conclude that Lane and his small band of cohorts did in fact make the right choice,[5] i.e., predicting that America's entrance into the European War would only compound an existing catastrophe. World War I was to shatter the equilibrium of Europe. Out of the ashes came the dictatorial regimes of Stalin, Mussolini and Hitler. As Governor Philip LaFollette of Wisconsin told Neuberger on the 21st anniversary of the war's declaration:

"It is fitting that we pay high tribute to Senator Harry Lane on this day . . . [He] made such a valiant effort to prevent the entrance of this country into the world war. History has proven . . . [him] right."[6]

Robert LaFollette, Philip's father, was one of the "willful" six who had opposed the war. Among the others was George W. Norris of Nebraska, one of the most renowned senators in American history. Norris came to the senate the same year as Lane and he was to compile a brilliant 30 year record before his death in 1943. Lane and Norris became close friends as revealed by a wire that he sent to Neuberger in 1938:

"I learned to love and admire him. I think he was one of God's noblemen. During his illness here I visited him almost daily. I got up in the middle of the night and went to the train with him when he left for his home. He knew that his days were numbered, and I remember the last conversation I ever had with him. He told me then that he knew he could not live and expressed the opinion that I probably would never see him again. He met his death as he met everything else in life without any fear and without trepidation. I thought then and I have always believed that in his death our country lost one of her best and most courageous statesmen. He always turned a sympathetic ear to anyone in distress and never considered himself when he believed it to be his duty to go to the aid of the downtrodden and poor."[7]

Senator William J. Stone of Missouri, a previously close associate of President Wilson and chairman of the Senate Foreign Relations Committee, joined with Lane, Norris and LaFollette in charging that America's war involvement would lead to "the greatest national blunder in history."[8] Stone was to suffer a fate similar to Lane and died within the year. One of Harry Lane's last letters to Portland, addressed to his good friend Henry Esterly, warned: "Be careful, Henry. We are in the war. Morgan [New York banker J. Pierpont Morgan] is in the saddle and he will ride without mercy."[9] Harry Lane would have agreed with Senator Gerald P. Nye of North Dakota when he charged that "the World War created 22,000 new millionaires."[10] But the immediate consequence of the war's declaration in the spring of 1917 was the generation of a different kind of spirit, the most intense feeling of patriotism that American society had ever encountered. And Portland became the patriotic center of the Northwest, achieving a per capita record of war bond sales unequalled in the United States.

Patriotic Fever

To understand the intensity of Oregon's response to the war, one must examine the roots of its population. Approximately 85 percent of the state's residents in 1917 were native born. The largest number had emigrated from the Middle West, with the second largest contingent from the South. The early New England influence, more one of quality than of quantity, was beginning to wane but the "covered wagon" complex was still prevalent. The pioneers had brought true Americanism with them and their descendants fought to preserve this purity in the face of an influx of foreign immigrants from the Orient and Southeastern Europe. With one of the most homogeneous populations in the country, Oregon was overwhelmingly white, Anglo-Saxon and Protestant. And it was the fundamentalist Protestant churches in the pre-war years that fathered the early patriotic organizations.[11] One of the most active groups, the Guardians of Liberty, was founded in 1912, and it proceeded to establish chapters in a scattering of Oregon communities, including Portland, under the fiery leadership of the pastors of the Christian Church.

World War I Poster

In the November 1916 election, several patriotic organizations fielded or supported candidates who publicly adhered to a strict pro-Americanism platform. More would emerge in subsequent months, including the Oregon Federation of Patriotic Societies which embraced strong Populist and "anti-corporate interest" sentiments. Existing fraternal associations of long standing like the Elks, Odd Fellows, Knights of Pythias, and the Scottish Rite Masons eagerly joined the patriotic fervor.

Under the stimulus of a well prepared national program of war propaganda, it was not difficult to transfer vaguely defined fears to a real live enemy, the German Empire. According to the Hearst press and other newspapers of similar ilk, the Kaiser and his generals were bent on destroying freedom, motherhood and everything else that was sacred in life. The Germans became the "Huns." Most news articles covering the war in Portland's leading papers printed "Huns" in their headlines when referring to battles with the German army. Pacifists became enemies and Socialist pacifists became the archenemies; "Onward Christian Soldiers" was the hymn to be sung by all true blooded American patriots. Under such pressure, it was not surprising that Portland's established families fell right into line. Although not a part of this group, Portland's new mayor, George Luis Baker, provided just the touch of drama and authority that Portlanders relished. He personified Portland's dedicated support of President Woodrow Wilson's "Crusade For Democracy."

George Luis Baker

"Goodbye and God bless you, boys," Mayor Baker would proclaim with tears in his eyes as he bade farewell to every contingent of Oregonians heading off to do battle against the Germans.[12] "Our George," as he was fondly called, used to hold breakfasts in the Civic Auditorium for all the boys going overseas. These were not contrived events although George Baker loved to put on a good act. According to one of his friends,"He became the biggest 'ham' in town."[13] George Baker was an emotional, gregarious man who loved people and loved his country more. America had been good to George and such acts of generosity were a means of expressing his appreciation.

Baker was an Horatio Alger character. Born of poor but hard-working parents in The Dalles in 1868, Baker had quit school at nine in order to help support his family. George's father was a German born shoemaker who had emigrated at the age of 17. His mother was a Vermonter of Irish extraction. The family moved around the west, from one job to another, until George left his school in San Francisco to shine shoes and sell newspapers. A night job at Morosco's Theater launched Baker on his first career. He ventured to Portland in 1889 and secured a menial position with John F. Cordray, Portland's leading theater owner. Within ten years he became the protege and associate of Calvin Heilig who had purchased some of Cordray's properties, including the Third Street Theater. In 1901, Baker acquired it and renamed it the Baker Theater. From this base of

GEORGE L. BAKER

Give the Town a Boost
Make BAKER Mayor

1917 Campaign Poster

141

operations, he built his famous Baker Stock Company which was to entertain Portland audiences for many years.

While assistant manager of Heilig's Marquam Grand Theater, George Baker took the first step that was to launch him on his second career. In the spring of 1898, he won a seat on the city council from district 4, the heart of the old downtown. Failing re-election in 1900, Baker went to Eastern Oregon and then returned. Forced into bankruptcy by a fire in 1905, he rebounded quickly with Heilig's help, and in short order became the proprietor of two downtown theaters. "Nothing or nobody could ever get him down,"[14] noted his friend Frank Sterrett years later. "No matter where this man was he always put on a good act. He had guts. . . . "[15]

As a reflection of his growing influence in the downtown, when railroad attorney G. S. Sheppard resigned from the council in April 1907, George Baker was selected by the other members to represent his old district 4. He was to remain on the council for six years, the last three of which he served as council president. During Harry Lane's second term as mayor, George Baker became one of his severest critics. Two more different people could not have confronted one another. Although both men loved children, flowers and animals, Baker was not issue oriented, except when the issue involved a patriotic cause like the World War. Whereas Harry Lane tended to be a loner, George Baker was a joiner. As Sterrett remarked: "George belonged to everyone. He joined every club and organization he could. He used to say, 'If you want to get elected to any public office join 'em all, those votes are all in the bag.' "[16]

Baker lost his bid for one of the new city commission seats in 1913 but came storming back in 1915 to defeat William L. Brewster. He spent two years preparing for his 1917 victory which came seven weeks after war was declared. Although the mayor's office was non-partisan, George Baker always ran with strong Republican backing which he made no effort to discourage. He counted most of Portland's important business and banking executives as supporters, particularly Franklin T. Griffith of the Portland Railway Light & Power Company. Baker was to remain in office for 16 years, a record unequalled until the four terms of Terry Schrunk. In 1931 he was to be elected chairman of the United States Conference of Mayors, an honor that Schrunk also received near the end of his term. Although his administration would occasionally be charged with graft and corruption, there is no solid evidence that Baker himself derived any personal emoluments from his position as Portland's first citizen. His friends did.

At the end of one year in office, Mayor Baker listed 15 accomplishments to which he could point with pride. For example, he had strongly backed the war effort in support of war bond drives; he had promoted the safety and health of soldiers billeted within the Portland area; and he had "enforced the laws" and taken the lead in resolving labor problems in the city's ten shipyards.

Portland had been inundated with thousands of shipyard workers "who labored in three shifts, turning the city into a 24 hour town. There were acute problems in housing, recreation, transportation, vice and crime."[17] The downtown hotels were busy and they took a physical beating. Guests brought bootleg liquor in their luggage and the parties often became wild, with broken furniture, lamps and often bruised bodies to repair and bandage. But there was only so much the mayor could do about such matters. With an undermanned force, the police were too busy tracking down German sympathizers and "reds," particularly after the success of the Bolshevik Revolution in November 1917.

An excerpt from Captain Lee V. Jenkins' autobiographical notes is revealing. Jenkins was to be Mayor Baker's Chief of Police from 1919 to 1933. He was to serve as the department's inspector from 1933 to 1947 and again as chief from 1947 to 1949.

"During the period of the World War, I had charge of outside police activities and had eighty men under my command. [27 percent of the active officers.] This work included the policing of all railroad shops, buildings, and tunnels, also all public docks and shipyards and other places where materials were assembled or manufactured for use in the war. My detail had charge of the registering of alien enemies in the city of Portland, and within a radius of four miles outside the city. During this special duty work I uncovered a number of plots against the Government, which resulted in several persons being sent to Federal prisons; also had charge of many raids on radical headquarters during this period. The United States Government appointed several outstanding citizens as secret service agents to assist me. I also worked in conjunction with, and made reports to, the Area Commanders of the United States Army and Navy Intelligence Service regarding alien activities."[18]

The Anti-Americans

All German residents in the United States who were not naturalized citizens were classified as enemy aliens. President Wilson's proclamation #416 forbade them from approaching within one-half mile of the armory or within 100 yards of the waterfront, an exclusion that played havoc with the hundreds of non-naturalized Germans who held jobs either in downtown Portland or in the shipyards. They all had to secure permits before being allowed entrance to the forbidden areas.

The fear of anti-American activity by Germans appears humorous in retrospect because in actuality it was almost non-existent. But the authorities were taking no chances. In the records of the United States Attorney for Oregon, there are hundreds of letters between Portland and Washington, D. C. referring to the loyalties of German immigrants in Oregon. One letter, dated March 8, 1918, mentioned the case of Mr. and Mrs. Richard Koehler, their son Kurt and daughter Ilse. Richard Koehler was one of Portland's most prominent elder citizens. He had come to Oregon as Henry Villard's personal representative and had just retired from a top management position with the Southern Pacific Railroad. His son Kurt was to become a leading member of Portland's business and social hierarchy. The problem related to daughter Ilse. She had returned to

Germany where she had married a German army private who was later killed on the Russian front. The Koehlers were suspect and were being kept under surveillance. In the words of Assistant U. S. Attorney General Clarence Reames, a former Jackson County district attorney who was appointed chief prosecutor of spies on the West Coast, "They have been well known as German sympathizers in this community. Their talk has been exasperating. . . . "[19]

A communication of July 1918 referred to a passage from a book being circulated by Portland's well regarded Blumauer & Frank Drug Company, entitled "People's Common Sense Medical Adviser." The passage contained a phrase about "pure-minded Teuton" women and their marriage relationships. This was considered obvious propaganda and the book was removed from sale. Everything with a German sounding title underwent a name change: Sauerkraut became "Liberty Cabbage" and hamburger became "Liberty Steak."

The case of German born J. Henry Albers, the "central figure in Portland's most vivid wartime criminal prosecution,"[20] was both tragic and totally indefensible. The president of the profitable Albers Brothers Milling Company was returning by train from a business trip to San Francisco. He had too much to drink in the lounge car before it crossed the Oregon border and he took to singing German songs in a loud tone that disturbed some fellow passengers. Upon his arrival in Portland, Albers was arrested, jailed and convicted for seditious conduct by a German alien. He was given three years in a federal penitentiary and fined $10,000. Albers appealed his case all the way to the United States Supreme Court which finally agreed to consider it in the spring of 1921. On the day of the actual hearing, the Solicitor General himself withdrew the case citing the fact that the government had erred in the initial proceedings. By this point, the much respected and beloved Albers was a broken man. The final indignation to befall him was his expulsion from his local Elks Lodge in Milwaukie. He suffered a paralytic stroke and died ten days later.

The records are full of similar stories. Local vigilante groups went on forays into the countryside, searching for Germans in haystacks. The noted American historian, David Muzzey, had his widely used United States history textbook removed from school circulation because he gave too much attention to the positive German influence on American history. If such treatment of German aliens and influence seems extreme, that accorded the self-proclaimed socialists, pacifists and religious non-believers was even more severe.

Floyd Ramp, a prominent Socialist farmer from Eugene, travelled to Roseburg with a load of wood in September 1917. He encountered a troop transport train that was being loaded with soldiers. As he related the episode recently, "I asked the boys if they knew what they were fighting for. Then I told them they were fighting to protect John D.'s [Rockefeller] money."[21] Ramp was arrested for violation of the Espionage Act. He was tried in Portland where he unsuccessfully defended himself with the aid of C. E. S. Wood. Found guilty, Ramp served 18 months in a federal prison.

Most of Oregon's jurists during the war seemed to share the feelings of one Judge Rossman who was quoted as declaring: "The time has come and is now here: When every good citizen's conduct, if not his conscience, must come into accord with the wishes and designs of the government of the United States."[22] Needless to say, when medical doctor Marie Equi, a long-time radical and women's liberationist, described the war as "The Big Barbecue," she was arrested, convicted and shipped off to San Quentin Prison in California despite a noble defense by C. E. S. Wood.[23]

One of the most amusing letters from Reames was a response to the U. S. Attorney General's inquiry about a pamphlet entitled "Ave! Caesar. Imperator. Morituri Te Salutant," written by Col. C. E. S. Wood. Reames was requested to submit all available information on Wood who was thought in Washington to be a personal friend of not only President Wilson but also former President Theodore Roosevelt.

"C. E. S. Wood is a man approximately sixty years of age and one of the leading lawyers of the state of Oregon. In times past he has in the public prints openly announced himself as an anarchist. Prior to the declaration of war when Emma Goldman visited Oregon he always stood sponsor for her and introduced her at public meetings. He is a very polished gentleman and moves in the best society and is generally considered as loyal. He tries to give the impression that he is erratic, both by his speech and dress and it is the opinion of the writer that he likes to have people believe that he is a very unusual, extraordinary and mysterious man.

His name appears on socialistic letterheads as an attorney to whom persons in trouble with the United States may safely go. . . . The very worst agitator we have in town is a Dr. Marie Equi; she is thoroughly disloyal and a woman of the Emma Goldman type . . .

I am of the opinion that he is rather insincere in his protestations of anarchy because he is the attorney for and a heavy stockholder in some of the biggest land grabbing corporations in the west.

He is a man of very pleasing personality, has a host of friends, and a great deal of influence in the community. I think the upshot of the whole thing is that he rather likes to pose as being erratic, unusual and obstreperous.

. . . In strictest confidence, and recognizing the delicacy of the statement, permit me to suggest that a few years ago Colonel Wood claimed that he was a very close personal friend to the President, and it is quite probable that the President did, a few years ago, take the colonel's advice relative to conditions in Oregon. With the greatest deference permit me to suggest that . . . the colonel is not a safe man to advise the President, especially relative to labor conditions."[24]

In Mayor Baker's mind, the threat of pro-German activity was nowhere near as serious as that of the radicals or "reds" as they were called. And the radical members of the IWW, the "Wobblies," seemed to become "redder" with each passing month. As one of his first year accomplishments, Baker noted that he had exercised "a firm hand in the extermination of the IWW members congregated in this city." He was proud of the police raids. "The IWW members fled to other cities."[25]

World War I Poster

Patriotic Efforts

Mayor Baker liked to boast about his wartime conservation and recycling efforts which were so successful that one is left wondering why it took almost 50 years to restore such practices. "Garbage has value," reported *The Oregonian*[26] in April 1918. As a wartime measure, the city was collecting and segregating free of charge all of the city's refuse. It then proceeded to sell it on the open market. Food waste — swill for hogs — went for $3.90 a ton. Other categories of waste were sold by the ton as follows: Paper $5, dried bones $18, mixed rags $50, woolen rags $120, tin cans $5 and scrap metal from $50 to $1100. The system proved so profitable that the garbagemen who were being paid a salary by the city wanted a 50-50 split of the net proceeds. One group of private citizens who organized the Patriotic Conservation League salvaged $59,450 worth of paper in two years.

Another wartime project, the brainchild of Commissioner Kellaher, was the city's entrance into the commercial fish business. In July 1914, Portland had assumed municipal ownership of the privately operated Carroll Public Market[27] on S. W. Yamhill Street between 3rd and 5th Avenues. It made sense to Kellaher that with the wartime shortage and high price of meat products, the city could catch its own fish and retail it from its own market. In February 1918, the city leased an old and battered pilot boat from the Port of Portland, carrying the distinguished name of publisher Joseph Pulitzer. For over a year, the schooner ventured down the Columbia River and out over the treacherous bar, filled its hold with whatever it could catch and returned eight days later. The end result of this cyclical effort was a plentiful supply of native fish at a greatly lowered cost to the consumer. The monopoly of "the Fish Trust" had been broken, Commissioner Kellaher claimed, but the operation was to be short-lived. The courts eventually ruled the practice unconstitutional. The *Joseph Pulitzer* was returned to the Port of Portland which later sold it to a local investor for $2500 after the city declined to purchase it. Within weeks it sank to the muddy bottom of the Willamette River.

The patriotic efforts of Portland's public and private citizenry were clearly proven by the extraordinary success of the first two Liberty Loan drives.[28] A third drive was set to be launched in the early spring of 1918. The campaign leadership hoped that by careful planning, Oregon and Portland might lead the nation in subscribing their quotas totalling $18,495,000. Of this amount, $10,050,000 was to be raised locally.

The campaign committee was drawn from the top level of Portland's business and banking community: Abbot L. Mills, John C. Ainsworth, Franklin T. Griffith, Emery Olmstead, *The Oregonian* editor Edgar Piper, Ladd & Tilton banker Edward Cookingham, banker-investor Dr. Andrew C. Smith, who was to purchase the ill-fated *Joseph Pulitzer*, and of course Mayor George L. Baker. The state chairman was Portlander Guy W. Talbot, president of both the Portland Gas & Coke Company and the Pacific Power & Light Company. Because of the chairman's supreme responsibility he was called "General" Talbot.

Someone, perhaps department store executive Julius Meier, dreamed up the

The Liberty Temple under construction in front of the Portland Hotel on Sunday, March 10, 1918.

Liberty Temple — April 1918

idea of constructing a "Liberty Temple" in downtown Portland as a symbol of Portland's democratic war effort. It would have to be finished in time for the April 6th kickoff, the first anniversary of the declaration of war. The Third Liberty Loan Drive Committee eagerly endorsed the project. Under Meier's direction, businesses and banks donated the necessary materials and funds, and organized labor provided the skilled construction crews. Everything was set for the weekend of March 9th and 10th.

The Oregon Journal proclaimed in its Sunday edition: "This Sunday is made doubly sacred by the erection of Liberty Temple."[29] The foundations had been laid on Saturday, and construction began at daybreak on Sunday. Using over 250 volunteers, it was to be completed in one day. Physicians were on hand, ready to administer first aid if necessary. Food and non-alcoholic beverages were served but no music was provided. This was a serious undertaking and of course Mayor Baker laid the cornerstone at the appropriate moment. Flood-lights were installed in case the workers needed to toil into the night. And they did. But the temple was completed on schedule, except for the plastering and painting which took two weeks. Located in the heart of downtown Portland, on Sixth Avenue between Morrison and Yamhill Streets, and flanked by Portland's two most renowned buildings, the Pioneer Post Office and the Portland Hotel, the Liberty Temple was a "monument to the city's patriotism," declared the *Journal*,[30] the "finest symbol . . . that the city has ever produced," exclaimed *The Oregonian*.[31] Patterned along the lines of a Grecian temple, it became Portland's Parthenon. But it was only to remain standing for ten months.

Liberty Day was proclaimed for April 6th. The campaign was kicked off with great fanfare: Parades, bands, floats and military marching units. The newspapers blazed forth with banner headlines beseeching one and all to subscribe immediately. Portland wanted to set a national record. Even the clergy, especially the Protestants, lent their enthusiastic voices to the crusade. "Fight or buy bonds" was the title of an address given by a Methodist minister before the Portland Rotary Club. "There is no place," said he, "on the top side of American soil for a Pacifist. . . . There is no room in this country for a Pacifist. If you have one, shoot him. Don't talk peace to me; I don't want peace, I want righteousness."[32]

"Disloyalty" at the Library

Within six days of the campaign's inauguration, Oregonians received word that they had achieved their goal: National honors for being the first to meet the state's quota. But on the same day, Portlanders were to learn with horror that one of their city librarians would not purchase war bonds. Miss Louise Hunt, an assistant to Portland librarian Miss Mary Francis Isom, was a quiet, scholarly New Englander; certainly not the type of person the public would have expected to assume such an obviously unpatriotic stance. She was known as an efficient professional who at no time had ever been heard to utter a disloyal statement.

149

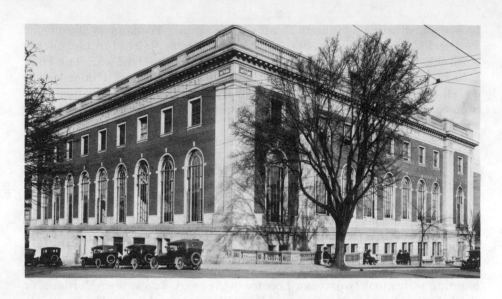

Portland Library

Under increasing pressure from several directors of the Library Association, the local newspapers and members of the Third Liberty Loan Drive campaign committee, board president Winslow B. Ayer was forced to call a directors meeting for the evening of April 12th.

This episode, that was to explode in Mr. Ayer's face, must have proved an agonizing experience for the generous public benefactor who was one of Portland's most enlightened and cultured business leaders. As the founder and president of the profitable Eastern & Western Lumber Company, W. B. Ayer had been instrumental in creating the Portland Public Library in 1902. Before that time it had been a private subscription library that served the public for a fee. Until the new central library building was constructed in 1913, the institution had been housed in various downtown locations none of which was large enough to provide adequate space to meet the growing demand. It was Mr. Ayer who persuaded the Ladd estate to donate the downtown block on which to build the new headquarters. He assisted William M. Ladd in selecting the architect, Albert E. Doyle, and he was responsible for choosing Mary Francis Isom to be the first librarian under the new public charter. So committed was Ayer to this project that he personally donated $300,000 to the library building fund. Upon his death in 1931, he was to leave three times this amount to the Portland Art Museum which he had served for years as a dedicated trustee. In truth, few could justifiably question W. B. Ayer's credentials, particularly his loyalty to Portland's cultural institutions.

The Library Association was, and still is, a private, nonprofit corporation. Under an agreement with Multnomah County, it was charged with providing library service to the public, not only at the central branch but at all other branches throughout the city and county. It received an annual operating subsidy from county tax receipts and for this reason the three county commissioners served *ex officio* on the board of directors. The remaining directors were elected by a small membership of approximately 50 local residents.

Except for the Hunt incident, and a few other episodes of a minor nature, the Library Association has maintained a low profile over the past 80 years. There have been two categories of membership for a fee, lifetime ($200) and perpetual ($250). The latter could be passed on by will or gift. The small membership has assured continuity, and usually longevity, to the board of directors which, in practice, has been a self-perpetuating body. Practically all of the directors have been male, with the leadership drawn heavily from the ranks of the Arlington Club.

In 1918, the directors included, besides Ayer: Richard W. Montague, law partner of C. E. S. Wood and close personal friend to the late Harry Lane; Robert L. Sabin, another prominent attorney; Elliott R. Corbett, younger brother of Portland Chamber of Commerce President Henry L. Corbett and vice president of both the First National Bank and the Corbett Investment Company; William M. Ladd, president of the Ladd & Tilton Bank; Robert H. Strong, administrator of the Corbett estate and future partner of E. B. MacNaughton; William L. Brewster, prominent Democratic attorney who was defeated for city commissioner by George L. Baker; Rabbi Jonah B. Wise of Temple Beth Israel who would later leave Portland to become rabbi of New York City's Central Synagogue; and William F. Woodward, a well known druggist, active Republican and chairman of the Oregon State Council of Defense, by appointment of the governor. This was generally a distinguished group, but not one of them was then a member of the Third Liberty Loan Drive campaign committee.

The directors meeting on April 12 began late. Chairman Rufus Holman of the Board of County Commissioners could not wait, but before leaving he placed on record his strong objection to Miss Hunt's continued employment. Taking a position that he would repudiate 20 years later, Holman did not believe that a public institution should employ someone who refused to support the government. In the course of the meeting, Miss Hunt was sharply questioned. She explained that she had always shown wholehearted concern for the best interests of the United States. She considered herself a loyal American who simply disagreed with President Wilson's aims and ideals. "At no time," she concluded, "have I desired to be an 'obstructionist,' I merely wish to claim the constitutional American right privately to hold a minority opinion."[33]

All of the directors, except for W. F. Woodward and Rufus Holman *in absentia*, voted in support of Miss Hunt. Woodward took Holman's position but he expounded upon it with public vehemence: "Patriotism . . . is in Miss Hunt a perfect vacuum."[34] The leaders of the Liberty Loan Drive reacted in shock.

151

Banker Emery Olmstead named a committee to request that the directors reverse their action, but President Ayer demurred. Explained Ayer: "We found nothing wrong with Miss Hunt's attitude toward the government so far as any overt act was concerned. She is a pacifist and is conscientiously opposed to war. She is not an obstructionist. . . . "[35]

The crusaders for democracy were not satisfied. The newspapers inflated the episode. Mayor Baker was quoted as saying that Miss Hunt was an insult to motherhood even though the good librarian was not married and most likely had not produced any children of her own. The mayor lashed out at the library board:

> "Nothing short of her dismissal from an institution where our boys and girls are compelled to go and must of necessity come in contact with a mind that is wholly un-American and unsympathetic to our common and vital cause will suffice in this case. The Liberty Board must . . . clear the stain from the name of our otherwise thoroughly loyal state."[36]

Mr. Ayer could not withstand the pressure. He called for a second board meeting to weigh a resolution requesting reconsideration of the Hunt affair. General Guy Talbot was quoted as saying that the directors had "taken an academic position . . . whereas . . . an active militant patriotism" was the need of the hour.[37]

Statements in opposition to Miss Hunt's continued employment were received from organizations all over Portland. Chamber of Commerce president Henry L. Corbett, considered one of Portland's more enlightened aristocrats and state chairman of the wartime Red Cross drives, signed a resolution declaring that "now was not the time for individual opinion."[38] *The Oregon Journal* and its publisher C. S. Jackson asked editorially how the library board and Miss Hunt earned the right to hold minority opinions in a time of national crisis.

At the second board of directors meeting Miss Hunt tendered her resignation before any other business was considered. Woodward and Holman moved not to accept her resignation but to dismiss her instead. After some heated argument, the motion lost and Miss Hunt's resignation was accepted. In her letter to the directors, Miss Hunt expressed her appreciation for their support. But she no longer wanted to be a burden. She felt it was best for all if she took immediate leave. Just before the end of the meeting, Woodward stated that he also doubted the loyalty of librarian Mary Francis Isom who had indicated that she might resign if the board did not support Miss Hunt. As one report described the ensuing melee, "Pandemonium then broke loose with the majority of the board all trying to talk at once." Miss Isom was described as angered beyond all restraint."[39] She apparently leaned across the table and told Woodward, "You are no gentleman."[40]

152

The Library Case in Retrospect

The library case presents a classic historical example of one of democracy's gravest weaknesses. A democracy is supposedly peaceloving. It does not like to go to war. It is slow to rise to provocation, but when stimulated to the point of action, it does not readily forgive the cause of its provocation. Democracy fights in anger. It fights to punish the adversary that supposedly forced it to declare war. Once aroused, a war to preserve democracy must be fought to the bitter end. George Kennan once likened a democracy to a prehistoric monster with a large body and a small brain. It was almost impossible to arouse. One practically had to "whack its tail off" to make it aware that its interests were threatened. But once worked up and cognizant of what it was experiencing, the monster would go on a rampage with such blind determination that it not only destroyed its enemy but often its own native habitat.[41]

Although tempers cooled off, a number of perceptive Portlanders pondered some grave questions that were raised by the whole episode. The late Harry Lane's close friend, lawyer Richard W. Montague, wondered "whether the people of Portland . . . were willing to yield to the rising tide of hate against all who disagreed with them,"[42] or whether they would come to their senses and oppose it. Oregon District Court Judge J. Hunt Hendrickson cautioned Portland against mob rule. To Hendrickson, it was "only a matter of degree that separated the action of the Illinois mob which strung up a man for refusing to kiss the flag and that of a committee which said buy bonds or lose your position."[43] The events of the next four years, culminating with the success of the Ku Klux Klan in the the November 1922 election, would lead one to believe that Portland's established leadership, or at least the majority of it, did not learn much of a lesson from the excesses of wartime patriotism. Insecurity and fear continued to dominate people's lives.

The library, however, came through with flying colors. It was to receive wide national attention in an article published by *Outlook* in March 1921. Entitled "A Library that Goes to the People," the article described six ways in which library service had been taken to the people of Portland instead of waiting for the people to come to it. As listed, they were:

1. Using advertising, especially in foreign language newspapers.

2. Holding six library parties a month, especially for the foreign born.

3. Compiling and distributing special lists of books for different interest groups, but especially for the foreign born.

4. Branch librarians visiting factories, shops and other large places of employment to talk to workers about the library.

5. Sending out travelling libraries into the neighborhoods.

6. Providing free auditorium space for local group meetings.

The Portland Public Library, reported *Outlook*, was a true community center, with the librarians actively working within the total community. Of course this

153

very kind of activity may have been what worried W. F. Woodward and Rufus Holman. They were fearful of someone like Miss Hunt venturing forth among the public. She might subvert those whom she encountered. Regardless, the Portland library staff viewed their operation as "a big business in which the taxpayers [were] the shareholders." A public library was "not a morgue of books."[44]

The person who was credited with this success was the librarian, Mary Francis Isom. She had come from the East in 1901 to catalogue the John Wilson collection that had just been bequeathed to the library. In 1902, when the library officially went public, she was appointed head librarian. She played the key role in directing the internal planning for the new building that opened in 1913. And she was the major organizer of the Pacific Northwest Library Association. It was unfortunate that Miss Isom did not live to enjoy the *Outlook* article. She died at 55, almost two years to the day after her distasteful encounter with W. F. Woodward.

She also missed the sorry spectacle of her library director, Woodward, stooping to accept the support of the Ku Klux Klan in his successful campaign to win election to the state legislative session of 1923. Woodward was a maverick of complex motivation: He strongly opposed private schools, he was a staunch patriot, and yet he favored equal treatment for Negroes. In 1925, he was to be one of the sponsors of the amendment which finally removed the state constitutional provisions denying Negroes their suffrage and legal standing — articles long superseded by the 14th and 15th Amendments to the U. S. Constitution.

The Flowering of Bigotry

The statewide primary election campaign of May 1918 witnessed the first of many politically inspired attacks on the Roman Catholic Church. Anti-Catholicism had long been quietly nurtured within the congregations of fundamentalist Protestant churches. Although concerns of this kind were more apt to be found in the rural areas of the state, Portland was not immune to such incitements. On a Sunday in June 1914, a number of Portland Protestant ministers directed their sermons to the growing menace of Rome. After war was declared, anti-Catholic fears increased, particularly in the districts of Portland that were most immediately affected by the vast influx of war plant workers, some of whom were originally from Southern Europe and of Catholic devotion. To established residents, such outsiders posed a threat. Because Catholics, like Jews, were suspected of maintaining international ties that transcended national loyalties, they became targets for the super-patriots. How could they be 100 percent loyal to the United States? Americans were dying in a war against German absolutism. Was not papal absolutism an equal threat to American democracy?

Three patriotic groups fielded slates of candidates: The American Patriotic Association, the American Patriotic League and the Oregon Federation of

Patriotic Societies. A number of the candidates, particularly for the legislature, made all three lists. One of the key planks endorsed by each of the groups favored free and compulsory education of Oregon's children in the state's public primary schools. This was to be the measure that the Ku Klux Klan would successfully latch onto in 1922. In 1918, however, it was taken seriously only by the leaders of the Catholic diocese, who correctly sensed that its purpose was to abolish parochial schools and thus cut away much of the church's influence over its youth.

As the election day approached, a number of prominent Portland Catholics took aim at the American Patriotic Association, charging that the APA in particular had injected anti-Catholicism into the campaign. The APA fired back with its own newspaper ads, linking Catholics together with pacifists, socialists and "radicals" like C. E. S. Wood and Charles H. Chapman, former president of the University of Oregon. Calling them "Bolshevik," the APA quoted Chapman as having publicly declared that "the sale of bonds is to pay tribute to a privileged class . . . a vain and empty show so far as supporting the soldiers is concerned."[45] Father Edwin Vincent O'Hara was singled out as a radical — with the implication that he was disloyal — overlooking the fact that at that very moment the good father was serving in Europe as an army chaplain.

The patriotic fervor of the 1918 primary campaign provided a number of the candidates with more than enough public exposure to guarantee their elections. But just how much actual influence the particular patriotic groups exerted on the individual races has long been open to speculation. The fact that the majority of the winners from Multnomah County were Republicans, with almost half being incumbents, tended to downplay their influence. On the other hand, over 50 percent of the winners in the years from 1916-1922 did receive the support of at least one patriotic organization.[46]

If nothing else, the campaign of 1918 gave two Portland incumbent legislators a real boost: Senator Gus Moser and Representative Kaspar K. Kubli. Moser had been in the senate since 1913 and had served as its president in 1917. He decided to seek the Republican nomination for governor against the incumbent James Withycombe, a kindly, dignified, middle of the road public servant. Moser sought out all of the patriotic society support he could find. As a self-proclaimed "patriotic American," he became the logical candidate of the American Patriotic League. Although unsuccessful in his quest for the state's highest office, Moser increased his name familiarity and was to become one of the most influential Republicans in Oregon. He was a "wheeler-dealer" manipulator of the most extreme sort and belonged to every organization that would take him. As the conservative *Oregon Voter* was to characterize him the following year: "He is a smart, cute, wiley [sic] resourceful, selfish politician of unquestioned ability."[47] Patriotism was in the saddle in 1918 and Moser rode it for all it was worth. Through a deal that he made in the legislature, Moser was to get himself appointed in 1919 as the attorney for the Port of Portland Commission, a lucrative post that he would keep for 16 years.

*Kubli's Campaign Ad
for the May, 1920 Primary*

Gus Moser's friend, K. K. Kubli, was to become the super-patriot of the legislature in the period from 1919 to 1923, serving as house speaker in 1923. He was to co-sponsor most of the anti-radical legislation that came out of those sessions. And because of his initials, the Harvard Law School graduate turned printer was to be awarded a free membership in Portland's Klan No. 1.

The end of the war that came in November 1918 did not diminish the internal tensions that had been building up over the previous three years. Ugly rumors continued to spread — a diabolical, radical conspiracy against the government and the institutions of the United States was in the making. There was actual fear, even in Oregon, that a Red revolution might begin, patterned after the successful Bolshevik revolution of November 1917. The ranks of labor were in turmoil, stimulated by the wartime inflation that had propelled beyond reach the prices of everything that the laboring man needed in order to live. The radical labor movements like the IWW wanted more than increases in pay. They were demanding a new industrial order that called for the displacement of capitalistic control by government control — in short, something approaching a socialist regime. With the local press giving wide publicity to such apparent threats, people easily became scared. The local flu epidemic was even viewed as a red plot. During the late fall of 1918 and the first four months of 1919, Oregon's death toll reached alarming levels. The Standard Insurance Company reported the highest death losses in the life insurance company's history.

Holding its annual meeting during the height of the flu pandemic, the Oregon

Bar Association unanimously adopted a resolution calling for the appointment of a committee to draft a law for the 1919 legislative session that would "check and stamp out . . . IWWism and all other isms."[48] Portland lawyer John H. Hall led the attack against the "Bolshevists, anarchists . . . [and] others of their ilk." Demanded Hall, "They must be put out of business once and for all." The attorney reminded his listeners that Oregon was currently enjoying a "stable, permanent" form of government. The people were "happy" and "prosperous."[49] Hall felt that radicals, like the Wobblies, should be exterminated both for their radical philosophy and for any overt actions that might threaten the security of the state.

Attorney John H. Hall had a spotted career. His stance against radicalism revealed him as the type of person Samuel Johnson must have had in mind when he cited "patriotism" as "the last refuge of a scoundrel." In 1905, President Theodore Roosevelt had removed him as U. S. Attorney for Oregon. There was substantial evidence to support this action. An early political associate of Judge Henry McGinn, in McGinn's pre-reform period, Hall had become involved in the fraudulent federal timber sales at the turn of the century. He was convicted, along with Oregon's U. S. Senator John H. Mitchell, but had managed to escape imprisonment through the appeal process until President William H. Taft could pardon him. Ten years later, with those ugly memories all but forgotten, Hall had built a prosperous legal practice and in the process had become an ardent super-patriot. He was particularly impressed by the federal conviction of 93 Wobblies in Chicago three months earlier. Oregon, declared Hall, needed its own law to produce similar results in the state courts.

It did not take long for the legislature to crank up the necessary machinery to introduce a criminal syndicalism bill. *The Oregonian* gave lukewarm support to it in contrast to the *Journal* which proclaimed: "We must hereafter have an Americanized America." The *Journal*, along with many of the bill's backers, felt that a tough law would "preserve Americanism. . . . Evil in the human heart . . . [was] the motive power of Bolshevism."[50] Not so, declared State Senator Walter Pierce who would be elected governor in 1922. Democrat Pierce, who was the only senator to vote in opposition, urged his colleagues to examine the causes of the social ills that were plaguing American society. It was not a matter of "evil in the heart," but of a decent standard of living for the average workingman. Under the prodding of Kubli and Moser, however, the legislature was in no mood to examine the issue rationally. Mayor Baker of Portland lent his support with a statement that declared "this law is the greatest need of the day." In so doing, Baker noted that 135 returned servicemen had already enlisted in the Bolshevist cause.[51]

After the bill was passed by both houses on January 30, 1919, *The Oregonian* changed position and asserted that the law was most likely unconstitutional — a violation of the guarantees of free speech, press and assemblage as embodied in the First Amendment of the constitution.[52] Such warnings, however, did not deter immediate enforcement. On February 9th, a man was arrested by the

Portland police for carrying a banner advertising a meeting of the "Worker's International Industrial Union." The headquarters of the organization were then raided and a large amount of literature was confiscated. Following these actions, the police department and Mayor Baker issued an order to prohibit persons from carrying banners on the street advertising strikes and workers' meetings in Portland.[53]

Late in February, as part of what *The Oregonian* came to call "a kind of recurring festivity,"[54] Portland police raided the IWW hall at 109 Second Avenue. They not only broke into the office but they smashed the furniture and carted off all of the literature and records that could be carried. Mayor Baker then notified the owner of the building that he would be prosecuted unless the Wobbly tenants were evicted. In the process, Baker failed to foresee the humorous consequences of the raid. The IWW wrote letters to the city fathers, the W. C. T. U. and all of the city's leading ministers telling them exactly "where all of the speakeasies and bootleg joints" were located. They then began to picket the thirteen outlets, carrying banners proclaiming, "This place sells poison bootleg liquor — All good IWW's will not patronize."[55] Within 24 hours, persecution of the Wobblies ceased. In future months, sporadic attempts would be made to harass the Wobblies but no organized campaign would be launched against the group as a whole until the waterfront strike in October 1922.

Instead of engaging in mass arrests of Wobblies, the police sought out particular leaders who also were affiliated with other radical organizations like the Communist Labor Party. Mayor Baker and the authorities were deeply concerned about the possibility of a general strike in Portland similar to the one that paralyzed Seattle in early February 1919. They kept a watchful eye on all the Portland labor leaders, especially those involved with radical organizations.

The ensuing months of 1919 brought much disquieting news from around the nation. On the 28th of April, "an infernal machine 'big enough to blow out the entire side of the County-City Building' " was found in Mayor Ole Hanson's mail at Seattle.[56] Mayor Hanson was an avowed enemy of the Red Menace. The following day, a bomb exploded at the Georgia home of a U. S. Senator who was chairman of the senate immigration committee. Then the next day, 16 little brown packages were discovered in a New York City post office addressed to some of the most important public and private figures in America. Hardly more than a month later, a bomb exploded on the front porch of Attorney General A. Mitchell Palmer's house in Washington, D. C.

Portland managed to escape the turbulence and destruction that afflicted other cities but Mayor Baker continued to be prepared for the worst, particularly after he learned that President Woodrow Wilson was planning to visit Portland on his swing through the West in September 1919. But as it turned out, everything went smoothly — without one "Red" protest. Even Baker was surprised. He was obviously pleased to receive the Secret Service report that "Portland was better policed with respect to the crowds than the other big cities President Wilson has visited on this particular trip."[57] Portland also scored on the size of the turnout and the degree of popular enthusiasm accorded the President.

In methodical fashion, Portland's leaders planned the Wilson reception with the precision of a military campaign. A school holiday was to be declared and businesses would close at noon. To determine who among the populace, excluding notables, would be permitted to hear the President's address in the Public Auditorium on the night of Monday, September 15th, the Shattuck Grade School children drew 7000 names by lottery, from a pool of names submitted by those who wished to attend. *The Oregonian* reported that Woodrow Wilson's forthcoming visit, his first as President, created "the greatest expectancy of any event in memory."[58]

The purpose of the President's trip across the country and down the coast was to stimulate public support for the League of Nations Treaty that was currently undergoing rough treatment at the hands of the U. S. Senate. He arrived on schedule, by special train, and spent the morning leading a parade through the downtown, stopping to shake hands and talk with hundreds of individual citizens.

A special luncheon for 200 local dignitaries was held at the Portland Hotel. A humorous story is associated with this event. Former Governor Oswald West, a long-time Democrat and loyal supporter of Wilson's, was the overall general chairman for the entire visit, but with particular responsibility for the post-luncheon entertainment. Having been detained, he arrived after all the guests were seated and not one place was left for him. The room was overflowing with guests. So West had to leave the hotel and walk down the street to his favorite lunchroom for a sandwich. Later, he did accompany the presidential party on a drive up the Columbia River Scenic Highway to Crown Point.

After a quiet dinner, the President gave a dynamic speech to the packed auditorium and seemed to win the enthusiastic support of both the audience and the local press. To those who observed him closely, he seemed tired and drawn. Ten days later, while travelling through Colorado on his way back to Washington, he collapsed and six days later suffered a paralytic stroke. He never recovered, and spent the remaining 17 months of his term as an invalid.

The reign of peace that followed President Wilson's visit was abruptly shattered two months later by the now famous "Centralia Massacre" which occurred on the first anniversary of the Armistice, November 11, 1919. Located 80 miles north of Portland, Centralia, Washington, was the coal mining center of the Pacific Northwest. It was also a center of unrest in November 1919, due largely to the fact that the miners had gone out on strike early in the month along with 400,000 other mine workers throughout the country. Under prodding from some IWW members, the Centralia mine workers planned a demonstration during the occasion of a scheduled parade to be led by the local American Legion post. What started out to be a disruption, however, soon turned into a shoot-out. Halfway through the parade in downtown Centralia, shots were fired from nearby buildings and four Legionnaires fell dead, including the post commander, a much decorated Army colonel who had also been a star football player at the University of Washington.

The reaction of the populace was instantaneous. Vigilante squads were organized and 40 Wobblies were jailed. In the process, one was strung up and lynched on the outskirts of town. Although ten men were to be charged with murder, after tempers cooled only four were convicted and sent to prison. None received the death penalty because conclusive identification of who actually fired the fatal shots was never established. Following the report of the violence, shock waves emanated in all directions, especially southward across the Columbia River to Portland, Centralia's nearest metropolis. Fears of further violence were generated. Would Oregon be next?

When the Oregon legislature met in special session in January 1920, however, a fear of a different kind appeared on the agenda: The Japanese aliens living and farming in Oregon. As the *Oregon Voter* wryly described the atmosphere in Salem: "The people of Oregon . . . despite the experiences of the late world war, are still in a scrappy mood and carrying a chip on their shoulders."[59] Both houses unanimously passed a resolution urging Congress to enact a law that would exclude from citizenship the American-born children of aliens who could not be naturalized, i.e., Orientals. "Patriotism and the influence of the Loyal Legion" were responsible for this united stand against the Japanese obtaining a stronger foothold in Oregon, charged the *Oregon Voter*. Fear was expressed that the Japanese were acquiring too much land. They were rumored to be circumventing the alien ownership laws by buying land and vesting titles in their children, most of whom were qualified for citizenship. K. K. Kubli quoted somebody as having estimated that within 30 years the population of California would be "equally composed of Japs and whites unless radical measures were taken." Kubli feared that the same pattern might prevail in Oregon. He ended his warning by asking loudly, "Why postpone action?"[60]

Portland business interests counseled a more thoughtful approach. William D. Wheelwright, past president of the Portland Chamber of Commerce and one of the city's most distinguished elder business leaders, wrote: "Before we join in a crusade against the Japanese it behooves us to enquire whether there be just cause."[61] He doubted that the Japanese were any more prolific than Americans. "Is there any one of the readers of *The Voter*," he asked, "who thinks that the interests of the sovereign State of Oregon are likely to suffer because its population of 672,765 (in 1910) included 4308 Japanese who operated 172 farms having a total acreage of 6477, of which they owned 2793?"[62] Wheelwright minced no words when he declared that "the argument against Japanese exclusion is an argument in favor of encouraging feebleness in ourselves instead of strength." Referring to the United States, he asserted: "The prosperity of this country is largely dependent upon its foreign trade. Commercial relations between individuals in the two countries are of the friendliest character. Portland and the coast generally are offering every inducement to the Japanese to deal with us."[63] Wheelwright warned his fellow Oregonians not to endanger this relationship.

Unfortunately, few of Portland's public and private institutional leaders spoke out as vigorously as did Wheelwright. K. K. Kubli did not change his mind. He wanted to keep Oregon pure. Others like Representative Eugene Smith were not worried about Japanese commerce being deflected from Oregon ports. "You can't insult a Jap when a dollar is in sight," he remarked.[64] The issue would keep reappearing in subsequent legislative sessions. When Republican Governor Ben Olcott addressed the opening meeting of the 1921 legislature, he strongly emphasized the need to curb Japanese growth in Oregon.

Whether it was the Japanese, the Catholics or the Reds, the fears of "an enemy from within" seemed to grow by the week. Many political leaders were concerned with lenient treatment accorded convicted IWW and Communist Labor Party leaders. Too many of them were being released with minimal fines and paroles. Because the 1919 law had only made it a crime to "join" an organization like the IWW, and since most of those arrested were already radicals of long experience, the judges felt obliged to reduce or cancel most of the sentences. Thus, the 1921 session of the legislature came under intense pressure to correct the apparent flaws in the 1919 law.

As historian M. Paul Holsinger has described the occasion:

"On January 11, 1921, a new and more comprehensive syndicalism statute was introduced . . . , designed to repeal the 1919 act while providing more restrictions against radicals. . . . The new act received enthusiastic and immediate support. . . . [It was passed unanimously by both houses on February 2, 1921.] Far from weakening the [old] act, as some observers had feared, the legislature gave Oregon one of the strongest and most flexible anti-radical statutes in the United States."[65]

The day following this fervent expression of super-patriotism, a delegation descended on City Hall for the purpose of requesting Mayor Baker to lift a ban that he had placed on any public appearance by the noted journalist Lincoln Steffens who had just returned from a trip to Russia. Steffens was considered a pro-Bolshevik, red Socialist by the local authorities and his anticipated visit to Portland after a lapse of 14 years was viewed with trepidation. Much to the subsequent horror of Oregon's Episcopal Bishop Sumner, the group was led by the chaplain of the diocese's Good Samaritan Hospital, together with the president of the Central Labor Council. Baker was unmoved. Speaking bluntly to the chaplain, he said:

"As a law abiding citizen, do you think it is good policy to allow an agitator the run of the city? Even to place a public building at his disposal in order that he may stir up trouble among that certain element which is ever the enemy of government? . . . I will keep Portland free from unnecessary radicalism and agitation."[66]

Baker had heard that Steffens' lecture was planned for the purpose of opposing the deportation of a Russian agitator. He simply did not want to deal with the matter. "I'm not a match in talking to a high class socialist," he concluded. Lawyer Burl A. Green, who was to become Portland's most famous labor and defense attorney over the next two decades, announced that he planned to file suit in the circuit court.

The following day, Mayor Baker received strong local support. The major veterans organizations backed him and the school board banned the use of the Lincoln High School auditorium. School directors Frank Shull and W. F. Woodward were adamantly opposed to Steffens' appearance. The leadership of the Episcopal diocese, including Bishop Sumner, disclaimed the hospital chaplain, stating that he spoke only as a private citizen. The meeting was set for the evening of February 7th; the group was going ahead with its plans despite the uncertainty of what the authorities would do. The injunction was filed and Judge Morrow ruled against the city. The entire police force was placed on emergency duty as the crowds flowed into and spilled out of the small Columbia Hall at Second and Oak, located, coincidentally, next door to the central police station. Even the Public Auditorium, closed by the city, could not have accommodated the crowd of over 7000 that flocked to hear the great Steffens.[67] The event went off smoothly, with no violent behavior evident except for some pushing and shoving to gain entrance to the hall. The next morning, attorney Green had breakfast with Steffens and apologized for "Portland being so stupid." What could one expect from "a city that kept a million dollar cow barn in the middle of town?" As Green recalled the occasion, Steffens "reached over and patted me on the back and said: "Green, quit bragging. All cities are that way."[68]

The Ku Klux Klan

As subsequent events were to reveal, Portland may well have been more "that way" than most American cities. Four months later, toward the end of June, Luther I. Powell slipped quietly into Portland from Southern Oregon where he had been the primary organizer of Ku Klux Klan activities. He registered at the Multnomah Hotel and surreptitiously went about his work enlisting local knights in behalf of the Klan. The groundwork had already been laid. Contrary to what many Americans might have thought about Oregon, the state was ripe for the Invisible Order.

The objectives of the Order, as stated in its constitution, were:

" . . . to unite white male persons, native born Gentile citizens of the United States of America, who owe no allegiance of any nature to any foreign government, nation, institution, sect, ruler, person or people; whose morals are good, whose reputations and vocations are exemplary . . . to cultivate and promote patriotism toward our Civil Government; . . . to maintain forever white supremacy, . . . to conserve, protect, and maintain the distinctive institutions, rights, privileges, principles, traditions and ideals of a pure Americanism."[69]

162

HIS FAVORITE CHILD.

That was the theory. In practice, the "pure Americanism" varied with the locality. For Oregon, opposition to Catholicism proved the best talking point. After all, the Negro population was less than one-third of one percent of Oregon's nearly 800,000 residents.[70]

Luther Powell was actually the second Klan organizer to hit Portland; the first one had been fired for talking to the press. On June 17, 1921, *The Portland Telegram* announced in thundering headlines: "Portland invaded by the Ku Klux Klan."[71] One recruiter certainly did not constitute an invasion, but the *Telegram* had been following Klan activities in Southern Oregon. It was the only Portland paper to show any critical concern about the Klan and it was the only local news medium that would publicize Klan activities for almost four months. Two weeks later the *Telegram* printed a whole page of photographs of garbed Klansmen in other areas of the country and again featured a massive headline: "Ku Klux Klan signs up 1000 here."[72]

On August 1st, King Kleagle Powell and his handpicked local leader, the Exalted Cyclops Fred L. Gifford, staged a mysterious event at the Multnomah Hotel. Several days previously, a number of local officials had received enigmatic invitations to attend a reception. When they showed up at the

From left to right: National Safety Council representative Coffin, Portland Police Capt. Moore, Police Chief Lee Jenkins, District Attorney Walter Evans, U. S. District Attorney Lester Humphries, King Kleagle Powell, Sheriff T. M. Hurlburt, U. S. Department of Justice Special Agent, Mayor Baker, P. S. Malcolm of the Scottish Rite Masons, and Exalted Cyclops Gifford.

appointed hour, they all stood around the room somewhat befuddled, until a stranger asked them to line up in front of a velvet curtain for a photograph. At the last moment, before the shutter clicked, the curtain parted and out stepped two hooded Klansmen, Powell and Gifford. When the *Telegram* printed the photo the next day, groans of agony were heard all over Portland, particularly from the two district attorneys present who were blazing mad about the deception.[73] The whole event was a "frame-up," but the Klan leaders had accomplished their purpose. Here was photographic proof that the Ku Klux Klan had achieved recognition as a *bona fide* civic organization. Unfortunately for the record, historians were to use this as evidence in subsequent years to substantiate charges that the Klan had taken over the "capital, city hall and the courthouse."[74] Such was far from the truth, at least in August of 1921.

As reported to the *Telegram*, Kleagle Powell informed his guests: "Ours is not an anti-organization of any kind. . . . We are not anti-Japanese, or anti-Jew, or anti-Negro, or anti-Catholic, or anti-anything else. . . . Ninety-five percent of the stories are false. . . . Stories of violence are unfounded." Powell tried to reassure his listeners that the Klan was merely supplying a "need for a national fraternal organization," a "secret" organization. The Klan's efforts were dedicated to a "clean-up of Portland — both moral and political. . . . Respect for the law," was its primary interest, he declared.[75] The *Telegram's* editors were unconvinced. "Do we need an Invisible Empire in the midst of our democracy? If so, then democracy is a failure."[76]

The Klan must have had some influence on police activities. Chief Jenkins reported that July 1921 was "a big crime clean-up month."[77] The morals squad had been reorganized and 384 offenders had been arrested, largely in the North End. Over $3500 in fines had been collected from bootleggers, gamblers, prostitutes, vagrants and lottery enthusiasts. Kleagle Powell was obviously pleased with this news when he informed District Attorney Evans that the Klan had already enrolled 150 members of the police force.

The Klan's appeal was directed primarily at the blue collar working class of largely non-union affiliation and of no more than a grade school education. The three local leaders, including Gifford, were former union electricians who had been booted out by their fellow tradesmen for taking management's side in a 1919 strike settlement. All three had subsequently been employed by management in low level administrative positions, Gifford with Northwestern Electric and the other two with Pacific Telephone and Telegraph. The record would seem to indicate that both companies gave tacit approval to their employees' "extra-curricular" activities. Cyclops Gifford was to spend an increasing amount of his time with Klan affairs and the company kept him on the payroll with no questions asked. In fact when Powell left to conquer untapped markets, Gifford was elevated to Grand Dragon and moved Klan headquarters to the Pittock Block, the home office of Northwestern Electric.

Keeping a low profile during the fall of 1921, the Invisible Empire went public just before Christmas with a widely promoted lecture at the Public Auditorium, delivered by the Rev. Reuben H. Sawyer of the East Side Christian Church. This was the opening attack of the Klan's campaign to gain public support for its compulsory public grade school program which was really the brainchild of the Scottish Rite Masonic order. *The Oregonian* now entered the fray along with the *Telegram*, but it was George Putnam's Salem *Capital Journal* that assumed statewide leadership in opposing such efforts. Throughout the month of February 1922, Putnam released one blast after another, particularly at the candidates for public office who were seeking the endorsement of secret societies which he accused of exploiting the politicians — a reversal of the customary practice.

Wrote Putnam on February 9th:

"Such fanatical organizations are unpatriotic to a degree and un-American. They are a recrudescence of the medieval intolerance which devastated Europe by civil war and deluged the land with the best blood of the people. Their revival in the 20th century in free America is an anachronism and a menace to democracy."[78]

The most prominent of the candidates to announce early was State Senator Charles Hall of Marshfield, the president of a local telephone affiliate of the

The TRUTH ABOUT THE INVISIBLE EMPIRE KNIGHTS OF THE KU KLUX KLAN

A Lecture delivered at the Municipal Auditorium in Portland, Oregon, on December twenty-second, Nineteen Twenty-one, to six thousand people.

BY R. H. SAWYER, GRAND LECTURER OF THE PACIFIC NORTHWEST DOMAIN

Pacific Telephone and Telegraph Company. In pursuit of the Republican nomination for governor, Hall received the endorsements of all the major patriotic societies including the Klan. The central plank of his platform read as follows:

"The public school is one of the fundamental factors in our system of government. I favor compulsory attendance in the primary grades. Teach pure Americanism to all pupils beginning at an early age. Continue to strengthen and build up this typical American institution."[79]

The battle was now on and as the May primary approached the broadsides from each camp became more bitter by the day. The Rev. Sawyer delivered a series of emotional addresses to thousands who packed the Public Auditorium. When Mayor Baker was confronted by a delegation asking why he allowed the inflammatory Rev. Sawyer to use the auditorium when he had closed the facility to Lincoln Steffens a year earlier, his honor replied with disarming inconsistency that "the government cannot regulate the minds and temperaments of its citizens." When queried, Baker denied that he was a member of the Klan. But few could doubt his desire not to alienate the Invisible Order. He had already indicated his intention to seek the Republican U. S. senatorial nomination in 1924. He was starting to mend his political fences early. There is no documentary evidence of Baker having joined the Klan with the exception of a statement, by ex-Klan editor Lem Dever, that Baker was, in fact, an enrolled member.[80] Knowing Baker's propensity for joining every organization in sight, excluding the likes of the IWW, one might readily conclude that Dever was telling the truth.

Like his fellow Republican cohorts, Gus Moser and K. K. Kubli, George Baker never did or said anything that might discourage the "patriots' " support. Dever characterized them as "political tom-tits and tin-horn four-flushers." He warned that "men who gain office through alliance with arrogant Klan Dragons are not to be trusted with public affairs of importance."[81] In public, at least, Baker kept just enough distance to protect himself. As the *Oregon Voter* had described him earlier, "Mayor Baker is . . . the champion loud noise of the Pacific Northwest south of Seattle, but along with his hot air and shouting he introduces a big lot of common sense founded on real patriotism. . . . The people sit up and take notice."[82]

Baker had an uncanny knack for assessing the public mood. By not taking an unequivocal anti-Klan position, he and his Republican business friends could not help but lend support to the Klan-backed issues and candidates. But Baker was more interested in protecting his Republican Party flank than in any adverse consequences that might result from Klan success. The Klan already controlled the county Republican organization and most of the Klan-supported candidates were also the official local Republican Party favorites. Neither Baker nor the local Republican leadership had much to fear from charges levelled by the Catholic diocese that both the Klan and its candidates were "exploiting ignorance and bigotry."[83] The Catholic vote was small.

The primary election of May 19, 1922, had to be considered a victory for the Klan with two exceptions. Republican Governor Ben Olcott barely nosed out Charles Hall after having strongly denounced the Klan six days previously with a proclamation ordering the state and local police to enforce an old Oregon law, forbidding the wearing of masks in public places. Republican Congressman C. N. McArthur from Portland also survived the Klan challenge. However, both would be knocked off in November by Klan-supported Democratic candidates — an example of the how the Klan was not adverse to switching parties when its interests were at stake. Within Multnomah County, 12 of 13 Klan-backed legislative candidates won nomination. But the sweetest victory for Grand Dragon Gifford was the election of two new members to the Board of County Commissioners: John H. Rankin and Dow Walker, who defeated veteran Rufus Holman.

In subsequent months, Rankin and Walker were to prove both incompetent and dishonest, leading to their recall in 1924. The one legislative candidate who did not seek or accept Klan support, and who also compiled the largest primary plurality, was banker, civic leader Henry L. Corbett. The moderate Republican would be elected in November and begin a decade of political leadership that proved to be an important counterbalance to the jingoism of the Gus Mosers and Kaspar K. Kublis.

By the middle of June 1922, enough signatures had been received to place the compulsory public school initiative on the November ballot. It was actually filed by Portlander Robert F. Smith, president of the Lumberman's Trust Company and a member of the Scottish Rite Masons. *Capital Journal* editor George Putnam was convinced that the Klan's success, with both the primary election and the filing of the school initiative, was due to "the cowardice and pusillanimity of the big Portland papers, which lacked the nerve and still lack the courage to vigorously combat the menace of the Ku Klux Klan."[84]

Over the summer and into the fall of 1922, the school measure attracted the major interest, both locally and nationally. It seemed to be almost a foregone conclusion that the initiative would pass. Republican incumbent Governor Ben Olcott staked his political future on its defeat; for this effort he deserves more credit than history has given him.

Olcott's opponent was Democrat Walter Pierce, a state senator from Eastern Oregon who had established a generally liberal record, especially in his early opposition to the private utilities and the criminal syndicalism laws. But in 1922, Pierce eagerly coveted the governor's chair and he apparently was willing to make a deal with the Klan in order to gain its support. Pierce was clearly the underdog in a state dominated by Republicans. Although he was running primarily on a tax reduction plank, Pierce announced in favor of the school bill two months before the election. "I am in favor of and shall vote for the compulsory school bill,"[85] he declared, much to the horror of many of his old

Reel I: 0%

Reel II: 10%

Reel III: 50%

Reel IV: 100%

liberal friends like Father Edwin Vincent O'Hara. Pierce was immediately accused by editor Putnam of deserting "Democratic principles for the sake of office."[86] The historical record seems to support Putnam's charge. Pierce and the Klan had an understanding. If Pierce would openly endorse the school initiative, Grand Dragon Gifford would assure the candidate enough votes to produce victory. The unanswered question, of course, was what did Pierce promise Gifford? Did he assure him patronage appointments? The question is still unanswered although former Klansman Lem Dever was convinced that Pierce promised far more than he delivered after his election to office.

The months before the election had been difficult ones, for both Mayor Baker and the business community. The city had to weather a national recession, the crash of the export wheat market, a national railroad strike, and a brief waterfront strike in May. Then on October 13, 1922, both the Longshoremen and the Marine Transport Workers (MTW) walked out, almost 1000 strong. Because the 235 members of the MTW were a branch of the IWW, Mayor Baker blamed the Wobblies for shutting down the waterfront. He branded the strike a "revolution," declaring repeatedly that the city was in the "throes of a revolution." He called upon all patriotic citizens to rally to the defense of law and order, and asserted that an army of 25,000 fully armed Wobblies was marching upon Portland to seize all transportation facilities in the city. The American Federation of Labor branded this as "hogwash"; the mayor was only playing the game of the Waterfront Employers Association.[87]

The night before he issued his proclamation of "revolution," Baker ordered the police department to raid the picket lines. Over 500 were packed off to jail. Every man affiliated with the IWW was held as a vagrant. All civil rights were dispensed with; no warrants were issued and all the men who were released had to suffer the indignity of a "kangaroo court." Labor attorney B. A. Green personally encountered "54 men packed in like sardines in the [police station] drunk tank with no toilet facilities." According to Green's autobiographical account of the episode, these men were not Bolsheviks bent on violent overthrow of the government. Green knew many of them from long acquaintance. They were "simply unemployed loggers and longshoremen" who had joined the strikers in a battle for their rights.[88]

Before the mayor was through, he ordered the arrest of every known IWW member in Portland. All trains entering and leaving Union Station were carefully searched. The city council appropriated $10,000 to stem the "revolution." Any man wearing workingman's clothes was subject to detainment and search. For ten days, the arrests went on, office headquarters were continually broken into, furniture smashed and records destroyed. More than 100 special police were hired. Most of the arrested IWW members were released after a hearing, forcibly taken to the city limits and told to "stay out of town," even some who were long-time residents of Portland. Then, suddenly, on October 25th, the raids were called off just as a battery of lawyers was preparing to file injunction proceedings against the city. The "revolution" ended because the waterfront

170

strike was settled. Not one case of IWW violence had been reported. Obviously, declared Green, the "revolution" had been conceived "in subservience to the Waterfront Employers Association, born in stupidity and nurtured in abysmal ignorance."[89]

The same characterization could just as easily have been applied to the compulsory public education campaign: "Born in stupidity and nurtured in ignorance." As the *Outlook Magazine*'s special correspondent reported, "The people were feeling mad when the Klan came along." They were upset by the strikes and still fearful of the radicals.

"They were mad at high taxes, mad at low prices for farm products, mad at the status quo in general. They wanted a change, and they didn't object to

They Brought Happiness to Many

Led by Mayor Baker and Chief of Police Jenkins, Portland's vigilantes gathered Christmas gifts from the city's merchants and distributed them among nearly 200 unfortunate families. The picture shows a group of the cheer dispensers with Mayor Baker and Chief Jenkins in the front row, just before they visited the families to whom Christmas would otherwise have been merely "another day." Two baskets were taken to each home and the particular needs of each family cared for in preparation of the baskets.

Photograph and caption, published in The Oregon Journal *and* The Oregonian, *December 26, 1922. Most of the men with stars were members of Mayor Baker's special police contingent. Rumor had it that many of them were also members of the Ku Klux Klan. At least this was the claim of former Klansman Lem Dever.*

171

smashing something . . . to get a change. . . . In Oregon, the 'thinking people' are in a hopeless minority. People in the mass don't think. They feel."[90]

The November election of 1922 provided just the opportunity to vent such pent-up, frustrated feelings. The compulsory public school initiative passed 115,506 to 103,685. It drew most of its support from Portland and Eugene south. Twenty-one counties, along with the capital city of Salem, rejected it. Much of the credit for Salem's opposition belonged to the *Capital Journal*'s crusading editor, George Putnam, who was the state's most outspoken critic of the Ku Klux Klan, excluding Catholic and Jewish editors. The *Capital Journal* put the Portland papers to shame in matters involving basic human rights.

In the governor's race, Democrat Walter Pierce won by 34,000 votes, despite Republicans outnumbering Democrats by three to one. Grand Dragon Fred Gifford immediately claimed the victory for the Klan. And *Outlook* correspondent Waldo Roberts concurred. After an extensive trip through the state, he reported:

"There is something new under the sun. Oregon, politically the most conservative and temperamentally the least romantic state west of the Rocky Mountains, is now under the control of the Ku Klux Klan."[91]

It was "the good people of Oregon" who were largely responsible, claimed Roberts. The Klan's appeal for "a moral uplift" had been highly effective. Roberts doubted that the Invisible Order had more than 10-15,000 members but their voting strength was obviously crucial. It was to exercise a pronounced influence in the 1923 legislative session with Kaspar K. Kubli as the Speaker of the House.

By the end of 1924, however, beset by internal bickering and the recall of Multnomah County's three commissioners, the Klan's power would begin to decline rapidly. The school bill, not scheduled to take effect until September 1926, was to be declared unconstitutional by both the U. S. District Court (in March 1924) and the U. S. Supreme Court, to which the state took the case upon appeal. The highest tribunal's unanimous decision of June 1, 1925, would be a complete vindication of the strenuous legal efforts undertaken by Father Edwin Vincent O'Hara, Rabbi Jonah Wise and their lawyer cohorts Dan J. Malarkey, John P. Kavanaugh, Frank J. Lonergan and Hall S. Lusk. Roger Baldwin of the American Civil Liberties Union was also to provide invaluable assistance.

As if it were all a bad dream, soon to be forgotten upon awakening, the decade of fear and bigotry would fade out of sight and memory, except for those who had personally suffered from its excesses. The Ku Klux Klan would evaporate into thin air and Grand Dragon Gifford into obscurity. George Luis Baker would survive in office until 1933. After being decisively beaten by incumbent U. S. Senator Charles L. McNary in the 1924 Republican primary, Baker would forsake higher ambitions and settle back into his mayor's seat to rebuild his former image of the people's man, "our George."

Chapter 8

Power and Politics (1):
Business in the mid-1920s

Business was booming in most areas of the country during June of 1923 when President Warren G. Harding undertook a two week trip that would land him in Portland on the Fourth of July. The crowds became larger and more enthusiastic as the President's special train moved westward. At a station stop in The Dalles late in the evening of July 3rd, Harding told his Oregon audience that he had met "a confident and seemingly happy people. . . . I am very much more proud of our country than when I started westward."[1]

The Harding-Coolidge Years

On average, the American economy had rebounded strongly from the severe recession of late 1920 and 1921. The dollar value of real estate sales and new construction showed a healthy gain, especially in Portland. The doubling of automobile ownership in four years created strong demand for street extensions and widenings, auto sales outlets, garages, filling stations, restaurants and highway stops. The local index of manufacturing production followed closely the national two year increase of 40 percent for all industries. Portland lumber mills maintained a steady growth in production. In five years, the dollar value of lumber exports increased five fold. By the end of 1924, it would rise another 200 percent. As economist Stuart Chase aptly remarked, business was becoming "the dictator of our destinies."[2]

The farmers, on the other hand, were not enjoying the 1923 business prosperity, especially those who raised wheat, corn and cotton. The national farm index had dropped from 205 in 1920 to 116 in 1921 — the worst slide in American history. By 1923, conditions had improved little, due primarily to weak foreign markets, overexpansion of agricultural lands during the war and the ending of wartime government subsidies. The price of wheat in the Northwest had dropped during the last six months of 1920 from an average of $3.50 to $1 per bushel, with dire consequences for Portland as the West Coast's major exporter of wheat and flour. In 1920, Port of Portland Commission President Max Houser was the world's largest individual grain exporter. Within less than a year, beginning in mid-1920, Houser was to be wiped out, losing as much as $15 million.

Houser received his first blow in 1919 when the dollar value of Portland's flour exports started sliding, dropping 65 percent in four years until it started to rise

173

slowly in late 1923. Unfortunately, Houser had purchased the Portland Flouring Mills from the Wilcox Estate in August 1918 for $7 million cash. Paradoxically, the year 1920 that brought Houser his second and fatal blow saw the actual dollar value of wheat exports rise 100 percent — a misleading statistic to say the least. The increased export crop was composed of cheap wheat, literally dumped on the market at a minimum profit and maximum loss to Max Houser.

Being a speculator, Houser had previously bought his wheat long at top market prices — almost 10 million bushels worth — and he had chartered an expensive fleet of ships for the European trade. When the wheat price started to fall in April 1920, Houser was stuck. No European would buy his costly wheat. Then the canny Scotsman Peter Kerr, of Portland's giant Kerr-Gifford Grain Company, entered the market by purchasing millions of bushels of surplus cheap wheat. Through his London brokers, he negotiated a profitable sale, to be split between Europe and China where it was needed to replace a rice shortage. As a consequence, the 1921 dollar value of cheap wheat exports shot up almost 800 percent. Houser's loss had turned out to be Kerr's gain.[3]

The grain business, particularly that of the speculative grain dealer, was plagued by such uncertainties and risks. With the exception of Peter Kerr, few derived any substantial wealth from the trade, especially in the twenty year period between the wars. By the time of President Harding's visit, the dollar value of wheat exports from Portland had declined over 60 percent from the 1921 high. The confidence and happiness that Harding encountered on his trip west

EXPORTS BY COMMODITIES AT PORT OF PORTLAND, OREGON, FOR FISCAL YEARS ENDING JUNE 30
(U. S. Custom House Records, Portland, Oregon)

Commodity	1917	1918	1919	1920	1921	1922	1923	1924	1925
Apples, fresh ....$	....	$........	$........	$........	$........	$........	$........	....	$2,683,762
Autos and cycles.....	....	....	101,931	92,228	101,758	105,522	156,941	272,952	301,346
Barley	....	....	....	....	49,000	109,848	....	....	565,828
Caustic soda	....	....	....	227,964	....	....	....	....	....
Coal	....	....	....	85,388	3,675	....	....	....	....
Copper	....	....	642,053	....	....	....	....	....	....
Cordage	....	....	8,058	....	....	....	....	....	....
Cotton	....	....	....	6,855,507	233,646	82,962	....	....	....
Fuel, gas and oil......	....	....	....	12,219	....	....	....	....	....
Fish	36,105	....	....	....	....	....	....	....	....
Flour	3,600	6,751,045	23,088,049	16,931,906	10,328,925	7,667,267	7,590,098	13,628,413	5,482,949
Fruits	....	....	....	....	155,384	1,861,285	2,921,623	2,486,941	1,543,089
Hides	....	....	....	....	84,993	433,386	290,146	904,228	1,030,292
Hops	....	....	....	217,768	120,315	21,090	5,745	....	811
Iron and steel mfgs....	163,025	102,150	1,136,280	2,999,506	1,295,017	824,892	110,373	97,051	112,461
Lead, in pigs, etc......	....	....	....	....	....	....	....	....	455,914
Lumber	830,808	1,835,117	1,550,953	5,304,302	5,375,302	9,108,117	8,946,323	17,953,715	11,884,448
Machinery	....	....	....	891,539	1,129,749	853,983	217,004	209,730	67,675
Miscellaneous	5,519	80,129	92,898	1,036,909	674,522	1,385,793	1,493,137	1,305,034	1,933,120
Milk, condensed	....	39,270	....	287,598	482,326	219,191	1,029	....	2,748
Oatmeal	....	253,193	....	....	....	....	....	....	....
Paper	131,928	....	121,928	488,066	343,366	270,702	....	123,408	227,110
Paraffin	....	....	....	....	106,414	....	....	....	....
Prunes, dried	....	....	....	....	....	....	....	....	1,098,209
Railroad ties	....	64,869	....	614,146	1,089,797	91,174	....	280,924	....
Salmon, canned	....	....	....	97,392	453,633	739,718	669,669	381,899	873,319
Tablefood prep'ts	....	121,679	85,417	....	....	....	....	....	....
Tallow	....	....	171,312	....	....	....	....	....	....
Tinplate	....	....	....	391,874	44,860	....	....	....	....
Tobacco	....	....	261,710	....	....	....	....	....	....
Wheat	3,019,710	957,993	3,237,930	6,298,579	47,057,289	42,346,440	18,039,685	27,535,376	19,759,933
Totals..........	$4,190,695	$10,205,445	$30,518,519	$42,812,891	$69,129,971	$66,101,370	$40,441,773	$65,179,671	$48,012,254

Multnomah Field on July 4, 1923. The special speaker's stand for President Harding can be seen in back of the old Multnomah Athletic Clubhouse that was built in 1911. Three years later a 20,000 seat concrete stadium would be built by the club. It was later sold to the city and stands today as the Civic Stadium.

was not uniformly shared, as most farmers and many labor groups were suffering. In fact, they would continue to languish for almost two decades.

But President Harding's friendly attitude toward business satisfied the conservative temper of Portland's Chamber of Commerce. On July 2nd, the chamber chartered a special train to take a large delegation to meet the President in Spokane and accompany him to Portland where a giant Independence Day celebration had been planned. Appropriately, Republican stalwart Charles H. Carey, the prominent railroad attorney, was general chairman for the event and Dr. Eugene Rocky was to provide the American Legion guard for the parade by virtue of his role as commander of the local post. Miss Henrietta Failing, Portland's most distinguished aristocratic spinster, was to loan the President her seven passenger Pierce Arrow complete with chauffeur.

In company with Mayor Baker, Herbert Hoover and other cabinet notables, President and Mrs. Harding reviewed the parade in front of the Armory and then moved to Multnomah Field where they faced a throng of 30,000 listeners, most of whom were wildly supportive. Among the minority of disenchanted were 74 Wobblies who were arrested and carted off to jail for distributing handbills during the speech. Assisted by Mayor Baker's loyal cadre of vigilantes, the police charged them with violating a little used ordinance that forbade distributing anything without a city license.

The President's address, which was carried on the new *Oregonian*-owned radio station and billed as "the greatest event in radio to date," discussed the imperative need for selective immigration to the United States. This was a topic that truly warmed the hearts of Portland conservatives. America, declared Harding, should admit only those who are "mentally and morally qualified" to become "true American citizens."[4] The Ku Klux Klan could not have said it any better. Ironically, Harding's administration would turn out to be the most corrupt and morally bankrupt of any in American history. Already the director of the Veteran's Bureau had left office in disgrace and rumors of graft, waste and mismanagement were beginning to float about the country, but they only attracted mild public interest.

As the presidential train headed to Tacoma where the Hardings were to board ship for Alaska, *The Oregonian*'s early July 5th edition proclaimed in banner headlines: "Hardings Take City By Storm."[5] Within a month, the President would be dead. Falling ill on shipboard while returning to Seattle, Mr. Harding was rushed by special train non-stop to San Francisco where he died on August 2nd, reportedly of an apoplectic stroke. According to *Harper's Magazine* editor Frederick Lewis Allen and his colleague, newsman William Allen White, Harding had been well aware "of what had been going on in his administration." They both felt that Harding "died a victim of the predicament in which he was caught." His "friends had betrayed him."[6]

Vice President Calvin Coolidge, who succeeded to the presidency, proved to be even more supportive than his predecessor in encouraging business development. No one was ever to question the integrity of the quiet New Englander who moved into the White House. But "cautious Cal," as Coolidge was aptly dubbed, was in no mood to rock the national boat. It took him ten months to replace the obviously dishonest Attorney General, Harding's close friend Harry Daugherty. To his credit, however, Coolidge chose one of America's finest legal minds, Harlan Fisk Stone, to be top man at the Justice Department. The former Columbia Law School Dean and future Chief Justice of the U. S. Supreme Court, Stone cleaned up the FBI and appointed young J. Edgar Hoover as director. He also prosecuted some delayed war fraud cases that Daugherty had quietly buried, and injected some much needed new blood into the ranks of the United States Attorneys, including that for Oregon. In February 1925, George Neuner would begin a long and distinguished tour of national and state public service that would later culminate in a ten year term as Oregon's Attorney General.

The congressional investigations that followed Harding's death — the most publicized of which involved the Teapot Dome scandal — were disquieting to the American business community. Business leaders became defensive, directing their harshest condemnation at the investigators rather than at those who had defrauded the government. The inquiries into the scandals threatened to disturb the *status quo*, the last thing that the dominant business sector wanted. The large newspapers — which were big businesses in themselves — tended to endorse the fears and concerns of the business community.

Portland business leadership reacted in a similar fashion. In a speech before the Portland Chamber of Commerce, First National Bank president Abbot L. Mills decried the investigations of Montana Senators Thomas J. Walsh and Burton K. Wheeler.

> "The demoralizing and disgusting spectacle of the highest legislative body in the land, the United States Senate, spending its time in mud slinging and muckraking, . . . for political reasons, to besmirch the character of men prominent in the councils of the nation, engenders not only loss of respect for the Senate, but shakes one's faith in our present form of government."[7]

Mills even cited the Portland bridge scandal investigation of April 1924 — an episode that would lead to the recall of the county commissioners — as unjustified muckraking. "Let us not forget that men are ever prone to believe evil of their neighbors, and that scandal-mongering is a popular pastime today."[8] Mills blamed his fellow businessmen for not having involved themselves in governmental affairs. "We have permitted ourselves to be represented in government by men other than those of the highest character," he declared. He encouraged the chamber members to run for office, or failing in that, to take an active interest in those who represented them.[9]

Implicit in such statements, of course, was the notion that successful businessmen would be honest. The bribe giver was not to be censored, only the avaricious bribe recipient. In the 1920s, business was regarded with a new veneration. A person was to be judged by his business success, not by his character, ancestry, inheritance or education. Business accomplishment was all that mattered; mistakes could be forgiven. It was almost unpatriotic to cast discredit on successful businessmen, even those who had entered government service for the primary purpose of protecting their own private business interests. As President Coolidge had said, "The business of America is business."[10] The fact that three of America's most successful oil executives had been charged with fraud and bribing a governmental official would soon be forgotten.

Business success and prosperity, rolling along with the throttle wide open, produced some remarkable attempts at self-justification — and even deification. When advertising executive Bruce Barton wrote *The Man Nobody Knows* in 1925, it became the number one best seller of non-fiction in the United States. In Barton's account, Jesus was the founder of modern business. Jesus was also the most popular dinner guest in Jerusalem, an outdoorsman and a great executive. "He picked up twelve men from the bottom ranks of business and forged them into an organization that conquered the world."[11] His parables became the "most powerful advertisements of all time. . . . He would be a national advertiser today."[12]

177

E. W. Scripps and the *News*

One man who had little love for advertisers, the new high priests of business success, was the eccentric multimillionaire Edward Willis Scripps. The English-born owner of more than 40 newspapers as well as the United Press, E. W. Scripps not only did not like advertisers, he distrusted rich men. As he once told Lincoln Steffens:

> "I'm a rich man and that's dangerous, you know. But it isn't just the money that's the risk; it's the living around with other rich men. They get to thinking all alike, and their money not only talks, their money does their thinking too."[13]

To isolate himself from such influences, Scripps used to seclude himself on his Miramar Ranch near San Diego where he could "think more like a left labor galoot." It was while he was in residence at Miramar that he decided to establish anonymously a newspaper in Portland. This was not an uncommon practice for Scripps, but in Portland's case, anonymity was essential. When signing up subscribers for his Newspaper Enterprise Association in 1902, Scripps had apparently promised *The Oregon Journal* publisher C. S. Jackson that he would not establish a competing evening paper in Portland. Just what prompted him to change his mind is not known. In any case, two reporters of his *Seattle Star* were provided with $25,000 to found a newspaper and secretly instructed to proceed to Portland. *The Portland Daily News* was launched in 1906 on a lively and reasonably successful career that would last until 1939. In 1931 it would assume ownership of the *Telegram* and be published as *The Portland News-Telegram*. In the 1920s, under the colorful and often disrespectful editorship of Fred Boalt, the *News* even more than the *Telegram* constantly attacked the "vested interests" that dominated Portland's public life. As Scripps described the process:

> "A newspaper fairly and honestly conducted in the interests of the great masses of the public must at all times antagonize the selfish interests of that very class [the advertisers] which furnishes the larger part of a newspaper's income. It must occasionally so antagonize this class as to cause it not only to cease patronage, to a greater or lesser extent, but to make actually offensive warfare against the newspaper."[14]

In contrast to most of the large urban newspapers, including *The Oregonian* and possibly *The Oregon Journal*, the Scripps newspapers were meant to serve the public, or at least the public as E. W. Scripps defined the word. He hoped his papers would make money, and most of them did, but he was prepared to publish without advertising if necessary. He felt that a good newspaper should

> " . . . keep the capitalist busy defending what he has got, and the very activity enforced upon him makes him a better citizen and more considerate neighbor

and employer. Capitalists resting secure behind the fortifications of ancient and obsolete, or modern, corruptly obtained laws, become vicious, arrogant and harmful alike to themselves and the community."[15]

Scripps' major concern was that most newspapers, excluding his own of course, were "subject to and dominated by capitalism." The *News* did not always attack the establishment with the degree of ferocity that would have pleased its owner, but it succeeded in creating enough local consternation so that when Abbot Mills charged the press with "muckraking," the *News* was his target. The paper would lose some of its bite after Scripps died in 1926 and Roy Howard began to assume management responsibility for the chain.

Edward Willis Scripps is best remembered today as the principal founder and supporter of the Scripps Institute of Oceanography at LaJolla, California. As a lover of the sea and a number of other enticements, he spent the last years of his life cruising the world on his luxurious yacht, drinking a bottle of scotch and smoking 30 cigars daily. Had he ventured to Portland, he might not have been too cordially received by the chamber of commerce despite his obvious business success and enormous wealth. His eccentricity, however, might have spared him. It could be a great asset, he once wrote, because the eccentric could usually escape the enmity of others. Colonel C. E. S. Wood had discovered this to be true. An eccentric was more apt to excite mirth and pity than indignation, animosity and antagonism.

Business Leadership and Growth

The expansive business growth and speculation that hit Portland in the years 1924-1925 created some disquiet for many old-time residents who had become used to the city's spinster image. A confident entrepreneurial spirit was at work: New energy and ideas, new businesses, and new investments in old businesses. A decade earlier, Reed College's ill-fated first president, William Trufant Foster, had sharply accused the city's business establishment of worshipping the Peter Apostle doctrine of "let there be no innovations except those which are handed down."[16] But English visitor John Leader noted some obvious changes occurring as early as 1923. "Portland is slow on the uptake," he said, "in the same way as an elephant is slow. An elephant is a leisurely beast, but in moments of excitement, is apt to break records."[17] In 1925, Portland was experiencing one of those rare "moments of excitement."

Historically, strong economic growth and high achievement motivation have gone hand-in-hand. According to Harvard psychologist David C. McClelland, the United States in 1925 was high on achievement motivation. By McClelland's definition, high achievers have normally been entrepreneurial in nature, "kind of driven — always trying to improve themselves, ... taking personal responsibility to solve problems and achieve moderate goals at calculated risks — in situations that provide real feedback."[18] McClelland has shown how the

179

drive for achievement has been a variable of key importance "within the 'mainstream' American culture — a culture in which status and self-respect come from what a person **does**, in the material world."[19]

Most of Portland's leading businessmen and bankers in 1925 were high achievers, particularly the younger ones. Some were oriented toward power while others were gamblers at heart. But as McClelland discovered, people with a high need for achievement were not apt to be gamblers; they were challenged to win by personal effort, not by luck. In Portland's history, the successful entrepreneurs generally embodied a complex of motives and values, including that of the speculator. The career of grain exporter Max Houser is a case in point.

Houser was born in the small southeastern Washington wheat town of Pomeroy. In his mid-thirties he had become a leading Northwest grain dealer, operating primarily out of Portland, and in his early forties he became president of the Pacific Grain Company and the world's largest individual grain exporter. When he acquired the Wilcox flour interests in 1918 for $7 million cash, he announced that he would distribute all net profits above six percent to the Red Cross and other war relief agencies, a pledge that he would be unable to fulfill. During and after the war, he volunteered his services to the federal government as a vice president of the Food Administration Grain Corporation and as president of the United States Grain Corporation. In March 1919 he was one of five new members to be elected by the legislature to the Port of Portland Commission which in turn chose him to be president. So that by the age of 46, Max Houser had reached the pinnacle of success, at least for Portland.

In all that he ventured, Houser exhibited extreme self-confidence. He did not know the meaning of the word defeat. He could lead people collectively to take risks that they might not assume individually. One example was the pending $1 million bond issue election on June 3, 1919. Designed to provide funds for harbor improvement, it did involve risks. Cautious Portland businessmen were concerned with what would happen when the government closed down the shipyards in September 1919, throwing 30,000 into the ranks of the unemployed. Houser's impatient response was brief and to the point: "What's the use of using up a lot of time worrying about the future? . . . The thing to do is to go ahead anyhow. That is what will come nearer solving the unemployment situation than anything else."[20]

As the *Oregon Voter* commented:

> " 'Go ahead anyhow' seems to be part of the secret of Max H. Houser's remarkable success in business. He is a doer, who believes in doing things as rapidly as they can be done, and whose busy brain is ever initiating some business move that results in more employment for labor and better markets for the producer. His courage and optimism have been put to the test many a time but have never failed him. . . . Max Houser has a good many dollars but he keeps them all busy. . . . An aggressive citizen . . . [he] is one of the best assets of a progressive community."[21]

Max Houser

About the time that the bond issue passed, Houser began to feel the ill effects of the decline in flour exports. But his spirits were not diminished. From his experience with the government, he became convinced that the post-war world would be starving for Northwest soft wheat. He began buying wheat futures as fast as he could — all that he could get his hands on. As described earlier, Houser was wiped out during the last six months of 1920. He resigned from the Port of Portland Commission and went into temporary seclusion.

Evaluating Max Houser is not easy. He was obviously highly motivated to succeed and yet he overestimated his chances for success. Had he thoroughly examined world market conditions he would have better understood that the Europeans did not possess the resources to pay for the wheat. By believing that he could do better than the facts warranted, he proved himself to be a gambler. He was really in the mold of the 19th century "entrepreneurial accelerator," one who continually over-responded to existing conditions and stimuli. He always felt that **his** chances were better than the stated odds if in fact he ever gave much serious thought to what the odds were.

Whether gambling and playing around with women inevitably go together would be hard to prove, but in Max Houser's case they did. His wife, who had been supporting him, filed for divorce and Houser moved into residence at the Arlington Club. He opened a small office in the Board of Trade Building next to the free-wheeling investment brokerage firm of Overbeck & Cooke. The Canadian Bank of Commerce, which was in the process of liquidating his business assets and paying his creditors, provided him a small monthly allowance which he promptly used to play the commodities market through Overbeck & Cooke. He obviously bought on margin and he was either lucky or smart. By the fall of 1924, he was prospering with an accumulation of almost $200,000.

Early in 1925, the bank informed him that the government had made a tax error in his favor and he was due for a refund of $1 million. But the bank refused to let him have it because he owed much more than that to his creditors. When the bank requested that he sign the refund receipt and endorse the check, he refused. After much wrangling, the bank agreed to split the refund if he would endorse the check. He thereupon took the check for $1 million back to his office and disappeared from Portland. The bank was in an uproar, particularly after it received word from grain exporter Mike Sanford's father that two days previously he had passed Houser driving in his car in Southeastern Oregon, heading in the direction of California. One week later, however, all fears subsided when the bank received through the mail a check for $500,000. Houser may have been a gambler but he was true to his word, even though he had no legal or ethical right to the other half of the refund that should have gone to his long-suffering creditors.

Houser subsequently established residence in Southern California and began to play the market again. He was doing very well until mid-October of 1929 when he became bearish for the first time in his life. He sold everything short, expecting the market to continue declining. Rumor had it that he was the "biggest short" on the Los Angeles stock exchange. Unfortunately for Max Houser, he sold one week too soon. The market climbed back up again before it finally crashed with a resounding thud on October 29th. Houser was heavily margined and his collateral reserves were exhausted. The banks and brokers called their loans. For the second time in a decade he was totally wiped out. He moved back to Pomeroy, Washington, and settled down on his old family farm where he quietly lived out his remaining years.[22]

Max Houser's experience was unique but there were others in Portland who flirted with similar dangers: Northwestern National Bank president Emery Olmstead, lumberman John Wheeler, the Wilcox Investment Company, the Ladd & Tilton Bank, bond promoter John Etheridge of Morris Brothers, a number of real estate developers and several investment houses like Clark-Kendall Company and Houser's broker, Overbeck & Cooke. Their misfortunes will be recounted later in this and subsequent chapters.

The greatest speculation was in unlisted local stocks that were being promoted

by Portland investment concerns. In late November 1924, Overbeck & Cooke reported local demand for stocks at 25 percent in excess of normal demand. Given as the chief reason for the outburst was "an emphatic confidence in business conditions as a result of the general election,"[23] when Calvin Coolidge was overwhelmingly returned to office. On the big board, railroads, oils and industrials led the list in that order. Among utilities, Franklin T. Griffith's Portland Electric Power (PEPCO) common stock was selling at 37½, up 425 percent in two years.

The *Oregon Voter*'s mid-November 1924 investment report noted the Oregon Portland Cement Company's first dividend in over eight years. Controlled until 1937 by the R. P. Butchart interests of Victoria (British Columbia), Oregon Cement had gone through reorganization in 1916-1917. Butchart had been indicted by the U. S. Government for anti-trust violations, and the company had found itself in need of new venture capital. A syndicate of local investors, comprising the cream of the Portland business-financial community, subscribed almost 50 percent of a $150,000 seven percent note:

Portland Railway Light & Power Co. (PEPCO)	$20,000
Joseph N. Teal	5,000
Dr. Andrew C. Smith	5,000
William M. Ladd (Oregon Iron & Steel Co.)	10,000
Abbot L. Mills (1st National Bank)	5,000
T. B. Wilcox	20,000
John C. Ainsworth (U. S. National Bank)	5,000

The largest investment, $65,000, was made by Charles Boettcher, prominent Denver banker, cement manufacturer and industrialist. Butchart himself put in $15,000. Under the management and then presidency of Canadian L. C. Newlands, the company began to prosper.[24] It became a major supplier of cement for the Columbia River dams in subsequent decades, and today it is the Northwest's leading cement manufacturer.

Oregon Portland Cement Company offers a prime example of a well managed, locally supported company which has maintained a solid, steady growth for over 60 years. In retrospect, however, it has proved unfortunate that the company's major local plant is located along the Willamette riverfront, adjacent to the attractive central shopping district of suburban Lake Oswego. The 20 acre site was sold to the company before the war by William M. Ladd's Oregon Iron & Steel Company in the days when Oswego was a tiny outpost of Portland. Adjacent to the Willamette Greenway project, the plant's location has had an adverse impact on the visual and recreational enjoyment of the river. As the lessons of history have shown, plants of this type and magnitude belong in industrial parks, such as the Port of Portland's Rivergate district. It is almost prohibitive to move them once they are built, let alone after they have been enlarged and modernized.

The mention of the Rivergate Industrial district leads directly to the two men whose remarkably successful business careers made this unique development possible: *The Oregonian* publisher and owner, Henry L. Pittock and his son-in-law, Frederick W. Leadbetter. Both men belong at the top of any list of high achievers. They were the quintessential entrepreneurs of Portland during the first quarter of the 20th century.

London-born Henry Pittock arrived in Portland in 1853 as an 18 year old assistant to Thomas J. Dryer, founder of the struggling weekly, *The Morning Oregonian*. Within seven years he had become the paper's owner and the following year he took the financial plunge and made it a daily. Hard times and increased competition forced him to relinquish control in the early seventies, but with changing conditions and the chance for additional financing, Pittock and his former editor, Harvey W. Scott, bought out the Corbett interests in 1877. "This resulted in a 2/3 ownership by Pittock and a 1/3 by Scott — a cause of irritation and some bitterness over the years by the Scotts toward the Pittocks."[25] In fact, when S. I. Newhouse was negotiating with the directors of the Oregonian Publishing Company to buy the paper in 1950. Harvey Scott's son, Leslie, unsuccessfully fought the sale to the bitter end. For years, Leslie had yearned to own and edit the paper, a chance that was denied him.

Pittock remained in control of *The Oregonian* for 42 more years, until his death in 1919 at 83. When Scott died in 1910, Edgar Piper was appointed editor, but he had no financial interest in the paper. Although as E. W. Scripps said, "There is no more valuable and substantial property in the world than a successful newspaper,"[26] Pittock did not by any means confine his business interests solely to *The Oregonian*. Like most of his peers, he became involved in a number of real estate and banking ventures, but the depression of 1893 nearly bankrupted him.

Oregon Portland Cement with Lake Oswego in the background

Office Building for the Pittock Block Inc.

It was not until he was almost 60 that Henry Pittock began to accumulate the basis for a substantial fortune that would total in excess of $8 million upon his death. And it was not until he was 73 that he revealed any outward signs of changing a life style that was austere and spartan, to say the least. In 1909 he began construction of his luxurious mansion on Imperial Heights. Four years later, he moved from his simple downtown six room cottage into a hillside setting of magnificence that has never been equalled in Portland's history. His former downtown residence lay on a block of land that he had purchased in 1856 for $300. Known as the Pittock Block, the land today is worth over $1 million. In 1912, he leased the site to Herbert Fleishhacker of San Francisco for 99 years for a total net ground rent of $8,310,000 — nearly 28,000 times the original cost. Fleisshacker was to construct a building for not less than $650,000 with the ownership reverting to the lessor at the end of the lease. The increasing yearly rent scale was based on Pittock's estimate of the increasing value of the land. As it turned out, *The Oregonian* publisher was amazingly accurate in his prediction. The land was donated to Santa Clara University some years ago and Fleishhacker donated his lease and building rights to a similar eleemosynary

186

institution.

Henry Pittock was a classic high achiever. He was "quiet, systematic, prudent, hardworking and tenacious. . . . He never seemed to tire, no matter how tough the going. And when he accomplished one objective, he always had a new one in mind."[27]

He did not encourage small talk. In personal as well as business face-to-face encounters, he came to the point at once, often with extreme bluntness. He had no time to waste. Banker E. B. MacNaughton recalled the time that he was summoned to Pittock's office in 1913 after the collapse of the old Marquam Building on S. W. Morrison Street. Before he had ventured into property management and banking, MacNaughton had practiced architecture for a decade following his arrival in Portland in 1903, two years after graduation from MIT. Pittock had hired his firm to renovate the recently purchased building, the site of the Marquam Grand Theater, as headquarters for a new bank. After work had begun, some interior structural supports of soft brick appeared to be unsound, and before they could be replaced, the corner on 6th Avenue collapsed. When MacNaughton appeared at Pittock's desk, the publisher looked up and said only five words: "My attorney will see you."[28] And indeed he did. Charles H. Carey fired him on the spot.

The irony of this episode is that some 20 years later, one of MacNaughton's sons married one of Pittock's granddaughters. And 35 years later, MacNaughton was appointed chairman of the board of the Oregonian Publishing Company for the primary purpose of salvaging what appeared to be an increasingly unprofitable operation. It was MacNaughton who arranged the sale of the paper to the Newhouse chain in 1950 at the behest of Pittock's heirs. Proving Scripps' point that "a newspaper cannot be a very great and successful newspaper without being worth several millions of dollars,"[29] Newhouse paid $5 million for the paper, excluding the new plant that had been sold previously to the Connecticut Mutual Life Insurance Company for $3.6 million. Newhouse also bought the paper's KGW radio station for $600,000.

The upturn in Pittock's fortune, following the depression of 1893, began with the marriage late in 1893 of one of his four daughters, Caroline, to a young Iowan named Frederick W. Leadbetter who had just joined the advertising department of *The Oregonian.* Over the next 25 years, Pittock and Leadbetter combined their talents to put together a vast timber and paper empire that by 1950 would be worth over $50 million. Pittock is often given credit for being the founder of the Portland area paper manufacturing industry. Beginning in Camas, Washington, and then Vancouver, the network spread not only to many parts of Oregon but even to Los Angeles. However, the really expansive growth and prosperity occurred during the 1920s.

The filing of Henry Pittock's will after his death in January 1919 created deep consternation within the family. He established a 20 year trust for all of his property, to be administered by two long time associates, neither of whom the family cared for. Named as trustees were C. A. Morden, manager of *The*

Oregonian and O. L. Price, confidential advisor and attorney. The trustees were given "full and complete power and authority" over his estate. The central provision of the will dealt with *The Oregonian*; if it was not obvious before, the newspaper had been nearest to his heart. Above all else, he wanted it protected for as long as possible. Price was also named the sole executor as Mrs. Pittock had died seven months before her husband.

Fred Pittock and Caroline Leadbetter filed suit in circuit court to set aside the will on the grounds that the trustees had exercised undue influence over Pittock at the time that the will was drafted, "that in fact it was their will instead of Mr.

The old Oregonian Building

Pittock's."[30] The charges also included: (1) That the trustees were vested with unrestricted and unlimited discretion; (2) that the will did not specify with sufficient certainty the beneficiaries of the trust; and (3), that the trustees were directed to vote the stock of the Oregonian Publishing Company in favor of themselves as directors (and in Morden's case as an employee) of the company, for 20 years.[31] The circuit court rejected the suit and the children appealed their case to the state supreme court. In July 1921, the supreme court unanimously affirmed the lower court's decision on the grounds,

" . . . that there was no evidence of undue influence on Mr. Pittock in the making of his will; . . . that he had greater influence over the defendants, O. L. Price and C. A. Morden, than they had over him; that his word was the law and that it was their place to obey and not to influence or dictate."[32]

The restrictions of the will did not seem to affect adversely the growth and profits of the Leadbetter-Pittock industrial enterprises. During his lifetime, Pittock had largely left the management of these assets to Leadbetter who took Pittock's substantial resources and developed them to their maximum potential. He was to continue to pursue these goals with even greater success for almost 30 years. In the process, Leadbetter established and developed a number of his own enterprises.

The crown jewel of the Pittock-Leadbetter properties was the Columbia River Paper Company, a holding company for three mills: Columbia River Paper in Vancouver (Washington), Oregon Pulp & Paper in Salem, and California-Oregon Paper in Los Angeles. In 1926, Columbia River Paper's net income after taxes increased 500 percent over that of 1925, to nearly $250,000.[33] The holding company, with extensive timber reserves, was sold to the Boise Cascade Corporation in the early 1960s. The family was reported to have derived $60 million from the sale, with Mrs. Leadbetter receiving $12 million in cash. Surviving her husband by 24 years, Caroline Pittock Leadbetter was an inveterate world traveller into her late nineties. When she received her check, she apparently stashed it away in a desk drawer and promptly forgot about it. The Bank of California had to dispatch a representative to find it and arrange for its deposit in order to clear its own accounts. Mrs. Leadbetter lived in splendor until she was 102 on her vast Santa Barbara estate that was maintained by 30 gardeners.

In addition to timber and paper resources, Pittock-Leadbetter money was invested in logging, railroads, banks and Columbia and Willamette riverfront property. In 1910, Pittock had acquired control of the Portland Trust Company of which he had been a major stockholder for 23 years. The Oregon Bank (ORBANCO) is the present day successor to that profitable asset. In 1913, Pittock and his son-in-law opened the Northwestern National Bank, to be located in the renovated Marquam Building. After the building collapsed, the two entrepreneurs erected a modern 14-story office building, perhaps the finest of its type ever constructed in Portland. Today known as the American Bank Building, the structure had some shaky tenants for two decades: Three successive banks failed, beginning with the Northwestern in 1927. This was the only major loss suffered by the Pittock interests following the depression of 1893.

Outside of the downtown Pittock Block and bank properties, and the various industrial and timber holdings scattered around the Pacific Coast, the Pittock-Leadbetter Company acquired 2700 acres of land on the Willamette and Columbia Rivers. Starting with a 750 acre industrial tract in North St. Johns, the property ran for six miles, north along the Willamette, and from the juncture with the Columbia, east along the south channel of the Columbia almost to the SP&S rail line. This was largely undiked, flood plain acreage with marshes and scrub vegetation — excellent for duck shooting, which is exactly what the Leadbetter family and friends used it for.

Excluding the Industrial Land Company property in St. Johns, Leadbetter bequeathed the remaining 2000 acres to Willamette University in Salem. Worth approximately $200,000 in 1950, the gift was arranged by Willamette trustee, lumberman Truman Collins, whose late father, E. S. Collins, had pledged his own personal resources to protect the depositors of the Northwestern Bank in 1927. One good deed had led to another. There was only one problem attached to the bequest: The land was not to be sold for 50 years.

The Port of Portland desired to buy the land for industrial site development but the university wanted to delay any sale, even by condemnation, in the hope that the land would appreciate in value. The Port responded that without costly improvements, filling and diking, no appreciation would occur. The university did not have the money and the Port would not improve privately-held property. After much litigation, the land was condemned in 1964. After further court delay, the sale was consummated in late 1965 for $1000 an acre. Over the last decade, with dredge fill and basic services added, the Rivergate Industrial District has become one of the largest and most complete industrial parks on the West Coast. Currently Rivergate property is selling for approximately $45,000 an acre. Leadbetter's magnificent duck blind has become an equally magnificent addition to Portland's economic life.

Fred Leadbetter was a much more outgoing, sociable person than his father-in-law. He was a hard driving, hard working, and hard living person with a dominant personality. The achievement motive was strong, but overlapping it was an obvious power motive — he enjoyed the control that went with his economic position. The late Capt. Homer Shaver, one of Portland's most active towboat operators and an influential member of the dock commission, had this to say about him:

> "One of the most interesting men that I ever did business with was Fred Leadbetter of the Columbia River Paper Mills at Vancouver who we towed for for years. He was a very smart operator and a man hard to deal with, but I always knew that when the deal was made, that was it, and there would be no

backing away from it, as far as he was concerned. I sometimes felt that I had not only lost my shirt, but my pants too, when I got through. . . . "[34]

Leadbetter did not involve himself directly in any political activities although he was a staunch Republican spiritually. He was an active club man and enjoyed tennis, golf and polo as well as fishing and hunting. He was a member of some of the most exclusive clubs in Portland, San Francisco, New York and Washington. Toward the end of his life, he spent most of his time on his lavish Santa Barbara estate, one of the show places of Southern California. His fortress-like stone-crafted home near Washington Park on upper King's Hill in Portland was donated to the Oregon Historical Society which in turn sold it for a fragment of its cost in the early 1950s. It was demolished and replaced by some undistinguished but profitable garden-type apartments.

A man of many talents, whose career overlapped those of both Henry Pittock and Fred Leadbetter, was the colorful Charles F. Swigert. Portland has produced few business executives who have been involved in so many varied activities as the Ohio-born Swigert who arrived in 1880, at the age of 18, to open and manage an office for the Pacific Bridge Company of San Francisco, a concern that was owned by his uncle, Charles Gorrill. Swigert's early career was thoroughly

F. W. Leadbetter home on S. W. Park

191

Charles F. Swigert
1913

covered in *The Shaping of a City*. To summarize briefly, by the time of his 46th birthday in 1908, Swigert had already been a major promoter of electrified railways, an early developer of the North Albina and Peninsula districts of North Portland, the leading constructor of bridges and bridge piers, and the president of both the Port of Portland Commission and the Portland Chamber of Commerce.

Few would doubt that Swigert was clearly achievement motivated, but it was the challenge of the task that seemed to hold the highest fascination for him. He had an inquiring, innovative mind that was continually searching out new areas for investments. In his younger days, he was not adverse to using the instruments of government to help him achieve his goals. Many of his construction projects, of course, involved government contracts, but in whatever he undertook, he did a thorough job. Making money as such did not seem to be of prime importance. As a matter of fact, seven years before he died, at the height of the booming twenties, his net worth was only $471,000, not a great deal considering his list of accomplishments. As often happens, it was left to his children to fatten the family fortune. Aided by good management and the second world war, the business seeds that C. F. Swigert planted grew into giant corporate trees. It is estimated that his surviving son, Ernest G. Swigert, is worth at least $50 million.

The Hyster Company

The story is told that while visiting France shortly before the first world war, Swigert observed an electric arc steel melting furnace in operation, one of the world's first. He dreamed up the idea of manufacturing cast steel products for the logging and sawmill industries of the Northwest that were using cast iron and forged implements. He bought plans and blueprints of the furnace, returned to Portland, and in 1913 opened the first electric arc steel melting furnace west of the Mississippi River. The youthful company, known as Electric Steel Foundry, grew rapidly and profitably, especially during the world war. For the four years from 1917 to 1920, it paid total dividends of over ten percent on gross sales of $2.7 million. During the late twenties and the depression thirties, the company profits dropped off and dividends were often omitted. The second world war gave the business a shot in the arm and it has continued to prosper ever since. Probably the largest family-controlled corporation in Oregon, the multi-million dollar ESCO, as the firm is called today, has plants and offices throughout the world. From 150 employees in 1925 it has grown to over 3000, with 1600 working in the Portland operation, centered in the Northwest district.

Another Swigert enterprise that is better known than ESCO, because it is publicly-owned, is the Hyster Corporation. Swigert and his sons started this company in 1929, as an offshoot of Electric Steel Foundry and Willamette Iron & Steel; ESCO owns 21 percent of its stock. Established as the Willamette Ersted Company, Hyster grew rapidly during its first two years. For its first eleven months in 1929, it showed profits of ten percent on sales of $628,000, manufacturing lifts and hoists for tractors and earth moving equipment used primarily in logging operations. The depression took its toll with several years of losses, but, as with ESCO, Hyster came charging back. By 1978, it had over $450 million in sales and plants all over the world. Its home plant is located on Sullivan's Gulch, a mile west of the Hollywood district of Rose City Park.

The other major industrial enterprise, besides Pacific Bridge, in which C. F. Swigert invested funds was the Willamette Iron & Steel Works, one of Portland's oldest and most prestigious enterprises. Organized in 1865, the company had prospered during the world war through its government ship building contracts. Its major products were large logging machinery, marine engines and industrial boilers. Swigert invested heavily in the firm over the years, to the point that the value of his Willamette Iron & Steel stockholdings in 1928 comprised 20 percent of his assets. Unfortunately, the company lost heavily in the late twenties. It was forced into bankruptcy and reorganized in 1930-1931. As chairman of the board, Swigert had to bear much of the worry and pressure that such difficulties presented. He was successful in installing new management but he died before the company regained prosperity. He obviously lost money in the endeavor, but like so much that he did, the challenge had proved stimulating. Renamed the Willamette Iron & Steel Company, the successful WISCO operation is now a wholly-owned subsidiary of the Guy F. Atkinson Company of San Francisco.

During the mid-1920s, C. F. Swigert was to play an important role in constructing the new Burnside Bridge and the Willamette River Sea Wall. He also owned the 1800 acre Sundial Ranch east of Portland, on the Columbia River, and was instrumental in establishing the first diking district in Multnomah County. The reclaimed flood plain was later annexed to Troutdale and became the site of the Reynolds Aluminum Plant and the busy Troutdale Airport.

The ever restless entrepreneur also invested in sand, gravel and concrete enterprises, timber lands and motor trucking. Perhaps his most exciting challenge, however, was his decision to have Pacific Bridge join the consortium of six construction firms that built the Hoover Dam on the Colorado River. Other members of his family joined in the effort that was later followed by the contract to construct the piers for the Golden Gate Bridge in San Francisco. In retrospect, one would have to say that Charles F. Swigert lived a busy and fruitful life of extraordinary achievement. He made a lasting impact on the growth of Portland.[35]

The mid-1920s was an encouraging time for the well managed company to raise capital funds through the issuance of new bonds and preferred stock. Portland's growing woolen industry highlighted this development.[36] As the second largest primary wool market in the United States — Boston being the first — Portland led the Pacific Coast both in the export of raw wool and in the manufacture of woolen textiles. Sheep raising was big business. In fact, F. W. Leadbetter was president of a company that owned 4000 acres on the Washougal River in Washington on which he grazed both sheep and cattle.

As to manufacturing, with eight mills and 1200 employees, Oregon ranked second to Wisconsin among all states west of the Atlantic seaboard in volume of production. Portland Woolen Mills, the largest of its type west of Ohio, was organized in 1901 at Sellwood by W. P. Olds, T. B. Wilcox, E. L. Thompson and the Ladd & Tilton Bank. Relocated in 1905 to St. Johns with its over 500 employees, the company did reasonably well until the depression of the 1930s. Its major competition from the early years, Oregon City Woolen Mills, did not survive the depression, but Portland Woolen lasted until 1960 when its ten acres and aged plant were sold for $125,000. The early success of these companies stimulated the formation of other enterprises, two of which, Jantzen and Pendleton, have grown to become national leaders in their respective product lines. Sound financial management has characterized their development.

In 1925, Jantzen Knitting Mills offered $250,000 in seven percent preferred stock to members of the founding families and to the employees of the company. Jantzen was booming. Incorporated in 1910 as the Portland Knitting Company, with an initial capitalization of $10,000, Jantzen's assets had soared to $784,000. Co-founder John A. Zehntbauer had arrived in Portland in 1901 to work for $3 a week in a local knitting factory. He joined forces with Danish immigrant Carl C. Jantzen in 1909 and they in turn were joined by John's brother Roy. They opened a small store downtown on S. W. Alder Street which housed a few knitting machines that were used to turn out hats and mittens. In 1913, the company designed its first lightweight swimwear and within four years the product was in high local demand. From an output of 600 swimming suits in 1917, sales mushroomed to over 431,000 suits in 1925. Manufacturing one product — in 17 styles, 10 colors and 11 combinations — the company made a net profit of eight cents on every sales dollar. In 1926, business was so good that the company paid an 18 percent dividend. By October 1928, sales volume reached 979,000 suits and the company's expansion needs required a public offering of seven percent preferred stock to the amount of $1.5 million.

Twelve years of explosive growth, involving eight moves, led to the construction in 1925 of a new main plant at N. E. 20th Avenue and Sandy Boulevard. Space was provided for 400 employees. Claiming that it made the suit "that changed bathing to swimming," Jantzen launched one of the first nationwide advertising campaigns using a newly devised diving girl trademark that was to become world famous. By 1928, the company had opened plants in Australia and Canada and was selling its swimming suits in 50 foreign countries. In the decade following World War II, Jantzen was to broaden its production to include a full line of sportswear. For the fiscal year 1976-1977, it reported gross sales of nearly $124 million and current assets of nearly $70 million. Although the company went public in 1928, the founding families still hold almost 25 percent of the stock which brought them $360,000 worth of dividends in 1977.[37]

Pendleton Woolen Mills, a national leader in classic fashions, fabric and blankets made of 100 percent virgin wool, has a history similar to that of Jantzen. It is slightly older, has gross sales lower than Jantzen's (approaching $100 million annually), but is reported to be a more profitable operation. Being privately held by members of the founding Bishop family, the financial data has always been closely guarded except in 1924 when the owners floated $100,000 in 6½ percent gold bonds to fund some reconstruction costs related to the repair of fire damage to one of their mills.

The widespread Pendleton operation, which has about 60 percent of its garment manufacturing in the Oregon-Washington region, grew indirectly out of the Thomas Kay Woolen Mills, established in Salem in 1889. Kay, a Britisher, was considered the pioneer woolen manufacturer of the Pacific Coast. He had opened his first Oregon mill in 1864. Kay's partner in the Salem mill was his son-in-law, C. P. Bishop, who with his two sons, Clarence M. and Roy C., bought the faltering Pendleton Woolen Mills of Pendleton, Oregon, in 1909. Clarence Bishop had resigned as a mill superintendent at Portland Woolen when he was requested by his boss, E. L. Thompson, to inflate the inventory in order to show higher assets on the company's balance sheet.[38] It was this type of practice that brought ruin to Ladd & Tilton, Portland Woolen's banker, and it was the abjuration of such practices that helped to assure Pendleton's success.

The Bishops put the Pendleton mills back in running order and developed the manufacture of the widely known Pendleton Indian blankets. In 1912, the family purchased the Washougal (Washington) Woolen Mills and in 1915 purchased the equipment of the Marysville Woolen Mills of California. The

Eureka Woolen Mills were acquired in 1920 and the Coast Mills Wool Company was established in Portland as the wool department for all of their mills. The Washougal mills were partly destroyed by fire in March of 1923 with the consequence that outside capital was needed to restore them to full operation. But the 1924 bond issue was considered only a loan; it was paid off in short order.

More than any of Portland's prominent firms, Pendleton has remained a Portland company. In 1924, Clarence Bishop wrote that the Portland climate had a controlling influence on the development of the Oregon woolen industry. The moist air permitted weaving under the same favorable conditions that had given British worsteds world-wide pre-eminence. Another positive factor was the area's pure water that was essential for the quality treatment of wool.

From its earliest years, the company proved profitable. The Bishop investments in their various factories increased from $30,000 in 1910 to $917,365 in 1923. By June of 1924, annual production had grown to well over $1 million. Following a practice that was characteristic of cautious, achievement-oriented entrepreneurs, the Bishops never declared any dividends. It was their policy to keep all earnings in the business to strengthen their manufacturing and financial position. By strict adherence to such practices, the company was able to weather the storms of depression and recession and to keep control entirely within the family. Furthermore, Pendleton developed the necessary mechanisms to exercise complete control over all that went into its products. The company not only has bought the raw wool from long time suppliers and woven it into cloth, but it has employed its own fabric designers to create new patterns. Currently, it makes all but six percent of its goods. The clothes that it does not make itself are usually produced in factories owned by Pendleton. Within the entire American textile and garment industry, Pendleton holds a unique spot. And the basic tone and direction were set 70 years ago.[39]

Of the number of new companies established in Portland during the mid-1920s, one in particular stood out in 1927 as a solid financial success, the Iron Fireman Manufacturing Company. It was well managed, with limited debt and with a product of high demand: An automatic coal stoker.

"From Scratch to $3,000,000 in four years and three months," declared the *Oregon Voter* in August 1927.[40] This was the record of the Iron Fireman Manufacturing Company, one that the *Voter* asserted shamed every Oregon manufacturer who said it could not be done. The fact that the company sold 99½ percent of its output outside of Oregon, with 75 percent of its output going east of the Mississippi River, was a major reason for its financial success. It was not dependent on a local cyclical market which in turn was dependent on an uncertain agricultural and lumber economy.

Iron Fireman had found a way to overcome what would have seemed to be two natural handicaps in marketing a bulky piece of equipment that weighed over a ton. It was far from the center of an iron producing territory and it had to compensate for the competitive disadvantage of freight rates to eastern consuming centers. The company had discovered, in its preliminary stage of

Dynamics of Capitalism

The Birth Process

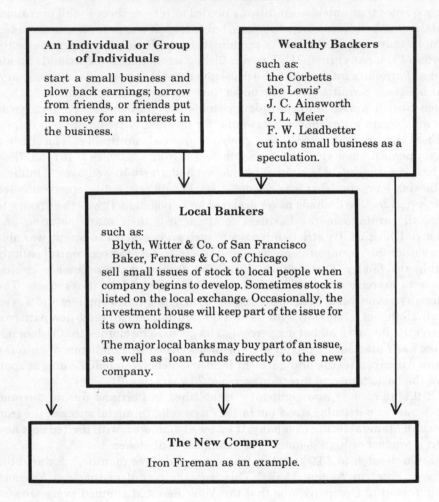

An Individual or Group of Individuals

start a small business and plow back earnings; borrow from friends, or friends put in money for an interest in the business.

Wealthy Backers

such as:
the Corbetts
the Lewis'
J. C. Ainsworth
J. L. Meier
F. W. Leadbetter
cut into small business as a speculation.

Local Bankers

such as:
Blyth, Witter & Co. of San Francisco
Baker, Fentress & Co. of Chicago
sell small issues of stock to local people when company begins to develop. Sometimes stock is listed on the local exchange. Occasionally, the investment house will keep part of the issue for its own holdings.

The major local banks may buy part of an issue, as well as loan funds directly to the new company.

The New Company

Iron Fireman as an example.

development, that even in Ohio, with its iron and steel industries, iron castings cost considerably more to make than in Portland. The major reason was the great quantity of scrap iron available in Portland, scrap that came principally from discarded agricultural implements. Heavy east-bound freight rates were avoided by the use of the Panama Canal in shipments to the Atlantic seaboard. A third benefit enjoyed by Portland was a 15 percent differential in the value of the labor dollar. Even with wage scales being equal, climatic and living conditions favored Portland over the Middle West.

Iron Fireman had a circuitous beginning. The two founders, T. H. Banfield and C. J. Parker, formed a partnership in 1909 to enter the construction business. Between them, they had $700 in capital. Over the next 14 years, they performed a number of medium sized jobs and picked up a sheet metal business in the process. In 1923, they bought the Portland Wire and Iron Works. Included in the deal were some tools and jigs for stoker experimental work — items that they paid little attention to until they began to get orders for coal stokers. They set about designing automatic controls which were then manufactured for them by L. R. Teeple of Portland, one of the region's leading producers of such equipment. As business picked up, the partners purchased a former government war plant and by 1925 they were beginning to show a profit from their new manufacturing enterprise. The construction business continued to thrive also. Although they lost out on the original county bridge contract in 1924, they managed to receive their largest contract in 1925 for the building of the Vista Bridge.

Iron Fireman was incorporated in 1926, a year that saw net earnings approach $150,000; by 1928 they would exceed $500,000. Also by 1928, the company had become the largest manufacturer in the United States of small automatic coal stokers, with offices in St. Louis and Cleveland where an assembly plant was later built.[41] For 17 years, the guiding spirit was to be Edward C. Sammons, who left his former position as a highly regarded young vice president of the United States National Bank to assume the role of vice president and chief operational officer of Iron Fireman in 1928. Partner C. J. Parker had recently died in an airplane accident. Sammons received a liberal allotment of stock in the company and his fortunes rose, along with those of Iron Fireman. In 1945, Sammons was asked to become president of the U. S. Bank, a task that he accepted and performed notably for some years. In fact, during the 1950s, E. C. Sammons was to become Portland's leading financial figure, a conservative and powerful man whose influence was felt far beyond the Northwest.

Sammons had known Banfield from boyhood days and during the early 1920s had become Banfield's banker. Banfield had supreme confidence in Sammons' ability and was thus released to perform other tasks that were offered him. He was to serve for 17 years as an active member of the dock commission (1930-1947) and for seven years as chairman of the state highway commission (1943-1950). After his death in 1950, at the age of 64, he was memorialized by the state's naming the first post-war freeway the Banfield Expressway. The family sold its large brick home in the King's Hill district in 1951 for $50,000 to a "mystery" buyer who turned out to be a Japanese-American physician — much to the horror of many nearby residents. This was the first such sale to an Oriental in the entire west hills section of Portland. The house was recently placed on the market for $395,000.

Iron Fireman prospered during World War II, manufacturing a variety of specialized pieces of military equipment. Following the war, with Sammons' departure and Banfield's desire to liquidate his holdings, the company was sold to some California investors who had plans to diversify its operations through a program of acquisitions modeled on the Textron corporate experience. But poor judgment and financial irresponsibility by the new owners soon terminated the company's existence.

Stable, prosperous growth was **not** a characteristic common to the local lumber industry, at least to the degree enjoyed by most of the city's metal and woolen manufacturing enterprises. But during the two decades following the first world war, one lumber firm achieved wide recognition for its extraordinary profitability: The Portland Manufacturing Company. Located on the St. Johns waterfront, Portland Manufacturing produced the first commercial plywood in the United States and pioneered the use of Douglas fir plywood in the fast growing automobile bodybuilding business. It sold the first laminated floor boards to the General Motors Corporation. It also pioneered the use of plywood wallboard.

When Peter Autzen acquired the company in 1905, it was a small plant engaged in the production of egg crates. Within a year, Autzen switched the

Portland Lumber Company Dock, St. Johns, 1947

operation to Douglas fir panels and the company began its meteoric rise that saw it become one of the major outlets for plywood products in the Northwest. After Peter's son Tom assumed command in 1919, the company continued to expand, to the point that by 1929, its products were exported throughout the world.[42]

Like many lumber firms during the depression, Portland Manufacturing found it necessary to seek additional funding through mergers and affiliations with other lumber interests. Tom Autzen joined forces with Harry Nicolai to form the Portland Lumber Mills and the Plylock Corporation. In all, the related Autzen operations consumed 1000 feet of St. Johns waterfront property. Some years later, Plylock was sold to the Malarkey controlled M & M Woodworking Company which became the world's largest plywood manufacturer. M & M was subsequently acquired by the Simpson Timber Company of Seattle.

In 1951, when the Autzens reorganized their various enterprises, the lumber manufacturing industry was beginning to move south, closer to the sources of supply. The Portland Lumber Mills plant was the oldest mill still operating on the Willamette River but its future was to be short-lived. In 1964, six years after Thomas Autzen's death, the St. Johns properties were sold to the Brand-S Corporation.[43] Thirteen years later, everything was liquidated and the last mill on the Willamette River was dismantled. Vacant for two years, the city is now planning to develop the 80 acre site as a subsidized housing project, using a $9 million Urban Development Action Grant from the federal government.

The Rise and Fall of Ladd & Tilton

From the Civil War to the end of World War I, the Ladd & Tilton Bank had played a distinctive role in Portland's business history. Not only was it Portland's first bank (1859) but it was a private bank. With the passage of the Oregon Banking Act in 1907, it was forced to incorporate and make its books available to public scrutiny. At the time of its 50th anniversary in 1909, Portlanders learned just how profitable a well run private bank could be: Its assets had grown 30,000 percent to $14.7 million. Under founder William S. Ladd's firm hand it had fulfilled one major purpose: To invest its bank resources in and gain control of potentially profitable business enterprises.

After William S. Ladd's death, the bank's control devolved to his children, particularly William M. Ladd who became president.[44] But W. M. Ladd was not a banker by temperament or interest so that the major investment decisions were really engineered by W. S. Ladd's protege, Theodore B. Wilcox. Being a director of the bank and president of the Portland Flouring Mills — controlled by the bank and the Ladd estate — the able, hard driving Wilcox used the bank as an instrument to enhance his own fortunes along with those of the institution. When the Ladd family's Title Guaranty and Trust Company collapsed in 1907, William M. Ladd was forced to sell his controlling Ladd & Tilton shares to his brother-in-law, Frederick B. Pratt of Brooklyn, New York, in order to raise $2.5

million to reimburse the Title Guaranty and Trust depositors. Pratt, who was married to Caroline Ladd, and who had attended Amherst College with her brother, installed Wilcox's associate, Portland banker Edward S. Cookingham, as vice president and chief executive officer of the bank.

Frederick Pratt was the son of Charles Pratt who had sold his oil refining business to John D. Rockefeller in 1874 for which he had received considerable Standard Oil stock in exchange. The Pratts became leaders of the Brooklyn community, endowing libraries and churches and establishing Pratt Institute in 1887. Not only was son Frederick Pratt a successful businessman in his own right, but he had a deep regard for family reputation and strong feelings of family loyalty that extended to the Portland Ladds. His main reason for investing in the Ladd & Tilton Bank was to help protect the good name of the Ladd family. But being 3000 miles away, he left the bank's operation to the local management.

In January of 1919, nine months after T. B. Wilcox died, the Wilcox Investment Company bought 63 percent of the outstanding Ladd & Tilton Bank shares from Frederick Pratt, using funds derived from the sale of the Portland Flouring Mills to Max Houser. Thus, a new ownership took control of Ladd & Tilton's assets and began directing the bank on a dizzy climb to previously unattained heights. Unfortunately, the spectacular growth would end abruptly in a shattering collapse during the summer of 1925. Most accounts of this episode have erroneously blamed the Pratt family for the trouble that developed at Ladd & Tilton.[45] The Pratts did repurchase the bank in December 1924. By that date, however, the damage had already been done and Frederick Pratt was not even remotely aware of it.

Pratt was sold a leaky ship that appeared to be seaworthy but which in fact was about to sink to the bottom. He deserved praise rather than criticism for being willing to risk as much as $15 million in order to preserve the good name of Ladd. After he discovered the truth, he could easily have written off his $3 million investment and forgotten about it. As it turned out, by agreeing to a quick liquidation of assets and a merger with the U. S. National Bank, his decision to protect local investors and depositors cost him only $7 million. Had he not followed banker E. B. MacNaughton's advice, the entire city would have suffered the consequences of the bank's failure.

For the decade following the war, Portland's other two leading banks, the First National and U. S. National, were administered with caution and soundness. Abbot L. Mills and John C. Ainsworth were similar in temperament and judgment. Both men were achievement oriented in performing their respective jobs. Occasionally they would take risks, but only as such actions were deemed necessary to conserve and enhance the results of other people's (and other businessmen's) successes.

Adhering to such a policy was the primary function of the banking profession. Historically, the fundamental blunder of bad bankers, large and small, was their effort to become enterprising businessmen. The record of the last decade of the 19th century was full of examples of unsound bank investments leading to disaster. Both William S. Ladd and his close friend Henry W. Corbett of the First National had indeed involved their banks in a number of business enterprises, but they were astute and basically conservative men. They did not enter into schemes and promotions of their own, expecting, as Max Houser had, that their judgment or success would be above that of others. They figured the odds carefully.

There were occasions when the city, and its public and private institutions, would have gained immensely if the leading bankers had been willing to extend their efforts beyond such self-imposed limits — beyond bottom line profits. Some real opportunities were missed. As E. B. MacNaughton used to say, businessmen and bankers should get "their noses out of their account books and take a long look at human values."[46] But given a choice between extremes, between the high flying Wilcox's and the cautious Abbot Mills, the better part of wisdom was obviously caution.

The Wilcox Investment Company, organized in 1918, was directed by Raymond B. Wilcox, oldest son of T. B. Wilcox. Educated at New Hampshire's Episcopal St. Paul's School and at Harvard, R. B., as he was called, immersed himself in a number of minor financial ventures after returning home from college. However, it was not until 1918, after the demise of his domineering father, that he, at the age of 34, really came into his own. His younger brother, T. B., Jr., showed little interest in the world of finance, preferring instead to concentrate his efforts on farm and livestock enterprises.

Cameron Squires

Cameron Squires' Portland Motor Car Company

The second in command was lawyer Isaac Hunt, formerly of the firm Wood, Montague & Matthiessen. Hunt had been T. B.'s investment attorney and had joined the Ladd & Tilton board of directors in 1915. Described by E. B. MacNaughton as "a cold-blooded calculating machine,"[47] Hunt was the mastermind behind many of the Ladd & Tilton speculations.

The third member of the triumvirate of ambitious speculators was Cameron Squires who had married R. B.'s sister, Claire, in 1917. The Minnesota native had graduated from the prestigious Hill School in Pennsylvania and had migrated westward to seek employment in the lumber industry. Stories are still told about Squires' announced intention to find a wealthy Portland girl and marry her. The 28 year old charmer wasted little time in achieving his first goal. He also wasted little time in putting the Wilcox money to work in his own behalf. He organized the Portland Motor Car Company and secured a Packard distributorship. He later added the Nash, Hudson and Essex lines. He joined all the important clubs and built one of Portland's more sumptuous homes near William M. Ladd's residence in Dunthorpe. As one published biographical sketch noted, Squires "was alert to his opportunities" which "he converted into tangible assets."[48]

Even before the Wilcox estate bought Ladd & Tilton, the bank had begun an aggressive investment program as part of the general postwar boom. In five years, the bank's assets were to increase 40 percent. Unfortunately, over 30 percent of the assets would be in unsecured notes. The board of directors had caught Max Houser's "Go ahead anyhow" spirit and Isaac Hunt strongly recommended that the bank should get involved in farm and forest products investments.

Among the many financially embarrassing ventures into which Ladd &

LADD & TILTON BANK

AT THE CLOSE OF BUSINESS

October 10, 1924

RESOURCES

Loans and Discounts	$14,301,041.25
Stock of Federal Reserve Bank	60,000.00
Bonds and Stocks	1,938,000.22
Customers' Liabilities on Letters of Credit	385,899.86
Customers' Liabilities on Account Acceptances	1,027,531.69
Customers' Liability on Foreign Bills	857,452.27
Bonds and Cash Securing Temporary Receipts	168,700.00
Real Estate and Claims	221,610.03
Other Assets	47,424.79
United States Bonds	1,263,565.29
Cash and Due from Federal Reserve Bank and other Banks	9,867,149.78
	$30,138,375.18

LIABILITIES

Capital Stock	$ 1,000,000.00
Surplus and Undivided Profits	1,673,286.47
Letters of Credit	385,899.86
Acceptances	1,027,531.69
Foreign Bills Sold	857,452.27
Temporary Receipts for Bonds Sold	168,700.00
Unearned Discount	44,199.24
Deposits	24,981,305.65
	$30,138,375.18

Our listed resources, enumerated in this statement, do not, and cannot, include those assets of friendliness and helpfulness which the Bank has in the personnel of its board of directors, its officers and employes. These are assets which pay dividends to our patrons in service and satisfaction.

LADD & TILTON BANK
Oldest in the Northwest

WASHINGTON AT THIRD   PORTLAND, OREGON

Tilton entered, the two most unfortunate involved the Bankers Discount Corporation and the King's Food Products Company. Bankers Discount, organized originally as Bankers Mortgage, was a livestock loan company with headquarters in Portland, but which operated as far away as Montana. Functioning with minimal stockholder equity, Bankers obtained most of its funds by selling its own obligations to commercial banks and, through local discount (investment) houses, to individual investors. Ladd & Tilton not only purchased the notes for its own account but enthusiastically recommended them to other Northwest banks. Essentially Bankers Discount made loans to cattlemen, using their cattle as collateral. The loans carried high interest rates. The notes were then endorsed by two officers — thus the title "two name paper" — and sold at a discount to the banks and local discount houses. MacNaughton described the enterprise as a "prairie fire."[49]

When livestock prices declined in 1920, defaults were inevitable. To make matters worse, it was discovered that many cattlemen had run the same herds of cattle through the counters, "over and over and around the hill."[50] The collateral began to evaporate. The bank became desperate. In an attempt to unfreeze its loans, it contracted with the major discount house, Dundas-Martin Investment Company, to promote the sale to local investors of its extensive portfolio of Bankers Discount notes. According to E. B. MacNaughton, who later had to unravel the mess, the guilty person was R. S. Howard, an officer of both Bankers Discount and Ladd & Tilton. He gave Dundas-Martin the names of wealthy Ladd & Tilton depositors, encouraging Dundas-Martin to sell them the "two name paper." The proceeds were forwarded to Ladd & Tilton for deposit to the bank's investment account. In a four year period, from 1918 to 1922, Ladd & Tilton had loaned Bankers Discount $2.8 million.[51] Less than 20 percent was ever recovered. After January 1919, every loan carried the approval of Squires and Wilcox.

The second and equally disastrous Ladd & Tilton venture was the King's Food Products Company affair. Drawing upon the wartime experience of the predecessor Wittenberg King Company, processors of dried vegetables, Cameron Squires and the officers of King's Food became overconfident, convincing themselves and friends that a world-wide market awaited the production of dried fruits and vegetables. The company, with plants in Salem and The Dalles, was run by the Clark brothers, one of whom, F. N., had become a leading Portland realtor before the war. F. N. Clark had assumed major responsibility for selling the Ladd estate's Eastmoreland properties. He was also involved in selling the Guild's Lake industrial properties that were platted on landfill taken from the Westover Terraces. The financing of the Guild's Lake- Westover enterprise makes an interesting side story to King's Food Products by revealing the kind of relationships that were involved.

Three months after Wilcox Investment bought the bank, Ladd & Tilton wrote off $200,000 of an original $391,000 debt that it had assumed from the Lewis & Wiley Hydraulic Company and the Westover Land Company. It turned out that Westover had floated $300,000 in bonds, secured by trust deeds to its property. The bank held $44,000 in bonds and Isaac Hunt and his father owned $127,000 worth. The bank decided to acquire the Hunt bonds in exchange for a 16 acre tract at Guild's Lake and $25,000 cash. The decision was made by Wilcox, Squires, Cookingham, Frederick H. Strong (a bank director) and Sam Eddy, an officer of the bank. Hunt refrained from voting, due to a "conflict of interest."[52]

Without doubt, Guild's Lake developer F. N. Clark had close associations with both the bank and the Wilcox Investment Company. Furthermore, Ladd & Tilton's vice president Sam Eddy was also vice president of King's Food

Products. Eddy was a "slippery character," as it turned out. In 1926, while the assets of Ladd & Tilton were being liquidated by the Pratts, he had the audacity to ask Frederick Pratt to guarantee $500,000 of a $1 million loan that Wilcox Investment had secured from the National Park Bank of New York City five years previously.[53]

By 1923, Ladd & Tilton had loaned King's Food Products $2.5 million. The company had a large accumulated deficit but its annual statement exuded nothing but confidence. Then a scheme was concocted to reorganize the company and issue additional stock in sets or packages of preferred and common. No dividends were ever paid. A subsequent investigation ordered by Governor Pierce and directed by former Governor Oswald West implied strongly that the bank had promoted the sale of these new shares through Dundas-Martin in order to unfreeze its own loans.

West's report called King's Food Products a defunct concern, hopelessly in debt when Ladd & Tilton assumed the work of reorganizing it and selling its stock to an unsuspecting public. Ladd & Tilton, declared West, was "responsible for the loss that has been brought to the doors of between 5-6000 innocent purchasers of this stock."[54] The only honorable course of action was for the bank to return to the stockholders every dollar taken from them. Almost $3 million in stock was sold during the reorganization, most of it to pay "the stale obligations of the old company, held largely by Ladd & Tilton." The Clark management was charged with "neither the appearance nor the capacity necessary for the successful conduct of its [the company's] affairs."[55] Further investigation revealed that most of the stock had been sold outside of Portland to people of small means. Dundas-Martin was also accused of charging the company excessive financing costs for the stock sale. When the bulk of the liquidation proceedings were terminated in 1929, the King's Food Products Company stockholders received only ten cents on the dollar. Many people were embittered and the Pratts and their liquidator, E. B. MacNaughton, received much of the blame.[56]

During the early stages of the liquidation in 1926, Dundas-Martin & Co., which had become the National Commercial Company in 1922, and F. N. Clark & Co. were accused by the Portland *Telegram*[57] of bilking 30,000 investors by selling them fraudulent Northwest securities. The Clark, Kendall & Co., founded by Willis Clark and Walter Kendall, was similarly accused. Before being sold to Seattle interests in 1922, Clark, Kendall had received $1.3 million in loans from Ladd & Tilton. Willis Clark subsequently became an officer of Ladd & Tilton. In actively soliciting stockholders whose equity would be used for underwriting and promotion, Clark, Kendall published a fancy brochure entitled: "Why We Want You as a Partner." Not surprisingly, Clark, Kendall went bankrupt in 1927.

Among the other local companies receiving Ladd & Tilton loans during the free-wheeling early twenties were: Oregon Portland Cement, Portland Woolen Mills, Multnomah Lumber Box Company, and R. B. Wilcox's own export-import

Ladd & Tilton Bank, "Oldest in the Northwest," was quietly liquidated in 1925 by E. B. Mac-Naughton. The investment of bank funds in a dehydrated food business and an "around the hill" cattle scam brought the bank down.

firm of Wilcox-Hayes Co. The latter received almost $2 million for its original trading enterprise.

Matters at the bank were going from bad to worse during the summer of 1924. First came the West report on security frauds. Then the state bank examiner became concerned when he found nearly $1 million of the bank's assets in uncollectable loans. But the bank kept up a good front with weekly ads in the newspapers and the *Oregon Voter*, all exuding confidence. The depositors were apparently not worried, but Hunt, Wilcox and Squires were. They finally realized that they were deeply in trouble.

They decided that they wanted to get out of the banking business while they could. In the late fall of 1924, they made contact with Frederick Pratt in New York and offered to sell him back the bank. The increased deposits of $30 million looked healthy, and, as MacNaughton later reported, Pratt thought that he was dealing with "honest gentlemen." The sale occurred before Christmas and immediately Wilcox, Squires and Hunt resigned from the board of directors. They had retrieved their money and they were out free and clear. All three should have been sent to jail, but Oregon justice was not prepared to incarcerate men of such power and influence. In fact, Raymond B. Wilcox was to be elected president of the Portland Chamber of Commerce in 1926.

Edward Cookingham, a rather weak and ineffectual man of high social prominence, remained as president, with William M. Ladd as the figurehead chairman of the board. As E. B. MacNaughton commented, "The foxes were guarding the chicken house," with Sam Eddy and R. S. Howard remaining as vice presidents. Within a month after the repurchase, Pratt discovered the truth about the bank and E. B. MacNaughton was summoned to see Pratt in New York. Pratt wanted MacNaughton to enter the employ of the bank as a vice president, uncover what was happening and report back to him. MacNaughton replied that he knew nothing about banking but that he was glad to oblige. He asked Pratt why he had called **him** in the first place as they had never met previously. Pratt told MacNaughton that Winslow B. Ayer had recommended him. "He knows black from white," said Ayer. And MacNaughton received the call.[58]

MacNaughton was not warmly received by the other Ladd & Tilton officers, with the exception of William M. Ladd. He installed a desk in a small office and began to research the records. He was horrified by what he found. He recommended that Pratt organize two corporations: The Nassau Company under New York laws, and the Manhattan Company under Oregon laws, with Manhattan being a subsidiary of Nassau. The purpose of Manhattan was to acquire certain assets belonging to Ladd & Tilton and liquidate them. As the months passed, MacNaughton became increasingly concerned over the survival prospects of Ladd & Tilton. The Deputy State Bank Examiner, O. B. Robertson, came to him to express similar concerns. He had long been worried, he told MacNaughton, but he was frankly afraid to do anything because Ladd & Tilton was the largest bank in the state system and he feared that any overt action on his part would totally disrupt the system.

In late June, MacNaughton visited Pratt in New York and told him unequivocally that the bank had to be sold immediately. "The storm clouds were gathering quickly." But the only way the bank could be sold was for Pratt to guarantee personally any losses that might result. "How much will it cost me?" inquired Pratt. "Fifteen million dollars on the outside," replied MacNaughton. Pratt "swallowed hard," then asked, "Can you sell it?" MacNaughton said, "Yes, I think so. It must be done within a week or ten days."

Returning to Portland and operating in the strictest of confidence, MacNaughton initially offered the bank to the First National. After a "wild" meeting, attended by Abbot Mills, C. F. Adams and Elliott Corbett, the answer was "No." He then approached John C. Ainsworth of the U. S. National with the same offer. The time was Friday morning, July 10, 1925. Ainsworth wanted a couple of hours to meditate and phone one or two out-of-state banking friends whose judgment he valued. At 4 p.m., he phoned MacNaughton and said, "We'll take it." An emergency U. S. National Bank directors meeting was held Saturday morning at which Ainsworth won the necessary support. In the meantime, all Ladd & Tilton employees had been instructed to be at their posts early Saturday morning. The bank's annual picnic had been cancelled. At one minute past noon, the Ladd & Tilton doors were locked and the transfer of records, money, securities and deposit boxes began. Luckily, the U. S. National had just completed a new wing, running west to Broadway, so it had the space.

The assets were transported in enclosed drays drawn by draft horses. MacNaughton recalled seeing William M. Ladd standing dejectedly in the Ladd & Tilton lobby, watching "the whole bank go down the chute like a dead ox." MacNaughton was extremely fond of Ladd who told him later that he "never should have been a banker." He had wanted to be a farmer, developing purebred livestock, but his father would not permit it. William M. Ladd was "a gentleman to the last ditch," asserted MacNaughton. Apparently Edward Cookingham looked upon the proceedings in horror. He had bitterly opposed MacNaughton for six months. After the move was over, although appointed an officer of the U. S. National, Cookingham was never allowed by John Ainsworth to touch anything. His banking days were over.

The Sunday morning newspapers of July 12, 1925, gave the story most of their front page space. *The Oregonian* noted in headlines that the "sale surprises the city." It was well that it did, otherwise Ladd & Tilton might have experienced a disastrous run on its cash reserves. As it was explained to the public, only part of the bank's assets were taken over in the deal. Real estate holdings, notes, claims and some of the bank's securities remained and would be liquidated under the direction of the Strong & MacNaughton Trust Company. On July 14th, the Ladd & Tilton Bank corporate name was changed to the Nassau Company. Officially, Ladd & Tilton ceased to exist. The former headquarters space on the first floor of the Spalding Building, at Third and S. W. Washington Street, was leased to the Portland Trust & Savings Bank which later was to become the Oregon Bank. All of the furniture and fixtures were sold for $16,500.

Not only was Portland surprised by the sale, but Governor Walter Pierce and his state banking department were equally unprepared. Pierce called MacNaughton and told him that the sale was illegal; that it needed the consent of the Oregon State Banking Board. According to MacNaughton, he replied: "Governor, the omelette's made — you try to unscramble it." No further official reaction was heard. The state was obviously unhappy. Their largest bank had been acquired by a national bank that was free of state jurisdiction.

President Ainsworth asked MacNaughton to become a director of the U. S. National but MacNaughton declined due to a conflict of interest involving his own Strong & MacNaughton Trust Company which was given full authority by the Pratts to liquidate all remaining assets. MacNaughton hired a young assistant whom he had spotted at Ladd & Tilton to be his agent and to handle personally all of the details involved in the liquidation. C. B. Stephenson was thereby launched on a successful career that would see him follow in E. B. MacNaughton's footsteps and become president of the First National Bank 25 years later. Liquidation negotiations were to consume almost five years of Stephenson's time.[59] And the resulting litigation was to consume the energies of some of Portland's largest law firms.

Less than a month before he died in August, 1960, E. B. MacNaughton recalled the meeting that he had with Frederick Pratt in New York after the bank sale was completed. It was on this occasion that Pratt appointed MacNaughton his agent with absolute authority to complete the liquidation. Apparently no mention was made of compensation. Finally, Pratt asked him what he thought his services would be worth. MacNaughton was hard put to answer. He told Pratt that $1000 in Portland was equal to $10,000 in Chicago and $100,000 in New York. An agreement was reached to pay MacNaughton $25,000 a year for a period of 12 to 15 years. The canny Portlander wanted the pay-out stretched for as long as possible to minimize its tax impact.

MacNaughton ended his long account of the Ladd & Tilton collapse with the statement that "the Pratt family saved Portland by cleaning up a hopeless mess. . . . They deserved a monument." Ladd & Tilton's operations had been so intermingled with those of most other Northwest banks that a precipitous collapse would have wrought havoc on the region's economic life. Fortunately, such did not happen. And fortunately for John C. Ainsworth, the U. S. National had become Portland's leading bank, with assets exceeding $60 million.

Considering the thousands of local residents who had suffered from the failures of Ladd & Tilton and other financial institutions, it was astounding that there were so few public outcries against the practices that allowed such disasters to happen. Tom Burns, the veteran socialist and long time "Mayor of Burnside Street" was not afraid to speak out. From his clock shop with a basement office stuffed with hundreds of books, Burns issued one of his many blasts on January 13, 1926:

WORRY KILLS
Remove the Cause!

Nearly all the ills of the human family are due to the worry about **Money**. Insane asylums are filled with human wrecks that have lost out in the struggle for existence. Our hospitals and sanitariums are the repair shops for thousands of men and women suffering with all sorts of nervous diseases, brought on by worry in most cases about money matters. Kidney and bladder troubles result from worry over business affairs and obligations that cannot be met. Worry will bring about indigestion and a whole string of consequent ailments.

What is Money, and why does it cause so much trouble in the world? Money should be simply a medium of exchange, but it has been made a tool to gamble with and to rob the people.

THE WHOLE MONEY SYSTEM OF THE UNITED STATES IS WRONG FROM THE BOTTOM UP. IT IS THE GREATEST SPECIAL PRIVILEGE INSTITUTION EVER FOISTED UPON THE PEOPLE—A GIGANTIC PRIVATE MONOPOLY, AND THE PARENT OF ALL OTHER MONOPOLIES. IGNORANCE ONLY PERMITS SUCH A SYSTEM TO EXIST.

211

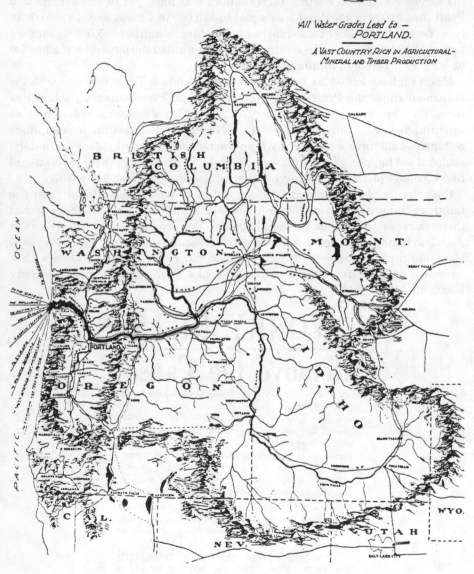

COLUMBIA COUNTRY
(Area Drained by Columbia River and Tributaries)

All Water Grades Lead to —
PORTLAND.

A Vast Country Rich in Agricultural-
Mineral and Timber Production

Chapter 9

Power and Politics (2):
The Rivers and the Port, 1919-1931

The Columbia and Willamette rivers made Portland. The city's earliest fortunes were derived from river transportation. Portland's location at the confluence of the two navigable waterways in the very heart of a region enormously rich in natural resources preordained its early growth and prosperity. Being the only water level gateway through the mountains to the coast, the Columbia opened up the entire basin and its valleys and made them tributary to Portland. Most traffic could reach tidewater by the route of least resistance. As the map of the "Columbia Country" reveals, Portland became the delivery end of a great funnel. And as a branch of the Columbia, the Willamette gathered the products of the Columbia's chief tributary valley.

The Port and Its Growth

Lying near the mouth of one of the great river systems of the world did not in itself assure the city of its future growth and prosperity, particularly after Seattle surpassed Portland in population following the turn of the century. By the start of World War I, the Puget Sound ports had become dangerously competitive. To retain its supremacy as the leading dry cargo port on the West Coast, Portland was forced to undertake a number of difficult and costly tasks, foremost of which were: (1) The continued dredging and maintenance of an adequate ship channel from the city to the sea; and (2), the improvement of the harbor and the expansion of public dock and ship repair facilities.

In 1891, the legislature had established the Port of Portland Commission to undertake and manage channel dredging and harbor improvement functions. The U. S. Army Corps of Engineers held primary responsibility for dredging the lower Columbia and the bar at the river's mouth. No attention was given in the early years to the need for publicly-owned dock facilities, with the exception of dry docking which was a Port responsibility.

Funds to operate the Port of Portland came primarily from tax levies collected upon property assessed in the area forming the Port of Portland corporation. Bonds were also issued since the activities of the commission at times required expenditures in excess of receipts. For the first 25 years of its existence, the Port of Portland spent roughly $7.2 million: $1.2 million from bond revenues and $6 million from tax levies. From 1919 to 1932, expenditures were to more than double, to $14.7 million: $4.8 million from bond revenues and $9.9 million from tax levies. By 1932, the Port of Portland would have spent nearly $22 million of

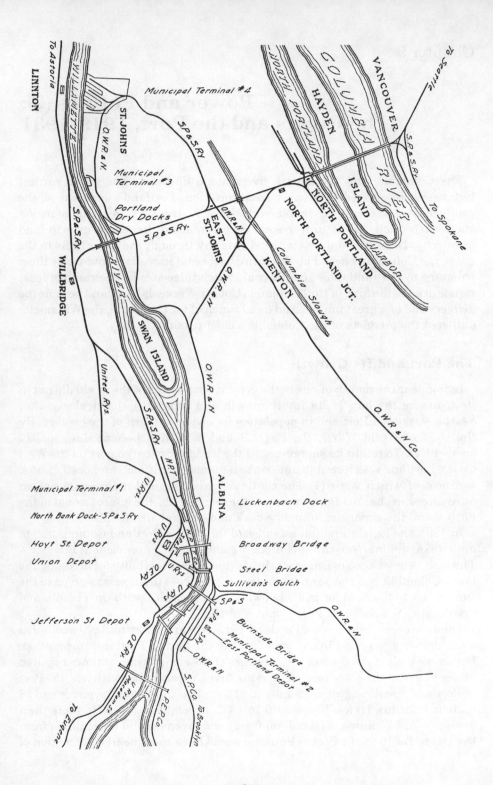

To Astoria

LINNTON

WILLAMETTE

Municipal Terminal #4

ST. JOHNS

O.W.R.&N.

Municipal Terminal #3

Portland Dry Docks

S.P.&S.Ry.

EAST ST. JOHNS

O.W.R.&N

S.P.&S.Ry.

COLUMBIA RIVER

VANCOUVER

To Seattle

HAYDEN ISLAND

NORTH PORTLAND

PORTLAND HARBOR

NORTH PORTLAND

NORTH PORTLAND JCT.

S.P.&S.Ry.

To Spokane

KENTON

Columbia Slough

O.W.R.&N

WILLBRIDGE

S.P.&S.Ry.

WILLAMETTE RIVER

SWAN ISLAND

United Rys.

S.P.&S.Ry.

N.P.T.

O.W.R.&N

O.W.R.&N Co.

Municipal Terminal #1

North Bank Dock - S.P.&S Ry

U.Rys.

Luckenbach Dock

ALBINA

Hoyt St. Depot

Union Depot

U.Rys.

Broadway Bridge

Steel Bridge

Sullivan's Gulch

Jefferson St Depot

O.E.Ry

U.Rys.

S.P.&S

S.P.&S

Burnside Bridge

Municipal Terminal #2
East Portland Depot

To Eugene

U.Rys.

O.W.R.&N

McAdams

PEPCo

S.P.Co

To Brooklyn

214

public funds in 40 years, of which $14.4 million would go for dredging and channel improvements. In the same period of time, the Corps of Engineers would spend $10.7 million of federal funds.[1]

The first task of the Port of Portland in 1892 was to construct and permanently maintain a 25 foot ship channel in the Willamette and Columbia rivers "at the cities of Portland, East Portland, Albina, St. Johns and Linnton and from these cities to the sea."[2] The legislation to create the Port of Portland was passed a few months before city consolidation. Since none of these entities had the tax base to develop and keep a shipping channel open, the Port was established as a state agency. In 1912, the channel depth was increased to 30 feet. By 1932, it would reach 35 feet.

During the early years of the Port's existence it was dominated by the railroads, a condition that did not encourage the growth of waterborne commerce. Furthermore, all of the docks and most of the accessible waterfront properties were owned by either the railroads or the grain companies. By 1910, when the Commission of Public Docks was established by the Portland voters, it had become obvious that the city needed to create its own terminal facilities if maritime commerce was ever to reach its potential. Wheat and lumber, although highly profitable exports, were not sufficient in themselves to make Portland a great commercial port. Furthermore, the old private docks were fading into disuse and the intercoastal trade was dropping off. As lawyer Joseph N. Teal had stated on numerous occasions, only multi-commodity foreign cargoes would provide the essential basis for a thriving Portland trade. The dock commission was to be a single-purpose body, promoting maritime commerce through providing warehouses, docks and wharves.

In 1912, two years before Municipal Dock No. 1 was ready for service, a number of Portland business leaders expressed concern with the apparent overlap of authority that they presumed would increasingly develop between the dock and port commissions. Which agency would exercise responsibility for straightening the harbor line? Who would decide ownership of the waterfront tidelands between low and high water? Was this public or private land? Who would tackle the railroads — a continual pain in the neck to any public body they could not control?[3] Friction and jealousy, it was feared, were going to develop between the two public bodies. Although the Port of Portland had long viewed itself as the major promoter of maritime commerce, it had acted indifferently, showing too much favoritism to the railroads. In 1912, Portland still had no trans-Pacific steamship line providing service on any regular basis. Pacific Mail, with its home port in San Francisco was owned by the Harriman railroad interests, and James J. Hill owned the major steamship service operating out of Seattle and Tacoma. The early dock commission members came under strong pressure to stimulate Portland-owned shipping companies that would enter international trade. But this development would not materialize for another decade, or until the world war emergency fleet was liquidated by the federal government.

Municipal Terminal No. 4, Slip No. 1

During the first decade of the dock commission's existence, the total annual tonnage of imports and exports through Portland rose by 60 percent, from 2.5 million to 4.1 million tons. In the immediate post-war period of 1919 to 1926, lumber exports increased five times.[4] Portland manufactured and exported by water more lumber in 1926 than any other single city in the world, and the bulk of the lumber activity was along the Willamette riverfront. By 1926, over 50 steamship lines were operating out of the port, being served by 6½ miles of docks — 85 in all, and four modern municipal terminals that were provided with elevators, storage plants, tanks and handling equipment. Visitors from around the world considered Portland's harbor one of the finest. It had the only fresh water on the Pacific Coast and was considerably nearer the Pacific Ocean than the ports on Puget Sound. While further inland than any other Pacific seaport, Portland was but 108 miles from the ocean, while Seattle was 140 miles and Tacoma 180 miles.

The Portland voters had enthusiastically supported the expansion of dock facilities that helped to stimulate the sharp increase in waterborne tonnage. In December 1917, early dock commission members and current chamber of commerce president Henry L. Corbett had written Joseph N. Teal that "it is now or never for Portland."[5] Corbett, who was later to spend 30 years on the Port of Portland Commission, worked with Teal to convince the federal government of the advantages of shipping Northwest commodities to the Atlantic Coast by water.

By 1925, the voters had authorized $10.5 million of bond issues for harbor and dock development. Four terminals had been constructed and put into service, each with a railroad connection. Terminal No. 4, with a large grain elevator, was the first to be located in the lower harbor, north of St. Johns. It was connected with the tracks of the Union Pacific and by common user agreement with all other railroads serving Portland. The smaller Terminal No. 3 in St. Johns, had the same railroad connection arrangements. Terminal No. 2, the smallest was located in Southeast Portland and connected with the Southern Pacific system. Terminal No. 1, in Northwest Portland, was served by the Hill lines: The Northern Pacific, Great Northern and their local operating subsidiary, the SP&S.

When the first unit of Terminal No. 4 was dedicated in April 1919, *The Oregonian* editorialized that the event marked a great stage in the commercial progress of Portland. Thousands of citizens attended the ceremonies, thronged the buildings and grounds and cheered the speakers who exuded "confident optimism" for the future. *The Oregonian*'s Lawrence Kaye Hodges, a veteran advocate of waterborne commerce, declared that:

" . . . the people of Portland have turned their backs on the past and have united in a purpose to lift their city to its rightful place among the ports of the

A complete dry dock plant with two dry docks with lifting capacities of 15,000 tons and 9000 tons was provided by the Port of Portland for the convenience of shipping. (1920)

Pacific coast and of the world. They will remember the past only to profit by its mistakes, and to avoid that hesitation, those doubts, that hypocritical frame of mind which caused their commerce almost to disappear from the sea."[6]

The tone of Hodges' remarks, which embodied his own brand of "confident optimism," was understandable for one who had felt frustrated by years of official indifference to maritime commerce. Max Houser, who was undoubtedly present at the dedication, would have agreed with Hodges' declaration of faith. Unfortunately for Houser, he was to get carried away by exceeding the limits of normal risk, and others were to do likewise.

Future progress was to result not so much from the avoidance of hesitation or even doubt, as from the avid pursuit of clearly and realistically defined goals. The first post-war goal of Portland's business leaders who were interested in furthering waterborne commerce was to convince the Interstate Commerce Commission in Washington, D. C., of the justification for reducing railroad freight rates from the Northwest hinterland to Portland.

One of the most active proponents of rate reduction, besides attorney Joseph N. Teal, was former Port of Portland president Samuel M. Mears, long-time chief executive of the Portland Cordage Company, importers of cordage from the Philippines. In a letter to U. S. Bank president John C. Ainsworth, Mears described the successful effort.

> "I venture to write you of my thoughts on the subject of the Columbia River Rate Case. It was largely due to my efforts that the $10,000 was pledged by the four public bodies and I can assure you it was discouraging work, due to the apathy on the part of the subscribers. . . . The Portland Traffic and Transportation Association after many years' effort succeeded, over every opposition from the railroad companies, in having the Interstate Commerce Commission recognize our cheaper water level routes. As a result, it gave Portland a 10% lower rate to and from all the territories south of the Snake River."[7]

The I. C. C. announced its ruling on November 5, 1920, to become effective on July 1, 1921. The commission recognized that railroad rates should be in proportion to cost of service, and, in the absence of other means of transportation, to distance. The railroads did not attempt to deny that it cost less to haul freight on a water grade, such as that from the intermountain country to Portland, than over a range of mountains. Yet the railroads using this water grade collected the same rate to Portland as other roads collected for hauling freight over the Cascade mountains to Puget Sound. The rate reduction stimulated increased shipments of wheat and other agricultural commodities to Portland's docks for transshipment overseas. But the railroads did not give up the fight. Mears noted in 1927 that the railroads, together with the Puget Sound cities, had already tried four times since 1921, under various excuses, to break down the differential. In every instance Portland won, but the battles were costly.

Mears acted as a watchdog to alert the Portland business community to any threatened loss of the ten percent differential. "Freight rates," he wrote Ainsworth, "are the foundation of all manufacturing and mercantile business enterprises, and have the same importance to business as a good foundation has to a building."[8] To lose the differential would be disastrous. Mears pointed out that 1617 deep sea vessels had loaded and departed from Portland in 1926, and that "the port disbursements of each ship, in the way of dues, labor and supplies, average[d] over $9888. . . . The loss of every 100 loading in this port [would] mean the loss of $900,000 in disbursements."[9]

Shipping

"Without a merchant marine this country cannot maintain its export business and we might as well face the facts," declared Portland attorney Bert Haney to the Portland City Club in March 1926. "If the merchant marine is a necessity, then let's face the facts and pay for it. If not, then let us abandon it. We've got to stop trading jackknives in our own little circle."[10] Haney had just resigned from the United State Shipping Board to run for political office. He described the difficulties encountered by American ship owners in competition with foreign carriers that were operating more economically. The problems he raised were the very ones faced by Portland business interests which attempted to develop their own locally controlled international shipping companies following the war.

Prior to the war, 92 percent of the nation's foreign commerce was carried by British, German and other ships which offered generally satisfactory service to the nation as a whole. Portland exporters had not been too happy, however. They wanted more choice, more competition. A Portland-owned shipping company, it was felt, would produce better service for Portland products. In 1916, facing the need to supply the Allies with war materials, Congress established the United States Shipping Board, the first such body in American history to be charged with the supervision of the merchant marine. During the war, it helped to direct the construction of 1275 steel vessels. As Haney recounted, "They were good steel ships but they were all of one kind and made for one purpose only. The cost was excessive."[11] When the war was over, the United States had the largest merchant fleet in the world. A number of the vessels had been built in Portland's wartime shipyards.

To put the ships into peacetime service while the government decided how it was going to liquidate the huge fleet, local companies were organized in American ports to operate ships directly for the shipping board. Thus was born the Columbia Pacific Steamship Company of Portland in March 1919. The directors included: Banker John C. Ainsworth, lumberman Henry Van Duzer, investor Drake O'Reilly, maritime lawyer Erskine Wood, and a young shipping executive, Kenneth C. Dawson, who was to become Portland's leading promoter of a home-owned shipping industry. Essentially, Columbia Pacific became a local manager for the United States Shipping Board.

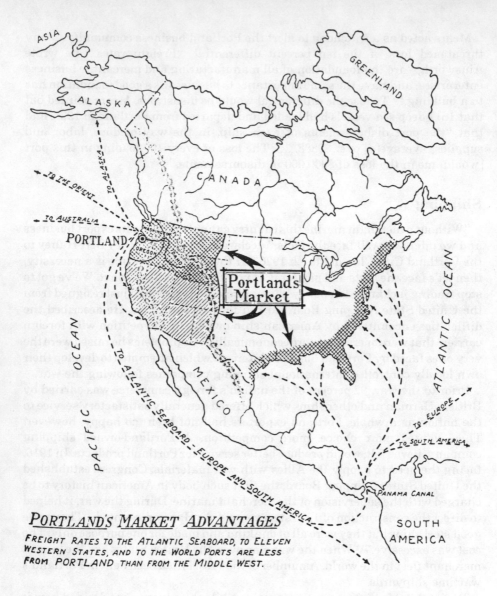

ASIA

GREENLAND

ALASKA

CANADA

PORTLAND

WASHINGTON
OREGON

Portland's Market

PACIFIC OCEAN

ATLANTIC OCEAN

MEXICO

TO THE ORIENT

TO ALASKA

TO AUSTRALIA

TO ATLANTIC SEABOARD - EUROPE AND SOUTH AMERICA

TO EUROPE

TO SOUTH AMERICA

PANAMA CANAL

SOUTH
AMERICA

PORTLAND'S MARKET ADVANTAGES

FREIGHT RATES TO THE ATLANTIC SEABOARD, TO ELEVEN
WESTERN STATES, AND TO THE WORLD PORTS ARE LESS
FROM PORTLAND THAN FROM THE MIDDLE WEST.

The Oregonian's Lawrence Hodges was worried. In August 1919, he wrote:

> "When the work of sale or lease to licensed companies begins, all of those
> vessels are liable to be withdrawn from their present service. That is true of all
> the shipping board vessels now running from Portland. We have no hold on
> them. . . . [We must] buy or lease them. . . . Portland must own its own ships
> in order to preserve and extend its commerce."[12]

Hodges warned Portland business leaders that they must rely chiefly on their
own resources to secure the ships. Outside capital would help, but control had to

rest with Portland "in order that the interests of this port may receive full consideration."[13] In September 1921, Hodges reported that Portland was now recognized by the shipping board as a port able to support a trans-Pacific steamship line. To gain such status had not been an easy task. San Francisco and Seattle had fought hard to squeeze Portland out of the trans-Pacific trade by confining Portland to a port-of-call (non-terminal) status. In the spring of 1920, the shipping board had allocated five steamers to the Columbia Pacific Company for operation to North China ports, and two more to a Seattle company for operation out of Portland.[14] Such actions represented progress, said Hodges, but Portland would not attain full equality with other Pacific ports until it had passenger as well as freight service across the ocean.

The struggle to achieve full equality in shipping paralleled Portland's battle with the railroads over freight rates. Although Columbia Pacific had been able to purchase two of the shipping board's largest freighters in 1923, Hodges accused the shipping board of playing into the hands of the few large companies that were endeavoring to buy up the emergency fleet and shut out any new enterprises that would be independent and competitive. Throughout most of the 1920s, Portland shipping interests found themselves locked into an unceasing contest just to survive. And the waterfront strikes of 1922 and 1923 threatened their already precarious financial condition.

In the spring of 1926, the shipping board's subservience to the large operators was revealed by the announcement that the board had sold the five ship Admiral Oriental line to the sizeable Robert Dollar Company of San Francisco for $4.5 million, $100,000 less than another bidder had offered. Oregon's Senator Charles McNary tried to get Congress to reverse the board's decision without success. The Scotsman Dollar was a powerful man. After his arrival in San Francisco in 1888, Dollar had put together a vast transportation and lumber network, including thousands of acres of Oregon O&C lands. In 1916, he had purchased the New York Shipbuilding Company for $11.5 million.

This was the kind of competition that Portland, with its more limited private resources, had to face. Hodges blamed Bert Haney for the Dollar sale. By resigning from the shipping board while negotiations were in progress, thus removing a member from the region affected, Haney allowed the California interests to prevail. It mattered little to Portland that 20 percent of the Dollar company was owned by Seattle investors. San Francisco interests would dominate its operation.

All was not lost for Portland shipping interests however. On February 15, 1928, the Columbia Pacific directors negotiated the sale of the shipping board's 11 ship Oregon Oriental fleet to a newly organized local company that was given the name States Lines. A total of 7500 shares were sold to ten stockholders for $100 per share. Majority control was purchased by Charles E. Dant, the founder of the Dant & Russell Lumber Company. Dant had been the major investor at the time that Columbia Pacific bought its first two freighters. By the time of the States deal in 1928, Columbia Pacific had negotiated the purchase of three more

221

freighters and all five became engaged in intercoastal trade to the Atlantic seaboard. The intercoastal fleet was renamed the Quaker Line and Charles E. Dant assumed majority control.

In acquiring the Oregon Oriental fleet, the States Lines inaugurated a trans-Pacific route to serve Japanese, Chinese and Philippine ports. Kenneth Dawson who had managed the Columbia Pacific and was also manager of the Quaker Line, was named vice president and general manager of the new States Lines. As Lawrence Hodges reported in *The Oregonian*:

"A prediction ten years ago that at the end of that period a Portland company would own sixteen large steamships with this as their home port would have been received with incredulity."[15]

Kenneth Dawson was the sparkplug of Portland's explosive shipping growth. In 1929, he organized a fourth local company with many of the same directors and investors who were involved with Columbia Pacific, Quaker and States Lines. Named the Pacific and Atlantic, it purchased 16 ships at auction from the shipping board. The major funding was provided by Kuehn, Loeb & Company of New York. Pacific and Atlantic operated intercoastal entirely and it carried only freight. In February 1930, an inauspicious time unfortunately, Kenneth Dawson developed a new project: To form a fifth locally owned steamship company to operate both intercoastal and trans-Pacific routes. To be known as the Pacific & Atlantic Navigation Company, the line planned to order the construction of five new passenger-cargo ships for $17 million. The federal government would loan $12 million at 3⅛ percent and the remaining funds would be raised locally. The company expected to receive a ten year mail contract, paying net $700,000 per year or $7 million over the length of the contract.

Although the depression killed the project, the attempt to raise $5 million from local investors was the most ambitious financial undertaking by private subscription in Portland's 80 years of existence. It is interesting to note some of those who were prepared to subscribe and for how much:

States Steamship Company	$1,000,000
Kenneth D. Dawson	250,000
Dant & Russell, Inc.	500,000
Corbett Investment Co.	200,000
Inman-Poulsen Lumber Co.	250,000
E. S. Collins	150,000
E. B. MacNaughton	50,000
Meier & Frank Co.	50,000
Mrs. Thomas Kerr	50,000
Durham & Bates Insurance Co.	30,000
H. B. Van Duzer	50,000
Franklin T. Griffith	20,000
Guy W. Talbot	25,000
Erskine Wood	20,000

J. C. Ainsworth   25,000
Eric Hauser, Multnomah Hotel Co.   30,000
W. B. Ayer   25,000
Drake C. O'Reilly   20,000
Cameron Squires   15,000
Aubrey R. Watzek   20,000

Out-of-state investors included: C. P. Stewart & Co. of New York, $250,000; and Williams, Dimon & Co. of San Francisco, $250,000.[16] The list of local investors reflected closely, but not entirely, the level of wealth distributed among

Volumes of Waterborne Commerce in Short Tons
1929

Class of Commerce	Portland	Seattle	Tacoma
Foreign	1,630,169	1,230,607	1,364,022
Intercoastal:			
Atlantic	644,926	648,579	488,471
Gulf	90,663	81,043	32,285
Coastwise	2,960,378	2,961,108	749,844
Alaska	3,071	553,775	83,298
Hawaii	16,366	99,226	49,662
Total Deep-Sea	5,345,573	5,574,338	2,767,582
Local	4,483,876	3,592,957	3,638,077
Total	9,829,449	9,167,295	6,405,659

Commodity Comparisons
1929

Commodity Group	Total Imports and Exports Handled through Port in Short Cargo Tons		
	Portland	Seattle	Tacoma
Lumber & Lumber Products	1,289,890	622,555	1,191,347
Pulp, Paper & Paper Products	213,924	126,018	104,804
Grain & Grain Products	872,860	330,428	298,328
Animal, Fish & Dairy Products	37,379	329,742	18,538
Other Food Products	318,300	407,103	78,910
Petroleum & Petroleum Products	2,022,142	2,489,113	357,651
Coal & Coke	7,588	103,288	11,953
Cotton, Wool, Silk & Manufactures	24,773	63,215	3,835
Ores, Metals, Metallic Products	276,156	455,414	635,395
Other Manufactures	233,434	447,438	59,344
Unclassified	48,400	129,021	4,742
Total Deep-Sea	5,344,846	5,503,335	2,764,847

(Day & Zimmerman Report, Dec. 1931)

the financial community in 1930. These were the individuals who at least had faith in Portland's future, and who had the resources and degree of interest to make substantial commitments to a risky cause. Like many other investment projects in the planning stage during 1930, Pacific & Atlantic Navigation was torpedoed before it was launched. The depression severely affected the security holdings of many on Ainsworth's list. Within four years, Pacific Power & Light president Guy Talbot would be nearly wiped out. And U. S. National Bank stock, the mainstay of John C. Ainsworth's and Mabel Macleay Kerr's investment portfolios, would decline from $440 to $35 a share.

Because it remained totally free of debt, the States Steamship Company rode through the depression in relatively healthy condition.[17] As its president until 1934, banker John C. Ainsworth provided the same kind of stable administration to the shipping company that he had long given to the U. S. National Bank. Kenneth Dawson was to succeed him as president, although Dawson had been the chief operating officer since 1928. Charles E. Dant remained in the background and served as a director. Toward the end of 1932, a long sought dream came true. States Steamship purchased three large 14-knot passenger ships from the debt-ridden United Fruit Company to use in its trans-Pacific trade. First class passenger service had finally arrived. Portland could now fully compete with the other Pacific ports.

Although approaching equality of service with San Francisco and Seattle, Portland's harbor would never be as spectacular as those of its two major competitors. Its bustling activity was largely hidden from the eyes of passersby. As *Oregon Journal* columnist Dick Fagan was to write several years later:

> "Portland primarily is a work harbor without the champagne and orchid atmosphere of the luxury liners. On an average of every six hours throughout the year an ocean-going vessel enters Portland harbor. This does not count tugs and barges and river craft, but only ocean-going vessels in the ancient business of exchanging the products of the world."[18]

The Port and Dock Commissions

From its inception, membership on the Port of Portland Commission was considered a high honor, reserved for representatives of the city's leading families. After the turn of the century, with the appointment power vested in the legislature, membership on the commission became increasingly political. This tradition has not changed appreciably in the past 70 years. Indeed, in January 1979, newly inaugurated Governor Victor Atiyeh appointed four new replacements to the Port of Portland Commission, three of whom had been his chief fund raisers in the election campaign.

In 1921, the governor was granted the appointive authority, only to have it retrieved by the legislature in 1925. In 1932, the voters of the district were empowered to elect the commissioners, but this procedure lasted only three years. Since 1935, the governor has enjoyed the right of appointment — a practice that has been challenged occasionally but never successfully.

During the 60 years of its existence — the dock commission was merged with the Port in 1970 — the dock commission members were appointed by the mayor, with inevitable political overtones. However, with one or two exceptions, the dock commissioners were not as directly involved in politics as their counterparts at the Port.

During the earlier years, each agency was dominated by a presiding officer of long tenure. Insurance agent John H. Burgard, for example, was chairman of the dock commission from 1921 to 1945, and wealthy fish packer Frank M. Warren was president of the Port from 1920 to 1934. By their very nature, public agencies, like the dock and Port commissions, were bound to become involved in conflicts of interest. The members have often had their own economic or professional interests which have related directly to commission functions. But it has been that very business or professional experience, paradoxically, that has given the members a working knowledge of the dock and port activities that the commissions have been mandated to regulate. For example, it was never any secret that John Burgard used the dock commission to help promote his insurance business. Historically, however, the greatest amount of interest conflict has been centered in decisions affecting the location and development of industrial sites.

One major conflict, involving both political and private interests, occurred less than five months after the war's end when the Port of Portland became involved in a legislative squabble. Five new commissioners out of nine were to be named in addition to a new Port attorney. Political wheeling and dealing were rampant. Frank M. Warren, Max Houser and Phil Metschan, Jr., were three of the five elected and Senator Gus Moser, the world war superpatriot, was instrumental in their selection. Metschan was Representative K. K. Kubli's brother-in-law, and of course Kubli and Moser had worked closely together for years and would join forces in support of the Ku Klux Klan in 1922. Having been president of the senate in the 1917 session, Moser carried much influence with his colleagues.

Phil Metschan, Jr., came into politics naturally. His father had been state treasurer from 1891 to 1899 and a bulwark of the Republican Party for years. Young Phil had a hankering for both politics and winning acceptance into Portland's establishment. A story was told that when *Oregonian* publisher Henry Pittock was searching for an appropriate spot for his mansion, he discovered a hillside location that was owned by young Metschan. Phil had decided to build a hotel on the hill which he named Imperial Heights, after the Imperial Hotel that his family and T. B. Wilcox had built downtown in 1909. It was to be Portland's grandest hostelry and he was going to name it the Imperial House. When Pittock persisted in his demand to buy the property, Metschan decided to make a deal. By secret agreement, he would sell the property to Pittock provided that the publisher would call the hill Imperial Heights. Second, and most important to Metschan's future, *The Oregonian* would give Phil its future

Gus C. Moser

editorial and news support in any political endeavors in which he might become involved. There was apparently a third stipulation, that Metschan could assume a financial interest in Pittock's new Northwestern Bank and sit upon the bank's board of directors.

Whether completely true or not, the story is plausible in the light of subsequent events. Metschan became a kingmaker in Oregon Republican Party affairs: Chairman of the Republican State Central Committee from 1924 to 1930 and the Republican gubernatorial candidate in 1930. He was also to remain on the Port of Portland Commission for 16 years, the last ten as its treasurer. And in all of these efforts, Metschan received solid backing from *The Oregonian*.

As a political payoff, Metschan convinced enough of his fellow Port commissioners to name Gus Moser as the Port attorney. Commissioners Drake

O'Reilly and Max Houser objected but they were outvoted. Commenting several months later, the conservative *Oregon Voter* declared:

> "Our port affairs should be rescued from political manipulation. The majority of our port commission have no use for politics. An intriguing minority succeeded in getting Senator Gus Moser appointed. . . . Senator Moser is a good trial lawyer — probably has won more cases of the kind that get into court than have most high-class Portland lawyers — but his appointment was due to politics and politics alone."[19]

Much of the Port's time in 1919 was taken up with the matter of finding cheap industrial sites along the river. Existing mills and other plants continually sought channel dredge fill to expand their sites. The commission refused to provide free fill or to dredge ship channels in front of private docks for free despite pressure to do so. However, questions would be raised subsequently about the level of rates that were charged. Were they high enough? Was the commission favoring its friends in performing some tasks ahead of others?

One of the most active petitioners for dredge fill was F. C. Knapp, president of the Peninsula Lumber Company of St. Johns and a veteran member of the dock commission. Cameron Squires petitioned the commission on several occasions in behalf of Ladd & Tilton financed projects that needed dredge fill. In several ventures, he and his Wilcox Investment partners were joined by Emery Olmstead, president of the Northwestern National Bank. Squires, in fact, became deeply involved in waterfront property during 1919 when he joined with R. B. Wilcox and Isaac Hunt in purchasing the unused 101 acre North Pacific Lumber Mill site just below Municipal Terminal No. 1. From their friends on the dock and Port commissions, they knew only too well of its long-term value. They would sit patiently on the land until 1926, accept cheap dredge fill to improve the site and then sell it for a handsome profit — more than three times what they had paid for it. Commissioner Metschan was close to the Wilcox Investment Company, and in fact he would buy out its interest in the Imperial Hotel in 1926. Also in 1926, R. B. Wilcox would become president of the chamber of commerce. And during the early 1920s, Isaac Hunt was on the chamber of commerce committee that was promoting the development of riverfront industrial sites.

Speaking before the realty board in June 1918, seven months before the Wilcox Investment Company bought control of Ladd & Tilton, Hunt had declared that "the development of the city is but incidental to the gratification of personal ambition." As if the realtors did not already know, Hunt advised them to "build your own fortunes and the growth of the city will follow."[20] Hunt's ambitions were to be fully revealed by his subsequent Ladd & Tilton activities. Isaac Hunt never married. He once told Pendleton Woolen Mills' Clarence M. Bishop, who did not marry until he was nearly 50, that a successful businessman had no time for marriage. It would impede his success. Of course, if his business associate Cameron Squires had not married R. B. Wilcox's sister, Squires would not have had the funds to invest in the first place.

One of the more interesting deals involving Messrs. Hunt, Squires and Wilcox related to a company called Portland Vegetable Oils. Early in 1921, Ladd & Tilton put together a syndicate to provide funding for a riverfront plant and site in the Guild's Lake Industrial District. Together, Ladd & Tilton and Emery Olmstead's Northwestern National Bank, with Phil Metschan as a director, sold a total of $500,000 in bonds to local investors. The company needed dredge fill, but instead of agreeing to pay the normal cost that in this case could have amounted to $25,000, it offered to provide free the required amount of dredge fuel oil plus $8000 in cash in exchange for the fill. In considering the matter, the Port of Portland Commission, with Metschan present, realized the irregularity of the procedure, but because the Port was short of operating revenues in April 1921, it agreed to accept the offer.[21]

Two years earlier, the Port had encountered another type of problem that it was to face continually throughout the 1920s: Removal of a dredge from channel work to handle a private request. In April 1919, the Union Meat Company on the Columbia Slough announced that it needed to lease a dredge to provide fill for a new livestock pavilion that was planned for construction near the Union Stockyards. The Port only had one available dredge, the Tualatin; the old dredge Sandy had just sunk. The commission agreed to postpone the harbor work and lease the Tualatin for $600 per day. A month later, it became obvious to the public that the proposed livestock pavilion was to be backed financially by Portland's leading banks and businesses.

To be called the Pacific International Livestock (PIL) Exposition Building, the facility was to cost $500,000. One-half of the amount was to be raised locally, with the other half to be provided by the large national meat packers like Swift & Company which owned Union Meat. Pledges of $5000 were received from the First National Bank, Ladd & Tilton Bank, Northwestern National Bank and Meier & Frank Company. The Olds & King department store and *The Oregonian* pledged $2500 apiece and the leading lumber, grain and wholesale houses pledged lesser amounts. Simon Benson came through with $1000.[22]

The project was worthwhile and the PIL Exposition Building was to play an important role in Portland's history, but the manner in which the fill request was processed was open to question. There was no emergency, and the channel dredging was far more important to Portland's commercial life in the spring of 1919 than the construction of a livestock pavilion. But from the commission's point of view, leasing the dredge for $600 a day to a private party could be justified because the Port needed the extra revenue for its general operation.

The expansion and development of new industrial sites concerned both the dock and Port commissions. The decided in February 1919 to invite each other to their regular monthly meetings. Both agencies were in a quandary. The dock commission's attempt to annex property in North Portland, bordering on the Columbia River, was ruled by the city attorney to be in violation of the city charter. The Port also had considered a similar project: To acquire, improve and dispose of riverfront factory sites. But counsel advised that such procedures were unconstitutional in the absence of specific legislative authorization.

Both commissions prevailed upon Mayor George L. Baker in April 1919 to appoint a blue ribbon committee to examine a number of common problems and to make appropriate recommendations for action. "The Committee of 15" was given broad scope to investigate the following matters that were considered crucial: The overlap of commission functions; potential industrial sites; the abandonment of the existing east channel and the dredging of a new main channel west of Swan Island; and the future of Swan Island itself. Other issues of lesser importance that the committee could study included the sewer problem, river pollution and the need to build a seawall along the west riverbank of downtown. Mayor Baker's committee of "disinterested individuals" — as he labelled the group — was loaded with business power. It included:

Emery Olmstead, Northwestern National Bank president, chairman
F. C. Knapp, lumberman and dock commissioner, vice chairman
James B. Kerr, railroad attorney and Reed College trustee
Ira Powers, furniture merchant and dock commissioner
John E. Wheeler, lumberman and owner of the *Telegram*
Max Houser, grain dealer and Port of Portland president
Frank M. Warren, fish packing executive and POP commissioner
John H. Burgard, insurance agent and dock commission president

On March 19, 1920, "The Committee of 15" issued four preliminary recommendations:

(1) An initiative measure should be placed before the state's voters at the November 1920 election, authorizing the merger of the Commission of Public Docks and the Port of Portland Commission;

(2) the Port, or the newly merged agency, should acquire Swan Island;

(3) the west channel of Swan Island should be dredged to create a new main shipping channel and the dredge fill should be used to extend the fill of Guild's Lake and to begin the fill of Swan Island;

(4) Mock's Bottom should be filled for use as a future industrial site. [A large portion of Mock's Bottom was owned by the Pittock-Leadbetter interests. It was considered one of the best duck blinds in Portland.]

The committee then addressed the problem of property acquisition. The city, through its own agencies like the dock commission, had the right, with council approval, to acquire land for industrial sites, but not to annex unilaterally any non-city property for that purpose. The Port could not purchase, develop and then sell property unless it was to be used for public, port-related purposes. An airport site would qualify. If recommendations 2, 3, and 4 were adopted, the city, primarily through the Port commission, could add 1530 acres of new industrial sites within the city boundaries. The committee emphasized that Portland's greatest economic need was for prepared industrial sites of 20 acres or more, with

229

flood protection and street access.[23] An industrial zoning requirement was endorsed by some committee members. The 1919 code, drafted by the city planning commission, had provided for such, but it was to be rejected by the voters in November 1920.

A month later, the city council approved the merger proposal and by ordinance agreed to sell the dock commission properties to the Port of Portland Commission. *The Oregon Journal* came out in favor of the merger in June.

> "The property at Mock's Bottom and Guild's Lake is undeveloped. Its owners are powerless to develop it. The same is true for Swan Island. All are wasted and will remain wasted until the city makes an expenditure that will reclaim them to use."[24]

Through the summer, the initiative measure seemed to gain support. Although some chamber of commerce criticism developed, the chamber's board of directors approved it. By the middle of October, however, strong opposition surfaced, threatening to defeat the merger initiative. The industrial bureau of the chamber registered its negative feelings by charging that the improvements resulting from Port consolidation would be too costly in proportion to the supposed needs for industrial sites. Seven of the 15 member chamber board of directors reversed their previous positions and voted against the measure. They may have been influenced by the much respected Winslow B. Ayer who feared the loss of home rule — giving away a city prerogative (dock commission) to a state body (Port commission), over which the people of the city would have no direct control. Ayer was joined by attorney Joseph N. Teal, former county assessor Henry E. Reed, attorney and French Consul Henry Labbe, and influential attorney Rodney L. Glisan, a descendent of the prominent Couch family. Teal not only feared loss of home rule, but he opposed any tax increases that would result from the merger.

Another ingredient entered the picture, that of a populist type of revolt. Ads appeared in the local papers, depicting the "little people" fighting for their rights against big business and big taxes. The merger was characterized as "a conspiracy by the professional politicians." Apart from the tax concerns, much of the opposition to port consolidation reflected a distrust of the legislature and of some members of the Port of Portland Commission. Teal and Ayer mistrusted people like Gus Moser, or even Phil Metschan for that matter. They had fought long and hard to secure the dock commission for the city and they did not want to deliver it to a state body that they did not totally respect. Emery Olmstead was also the subject of some latent criticism. He was too much of a "go-getter" for many old time Portlanders who were suspicious of his true motives. Seven years later, such fears would be justified.

The November 1920 election, that bestowed the presidency on Warren Harding, produced a number of negative votes: Not only were the people opposed to Port consolidation, but they voted against all tax increases and Portland's first zoning code. Oddly enough, the Port bill carried handily in the tri-county metropolitan area of greater Portland, but it suffered defeat in 20 counties. One could argue that the residents of the state who were not affected should not have been allowed to vote. But being a creature of the state legislature, the agency was made responsible to the people of Oregon and not just to Multnomah County residents. The vote was close: 66,500 No; 62,900 Yes.

In 1921, the state legislature, under Senator Gus Moser's prodding, enacted a bill authorizing the Port to acquire the dock commission properties. But the dock commission opposed it in 1922, as did the city council. Their continued joint opposition effectively killed all further merger attempts until 1969-1970.

In retrospect, it would appear that personal differences and mistrust were important, if not primary, factors in the defeat of Port consolidation. Carrying additional force were the generally negative reactions that were widespread in 1920. With united leadership in Portland, an increased majority of local votes would have more than offset the heavy downstate opposition.

The Big Landfills

The Port of Portland was in a state of crisis by late 1920. With consolidation defeated, Max Houser's resignation as president and a shortage of operating revenues, the future was not overly bright. But by mid-1921, under the strong leadership of President Frank M. Warren, the Port found itself deeply involved

Frank M. Warren

in three major projects which would consume most of the decade — projects that were to have significant impact on the future shape of Portland. Following the recommendations of the "Committee of 15" report, the commission directed its efforts to: (1) The purchase and development of Swan Island; (2) the dredging of the west channel; and (3) the filling of Guild's Lake for industrial sites and railroad freight yards.

Frank M. Warren must be given the major credit for picking up the pieces that were left in disarray after the November '20 election. He was to be president for nearly 14 years. A man of high ability and forceful drive, Warren's presence dominated all facets of the Port's operation. As the *Oregon Voter* commented: "He is the kind of man who is selected because those who do the selecting want the man who can do a big job in the right way."[25]

Born in Oregon (1876) of a pioneer family from New England, Warren was raised in close association to the river and river life. His grandfather had founded the Warren Packing Company which was one of the earliest salmon canneries in the Pacific Northwest. His father, who went down on the Titanic in 1912, expanded the business in association with James W. Cook and Sylvester Farrell, both of whom played prominent roles in Portland's business life at the turn of the century. Frank Sr. organized the profitable Alaska-Portland Packers Association which the family was to sell in 1930.[26] The Warrens had invested heavily in downtown real estate, including the property on which the present Arlington Clubhouse was built. When Frank Jr. retired from the fish packing business, he was cited as "one of Oregon's wealthiest men."[27]

After graduating from Amherst College which awarded him a Phi Beta Kappa key, Warren returned to Portland to assist his father. Before the war, he was instrumental in establishing the Oregon State Fish Commission. During the war, Herbert Hoover requested his services in Washington to help with the U. S. Food Administration. And following the war, concurrent with his election to the Port of Portland Commission, Warren helped to draft a bill establishing a motor vehicle revenue system for the state. Obviously oriented toward high achievement, Warren was quiet, methodical and well organized. He was known as "a man of decision" who enjoyed using the authority of his office.

From his first days on the commission, Warren knew that Swan Island needed immediate attention. It was the key to the inner harbor. In January 1919, the dock and Port commissions had actually considered eliminating the island by widening the east channel. The Corps of Engineers objected. Col. Zinn told the two commissions meeting jointly that the island should be built up and connected to the mainland by a causeway. "The west channel is far the best one to develop," Zinn declared.[28] When Warren took his seat on the Port commission two months later, he supported Zinn's position.

No one knows who first named Swan Island. The early donation land maps show the property to be unclaimed. No longer an island — but still called one — Swan Island has more than fulfilled Col. Zinn's wildest hopes. It has become one of the most important pieces of real estate in Portland. The site of the city's first

commercial airport in 1927, the island housed the Kaiser shipyards during
World War II and has since become the service headquarters for the Port of
Portland, containing the dry dock and ship repair facilities worth millions of
dollars.

Pioneer merchant William Sherlock owned the island for some years before he
organized the Swan Island Realty Company in 1889. He issued 1000 shares of
stock, kept 350 shares for himself, sold 350 to Simeon Reed and 300 to Reed's
nephew, Martin Winch, for a total of $90,000. Except for duck shooting, the
property had little use. It was scrub and marsh land that was usually under
water during flood season. It was first offered for sale in 1906 for $200,000. In
October 1913, when the dock commission considered its purchase, the price had
risen to $525,000. Fortunately for the public treasury — but unfortunately for
Reed College — the price was deemed much too high. The college owned the Reed
and Winch shares and the trustees were apparently desperate to liquidate them.
They had to wait eight more years. In December 1921, despite the owners'
appraised value of $450,000, Warren negotiated a sale price of $120,577 for 270
acres. The Port issued five percent bonds and took possession in January 1922.[29]

One artist's depiction of Portland's future growth with Swan Island
eliminated. Note the landfills all dedicated to industrial development.

233

Swan Island became the first recipient of the millions of cubic yards of spoils that would be dredged from the west channel.

The disposal of the dredge fill presented a number of problems. Initially, the Port figured that it would have to excavate five million cubic yards to open the west channel. But by the end of 1928, the total cubic yards excavated amounted to over 38.6 million. Some 1300 acres of Guild's Lake were reclaimed. Because the owners of Mock's Bottom did not want to pay the Port's charges, the balance of the dredge spoils were added to increase the size of Swan Island and build a connection to the mainland.[30] The whole undertaking proved to be far more complex, costly and time consuming than originally planned.

In pursuing the course that it followed to redevelop the Portland harbor, the Port of Portland Commission was guided by a report submitted to "The Committee of 15" in March 1921. Written by consulting engineer George W. Boschke, the document is worth serious consideration. Boschke raised a question that has been central to the Port's operation over the past half-century: As to the proper use of Port developed land for private industrial sites, should the property be leased or sold? Referring particularly to the property owners within the Guild's Lake district, Boschke had this to say:

> "From a study of the list of individual owners it will readily be seen that the property so divided and held is not susceptible of being developed economically to its maximum efficiency by private individuals; that it now practically is not revenue producing nor is it of value to the port, but that when the project regarded as a whole shall be designed broadly and logically developed as a municipal enterprise, it will materially add to the prosperity of the city and of its citizens.
>
> In the purchase of property, prospective or inflated values should not be considered, for it is of but little value unless developed as a whole. Considering this statement to be correct, I am of the opinion that the property should be secured at reasonable figures and that the enhanced values due to shore filling the partially submerged lands, together with the development of water frontage and rail facilities, whereby industrial activities may be concentrated, will in the future, reimburse the city for all of the original expenditures of money, besides affording building sites for industries at *reasonable rentals*, whose payrolls and purchase of materials and supplies will greatly add to both population and prosperity of the city. . . . "

Under "Conclusions Derived," Boschke stated:

> "Being municipally owned, [Boschke apparently did not know that the Port was a state agency or he got his terms confused because the dock commission was municipal] prospective industries could *acquire leases* at rates which would be remunerative to the municipality, but which would be ruinous to privately owned developments, therefore to insure the location of new industries in this city, it is necessary that *the project be taken out of private hands.* . . . After all the property shall have been acquired and the channel improvements shall have been made, together with the shore filling incidental thereto, the further development of the project may be made as occasion warrants and funds become available."

Under "Recommendations," Boschke urged:

> "That private property embraced in this report (1550 acres valued at $1.7 million) . . . be acquired by either purchase or condemnation . . . ; that proceedings be started as rapidly as authority can be obtained to acquire lands and rectify the harbor lines; that dredging and shore filling operations herein specified be commenced and prosecuted . . . to a speedy completion."[31]

The implication is clear from the italicized words[32] at least, that Boschke strongly encouraged the Port to acquire and keep the landfilled harbor properties for future lease, not sale. This was the European tradition. It was to be a long-term program that required front-end investment by the public substantial enough to support the program until lease revenues could begin to amortize the investment. The crucial properties in this regard were at Guild's Lake. With Swan Island destined to become an airport, public grants, subsidies and user fees would assure reasonably quick repayment of dredging and development costs. The filling of 900 or more acres at Guild's Lake — appraised conservatively by Boschke at $1.2 million in 1921 — was a considerably more expensive undertaking. It is worth noting in this regard, that Boschke's appraisals proved to be fairly accurate. He valued the Swan Island property at $90,000, one-fifth of the amount asked by the Reed College trustees. At the time of purchase, a board of disinterested appraisers set the value at $120,577.[33]

As the following account will reveal, the Port of Portland Commissioners were either unable to raise the front-end capital or unwilling to try. By legislative authority, the commission was empowered to issue up to $2 million in bonds in any one year without the approval of the people of the Port district. Over a seven year period, a maximum of $14 million so raised would have provided more than enough capital to purchase both the Guild's Lake and Swan Island properties and fill them with 38 million cubic yards of dredge spoils. But a total of $14 million of issued bonds — 75 percent of the authorized limit (5 percent of the district's assessed valuation) — would have required increased tax levies for principal and interest payments, and the voters had strongly opposed any tax increases in November 1920. Thus, although the commission had the authority to raise the required funds, it must have been under severe pressure not to incur the wrath of the majority of voters who were already on record as unhappy with existing tax rates. Throughout its first 40 years, in fact, the commission always pursued a conservative course in raising operating and capital funds. Rarely did the total ever exceed 50 percent of the authorized limits. In 1920, only $340,000 of issued bonds were outstanding.

The Port of Portland Commission accepted Boschke's general proposition that all of the filled lands should be treated as a whole to be integrated into a broad program of harbor related developments. But to achieve their goals, they elected to pursue a totally different course of action than Boschke recommended. The Boschke report was not well received by some leaders of the chamber of commerce like former Port president Max Houser and the officers of the realty

1927 aerial survey of the Guild's Lake industrial district. Municipal Terminal No. 1 is on the lower right. Swan Island is in the upper background. Two dredges are at work. Portland Flouring Mills can be seen on the east bank and Mock's Bottom at the upper right corner. The northern Pacific Railroad bisects the scene. To its right is Front Avenue that was being extended to the partially cleared site, below the nearest dredge, owned by Wilcox Investment.

board who characterized its recommendations as nothing more than "socialism." Several members of the Port commission also held the same opinion, namely that a public agency should not enter into the rental real estate market in competition with private enterprise.

It was one thing for public money to finance the improvement of marginal lands and then sell them at reasonable prices to private operators. But it was quite another matter to maintain public ownership of the land and lease it at competitive rates that would force down values and rentals on adjacent privately owned property. After all, the *raison d'etre* of owning real estate was to realize profits in sales and rentals, not to serve any public purposes *per se*. Public agencies were not expected to make a profit. Public ownership was therefore tantamount to socialism, unless of course no profits were considered inherently possible.

Instead of outright purchase, the commissioners decided to negotiate with the major property owners, including the railroads. They would charge eight cents per cubic yard for dredge fill placed on private property. However, they would cut

236

the charge to four cents if the property owners would agree to grant waterfront ownership rights to the Port of Portland. The property owners requested that the Port finance the entire project through the issuance of 20 year bonds, with interest to be carried by the Port for ten years. After ten years, the accumulated interest and principal would be amortized, payable by the property owners in ten annual installments. The Port of Portland Commission rejected the plan on the grounds that the property owners, not the taxpayers, should carry the costs of improvement even though it was not necessarily in their best interests to do so.

In forcing the Guild's Lake property owners to carry 50 percent of the landfill costs, payable upon completiion of the fill, the Port encountered numerous difficulties. Some owners did not want any fill unless all of their holdings were filled to the waterfront grade level of 32 feet. They refused to pay for a partial fill job. Others refused to pay even though they had agreed to accept fill. In some cases, the Port was to end up owning land that it had no intention of possessing in the first place. Several of the larger tract owners who accepted fill and duly paid for it, were to find themselves obligated to pay property taxes on improved lands that no industry wanted to lease. In a few instances, most notably that of the 643 acre Cook tract, properties were to be auctioned for tax arrears, wiping out most of the property owners' investments.

From the vantage point of 50 years later, it would appear that the Port of Portland Commission, perhaps through no fault of its own, committed a basic error. In its effort to find dumping grounds for its dredged channel spoils and at the same time to secure for itself an extensive strip of land along the west riverbank, it encouraged the filling of land far in advance of the perceived need for industrial sites. Had the commission been able to purchase all of the properties, as recommended by Boschke, it could have filled the land with the excess spoils and not have worried about the immediate financial consequences. It also could have developed its own waterfront strip simultaneously.

The Port of Portland, and its business establishment allies, tried to do an adequate job too cheaply, and it found itself continually short of funds. It was forced to lease two dredges to the Long Bell Lumber Company at Longview, Washington, for two years because it needed the net income of $12,000 per month for each dredge. In so doing, the Port needlessly extended by at least two years the channel improvement project as well as the filling of Swan Island and Guild's Lake.[34] Financial stringency was to become so acute in the late 1920s that the Port would find it necessary to sell pieces of equipment, including dredges, and then lease them back from private operators.

The path of least resistance, based on the lowest public expenditure, was in the long run to produce excessive waste of economic resources. Unfilled land that could have been purchased at Guild's Lake for $1000 an acre now sells for as much as $45,000 an acre. During the 1920s, dredge spoils cost approximately $2000 an acre. Fifty years ago, few could imagine that comparable waterfront acreage, filled but not developed, would increase in value at least 15 times.

Some Package Deals

The largest package deal involving Guild's Lake property was negotiated with the Northern Pacific Terminal Company in behalf of the railroads, largely the Hill lines, which had long been planning an extension and unification of railway terminals and freight switching yards. Signed in December 1921, the contract called for a million cubic yards of fill at eight cents per yard. The amount of fill was doubled in 1922 and the Port received a total cash payment of $160,000. In lieu of accepting half-payment, as was done with the other Guild's Lake property owners, the Port arranged with the city to exchange street vacations for frontage on the west channel. In the area around the Union Station, the city, working with the Port, agreed after extensive negotiation to grant the railroads 34 street vacations in exchange for land that the city needed for construction of: (1) An approach to the Broadway Bridge; (2) elevated passageways from the Broadway to N. W. Tenth Avenue and along Lovejoy Street to the area west of Fourteenth Avenue; and (3), a new approach to the Steel Bridge leading onto N. W. Glisan Street.[35]

The Guild's Lake property owners divided themselves into two groups. The earliest and largest group consisted of those owners whose property was located immediately north of the areas that had been filled and developed before the war. Representing the owners were attorney, James B. Kerr, president of the Board of Trustees of Reed College and lawyer for the Hill railroads, and Robert H. Strong, a professional property manager who was E. B. MacNaughton's partner as well as the manager of the Corbett estate. He was the brother of Frederick H. Strong, the managing director of the Ladd estate. In addition to acting as agents for the Cook estate which owned the largest tract of 643 acres, Messrs. Strong and MacNaughton also managed 130 acres for other property owners. When Robert H. Strong accepted membership on the Port of Portland Commission in June 1923, he immediately placed himself in a position of severe conflict of interest. E. B. MacNaughton found himself in a similar position when he accepted the chairmanship of the Port's development committee, established to promote the leasing of industrial sites. MacNaughton was also a veteran member of the city planning commission. In 1926, Strong assumed the leadership of the Guild's Lake Improvement Association, representing all of the district's property owners.

Obviously, MacNaughton and Strong found themselves serving conflicting interests. The Port commission and its development committee were pushing land fills and industrial site leases, while Strong & MacNaughton were also supposedly counseling their clients as to what was in their best interests. The handling of the Cook property was a case in point. In the early 1920s, Strong had advised Mrs. James W. (Iolanthe) Cook to agree to accept landfill for a portion of her 643 acres. In May of 1924, the Cook estate sold 65.2 acres to the Port for $10 and "other considerations" — this being a commonly used term when the sales price was not disclosed. The deed carried the approving initials of Commissioner R. H. Strong.[36] Subsequent events revealed that the "other considerations" did

238

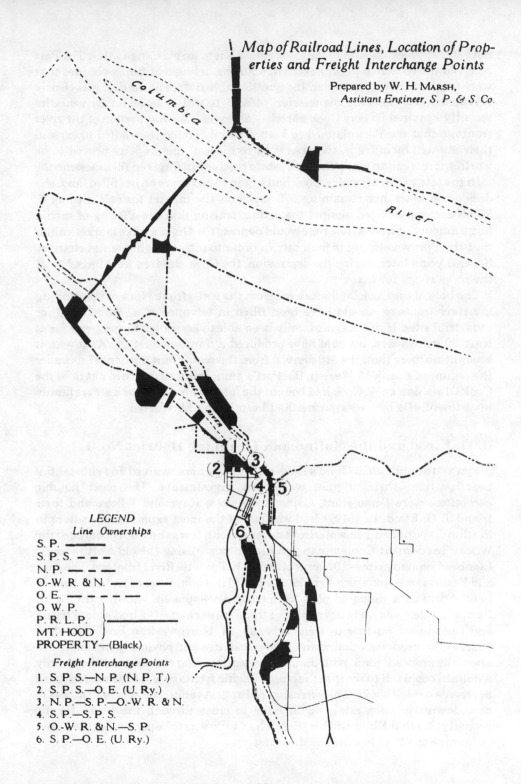

Map of Railroad Lines, Location of Properties and Freight Interchange Points

Prepared by W. H. MARSH,
Assistant Engineer, S. P. & S. Co.

Columbia

River

WILLAMETTE RIVER

LEGEND
Line Ownerships

S. P. ——————
S. P. S. — — —
N. P. – – – –
O.-W. R. & N. —— ——
O. E. – —— – ——
O. W. P.
P. R. L. P.
MT. HOOD
PROPERTY—(Black)

Freight Interchange Points

1. S. P. S.—N. P. (N. P. T.)
2. S. P. S.—O. E. (U. Ry.)
3. N. P.—S. P.—O.-W. R. & N.
4. S. P.—S. P. S.
5. O.-W. R. & N.—S. P.
6. S. P.—O. E. (U. Ry.)

not refer to proceeds paid to the Cook estate but to an exchange value. The Port received the 65 acre parcel in exchange for the delinquent filling charges that were forgiven. Four years later, the questionable nature of the deal was clearly revealed when the Port commission offered to sell or lease for 30 years its recently acquired 65 acre Cook parcel — all except for that portion of the river frontage that the Port planned to keep. The oil companies wanted to expand their storage facilities in the area.[37] In retrospect, the property proved to be worth far more than what the Cook estate received in forgiven fill assessments.

In the late 1920s, after Mrs. Cook had begun to pay taxes on her filled land, she decided to place her remaining 570 acres on the market for sale. Strong & MacNaughton advised against the action, fearing that the offering of such a large amount of land at one time would depress the Guild's Lake market values that the Port was trying to maintain in order to attract higher rental charges. Several years later, during the depression, the Cook children were forced to let the property go for taxes.[38]

The bulk of the Cook land was back from the waterfront. None of it, including the river frontage, should have been filled in advance of a proven need for industrial sites. Had the Cook family been able to keep all of the property for at least 20 more years, it would have produced a handsome return. As it was, it brought no more than the $10 derived from the waterfront portion. Thus under the regime of Frank M. Warren, the Port's gain, ironically, turned out to be the Cooks' loss. James W. Cook had bought the land years earlier as a secure family investment. His business partner had been Frank M. Warren Sr.

J. O. Elrod and the Multnomah Drainage District No. 1

Few of the individual Guild's Lake property owners received any substantial benefits from their original waterfront investments. The most notable exceptions were Isaac Hunt, Cameron Squires, Raymond Wilcox and their friend J. O. Elrod. In 1919, Elrod was one of the most experienced realtors in Portland, specializing in waterfront development. It was he who encouraged the Wilcox Investment Company to join him in purchasing the old North Pacific Lumber Company site — 101 acres of choice Willamette River frontage. The dock and Port commissions, through the work of "The Committee of 15," had already jointly drafted a proposed plan for harbor development, showing the North Pacific property as an integral part of the whole scheme.[39] Elrod's close friend and investment partner in some other deals, Northwestern Bank president Emery Olmstead, was chairman of the committee and obviously well informed about the proposed plan. With the anticipated dredging of the west channel, only a dullard could fail to see that the North Pacific frontage would be the first area to receive dredge spoils. The extension of Front Avenue, the sole road access to new downriver dock sites, would have to cross through the North Pacific property. All that Elrod and his friends had to do was to be patient, sit tight, and encourage the Port to continue dredging.

In October 1926, the Wilcox Investment Company sold its interests in the North Pacific site to a syndicate headed by Elrod, who kept his share. The other principal and major owner was J. H. Trimble, an Indianapolis oil refiner. The 101 acres sold for $1.8 million, or at an average of approximately $17,000 per acre. This was one of the better investments ever made by Hunt, Squires and Wilcox. Elrod derived some profit but not of the same magnitude. After the sale, Elrod was quoted as saying that "he himself believed the Guild's Lake district to be the future industrial center of Portland."[40] The property was temporarily deeded to Emery Olmstead's Portland Trust & Savings Bank which was affiliated with the Northwestern National Bank on whose board of directors J. O. Elrod was serving in 1926.

In a stock prospectus that was issued by Blyth & Co. early in 1927, Elrod announced his plans for the site. Over $1.5 million were to be spent in constructing the modern Oregon Terminals that would include warehouses and much needed cold storage facilities. Three berths could accommodate simultaneously any three of the largest ships entering the Portland harbor. The whole facility was to be leased for 15 years to the Oceanic Terminals Company, headed by George Powell, for $175,000 a year.[41] The prospectus described J. O. Elrod as "one of the leading business men of the Pacific northwest" who "for many years has been successfully identified with large enterprises. As a member of the Commission of Public Docks of Portland, Mr. Elrod learned the shipping problems of the Port, and fully appreciates the benefits that will accrue to the city"[42] and, it should have added, to himself.

James O. Elrod was born in Iowa in 1875, attended school in Minnesota and moved to the wheat country of Sherman County, Oregon, in 1895 in company with his father. In Minnesota, he worked in his father's lumber camps while attending high school. Foresaking college, Elrod joined his father in Eastern Oregon wheat farming, served as a young mayor of Moro, Oregon, and moved to Portland in 1905 where he engaged in the lumber business and real estate development.

During the world war, Elrod became interested in the possibility of creating a drainage district along the south bank of the Columbia River, just west of C. F. Swigert's 1800 acre Sun Dial Ranch property that Pacific Bridge Company had successfully diked and drained. He enlisted the support of a group of local bankers and businessmen who had affiliated with the United States Employment Service, a national organization dedicated to finding employment for returning servicemen. Being an ex-farmer, real estate developer Elrod had the notion that over 8000 acres could be reclaimed from the flood plain and converted into productive farmland to be worked by war veterans. His local supporters were an impressive group: Guy Talbot, W. F. Woodward, Emery Olmstead, Julius Meier, Edward Cookingham, Edgar Piper, Fred Boalt and J. E. Wheeler. In this regard, his efforts were assured the endorsements of *The Oregonian*, *News* and *Telegram*.

The Multnomah Drainage District No. 1 (MDD#1) was organized in 1918 with

James O. Elrod

J. O. Elrod as president. It faced a number of problems. First it had to secure the approval of the Port of Portland, the city and the U. S. Army Corps of Engineers to erect two dams on the Columbia Slough; one near the Interstate Bridge and the other at the intake of the Columbia River to the east. Second, it needed to raise funds through the issuance of bonds. In 1917, the Oregon Legislature had created the Irrigation and Drainage Securities Commission with authority to certify irrigation and drainage bonds as legal instruments for trust funds. A companion measure, authorizing the state to guarantee the interest on all bonds for the first five years after issuance, was referred to the Oregon voters and passed in June 1919. In the two year period following this enactment, MDD#1 issued two bond offerings totalling $600,000 with Ladd & Tilton underwriting both issues. Elrod's co-investors in the North Pacific Lumber property proved helpful when he needed their assistance. Local funding efforts were supplemented by the congressional passage of the Sinnott Bill which provided $113 million for national reclamation, drainage and diking projects. Representative Nicholas J. Sinnott from The Dalles was a long-time friend of the Elrod family.[43]

By the summer of 1921, *The Portland Telegram*[44] reported that MDD#1 had already increased the wealth of Multnomah County by $3.5 million, with the county's farm production up by more than 50 percent. Property tax receipts were providing the county over $40,000 annually. Then the farm depression hit and

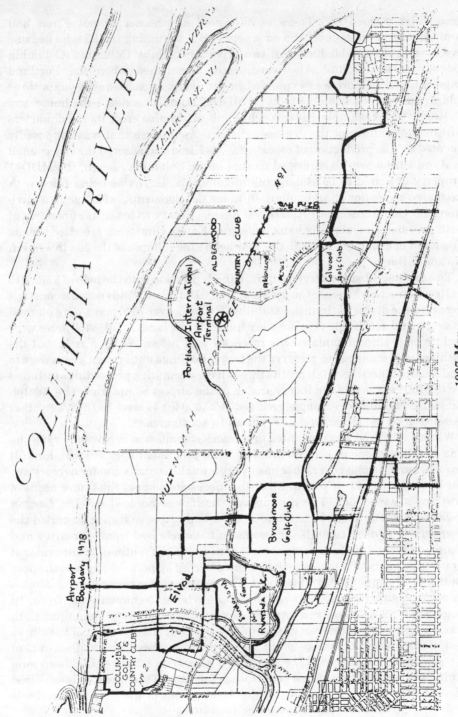

COLUMBIA RIVER

1927 Map

Portland International Airport Terminal

ALDERWOOD COUNTRY CLUB

DRAINAGE DITCH

No.1

MULTNOMAH

Calwood Golf Club

Broadmoor Golf Club

Riverside G.C.

Columbia Slough Farm

Airport Boundary 1978

COLUMBIA GOLF & COUNTRY CLUB No.2

land sales tapered off. There is no record of whether or not Elrod had contingency plans to meet the emergency. But beginning in 1924, he became involved in the establishment of two private golf clubs: Columbia (Columbia Edgewater today) and Alderwood, later demolished when the Portland International Airport was expanded in the 1950s. In subsequent years three additional courses would be built on MDD#1 land: Riverside, Broadmoor and Colwood. The Columbia River Yacht Club would also erect its headquarters within the confines of the drainage district. As an area that was supposedly devoted to "the production of foodstuffs," as Elrod had assured the city council in June 1918 when he requested closure of the Columbia Slough, the MDD#1 property appeared to be undergoing metamorphosis. It was being filled with exclusive recreational and suburban home developments, with such subdivisions as "Golf Acres" and "Alderwood Acres." Elrod was to become president of both private golf clubs. His bank colleague, Emery Olmstead, preceded him as president of Columbia in 1926, the year before the collapse of the Northwestern National Bank.

The drainage district survived during the depression with the help of $272, 315 in Reconstruction Finance Corporation loans. Defaulted bonds posed a constant threat to the district's financial stability. By 1935, over 7000 acres were planted in crops and nearly 900 farmers were living on the land. In all, 8400 acres were reclaimed.[45] Elrod liquidated his interests well before World War II, but the farmers who managed to preserve the larger holdings until recent years were to realize substantial windfall profits through condemnation proceedings initiated by the Port of Portland in its expansion of the airport boundaries. The Adolph Cereghino family, for example, received $622,000 for 44 acres in 1972. Ten other families received lesser amounts, but all in six figures.[46]

When J. O. Elrod was appointed to the dock commission in November 1924 he was considered one of the Northwest's most prominent specialists in landfill acquisitions. He played a rather passive role on the commission for over a year, but he had a front row seat at all of the discussions about the future needs of Portland's waterfront. The commission itself was accused by *The Oregon Journal* in January 1926 of assuming an equally passive stance. Reported the *Journal*: "The dock commission seems to have relapsed from a creative and commercial building factor into the less thrilling role of routine administrator of a public property."[47] One issue that seemed to crop up periodically was the poor condition of some of the private docks. The commission was urged to condemn a number of structures and to redevelop the whole downtown waterfront. In August of 1926, despite a strong protest from property manager E. B. MacNaughton, the dock commission did order the condemnation of the Burke Fish Company's cold storage plant. Elrod must have been personally aware of the problem. Furthermore, *The Oregonian*'s Lawrence Hodges had been long urging the construction of new cold storage facilities. Three months later, Elrod assumed the challenge and began the development of the Oregon Terminals project to provide modern cold storage facilities.

At the same meeting at which the Burke facility was ordered removed, the dock commission granted a permit to the Ross Island Sand & Gravel Company to construct a gravel bunker on Hardtack Island in the Willamette River. Hardtack was one of two islands, actually, that were usually combined in the public's mind as one Ross Island. Both islands had been bought five months earlier by a syndicate headed by J. O. Elrod. Sometime in June, the company was formally organized and the directors announced. They included ex-governor and prominent Republican attorney Jay Bowerman, young and wealthy lumberman Coleman H. Wheeler, utility executive Franklin T. Griffith and Elrod. Although a lawsuit was filed with the state attorney general to prevent the island from being used for commercial purposes, the state ruled that it had no authority in the matter. The dock commission was empowered to grant permits for any dredging activity in the upper harbor and J. O. Elrod was sitting in the right spot. The rumored price was $215,000 for 290 acres.

Ross Island had long been viewed as a possible city park site. In 1912,

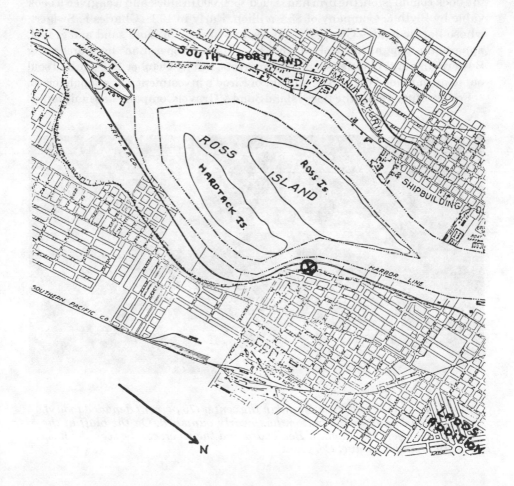

Portland voters had decisively defeated a bond measure that would have provided funds for its purchase. The matter came up again in 1924 when a private syndicate evidenced interest in buying and developing the site as a tourist park. The city council was encouraged to acquire the property before it was too late. But a Portland City Club committee opposed the action. "Because of water pollution, Ross Island is not suitable for a park for aquatic sports." The City Club members did indicate, however, that at some future date, the island might be desirable "as a general purpose park."[48] The city council agreed. In 1924, city funds could be better used.

Three weeks after Elrod acquired the site for a future cold storage terminal, the dock commission, with Elrod voting "aye," passed a motion to allow the construction of a tramway and hoppers to service sand and gravel bunkers on Hardtack Island.[49] The Ross Island Sand & Gravel Company was now off and running. It bought control of the Beaver Portland Cement Company of Portland and Gold Hill, Oregon, for $850,000. By early 1927, when Elrod resigned from the dock commission, the firm had issued $550,000 in stock and was given a book value by Blyth & Company of $3.7 million. Early in 1928, Charles F. Swigert, whose Pacific Bridge Company was always in need of more sand and gravel, apparently bought control of the Ross Island operation by purchasing Bowerman's and Wheeler's majority interests. But by October 1928, he had sold out to an unnamed party. The amount of Elrod's investment was not publicized.

For over fifty years, the Ross Island Sand & Gravel Company has maintained

1947 aerial showing Ross Island in the center (75 percent denuded today). Hardtack Island at the bottom has nearly vanished. On the bluff at the right, between McLoughlin Boulevard and the river, can be seen the Ross Island Sand & Gravel Co. plant.

a love-hate relationship with the Portland community. Admired by business leaders as an aggressive, well managed enterprise, the company has often aroused the ire of both the city planning commission and the residents living adjacent to its large plant. To begin with, in 1926 the company constructed its office and operation buildings on the river bluff, adjacent to what has since become McLoughlin Boulevard, without benefit of a building permit. They were nonconforming commercial structures in a residentially zoned area. Furthermore, the city zoning code of 1924 required that an affected neighborhood should be consulted before a nonconforming use could be considered. The procedure was not followed. Five years later, when the city council officially discovered what had happened, it decided not to disturb the *status quo*. The buildings were allowed to remain. In 1937, both the company and the Southern Pacific Railroad were charged with violations of city ordinances for erecting buildings along the riverfront, below the bluff on which the original buildings were placed. Again, they were not ordered removed.[50]

The company received its only official rebuff in April 1941 when the city council denied issuance of a permit to construct additional buildings along McLoughlin Boulevard. Over 150 property owners had filed remonstrances. After the war, the company grew rapidly under the ownership of Walter H. Muirhead, an original officer who had gained control of the firm in 1942. Buying war surplus equipment, Ross Island Sand & Gravel became the largest pre-mix concrete company in Oregon.

In 1959, when the city was considering a new comprehensive zoning code, the company had grown so powerful that it was able, through city council influence, to preserve its nonconforming industrial use in a designated special residential zone 1 area. Potentially one of the most beautiful views in the city was to be blocked permanently from public enjoyment by a strip of ugly, but highly profitable, commercial construction.

Befitting its past history as a child of power and politics, the company was bought in 1976 by Robert B. Pamplin, one of the powers of the Portland establishment and the retired chief executive officer of the Georgia Pacific Company, the nation's largest lumber products corporation. When Pamplin was approached by both the governor and the mayor in September 1977 to see if he would consider donating to the city as a park the outer shell of Ross Island, the only remaining portion not denuded, he hedged his response. At some future date he might be so inclined. "It depends on how everyone behaves himself," Pamplin declared,[51] referring to the future actions of governmental officials.

Eighteen months later, the state and county governments gave their blessings to the issuance of $5 million in Oregon State Revenue Bonds for financing a major expansion of Ross Island Sand & Gravel's Willamette River operations, environmental drawbacks notwithstanding. It remains to be seen what will be left to donate as a future city park site — possibly a narrow sandbar. Regardless of what happens in the future, however, Ross Island of the present bears little resemblance to the Ross Island of 30 years ago.

Municipal Terminal No. 2, the former Oregon Terminals.

In retrospect, James O. Elrod's ambitious career had an obviously significant impact on the shaping of Portland. The Oregon Terminals were to be sold to the dock commission during World War II, to be converted into a new Municipal Terminal No. 2. And the Multnomah Drainage District No. 1 acreage became the site of Portland's ever growing international airport. Elrod had other interests including some bank investments and several downstate timber and logging companies, but his river-related properties in Portland had consumed his major attention. Although he did not die a wealthy man, leaving an estate of less than $85,000, he must have made — and lost — a good deal of money during the course of his active working life. He was probably not the major investor in those projects to which his name was attached. But he was the initiator, the classic promoter, who was able to attract other people's money, including that of the banks with which he was associated. And he knew how to employ the instruments of government to achieve his economic ends, or those of his wealthier business associates who made good use of his talents.

Some Problems at the Port

In February 1925, Portland maritime interests found themselves faced with a serious threat to their future. The U. S. Congress passed a law, granting a franchise to a private corporation to build a toll bridge across the Columbia

River at Longview, Washington, provided that the plans secured the approval of both state highway commissions. The franchise expired a year later without formal action by the Oregon agency. The chamber of commerce and the Port of Portland had both opposed the bridge on the grounds that the horizontal and vertical clearances were insufficient to allow passage for the largest ships that could be expected to use the Portland harbor.

A new bill was introduced in 1926, removing the authority of the two highway commissions and substituting that of the U. S. War Department Board of Engineers. Under the leadership of Frank L. Shull, a local grain merchant and co-founder of the Benjamin Franklin Federal Savings & Loan Association, the chamber of commerce mounted a strong counterattack in which it was joined by the major agricultural and trade organizations of the Inland Empire and Willamette Valley. The authority to make a final decision was later granted to the Secretaries of War, Commerce and Agriculture and hearings were held in both Portland and Washington. In January 1928, the dock and Port commissions agreed to split a $5000 fee and hire the famed New York lawyer John W. Davis to plead Portland's case. A former ambassador to Great Britain and the 1924 Democratic presidential nominee, Davis knew his way around Washington and had the reputation of being one of America's top trial lawyers.

By March of 1928, the issue was settled to Portland's satisfaction. The bridge was to be built, but with a clearance of approximately 190 feet, 55 feet higher than originally planned. Davis had done his work and earned his fee, and the Port of Portland commissioners breathed a collective sigh of relief. Much time, effort and money had gone into the successful effort. And Frank Shull gained sufficient public acclaim to win a seat on the Board of Multnomah County Commissioners in 1931.

During the early months of 1927, the Port of Portland sought additional help from Washington, D. C., in its rush to complete the Swan Island airport. In March, Congress granted the Port the right to fill in the south end of the east channel in order to connect the island to the mainland. A strip of land was acquired on the east side of the east channel and the construction of a paved causeway was begun. The airport did not become fully operational until the summer of 1928, but it was available for limited use in September 1927, when Charles A. Lindbergh planned a visit to Portland in the course of his triumphal tour of the United States, following his solo flight to France in May 1927.

Much preparation went into the Lindbergh reception that was planned for September 14th. Two weeks in advance, an agent arrived to check out the landing conditions. He was assured by the Port's manager, James H. Polhemus, that the field was "among the best in the country." Polhemus even agreed to remove a pipeline that occupied a center strip. Pearson Field wanted the landing in Vancouver because more people could view the plane, but Mayor Baker would not hear of it. "We're going to have a Portland celebration," declared the mayor.[52] George Baker never missed an opportunity to stage a good show and place Portland in the national limelight.

Flying down from Seattle, Lindbergh arrived over Portland on schedule. All planes had been cleared from the airspace. By pre-arrangement, Lindy circled low over Marquam Hill to honor the war veterans who were still hospitalized in temporary quarters at the site, and then he made two low swoops over the Swan Island airfield to inspect the conditions. At 1:59 p.m. he landed "like a feather," reported the *Journal*, "with the punctuality of a crack railroad train."[53] Crowds lined the bluffs to the east to watch their hero. A pontoon bridge would be available the next day for public crossing to view the *Spirit of St. Louis*, but on the great day itself, only the official welcome committee of 400 dignitaries were on hand. They had arrived on the steamer *Portland*, an hour earlier. After official greetings were exchanged, Lindbergh was taken on board Julius Meier's yacht, the *Grace*, and transported across the river, passing the battleship *Oregon* on his way to the awaiting parade bands. Speeches and a formal banquet were to follow. All in all, George L. Baker had arranged a spectacular occasion for those who participated. The *Spirit of St. Louis*, destined for preservation at the Smithsonian Institution, was treated with even greater care

Colonel Lindbergh Banquet, Multnomah Hotel, September 14, 1927

250

than its pilot. A special hangar was constructed and 24 hour guard service provided.

By the fall of 1929, the dredging of the west channel was largely completed. Over 39 million cubic yards of spoils had been excavated from the river, and the east channel had been made into a still water basin. The west side fairway, with a width of 1500 feet, was as wide as the lower Willamette at any point except in the basins at the upper and lower ends of Swan Island, where the width reached 2200 feet. Not only had Swan Island been enlarged three times to 900 acres and converted into a modern airport, but Guild's Lake had also been converted into 1300 acres of available industrial sites. Approximately 65 percent of the dredge fill had been allocated to the district. In October, prominent industrial realtor Henry J. C. Quin announced optimistically to the press that the "Guild's Lake lands are becoming more valuable by the day."[55]

Before the filling began in 1921, the district's properties had been assessed at roughly $1.2 million. In 1929, the total value was placed at $5 million. Property taxes had increased two and one-half times, to over $250,000. The Port of Portland itself owned 120 acres of river frontage appraised at $1.1 million. Some 20 percent of this valuable property came into Port hands through default actions. In addition to the Cook property, the Port took title to ten acres of land belonging to Scotsman Percy Blyth, a prominent Portland realtor and clubman. Blyth owed the Port $3600 for improvements for which he refused to pay. The going rate for improved land ranged from $3500 to $7600 an acre. Unfilled land could still be acquired for $1000 an acre, but there were few takers. In truth, the Port was disturbed by the slow pace of sales and leases, and the trend was to grow worse as the depression became more severe. Most of the industries that

Acres Available For Industrial Development

Prepared by Day & Zimmerman of Philadelphia,
for The Dock Commission, 1930
Report #2863

Area	# Acres	Average Assessed Value Per Acre
Guild's Lake (filled)	926	$2300
Linnton	177	1100
St. Johns (partially filled)	1172	850
Mock's Bottom (unfilled)	492	815
South Portland	113	5000
Outside of City Limits		
North Portland (unfilled)	3120	70
Ramsey Lake (unfilled)	1411	75
Highest Recommendation		
South half of Guild's Lake	400	4000

located in the district, excluding the rail freight yards, were in the south half, close in to Northwest Portland, situated on land that had required only partial fill. Besides the Elrod Terminal, they included: The MacMar Company, Jones Stevedoring, Soule Steel, Paper Makers Chemical, Fuller Paint, PEPCO and Texaco which had just erected a huge oil distribution plant.

The Supreme Conflict of Interest

In order to raise additional operating revenues, the Port of Portland Commission decided in 1927 to begin a program of selling off equipment which was either not used too often or considered too old to be of much value. Most of the deals were made by the Port's general manager, James H. Polhemus, acting under the direction of Port president Frank M. Warren. The commission minutes recorded the actions, all of which appear to have been *pro forma*.

The most interesting sale was approved in September 1929. President Warren submitted a letter from the Portland Dredging Company offering to purchase two diggers with complete equipment for a total of $21,000. Warren then produced a sales contract containing the provision that the Port reserved the right to lease back the equipment for three years at the rate of $50 per day. Maximum use for three years could cost the Port more than $40,000, not including operational costs, but Warren did not tell the commission this fact. Apparently no one bothered to compute the figures to see what the total bill might run to. The actual cost was to exceed $47,000.

To the historical investigator, the intriguing aspect of the matter is a recorded

The Airport on Swan Island

252

comment made by Warren that the Port had purchased these very same diggers from the Portland Dredging Company "about four years ago" for $20,000,[56] or approximately the same amount that the company was prepared to pay for their repurchase. An examination of the Port records shows no mention of any such purchase by the Port at any time prior to September 1929. And in fact, the Portland Dredging Company was not even organized until 1929.[57] The Portland Dredging Company was to give birth to the present-day giant Willamette-Western Corporation, a firm that currently grosses over $100 million a year. Herein lies an interesting tale.

In the late fall of 1932 and early winter of 1933, the Port of Portland Commission and its general manager, James H. Polhemus, received sharp criticism from both an official investigator, appointed by Governor Meier, and Scripps' *News-Telegram*. (The actual investigation and its outcome will be discussed in Chapter 15.) One of the charges accused Polhemus of direct conflict of interest relating to the Portland Dredging Company's formation in the period 1928-1930. Polhemus was accused of establishing a dummy corporation as a front for his father's dredge equipment manufacturing company located in Longview. Polhemus denied the charge and also denied that he had ever derived any personal profit out of his position as the Port manager. President Warren called the charges "dastardly."[58] Three months later, however, Polhemus did admit that he had accepted private compensation from different companies, including his father's, for "consulting work."[59]

From an examination of the available records, including James H. Polhemus' probated will, it would appear that the charges were indeed valid. The man who is remembered as the founder of the Willamette-Western Corporation was Arthur A. Riedel, Sr. During the war years and the early 1920s, Riedel had been a dredge foreman for the U. S. Army Corps of Engineers. Also during the war years, young Stanford engineering graduate Polhemus had been in charge of all Corps dredging on the Columbia River. Up through 1927, Riedel was listed as a Corps dredge foreman. In 1929, the city directory listed him as a Port of Portland dredge foreman. In 1930, he was listed simply as a dredge foreman. The first listing for the Portland Dredging Company was in 1931 and its president was Henry L. Shepard, a manufacturer of electric dredge boosters and close friend to Polhemus. Riedel did not appear under the dredge company's name until 1933 at which time he was called the superintendent. By 1937, he was president. But in 1939, when the Willamette Tug & Barge Company was organized out of the Portland Dredging Company, he was listed as vice president and general manager. He later became the president and remained in that capacity until he died in 1957. After the second world war, Riedel organized a subsidiary company called Willamette Hi-Grade Concrete, a pre-mix concrete firm that went into competition with Ross Island Sand & Gravel. The Portland Gravel Company had been absorbed earlier.

After A. A. Riedel, Sr.'s death, the company reins were assumed by Arthur A. Riedel, Jr., age 26. In 20 years of explosive growth, the corporation has developed world-wide operations with 12 specialty divisions. Gross annual sales have risen from $750,000 to well over $100 million. The firm is still privately controlled with the Riedels owning most of the common stock.

An examination of the Polhemus estate raises some interesting questions. Out of a total valuation of $2.8 million, Polhemus had $480,000 in Willamette-Western and Willamette Hi-Grade securities.[60] The remainder of his portfolio was in blue chip stocks and bonds.[61] One is left wondering how a man who had never earned much in the course of his working life was able to leave such a sizeable estate — over twice that left by his former boss, Frank M. Warren, and that of his next boss, Portland General Electric executive, Franklin T. Griffith.

During his 16 years with the Port, with a salary that ranged from $5000 to $10,000 at the most, Polhemus became a protege of Frank M. Warren's. As a director of PGE, Warren exercised considerable influence within the utility company. In 1936, Warren rescued his associate Polhemus from the entanglements of the Port and got him appointed a vice president of PGE. Although Polhemus was elected PGE's president in 1940, the company was to be ensnarled in bankruptcy reorganization for a decade and in no position to pay even its president much more than $25,000 a year. During his executive tenure, Polhemus acquired less than $50,000 of PGE stock, so that there were few, if any, windfall profits in that relationship.

The estate appraisal indicated that Polhemus' 600 shares of Willamette-Western stock were originally issued in the name of the Willamette Tug & Barge Company. Carrying certificate #38, they must have been some of the earliest issued. His stock in the Hi-Grade Concrete Company carried certificate #6. After Polhemus' death in 1965, the executors of his estate spent several months negotiating a fair market value for his Willamette-Western stock which was closely held. Being childless and with his widow well provided for, Polhemus left 95 percent of his estate to his beloved *alma mater*, Stanford University. The executors drafted an agreement in the form of a four percent note which provided that the company purchase the stock held in trust by Stanford at the rate of $22,000 a year. With each of the 600 shares worth close to $700, it would take 20 years to conclude the transaction. Considering the fact that the note was executed in 1967, carrying a four percent annual interest payment to the university, unless the interest rate was subsequently negotiated upwards, Stanford came out on the short end of the deal. Commercial loan rates are currently more than double the 1967 rate.

In summary, it would appear that Polhemus and his father loaned money to A. A. Riedel, Sr., to establish the original Portland Dredging Company as a vehicle for purchasing equipment from the Port of Portland. The Port was under pressure to raise operating revenues and Portland business interests were continually chiding the Port for competing with local enterprise. In a strongly worded editorial, the *Oregon Voter* declared: "Our Port Commission is committing a serious error of policy in undertaking or supporting anything that tends to discourage private enterprise. . . "[62] By 1931, the commissioners were

254

officially on record as favoring private business operation "if and when private business can do the job being done by the Port."[63] The particular issue at stake related to tow boat service. The shipping interests, especially the States Steamship Company, and the private tow boat operators like Shaver Transportation wanted the Port to discontinue tow services. Later in the decade, Willamette Tug & Barge became a major lessor of harbor towage operations, particularly after Polhemus himself became a Port commissioner.

Selling publicly-owned equipment to private operators and relinquishing a long established public service such as towage to private operation were apparently considered good business practices by many of Portland's leading corporate executives. The 1933 investigations were to accuse the Port commission of wasting hundreds of thousands of dollars of public funds by pursuing such policies. It is difficult to believe that Polhemus' boss, Frank M. Warren, was not aware of what his protege was up to. For years, in fact, a story has been told that Warren himself had also loaned Riedel money, receiving stock in exchange, and that a portion of his wealth was also tied up in Willamette Tug & Barge stock. An examination of Warren's estate indicates otherwise. At least by the time of his death in 1947, there was no listing of Willamette Tug & Barge stock, or any reference to the company, in the estate appraisal.[64]

James Polhemus, on the other hand, through either direct investment or inheritance, ended up with a large block of Willamette Tug & Barge stock. It is not inconceivable to conclude, therefore, that much of Polhemus' wealth came from that original series of loans to Art Riedel's small tug and barge operation; and that over the years as the stock appreciated in value, Polhemus sold portions of it back to the Riedels and invested the proceeds in blue chip securities.

As a postscript to the story, it is worth noting that Frank M. Warren's son followed in James Polhemus' footsteps and attended Stanford University. Upon graduation, young Warren went to work for PGE, as an assistant to Polhemus. When Polhemus retired as president, Frank M. Warren, Jr., succeeded him in that capacity. To maintain the tradition, Polhemus was appointed to the Port commission in 1939 to be followed by Frank M. Warren, Jr., in 1951. Today, although no longer on the Port commission, Frank M. Warren, Jr., is chairman of the Board of the Portland General Electric Company.

THE BRIDGE BUILDER

Oregon Journal, April 13, 1924

Chapter 10

Power and Politics (3):
Government in the 1920s

Portland's urban society in 1925 was developing many of the same characteristics that had long marked the older, eastern cities of the country. Although not an industrial city, in contrast to Buffalo or Cincinnati, Portland was an integral part of the emerging industrial order. It felt the impact of forces that were nationwide in scope: Population changes, transportation and technological innovations and economic growth. The city was also affected by "the competitive drive for entrepreneurial success"[1] that tended to fragment cities functionally, politically and socially. The greater Portland community was being gradually divided, and even segregated, by class and race. Driven by the never ending quest for the dollar, economic growth and urban expansion became unplanned and unregulated. Government, which had traditionally served the interests of private property, was so fragmented and beset by personal and economic conflicts that it was incapable of exercising any meaningful control.

A Fragmented Government

Metropolitan fragmentation originated in the pre-industrial era. (Currently there are over 370 units of local government within the region.) When county boundaries were established 125 years ago, they created many overlapping political jurisdictions. Within the City of Portland alone, the government was divided among six governing bodies: A city council, a board of county commissioners, a port commission, a dock commission, a school board and a library board. At least two efforts were made in the post-war years to simplify this arrangement by means of consolidation. One was the proposed merger of the dock and port commissions in 1920 and the other was a proposed consolidation of city and county that the legislature refused to pass in 1919. A subsequent effort failed in 1927.

President C. C. Ludwig of the Portland City Club addressed the problem in an article in the *National Municipal Review*. How did Portland, he asked, meet the tests for the government of a large city?

"Three of the important criteria which Charles A. Beard has laid down for testing the government of a metropolitan area are:

1. Is the political jurisdiction of the city extensive enough to cover the entire urban area?

257

2. Are related functions performed by single or closely co-ordinated departments rather than by independent agencies?

3. Does the overhead control rest in a central accountable legislature which has available for use an ensemble of information on accounts, budgets, taxes, and indebtedness?

Portland cannot meet these requirements,"[2] concluded Ludwig. The only locally created public body that provided some measure of coordination was the Tax Supervising and Conservation Commission which exercised a limited jurisdiction over budget and tax levies.

Fifty years ago, the City Club was the only established organization in Oregon that showed any basic concern for the services not available to the suburban fringe. Police and fire protection were inadequate; building codes and health inspections were almost non-existent; street improvements were not subject to practical assessment procedures and proper sewer and water systems were scarce. Financial support for the port and dock commissions was inconsistent. Suburban taxpayers were not required to contribute to dock terminal development whereas they were compelled to support channel dredging and maintenance.

Wide diversity existed as to the method of selecting the six governing bodies themselves: Three were elected, two were appointed and one was a combination of *ex officio* and self-perpetuating. Similar variety existed in the method of selecting administrative officers. In the main, the city administrators were appointed while those in the county were elected. For example, the city police chief was appointed while the county sheriff was elected; the city treasurer was

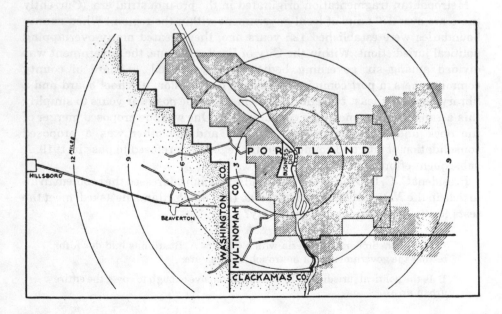

appointed and the county treasurer elected; and the same procedures applied to the engineers and attorneys.

One of the shrewdest schemes that was performed occasionally related to street improvements. County road improvements were paid for by the general taxpayer while the city street improvements were charged to adjacent property owners. On several occasions, city streets were converted temporarily into county roads. Once paved they were reconverted into city streets. It was obvious to the City Club's C. C. Ludwig that "it would be much better if all the streets of the city were under one legal jurisdiction."[3]

For diversity of control, the Willamette River bridges provided the choicest examples. The year 1925 was an important time for bridge development in Portland, with three under construction: The Burnside was being replaced and the Ross Island and Sellwood were being added. By 1926, Portland was to have three bridges owned by the city: The Broadway, Morrison and Hawthorne; three owned by the county: The Burnside, Ross Island and Sellwood; and one owned by the Union Pacific Railroad: The Steel Bridge. All were subject to a degree of fragmented authority.

The city-owned Morrison Bridge, for example, was built in 1904-1905 (replacing the first one of 1885) with the proceeds of a city bond issue. Major structural repairs were made at the expense of the county. The operation of the bridge span was a county expense while any repaving was done under the direction of the city owned municipal paving plant. The policing of the bridge was handled by the Portland Police Department.

In matters of tax and debt limits, similar diversity existed. Some of the levying bodies were subject to fixed mileage limitations while others were restricted by constitutionally established percentage limitations. A variety of bonded debt limits also prevailed. In most cases, bond revenues could be used only for capital purposes, while the Port of Portland could spend money for current operations. Again, in most instances, bond issues were subject to popular authorization, but in the case of the Port this was not true as long as the Port issued no more than $2 million worth of bonds in any one year.

Finally, there was greater diversity in matters of personnel control. The city and the school district operated under civil service while the county did not. City police were under civil service while their counterparts in the sheriff's office were largely political appointments. The county, in fact, was much more politically oriented than the city. The events of the 1920s and 1930s clearly revealed the politicization of county government. In many cases, county commissioners looked upon their "political" offices as a means of fattening their pocket books or of serving particular private economic interests.

The County Bridge Scandal

Running counter to the widespread anti-tax movement of the early 1920s, Multnomah County voters approved a total of $6 million in bonds for three new bridges. Traffic congestion on the existing five trans-Willamette bridges was severe. With 75 percent of Portland's residents living on the East Side, the pressure for more crossings easily won popular support. Between the summers of 1919 and 1924, trans-Willamette bridge traffic doubled, from 45,000 to 90,000 daily crossings. In the same period of time, county automobile registrations tripled, from 25,000 to 75,000. By 1925, the daily crossings would increase to 130,000 vehicles.

Apart from the need for additional bridges to serve the fast growing southeast sections of Portland, the Burnside Bridge (built in 1894) was badly deteriorated. Connecting the West Side's Washington Street thoroughfare with the East Side's Sandy Boulevard, the Burnside Bridge was the central structure of the whole trans-Willamette traffic configuration. When it was closed during the severe flood of January 1923 out of concern for its durability, traffic congestion reached crisis proportions.

Illustrating the problem of fragmented authority, the city council became increasingly angered by the county commissioners' unwillingness to take action once the voters had approved the bond issues. Delay followed upon delay until the bids were finally opened, appropriately, on April Fools' Day, 1924. To the surprise and dismay of the public, the county commissioners had accepted a joint bid by three companies and in the process had rejected a single bid for the Burnside job that came in $500,000 lower than the amount allocated for the Burnside Bridge in the joint proposal. The accompanying letter from the joint bidders stated:

"The enclosed proposals are to be considered as a whole in comparing them with any other proposal, or combination of proposals that may be submitted and these proposals are to be accepted or rejected on the basis of all or none."[4]

It was signed by the leader of the group, local contractor J. H. Tillman, a person with no bridge building experience, by an officer of the Union Bridge Company of Tacoma, and by T. Harry Banfield of the firm of Parker & Banfield. Banfield would later deny all charges of connivance and collusion directed at the bidders by investigative authorities. He and his partner had just launched their careers that would lead them down the road to prosperity and civic prominence. Banfield was to found the Iron Fireman Company in 1927 and be appointed to the dock commission in 1930.

With only a few hours of deliberation, the county commissioners approved the joint bid. According to some observers, such action revealed "a grievous want of elementary business knowledge and judgment."[5] The public reaction was vehement. Former governor Oswald West demanded the recall of the entire board of commissioners.[6] On April 4th, Pacific Bridge President C. F. Swigert filed suit against the three county commissioners, charging that the bids were "illegal, irregular and accepted without competition."[7] The following evening, the *News* headlined its front page with "Throw out the Rotten Bridge

Contract."[8] Three days later, Governor Walter Pierce ordered a state investigation of the whole matter. The *News* and *The Oregon Journal* took the initiative locally in giving "the span graft quiz" maximum publicity.

Of the three undistinguished Multnomah County commissioners, Dow V. Walker was the most prominent if for no other reason than his immense size. Walker had been a football star at Oregon State College early in the century. During and after his college years, he had played for the Multnomah Athletic Club which, like many similar athletic organizations, fielded competitive football teams in those days. Walker became so popular at the club that he was hired as a staff member and eventually secured appointment as club manager in 1908. Walker was a big, jolly, "hail fellow-well met type" who energetically

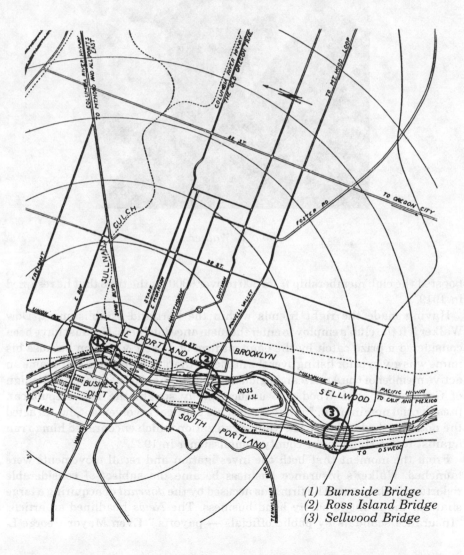

(1) Burnside Bridge
(2) Ross Island Bridge
(3) Sellwood Bridge

261

Dow V. Walker

boosted the club membership from 800 to over 6000 by the time that he resigned in 1919.

Having made the right friends within the Portland establishment, Dow Walker left the club's employ to enter the insurance business. He must have been considered a prize catch by the eminent firm of Jewett & Barton because his name was given prior listing over the names of the other partners. He became an active member of the American Legion and then managed the Oregon campaign of General Leonard Wood who unsuccessfully sought the 1920 Republican presidential nomination. In the course of his political involvement, he attracted the notice of the local Ku Klux Klan organization which encouraged him to run against Rufus Holman for county commissioner in 1922.[9]

From the moment that both the investigation and recall movements were launched, Walker's insurance business became the subject of considerable reportage in the press. The firm was accused by the *Journal* of acquiring a large share of the county's surety bond business. The *News* headlined an article: "Insurance scandals by public officials — payoffs." Even Mayor George L.

INQUIRY BEGINS MONDAY,
RECALL MOVE POPULAR

INVESTIGATORS TO SEEK FACTS

Official Inquiry Into County Mess and Insurance Scandal Starts Tomorrow.

Official investigation into the Multnomah county mess precipitated by the Willamette river bridge deal will be begun at the courthouse Monday, under direction of Attorney General Van Winkle, District Attorney Myers and John Collier, special counsel.

The investigators will take sworn testimony of persons who can throw any light on alleged irregularities practiced by any officials or others having dealings with them.

While the bridge deal is the primary reason for the inquiry, the many and persistent rumors of privileges enjoyed by insurance men and others because of alliances, open or hidden, with officials, will be investigated.

From this mass of testimony such facts as appear pertinent will be sifted for presentation to the grand jury.

Portland people have in the past 12 days been treated to an almost unequaled demonstration of what aroused public sentiment can do.

It is remembered that on April 2 the county commission opened the Willamette river bridge bids and six hours later awarded the contracts to a group of three contractors, who asked either that the bid of each be accepted or that all three be thrown out. There were no alternate bids on the Ross Island and Sellwood bridges. The bid of J. H. Tillman for the Burnside bridge was about $530,000 higher than the bid of the Pacific Bridge company, the only other bidder for the construction of this span.

JOURNAL SPEAKS FIRST

The first newspaper to voice the resentment of the public was The Journal. The resentment became a tidal wave of wrath. The commissioners bowed before it. Four days later they withdrew their signatures to the contracts. They endeavored to restore the bids to their status when the offers were first opened. They received to do what they had before omitted, secure the advice of the district attor-

(Concluded on Page Sixteen, Column Four)

County Mess Calendar

Forecast for this week in the investigation of the county mess includes:

Series of special hearings by official commission of inquiry to open in courthouse Monday. Grand jury investigation to get under way on basis of preliminary facts brought out at hearings.

Recall petitions directed against County Commissioners Rudeen, Walker and Rankin now bear 5000 signatures each after two days of circulation. Recall leaders predict that the rest will be obtained this week in time to file April 20 so that recall election may be held coincident with primary election, May 16.

County Commissioners Rankin and Rudeen arrange for public hearings on bridge deal at Central library hall, the first to be held Wednesday evening.

TILLMAN STATES HE WILL NOT QUIT

Contractor Declares He Is Ready to Begin Work on Burnside Span at Once.

"I do not intend to quit. I am ready to begin work on the Burnside bridge and complete the job on contract time."

Such is the pronouncement of J. H. Tillman, with whom the county commissioners signed a contract to build the Burnside bridge a few hours after opening the bids on April 2, and from which contract they withdrew their signatures a week ago.

Tillman declared to The Journal Saturday evening: "I have not surrendered the contract which I entered into with the county commissioners in good

(Concluded on Page Twelve, Column One)

5000 SIGNATURES ALREADY SECURED

One-Third of Requisite Number of Names Signed in Two Days.

Five thousand names have been secured for the petitions to recall County Commissioners Rudeen, Walker and Rankin, according to announcement late Saturday from Chester Fuller, recall campaign manager, from headquarters, 608-9 Medical building.

Fifteen thousand names are needed; 20,000 will be secured, Fuller added. The recall petitions had been in circulation two days. It was estimated that about 125 circulators were at work, of whom 23 were employed by the day by the recall committee. All others had offered their services without charge.

"At the present rate," Fuller continued, "we will have all the signatures desired within the next six days. I am inclined to believe that four days more may be enough, because the recall movement shows a gathering momentum that is remarkable."

The circulators of recall petitions also report unusual experiences.

"I secured 100 signatures Friday afternoon and Saturday," said one volunteer circulator. "To do this I interviewed 117 people. Only five declined to sign. Twelve were ineligible for one reason or another.

"But in nearly every instance I got a welcome that warmed my heart. People would ask me for the pencil as soon as they learned I had the recall petitions. I would hear expressions such as, 'I never heard of such high-handed procedure in my life as the county commissioners put us up against.' The commissioners have lost public confidence; now is a good time for them to stop. If they won't resign we will recall them.' The bridge program is big public business. Let's get men in as county commissioners whom we can trust.'"

IN OUTLYING DISTRICTS

Another circulator of the petitions had been out in the Woodstock and Lents districts. "I got 100 names," said he, "in little more than one day's working time. Out of the total number whom I interviewed not more than

(Concluded on Page Sixteen, Column Three)

Front page, Oregon Journal, April 13, 1924

Baker became involved. He was linked to another insurance agency, that of the Harvey Wells Company, in which his stepson had a major interest. City Commissioner S. C. Pier was likewise accused of conflict of interest involving the Wells agency. The *News* printed a front page editorial entitled: "Cure that's needed for Bridge Eczema and Insurance Pimples."[10] Walker was reported to have struck a deal with the large local Davidson Baking Company: The county would buy its bread if Walker, Jewett & Barton received the company's truck insurance. Walker's partner, Charles Barton, was charged with promoting a similar arrangement with a large printing firm. Barton was also accused by a former state deputy treasurer of offering to get the state to deposit $2 million of state funds in the U. S. National Bank if the bank would allow him to handle the matter for a $10,000 fee. Barton had been authorized previously to write surety bonds to protect the state on any funds placed in state depositories of which the U. S. National Bank was one.

By the date on which the state attorney general launched his official investigation, the charges were flying all over the county. The same day, the City Club endorsed a report that concluded: "The County Commissioners have forfeited the confidence of the public."[11] The most popular recall effort in Portland's history had already produced 70 percent of the required signatures. Attorney General I. H. VanWinkle heard charges that Walker and his partner Barton had an agreement with one of the bidders, the Union Bridge Company, that if the combined proposal was accepted by the county, Walker, Jewett & Barton would get the surety bond business. Charges were also made by witnesses that a $50,000 pay-off was involved if the three combined bidders were successful. A firm of consulting engineers, in collusion with the bidders, had already been paid $124,000 out of a $200,000 budget and the bridge construction had not even begun. A normal fee at that stage would have been $40,000.

One of the most serious charges related to the Ross Island Bridge contract. A sum of $500,000 had been added over and above the authorized bond total to change the location, width and structural material of the bridge. At the hearing on May 2nd, Commissioners Walker and Charles Rudeen, realtor Ferdinand Reed and City Health Officer Dr. George B. Parrish were revealed to have bought the two blocks in the Caruthers Addition on which the west approaches of the newly located Ross Island Bridge were to be built. Walker and Rudeen had sold their shares just before the bid opening to the same consulting engineering firm that had been overpaid. The hearing concluded that had the original bids not been rescinded, the county taxpayers would have been liable for $1 million of additional costs. It came out in the hearing that Dr. Parrish had made a similar investment on the east end of the Broadway Bridge a decade earlier. And according to a former member of the Walker family, as revealed to this author, Walker had purchased and kept several properties at the east end of the new Burnside Bridge. The income from these sources was to provide him his major financial support during the later years of his life.[12]

A grand jury was formed on May 5th and five days later the following

264

indictments were handed down: Commissioner Walker charged with bribery; Commissioner Rudeen charged with malfeasance and bribery; and consulting engineer R. C. Kremmers charged with accepting and offering a bribe. Commissioner R. H. Rankin was not indicted initially. Six days later all three commissioners were overwhelmingly recalled from office in spite of the efforts of the local Ku Klux Klan organization to generate support for its three proteges.

The trial began on June 6th and Walker had the services of one of Portland's most experienced trial lawyers, Robert F. Maguire. The blame seemed to fall more heavily on Rudeen as the initiator of the $50,000 bribe attempt. A sordid tale of influence peddling was related, depicting each commissioner holding out his hand for some kind of a pay-off, but the state had a difficult time establishing direct connections involving bribery. All of the evidence, relating to the bridge bids at least, was inferential. Witnesses supported Walker's contention that he was opposed to any money changing hands. One quoted Walker as declaring that "any man offering money for this is a fool." As someone commented, Walker did not need the bribe money because he was getting his pay-off through the insurance business. Judge Campbell implied as much when he acquitted Walker on June 11th. Walker had obviously known what was transpiring and he had still voted with and supported his fellow commissioner Rudeen. Even his lawyer Robert Maguire admitted that Walker had shown poor judgment, but that was all.

Commissioner Rudeen was also acquitted — rescued by a legal technicality. Defended by another of Portland's top trial lawyers, former senate president Dan J. Malarkey, the judge accepted Malarkey's contention that only the legislature had the constitutional right to authorize the governor to supersede the district attorney with the state attorney general who had signed the original indictments. By state constitution, the attorney general could not be a party to the proceedings.[13]

The recall election that had banished Messrs. Walker, Rudeen and Rankin brought three new faces to the county commission. The most prominent, socially and civically, was Amadee M. Smith, a long time associate of C. F. Swigert, J. O. Elrod and Franklin T. Griffith. An active real estate investor, Smith was to assume top executive positions with both Hyster and Willamette Iron & Steel after leaving county office in 1928 and then to be elected chamber of commerce president in 1933. Erwin A. Taft, who would serve for two years, was a grain merchant and close friend of former governor Oswald West. The third new member was Grant Phlegley who was to remain on the commission for ten years. A former clothing merchant, Phlegley had most recently been involved with a series of building and loan associations.

As with previous commissions, the new board was closely allied to the real estate trade. In fact, Smith would be succeeded in 1930 by Fred German who was one of the most active Portland realtors during the 1920s. Frank Shull would succeed Clay Morse in 1931. By that date, two of the three county commissioners, German and Shull, would also be officers of the Benjamin Franklin Savings &

Loan Association. County commission responsibility had never been — and would not be for many years — a full time effort. County commissioners were not prevented from carrying on their own business enterprises. Thus, although the command would change, the same kinds of problems would remain. Conflicts of interest were to be inevitable.

The new board of county commissioners addressed the bridge problem immediately. One of the world's leading bridge authorities, Gustav Lindenthal of New York, was hired to visit Portland and advise the commission on what steps to follow. He inspected all of the plans and made several suggestions including the provision for adequate approaches which he deemed crucial. New bids were let separately and the total amounted to almost $6 million, including the added costs of the newly designed approaches. C. F. Swigert's Pacific Bridge Company won the Burnside contract for $400,000 less than the original Tillman bid, but the cost of the new bridge did not include $800,000 for the removal of the old bridge. Approximate costs for the three bridge projects were as follows: Burnside, $3.4 million; Ross Island, $1.9 million; and Sellwood, $541,000. The Sellwood Bridge was limited to two lanes for reasons of economy despite professional advice to the contrary; it became totally inadequate within 40 years.

As often happened in Portland's history, the guilty who escaped conviction were not daunted by their past mistakes. Five years after his acquittal, Dow Walker was in trouble again. He was to be convicted in March 1929 of collusion with a government attorney who worked for the U. S. Alien Property Custodian's office, to obtain for less than true value the stock of the German heirs of E. Henry Wemme, the late founder of the Willamette Tent and Awning Company.[14] Walker was found guilty only of mismanagement, not the fraud and conspiracy for which he had been indicted. He was ordered to pay the Wemme estate $67,545 (see Chapter 13). Being insolvent, Walker hastily retreated across the Columbia River to Vancouver, Washington, where he could not be touched. Four years later he returned to Oregon and filed a voluntary petition for bankruptcy. In subsequent years, he managed to survive, free of jail, and gradually work himself into positions of some responsibility. He was living on the coast in 1945, at Newport, Oregon, when he was elected the National Commander of the Disabled American Veterans. Two years later, when he died of a heart attack, no mention of his previous troubles was recorded in the published obituaries.

Aspects of City Life

Was Portland a good city in which to live and work? Did it have a high quality of life? These and similar questions were continually posed and answered with strong affirmation by both the Portland Chamber of Commerce and its renowned ambassador of good will, Frank Branch Riley. Lawyer Riley was an eloquent speaker who made annual pilgrimages across the country, delivering

266

*Columbia Theater on S. W. Sixth Avenue, between Stark and Washington.
Current site of the First National Bank, Main Branch.*

his famous illustrated address, "The Lure of the Great Northwest." Each trip
cost approximately $45,000 and the money was raised from local business
enterprises under the direction of the chamber of commerce.

In a further effort to attract new business to Portland, the chamber drafted a
series of special reports, each tailored to a particular company. The Hooker
Chemical Company Report of 1928[15] was one of its most extensive undertakings.
Unfortunately for the chamber, the Niagara Falls corporation elected to locate
in Tacoma, Washington. The chamber suffered a similar rebuff from the Ford
Motor Company which was contemplating erecting at least one new plant on a
waterfront location somewhere in the Pacific Northwest. The original small
Ford plant on S. E. Division Street in Portland was destined to be phased out as
obsolete. Following a visit to Michigan, chamber manager W. B. Dodson wrote
Senator Charles L. McNary:

"There is a strong prejudice in the minds of the Department heads of the Ford
Company against Portland, and against this territory generally. They
seemed imbued with the thought that Portland had no future, that it was a

quiet, delightful place to live in when one desired peace and complete rest, but was not a city or a center of business."[16]

The chamber itself may have been partially at fault for creating Portland's peaceful image. Riley's lectures strongly emphasized the wildlife and mountain scenery. Even the special company reports highlighted the city's liveability. The qualities that seemed to receive the greatest attention were: The clean environment, the low cost of living, i.e., low taxes and utility rates, low mortality rate, high percentage of owner occupied homes (sixth in the U. S.), and a stable labor market.

"Among the important advantages which Portland offers for the development of manufacturing are its sound and stable labor conditions. Portland is an open city. The city has always been free from radical sentiment. The American worker predominates. A wide labor market of trained, serious minded, reliable, anti-radical workmen, has been built up. A large percentage of these workmen are home owners with the responsibility of families. Portland employers declare that strikes or lockouts of any serious proportions are impossible with the working conditions in Portland."[17]

Mayor George L. Baker could not have phrased it any better. The statement was hardly accurate but it revealed the extent to which Portland's business leaders had become prisoners of their own propaganda. Although the "American worker" may have predominated, nearly 20 percent of Portland's population was foreign born. According to the 1920 census, the number of foreign born Portland residents listed by place of birth were as follows:

Canada	6,458	Denmark	1,365
Germany	5,384	Japan	1,345
Russia and Lithuania	5,218	Switzerland	1,283
Sweden	5,060	China	1,244
England	4,021	Poland	909
Norway	2,915	Greece	896
Italy	2,847	France	529
Ireland	1,969	Hungary	519
Scotland	1,809	All other countries	3,014
Australia	1,599		
Finland	1,394	Total	49,778

The percentage of Oregon born Portland residents was 37.[18]

In the chamber publications no mention was ever made of Portland's non-white population. With the lowest percentage (2.1) of any major West Coast city, Portland's 2500 blacks rarely entered the consciousness of Portland's business and political leaders except when problems arose that related to public accommodations and residential districts. During the 1920s, several bars and restaurants had their licenses revoked by the city for permitting racial intermingling among the customers. Separate but not necessarily equal facilities was the unwritten rule enforced on the city's public accommodations.

Racial separateness was also a fact of life in Portland's impressive Community Service program which served the interests and needs of thousands of children and adults on an annual budget of only $8000. As an article in *The Playground* noted:

> "The colored citizens are not forgotten in planning the recreation program. With the assistance of the Park Board and the Young Men's Christian Association a tennis court was built for the exclusive use of colored players. Community Service received a request for assistance from a colored colony in Montavilla and a club was organized for the boys and girls of that district. The colored churches have helped by giving space for club meetings. They in turn have been assisted in giving entertainments and have been furnished with song leaders and loaned motion picture equipment. This last is much appreciated as most of the local motion picture theaters do not cater to colored patronage."[19]

After the first world war, when the center of the black community shifted to the northeasterly districts of Portland — in the vicinity of Albina — the Portland Realty Board became worried. An article appeared in the March 6, 1919 issue of *The Oregon Journal* with the headline "Realty Board Intends to Stop Sales to Negroes, Orientals." The members were instructed by the board's executive committee not to make any sales to such groups in "white residence districts." The rule was adopted, reportedly because of "the depreciation in property values which follows an influx of colored or oriental population." The realtors were quick to point out to the press, however, that they did not take this action "because of any prejudice against members of these races."[20]

It was purely a matter of good business. The preservation of property values for Portland's white population was clearly more important than any human concern for the feelings of non-white minorities or even of Orientals. This custom was embedded in the American tradition, wherein wealth, white power and influence determined the physical, cultural and social shape of Portland.

Local labor unions were equally prejudiced against the acceptance of black workers. The Portland Hotel fired its Negro waiters in its grille room because of union insistence that such jobs be reserved for white "American" waiters. Discrimination within the shipping industry was even worse. It was absolute. A letter answering a prospective longshoreman's application for employment, written May 8, 1922, stated unequivocally: "We employ white labor only."[21] Such a policy on the employers' part "firmly established the tradition of Negro exclusion from the longshore union."[22]

With the Pullman porters, however, conditions were to improve gradually after 1925 when A. Phillip Randolph in New York secretly organized the Brotherhood of Sleeping Car Porters. With a high proportion of Portland's adult black male population working for the railroads, the *sub rosa* establishment of a

Although a local chapter of the Brotherhood of Sleeping Car Porters was organized in 1926, it wasn't officially recognized until the mid-30s.

local chapter in 1926 must have been a welcome event. Black porters, like most other black workers, were often required to work under inhuman conditions for little pay. If they objected they were apt to be fired. Randolph was forced to keep his union membership list concealed until the Brotherhood received official recognition by the National Labor Relations Board in the mid-1930s. Premature publication of memberships in such a "radical" organization would have guaranteed dismissals.

In 1927, a prominent woman in the black community publicly described conditions that she observed in Portland. She sensed some limited progress:

"We have three thousand colored people, and we are gradually increasing. For the most part we are buying our homes in all parts of the city. We have one large hotel, a newspaper, three modern barber shops, a confectionary, beauty parlor for the wealthy people, a branch YWCA, three churches and two missions. From the economic standpoint it is very difficult for one of our race to find other than menial work, yet we have two postal clerks, one shoe clerk, two stenographers in white offices, a clerk of the Child Labor Commission in the Court House, three men in the express business, one dentist and physician, and two attorneys."[23]

270

Three months previously, the voters of Oregon had approved the repeal of a state constitutional provision — superseded 60 years earlier by the 14th and 15th Amendments to the U. S. Constitution — denying the right of suffrage to Negroes, Chinamen and mulattoes. A year earlier, the voters had repealed another provision that had denied the same groups any legal standing in the state. These were symbolic gestures, to be sure, but the fact that it took 60 years to erase them indicated the depth of prejudice against minorities that had so long existed in Oregon.

Most of the members of the Portland white community who inhabited the upper strata of business and society were probably unaware of their prejudices, at least against non-white minorities and Orientals. Anti-Semitism was a fact of life but rarely mentioned in polite society. Rumor had it that some club members of distant and diluted Jewish blood had found acceptance into the Arlington and Waverley Country Clubs, but few took such tales seriously. As visiting Englishman John Leader had commented in 1922, Portland's traditional leaders were "typical aristocrats." They were not really snobs, because they could not imagine that "anyone could look down upon them."[24]

A written response from one of Portland's "typical aristocrats" was revealing in this respect. Banker John C. Ainsworth, the veteran chairman of the city planning commission in 1930, was answering an inquiry from the exclusive Pacific-Union Club of San Francisco. Was former Portlander, Walker Kamm, of Jewish extraction? Ainsworth replied:

> "I beg to say that the family of course is very well known to me, as the grandfather [Jacob Kamm] was my father's partner in the transportation business on the Columbia River for over thirty years.
> He is the son of Charlie Kamm, only son of Jacob Kamm. There were three boys, the oldest was Jacob Kamm, Jr., polo player, a boy with red hair; Walker has dark hair and is the middle son; and Phil is the youngest of the three.
> There is no Jewish blood in any of his family. I think two brothers married two sisters — California girls."[25]

Ainsworth was no snob. In fact, he was one of the most enlightened and public spirited people in Portland. He was neither a clubman by temperament nor one to harbor obvious prejudices, but he was a product of his times. In 1930, clear lines of distinction were drawn between Jew and gentile, Caucasian and non-Caucasian. According to the authors of a study of Episcopal Church members whom they labeled "the Episcocratic class":

> "Anti-Semitism and the country club bloomed vigorously during the 1920s, one fertilizing the other. It was the high-water mark of the xenophobia of the Anglo-Saxons in America — their moments of most public power and also of greatest fear."[26]

Unlike most "Episcocrats," Ainsworth was secure personally and financially, living with his family unpretentiously in a comfortable, unextravagant city

**Business and Civic Affiliations of
John C. Ainsworth**

U. S. National Bank

Columbia Pacific Steamship Co.

States Steamship Company

Clark County National Bank

Pacific Telephone & Telegraph Co.

Portland General Electric Co.
(Portland Railway Light &
Power Co., PEPCO)

Pacific Power & Light Co.

Federal Reserve Bank of San
Francisco

Hawley Pulp & Paper Co.

Title & Trust Company

Portland City Planning Commission

Oregon Roadside Council

Oregon State Highway Commission

Save Oregon Scenery Association

Portland Symphony Society

YMCA

General America Corporation

Mid-Mountain Oil Co.
(Wyoming Western Oil Co.)

home. In all of Portland's history, few businessmen or bankers could equal his record of devotion to worthy civic endeavors.

In 1928, Ainsworth was interviewed for a biographical sketch and some of his responses are worth noting:

" 'What would be your definition of success?' this banker was asked. J. C. Ainsworth, University of California graduate, broad shouldered, athletic, smooth shaven, a dapper dresser, has an engaging personality. His hair is heavy and black and his hazel eyes are steady and observing. His smile is a particularly attractive one.

'Success to me is just the achievement of one's particular native propensities and disposition — sometimes called the vital urge. It has nothing to do with money making any more than with a lot of other things. Of course, if one's peculiar native propensities and dispositions are basically acquisitive and self-centered, then money making will be the achievement desired by that individual. It will become the one goal in life. . . . I think our trouble in the United States has been that we have judged success far too much by the money making yard stick. For it is only one of hundreds of success yard sticks. . . . The leaders of art and literature and religion and humanity have occupied far more imposing places in the world's history than the men whose only claim to distinction has been in wealth accumulation. Money making is perhaps an art and it requires industry and perseverance, but based on its influence on world life and thought in itself, it does not stand up with the other achievements of man.' "[27]

Wealth was obviously as important to Portlanders as to residents of any other city. In 1921, the per capita wealth of Portland was reported to be "probably greater than that of any city west of the Mississippi."[28] As in most of America's major cities by the mid-1920s, money making and affluence had exercised a fragmenting effect on community social life. The resultant social stratification was reflected in the upper income real estate developments in districts such as Dunthorpe, Eastmoreland, Westover Terraces and Portland Heights. To most of Portland's elite, business and society leaders who tended to live and work in an isolated world, quality of life was measured largely by private experiences and appearances, by formal social engagements and the close fellowship of church, club and outdoor activity. The establishment's civic endeavors were focused on the Art Museum, YMCA, Portland Symphony Society, Library Board, Reed College, and to a lesser extent on the Portland Public School Board. The city's leading Jewish families, drawn largely from the German ethnic element, followed a similar pattern of life except for their exclusion from the prestigious gentile clubs. The men's Concordia Club and the Tualatin Golf Club became centers of Jewish secular social activity. The symphony society was the one prestigious social organization that intermingled prominent Jews and gentiles.

For at least two of the society's board members, Ben Selling and John Ainsworth, Portland's quality of life was defined in broad terms, including a public dimension that transcended private experiences. Ainsworth's long service on the city planning commission kept him in contact with the diverse elements that comprised the city's urban fabric. His relationships with Mayor Baker were not always harmonious, but he stuck to the task patiently and doggedly — winning and losing battles for 15 years. The planning commission's early history will be discussed in the following chapter.

Baker's City

George L. Baker and John C. Ainsworth were men of markedly dissimilar background, personality and temperament. But despite their differences, they both intensely loved their home city of Portland. Each in his own way dedicated years of time and effort to making the city more liveable for its citizens. Never financially secure and largely self-educated, Baker identified easily with "the man in the street" whose aspirations and values he thoroughly understood.

"What kind of a man was Baker?" asked *The Oregonian*'s Frank Sterrett some years ago. "Well," said Sterrett, "you had to know him to really appreciate him.

> "He was a big man, very big. He had a large mouth and always had a pleasant smile. His hands always reminded me of a 12 to 14 pound ham. The most outstanding feature about him was his eyebrows. They were coal black and heavy. There was enough hair in that pair of eyebrows to stuff a pillow. Well, almost. George had many interests but the one closest to his big heart was the Shrine Hospital for crippled children. . . . He loved children."[29]

Baker's "pleasant smile" could vanish instantly, however, if and when confronted by those whom he considered "un-American." He had no use for the educated liberals who seemed to thrive on criticism of American life and its traditional values as he interpreted them. He strongly endorsed the city's policy of movie censorship. Although a lover of grand opera, he engaged in periodic confrontations with the city's arts organizations. The Portland Art Commission drew his ire in March 1926 when it criticized a gift of statuary that was placed in the Park Blocks across Salmon Street from the Arlington Club. Portland businessman, Joseph Shemanski, not himself an Arlington Club member, had donated a "little temple" that combined a fountain and a well. The commission questioned both its artistic merits and the cast stone material used. Baker responded with a blast, warning the commission that it would find itself out of business if it continued to criticize private gifts of this kind.[30]

A poor immigrant upon his arrival in Portland, Shemanski had wanted to show his feelings of gratitude to the city in which he had prospered. He was one of several who responded belatedly to Mayor Baker's proclamation to "make 1921 a year of gifts to Portland." Sponsored initially by the city planning commission, the proclamation was later printed with the addendum: "An inspiring appeal to the citizens of Portland, Oregon. From ancient times, public-spirited citizens have found satisfaction in offering gifts to their native cities."[31] Invocations of this sort, including his annual proclamations of "Beautification

Proclamation

Make 1921 a Year of Gifts to Portland

————

To the People of Portland:—

Let us make 1921 a year of gifts to Portland.

We are building a great city. Nature has endowed us with greater scenic gifts than are possessed by any other large city of our country. To make our city now as accessible, useful and beautiful as it should be is a task which commands the best efforts of every citizen

Automobile tourists and travelers are just discovering Portland Splendid state highways are nearing completion. Our Portland traffic ways and boulevards should be linked up with them without delay. We need more base-ball grounds, and larger playgrounds at our schools Every child, and adult, too, anywhere in Portland should have full opportunity for healthy recreation We need large, wild parks, and more mountain parks. We must depend upon the generosity of our citizens to save such spots and present them to Portland before the desired tracts are broken up or built upon.

In the past we have had some splendid benefactions The man of modest means who gave us the beautiful ten acre Shepherd's Dell Park, on the Columbia River Highway, did no less a permanent public service than he who gave us for all time the wonderful Multnomah and Wahkenah Falls, with their 740 acres of Park, or Terwilliger Boulevard, or the beautiful fountain at Second and Ankeny Streets.

The City Planning Commission for two years has been carefully listing the city's needs, and with the help of the Advisory Park Board has perfected a general boulevard and park system plan which should be completed as fast as possible All citizens who will participate in the campaign are requested to get in touch with the Commission's office, Room 424, City Hall, and see what the needs are Gifts to the city should be outright, without restrictions

I ask civic organizations to name committees to seek gifts for the city in cooperation with this Commission. At the end of the year public acknowledgment will be made to the organization bringing in what, in the opinion of the City Planning Commission and Advisory Park Board, is the most important gift to Portland in 1921.

Portland today is entering its greatest and most important era The recent order granting justice, so long denied the city, in freight rates to and from the Inland Empire, inauguration of the world port program authorized by the city and the legislature, the location of many new industries here, and other constructive steps being taken by city, county, and state, including plans for the 1925 Exposition in this city, bring promise of equally increased prosperity and responsibilities to all

Let us now do these generous and public spirited things, for which the city must wait many years unless it has unusual aid from its citizens.

February 23, 1921.   GEO L BAKER, Mayor

Week," came naturally to the showman Baker who loved nothing better than to stage a good performance.

Even though he could become easily angered and lose his temper, George Baker was never known to be arrogant in public encounters, not even with his adversaries. At a city council session during his last term of office, Baker was addressed by some of his former neighbors who lived near his old home on S. E. 28th Avenue. They complained because the mayor had sold his house to the Volunteers of America, an organization whose purposes they did not understand. They feared the "presence of diseased or vicious women," who would bring harm to the neighborhood. They asserted that they were prepared to file suit against both the city and the mayor personally. Baker left his chair gracefully and walked over to his irate former neighbors. He told them that the house was being used for widowed or deserted mothers, not "fallen women." They were working women who needed a place to live and leave their children with proper care while they were employed. Then Baker began to describe some conditions in the neighborhood to which he had never objected. He reminded one of the protestors that he (the protestor) had kept a cow and bull on his property. Another had sold a lot to someone who had built a small wood planing mill. Were not these activities more disruptive to the neighborhood than a home for needy mothers? The message got through. Baker smiled and the neighbors went home.

Each time that George Baker ran for re-election, he encountered some opposition, but the election of 1924 was probably the most bitter of his four campaigns. There were pockets of resentment over his handling of the IWW and his general attitude toward radicals. There were some who could never accept his tolerance of the Ku Klux Klan. But the most damaging criticism was directed toward the police department. As Commissioner of Public Safety, Mayor Baker had jurisdiction over police affairs. As early as the fall of 1920, *The Oregon Journal* had accused the police department of entering into a conspiracy with the bootleggers. Baker was charged with mismanagement and ineffective enforcement. On other occasions the police department was accused of "making a monkey out of the mayor" and "a goat out of Chief Jenkins," by willfully disobeying regulations and providing tips on raids. Regardless of what was charged, however, prohibition created a "no-win" contest for city and police officials. It bred police corruption and produced a number of wealthy crooks.

According to the late former police officer Floyd R. Marsh who served in the department in the mid-1920s, a certain amount of corruption existed even among city hall officials. On one occasion, Marsh was ordered to take some whiskey to a city commissioner who had a summer home near Mt. Hood. As a member of the vice squad, he delivered numerous cases of liquor to city hall. The basement of the city police station on S. W. 2nd and Oak became a wholesale liquor warehouse for the whiskey that was confiscated during the raids. Marsh was disheartened by having to arrest and jail people for possession of alcohol and then find "the city hall crowd" drinking it up.[32] On one occasion, the local W. C. T. U. discovered that a particular haul of high quality contraband had been stored in the basement of police headquarters for over three years. Chief Jenkins was compelled to order the dumping of 291 quarts of "fancy assorted liquors" into the sewer in front of the station.[33]

From the annual police reports, it would appear that the vice squad was sufficiently active. The public criticism stemmed primarily from the disposition of the seized goods. The 1923 report seemed average for the decade. Listed as confiscated were: 3227 quarts of beer, 160 gallons of hard cider, 17,572 gallons of mash, 92 stills, 18,695 pints of whiskey, 14,141 gallons of wine, 15 opium outfits, "many" packages of morphine, 15 ounces of cocaine. The report concluded with a statement that "there was introduced this year a 'sledge hammer squad' for the purpose of smashing known bootlegging places which could not be stopped by ordinary methods."[34] Throughout the 1920s, drugs were in constant supply. In 1925, the police confiscated 47,275 grains of narcotics. The Chinese were the chief offenders, but most Caucasian bawdy houses that were raided were reported to be in possession of extensive drug supplies, particularly cocaine and opium. Vice arrests averaged over 400 a year.

Portland was apparently a distribution point for bonded liquor coming in from Canada as well as moonshine made in local wooded areas. As many as ten bonded whiskey dealers operated within the city. The Canadian whiskey was brought up the Columbia River by high powered motor launches and taken to pick-up spots on Sauvie Island. Marsh reported as many as 100 speakeasies and 100 beer and wine parlors within the city. There must have been at least that many if the record of arrests for drunkenness was accurate. During the 1920s, annual arrests of this nature ranged from 2800 to 3600. Most of the speakeasies paid police protection money totalling over $100,000 a month. The patrolman on the beat normally received $10 a month. City Hall received its cut via two plainclothesmen who were regularly stationed around police headquarters, reporting directly to their bosses up the street.[35]

Officer Marsh was distressed by the treatment accorded "the poor working class of the Italian people" of South Portland who were unable to pay off the authorities. They were usually the ones arrested and prosecuted. One episode was instrumental in convincing Marsh to leave the department. He had arrested an Italian widow with three small children for being in possession of a 10 gallon keg of wine that she had made from her own grapes. She was unable to appear in court for her hearing because one of her children was sick. The judge nearly sentenced Officer Marsh to jail for failure to produce the accused.

Marsh's account noted that gambling payoffs totalled about $50,000 a month and that the city's 35 "sporting houses" spent $20,000 a month for protection. Although the vice squad encountered moments of distress and discouragement, Marsh concluded his narrative with the assertion that "the work was interesting and exciting."[36]

Despite the corruption, the police did a comparatively adequate job of generally enforcing the prohibition laws. During the national Shriners' convention in Portland in June 1924 — when Mayor Baker was the Illustrious

Essex police radio patrol cars — on S. W. Oak
Front door to headquarters

Potentate of Al Kader Temple — *The Oregon Journal* quoted one of the visiting officials as remarking that prohibition was so well enforced in Portland that whiskey was "$30 a case higher than in Seattle."[37] One might deduce from this remark that Portland's police were simply asking and getting a higher than normal price per bottle from their well stocked basement warehouse.

Neither Mayor Baker nor Chief Lee Jenkins was ever connected personally with either receiving or condoning payoffs, but they did face criticism for not effectively stamping out the practice. One incident a month before the November 1924 election date threatened to hurt the mayor's campaign. John L. Lowe, cited as a "notorious colored bootlegger," was known to have some influence within the police department. His wife was arrested for drunken driving and hitting another motorist. A police captain, assigned to Mayor Baker's office, interceded in her behalf. When the press reported the affair, Baker suspended Capt. Harry Circle for ten days.[38] No further action was reported in the newspapers.

It has never been possible to rate the overall efficiency of Portland's police department during the 1920s because the city did not keep an adequate record of crime statistics. As reported in one national study published in 1929, using 1925-1927 data, only Baltimore, Berkeley, Cleveland, Detroit, Los Angeles, Pontiac and Rochester, N. Y., made any effort to keep detailed records.[39] According to the police data that were published annually, Portland arrests averaged approximately 23,000 a year during the decade. For whatever it is worth, the Auto Theft Division reported an amazingly high level of recoveries, nearly 98 percent. In 1926, for example, 1422 automobiles were recovered out of a reported number of 1445 stolen. Chief Jenkins was proud of this record and credited his auto patrol system for the achievement. He also instituted the use of radio prowl cars, manned with plainclothesmen, "to pick up suspicious characters on the street and bring them in for investigation and identification by fingerprinting."[40] Whenever crime was expected "to be at its peak," during the fall and winter months, relief officers were ordered to duty. Shotgun squads were also organized to guard bank and payroll transfers. A Night Squad was put into service with two radio cars to prowl public places, "such as athletic events, wrestling matches, etc."[41]

Considering the size of its force, the Portland Police Department probably did as effective a job as any in the country. For over 30 years, Portland had been told that it had fewer policemen per thousand of population than other cities of its size or larger. During the decade of the 1920s, the force averaged 375 in number. Seattle, with a 15 percent greater population, had 65 percent more policemen. Some might argue that perhaps Seattle had a higher crime rate necessitating a much larger police force, but crime statistics would not bear out such a contention. In fact, the press was continually critical of Portland's crime incidence. In January 1921, the *Telegram* had cited the force's numerical deficiency when it claimed that people were afraid to walk the streets at night.[42]

Mayor Baker was able to dispel most of the criticism of police operations but two articles in the local press threatened to undo him. The *Journal* published an account in April 1924 describing how the police department had been providing a daily list to the Harvey Wells Insurance Company of names and addresses of all uninsured automobiles figuring in traffic accidents. The practice had begun in 1921 when Baker's stepson, Brace Galloway, had visited Chief Jenkins and received authorization to inspect the daily accident rosters. Galloway had a 40 percent interest in the agency. The practice was allowed to continue until Galloway's death early in 1924. The competing insurance companies and their agents, led by young Phil Grossmayer, loudly complained and an investigation resulted. Baker vehemently denied any conflict of interest on his part. He stoutly maintained that he had no personal involvement in the company although he was quoted as having told a friend that he was receiving some insurance business income. Ironically, the same Phil Grossmayer, who cried "foul" in 1924, was himself to play the same game for even larger stakes during the mayorship of Earl Riley in the 1940s. It came out subsequently that Galloway had also pressured the police department to lease space in the large new Imperial Garage for its fleet of cars. The Wells agency carried the insurance on the whole operation.[43]

The second blast at Mayor Baker, launched by the *News*,[44] concerned a $7100

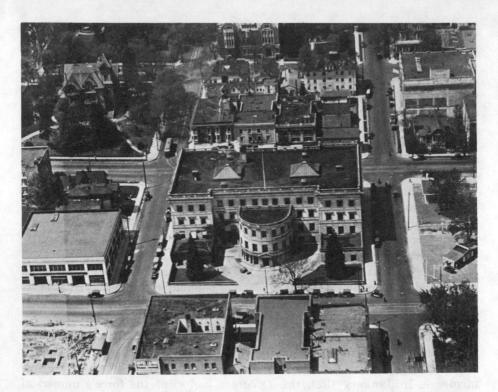

City Hall in the 1920s. The University Club can be seen at the top center, and the late Sen. J. N. Dolph home on the upper left, current site of the Equitable Savings & Loan Association.

slush fund raised by Portland business leaders under the direction of PEPCO president Franklin T. Griffith. According to the *Oregon Voter* which thoroughly investigated the matter, the business leaders had heard rumors that Baker might not seek re-election because he could not afford to live on his $6000 salary. When Baker was informed of Griffith's intentions he felt that it would be improper to accept such a contribution. Griffith and his associates decided they would instead pay off Mayor Baker's home mortgage which amounted to $7100. After completing this task, a committee went to the mayor's home and burned the mortgage in Baker's fireplace. Although the *Voter* editor questioned the propriety of the procedure, he asserted with confidence that had the public known the truth about the mayor's financial hardship, thousands of dollars would have flowed into the coffers to help a mayor "whom we all love in spite of his shortcomings." The "ordinary people were given no chance to participate. . . . The privilege of giving to a good cause was monopolized by the few."[45]

Baker's opponent in the mayoralty race, Rufus Holman, did not look upon the contribution with such charity. "They may call it a tip; a gratuity, or explain it any way they can; but I call it a bribe. Among those who made up the swag was Franklin T. Griffith, president of the PRL&P Co., whose franchise is soon to expire."[46]

Baker had been too close to Griffith, some critics like Judge Henry McGinn had long claimed. Griffith had been one of the major backers of the Chicago Opera Company's tour to Portland the previous February. The famous visit of the world renowned opera star Mary Garden received even more notoriety when Baker kissed her publicly upon welcoming her to his city. Baker had promoted the musical event and in true showman fashion had exploited it to his own advantage.

The *Oregon Voter* summed up the feelings of a majority of Portland's electorate when it officially endorsed Baker in August 1924:

> "In spite of his press-agented grandstanding, in spite of his sporadic and political police raids, and in spite of his issueless senatorial campaign . . . Mr. Baker has given Portland an administration that compares favorably with the administration of other large American cities. Since he is no student of government, he may miss many fine points in management of the city's affairs, but he has assisted in keeping Portland in a favorable light before the country. That has come to be a function of American mayors. The people expect it from their mayor. Mr. Baker has supplied the color and dash which a more prosaic but nevertheless efficient business man might not possess."[47]

Whether John C. Ainsworth and his right-hand man on the city planning commission, Pacific Power & Light executive John A. Laing, would have fully endorsed the *Voter*'s editorial is difficult to determine. Both men must have voted for Baker who had appointed them to the commission. On the other hand, Ainsworth and Laing became increasingly disturbed by Baker's attitude toward the role of city government. On more than one occasion, Baker had stated that the council was merely a clearing house for public opinion, and he included himself as a member of the council. The planning commission leaders believed that plans had to be "translated into common good, crystallized and developed intelligently." No plan could be undertaken without leadership. If the mayor and council waited upon public opinion to express its demands, declared Laing, they would not take any active part in the city's development.[48] In spite of Baker's showmanship and "color," he was a passive mayor when it came to promoting new policies and programs designed to solve pressing urban problems. Mayor Baker seldom initiated any program of substance although he took credit for some of the more imaginative developments undertaken during his administration. One such activity was the city's public market on S. W. Yamhill Street.

The Central Public Market, originally named the Carroll Market after the *Evening Telegram*'s editor John Francis Carroll, opened initially in May 1914. Within two months the city assumed control and before long both sides of Yamhill Street from Fifth to Third Avenues were covered with open stalls. Baker was a city commissioner at the time and took credit for the city's purchase of the successful commercial enterprise. It was here in 1915 that Fred G. Meyer, who was subsequently to become the Northwest's largest food shopping center operator, launched his illustrious career. Before changing his name during the war, Meyer was known as Fred Grubmeyer. He opened the Java Coffee Company in a market stall and lived at the nearby YMCA. In 1916, he opened another stall under the name of Grubmeyer & Hogan to sell tea, and in 1917 groceries were added in a third stall.

Portland's Yamhill market became nationally famous. One Portland visitor in 1924 was quoted as saying that "I have seen markets in many cities in both America and Europe, but I have seen no market that compares in all ways with the Yamhill market." One could find almost anything to buy, "from brooms to radishes. . . . American markets are more carefully operated than the French."[49] Some years later, Oregon writer and historian Howard McKinley Corning recalled with relish his early experiences at the "colorful Yamhill Market. Here much of the Portland populace shopped for farm produce, fresh vegetables and flowers. . . . It was a . . . teeming strip of small commercial activity."[50]

The Yamhill Public Market

282

Chaos would have reigned on Yamhill Street were it not for another local institution, Traffic Officer Pasquale Tusi. Officer Tusi directed the activities of thousands of cars and people daily as they squiggled their way through the crowded labyrinth. He kept cars from becoming tangled up, cross-tied and telescoped. He was noted for his efficiency, kindness, consideration and uncompromising execution of the law. His major duties were six in number: (1) Compelling one-way traffic (introduced earlier in 1924 throughout the downtown); (2) enforcing the 15 minute parking limit; (3) keeping the peace between disputants over parking privileges; (4) maintaining an eye on babies left in the cars while their mothers went to market; (5) showing inexperienced drivers how to back into small holes; and (6) directing strangers to particular market stalls.[51] Tusi was only a three year veteran in 1924 but he was one of the most professional officers on the force. He knew everyone — their names, faces and children. He obviously cared about his job and the quality of his performance.

Unfortunately, the market's city management did not match the quality of service provided by traffic officer Tusi. The sanitary conditions were appalling, and Mayor Baker was partially responsible. Under pressure from several citizen groups, the mayor appointed a public commission to survey the market operation. The report was so damning that it was not published — not even dated for that matter. But Mayor Baker did institute a few changes, including the hiring of an experienced non-political market master. The report cited the following conditions:

(1) It was not an uncommon occurrence for unsuspecting purchasers to have palmed off on them spoilt fruits and vegetables.

(2) When the early morning garbage wagons arrived, the entire street presented a filthy appearance, with the air exuding an indescribable stench. The street was piled with garbage, less than half of it having been placed in cans.

(3) Stall renters threw their trimmings on the street.

(4) It was a common practice of the Japanese and Chinese to wash their vegetables in the polluted gutters. Equally unsanitary was the amount of expectoration on the streets with food not far out of reach.

(5) Storeroom conditions were found to be worse than those on the streets. Rotten vegetables and fruit were thrown about in boxes of paper and the floors were littered with decayed matter of every description, with innumerable flies buzzing and crawling all over everything. So much rotten garbage was found in one spot that the stench nauseated one of the commission investigators.

The commission cited other abuses. Growers were using the markets as wholesale distribution centers in violation of the purposes for which the market was originally established, namely, to bring the consumer into direct business relations with the producer in order to reduce consumer prices. The commission recommended that the market master have authority to fix maximum prices

283

only. "There must be no minimum." The report concluded with the demand for "a competent administrator."[52] Under any set of conditions, managing the Yamhill Public Market was an exhaustive and complicated responsibility. In a given year, over 75,000 producers used the facilities.

General City Services

The first comprehensive comparative rating of American city services appeared in the July 1929 issue of *The American City*. Using data from the two year period 1926-1927, Portland ranked 22nd among 159 cities with populations of 30,000 or over. But among the top 25 cities in total population — of which Portland was number 25 — Portland ranked fourth, behind San Francisco, Seattle and Cleveland. Generally speaking, the larger cities ranked higher and those on the Pacific Coast the highest. As a group, the southern cities ranked lowest, with Nashville, Tennessee, at the bottom. With a maximum possible score of 100, Oak Park, Illinois, led with 87.84. Portland received a score of 84.0 against a national average of 77.82. As might be expected, Portland received its highest points in low death rate, and school and library services. It was above average in parks, total street paving and garbage collection; average in street cleaning and below average in sewer services and fire losses. Eliminated from consideration along with police services were waterworks, charities, hospitals and street lighting,[53] although the *American City* three years previously had cited S. W. Broadway as "one of the best lighted streets in America."[54]

The highest rated cities were spending approximately 40 percent of their total tax revenues on schools. According to a Federal Bureau of Education study, Portland had "developed one of the finest and most progressive school systems in the country."[55] The school "atmosphere" was cited for its "progressive people." Superintendent Rice was "considered in the East to be one of the best in the country" and the board of school directors was "one of the best."[56] In 1927, Portland contained approximately 200 public and private schools and institutions of higher learning, including Columbia University (now the University of Portland), Reed College, the University of Oregon Medical School, and the colleges of Dentistry, Optometry and Pharmacy of North Pacific College. Pre-collegiate school enrollment totalled approximately 65,000 students.

The school expansion of the 1920s reflected the growth in residential construction, most of it on the East Side of the city. According to Mayor Baker's figures, over 26,000 residences were built in the period from 1920 to 1928.[57] A development of this magnitude necessitated the expenditure of approximately $12 million in sewer and street construction, with special attention given to street widenings.[58] As City Engineer Olaf Laurgaard commented in 1931, "No other city engineer in the country has widened as many streets as I have."[59] This judgment was confirmed by St. Louis consultant to the planning commission, Harland Bartholomew, when he wrote: "No city of Portland's size did so much in

Lincoln High School (1911-1951), served the West Side and Portland Heights. When the new Lincoln High School was built, the original building became the site of Portland Community College and the main building for Portland State College. Located in the Park Blocks, "Ol Main" anchors the northeast corner of the extensive Portland State University campus.

Miss Catlin's School for Girls in 1926, located in the Westover Terraces development of Northwest Portland. The Catlin School became a nationally prominent independent school, known today as the Catlin Gabel School. The school moved to the suburbs in 1968, the buildings were demolished and a city park occupies the site.

the way of street openings and widenings in the period 1917-1931."[60]

Beginning in 1924, the cost of street widenings was financed on "the 75-25 plan." The plan placed 75 percent of the improvement cost upon the entire city through bond issues, while 25 percent was assessed against the benefited property. With sewer construction, however, the benefited property owners were often expected to assume a larger financial responsibility, depending on the nature and location of the project. The Front Street Intercepting Sewer and Drainage Project, also called the Waterfront Improvement Project because it combined the construction of the sewer with the building of the harbor seawall from Jefferson to Glisan Streets, was assessed entirely to the property owners benefited. No portion of the $2.5 million cost was paid from the general fund or by the city's taxpayers.

Excluding this project, in which considerable pressure was applied against the reluctant property owners, no sewers were constructed unless 50 percent or more of the affected property owners so petitioned or unless the public health absolutely required the immediate construction of a project. Adhering to a policy of this sort may have been responsible for Portland's lower than average rating in sewer services. Baker defended Portland's traditionally conservative sewer construction policy when he declared in 1929: "I have consistently followed the policy of not burdening the property owners or taxpayers with unnecessary expenditures."[61] Three years later, however, the mayor was to be accused of having made a secret deal with Julius Meier, and the Ladd, Corbett and Mead estates, for the city to reimburse them for their Waterfront Improvement expenditures through public acquisition of their waterfront properties on which was built the new Public Market Building, later known as the Journal Building. This controversial matter will be discussed in Chapter 16.

The person who deserved credit for Portland's above average rating in street paving was commissioner A. L. Barbur, after whom Barbur Boulevard was named in the 1930s. Barbur served with distinction for 16 years as Commissioner of Public Works. Prior to his city council tenure, Barbur had been city auditor for a decade. He was a truly dedicated public servant who was not afraid to provide positive leadership, often in the face of severe obstacles and stubborn opposition from private interests.

Barbur's pet project was the municipal paving business. Post-war costs and increased demand for repair work moved the council to experiment with its own municipal paving operation. A site was leased and a small repair plant built. After the plant had been in operation for several months, it was requisitioned by the Bureau of Parks to pave Terwilliger Boulevard, the scenic parkway that ran south through the lower West Hills. The job was completed, for a distance of one and one-half miles, for $.622 per square yard as compared with the prices asked by private contractors for bitulithic surfacing that ranged from $1.25 to $1.45 per square yard. The savings to the taxpayers on this piece of work alone was more than the total cost of the original paving plant.

Because of persistent demands from the public for lower prices, Barbur convinced the city council to go more deeply into the paving business. A new and fully equipped paving plant was erected on city-owned waterfront property adjacent to where the Pacific Power & Light Company's steam generating plant is currently located. Opened in 1920, the plant saved the city taxpayers $175,900 in the first two years. Private contractors accused the city of promoting "socialism" by competing with private enterprise, but Barbur was unperturbed. The city costs were 50 percent under what private contractors would have charged. During the same two year period, the city not only paid off the $93,000 cost of the plant but showed a $40,000 profit as well.[62] Upon his retirement in 1933, Commissioner Barbur was proud to announce that the asphalt operation had saved the city over $1 million in 15 years of service.

Garbage collection was another matter. Despite the city's fairly high rating nationally, garbage disposal was a continual problem that drew local criticism from all directions. In a lengthy report issued by the City Club in November 1922, the methods of collection and incineration were sharply condemned. The method of collection was "a form of the scavenger system," described as "a collection of licensed individual contractors." Licenses were a mere formality. There was no actual control over the 82 collectors, no control over their character, equipment, routes or charges which ranged from 50 cents to $1 per month for weekly collections. The city had no record, furthermore, of the routes

Terwilliger Boulevard (Hillside Parkway) in the mid-1920s

being serviced. All the city authorities knew was that the incinerator plant was completely inadequate. To accommodate the excess, mixed wastes were dumped in various locations "in a manner so unsightly and unsanitary that any private concern doing the same thing" would have been "liable to prosecution for maintaining a nuisance."

After the war, the price of garbage for swill had dropped 75 percent; nobody wanted it. The principal dump was north of the incinerator plant at Guild's Lake, but due to the Port's dredge fill project the available space was limited. Inflammable rubbish was burned in the open and since it was usually mixed with garbage, offensive odors were created. Decaying garbage was not covered and the water of the lake was foul "beyond description." Furthermore, the whole place swarmed with flies and was alive with cockroaches.[63]

Mayor Baker and the council majority did not favor a new, enlarged incinerator plant as long as there were enough gulches available to receive the garbage. Marquam Gulch was the second principal dump. The area was later reclaimed as Duniway Park. Other dumping grounds included the Greeley Avenue Cutoff and areas adjacent to Alberta and Fremont Streets in Northeast Portland's Albina district. The neighborhoods complained but to no avail. Nearby homes were not safe "from migrating rats, bed-bugs and cockroaches." The City Club strongly recommended the construction of a new incinerator of at least 200 ton capacity — 25 percent larger than the old one — a plant that would generate steam for heating and industrial purposes. In 30 years time the plant would be fully amortized through annual net revenues of approximately $5000.

The City Club recommendation was not followed, at least insofar as municipal construction of a steam generating plant was concerned. But in 1927, the city did contract with the Nye Odorless Company to build a new incinerator that Mayor Baker was confident would serve "all West Side garbage for many years." At the same time, the mayor encouraged the planning for a second incinerator to serve the East Side. He suggested a site at N. E. Columbia Boulevard and 42nd Avenue that was termed "ridiculous" by the *Telegram*. Foreseeing the city's future problems more clearly than most, the *Telegram* urged the city council to "make a serious study of the whole matter of garbage disposal on a metropolitan scale."[64] It would be decades before this recommendation was implemented. As *The Oregonian* had remarked 30 years earlier: "The old, old question of 'What shall we do with our garbage?' which, like Banquo's ghost, or the smell of a garbage dump, 'will not down', nor be downed, is . . . coming to the surface again."[65] It is still coming to the surface in 1979.

Taxes

Like garbage disposal, taxes and tax rates were continually under fire during the decade of the 1920s. Oregon's bankers and business leaders were made particularly unhappy when the state's voters narrowly approved — by a margin of 516 — a state income tax referendum in 1923. A well financed repeal campaign was successful in 1924. The issue arose again in 1926 and 1927, and in both cases, the voters narrowly rejected a return to a state income tax. It was not until Governor Meier's administration during the depression that the income tax became a permanent mechanism for raising major state revenues. It may have dawned on a majority of Oregon's voters that the top five percent of the state's population had over 30 percent of the state's disposable income. Although nobody liked taxes, the progressive income tax was still the fairest method to raise needed state revenues and the rich were the ones most able to pay the higher rates.

In 1931, corporations complained that their rate was far too high; that it discouraged industrial investment and development. In proportion to individual income taxes, corporate taxes totalled nearly 30 percent more. But total revenues raised from both income tax categories were relatively minor when compared with the total raised by property taxes. As several studies during the decade indicated, the major reason for voter dissatisfaction with Oregon's taxes was "not in the size of the load, but in the maldistribution of the burden."[66] Oregon's public bodies, including the City of Portland, relied much too heavily on the property tax as a source of revenue. Given the imbalance of the tax burden, however, Portland still ranked low on a national scale. In 1924, for example, Portland's property tax per capita was $27.14, as compared with Seattle's $41.00, San Francisco's $40.17, Los Angeles' $45.32 and Boston's $54.21.[67] The comparative ratios remained fairly constant until the early 1930s when assessed property values decreased rapidly.

Regardless of what the rest of the nation was paying, Portlanders always felt overtaxed. In a meticulously documented study, University of Oregon economist James H. Gilbert showed in 1924 that Oregon voters were "not overtaxed, overburdened and overbonded." Gilbert was making a case for transferring the load from the property tax to income and business taxes which he felt to be more equitable. But the voters felt otherwise in 1924 at least. They were unable to lower their property taxes and so they wiped out their income tax. Gilbert blamed part of the property tax problem on the fact that Oregon's assessed values were unduly low, more so than the average American state. In many western states, i.e., Colorado, Utah and Nevada, assessments approximated 100 percent of market value. In Oregon they fell to as low as 60 percent.[68]

For almost seven years following the end of the war, Portland's city revenues became increasingly inadequate to perform the required services. The 1913 reform charter limited taxes to 8.0 mills for general purposes, but it authorized levies for special purposes — levies that required special elections. In 1926, the general fund budget was $6.9 million and the total expenditure budget was $12.8 million. The city was facing some serious reductions in essential services, of as much as 20 percent, unless the 1927 general fund revenues were increased beyond the existing charter limit. Not only did the post-war inflation take its toll, but in the ten years of prohibition the city had lost $4 million in liquor license fees and an additional $1.6 million in related miscellaneous revenues. To counter this loss, special levies had raised $5 million, but the city was still left with a net loss of $600,000 during a period of spiraling inflation.

The voters had rejected any further levies in May 1926, so a new package was put together and offered to the city electorate on July 1, 1926. The chamber of commerce, the business community and the City Club worked hard for its passage. In essence, the 8 mill limitation was to be repealed. In its place was to be inserted the state constitutional provision allowing a six percent annual increase on the base levy of the previous year without further authorization from the electorate. In addition, certain maximum special levies were to be approved for the years 1927 through 1936, scaled down each year from 3 mills to .2 mills. The measure carried by a margin of three to one. Many ads had been run in the newspapers, but perhaps the best tactic used was the placing of placards on all the light poles with the words writ large: "Shall this and 900 other street lights be discontinued for lack of funds?"[69]

Portland city services had been saved in the nick of time. By 1928, general fund revenues reached $9 million with the total budget hitting $16 million. The Johns Hopkins study of city services did not attempt to relate tax rate with quality of service, but given the fact that 1927 financial data were used for most of the study, had Portland not passed the new tax amendment, the city most likely would have ranked lower on the national scale. As a matter of interest, for the sake of comparison, in the fifty year period following 1928, the city's population was to increase by 20 percent, the general fund expenditures by 1300 percent and total budgetary expenditures by over 2000 percent.

Taxes and Utilities

In August 1930, the *Oregon Voter* published a detailed comparison of Portland and Seattle tax rates. "If Seattle had enjoyed Portland tax rates during the last ten years," explained the *Voter*, "the taxed property within its city limits would have paid $45,467,000 less property taxes than it did pay within the same ten years." The *Voter* went on to point out that the reported combined replacement cost of Seattle's municipal lighting and street railway systems was $47 million.

> "They were built or acquired 'without cost to taxpayers.' It is a mere coincidence that the excess taxes in a municipal ownership city in ten years aggregate a sum equalling the entire cost of its municipal ownership projects."[70]

The *Voter* was raising an issue that was going to be debated every time the question of public ownership was to surface in subsequent years. The Portland Chamber of Commerce, through its own publications and that of the *Oregon Voter*, used every opportunity to point out that public ownership of a utility did not save the rate paying taxpayer any money; that in fact, publicly-owned utilities cost the consumer more in the long run. Publicly-owned utilities paid no

290

taxes, whereas the private utilities paid millions of dollars annually to state and local taxing authorities. An additional advantage of the private utilities, declared Franklin T. Griffith on numerous occasions, was the wide opportunity for investment offered to Oregon citizens, an opportunity to become a partner in a great enterprise and to share in its financial rewards. One ad in the *Oregon Voter*, run by the Portland Railway Light and Power Company, was headed "Invest at Home." Portlanders were told: "If you can save 34¢ a day you can become a profit sharer in this big and growing Public Utility."[71] Implied in such ads was the notion that the electric power consumer who became an investor in his local utility actually saved on his utility bill an amount equal to his seven percent annual dividend. For one who could not afford such an investment, such a saving was obviously impossible.

Oregonians were to be torn in every direction over the question of private versus public ownership of utilities. Julius Meier was to win the governorship on a public power plank in 1930. But the private utilities were to fight back with a vengeance. The issues that most private utilities rarely mentioned — matters that concerned the Oregon State Public Service Commission — related to the value of the service to the patron who was not an investor, the patron's ability to pay, and the service afforded for the rate received. All of these matters and more will be considered in Chapter 14.

The arguments used by the private power companies were never applied to Portland's municipal water system because the city acquired its waterworks in the days before large private utilities were organized. The Portland Gas and Coke Company was the only major utility to antedate the organization of the Portland Board of Water Commissioners. The city's municipal water system was developed slowly and soundly, financed by bonds that were amortized out of user fees. At no time were the capital needs ever so large that they posed a burden to the taxpayer. Portland had its chance to acquire a municipal lighting system for less than $200,000 in 1901.[72] Had it done so, it might have been able to finance a full blown public power operation out of user fees, following the practice of the city water department. Taxes would have played a minor role, if any, in the whole development.

In 1926, Portland's municipal water system was considered to be one of the finest in the United States. Not only was it one of the cheapest in user charges but it was unequalled in quality and quantity for a city of Portland's size.[73] The same could not be said for the services supplied by the private utilities, especially by the Pacific Telephone and Telegraph Company. Throughout the 1920s, that utility was accused of gross overcharges and poor service. The gas and electric power utilities were in turn to be accused of watering their assets and of deriving excessive profits from their operations. But they all managed to survive, relatively intact. Along with the railroads, they became the largest property owners in Portland.

Throughout the decade of the 1920s and for many years thereafter, taxes, rates, services and profits would be intermingled with the arguments in favor and against public ownership. The debate is still going on.

292

Chapter 11

Planning for the Auto:
City Planning and Development
in the 1920s

City planning became a recognized function of government in the years following World War I. In the minds of Portland's city fathers, city planning's primary task was twofold: First, to diagnose the traffic troubles — the traffic tangle — born of the automobile; and second, to determine the best means of correcting them. In company with other large American cities, Portland found itself immersed in what Lewis Mumford called "The Fourth Migration" — the technological revolution that had taken place since the turn of the century.[1] The explosive growth of automobile use created crises of severe proportions for the central business district in the form of extreme congestion, decreasing property values close to the waterfront and bridgeheads, decaying dock and deteriorating buildings.

Earlier attempts at city planning, such as the Olmsted Plan of 1904 and the Bennett Plan of 1912, were products of the "City Beautiful" movement that was aimed at rescuing Portland from the "slough of ugliness into which utilitarianism seemed to be dragging it."[2] Although Portland voters overwhelmingly approved the plan's concept in November 1912, followed by the city council's formal adoption of the plan in 1917, nothing substantial resulted from the grand scheme. Chicago planner Edward H. Bennett had recommended the widening of arterials, the construction of boulevards and parks, and the creation of a waterfront embankment patterned upon London and Budapest, but he had not foreseen the crush of automobile traffic that was to occur after the war. As veteran city commissioner Ormond Bean later described the plan:

> "It was a general and visionary plan of the development of the city as a whole with no thought of the practical carrying out of the exact plan. It was hoped that in a general way the city would follow out the suggestions made, and I believe it was very unfortunate that the old city administration [Baker's] did not see fit to consider the Bennett Plan in its development program. It was logical in its general conclusions but needed more careful engineering study in details."[3]

Probably no plan devised before 1919 could have been expected to recognize the full impact of the automobile. Banker E. B. MacNaughton, an early member of the city planning commission, confessed in 1929 that "none of us, no matter how forwardlooking we may feel ourselves to be, can accurately forecast the growth of traffic."[4] In a letter to *Oregon Journal* editor Donald J. Sterling, MacNaughton cited three different reconstructions of Canyon Road within 25 years, each one more costly. The major highway leading west out of Portland — the present U. S. 26 — was to be rebuilt two more times within the next 40 years. In 1979 its designed capacity is already exceeded at rush hour.

Eight years after the planning commission was established, the city's chief planner noted few improvements. "Conditions in Portland are decidedly muddled because of a lack of a city plan in the past. The larger the city becomes without serious attempt to direct the growth, the more chaotic the conditions become."[5] In 1927 alone, the city was required to spend $4 million "to get half of what should have been done" earlier without any appreciable cost. As the City Club noted in an extensive review of downtown traffic patterns in 1921, "attempts to plan . . . in advance have proven a sorrowful chapter of community development."[6] Concerns for property rights, fears of property value loss and taxpayer reluctance all combined to thwart constructive action. Toward the end of the decade, the planning commission staff seemed to react philosophically to the hard political realities when it declared:

> "The history of the race is a story of civilization bred in cities and overrun by barbarians reared in the open. Today we have no barbarians left to overturn our civilization, but we are threatened with internal decay which may end our culture and leave no conquering barbarians to pick up the smoky torch of progress, to trim the wick and replenish the oil and carry the renewed flame to greater heights than ever before."[7]

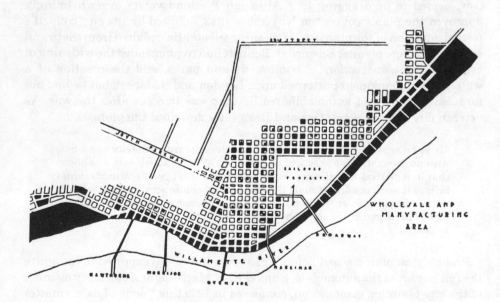

WHOLESALE AND MANUFACTURING AREA

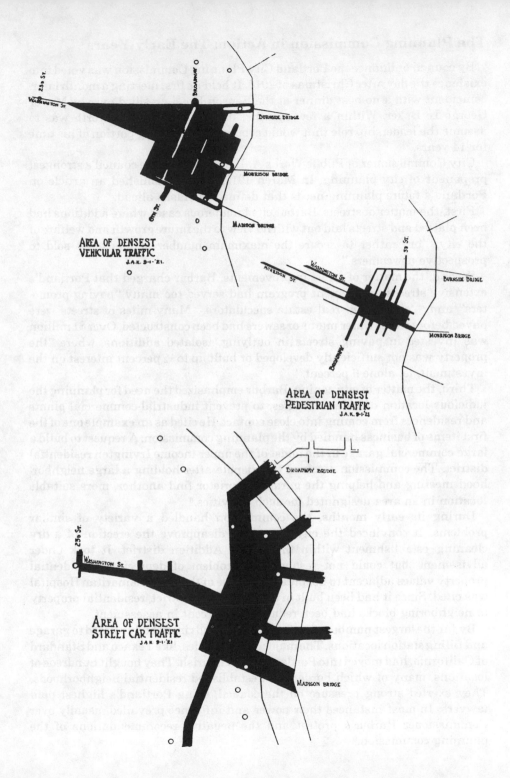

AREA OF DENSEST
VEHICULAR TRAFFIC
J.A.K. 9-1-'21.

AREA OF DENSEST
PEDESTRIAN TRAFFIC
J.A.K. 9-1-'21

AREA OF DENSEST
STREET CAR TRAFFIC
J.A.K. 9-1-'21

The Planning Commission in Action: The Early Years

By council ordinance the Portland City Planning Commission was voted into existence the day after Christmas of 1918. It held its first meeting a month later, coincident with a no-host dinner at the Benson Hotel presided over by Mayor George L. Baker. Within a few months, banker John C. Ainsworth was to assume the leadership role that would occupy an increasing portion of his time for 14 years.

City Commissioner of Public Works A. L. Barbur was the council's strongest proponent of city planning. In March 1919, Barbur published an article on Portland's future planning needs that defined the tasks ahead.

First, the matter of streets. Barbur cited numerous cases where additions had been platted and streets laid out with no view to the future growth and welfare of the city, "but rather to secure the maximum number of lots to be sold to prospective newcomers."

Second, the matter of street improvements. Barbur charged that Portland's extensive street improvement program had served too many "paving promoters" and " 'shoestring' real estate speculators." Many miles of streets were paved before either water mains or sewers had been constructed. Over $1 million was invested in paving streets in outlying, isolated additions, where "the property was not sufficiently developed or built up to ½ percent interest on the investment, let alone 6 percent."

Third, the matter of city zoning. Barbur emphasized the need for planning the judicious location of industrial sites, to prevent industrial-commercial plants and residences from coming into close contact. He cited as an example one of the first items of business handled by the planning commission: A request to build a large commercial garage in the midst of the upper-income Irvington residential district. The commission resolved the dispute after holding a large neighborhood meeting and helping the garage proprietor find another, more suitable location in an area designated for such activities.[8]

During its early months, the commission handled a variety of similar problems. It convinced the city council to disapprove the erection of a dry cleaning establishment within the Ladd's Addition district. It took under advisement, but could not resolve, the problem of depreciated residential property values adjacent to hospitals. The case of the Good Samaritan Hospital was cited. Since it had been built in the Northwest district, residential property in neighboring blocks had been reduced ten percent in assessment.

By far the largest number of issues to face the advisory body related to garage and filling station locations. The major oil companies, like Texaco and Standard of California, had moved into Portland with a flourish. They bought hundreds of locations, many of which bordered on established residential neighborhoods. They exerted strong pressure on the council, using Portland's highest paid lawyers. In most instances their power and influence prevailed, usually over Commissioner Barbur's protest and the negative recommendations of the planning commission.[9]

As an appointive body dealing with land use matters, the planning commission soon encountered the same kinds of criticism that have traditionally been levelled at all such non-elected semi-regulatory agencies. In July of 1919, the East Side Business Men's Club addressed a communication to the city council with the request that it not be "passed up to the so-called Planning Commission. . . . We have confidence in the members of the Council; we picked and elected the Council . . . , we had nothing to do with the Planning Commission; they are proving, so far, to be idealistic in a way, but not practical idealists."[10]

The *Oregon Voter* was amused by the use of the word "idealist." As its editor commented:

> "Maybe J. C. Ainsworth, president of the U. S. National Bank, is an idealist, but he insists on rather material security when a loan is sought. His *idealism* may however be confined to the depositor's phase of the business. . . . E. B. MacNaughton may somewhere in his system have a strain of idealism, but it doesn't crop out strongly on the outside and if the labor unions ever were told that their representative, B. W. Sleeman, was an *idealist*, they'd mob him. [The *Voter* opined that] society needs *idealists* to maintain its proper balance and perspective. . . . The idealist, more commonly called the crank, is responsible for the majority of the world's greatest reforms and substantial progress. . . . Portland has plenty of materialists, plenty of selfish, narrow visioned realists, who will always offset any danger of the *idealists* running rampant."[11]

Portland's history would tend to support that judgment.

For four years, beginning in 1917, Portland was fortunate in being able to acquire the consulting services of Charles H. Cheney who was secretary of the California Conference on City Planning. Cheney was hired initially to assist the city with its war housing problems. After the war he drafted the state enabling legislation that authorized the formation of city planning commissions. In 1919 he began work on two extensive projects: (1) A major traffic artery and park plan; and (2), the city's first zoning ordinance. In the course of his work, he compiled a report on zoning and city planning that was submitted to the planning commission in June 1919. In the light of recent history, some of his comments are worth noting.

"Zoning is the first fundamental step in any city to establish a practical basis for constructive city growth," Cheney declared. It "saves public funds . . . and stabilizes values." In an amazingly prophetic statement that city authorities would have been wise to heed in recent decades, Cheney proclaimed that "the skyscraper is the stepbrother to the vacant lot. . . . It is unhealthy and uneconomic." The mushrooming of parking lots in downtown Portland since the 1950s has verified the truth of this observation.

In great detail, Cheney documented the growth of blighted neighborhoods resulting from a poor mixture of land uses. Too many stores were located in the wrong places. The unlimited scattering of industries in retail and residential areas, along with the extensive intrusion of garages, had lessened property values. Cheney discovered "thousands of rooms in local hotels and lodging houses, where men, women and even children are sleeping nightly without even a single window, built in defiance of all modern principles of health, light, air and sanitation." His conclusion was obvious: Portland's recently enacted housing code was totally inadequate. Cheney contended that an adequate housing code was impossible to attain without the prior enactment of a city-wide zoning code that would regulate land uses.[12]

The Zoning Code Battle

Beginning in June 1919, the planning commission spent over four months holding neighborhood zoning meetings throughout Portland. A number of citizen suggestions were incorporated into the final ordinance that was presented to the council in March of 1920. One authorized the planning commission to establish 29 advisory neighborhood associations comprising property owners who would be consulted prior to any planning commission decision affecting a neighborhood's existing zoning classification. It was this provision, more than any of the others, that provoked such heated opposition from the Portland Realty Board and the Citizens Anti-Zoning League. Although neither group ever mentioned the matter publicly, the planning commission's zoning commission informed the city council of the fact on March 17th:

> "We found most of the [Realty Board] committee . . . very loath to have the people of any neighborhood be allowed to say whether they wanted to keep stores and apartment houses as well as industries out of their home blocks. . . . This right of neighborhoods to be consulted . . . is well recognized. . . . These regulations resulted from the gravest abuses of unwarranted scattering of such buildings through residence districts."[13]

The Citizens Anti-Zoning League was formed as a front organization for the realty interests. The majority of the Realty Board members opposed the zoning code. But because the opposition did not want to be identified directly with realty interests, and because a few prominent Realty Board leaders like E. B. MacNaughton and Frederick H. Strong favored the code, the anti-zoning group took the initiative in the name of "the small property owners" who, they declared, were being victimized by the code. The facts revealed otherwise. Many of the opponents represented "large property owners." The league president was wealthy former Republican U. S. Senator Frederick W. Mulkey. The executive committee included railroad attorney William D. Fenton and utility attorney Frederick V. Holman. It also included wealthy lumberman Louis Gerlinger and prominent realtors A. R. Ritter, Dorr Keasey and Coe McKenna, who was subsequently appointed to the planning commission by Mayor Baker. The leading anti-zoning spokesman, however, was realtor Fred W. German, chairman of the Citizens Anti-Zoning League Executive Committee.

298

It was Fred German, in his capacity as the 1920 president of the Portland Realty Board, who spearheaded the opposition before the city council. German took aim at consultant Charles E. Cheney. "The hiring of Cheney," he declared, "at $300 per week, and the expenditures of thousands of dollars of the taxpayers' money for propaganda work in an effort to gumshoe an unjust and inefficient zoning ordinance through the city council is not only sheer waste of public funds but an insult to the public intelligence." German criticized the paying of "an out of state novice." There were, he said, "plenty of public spirited citizens of

NEIGHBORHOOD ZONING MEETING

Property owners and residents of the district, between:

The City Boundary on the north and the Willamette River on the south and west and extending to Dana Street on the east, known as the St. Johns and University Park districts.

are invited to be present at a conference with representatives of the Portland City Planning Commission on the zoning of your neighborhood to be held:

in the St. Johns Branch Public Library at 7:45 P. M. Friday, June 27, 1919.

The purpose of this meeting is to recommend what part of this district should permit new business buildings, what part should permit new apartments, and what part should hereafter be restricted to single family residences only. A committee of property owners will report its recommendations at this meeting.

All written communications from residents or property owners of said district, filed with the City Auditor within ten days after the above neighborhood meeting will be reviewed by the City Planning Commission.

PORTLAND CITY PLANNING COMMISSION

Portland more knowledgeable of local conditions and better qualified." German reminded the council that planning commission members served without pay; was it necessary to pay an outsider?[14] German was either unaware, or unwilling to accept the fact, that Cheney was one of the most highly qualified city planning consultants in the country. But in 1920, city planning was a suspect profession, "identified as a long-haired attempt to invade private enterprise."[15]

German attacked one of the basic principles of the zoning code: The establishment of restricted centers for commercial and industrial purposes. Such a principle was "socialistic and un-American," he charged. Every property owner should be allowed to use his own judgment without the necessity of consulting city government. "No zoning code should reduce the potential value of any property in the city."[16] A week later, Mayor Baker publicly accused certain members of the Realty Board "of acting from selfish motives." The city had already spent $16,000 on the preparation of the zoning ordinance. The code was needed, declared the mayor. Baker was angry.[17] He rarely became so exercised in matters of this sort, especially against an organization to which he had close personal ties.

The council passed the zoning ordinance by a vote of 3 to 2, with Mayor Baker joining Commissioners Barbur and Bigelow. Ten days later, in an attempt to thwart a referendum petition by the anti-zoning league, the council voted unanimously to refer the ordinance to popular vote in the November 1920 election. This move turned out to be a tactical error. The anti-zoning forces proceeded to file their referendum petition anyway, and they were given over six months to generate support. The code was rejected by only 219 votes out of over 61,000 that were cast.

The defeated ordinance had provided for eight classes of property use: Two involving residential dwellings, four regulating the location of businesses and public facilities, and two establishing specific districts for factories, warehouses and "noxious industries." An additional provision had established districts with defined height limitations. Had the voters approved Cheney's plan, Portland would have joined New York and St. Louis as the only American cities to have adopted comprehensive zoning codes by 1920.

It was to take four more years before Portland voters would approve a zoning code — a diluted and simplified version of the 1919 plan. In the interim, uncontrolled development proceeded at an increasing pace. Commercial and industrial enterprises invaded residential districts in Rose City Park and Northwest Portland. Sullivan's Gulch became an established industrial zone and Sandy Boulevard exploded with strip development. The area north of Hoyt Street in Northwest Portland lost much of its residential identity to expanding commercial enterprises. All of these developments, together with others in Southeast Portland, proved to be irreversible even after the 1924 code was finally approved.

The 1924 zoning code, to remain in effect for 35 years, became a realtor's dream. In fact, it was drafted by the realty interests. Charles Cheney was dropped as an active consultant, and Mayor Baker appointed a special joint committee to formulate the code. It was composed of seven members from the Realty Board and six from the City Planning Commission. However, three of the new planning commissioners were themselves active members of the Realty Board, and two of the three had opposed the 1919 plan. The chairman of the joint committee was Fred W. German.

The "realtor's code" provided for four zones. Zone 1 was restricted to single family residences. It covered 18 percent of the city's area and included all of the wealthier residential districts. Zone 2, covering 41 percent of the city, provided for a heterogeneous mix of lower valued residential properties, multi-family structures and incidental commercial uses. Zone 3, allotted 26 percent of the city, was designated for commercial and light industrial use. Zone 4, the remaining 10 percent, was unrestricted. When outlining the four zones, the joint committee followed one basic rule: "All streets, upon which main or through streetcar lines were located, were zoned business"[18] — zone 3.

The new ordinance ignored all area, height and density controls, factors which in subsequent years became recognized as essential ingredients of effective zoning legislation. The major consequence of zoning 41 percent of the city's area for possible apartment and commercial use was the gradual blighting of older single family homes. The areas that were to suffer the worst consequences, however, were those adjacent to the Willamette River frontage. Both banks from Sellwood in the south, past the downtown district, and past St. Johns to the northern city limits were zoned either manufacturing or unrestricted. All of South Portland's Lair Hill Park, Corbett and Terwilliger districts to the base of the hills were placed in zone 3. Ross Island and the other islands were zoned unrestricted.

The fraudulent nature of the Realty Board's strongest public attack on the 1919 code — as a detriment to the small property owner — was clearly documented by veteran Commissioner William A. Bowes in 1945. "It was the people of modest means who suffered the most" from the overly permissive 1924 code. "This condition reflected itself in the lowering of property values in many areas and in handicaps in obtaining loans for construction of homes." Bowes cited the effect of overzoning for commercial use along Union Avenue, Sandy Boulevard and S. E. 82nd Avenue. Many of the commercial establishments that were erected were flimsy and underfinanced. In later years, they would be abandoned or simply allowed to deteriorate while in use, resulting "in the depreciation of adjacent residential property values."[19]

Few realized in 1924 what many have come to recognize as a self-evident truth in 1979, that only a limited street frontage of any city can profitably be devoted to business use. As Los Angeles architect George H. Coffin told the planning commission in 1934 — speaking from personal experience in his native city:

"Unfortunately, most of the so-called business frontage was born of the wedlock between ignorance and speculation and the naked miles of vacant

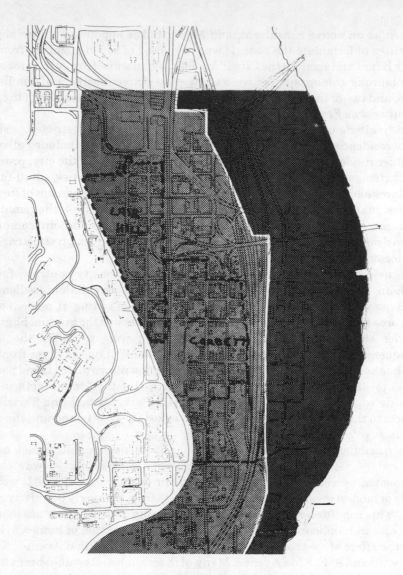

1924 Zoning

Zone I: Apartments - *Not Shown*

Zone II: General Mfg./Commercial

Zone III: Unrestricted Mfg.

lots along our arteries of travel are mute testimony to an economic waste of such proportions that the imagination is startled at the farce of perpetuating this needless waste into the eternity of tomorrow."[20]

Seven years earlier, the planning commission staff had directed similar comments to Portland:

"The . . . zoning ordinance has established potential business of a little over 750,000 lineal feet. This is exclusive of the main business area of the city. Portland therefore has potential business frontage for a city of more than one and a half million people. Yet every little while some citizen complains that the zoning ordinance is stifling business development."[21]

Another unfortunate aspect of the 1924 zoning code was its failure to deal adequately with housing conditions. Housing facilities for the poor became worse through ineffective provisions for code enforcement. The Portland Housing Association found no improvement in the conditions that it had described in January 1923 as "ramshackle, airless buildings, mildewed walls, stagnant water in basements, useless plumbing, dark hallways blocked with firewood, attic rooms occupied by men, women, children, unclean, no water or ventilation."[22] Dozens of apartment houses, many owned by prominent realtors and investors, did not meet the code and nothing was being done to enforce compliance.

The 1924 zoning ordinance created an Advisory Board of the Housing Code that was nothing more than a front for realtors and homebuilders. Only one member represented the public. A second represented the builders and the third, supposedly an architect, was also a builder. In other words, the very class which the code was designed to check was in control of its enforcement. As former Portland Rabbi Jonah Wise later wrote to Jesse Short from New York:

"I resigned from the Advisory Board . . . because of the total inadequacy of the project. There was no way of really checking building enterprises which were definitely against public interest. . . . We had the sympathy of Mayor Baker and the cooperation of some very good men, but the code itself was of such a nature that it allowed many evasions."[23]

For the three year period from 1924 through 1926, Portland experienced a record growth in homebuilding and new commercial construction. It was two years ahead of the rest of the country, based on percentages, and the homebuilders and realtors like Fred W. German thrived accordingly.

German's public stance enabled him to secure election to the Oregon House of Representatives for the years 1925 through 1927. Realizing that pastures were greener in county government, he was elected a county commissioner in 1929 to succeed Amadee Smith. The following year, he became vice president of the young Benjamin Franklin Savings and Loan Association. Never one to pass up

I.
HISTORY OF PORTLAND HOUSING CODE
Relative to Depth of Rear Yards for Dwellings and Apartment Houses
Minimum Requirement in Feet, Based on 50x100 ft. Lot

	CORNER LOT—NUMBER OF STORIES						INTERIOR LOT—NUMBER OF STORIES					
DATES	1	2	3	4	5	6	1	2	3	4	5	6
Portland, 1919	15	15	15	20	25	30	15	20	25	30	35	40
Portland, 1920	12	12	12	15	18	21	12	15	18	21	24	27
Portland, Dec. 1927	10	10	10	11	12	13	10	11	12	13	14	15
Proposed for Portland	10	10	10	11	12	13	10	10	10	11	12	13

II.
WHERE WE STAND IN COMPARISON WITH OTHER CITIES
All Data Available Showing Rear Yard Requirements of Cities Having Housing Codes
Minimum Requirement in Feet, Based on 50x100 foot Lot

	CORNER LOT—NUMBER OF STORIES						INTERIOR LOT—NUMBER OF STORIES					
NAME OF CITY	1	2	3	4	5	6	1	2	3	4	5	6
Berkeley	10	10	10	15	20	25	10	10	10	15	20	25
California	10	10	10	10	10	10	10	10	10	11	12	13
Columbus	15	15	15	15	15	15	18	18	18	18	18	18
Detroit	10	12	14	16	20	24	10	12	14	16	20	24
Duluth	12	14	16	18	20	22	12	16	16	18	20	22
Indiana	15	15	18	21	24	25	25	25	28	31	34	
Iowa	10	12	14	16	18	20	10	12	14	16	18	20
Louisville	12	13	14	15	16	17	12	13	14	15	16	17
Michigan	10	12	14	16	20	24	10	12	14	16	20	24
Massachusetts	15	15	15	20	25	30	25	25	25	30	35	40
Minneapolis	15	15	20	25	30	35	15	15	20	25	30	35
Minnesota	20	20	22.5	26.5	29.5	31.5	20	20	22.5	26.5	29.5	31.5
Sioux City	10	12	14	16	18	20	10	12	14	16	18	20
Average	12.6	13.5	14.8	17.3	20.2	23.0	14.4	15.2	16.7	19.3	22.1	24.9

III.
HISTORY OF SPECIAL PERMITS RECOMMENDED BY THE ADVISORY BOARD AND PASSED AS EMERGENCY MEASURES BY THE CITY COUNCIL
Yearly Increase of Permits and of Buildings

DATES	Numbers of special permits	Rates of special permits to 1920-21 base	Dwellings and apartments built, rates to 1920-21 base
April 1920—April 1921	9	1.0	1.0
April 1921—April 1922	19	2.1	3.0
April 1922—December 1923	95	6.3	3.3
December 1923—December 1924	127	14.1	4.2
December 1924—December 1925	130	14.4	3.9
December 1925—December 1926	147	16.3	3.5
December 1926—December 1927	167	18.6	2.4
Total	694		

TYPE OF INFRINGEMENT OF CODE GRANTED BY SPECIAL ORDINANCES
(Estimated from sample periods totalling 4 years distributed through the 8 years.)

	Number of special ordinances	TYPE OF VIOLATION OF CODE					
DATES		Light and ventilation	Size of yards and courts	Cellar apartments	Other sanitation	Fire protection	Other Items
Apr. 1, 1920 to Apr. 1, 1928	694*	172	451	142	24	177	26

* By actual count.

a profitable deal, German maintained an active personal real estate business during his term in county government. In fact, it was while he was rushing from his county courthouse office to complete a real estate transaction that his car hit and killed a 78 year old janitor who was crossing Sandy Boulevard at N. E. 52nd Avenue. At least two witnesses described his speed as excessive; one noted that he had sped through a red light. German protested that he was only travelling at 25 miles per hour even though the victim had been dragged 75 feet. The two investigating officers did not sign a complaint even though their accident report validated those of the witnesses. Coroner Earl Smith, along with the police officers, proved to be most accommodating to the powerful politician. A coroner's jury cleared German of any legal responsibility. It was "an unavoidable injury." All charges were dismissed.[24] Two months earlier, German's son Frank had been involved in a similar occurrence and had won similar exoneration.

Justice finally caught up with both father and son when they were indicted in April 1937 on eight counts of larceny. Their family real estate business went into

*Buckman district during
World War I*

receivership and seven months later they were indicted on six additional counts of larceny. In both cases, the Germans were accused of embezzling client funds, although the first charges were later dropped. After a lengthy trial in July 1938, Fred W. German was convicted and sentenced to two years in jail. His son Frank received a heavier sentence of five years.

Following the passage of the 1924 zoning code, the city council continued to buckle under to realtor pressure despite the protests of the planning commission. Even with a code that was overly flexible, the council was besieged with requests for changes in zone classifications. In the nine year period from 1925 to the end of Mayor Baker's term, 275 zone changes were approved and 164 revocable permits were granted. In seeking to determine the reasons for these changes, the Portland Housing and Planning Association discovered that most of the property owners involved were encouraged by realtors to place their property in a zone classification that would ensure its future sale as a business property. The property would be held and not developed further until the time was ripe for a sale at commercial use prices that were higher than those for residential use. At stake were residential properties that were gradually being engulfed by commercial activity.[25]

The present day Buckman neighborhood in near Southeast Portland bears witness to this pattern of development. As one of the oldest communities in the city, the 1924 code zoned it "as a medium density residential area with commercial cores developing around through portions of the neighborhood."[26] As a recent planning commission study noted:

"The housing stock in the neighborhood, particularly single family units, began to deteriorate as owners anticipated offers from developers of

A dilapidated residence, replaced by an apartment, resembling a motel with its asphalt parking area.

apartment buildings. As single family units gave way to apartments, and the population became highly transient, the character of Buckman began to change. These changes are symbolized by deteriorated housing, crime, noise, traffic problems and a general state of instability within the community."[27]

Since 1960, over 200 homes have been demolished and 100 apartment complexes erected, many of which have the appearance of motels. Although 70 percent of the Buckman population lives in single family homes or duplexes, the ratio of renters to home owners is two to one.[28] The transient population has produced the city's highest rate of juvenile delinquency and the largest incidence of school enrollment turnover, particularly at the Buckman elementary school.

Downtown Development

The physical shape of downtown Portland underwent extensive reconstruction during the decade of the booming 1920s. Property values began to rise rapidly as the commercial headquarters of the city expanded, moving south from the congested old central business district adjacent to Meier & Frank's department store. In one seven block area, over $10 million was spent on new buildings in the period from 1923 to 1927. City-wide, total yearly construction expenditures rose by over 400 percent. As with the rest of the city, however, the downtown development occurred without benefit of any public plan — without regard for any particular order or system. There was planning, to be sure, endless planning, but 90 percent of it was executed by individual owners, anxious to derive the largest possible profit out of the fewest possible acres.

No one was better prepared to promote an increase in property values than E. B. MacNaughton, one of the most astute property managers in Portland. Planning commissioner MacNaughton, and his partner, Port of Portland commissioner Robert H. Strong, dedicated a portion of their time to directing the affairs of the Corbett Investment Company. Totalling over $3 million, the combined downtown Corbett properties ranked seventh on the city scale of total assessed property values, exceeded only by those of the major utilities and railroads. MacNaughton clearly perceived the future growth pattern in downtown Portland. This may have been the reason why he and Strong convinced the First Unitarian Church, of which they were both active members, to sell them its building and quarter block on S. W. Broadway and Yamhill and to move to Twelfth and Salmon Streets. For the church, this was probably a wise step. It also proved to be a wise decision for the Strong & MacNaughton Trust Company which purchased the old church site in 1923 for $200,000.

Seventy years earlier, the land had been acquired by Henry W. Corbett for $2.50 plus delinquent taxes. The church bought it from Corbett for $2000 in 1866. The 57 year old structure would be replaced, thus its value was only a fraction of the property's total sale price. Strong & MacNaughton erected a single story

307

New First Unitarian Church — 1924
S. W. 12th and Salmon
Designed by Jamieson Parker

building to house a few retail shops, for a total cost of close to $85,000, and then sold the land and building in 1925 for $385,000 to the Realty Associates of Portland, a prestigious group of local investors that included Franklin T. Griffith, county commissioner Amadee Smith and Charles F. Swigert. Strong & MacNaughton cleared close to $100,000 on the deal and succeeded in pushing up all of the property values on the adjacent blocks. Not only could the firm expect to gain by increased commissions from potential future sales, but its fees could be increased proportionately for any of the nearby properties that it managed.

This series of transactions provides a prime example of how real estate deals could be executed profitably if the participants had "inside" connections. The only possible loser was the church. Yet, assuming that the sale price to Strong & MacNaughton was fair market value, without this kind of manipulation, the church property might not have appreciated by more than 10 or 15 percent had the sale been delayed for a year or two. And as for Franklin T. Griffith, being the chief executive of the city's largest utility carried certain inside benefits. Portland Electric Power Company advanced Realty Associates $40,000 to complete the purchase, "borrowed" at six percent.[29]

The Strong & MacNaughton Trust Company was instrumental in promoting the sale of several key pieces of downtown property containing some of Portland's fine early mansions, and the prices reflected the inflated commercial market that the firm had helped to stimulate. In 1924, the Failing sisters sold the old family homestead on S. W. Taylor and Sixth for $450,000 to a Los Angeles capitalist who planned to build a new, first-class hotel on the site. But with an unexpected decline in the downtown hotel trade during the early months of 1925, the purchaser reconsidered his plans. Before the year was out, the property was resold for $550,000 to the Electric Bond & Share Company in behalf of the three local utility subsidiaries of its American Power & Light affiliate. In less than 12 months, the block had appreciated $100,000 in value.

Under the direction of architect Albert E. Doyle, plans were prepared to erect Portland's highest edifice, the 15 story Public Service Building. To cost $1.5 million, the structure was designed to serve as a permanent home office for the Portland Gas & Coke Company, the Northwestern Electric Company and the Pacific Power & Light Company — all headed by the veteran utility executive Guy W. Talbot. The financing was provided by the U. S. National Bank. Selected as the general contractor was L. Hawley Hoffman, a man with prominent attachments to the older Portland establishment.

Hoffman's father had been one of Portland's early bridge builders, an associate of Charles F. Swigert and one of the original developers of Albina. Hawley Hoffman received his degree in architecture from Harvard and returned to Portland to practice his profession. He married the daughter of prominent grain merchant Walter J. Burns and thus became a member of the famous Couch-Lewis clan, Portland's oldest and largest dynasty. Like E. B. MacNaughton, Hawley Hoffman decided, after more than a decade, that there was more money to be made in other fields than architecture. Instead of property management he opted for general construction. By establishing his own firm in 1922, he found himself in the right place at the right time and with the right connections to cash in on the various large scale projects that were about to be launched. As with most successful contractors, he also found it profitable to acquire a "piece of the action" himself.

Who knows what went through his friend Guy Talbot's mind when he chose to give the novice contractor the entire job for a fixed fee of $50,000. Hoffman had built only garages and small apartment houses prior to securing his first major contract six months previously: The $400,000 Terminal Sales Building, owned by the Mead estate whose properties were managed by Frederick H. Strong.

There appeared to be more involved than friendship, however. It was to be revealed later that Hoffman, Talbot and some associates had purchased the eastern half of the old Failing block for less than one-half of the original sale price. They organized a company called Pacific Properties and constructed a large garage that would serve the building's tenants and at the same time produce a handsome return for many years.

No one could fault the quality of Hoffman's workmanship. For over 30 years he was to build many of Portland's finest commercial structures. Success followed upon success so that by the end of his first decade in business his contracts were to total nearly $11 million. As banker Ainsworth remarked to a friend in March 1928, "Hoffman is drawing most of the big work in the city."[30] Hoffman had launched a company that was to grow into one of the Northwest's leading construction firms under the guidance of his sons. In the process, he became a wealthy, powerful and conservative force within the Portland community. He served as a long-time trustee of the Portland Art Museum and was an influential member of the Port of Portland Commission for nine years prior to his death in 1959.[31]

The sale and destruction of the Failing mansion was the first of many similar developments that marked the mid-1920s. The former Henry L. Corbett and William M. Ladd homes on the Park Blocks were replaced by the Masonic Temple. The Burrell homestead on S. W. Tenth and Jefferson, a major streetcar junction, was sold by Strong & MacNaughton for $200,000. A Standard Oil filling station was erected, to be followed much later by a large Safeway grocery store. The William S. Ladd home, between Jefferson and Columbia, Broadway and Sixth, was sold for $185,000 to C. S. Jenson, a California theater developer who demolished the mansion in April 1926. Twenty-two years later, the block became the site of the new Oregonian Building, constructed by Hawley Hoffman, whose offices were across Broadway in the old Ladd Carriage House which still survives.

One of the more interesting transactions engineered by Strong & MacNaughton was the decision of the Corbett Investment Company to construct a large office building on the north half of the old Henry W. Corbett property that overlooked the Pioneer Post Office, one of the choicest locations in Portland. Henry Corbett's widow, who maintained the famous cow pasture, had already survived her husband by 22 years. As the pioneer financier's second and much younger wife, she would live into her nineties and continue residing in the mansion until 1935.

With the real estate boom in full swing in 1925, her step-grandsons became concerned over the steady increase in property taxes that were being levied against one of Portland's most valuable sites. A plan was formulated to preserve widow Corbett's life style by building a large office structure to generate sufficient revenues to carry the taxes on the entire block. So desirable was the space commercially that even before groundbreaking in May of 1925, three entire floors had already been leased, two to the Southern Pacific Railroad and

Corbett Mansion — 1885   *Today*

1927

one to the Standard Oil Company of California.[32] Over $1 million were to be spent on the ten story Pacific Building, one of the two or three finest edifices ever to grace the Portland skyline. When the building and its half block were last sold to the current owners in 1968 for $3,750,000, the event was noted as one of the largest real estate transactions in the history of downtown.

Much sadness was registered when the cow pasture and its unique grove of trees were removed in July; in fact *The Oregonian* devoted an entire page to the proceedings.

> "Logging operations in the heart of a metropolis were staged yesterday when buckers, sawyers and fallers began the deforestation of the Corbett block on Yamhill Street. . . . Everyone who lives in Portland is familiar with the grove of majestic trees sprinkled over the lawn."

Henry Corbett had replaced the native fir with a number of more ornamental trees: One flowering tulip, three maples, one horse chestnut, a few holly and one distinctive almond, which most observers thought to be a peach tree. The twelve elms had been carried as little slips by Corbett himself on one of his return trips from the East in 1855. They came from his sister's home in the upstate New York town of Lansingburg. They would all have to go, except for the almond; its stump and roots were to be replanted in Washington Park. *The Oregonian* account continued:

> "Nestling now in a forest of towering buildings, the old trees. . . are a breath from the past, but must leave now — no pun intended — so that another pile of brick and mortar and concrete and steel can have room. Man can make office buildings, but he never yet made a single tree. Considering the size and value of the site, probably $500,000, it is the most expensive logging operation that has been conducted in this region."

The Oregonian concluded its essay on a philosophical note:

> "This is a way that cities have. . . . We take delight in cities, for they, too, are pleasing to the eye, and essential to the comfort and welfare of man. Yet often it seems to some of us that a city in its growth might sometimes grow round the trees and leave them there. For though land is valuable, and is priced by the foot, and is needed for commerce, the destruction of its esthetic values is wholly without an appraisal. But we know this tribute to sentiment is forbidden — now. The city is in haste."[33]

Indeed, the city was in haste. This was the age of new theaters and the proliferation of garages, filling stations and auto sales outlets. Most of Portland's leading families could not resist the temptation to invest in such instruments of progress — the potential rewards were tempting. Public investment in building enterprises became popular ventures in the mid-1920s. Blyth & Company managed over 20 stock and bond issues ranging from

$250,00 to $1 million. Medical buildings, concentrating doctors' offices and clinics, were in demand. Existing commercial office structures such as the Morgan and Wells Fargo Buildings sought refinancing through security promotions — in many cases for the primary purpose of bailing out major investors while the market was high.

The need for new downtown hotels came under study by the chamber of commerce. California investors showed some interest and the Spokane-based owners of the Portland Hotel even considered tearing down the 32 year old crown jewel of Portland's hostelries to make way for an updated, modern facility that would provide space for retail stores at street level. At one point, the chamber advocated purchasing the Pioneer Post Office block from the federal government in order to erect a new superhotel of which the whole Northwest could be proud. The concerned proprietors of the existing major hotels, including the Portland, did a quick study and found that their establishments had been running at only a 50-60 percent occupancy rate during the first half of 1925. The message was clear: Beware of overbuilding just to accommodate seasonal conventions. Portland already had 45 hotels with 50 or more rooms. The Multnomah was the giant with 534, almost twice the size of the Portland. The city had a reservoir of over 6000 hotel rooms, a total that seemed to be adequate for all but the largest conventions.

Once these facts became public knowledge, it proved increasingly difficult to interest local investors in any new hotel project. Banker John C. Ainsworth tried for four years to put together a syndicate that would buy the old Oregon Hotel next to the Benson and build either a new hotel or a new annex to the Benson. As with his ambitious States Steamship Company proposal, he nearly succeeded, but the increasing severity of the depression killed the project. California oilman Ralph B. Lloyd would also try, but fail, to enlist local investors for a new superhotel on the East Side.

In fact, by mid-1927, downtown commercial development had peaked. Wealthy Michigan lumberman John W. Blodgett, who owned extensive Portland properties, noted in August "that there is no demand at present . . . for additional office space."[34] He expressed the same feelings about new hotel and department store space. Local investors like Blodgett, who maintained a home in Portland, were happy with the "very good revenues" that they were then receiving from their existing properties. They saw no need to take any risks beyond what normal caution and prudence would dictate. This was the Portland tradition that California oilman-developer Ralph B. Lloyd was to encounter. The Lloyd story will be related in Chapter 12. It raised an explosive question that was to be debated for over 40 years in Portland: What should be done with the old federal post office site that was located north of the Corbett home?

The Portland community entertained mixed emotions about the 50 year old structure that rested on one of the most valuable pieces of real estate in the city. Following the war, the federal government initiated plans to build a new federal office building in Portland and the post office block was considered a prime site.

The reactions were immediate. Practically no one argued to preserve the building as a valuable historical landmark. This type of thinking was non-existent in the 1920s. However, there were many in Portland who were opposed in principle to a new federal building on the site, out of fear "that the government might be inclined to build a federal office building not in keeping with the character of the surroundings, a plain, utilitarian edifice, massive but misfitting in appearance."[35] Furthermore, the local business establishment did not regard federal offices "as high class occupancies." Beyond that, the government was not known for maintaining its buildings in first class condition. In 1927, the *Oregon Voter* described the post office as an out-worn and out-grown . . . sub-post office, surrounded on three sides by grass struggling to stay green."[36]

From the earliest days of debate, a number of prominent citizens advocated that the government donate both building and site to the city for use as a public park. The city needed "an oasis of rest and beauty, . . . a breathing space in the rapidly growing district south of Morrison Street."[37] This suggestion provoked even more heated opposition from downtown business groups, except, that is, for those whose properties bordered on the block. They would benefit, they thought, "from the existence of an adjacent ornamental plaza."[38] Congressman C. N.

Pioneer Post Office

314

McArthur from Portland disagreed. "I am unalterably opposed to the plan of turning this property over to the City of Portland for park purposes," he wrote in March of 1921. "I am heartily in favor of parks, . . . but I believe that parks should be provided by the local municipal government." McArthur feared the setting of "a very bad precedent." Within ten years, he warned, such a policy could cost the federal government "a billion dollars."[39] Future leading shopping center developer Fred G. Meyer, who would later acquire a store across from the post office, wrote realtor Chester A. Moores that "the block would best serve the city if put to business uses."[40] Meyer never did place much value on anything that he considered an impediment to business progress. Other downtown retailers feared that a park would attract too many women and children to the already congested center of the city. Parks belonged in "outlying residential districts."[41]

The debate would go on until 1968 when the federal government was persuaded to preserve and restore the post office. The building had been saved miraculously by the depression and two wars. As an historic landmark in the National Registry of Historic Places, it now houses the local offices of United States Representatives and Senators as well as the local headquarters for the federal District Court of Appeals. Today the building thrives in splendor as the Pioneer Courthouse. Within a short space of time, it can expect a new neighbor to the west, a public square on the site of the Portland Hotel, for the past 28 years the Meier & Frank parking lot.

The Waterfront Plans

From 1912 to 1972, over ten major waterfront plans were presented to city authorities. Of the numerous recommendations submitted, only four projects found acceptance and were executed: (1) The construction of a harbor seawall and sewer interceptor; (2) the widening of Front Street and the elevation and extension of bridge approaches; (3) the removal of all buildings east of Front Street and the construction of a large public market and a harbor drive along the seawall; and (4), the removal of both the market (later known as the Journal Building) and the drive in order to create a landscaped waterfront esplanade.

Each of the ten plans had meritorious features as well as severe drawbacks, and each was to cost millions of dollars. The cost factor may explain why the first projects chosen involved the least public expenditures. The seawall and sewer line were to be funded largely by the private property owners affected. Several refused to participate. In fact, the Northern Pacific Terminal Company, owned by the Northern Pacific, Great Northern and Union Pacific Railroads, unsuccessfully appealed its $99,000 sewer assessment to the Ninth Circuit Court of Appeals in San Francisco.[42]

The plan that stimulated the seawall and sewer projects was part of an ambitious scheme submitted by City Engineer Olaf Laurgaard in 1923. Additional features included a large central public market building to the south,

Tearing out the docks — early 1928

consolidated interurban passenger terminals in the center section and a permanent warehouse district to the north, all bordering on the waterfront. The bridge approaches were to be elevated over Front Street, which in turn was to be widened into a major traffic artery. Finally a 25 foot strip was to be dedicated for a public levee, or esplanade, for the entire length of the seawall from Glisan to Jefferson Streets. The total cost was projected at $11 million.[43]

It was ironic, historically, that the property owners were expected to pay for their share of the $2.7 million seawall and sewer projects, considering the fact that 60 years earlier private interests had defeated city efforts to preserve public ownership of the waterfront. Had the city owned the waterfront in 1923, assuming that it was in a similar condition, public funds would have had to pay for the needed improvements.

The attempt to eliminate most train traffic from downtown streets had obvious merit. It would have helped to relieve traffic congestion and restore stability to property values. But the consolidation of tracks and terminals close to the river would have created a formidable barrier to public accessibility despite the existence of the 25 foot esplanade. As architect Ellis Lawrence commented: "In no sense of the word can it [the plan] be considered satisfactory from the humanitarian point of view, which capitalizes the water fronts of other great ports. It is inadequate as to width and should be carried farther into the city."[44] Lawrence contemplated an open landscaped embankment 200 feet wide,

316

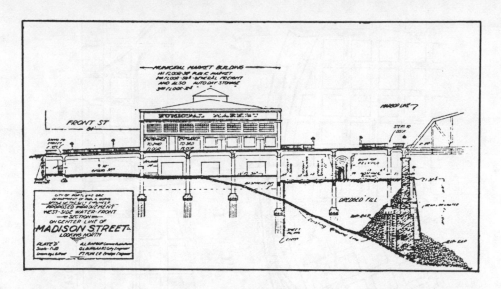

Laurgaard Plan for Seawall

Seawall today

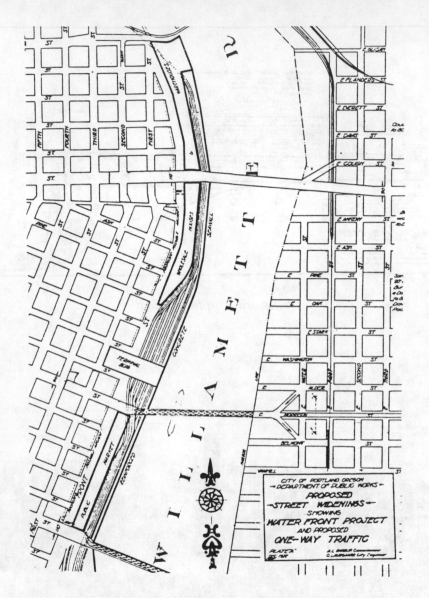

The Laurgaard Plan — 1923

from the harbor line to Front Street. Portland was to realize this goal 50 years later.

It was to take the city nearly three years to complete negotiations with the waterfront property owners. The project was backed heartily by most civic and business groups. *The Oregonian*'s Laurence Hodges wrote glowingly:

> "Construction of a river wall on the main west water front of Portland will be the first unit in a great work which is to contribute to the making of a new Portland. . . . The port has simply far outgrown the present structures along the river between Jefferson and Glisan streets, and they have become mere relics of a long past era in the city's development. . . . Discharge of sewage directly into the river served for the city's infancy but is offensive to health and to the nostrils when population has passed a third of a million and is evidently destined soon to reach half a million. . . . If this evil is not checked early in its growth our 'beautiful Willamette' will become as repulsive to the eye and nose as some river flowing through industrial cities of the old world and will be deserted by its abundant fish."[45]

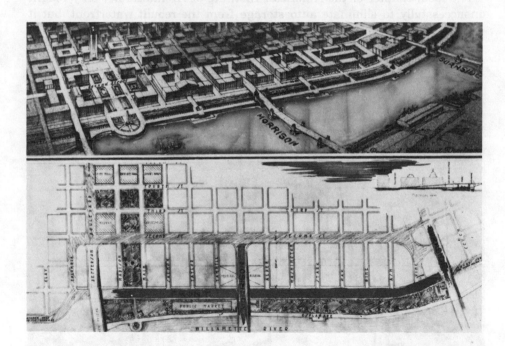

1929 prospective prepared by an Oregon Chapter committee of the American Institute of Architects showing the waterfront from Jefferson to Glisan Streets as planned by the Oregon Building Congress. First Street has been abandoned, and a park between Front Street and the esplanade is shown. A proposed civic center is shown between Main and Madison Streets, running from the river to Fifth Street. Note the public market in the park area just south of Morrison Street.

The bids were opened in October 1926 and came in at $200,000 above the engineer's estimate. Inflation was taking its toll. C. F. Swigert's Pacific Bridge Company was the major subcontractor, and the project turned out to be highly profitable for the veteran Portland entrepreneur. Through June of 1928, Pacific Bridge realized over $200,000 in profits, amounting to 20 percent of the expenditures to that date.[46] The project was completed in 1929 at a final cost of $2.7 million.

One feature of the waterfront clearance that established a precedent with unfortunate future consequences was the city council's decision to use the area for the day storage of automobiles. This trend was to continue until recent years, to the point where over 50 percent of the land from Front to Third Avenues became devoted to asphalt parking lots.

A Civic Center

The local chapter of the American Institute of Architects not only fought unsuccessfully to eliminate auto storage from the rebuilt waterfront, but it

Proposed City-County-State Office Building
1929

opposed all efforts to divert total dedication of the area to park use except for the inclusion of a public market. The A. I. A.'s major interest, however, was in a proposal to integrate the redevelopment of the riverfront with a new civic center to be located between City Hall and the Multnomah County Courthouse. Two plans were drafted, one in 1924 and a more expansive one in 1929, that envisioned extending the civic center through Lownsdale and Chapman squares to the riverfront. The latter plan won little support in the city council due to both the high cost of the land involved and the size of the projected city-county-state office building. To the planning commission, the plan had one basic flaw: It did not provide an effective solution to the parking and traffic congestion in the downtown.

Traffic Congestion

During the 1920s, the automobile was proving to be a leveller of property values. Its ability to produce street congestion not only limited traffic flow but also restrained the tendency of central business district property to increase in price. Its mobility, on the other hand, made possible a greatly widened radius of commutation that raised the value of outlying city and suburban acreage. Much of the argument for waterfront improvement, and for new bridge approaches, was based on the realization that if downtown congestion were not relieved, the central business district would not remain the geographic center of Portland's commercial life. The population center had already moved to the East Side and business was moving with it.

It would have made more sense, geographically, to develop business and population centers to the west, in areas of the nearby Tualatin Valley that were closer to downtown Portland than Laurelhurst, Irvington and Rose City Park to the east. Such a move would have relieved the severe bridge congestion that actually worsened when the two new bridges were opened in 1926. After studying the problem, a City Club committee ascertained that it was **not** the western hills that retarded development so much as it was "the lack of legal machinery for financing plans and construction of arterials." It was "absolutely impossible for commercial vehicles to get out of Portland" onto West Side state highways. The State Highway Commission was prohibited by law from building any roads in Multnomah County. It was, therefore, "powerless to connect its expensive state highway system to the city streets by roads" that would conform to state standards.[47]

The city planning commission gave much of its early attention to the problems of traffic congestion within the city, but it was powerless to deal with the matter of proper access to the state highway system. In 1921, the city council approved the "Major Traffic Street and Boulevard System Plan." It was designed by Charles H. Cheney to complement the waterfront and "West Side Flat" plans. It was also designed, in the words of John Ainsworth, to "save thousands of dollars of needless overwide street paving by designating the 85

321

percent of the streets" that were not needed as through traffic streets. It would help the small home owner by clearly establishing the minor residence streets, and it would increase safety and reduce accidents. One of its major purposes was to stabilize downtown centers of traffic and thereby prevent an "unwarranted" shifting of the retail center.[48]

The widening of Burnside Street west to the city limits was given a high priority but it would be years before that dream was fully realized. The "Uptown Portland Association" was organized to promote the project and it was composed of some of Portland's leading business executives. Another group, called the "Stark Street Improvement Association," drafted an extensive plan to build a major arterial from Burnside and Stark Streets diagonally across the Northwest district, leading through to a new highway to Linnton that would cut through lower Macleay Park. There was more to this scheme than the alleviation of traffic congestion, however. Real estate developers had long had their eyes on the extensive hillside acreage that could be opened up to development were direct access provided. The future growth of both the Northwest district and Linnton would have been altered radically had this plan been executed and Forest Park might never have been created.

Another suggestion that was spawned by the city's street and boulevard plan related to Sullivan's Gulch in the Rose City Park area. Close-in northeast traffic congestion was approaching the density of downtown. The City Club study found need for a new by-pass route and recommended, that for a short distance, Sullivan's Gulch be used "for all fast moving traffic going to the northeast portion of the city, and out the Columbia River Highway."[49] By following the gulch, from the east end of the Burnside Bridge to N. E. 28th Avenue, all danger of cross traffic would be removed. It would be 20 years, however, before the Oregon State Highway Commission would choose this path as the route of the city's first freeway, but at least in 1925 some thought was being given to the idea. The Union Pacific Railroad had enjoyed sole use of the gulch for 40 years. Eventually it would acquire much more company within the confines of the narrow ravine than it had ever anticipated when it agreed in 1916 to pay its share of the city's viaduct construction costs.

Possibly the most distinctive consequence of the street and boulevard plan was the construction of the Vista Avenue Viaduct, better known as the Vista Bridge. Approved initially in 1925, the $200,000 structure was completed in December 1926. The bridge provided a direct automobile link between upper Burnside Street and Portland Heights, replacing the old Ford Street streetcar bridge that was moved to the Burlingame district to carry the southward extension of Terwilliger Boulevard over the Oregon Electric tracks. Showing a degree of civic responsibility and generosity not evidenced by most other citizen groups, the affluent Portland Heights Association paid half of the construction costs, an arrangement that the city government happily accepted. Over 120 feet in height and 550 feet long, the sturdily built concrete structure has withstood its 50 years of heavy use with no signs of deterioration. Carrying over 11,000

Vista Avenue Bridge — December 1926

The Council Crest Streetcar, the last to operate in Portland, was taken out of service in 1950. It is shown here at the intersection of S. W. Vista and Patton Road.

Deluxe Cottages, Portland Auto Camp

vehicles a day, the Vista Bridge offers an unparalleled view of the central city with Mount Hood framed in the center background. The bridge's opening also assured the further development of Portland Heights as a prime residential center. The Council Crest streetcar continued to use the Vista Avenue route until the service was discontinued after World War II.

The automobile had made its mark on Portland by the end of the decade. Over 30 percent of the city's land was now related to automobile uses and Oregonians spent nearly $100 million in 1928 on automobile related expenses. In fact, one 1927 report noted that Oregonians annually consumed more gallons of gasoline per motor vehicle registered than any other northern or western state — 262 to be exact.[50]

Increased automobile use spawned another commercial activity that was to become one of America's largest service industries 50 years later — the auto camp, better known today as the motel. In most cities on the west coast, the first auto camps were municipally owned. Portland's single auto camp in the early 1920s was located on North Union Avenue, north of Columbia Boulevard, the main north-south interstate route. Although it was self-supporting for several years, Portland decided, in company with other major west coast cities, to turn such business over to private management. The project had proved its worth financially and the need for additional camps was beyond the means and scope of city government to provide. But the seeds of the future had been planted.

Chapter 12

West Side vs. East Side:
Ralph B. Lloyd Enters Portland

On a Sunday morning in the spring of 1923, Ralph B. Lloyd, a multi-millionaire oilman from Ventura, California, purchased a quarter block at the northeast intersection of Grand Avenue and Glisan Street for $5000. This was the site on which Sears, Roebuck was to build its Portland store in 1929. The purchase marked the launching of the most ambitious program of urban land acquisition by one person in Portland's history. Lloyd told local realtor Albert R. Ritter that he was prepared to spend upwards of $25 million over a period of 25 years to build America's greatest "little city within a city" if Ritter could secure for him a vast area on all sides of Holladay Park embracing some 50 or 60 solid blocks of property.

During the decade from 1923 to 1933, from the boom years through the bottom of the depression, Lloyd was to spend only $3 million of the $25 million he expected to invest, but he acquired the basic properties that would create the giant Lloyd Center 27 years later. When it opened in 1960, the center included not only a major Sheraton Hotel and numerous governmental agencies including the Bonneville Power Administration, but the largest shopping mall in the world — a commercial complex that is today rated among the top ten centers in the nation in dollar volume.

The story of the Lloyd Center's genesis, coupled with the account of Ralph Lloyd's first decade as a Portland investor, adds an interesting dimension to the history of Portland's boom and depression eras. It also serves as an invaluable case study of Portland attitudes toward California investors and of traditional West Side attitudes toward East Side developments.

The Near East Side: The Holladay and Irvington Districts

The Holladay Addition to East Portland owes its name to the colorful railroad magnate Ben Holladay who purchased the property in 1868. Although he had little to do with any actual development, Holladay was convinced that Portland's future would be centered on the East Side. Some years after he had left Portland, Holladay's former associates, headed by George Weidler, began to develop the addition as a middle to upper class residential area. It grew rapidly until World War I. Most of the land that Lloyd bought was in Holladay's addition. It was purchased from private owners, the largest being the Larrabee family and the Balfour Guthrie Company of London, which had previously acquired 170 lots on both sides of Sullivan's Gulch.

The Irvington Addition, several blocks to the north, was platted in 1887 and underwent its initial development in the 1890s. A number of prominent West Side Portlanders were involved in Irvington's future, but the leading developer was Ellis Hughes who founded the Irvington Investment Company. From its earliest days, Irvington was planned as a self-contained middle to upper class residential district of approximately 120 double blocks, eleven of which were set aside for a park. Commercial activity was to be prohibited. After a period of normal growth, competition from the newer Rose City Park and Laurelhurst developments slowed down the pace of sales in Irvington, and the advent of the European war reduced activity even further. The post-war period, from 1920 to 1923, found all Portland developers anxious to move their properties as quickly as possible. Intense sales competition ensued, complicated by the city's attempt to auction over 4000 lots city-wide for delinquent taxes.

For a potential purchaser of large acreage like Ralph B. Lloyd, the year 1923 was a propitious time to enter the real estate market. Lots that would normally sell from $1000 to $1600 could be bought for one-third of their market value. Although Lloyd did not purchase any property in Irvington proper, in many people's minds his development **was** in Irvington.[1] By 1923, the Holladay Addition property had already been invaded by both commercial activity and multi-family construction whereas Irvington had largely maintained its residential uniformity. And the person most responsible for this condition was Major General Charles H. Martin, the late Ellis Hughes' son-in-law, the president of the Hughes Investment Company and the future governor of Oregon.

During the years that he was serving in the Canal Zone, Martin was in continual contact with his Portland realtor, E. J. Lowe, Albert Ritter's partner. In trying to meet just the needs of both Ralph B. Lloyd and General Charles H. Martin, the firm of Ritter & Lowe was kept fully occupied. Martin had 120 lots he wanted to sell, but strictly for residential use. In May 1920, he wrote Ritter & Lowe: "It is necessary that we leave no stone unturned to move Irvington."[2] Through his friendship with banker John C. Ainsworth, who was chairman of the city planning commission, Martin exerted pressure to prevent the city from auctioning any Irvington properties — actions that could reduce the value of his own lots. The quality of the older Irvington district was going to be maintained at all costs. Realtor Lowe wrote Martin that the cheapening value of lots in Laurelhurst was "putting it in a class with Rose City Park instead of Irvington."[3]

As early as 1921, realtor Lowe clearly perceived the changes that were going to occur on the southern fringe of Irvington, three blocks north of the property Ralph B. Lloyd would be acquiring. In a letter to Martin, Lowe wrote: "Business is encroaching on this property. . . . It will eventually be flats and apartments."[4] Lowe was concerned about encouraging prospective purchasers who might build fine homes only to have to sacrifice them later. "They would prefer to go further out and get property where they are sure of not having business property

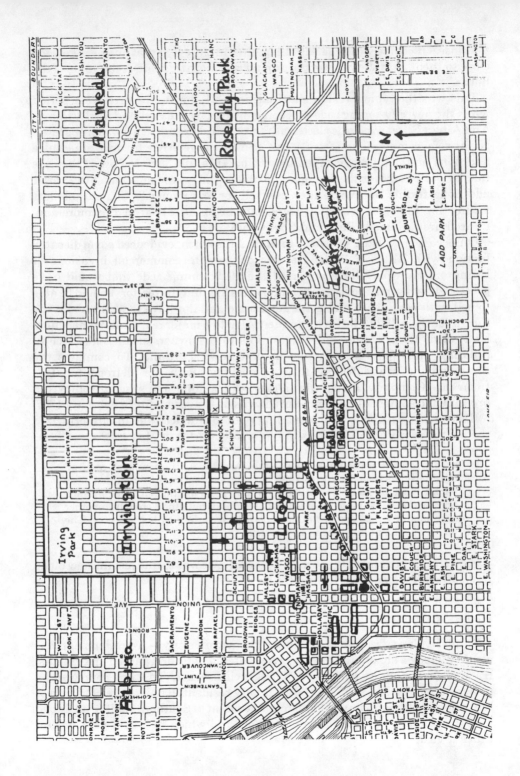

too close. Of course we argue with them that in the event that business gets too close to them, that the value of the ground will more than offset the value of the house."[5]

This was the typical realtor's attitude in 1921, during the three year period when the new city zoning code was being drafted by the Portland Realty Board. And Albert Ritter was to be elected as realty board president a few months later. Numerous communiques from Lowe to Martin referred to the "other nice additions on the market competing with us. It is true," wrote Lowe, "they are farther out but this is the day of automobiles and we are up against the newer additions further out where they can sell for less money."[6] Comparable lots selling for $1500 in Irvington were only bringing $1000 in Eastmoreland, Laurelhurst, Alameda Park and Rose City Park.

On occasion, Martin, in letters to John Ainsworth, evidenced some dissatisfaction with Ritter & Lowe. He was opposed to commercial invasions of Irvington. He would have preferred the 1919 zoning code that would have protected Irvington's southern boundary. He felt that the realtors should be able to sell with confidence and get a good price and not have to worry about the future. Early in 1922, Martin's impatience led to a major real estate transaction. He traded 80 percent of his Irvington lots to the owners of the Blake McFall Building on S. W. Fifth Avenue in downtown Portland. To complete the financing, he negotiated a $100,000 mortgage with the Metropolitan Life Insurance Company. Renamed the Hughes Building, the structure enjoyed a prominent commercial existence until it was destroyed by fire in February 1977.

Realtor Lowe defended the prevailing realtor practices and in turn criticized the attitudes of Portland buyers. As he wrote Martin in May 1922:

> "I look forward to the day when we get in Portland a little new blood, as I find that outsiders appreciate the values here a great deal more than the old moss backs. We have no trouble in selling a man from another city if he wants a home site because he does not object to telephone buildings, churches or other surroundings that are not exactly perfect according to his ideas. . . . The buying public at this time is very finicky."[7]

Exactly one year later, the firm of Ritter & Lowe was to find just the new blood it sought in the person of Ralph B. Lloyd.

Lloyd's Dream

Ralph B. Lloyd dreamed of building a city within a city — a development that would include a shopping center, a civic center, a hotel and garden apartments. He also contemplated some recreational facilities, such as a golf course and a professional baseball stadium. Single family residential units were not a part of his scheme. Although he would remain a resident of Southern California, Lloyd was to maintain an active interest in Portland which he would visit several times a year.[8]

Ralph B. Lloyd (1875-1953)

Beginning in October 1926, Lloyd made the U. S. Bank his Portland headquarters. He was pleased with his reception at the bank and took a personal liking to President Ainsworth. To solidify his relationship, he bought 100 shares of U. S. Bank stock which was selling for approximately $250 a share in 1926. For ten years, Lloyd carried on a lengthy correspondence with Ainsworth. His letters provided a detailed account of his hopes, plans, accomplishments and problems.

In February 1927 he reported to Ainsworth:

> "During the past six months I have invested in Portland about $1,600,000, making a total investment of approximately $2,000,000 in properties all the way from Sandy Boulevard to Kenton. I have paid in full for all properties with the exception of two lots . . . and feel that I have laid the foundation for my real estate investment and should now adopt my policy as to the handling of this real estate. . . . "[9]

Lloyd had to decide whether he would sell some of the property "at the most appropriate time or spend considerable sums of money in the development of it

The Irvington Residential District

From its earliest days, Irvington has contained some of Portland's largest homes. As realtor E. J. Lowe wrote General Martin, it was a "great place for the lumber people." Andrew Porter was a prominent Portland investor, lumberman, director of the U. S. Bank and owner of the Porter Building — formerly headquarters for the Wells Fargo Bank, later

The Andrew Porter home at the corner of N. E. Tillamook and 22nd

The Willard P. Hawley home at the corner of N. E. 22nd and Hancock

acquired by the U. S. National Bank and now the U. S. Bank Building. Utility executive Franklin T. Griffith was to move to Irvington in 1928 from Ladd's Addition. In 1935, Griffith's antagonist — and Governor Martin's chief critic — Public Utilities Commissioner Charles M. Thomas was also to move into the neighborhood.

Willard P. Hawley was the founder of the Hawley Pulp & Paper Company of Oregon City. He sold the company in 1926 and it was later acquired by the Publisher's Paper Company in 1948. Hawley also had an interest in the St. Helen's Pulp & Paper Company, purchased in 1952 by Crown Zellerbach. Hawley's son married the daughter of Oregon Republican leader Phil Metschan, Jr. Both the Hawley and Porter homes, along with the prestigious Irvington Tennis Club to the north, were located on the southeastern fringe of Irvington, in an area currently designated for high density residential use, three blocks from a designated apartment zone.

The western third of the Irvington district has experienced an influx of minority families — mostly blacks — who have moved eastward out of the Albina "ghetto" area. The ratio of blacks to Caucasians is approximately 10-1. Irvington's housing stock is mixed, ranging from older type mansions to modest tract-type dwellings. Median housing values place Irvington between Laurelhurst and Rose City Park. A 6-1 ratio of owner occupied to renter occupied residences ranks Irvington almost equal to Laurelhurst but well above Rose City Park.[10] In recent years, the district has undergone a considerable renovation of its older housing stock as younger professional couples have moved into the area. When President Jimmy Carter visited Portland in 1978, he spent the night in Irvington at the home of a young family.

Tract-type dwellings in the northwestern section of Irvington, adjacent to Irving Park. Built before World War I, several of these homes are black occupied.

and the development of the city in general by this work." He told Ainsworth that he was "inclined toward the development program." He already had plans to erect a combined theater, store and office building on the southwest corner of N. E. Union Avenue and Killingsworth, on land acquired from the Francis M. Warren estate. At a cost of $300,000, the structure was expected to "exceed in beauty any building of this type in the city." The Walnut Park Building occupies this site today.

Lloyd informed Ainsworth that he had already been approached by two different parties to open a bank at the Killingsworth location. But he expressed little enthusiasm for the banking business if he would have any of the details to look after. He was agreeable to investing in a bank — to take 50 or 51 percent — if the bank's management could be assumed "by some institution experienced in this line of work." Ultimately, the managing institution could absorb the bank as a branch. Lloyd was hopeful that the U. S. National might be interested and indeed it was. The Union State Bank opened for business in November 1927 with Lloyd as president and J. O. Elrod and L. T. Merwin, president of Northwestern Electric, as directors. Elrod, who had suffered from the recent Northwestern Bank collapse, was named a vice president. A majority of the stock was held by the Lloyd Corporation. The bank became a unit of the U. S. Bank's West Coast Bancorp and achieved full branch status in April 1933. Shortly after assuming the presidency, Lloyd discovered that Oregon law required state bank presidents to be residents of the state. He relinquished the post to his local Lloyd Corporation manager, C. W. Norton.

In 1928, Ralph Lloyd became increasingly involved in local governmental affairs. He was going to need city council approval for the various street widening projects that he was planning for his major East Side development. He wrote Ainsworth in October:

"Personally I am in hope that the Union Avenue widening, the widening of Burnside from the bridge to at least the park blocks, the widening of Sixth Street to the depot and from the steel bridge on Glisan to Sixth Street will be approved. I believe these four projects would add more tone to the city than any similar widening projects in the entire district of the city's incorporated limits.

While I may be called an East Side man, I see that a great city must be made by the building of both sides."[11]

Lloyd also knew that the building of "a great city" required the active support of the city council. With this point in mind, he wrote Ainsworth in September 1928 about the forthcoming municipal elections.

"As I understand it, Mayor Baker and Commissioners Mann and Barbur are all up for re-election this year. I do not know exactly how you people in Portland handle your campaign funds, but I presume each of these gentlemen has his campaign expenses to take care of. . . . I feel that I should show my

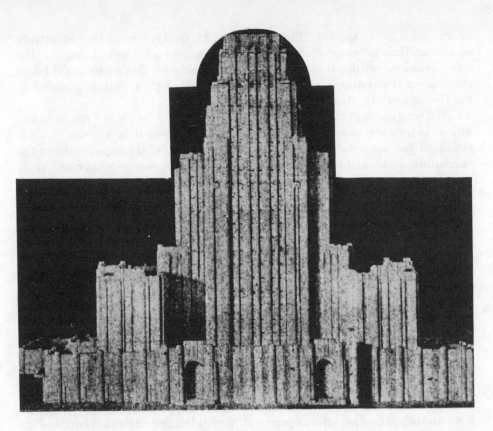

Original plaster model of the hotel — September 1930

appreciation at least in a modest way of the co-operation of the Portland
people, and I am agreeable to send my check for $300 to you or to whom you
may designate, to be applied upon the respective campaign funds of the
gentlemen mentioned above."

Lloyd assumed that Ainsworth was in sympathy with the re-election of
Messrs. Baker, Barbur and Mann and told his friend that he was sending them
copies of the letter.[12]

An East Side Superhotel

During much of 1929, Lloyd was occupied with his business affairs in Los
Angeles, particularly after the stock market crash in late October. Despite the
problems of the oil industry, he gave considerable thought to the construction of
a new hotel in Portland — to be the "center" of his "new city." He was hoping to
begin the foundation work in the summer of 1930 and he was prepared to expend
upwards of $3 million on the whole project. He felt that the city government was

333

dragging its feet in the widening of Union and Grand Avenues. He had already done more than his share of street improvements and believed strongly that the city should be willing to meet him at least half-way. Before he could begin excavation, it was necessary for the city to vacate streets in the center section of the Holladay Park area.

Lloyd wrote Ainsworth in June that the "multitude of details in a structure like this is something almost oppressive, especially when it is a desire to set a standard for the coast in this particular structure."[13] He hoped to have the excavation and foundations in before the "heavy rainy season is upon us." To do this, it was absolutely essential to begin work by August at the latest.

Lloyd came to Portland for the earthmoving ceremonies on August 16th. He told *The Oregonian* that he was planning a $2 million, 21-story hotel on a 30 acre tract that would be finished in 18 months. He wanted it "ready for the crowds of easterners and Europeans" who were expected to flock to the Pacific Coast "for the 1932 Olympiad to be held in Los Angeles."[14] Within four weeks he was back again, this time to host a conference of leading American hotel men who were invited to view the unveiling of a model. Described by *The Oregonian* as a "mountainous structure of stone and steel," the hotel looked like a small replica of New York's Waldorf-Astoria or Woolworth Building.

Speaking to the assembled group that included a number of local leaders like J. C. Ainsworth, R. H. Strong, L. H. Hoffman and the owners and managers of the Benson and Multnomah hotels, Lloyd indicated for the first time that it might be necessary to modify the plans "in some respect to make the hotel an economically sound proposition." He also used the occasion to discuss with Portland financiers and investors a proposal "for the leading citizens of Portland" to subscribe $500,000 to be applied upon the furnishing and equipment of the hotel."[15] He was considering the issuance of six percent preferred stock. As he later described the plan to Ainsworth:

> "We naturally feel that the next step is to have definite subscriptions made by the Portland group and we are writing you this letter to ask that you talk this matter over with the group proposing to make this subscription."[16]

Lloyd's proposal for some local financing, after he had announced originally that he was underwriting all of the costs, unsettled his Portland friends. William Hemphill of Commonwealth Securities wrote Ainsworth in October that "it would be practically impossible at this time to market a six percent preferred stock." Too many other issues were paying a higher return. Hemphill concluded with a statement that was in keeping with an old Portland tradition:

> "If it is local support and good will which Mr. Lloyd desires more than financial strength at this time, I am sure an excellent group of local men, possibly ten or twelve, would be very glad to serve on the Board of Directors of the new Hotel Corporation. This, in my opinion, would accomplish more than would the sale of any type of security to the investing public."[17]

The message was loud and clear: "We will be glad to lend you our name rather than our money. You take the risk!"

During the fall of 1930, the planning for the hotel moved at a slow pace. The excavation work had been completed and L. Hawley Hoffman had been awarded the construction contract. The reticence of local investors to back the Lloyd project was revealed by some exchanges between Robert H. Strong and John Ainsworth. The Commonwealth president, along with some of his close associates like E. B. MacNaughton of the First National Bank, really favored a major new hotel on the West Side, preferably on the site of the old Portland Hotel. Strong even wrote the president of the United Hotels chain seeking advice and support were a new West Side structure to be built.

Strong was a perennial optimist who was convinced that he could market a $2.5 million stock issue because "the Portland Hotel site will command more public interest . . . than any other site." Strong was also convinced that "the mental health of Portlanders" in December 1930 was "healthier than it has been for a good many years. . . . This city will respond . . . when business conditions revive."[18] Strong's optimism had driven him to persuade Commonwealth to pay $800,000 in cash for a half block on S. W. Sixth, "the largest single real estate deal"[19] of the year in the downtown. He had grandiose plans to construct a 20-story headquarters and general office building on the site. Although the structure would be delayed for 18 years and Strong would shortly be out of a job, Strong's feeling toward the desirability of West Side development, versus the liability of an East Side project like Lloyd's, reflected Portland's traditional attitude toward ventures across the river.

From the correspondence it is difficult to evaluate John Ainsworth's true feelings about the Lloyd hotel project. It is obvious that he was anxious to see the West Side undergo a renaissance of new construction. He certainly did not discourage Robert Strong's efforts. And yet he continued to give encouragement to Lloyd as he struggled to win local financial support. However, one is left with the feeling that Ainsworth's heart was really not in the Lloyd hotel project. He must have realized that Portland would not have suported the financing and construction of two new hotels during the bleak years of 1930-1931. He may also have been dismayed, along with many other Portlanders, by Lloyd's projected plans. The structure was way out of scale for its setting, and it was on the East Side.

Toward the end of December 1930, Ainsworth wrote Lloyd that he was excited by the prospect that the Biltmore Hotel chain might elect to operate the hotel and even invest some money in the project. "The Lloyd-Biltmore" pleased him. The name was "euphonious."[20] But such notions were premature until the hotel actually underwent construction. No chain, or any investor for that matter, would make a commitment before a definite completion date was established. Lloyd replied that the plans had been modified extensively but he still hoped to "be underway in a very few weeks."

On January 17, 1931, Ralph Lloyd wrote John Ainsworth an astounding letter about the frightening conditions of the oil market in California. This was the first mention of a serious problem that must have consumed an increasing amount of Lloyd's time over the previous six months. The oil industry in 1931 was facing the consequences of overproduction and underconsumption.

Moving on to a discussion of the hotel, Lloyd declared that a project of the type he was planning — "a little city within itself" — was overwhelming for a single individual to undertake and complete "under present conditions. . . . . "

> "Though it may force me to make some sacrifices, I feel that the example set in so doing will be beneficial not only to the entire city of Portland but to the State of Oregon . . . as well, for all value and the idea of prosperity or depression are to a great degree mental attitudes.
>
> Personally, I believe that there are three factors which have more to do with our present depression than anything else and I would rate them as follows: First: A break in the standards of integrity and morality in business, which has caused distrust. Second: Extravagance in management, which has caused waste and leads to a sudden check when the end of the rope is reached. Third: Fatigue. The wild rush of the past five or ten years has created a state of fatigue in the managerial brains of the nation.
>
> We are going into this hotel project depending upon you Portland men to stand by us up to the $500,000 and also to cooperate with us in the managing Board of Directors of the operating company.

PROPOSED·CIVIC·CENTER·FOR·THE·CITY·OF·PORTLAND·OREGON

Lloyd's new 1931 plan for an East Side civic center

336

A number of my friends seem to think that I am foolish to go into an enterprise of this type in a city as far away from my home as Portland and which will involve when complete, with land, golf course, etc., approximately $5,000,000. While I see their viewpoint to a large extent, I still believe that by cooperating with all of you this project can be made one of the unique developments upon the Pacific Coast and that it will have the entire City of Portland behind it. If I were to carry on a similar development in our area here in Los Angeles there would be a number of competitive institutions while in Portland, for some years to come at least, no one can afford to spend the money involved in a competitive structure, so that, irrespective of my friends' opinions, I believe it will be shown that even though Portland is a smaller city than Los Angeles, the feeding area that will be present for the hotel project will compare favorably with what would be present for a similar institution in the Los Angeles district on account of the many competitive institutions present here at this time. As a good citizen, I think my money will do more for the Northwest thus expended than it would for the Southwest."[21]

It is doubtful that anyone to date in Portland's history has expressed a greater faith in the city's future and at the same time made a commitment to provide the funds to finance such dreams. The desire to put one's money where it would do the most good was unique in a society governed by the precept of investment for highest return or largest profit. Unfortunately for Ralph B. Lloyd, Portlanders did not respond positively. It has been reliably reported[22] that some West Side establishment figures even wanted Lloyd to fail and leave town. His money— and his presence — were resented. Some Portlanders were still smarting over the sale of the First National Bank to California interests in 1930. They wanted to keep control for themselves. But the final straw for the old "moss backs" was the East Side location of Lloyd's hotel.

The next few months proved discouraging for investor Lloyd. He received word that many property owners in the Irvington and Holladay Park districts were attempting to pressure the city council to abandon the street widening that had been pending for two years. C. W. Norton warned the council that "Mr. Lloyd is not going any further to educate the people of Portland." If the street were not widened, he would abandon all his plans.[23] The Lloyd Corporation was prepared to pay for over 60 percent of the total costs involved, with the individual property owners sharing the remainder, with ten years allowed for completing payments.

Early in March, Lloyd for the first time began to wonder whether he had picked the right city for his major out-of-state development. Had he misplaced his faith in Portland? What brought such concerns was his discovery that the major Portland building suppliers had willfully entered into collusion to raise the bids on materials that would be needed for the hotel. He wrote C. C. Hall of the East Side Commercial Club:

"We have been sounding out the market in Portland for about $100,000 worth of material and are greatly disappointed and in a way discouraged by finding

337

that we can go into practically any city on the Pacific coast and buy material, pay the freight and lay it down in Portland cheaper than we have been offered it in Portland. . . . . We must frankly admit that if this is the reception that anyone attempting to do creative work in the City of Portland is to receive, then we are fearful the advantages of making investments in other cities will become very apparent by the difference in the cost of materials in your city as compared with other cities on the coast.

We would regret very much to have to build the hotel with out-of-state material, but if the prices we have received to date are indicative of what we may expect in the future, then we will have to admit that it will have to be built from materials purchased in other states.

In closing we wish to assure you that it was our desire and intention to buy everything in Portland and in Oregon that we possibly could in justice to ourselves and the future earning power of the money we have been pouring into Portland, but, of course, you realize that no one will pay a bonus for the opportunity to make investments in any city, and Portland is bound to be outranked by other cities if she offers economic advantages to other cities by holding of a higher level of operating or building costs."[24]

Lloyd wrote Ainsworth in June 1931 that plans for the hotel were 95 percent complete and a new model was to be finished by July 1st.

"I have already spent in the neighborhood of $100,000 on the hotel plans, but will have to admit that I am disappointed in the tendency of the country in showing such extremely slow recuperative power, and I am fearful that it is going to be quite some time for business to get back to the activity and volume to which we have been accustomed."[25]

A month after the stock market hit bottom in the summer of 1931, Ralph Lloyd had already made up his mind to effect some basic changes in his various Portland and California enterprises. He decided that it would be "folly" for him to provide more than the "junior financing" for the hotel. If he were to fund the project in its entirety, "the capital thus tied up" could not be used for other improvements in both California and Oregon that he felt should be made on properties that he owned.

Lloyd wrote John Ainsworth on August 13, 1931, reporting his change in plans and recapitulating all that he had spent on his Holladay Park projects. Excluding land purchasing costs and property taxes, he had expended $40,000 on the nine hole golf course, with $20,000 more committed to complete it with a fence and shrubbery. He had signed an agreement with both the city and the Union Pacific Railroad to stand one-third of the cost of building the 16th Street viaduct over Sullivan's Gulch. Projecting his share at $50,000, Lloyd was led to understand that the bridge was expected to carry "traffic from the super highway from Oregon City through Portland to the Interstate Bridge over the Columbia." The bridge was never constructed after the state abandoned its plans to convert 16th into a major north-south arterial to be incorporated into the state highway system.

In addition to the $100,000 spent on the hotel plans, including a kitchen layout described by the Dohrman Company as the "finest . . . of any hotel in the United States," Lloyd had expended approximately $250,000 on Lloyd Boulevard and other streets leading to the hotel project. In all, he had sunk nearly $400,000 into the endeavor and had commitments for another $70,000. He informed Ainsworth that he could invest no more than $1 million of additional funds; the rest would have to come from Portland backers and/or from a first mortgage.

> "Under the present depressed condition of the country I am not justified in attempting to handle this matter alone, for the very nature of the institution, its location and environment make of it at least a semi-civic project and I must have the united city behind me."[26]

Two new elements had been injected into the picture. The hotel was to assume a "semi-civic" character and the local lenders were being asked to provide more than $1.5 million to complete the project. Obviously, for Portlanders at least, such expectations were hopeless. Ainsworth had already seen several of his own local investment proposals collapse as the market hit bottom. The one closest to his heart had been the States Steamship Company venture. He really could offer no encouragement to his friend in Los Angeles.

The hotel was placed on a back burner for the next 21 months. The excavation ditch lay open and unimproved as a reminder of unfulfilled dreams. It later became the Holladay Bowl, a site for outdoor musical productions. In the intervening months, Lloyd finished the golf course and built the clubhouse, to be converted later to Ireland-at-Lloyd's Restaurant. He also constructed a store on N. E. Broadway that was leased to Ross McIntyre. Both buildings cost a total of $200,000. In California, reflecting his change of interest, he invested over $1 million on land improvements and new purchases.

Ralph Lloyd returned to Portland in early May 1933, carrying a number of new proposals and sporting an air of exuberance. The oil market had rebounded and his confidence had been restored. In mid-1931, his company had "opened up the deepest oil sands ever discovered by man." Over the succeeding months prior to his Portland visit, Lloyd learned that the new find was expected to become one of the great oil deposits of the world. He had good reason to be optimistic about the future.

In a lengthy interview granted to *The Oregonian*,[27] Lloyd discussed some of his revised plans and hopes for Portland. He believed that "his district will be the sleeping quarters of the West Side in time, and with this in mind, the hotel will be so designed that 50 percent will be residential." He envisioned an "English type," eight-story hotel to cost between one and two million dollars, to be built on the earlier already excavated site that would encompass five acres. With this, as with the other projects he had in mind, he hoped to receive some federal emergency relief funds to supplement his own resources.

Additional plans called for the erection of an East Side public market building, similar to the one that was then under construction on the West Side waterfront.

Lloyd also offered to contribute four blocks of his property for a new baseball park and to replace the old Vaughn Street Stadium with a new one. Portland needed a modern armory and he would be happy to donate the required land. Several of Lloyd's suggestions related to arterial improvements: A diagonal connection between Union and Grand Avenues and new ramps for the west end of the Steel Bridge. Not to be left out, of course, was the construction of a permanent Lloyd Corporation headquarters building.

Perhaps the most unusual suggestion related to Sullivan's Gulch which cut diagonally through the southern portion of his land. He wanted to beautify it by creating a mile-long park that would be deeded to the city. To fully accomplish such a goal, Lloyd told the press, he hoped that "the railroad tracks in Sullivan's Gulch will be buried." He failed to spell out what he meant. Possibly, he may have contemplated constructing a tunnel and then filling in over it with dirt, grass and trees. In any case, the idea intrigued his listeners. Had such a proposal become a reality, it would have radically altered the freeway configuration of present-day Portland. It also might have produced a different development pattern for the Holladay Park property. The building of the Banfield Expressway through Sullivan's Gulch 20 years later was the major determinant in the Lloyd Corporation's decision to build the Lloyd Shopping Center — a commercial labyrinth designed to serve the automobile.

Lloyd concluded his lengthy press conference with some thoughts about Portland and the oil industry. "I have not lost faith in Portland," he declared. "If Portland does not succeed, then there is no hope for the rest of the country." Referring to the nation as a whole, Lloyd asserted that "this country is deficient in but one thing — honesty! If the oil industry is any example, dishonesty and deception are rampant in this country, and that is largely responsible for the present conditions."[28]

Lloyd's Dashed Hopes

The total cost of Ralph Lloyd's new proposals for his Holladay Park property came to over $3 million. Lloyd failed to indicate just what funding he would provide. It would depend, he said, on how much federal emergency relief money he could secure. He made personal contact with Senator Charles McNary and Representative Charles Martin to see if they could be of assistance. Both indicated some interest but unfortunately both McNary and Martin were first committed to securing financing for the Bonneville Dam. Local governmental officials, with their own lists of pet projects most of which were on the West Side, highly complimented Lloyd without offering him much encouragement. Said Commissioner Earl Riley: "The proposals were the most constructive that had been brought before the committee," referring to the group of governmental officials and businessmen who were evaluating emergency relief applications. County Commissioner C. A. Bigelow said that "the proposals of Mr. Lloyd were the brightest ray that has come to Portland in the last four years."[29]

Over the next few years, Lloyd would return to Portland and declare that he still hoped to build a hotel on his East Side property, but nothing was to result from such pronouncements. He confined his new investments to smaller and more specialized projects that involved lessees who were willing to sign long term contracts. During the course of his visit in May 1937, he declared: "I am going to strain every facility to build the hotel and get it out of my system. It is going to be built for the middle classes instead of the rich and will give them a beautiful environment at a minimum cost." He particularly hoped to complete the facility in time for a projected Bonneville Dam celebration in 1939. Obviously, he was disappointed by his inability to generate sufficient local investment to make the hotel an economically viable enterprise. He told his friends in Portland that all the city needed was "a restoration of confidence for the future."[30]

He could not help but contrast the spirits of Portland and Los Angeles. The Los Angeles economy was booming. During the first four months of 1937, over $20 million of new construction had been launched. He was well aware that the waterfront strikes and the teamster violence had seriously disrupted Portland's economy. But what discouraged him was the attitude of mind that he encountered within the Portland business and financial community. He detected both a sense of inferiority and a feeling of insecurity that impeded healthy economic growth. Although he realized his inability to change such mental attitudes, he was still prepared to move when the proper signals were received.

Developments Further to the East and South

The anticipated opening of the new Ross Island and Sellwood Bridges, together with the rebuilding of the Burnside Bridge, provided the impetus for swift growth on Portland's East Side. And when the city's voters approved a street widening bond issue in May 1926, the real estate developers moved quickly to take advantage of their opportunities. The main arterials for growth were Powell Boulevard, Foster Road and Division Street in the Southeast, and Glisan Street and Sandy Boulevard in the Northeast. The major north-south arterial, extended and improved to connect with the other arterials, was S. E. 82nd Street — or 82nd Avenue as it was later renamed. S. E. 82nd became the first north and southbound artery to extend from the city's southern boundary near Milwaukie to Columbia Boulevard on the city's northern boundary, adjacent to the town of Parkrose. It became the eastern feeder for the coast-wise Pacific Highway and eventually received state highway designation. Within less than a decade, S. E. 82nd was to become a commercial strip, a development that has continued unabated. S. E. 60th, on the other hand, which was to be developed as a thoroughfare north from Division, running adjacent to the Mt. Tabor reservoirs, did not lose its residential zoning which it has kept to the present day. No commercial inroads were permitted.

341

Homes on S. E. 28th Avenue, some under construction, in Eastmoreland during the late 1920s. The public golf course is in the foreground.

The widening and extension of East Side arterials bode well for existing developments like Eastmoreland. The preliminary plans for a river highway leading to Oregon City indicated that before too long direct access would be provided to many of the Ladd properties that were still undeveloped. It became apparent to the hard pressed Ladd estate — still suffering from the effects of the Ladd & Tilton Bank debacle — that the appropriate time had arrived to liquidate most of its Portland area properties.

On October 1, 1926, the Ladd estate sold, for an undisclosed sum, later rumored to be approximately $5 million, undeveloped real estate in Lake Oswego, Dunthorpe, Westmoreland and Eastmoreland, Canyon Road (the Highlands), Terwilliger Boulevard (Burlingame-Fulton Park), Guild's Lake and the Brooklyn Industrial district. The purchasers were former associates and employees of the Ladd estate, in particular its managing director, Frederick H. Strong and Paul C. Murphy, manager of the Laurelhurst development. Ten days later, Strong and Murphy sold the Eastmoreland properties to a newly organized company, controlled by 49 home owners and residents of the district. The purchase price was not announced, but an appraisal of the 401 home sites came to $728,000. According to veteran Ladd employee Frank B. Upshaw, president of the new Eastmoreland Company, the venture was "unique in real estate development." The residents were "assured development in keeping with the present high standards of the district."[31] More than $3 million had already been invested in Eastmoreland's homes, ranging from $5000 to $40,000 in cost. Within three years, the company was to issue $345,000 in short term gold bonds, and within four years, over $1.5 million would be further invested by 225 new home owners.[32]

Four months after their purchase of the Ladd estate properties, Strong and Murphy sold the bulk of their remaining Portland holdings for a reported $2 million to L. B. Menefee, a prominent Portland lumberman. Menefee in turn would sell all but the Canyon Road-Highlands property that he planned to develop into a restricted "high class" residential district, with houses costing up to $20,000. The present day Racquet Club inhabits the building that Menefee opened inauspiciously in October 1929 as a community center for his new development.

The properties retained by Strong and Murphy were considered the most prestigious: The Dunthorpe and Lake Oswego Country Club districts, all located on land formerly owned by William M. Ladd's Oregon Iron & Steel Company. The Dunthorpe tract had been selling well. As John C. Ainsworth wrote a friend in February 1926: "It is a beautiful piece of ground, and the whole tract is developing very rapidly, some twenty of the finest homes in Portland having been built out there in the last three years and more building all the time. It has just started to develop rapidly . . . "[33]

Before the sale to Strong and Murphy, the Ladd estate had already invested considerable funds in the Lake Oswego district to the south. An 18 hole golf course and country club had been constructed and homesites developed along the southeast side of the lake. "Of all Lake Oswego's districts," declared one large ad, "Lakewood is the most accessible — the nearest — possessed of modern advantages. There is no more beautiful spot anywhere. . . . An easy 25 minute ride from Portland's business center."[34] The advertisement also emphasized the Red Electric station nearby and the availability of the Oregon City and Salem bus lines. In fifty years, Lake Oswego was to grow from a few hundred to over 22,000 in population and become the second richest town per capita in Oregon. City authorities now project a population of 50,000 by the year 2000. The original investment by Murphy and his major partner Frederick H. Strong, whom he later bought out, proved to be a bonanza over the long haul.

At the opposite end of the Portland metropolitan region, at its northeast extremity, the small farming and residential town of Parkrose received a boost by the widening and extension of Sandy Boulevard that resulted from the rebuilding of the Burnside Bridge. Traffic could be expected to flow directly into downtown Portland, a distance of only six miles. As *The Oregon Journal* noted in May 1926, "Parkrose is a primary commuting center. . . . It is one of the most progressive and promising commuting districts on the eastern border of the city."[35] Until the middle of the decade, Parkrose was considered "too far" from the center of Portland even though most of its working population was employed in Portland, with many of them using the Sandy Boulevard-Parkrose streetcar line.

Public curiosity about Parkrose was stimulated in 1921 when the Portland Planning Commission and the Portland Ad Club jointly unveiled a proposal to make Sandy Boulevard "The Roseway" — five miles of rose-bordered thoroughfare, extending from East Twelfth Street along Sandy Boulevard to the Parkrose limits. The city agreed to produce 15,000 "choice Caroline Testout rose plants"[36] to be used in beautifying the thoroughfare. Before the year was out, Paul Keyser of the park department had already planted 3000 of the plants.

343

Proposed entrance to Portland — N. E. Sandy Boulevard — 1932

Unfortunately, few of the rose enthusiasts could predict the impact of the commercial realtors on Sandy Boulevard's future growth. The 1924 zoning code placed most of the route in zone 3 — commercial. And as more commuters drove their autos into Portland, gas stations and stores proliferated along the "Roseway." By 1926, the *Journal* noted that Sandy Boulevard was "vital to autos" and the commercial trend was growing.[37] Beginning in the Hollywood district of Rose City Park, large chunks of frontage were being sold for commercial use and the lavish Hollywood Theater had been built. As late as 1932, the planning commission staff still hoped that the city could build a "grand entrance to Portland" on Sandy Boulevard, but the commercial interests proved too powerful. Anyone who drives the route today can witness the result — few roses are to be observed.

As Sandy Boulevard became a commercial thoroughfare, Parkrose also became a commercial center. Industry began to locate there, aided and abetted by the Union Pacific Railroad which owned large tracts adjacent to its right-of-way. The new housing stock built in the early 1930s was cheap by Portland standards, about 50 percent of the average cost of a new city home. One prominent ad noted that new five room houses along the "Roseway" at N. E. 91st Street in Parkrose could be bought for as little as $1500 in October 1932, or they could be rented for $30 a month, or better yet, for $17.50 a month with a $100 down payment. All rental charges included mortgage interest and taxes.[38]

Parkrose became a site for World War II temporary housing, and in 1946 it became one of the largest post-war centers for tract housing. Within a fifty year period, the little town of 2000 has grown large enough to serve a regional commercial-residential population of over 40,000, all without benefit of any systematic land use planning. As one local newspaper recently declared: "Parkrose is victim of urban crunch."[39] Its housing stock is diverse: Apartments, duplexes, condominiums, planned unit developments and mobile homes — all intermixed with assorted industrial and commercial enterprises which dot the landscape formerly occupied by dairy farms and rose gardens. The community is bordered on the south by the 20 year old Interstate 80N freeway that runs east and west. It is also bordered on the west by the new Interstate 205 freeway.

The projected widening of Sandy Boulevard in 1926 led to another development that was in stark contrast to Parkrose. The small residential community of Maywood Park was platted on the western border of Parkrose in a densely wooded area of fir trees. Planned strictly for residential use, the community was never intended to be a city. The original homes were priced from $4000 to $8000, designed to appeal to the same class of prospective buyer who could be expected to move to Laurelhurst or Eastmoreland. The onset of the depression created financial problems for the developer, Columbia Realty. When Commonwealth Inc. was organized in 1930, with Robert H. Strong as president,

Tract housing — N. E. 112th and Prescott
Parkrose — 1946

East Parkrose, bordered on the south by Interstate 80N, late 1950s. Farmland on the right (south) is now an industrial park served by the Union Pacific Railroad.

it negotiated the sale of Maywood Park's 167 unsold building sites to some clients who paid a total of $100,000 for the property. Commonwealth also assumed exclusive sales management for the development that had been platted originally for approximately 700 homes.

During the early 1960s when it became apparent that the new Interstate 205 freeway might penetrate its exclusive domain, Maywood Park's residents voted to incorporate as a city in the hope of blocking the freeway. They only partially succeeded in their efforts. The freeway has removed some houses along the western edge of the city, but it has been depressed below grade level and great care has been taken to preserve every tree possible. Maywood Park is a unique city: It has no commercial activity and it contracts for all of its services from Multnomah County and surrounding special service districts. It has no paid employees and is administered by an unpaid mayor and city council.[40] The freeway's intrusion has only had a minor negative effect on current housing prices which are in the same range as Eastmoreland homes, at least 50 percent more than the average price of a Parkrose home. Despite the disruption by the freeway, Maywood Park has kept its life style intact. But at some future date, the community might decide to annex itself to Portland. As the costs of contracted services increase, such a move could prove economically advantageous.

Developments to the North

As early as 1924, the Peninsula Bridge Company of St. Johns was organized to generate public support for a high bridge across the Willamette, to connect St. Johns with Linnton, replacing a ferry that carried over 1000 vehicles a day. It took four years to win voter approval for a $4.2 million bond issue. St. Johns and Linnton were the forgotten stepchildren of Portland, especially in the years following World War I. Both places were considered "Siberia" to police recruits and both were the butts of many jokes. When the bridge issue was first raised, someone remarked that it would "start from nowhere and lead to limbo."

Both communities had avid boosters who were generally the executives of businesses and banks located in the areas. As Sinclair Wilson, president of the First National Bank of Linnton and a member of the Wilson lumber family, wrote planning commission chairman John Ainsworth in October 1928:

> "St. Johns and Linnton are important industrial districts — both growing and possible of extensive development. Both have large unused residential areas but far in arrears of growth shown elsewhere in Portland. The average wage paid per individual is small, too small indeed to support the modern family."

Wilson was making a case for treating the two communities as one. Greater diversity of occupation could be achieved.

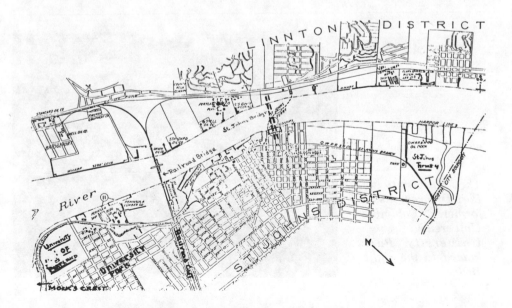

347

The old St. Johns City Hall. It became a fire station in 1915 and is being restored in 1979.

The Star Hotel, built in 1908. It became the Chicago Rooming House for shipyard workers during World War I.

The University of Portland campus — formerly Columbia University. University Park homes to the right. 1920s.

1926 aerial of Mock's Crest, overlooking Swan Island, south of the University of Portland. Large scale development began in 1925. Twenty years later it was completely filled in.

1947 Aerial

The Union Pacific track can be seen exiting from the tunnel under St. Johns. Swan Island is in the upper corner.

Mock's Bottom in 1979, being prepared for industrial sites. Swan Island facilities are to the left; Mock's Crest to the upper right.

"Accessibility to work is of prime importance. Walking distance is desirable despite the automobile. A well located bridge would promote interchange of labor and family wage. This in turn would rapidly tend to dislodge the undesirable floaters in our factories by substituting self supporting families and would bring about a building up of our residential areas."[41]

Wilson's description of the working force pertained more to Linnton than to St. Johns, which traditionally enjoyed a more stable, independent, hardworking and community-spirited residential population. In fact, before the location of several large war housing projects in the St. Johns area during World War II, the district was largely single family residential in character. It was the site of three lumber companies — Portland Manufacturing, St. Johns and Peninsula, an iron works, a shipyard, and the large Portland Woolen Mills. In addition, the community contained important harbor facilities with the Port of Portland dry dock and Municipal Terminals 3 and 4. Most of the industrial working force resided in the area, a characteristic that has remained fairly constant over the past fifty years.

Linnton's population of approximately 2000 was barely a quarter of that of St. Johns. Little strong community feeling had ever been generated among the unstable working force. The physical characteristics of the community, pinched into a narrow strip of waterfront, militated against the creation of such a spirit. In fact, the community's liveliest spirits were generated in its speakeasies; Linnton was a major recipient of liquor bootlegged into the state from Canada. Sinclair Wilson's letter implied that Linnton had really much more to gain from the bridge than St. Johns. Linnton's industry — the gas company plant, three large oil companies, four sawmills, two shingle mills and a furniture factory — was highly concentrated geographically. The logical shipping point for its large and bulky output of manufactured products was across the river at Terminal 4.

Once the bond issue was approved in November 1928, the only matters to be resolved were the bridge's exact location and width. E. B. MacNaughton and John Ainsworth strongly favored a four lane structure. In securing the support of the major newspapers, MacNaughton cited the past history of Canyon Road that had never been built wide enough to carry the traffic load. The county commissioners had the final decision and they were at odds over the matter. As might be expected, Commissioner Fred German wanted to follow the cheapest route, to build three lanes instead of four and save $400,000 for the county.[42] The bond issue approved by the voters was more than ample to cover the cost of four lanes, but German was adamant. After two months of haggling, together with the application of strong pressure from downtown business leaders, the commission voted two to one to build the four lanes. After all, the majority of the large business enterprises in Linnton and St. Johns were owned by men with strong downtown Portland attachments. They were apt to be members of the Arlington Club and reside in Alameda, Irvington or the West Hills. Under the influence of men like MacNaughton and Ainsworth, they were united in their intention to build the finest bridge possible.

350

1940 shot of an apartment over a garage on N. W. St. Helens Road, the main street. The widening of U. S. 30 to St. Helens in the 1960s brought disaster to the town, leaving a commercial strip in devastation. A few small buildings, many of them decaying, survive, along with the Linnton Plywood plant, and oil and chemical storage plants. The waterfront acreage, mostly owned by the Burlington Northern Railroad, is in an equal state of deterioration.

351

The siting of the structure also presented some problems. It was decided to run it just north of the old Municipal Dock No. 3. When C. F. Swigert's Pacific Bridge Company began to construct the piers on the east side in September 1929, it was discovered that there was only three feet of work space between the nearest pier and the dock. Swigert informed Ainsworth that part of the dock would have to be removed. The county commission refused to buy the old structure from the dock commission even though the county had excess bridge funds available. Ainsworth recommended that the dock be torn down at the dock commission's expense. It was of no real value to anyone in 1929. As he wrote to fellow planning commissioner John Laing: " . . . it has stood all of these years as a sort of white elephant, and was originally built for St. Johns before it came into the city limits of Portland."[43]

Portland's public authorities may have been overly thrifty at times — some thought much too thrifty — but the appointed St. Johns Bridge Commission showed excellent aesthetic taste when it selected the New York firm of Robinson & Steinman to design the St. Johns Bridge. In 1929, David Steinman was already being cited as the foremost bridge designer in the world. He had just

The St. Johns Bridge in 1947, with Linnton in the foreground. The Portland Lumber Company mill and dock can be seen in the center of the St. Johns waterfront under the bridge.

352

completed the largest eyebar-cable suspension ever built, at Florianopolis, Brazil. Before receiving the Portland commission, he introduced prestressed twisted wire rope-strand cables for the Grand Mere Bridge in Quebec. "This new system eliminated the time-consuming process of spinning the cables in place."[44] However, the economic benefits of the rope-strand cables were limited to spans up to 1600 feet in length. The St. Johns Bridge was designed for 1207 feet. Using the new method resulted in considerable savings to the Portland taxpayers, despite the $400,000 cost of the fourth lane. The total expenditure came to $3.9 million, over $300,000 less than the approved bond issue.

When the bridge opened during the Rose Festival of June 1931, everyone remarked on its beauty. Steinman himself was particularly pleased, especially with the towers which he described as " . . . architecture in structural steel where beauty is secured without camouflage or ornamentation."[45] Steinman may have had another bridge in mind when he made this remark. In the Gothic towers of the St. Johns Bridge there was "something vaguely reminiscent of those for the Brooklyn Bridge."[46] For many years the bridge's 1207 foot main span made it the longest bridge of its type in the world, and its 205 foot clearance made it one of the highest of the long suspension bridges.

The bridge's opening during the bottom of the depression temporarily brightened the spirits of Portland's citizenry. It was a magnificent public investment of which all could be proud. But that was the extent of such ambitious enterprises for some years to come. In fact, the voters had already registered their disapproval of spending any more taxpayer money on bridges. In May of 1930 they overwhelmingly defeated a $6.5 million bond issue to build the Fremont Bridge, to be located one-half mile north of the current Fremont Bridge, constructed 40 years later. It had proved fortunate that the St. Johns bond measure had come before the voters during the height of the American business boom in 1928. Two years later, all such efforts would have been doomed. The depression years, followed by World War II, precluded the construction of any new trans-Willamette bridges for nearly 30 years, or until the replacement of the 50 year old Morrison Bridge in the late 1950s.

Parks

In the growth years of the 1920s, Portlanders were less inclined to finance new parks than they were to spend public funds on new transportation, traffic and bridge accommodations. The reason may have been partially psychological. Traffic pressures were obvious and apparently worsening. People could see and feel them. With parks, the crunch was apt to lay in the future, when it was too late or costly to acquire them. Even 75 years after the city's founding, unspoiled natural scenery could still be found close at hand. The idea of spending money for parks seemed to many people to be impractical and unnecessary, particularly if the real need was ten years away.

Beginning with the Cheney Plan of 1921, the planning commission and the

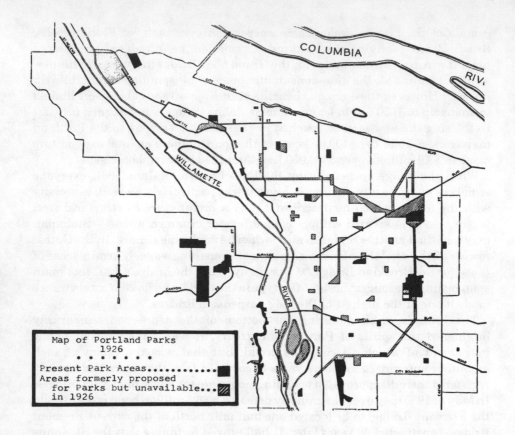

Map of Portland Parks
1926
• • • • • • •
Present Park Areas..............■
Areas formerly proposed
for Parks but unavailable...▨
in 1926

city park department, under the able leadership of C. P. Keyser, gave increased attention to the recreational features of urban park development, rather than to the more traditional concepts that were associated in people's minds with pleasantly landscaped areas.

Although Portland had been one of the national leaders in the playground movement that began in America before World War I, it was falling behind as the years advanced. The city did not own a baseball field, for example, and it possessed only two community athletic houses, one of which was borrowed. Portland's more affluent families could enjoy the Multnomah Athletic Club, but it directly benefited only a fraction of the city's population. And with all of its river waterfront, the city did not own or operate a river park, nor even a bathing beach.

The consequences of inaction and delay were clearly documented by the planning commission when it published a map in 1926, showing the locations for park use (recommended by the Bennett Plan in 1912) that had subsequently become practically unobtainable (the hatched areas on the map above). The areas in black constituted the current park system of the city. Realizations of this sort drove C. P. Keyser to explode:

354

"If there be justification for the expenditure of millions for bridges and arteries, and docks and waterworks — any of which my be provided according to demand, if, as, and when, — there is dereliction somewhere if the body politic does not preempt land for parks, which are never in full demand until the cost has become prohibitive."[47]

Keyser had been stung in 1926 by voter rejection of a $600,000 levy for park and playground acquisition. Only 212 acres had been added since 1919 — 22 of those by gift — to make a total of 1085 acres excluding the three city-owned golf courses. Comparatively Portland was not too far out of line: It was the 24th largest city in the country and it ranked 28th in park land. But Keyser was worried about the future and felt that Portland's rating would worsen if action was not taken immediately. The land was available within the city boundaries as Portland ranked 13th in area size. But only three percent of city land was devoted to parks, with another one and one-half percent dedicated to school use. In comparison, 28.5 percent of the city's land was devoted to streets and auto related uses. "There should be a concerted effort," declared Keyser,

" . . . to provide public playing fields within the city so that the following standard might be observed: Every child in Portland as it will be fifty years hence, should be within three-eighths of a mile of a playing field large enough to insure him 100 square feet of play area."[48]

Keyser also reported on numerous occasions that Portland was the only major city in America with no park police. Park employees were expected to handle such problems. And as to the city zoo, Keyser's true feelings were unprintable. Many years later, Keyser was to tell the city council that Portland never really had a zoo in the true sense of the word, only a "menagerie — a managed exhibit."[49] Throughout the decade of the 1920s, the zoo was in "a deplorable condition." The small animal compound in Washington Park had never really recovered from Mayor Harry Lane's administration. Lane was opposed to caging animals and he had tried to abolish the zoo by limiting and curtailing appropriations. Keyser was the first official to single out the site currently occupied by the zoo. In 1924, he advocated acquiring "the sector between Washington Park, the West Hills Golf Course and the Canyon Road" and developing "a park which might adequately provide a layout for the zoo."[50] Some 30 years later his dream was fulfilled, but at the expense of eliminating the golf course.

During the decade, Portland parks received national recognition for a number of "convenience buildings" and pavilions that had been constructed with the first post-war park levy proceeds. Ellis Lawrence's design of the Sellwood Park pavilion won national attention, as did L. L. Dougan's design[51] of the Duniway Park convenience facility. The only problem with some of the latter structures was that they were often placed in the centers of the parks, an idea that seemed good at the time. In later years, however, when needs and uses changed, requiring the construction of ball fields for example, the central location of the restrooms created severe space utilization difficulties. A long range master plan, detailing possible future uses, might have provided for a more efficient expenditure of public funds over the length of time that such facilities have been in place.[52]

Acropolis on Marquam Hill

Historically, long range master plans have proved reasonably popular in concept, but difficult to follow in practice, especially if they have been interpreted as restrictive on freedom of choice. The entrepreneurs of pre-World War I obviously planned for the future of their own enterprises, but they rarely considered the broader public consequences of their own private decisions. Whether they were businessmen, industrialists, government officials, or even physicians, if they were inclined to build empires they did not welcome restrictive interference from the outside, especially from plans or programs that they had not themselves devised. The good of their enterprise became identified, in their minds at least, with the good of society. The building of the University of Oregon Medical School on Marquam Hill is a case in point. It makes an interesting story that covers the period of years from 1913 to 1928. It is particularly relevant today in the light of the federal government's announced intention to replace with a new structure the 50 year old Veterans Administration Hospital that was built adjacent to the medical school.

In 1913, Dr. Kenneth A. J. Mackenzie, a prominent Canadian-born surgeon, was completing his first year as the second dean of the University of Oregon Medical School. The school building was located in Northwest Portland within walking distance of Good Samaritan Hospital. Mackenzie had practiced in Portland since 1882 and for 20 years had acted as chief surgeon for the Union Pacific Railroad's Oregon Railway & Navigation division. This was only one of his duties. Since its founding in 1887, the medical school had employed him as a professor of surgery. He led an active social life, joined the Arlington Club, and built a ruggedly handsome mansion which survives today as the William Temple House of the Episcopal diocese. His daughter married Roderick Macleay, son of the founder of the U. S. National Bank. After Macleay's death, she married John Laing.

Dr. Mackenzie was a man of high achievement motivation. He had a strong will and tended to dominate those around him. He also had a long cherished dream: To build a new medical school, a health center, not centrally located but at a site far removed from the hurly-burly activity of the Northwest district. There were some other reasons as well. It was rumored that Dr. Mackenzie was having problems with his faculty and he wanted to rebuild the staff as well as the facilities according to his own specifications.

In 1913, he personally secured a gift of 22 acres from the Union Pacific's extensive tract of Marquam Hill property that Henry Villard had purchased in the late 1870s. Mackenzie wanted it clearly understood that the land was donated "specially to the Medical School and **not** to the University of Oregon" — an interesting distinction considering the fact that the university owned the medical school. It was an important distinction for the dean, however, because he therefore felt justified in hiring his own architect, thereby circumventing the normal procedure of involving the dean of the school of architecture in the preliminary planning stages. The first of many confrontations resulted between the two deans, between Mackenzie and the university president and between Mackenzie and the president of the board of regents.[53]

Although the property deed was not received until November 1916, preliminary planning began as soon as the gift was announced. The offer, made personally by Union Pacific chairman Robert S. Lovett to Dr. Mackenzie, restricted one parcel of 12 acres specifically to the medical school. It would revert to the railroad if the "seat of the institution" was ever moved. The smaller parcel of ten acres was conveyed to the board of regents to hold in trust for future hospital development. Within weeks, Mackenzie had contracted with the architectural firm of Whitehouse and Fouilhoux, a Portland partnership that also maintained an office in New York. Preliminary cost estimates totalled $75,000 and construction time was figured at three years.

Mackenzie knew that he was going to have to raise private funds to supplement an anticipated legislative appropriation. He therefore had Whitehouse and Fouilhoux sketch a projected plan — an acropolis, dotted with Parthenon-type structures — depicting a serene setting with imposing buildings nestled among verdant growth. As soon as dean of architecture Ellis Lawrence saw the plan, he wrote regent president A. C. Dixon to register some general concerns. In the light of the present day controversy over the adequacy of site for the new V. A. hospital, Lawrence's thoughts are worth quoting:

> "If I am correctly informed a large portion of the present 25 acres is unavailable for building purposes being extremely steep. The latest rumor has it that a piece of this property is to be donated to the County for its Hospital. From our experience in planning County Hospital grounds we are quite sure there will not be sufficient ground available to properly house the Medical School and the County buildings."[54]

Of course in 1915 there was no thought of a veterans' hospital. That project was 13 years away. But there was concern about accessibility and sufficiency of space for a county hospital. As Lawrence related to Dixon: "I have secured from a man very well versed on the topography that the subject should not be allowed to go too far until a careful study of the block plan is made."[55]

There is no record of any further thought being given to the topographical limitations of the site. The project picked up momentum and Mackenzie secured an appropriation of $50,000 from the 1915 legislature. He wangled $40,000 more in 1917 and raised $25,000 by public subscription. He also won legislative assurance of a $40,000 maintenance appropriation once the facility was constructed.

In the spring and summer of 1917, with construction about to begin, Dean Mackenzie stumbled into a few roadblocks. He encountered his first open opposition from his faculty. Regent president Dixon reported on a meeting that he had attended with the dean and six of his faculty members:

> "Dr. Mackenzie stated that he had been acting and speaking at all times in behalf of the faculty as well as himself, but the faculty did not seem to back him up very strongly and I think he was a little embarrassed."[56]

Then, early in July, Mackenzie received a letter from Dean Lawrence who had become involved in the project upon the insistence of the board of regents. "We find," wrote Lawrence,

> " . . . that the deed dedicates the West portion of the tract for Medical School purposes and the East portion is given in trust for Hospital purposes. You will note that this reverses the preliminary scheme which has been under consideration."[57]

Needless to say it was easier to change the plans than to request the Union Pacific to change the deed, and in Lawrence's judgment anyway, the west tract provided a better and more level space for the medical school at much less cost. The final design bore little resemblance to the preliminary sketches. The city had no planning input, but the buildings were required to conform to city building regulations. In the course of construction, Dean Mackenzie continued to explore the matter of future hospital facilities. He had every intention of making Portland the medical capital of the Northwest.

The medical school moved up to the hill in 1919, but within a year Dean Mackenzie was dead at the age of 61. Although he did not live to see his dream fully realized, he had accomplished the major task and had secured the funding for the county hospital that went into construction during the summer of 1920. He had won the enthusiastic support of Rufus Holman, chairman of the Board of County Commissioners.

In December 1924, four years after Dr. Mackenzie's death, *Oregon Journal* publisher Charles Samuel Jackson, his wife and son Philip donated 88 acres of Marquam Hill property to the state of Oregon to be used for additional medical facilities and for a public park on those parcels not needed by the university. The land was purchased from the Union Pacific for $100,000 and donated to the state as a Christmas gift on December 24th.[58] C. S. Jackson died three days later at the age of 64 and his widow and son thereupon stipulated that the property should be named the Sam Jackson Park in his memory. For some time, C. S. Jackson had been planning to establish a hospital for the treatment of crippled children. Thus, it was not long after his death that the Doernbecher furniture family contributed sufficient funds to construct just such a facility adjacent to the medical school.

The Medical School in 1933

Early 1950s — The V. A. Hospital is to the right.

359

With the Jackson land available for use, negotiations were worked out with the United States Veterans Bureau to build a major facility on a 25 acre site to the east and down the hill from the medical school. The planning commission granted a zone change from 1 to 3 in November 1925. Being state land, this procedure was probably not required in 1925 but the federal government was anxious to work closely with the city in planning the new $1.35 million complex. Ground was broken in February 1928 and the veterans moved in three years later.

Over time, "pill hill," as it was jokingly called, expanded into the present multi-million dollar University of Oregon Health Sciences Center, incorporating the dental school and in close association with the veterans hospital. But with such growth, however, came a number of problems: Congested traffic and excessive concentration of auto emissions, to name two. The U. S. Veterans Administration has decided to replace its 50 year old hospital with a new structure, not much larger but 100 times more costly. The city would prefer that the complex be located more centrally, in the Northeast section on flat vacant urban renewal land adjacent to the Emanuel Medical Center. But the Health Sciences Center, in no position to move itself, wants the new hospital to remain on the hill for inter-institutional medical treatment and instructional purposes. Regardless of how the issue will be resolved, restricted accessibility and topographical limitations will always plague Dr. Mackenzie's monument. In retrospect, it never should have been built there.

Planning and Development in Retrospect

The history of city planning and development in the 1920s is a record of struggle, confrontation and frustration. Many plans were drafted but few were executed except in piecemeal fashion. Most of the battles were won by the private developers. Ideally, a condition that has rarely existed in our society, city planning embodies the coordination, within a conceptual framework, of the different activities that go to make the growth of a city. From its inception, the city planning movement has been an attempt to take the work of the various architects, contractors, engineers, realtors, investors and businessmen of a thousand sorts, and to make of that work a creation which will endure, providing rewards to the builders and benefits to the general public.

The process has seldom worked smoothly. Public input has tended to be fragmented, diffused and inconsistent while private input has been more highly structured, better organized and more adequately financed. The history of Portland planning and development, as illustrated by the experiences of the 1920s, has been a record of private interests exercising dominion over the public interest. In this respect, at least, Portland's experience has been similar to that of most other large American cities.

The main reasons for Portland's generally ineffective attempts at city planning during the 1920s were: (1) Inadequate public funding and staff support; (2) uneven political leadership from the mayor's office; and (3), conflicts of interest within the planning commission itself.

After the first zoning code was defeated in November 1920, the city council refused to appropriate any money for planning commission staff and general operation. John Ainsworth himself had to raise the necessary $6000 from private individuals and organizations. This condition led to the dismissal of Charles Cheney and to the appointment of the realtor dominated special joint committee that spent only $300 to draft the 1924 code — as opposed to the $16,000 spent by Cheney in drafting the 1919 code. The old saying that "you get what you pay for" could be applied to the revised code.

Immediately after the adoption of the zoning ordinance in 1924, the city council provided the planning commission with minimum funds to maintain a paid technical staff of from one to four persons. But in comparison with other cities, Portland's appropriations for city planning were "very inadequate."[59] In 1926, Portland appropriated $7180, as opposed to $14,000 in Minneapolis, $18,000 in Indianapolis and $100,000 in Pittsburgh. By 1928, the budget was increased to $9865, but with the onset of the depression it was to decrease to a low of $5665 in 1934. During the period of Ainsworth's leadership, all planning commission meetings were held in the board of directors room of the U. S. National Bank because there was no space in city hall.

As to political leadership and support, it would appear that Mayor Baker was beginning to tire of his responsibilities in 1929 although he did seek and win a fourth term. While running for re-election in the May primary, he was quoted as declaring "that the city council would not promote any plan for the development of the waterfront because it had fathered too many projects already and 'does not want any more babies left on our doorstep.' "[60] In response to the urgings of a number of West Side civic organizations that the city move ahead and develop a plan to rejuvenate the riverfront district, Baker suggested that the promotion of such a plan "come from the organizations interested in the development rather than from the city council."[61] The *Oregon Voter* picked up the issue by asking the property owners along the seawall what they were prepared to do. Nothing for the moment was the answer. The decade of the thirties would see more studies but little action except for the construction of a public market building, a project fraught with dangers and interest conflicts from its very inception.

A prime example of interest conflict within the planning commission membership involved the commission's issuance of a revocable sign permit to the Richfield Oil Company in 1928. By an action that turned out to be an environmental disaster, the company was granted permission to erect the largest electric sign in America — perhaps even in the world — on a high verdant ridge behind the medical school, a residentially zoned expanse known as Healy Heights. Overlooking most of Portland, with a length of 725 feet and a height of 60 feet, the sign was designed to be readable for ten miles and visible for 50 miles. In addition to advertising Richfield Oil, the sign was to serve as an air beacon. More than three-quarters of a mile of timber was used to construct the edifice.

The reaction of the planning commission staff is worth noting:

"It will be one of the largest electric signs in the world, costing over $60,000. The electric signs on the roof of the Utility Building cost over $20,000. If business can afford to pay such sums for the abstract idea of having its name "shine before men," is it not reasonable to think that thousands of dollars of the cost of proposed street widenings on future business arteries might well be charged to advertising and know that it was money well spent?

Even factory owners of today are finding that it pays to embellish their grounds with shrubbery and flowers. No amount of paint or ornamental finish or shrubbery can give the effect of spacious design, and after all the most powerful element that the artist can handle is space or mass. Nothing can convey the idea of power and grandeur like height or bulk. There is a feeling of elation and expansion of the spirit that comes over the person who enters a room of wide proportions or passes through a street of imposing width. This has an advertising value which can not be obtained for the same investment in many other directions."[62]

The Richfield sign was designed to use the new neon tubes, introduced to Oregon the previous year by the Electrical Products Corporation. Established for the purpose of manufacturing and distributing the Claude Neon Light products, Electrical Products held an exclusive Oregon franchise and was affiliated with 26 other manufacturing distributors of neon products throughout the United States.

Its board of directors comprised some of Portland's most powerful business leaders. It included: Cameron Squires of Wilcox Investment, company president; Eric V. Hauser, owner of the Multnomah Hotel; L. H. Hoffman, leading contractor; John Laing, of Pacific Power & Light, company secretary; David T. Honeyman, prominent hardware merchant whose wife Nan was one of C. E. S.

Wood's daughters; Guy W. Talbot, head of the Pacific Power & Light group; and J. C. Zanker, company general manager and vice president.

Parisian inventor George Claude had begun to extend his operations to America after the war. He advertised his type of lighting as the most powerful and penetrating in the world. By the end of 1927, Claude's United States affiliates were doing a volume of business that exceeded $18 million. Most airport beacons were using the tubes exclusively and the Richfield Oil Company was installing neon beacon lights at all strategic points on the Pacific Coast. Many of Portland's leading firms were already leasing neon products — all neon tubes were leased, not sold.

At some point in the company's early growth, before June of 1929 at least, John C. Ainsworth invested $9600 in the Electrical Products Company. This sum represented a large amount for Ainsworth to invest in an enterprise in which he had entertained no apparent previous interest. But the U. S. Bank had loaned money to the company initially, and one of the purposes of a 75,000 share stock issue in March 1929 was to retire the loan.[63] There is no record to indicate that Ainsworth actually held his investment at the time that the Richfield Oil Company secured its sign permit from the planning commission in the summer of 1928 while Ainsworth was president of the agency. In fact, no record exists in the commission minutes of any such request. But Ainsworth must have found himself in an awkward position when the permit matter came before the commission. Either he, personally, or the bank, of which he was a major stockholder and the president, had a private interest in the public decision. On the planning commission, in addition to Ainsworth, was John Laing, secretary of Electrical Products in 1929. It should be noted, furthermore, that both Ainsworth and Laing were directors of Pacific Power & Light, whose president Guy Talbot was the major promoter of Electrical Products' growth.

The financial results of 1928 proved rewarding to the Electrical Products Corporation. Gross profits totalled nearly $500,000. In June of 1929, the company reported that it had retired $100,000 of seven percent preferred stock and had accumulated assets in excess of $1.4 million. But no dividends had yet been paid on the common stock.

The depression that began four months later must have adversely affected the company's earnings. For one thing, Richfield Oil went into bankruptcy in January of 1931 and the beacon on Healy Heights went out. It remained unlit for two and a half years, serving as a grim reminder of the foolishness of a public body granting to a private group the right to despoil one of the most beautiful landscapes in Portland with an eyesore which lost what little use it had ever possessed. When the lights came back on during the winter of 1933, Portland Chamber of Commerce president Arthur L. Fields glorified its return to life. He was reported to have exulted:

> "Its brilliance will be a decided asset to the city, since Portland is known as one of the most brilliantly lighted cities in the world."

A symbol of the loss of respect for Wall Street brokers and the New York Stock Exchange was Rollin Kirby's cartoon, poking fun at the staid old institution.

Chapter 13

The Crash of 1929:
Its Causes and Consequences

If the New York Stock Exchange were an accurate indicator of economic health in the United States, the two year period leading up to October 1929 should have been viewed as one of the most salubrious in American history. A seat (membership) on the exchange sold for $525,000 in November 1928, up $225,000 in one year. In the same year, total number of shares traded on the exchange increased from 451 million to 577 million. In the 18 months following March of 1928, American Can rose from $77 to $182 a share; American Telephone & Telegraph, from $179 to $304; General Electric, from $128 to $396; and Electric Bond & Share, from $90 to $187. During the decade prior to October 1929, the total assets of America's 200 largest corporations increased from $43.7 billion to $81 billion.

Oregon's Economic Conditions Before the Event

Conditions on Wall Street, as it later turned out, did not faithfully reflect the general state of the American economy in a number of regions including Oregon. Unemployment began to grow in the early part of 1927, especially in the heavy industries, building trades and lumber production. And a decided weakening was evident in agricultural prices. National statistics from the U. S. Bureau of Labor, for those who bothered to examine them, showed that from 1919 to 1925 machinery had displaced 600,000 workers in agriculture, 900,000 workers in manufacturing and mechanical industries, and 175,000 workers on the railroads. It was paradoxical that with an increasing population, there were fewer people in factories and yet production was increasing. From 1919 through 1927, factory employment dropped ten percent while total production increased 15 percent.

Former Reed College President William T. Foster, a prominent economist who had left an unappreciative Portland in 1919, published several books during the 1920s that forewarned of troubles ahead. In *The Road to Plenty*, issued in 1927 in collaboration with Wadill Catchings, Foster documented clearly that an increase in production did not necessarily produce an increase in wages. In fact, Foster pointed out that Henry Ford's workers — Portland's Ford plant was shut down the last six months of 1927 for a production change from the Model "T" to the Model "A" — did not earn enough money to buy the cars that they were producing. Too much corporate money was going into security speculation on the stock exchanges and too little into wages. A few months earlier, U. S. Supreme

Burned Fingers

Court Justice Louis Brandeis had expressed wonderment as to "why a lot of folks don't go broke."[1] He was concerned by the number of business consolidations, security flotations and building booms.

Harvard economist William Z. Ripley created some momentary excitement with his *Main Street and Wall Street* which charged that vast holding companies were endangering the American economy by aggrandizing wealth. Although the supposed ownership of corporations was invested in common stock distributed among the masses, actual control rested with a small number of powerful holding companies. One-half of the nation's corporate wealth and 40 percent of all business wealth was concentrated in the hands of 2000 individuals who controlled the 200 largest American corporations. As Will Rogers colorfully described the phenomenon: "A Holding Company is a thing where you hand an accomplice the goods while the policeman searches you."[2] Professor Ripley had cited such questionable enterprises as "anonymous industrial autocracies." The practice was most prevalent among the utilities.

366

Organization of Some Bank Holding Companies
Affecting Portland Banks
1928-1930

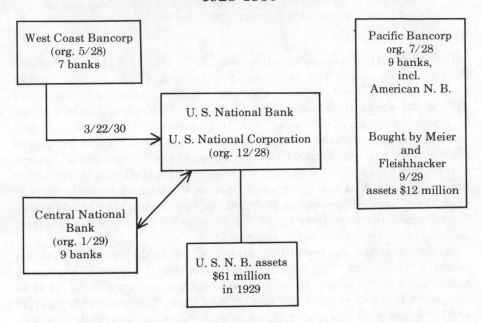

By 1927, as few as ten giant utility systems were in the process of absorbing nearly three-fourths of the total electric light and power business in the nation, and Oregon's private utilities were enmeshed in the financial entanglement. One of the two largest growing utility groups was Electric Bond & Share of New York, and one of its major holdings was American Power & Light which owned Pacific Power & Light and Portland Gas & Coke. In March of 1925, through a syndicate of Eastern investors, American Power & Light had acquired Portland's Northwestern Electric from the Herbert Fleishhacker interests of San Francisco. In 1927, American Power & Light reincorporated all of its Oregon holdings under the general jurisdiction of Pacific Power & Light. With headquarters in the new Public Service Building, the three companies continued to operate publicly as independent entities. Each time a reincorporation or reorganization occurred, millions of dollars of new securities were issued and the assets were inflated accordingly.

The nation's banking system became afflicted with a similar kind of frenzy during the late 1920s. Although branch banking had not yet become a permissible practice in most states, including Oregon, it was generally legal for individual banks to be bought by corporations organized solely for that purpose. Bank holding companies and chain banks became popular ventures throughout the country. Commenting upon this phenomenon, *Fortune* concluded that:

" . . . the development is entirely consonant with the kind of civilization we are erecting. . . . Consolidation in nearly everything else radically changes the kind of civilization which banking must serve. . . . The factors causing consolidation in all else **do** apply to banking with sufficient force to make further consolidation (and branching) not only inevitable, but, in the circumstances, wise."[3]

The man who personified branch banking in the United States was Amadeo Peter Giannini of San Francisco, founder of the Bank of Italy. By 1924, after 20 years of growth, Bancitaly had opened over 300 branches in California, one of the few states permitting this practice for state banks. National banks were not to enjoy similar privileges until 1933. But by creating holding companies, national banks could acquire other banks, and vice versa, holding companies could acquire national banks. Giannini organized the Transamerica Corporation in 1928 as a holding company for a variety of subsidiaries including his Bancitaly chain. As a $2.8 billion conglomerate, Transamerica bought the New York based Bank of America in 1928 and the First National Bank of Oregon, among others, two years later. By 1930, *Fortune* called Transamerica "the most gigantic of American holding companies."[4]

In an attempt to compete with Giannini in California, the famed Fleishhacker brothers, "Herb" and "Mort," formed the Anglo National group of 21 banks with resources of $278 million. Oregon likewise became an active field for bank mergers in 1928 with the establishment of West Coast Bancorp, Pacific Bancorp and U. S. National Corporation. Of the 18 banks represented in the three chains, only five were located in Portland. The new trend toward bank consolidations was sparked by an enormous increase in personal savings. Surplus income reached $14 billion nationally in 1928. As Lawrence Hodges noted in *The Oregonian*, "We seem about to have really big business in banking."[5]

From 1928 to 1932, the number of independent banks in Oregon declined from 260 to 160 and bank consolidations were responsible for most of the reduction. Bank failures, however, were also a factor. They became increasingly common in 1927, an average of two a day nationally. Over 80 percent of the failures involved banks that had less than $100,000 in capital. Among the larger 20 percent were several nationally prominent institutions, including Portland's third largest bank. By the end of 1931, two years into the depression, over one-third of the nation's banks were to have failed.[6]

The Lumber Slump

In the two year period before the depression struck nationally, a number of weak spots began to develop in the Oregon economy that was so heavily dependent on lumber and agricultural products. Not only were agricultural prices down in June of 1927 but lumber was in one of its periodic sales slumps. Several mills closed temporarily, including the large Eastern and Western operation on the west bank of the Willamette River adjacent to the Elrod

Terminal. The major reason for the lumber recession was overproduction and poor merchandising.

In November 1927, Michigan lumberman John W. Blodgett, who had extensive Oregon and California holdings, wrote banker John Ainsworth:

> "It is lamentable to sit back here and see the way Fir lumber is merchandised. . . . I do not mean to say that the faults are confined to the Fir industry, because that is far from the truth. Members of the Pine industry occasionally demoralize things as badly as the Fir people.
>
> When a small operator makes a [timber] cut, the damage, while severe enough, is not so extremely serious as it is when a big operator . . . makes these radical cuts. Then there is at once created an unsettled feeling that the bottom has not yet been reached, and dealers hesitate to buy for even the normal demands."[7]

Ainsworth replied to Blodgett the following week:

> "Something surely must be done before long to prevent this wholesale slaughtering of our timber. It would appear to me that the most feasible plan yet offered is the Fir merger."[8]

Along with a number of large timber operators and wealthy lumbermen of Blodgett's persuasion, Ainsworth had been advocating mergers among the Fir group as a means of stabilizing the industry. In the fall of 1927, he had dis-

The Clark & Wilson Mill at Linnton — one of the city's largest

John E. Wheeler

patched his young assistant, E. C. Sammons, to the East Coast to sound out New York bankers on the possibility of "welding the industry into some sort of consolidation." Although the lumber industry represented an investment of over $12 billion nationally, it was a fragmented industry wherein even the largest firms were small by comparison to other industrials like automobiles, steels and electricals. In a sense it was too competitive and there were all kinds of irresponsible "cut-throat" operators who were motivated to squeeze every possible nickel out of whatever timber they could acquire.

Ainsworth and Blodgett were suggesting a system of mergers and pricing policies similar to those that would be contained in the New Deal's National Recovery Act of 1933: Limitations upon competition and the formation of price agreements. In late 1929, Baker, Fentress & Company of Chicago was to warn: "There must be a lumber merger or there will be some funerals."[9]

Baker, Fentress was the nation's leading investment house dealing exclusively in forestry securities. It promoted many Oregon issues and in the process it acquired major investment holdings in several Oregon lumber companies. The Portland office was run by vice president Henry F. Chaney who became a power in the Oregon lumber industry.

By October of 1929, Baker, Fentress had already witnessed the "funerals" of several firms that it had helped to finance, including the Trask Timber Company headed by John E. Wheeler of Portland. In January 1927, Trask Timber issued $800,000 in six percent first mortgage bonds, secured by a first lien on the company's holdings that were appraised at $2.6 million. Baker, Fentress purchased the entire issue, keeping a portion and peddling the rest to customers around the country. To the investment house the issue looked sound. Prompt payment was unconditionally guaranteed by Wheeler and his brothers, one of whom resided in western Pennsylvania where the family fortune originated. A much younger brother, Lawrence, also lived in Portland and ran the *Telegram* that John had bought in 1919. The Wheeler brothers affixed their names to a statement reporting combined net worth at approximately $16 million.

Two months earlier, John Wheeler had executed $350,000 in one year six percent gold notes for the primary purpose, so the prospectus stated, of purchasing the outstanding stock in the *Telegram*. Subsequent evidence was to indicate that this information was not correct. What proved to be correct, however, was the concluding clause of the prospectus: " . . . and to fund current indebtedness."[10] Although Wheeler announced his net worth as "in excess of four million dollars," he was in shaky financial condition in November 1926, heavily in debt. Only a month earlier he had tried to sell the *Telegram* to *The Oregon Journal* but he refused to accept a cash offer of $600,000. He then went to San Francisco and tried, but failed, "to get a better offer from Hearst."[11] Wheeler's financial problems that were mounting rapidly in the early months of 1927 were to have an earthshaking effect on Portland in the weeks to follow.

The Collapse of the Northwestern National Bank

John E. Wheeler came from a region of western Pennsylvania rich in coal and oil. After graduating from Yale in 1900, he migrated to the West to invest some family funds in timberlands, ranging from McCormick, Washington, to the Redwood country of northern California. Wheeler was one of many Ivy League alumni from the East and Middle West who came to Oregon in search of natural riches, bankrolled by wealthy families who had struck it rich in coal, oil or timber in the older, more settled parts of the country. George Markle of Hazelton, Pennsylvania, Portland's leading entrepreneur in 1890, came from a similar background. However, he escaped the consequences of his indiscretions by fleeing the state.[12]

Citing the misfortunes of Wheeler and Markle is not meant to imply that all such refugees from the East were propensive crooks. Very few were, or at least very few were caught. But as the timber fraud trials of 1905 revealed, most of the large timber tracts in the west were acquired by some form of legerdemain.[13] The Wheeler Timber Company of California, by one device or another, had acquired one of the largest stands of redwood timber in the world, more than 31,000 acres worth. The Trask stand, located 45 miles west of Portland, comprised nearly 20,000 acres. John Wheeler's brother, William, directed the affairs of the

California operations, while John, or Jack as he was called by family and friends, managed the Northwest properties that included, besides Trask, the McCormick Lumber Company of Washington and the Wheeler Pine Company of Klamath Falls, Oregon.

Jack Wheeler found ready acceptance in Portland's business and social circles once he had established himself in the timber industry. He joined the Arlington and Waverley Country Clubs and built an imposing home on Portland Heights.[14] He also found a ready and willing friend in banker Emery Olmstead whom Henry L. Pittock had brought to Portland in 1910 to manage the Portland Trust Company. When the Northwestern National Bank was organized by the Pittock-Leadbetter interests in 1913, Olmstead was installed as president. Olmstead was an aggressive banker, and under his management, the Northwestern rapidly increased its assets.

In the course of his rise to the top ranks of Portland's business and financial world, Olmstead made a number of close friends and involved himself and the bank in a variety of business deals. He became associated with Cameron Squires, Raymond B. Wilcox and Isaac Hunt of the Wilcox Investment Company which bought control of his major bank competitor, Ladd & Tilton, in 1919. He also became a financial partner of James O. Elrod who in turn had business ties to the Wilcox Investment Company. And in 1919, he arranged for the bank to loan Jack Wheeler sufficient funds for Wheeler to purchase *The Portland Telegram*.

In an attempt to cement most of these relationships, Olmstead secured the election of Elrod and Wheeler to the bank's board of directors. And the bank in turn became more deeply involved in the various Elrod and Wheeler enterprises. Olmstead was following the same fateful path as his friends and competitors over at Ladd & Tilton. As *Fortune* magazine concluded after a study of bank failures:

> "The fundamental blunder of bad bankers large and small has been their effort to become enterprising businessmen. It is for the businessman to initiate ventures, to take risks. . . . But banking is a profession whose occupation is to conserve the result of the businessman's success. . . . If the banker goes into schemes and promotions of his own, it is not to be expected that his judgment or success will be above that of others. So long as our bankers have that failing, we shall have some banks that fail."[15]

Although Olmstead had become a prominent civic and financial figure, he was regarded by the more conservative establishment as being on probation. He had yet to make good as a sound banker in the minds of men like Abbot Mills and John Ainsworth. The Pittock trustees also had some qualms about his judgment. In fact, during the fall of 1924, the Pittock trustees on the Northwestern's board of directors instructed Olmstead not to allow any overdraft funds to Wheeler — a practice that he had apparently followed for some time. A short while later, the Pittock-Leadbetter interests attempted to force Olmstead's re-

Emery Olmstead

moval, but because they only controlled 43 percent of the bank's stock, the effort proved futile. Olmstead outmaneuvered them. Together with Elrod and Wheeler, who owned considerable shares, Olmstead secured the backing of San Francisco banker Herbert Fleishhacker who had just sold his Northwestern Electric Company to American Power & Light, and the four of them bought out the L. B. Menefee bank stockholdings. The Pittock interests were visibly upset. The coup had left them as a minority, but with a moral responsibility for the soundness of the bank. In the public's mind, the Northwestern was a Pittock bank. The Pittock trustees attempted to sell their shares to the First National Bank but Abbot Mills would have nothing to do with the matter.[16]

Mills and Ainsworth had a good idea of what was happening over at the Northwestern. As the city's leading competitive bankers they nevertheless remained in close and confidential communication with each other. They were also related by marriage: Abbot L. Mills, Jr., was married to Katherine Ainsworth. In February of 1925, Ainsworth wrote a confidential memorandum showing concern about Jack Wheeler, his nearby neighbor on Portland Heights. Wheeler had endorsed more than $40,000 of U. S. National Bank notes that had proved uncollectable and the bank chose to write them off rather than create a

Full page ad — Oregon Journal — February 4, 1920

public fuss.[17] Mills and Ainsworth were always careful not to take any action that might create lack of confidence in another bank, engendering in turn a possible lack of confidence in their own banks. Mayor George L. Baker proved his shrewdness in this respect. As a friend later recounted the episode, he and Baker were riding downtown together one day in 1925 and Baker asked his driver to stop at the Northwestern to make a deposit for him. When the driver returned, Baker asked him to stop two blocks down the street at the First National for the same reason. "I know what you are thinking," Baker said, "I keep two bank accounts so in case one goes broke I will not be washed out."[18]

For over two years, Wheeler's debts had been mounting and he had entangled his banker Olmstead in the web. His contingent liabilities were excessive and he was having a difficult time meeting his current requirements. Through his McCormick Lumber Company, he was borrowing heavily to buy logs. But the slump in the lumber market made it impossible for him to repay his debts. At one point he borrowed $100,000 from the National City Bank of New York, secured by 500 shares of Northwestern National Bank stock and an equal dollar amount of stock of his McCormick Lumber Company to which he was, at the time, personally in debt by over $500,000.

As subsequent investigations revealed, Wheeler and Olmstead devised a scheme to deposit checks in McCormick Lumber's Northwestern bank account, drafts drawn on a Pennsylvania bank in which Wheeler had supposedly established sufficient credit through the deposit of "trade acceptances" on log purchases. At no time, however, did his eastern credit ever exceed $16,000. And yet, millions of dollars in checks were drawn on the account and deposited in the Portland account, with most of them bouncing back to Portland because of insufficient credit balances. While this gigantic kiting operation was going on, it always appeared that Wheeler had an ample balance in his company's Northwestern account against which he could draw for his personal or other business needs. By stretching the process out and covering it up deftly, Olmstead and Wheeler were able to prevent their fraudulent behavior from being detected, that is until a sharp-eyed banker examiner discovered an actual $800,000 cash shortage on February 28, 1927. Then the roof fell in.

The examiner threatened to close the bank that afternoon unless the shortage was made good. O. L. Price, manager of the Pittock estate, took $1 million worth of bonds to John Ainsworth's office at the U. S. National Bank, and the U. S. gave Price the money which was delivered to the Northwestern. The immediate crisis was over, but much more was to come. Olmstead was fired after admitting what he had done. It later came out that bank director Phil Metschan had been told what was going on but had taken no action. Metschan denied the charge.

During the month of March 1927, Ainsworth and Mills knew that they were faced with a serious problem that would most likely require them to rescue the Northwestern depositors in some manner. At least $2 million of bad loans were discovered and a quiet run developed on the bank. Word leaked out that the institution was not in good shape. Meier & Frank Company was later to be

375

Run on the Northwestern National Bank
March 28, 1927
S. W. Morrison Street entrance

accused of promoting lack of public confidence by declining to accept Northwestern Bank checks at the store. There were charges levelled that depositors all over the city were being warned by anonymous phone calls to withdraw their money while they could. Finally, on Monday, March 28th, an active run occurred. As reported by *The Oregon Journal*:

> "Frantic depositors swarmed in and around it [the bank], clamoring for their money. The drawn and serious faces of depositors around a bank, struggling to get their money, is a pitiful sight."[19]

Former *Oregonian* publisher Robert Notson remembered the scene vividly when he later described the crowd that he witnessed "pushing and shouting . . . to get inside. I watched as a butcher from Yamhill Street ran up with his bloody white apron still on. In his hand he held his bankbook. He joined the pushing. A half-hour later he emerged with a triumphant shout, 'I've got it! I've got it!' "[20]

To John Ainsworth, it was a day he would never forget.

> "They kept open until six in the evening. . . . When they closed there was a larger crowd than ever.[21]

376

We were notified at six o'clock at night that they could not open the following morning. We had a real problem on our hands to pay off 18 millions of demand deposits in addition to properly protecting some 96 millions of demand deposits of the First National Bank and ourselves. In fact, there was not enough money in the town to care for it, and we brought in all the money they had in Spokane and Seattle, and brought other funds up by airplane from San Francisco. This, however, was not called upon."[22]

The officers of the two major banks, led by John Ainsworth, worked all night, until 7:30 a.m., to determine what the Northwestern's true assets really were. They removed $4.5 million of bad notes. At that point, the Pittock estate brought over $2 million in cash and bonds. O. L. Price and Northwestern director E. S. Collins, a wealthy lumberman who was only a minor bank stockholder, both agreed to guarantee another $2 million to cover contingent liabilities. Thereupon, the U. S. National and the First publicly announced that they would guarantee all deposits and the furor subsided. Although the Northwestern National Bank did not open for business on the 29th — or ever again for that matter — the community had been reassured and feelings remained calm. Liquidation proceedings, consuming over six months, were handled by E. C. Sammons of the U. S. National and C. F. Adams of the First.

John Ainsworth summarized the episode succinctly when he wrote: "The Northwestern National blow-up was a terrible thing, but a failure would have been very much worse."[23] Ainsworth cited the Pittock estate trustees, O. L. Price, C. A. Morden, and wealthy lumberman Everett S. Collins as "heroes." They did what they felt they had to do, voluntarily. Reacting in the same manner as Frederick Pratt, the preservation of the family's honor did not carry a price tag. The Pittocks lost over $2 million and Collins nearly as much. The stockholders were wiped out after having volunteered to accept a 100 percent assessment against their holdings. A. D. Charlton of the Northern Pacific Railway, an elderly and respected Portland businessman, believed on February 28th that he had a nest egg investment of $25,000 that would be worth $40,000 upon his retirement. He willingly paid in his assessment of $25,000 and then lost the entire $50,000. Emery Olmstead had cost his former associates over $5 million.

All was not dark for banker Ainsworth, however. As he wrote Jack Blodgett: "Naturally a good deal of the business [from the Northwestern] drifted to us, and we have added some seven or eight millions to our deposit line — all desirable business. . . . Our stock . . . sold this week at $400,"[24] a record high. And the U. S. National Bank clearly commanded the top ranking among Portland banks with total assets of $60 million. Even Jack Wheeler was to salvage some residue from the mess, but he succeeded in reducing the family fortune, including the assets of his brothers, by at least 80 percent. The *Telegram* went into receivership and was rescued by Herbert Fleishhacker and Carl Brockhagen of San Francisco who kept control until the paper was sold to E. W. Scripps' *News* in 1931.

Right Over the Barrier

Wheeler and Olmstead went on trial in January 1928. Summarizing the government's case, U. S. Attorney George Neuner declared that:

> "The defendants built up worthless, fictitious and fraudulent credit which they knew to be drawn on banks and on accounts which they knew to possess no funds for payment."[25]

Wheeler and Olmstead were found guilty on 22 counts of fraud. The conspiracy indictment had been dropped. In March, Wheeler received a sentence of three years and Olmstead five years, both to serve their time at the MacNeil Island Federal Penitentiary. In addition, both men were fined $1000. Considerable feeling was generated within the community that Olmstead deserved a heavier sentence and a much heavier fine.

Two years later, to the surprise of many Portlanders, both Wheeler and Olmstead were released from prison, not by parole as was the normal procedure, but by pardon of President Herbert Hoover. The *News* and *Telegram* printed some uncomplimentary remarks about how easy it was for powerful persons, or persons with powerful connections, to gain a presidential pardon, particularly if

378

they had been strong Republicans. But the other papers more or less treated the matter as a straight news release. The *Oregon Voter* welcomed them home. They were men who had "great capacities for useful citizenship."[26] Wheeler removed himself to California where he died in 1943. Olmstead stayed around town, and amazingly enough, within two years was to convince 26 local investors to underwrite an optical system for movies. He had the cream of Portland's business and financial establishment committed to support the project. Perhaps this was a way for Portland to provide rehabilitation to a man whose past indiscretions were not totally his fault.

An interesting side story to the Northwestern crash involves the attempt of the U. S. National and First National Banks to force the Fidelity and Deposit Company of Maryland to pay them $700,000 on a surety bond that the Northwestern National Bank had carried. Because both banks had guaranteed Northwestern's deposits, they wanted reimbursement for the cash shortage incurred by Olmstead. The company balked at paying off the bond. E. C. Sammons went back east to a meeting of the American Bankers Association Executive Committee and told his story to A. P. Giannini, chairman of the Board of Transamerica and one of the most powerful bankers in the world. Giannini made some uncomplimentary remarks about the Fidelity and Deposit Company to the assembled committee members and thenceforth the red carpet was rolled out for Sammons. He attended a special Fidelity directors meeting in Baltimore and "let them have it." In attendance was Franklin Delano Roosevelt who had been employed since 1920 as a manager of Fidelity's New York office. One year later, Roosevelt would be elected governor of New York. Needless to say, Sammons effectively stated his case and the Portland banks received their money.[27]

The Failure of Overbeck & Cooke

The demise of the Northwestern was not the only financial disaster to strike Portland in the period immediately preceding the 1929 stock market crash. Several small neighborhood banks collapsed, including the Bank of Kenton. In March of 1929, two years after the fact, Kenton's former president, J. V. Burke, was convicted of misappropriating funds, fined $2500 and sentenced to jail for seven years. Burke's misconduct was neither as serious nor as costly as that of Olmstead and yet he received a far heavier sentence. Burke did not enjoy Olmstead's stature within the community.

Two weeks after Wheeler and Olmstead went on trial, the Portland financial and social establishments were struck another blow when it was announced in the press that the pioneer stock brokerage house of Overbeck & Cooke Co. had closed its doors to business. Word went out to the community not to worry. The company was generally believed to be in strong shape; furthermore, it enjoyed the favor and confidence of the major New York banks. President James P. Cooke, a well regarded member of the Arlington and Waverley Country Clubs,

ACCUSED BROKERS DENY THEIR GUILT AND PLEDGE AID

Charles
Goodwin

Howard F. Philpott

Two sketches of James R. Cooke

Sketches drawn in court of principals in smashed brokerage firm of Overbeck & Cooke, by Howard Fisher, staff artist of The Journal.

was known for his ability and integrity. Few could imagine any indiscretions occurring in such an old and respected firm.

The truth began to emerge early in February 1928 when Overbeck & Cooke filed for bankruptcy. It was hopelessly insolvent with losses exceeding $1.5 million. The story that filtered into the press made fascinating reading, especially for those to whom stock market transactions had always been viewed as mysteriously shady practices. The tabloids had a field day.

The Cooke family had apparently been "living high" for seven years before the firm closed. Most of the family's bills, including large expenditures for liquor, were paid out of company funds by the company's cashier. James Cooke bought a Rolls Royce and Mrs. Cooke drew out vast sums for clothing expense. To keep ahead of the game, Cooke began to play the stock market with abandon, speculating heavily on risky issues. He made his fatal error by using customers' funds through a fictitious account registered to a "J. R. Smith." He created two sets of books and started to falsify his annual state reports. In the process of entangling himself deeper and deeper, he involved his two fellow officers, Charles Goodwin and Howard F. Philpott.[28]

Although his annual salary was only $18,000, Cooke withdrew $180,000 in one year for his own use, all from customer trust funds. His was a classic case of securities fraud. On big orders from his customers, he gave them false certificates of purchase. He took their money and instead of executing a normal purchase he assumed a short position on the market. He executed agreements to sell securities that he did not possess but which he agreed to buy within a specific period of time, hopefully at a price lower than the market value at the time of sale. Instead of just making a regular commission on a normal sale, he was using his customers' money to speculate in the expectation of making a large profit. At the time of purchase he would then register the securities in his customer's name. Unfortunately for James Cooke, the market kept going up so that every time he executed a short sale in the name of "J. R. Smith" he lost money, his customers' money. The books were falsified to hide the transactions. In all he expended over $1.2 million of customer funds and lost most of it.

All three officers were indicted for fraud on February 17, 1928, and all initially pled not guilty. Cooke hired the services of one of Portland's leading trial lawyers, Dan J. Malarkey, and Philpott secured an attorney of equal color and ability in John Logan. Goodwin changed his plea to guilty. In November 1928 all were found guilty and Cooke received seven years in the Oregon State Penitentiary. It was to be several years before the firm's affairs were untangled. One creditor, Frank Kiernan, a prominent real estate investor, had to wait nearly two years before the court approved payment of his $260,000 claim, the largest of all.

George W. Joseph and Julius L. Meier

The collapse of Jack Wheeler's ventures, together with that of the Northwestern National Bank, had consequences that reached far beyond the world of finance and lumber. It led to a political upheaval in state and local politics — a human drama with a cast of extraordinary characters. The catalytic event that helped to produce the "revolution" was Herbert Fleishhacker's purchase of *The Portland Telegram* in the fall of 1927. The San Francisco banker had long-standing ties to Portland, going back well before 1911, the year in which he established the Northwestern Electric Company, signed a 99 year lease on Henry L. Pittock's downtown block and agreed to construct thereon a building for no less than $650,000. He later installed an oil-fired electric generating plant in the basement of the Pittock Block. In 1924, he extended his Portland holdings by increasing his investment in the Northwestern National Bank, a fateful decision that was to lose him some money. Notwithstanding this distressing experience, he appeared willing to sink $226,000 in another Portland venture by acquiring two-thirds control of the city's third largest newspaper. The key figures in promoting this action were Portland attorney George W. Joseph and Meier & Frank vice president Julius L. Meier. In the words of *Oregon Voter* editor, C. C. Chapman, there was thus created a "labyrinth of relationship between a big advertiser [Meier & Frank], a big banker [Fleishhacker], a big attorney [Joseph] and a big daily paper [the *Telegram*]."[29]

George Joseph, born in California in 1872 of Basque extraction, moved to Eastern Oregon as a youth. He herded sheep while attending school, by-passed college and began studying law in a Lakeview law office in 1890. He moved to Portland in 1890, continued his law study and was admitted to the Oregon State Bar in 1893 at the age of 21. Two years later he entered into law partnership with Julius Meier who had just received his law degree from the University of Oregon. Although Meier joined the family business in 1896, he kept his partnership with Joseph for many years. The professional relationship developed into a life-long friendship and led to Joseph becoming the attorney for the Meier & Frank Company. Meier removed his name from the law firm although he kept a financial interest in its affairs. When Meier became vice president and general manager of the store in 1910, Joseph acquired a new partner, Bert Haney, who was to play a prominent role in shipping and Port of Portland activities in subsequent decades.

George Joseph's political career was formally launched in 1910 when he was elected as a Republican state senator from Multnomah County. Serving only one term, he was again elected to the same spot in 1920 and served two consecutive terms. During this time he established a reputation as the state's leading proponent of cheap hydroelectric power. He introduced many bills that called for public power development, but all were defeated. In the process, however, he succeeded in converting his friend Meier to the public power cause. When the *Telegram* became available for purchase, Joseph saw his opportunity to acquire an instrument that could publicize and promote a number of issues, including

George W. Joseph, Sr.
(1872-1930)

that of public power. The Meier family's close friendship with the San Francisco Fleishhackers proved invaluable.

Under its new ownership, the *Telegram* wasted little time in publishing a series of sensational articles disparaging some prominent local reputations. Written by Joseph's close friend Henry M. Hanzen, the political editor, the articles detailed a number of court cases involving Joseph, instances in which the outspoken attorney felt that justice had miscarried. One such case in 1923 concerned the Henry E. Wemme estate and Oregon Supreme Court Justice John L. Rand.

Henry Wemme had been one of Oregon's most colorful business figures before his death in 1914. He had left half his fortune, derived from the manufacture of tents and awnings, to the establishment and maintenance of a large home for "unfortunate girls during the period of their confinement and convalescence."[30] According to one who knew him well, bachelor Wemme was "a delightful and charming man, especially with the ladies. He had slept all over town. Maybe that was the reason he left his money for a home to care for pregnant young ladies."[31]

George Joseph had been Wemme's attorney. "Little did he then dream," reported Henry Hanzen, "that the charity he [Joseph] had provided for in the will in language so simple and clear . . . would be nullified by the high court of the state through legal legerdemain and subterfuge."[32] The case had been heard by Justice Rand in late 1923 and lawyer Joseph had been fuming ever since. Rand was up for re-election in 1928 and the *Telegram* launched an early attack in the hope of securing his defeat, thus validating the *Oregon Voter*'s assertion.

Wemme had left the other half of his $700,000 estate to his closest relatives in Germany. They seemed to accept this beneficence with gratitude until they received word from some sharp lawyers in Oregon that there might be more coming to them if they would join in a scheme to acquire control of the Wemme Company, the bulk of the estate being in Wemme Company stock. A legal door had been opened when the Christian Science Church, the recipient of the first half of the estate, elected not to operate the new girls home but rather to sell it to the Salvation Army which then renamed it the White Shield Home. The unscrupulous attorneys, in cahoots with Wemme's German brother and with Dow V. Walker, the discredited county commissioner, brought suit to remove the bequest from the church which they accused of breaking the provisions of the will. They wanted the stock assigned to them as the legal agents of the German heirs. The lawyers also requested legal fees amounting to one-fifth of the total estate. Although Judge Rand removed the church from the will, he denied the motion to reassign the stock to the contesting lawyers. However, he did approve excessively high legal fees for the attorneys. Joseph viewed this action as an unwarranted invasion of the estate's capital.

Lawyer Joseph instituted an investigation and discovered that Justice Rand, a resident of Eastern Oregon, owned some mining property near Baker that he had been trying to sell. "Coincidentally," the attorneys who had been contesting Wemme's will had made an offer to purchase the property. The sale was never consummated. But nearly four years later, when the *Telegram* articles began to appear, running periodically over a span of four months, the state supreme court decided that it had better investigate the matter for itself. It appointed a special Bar committee comprising prominent Republican lawyers. Rand, who had just won re-election, had long been identified with the conservative wing of the state Republican Party. Even Joseph was not surprised when Justice Rand was exonerated. But what was not expected was the subsequent decision of the Oregon Supreme Court to disbar George Joseph for life, while one of the attorneys who had tried to gain control of the estate only received a three year suspension of Bar privileges!

Joseph was notified of the action early in January 1930. He was so incensed that he decided to seek the Republican nomination for governor — a quest that was to prove successful. In all of these efforts he was closely supported by Julius L. Meier and *The Portland Telegram.* Joseph was to use his disbarment to stimulate public support and at the same time to undermine the stature of the party's traditional conservative leadership which feared him. Joseph was an enigma to many people, including the *Oregon Voter*'s C. C. Chapman. Joseph was admired for "his brilliance of intellect, . . . force of personality," and "daring" of mind. But his methods were suspect.[33] Had the thrust of the *Telegram* articles not been directed against the person of Justice Rand, Joseph would not have been disbarred. However, had he not been disbarred, with all of the attendant publicity, he probably could not have secured the Republican nomination. And had he not dropped dead in the middle of the campaign, Julius Meier would never have run in his place and been elected governor. George Joseph did not live to enjoy the restitution of his Bar privileges — approved posthumously by the very same state supreme court.

Julius L. Meier
(1874-1937)

Julius Meier — Investor and Banker

Julius Meier became vice president and general manager of Meier & Frank Company in 1910 when his older brother, Abe, assumed the presidency upon the death of Sigmund Frank. Although Julius was to spend an increasing amount of time at the store, he always seemed to have plenty left over for a variety of civic and private ventures. Beginning in 1912, he became one of the chief promoters of the Columbia River Scenic Highway and a major opponent of outdoor advertising signs. During the war, he directed the effort to construct the Liberty Temple on S. W. Sixth Avenue. After the war, he became an active promoter of vacation resort hotels at Gearhart, on the Oregon Coast, and at Breitenbush Hot Springs in the lower Cascade Mountains. He also involved himself in the construction of new hotels in Eugene and Vancouver, Washington. For all of these projects, Meier & Frank provided the interior furnishings, to be paid for over a period of years. Meier, rather than the store, assumed personal responsibility for the debts incurred. During the depression, when the hotels defaulted on their obligations, Meier was to find himself the principal owner of four unprofitable hotel properties.

In 1921, Meier became excited over the prospect of Portland hosting a world's fair in 1925. The official title of the event was to be the "Atlantic & Pacific Highways and Electrical Exposition," to be held in commemoration of the 100th anniversary of the founding of Fort Vancouver. Hayden Island was chosen as the most appropriate location even though it would have to be filled extensively in order to prevent flooding. As the promotional literature declared with great confidence, the exposition would "show to the world the best that the West has in scenery, in industry, in shipping and in undeveloped natural advantages."[34]

With strong City Club support, the Portland voters in November 1921 overwhelmingly approved a measure to tax themselves $2 million over a period of three years provided that the state vote a $3 million tax and that $1 million be raised by private subscription. Banker Emery Olmstead was chosen head of the finance committee to seek the private funds. Meier, as general chairman, offered to use his influence at the legislature to seek the passage of a state tax referendum. In so doing, he incurred the criticism of a number of Portland establishment figures, including the editor of the *Oregon Voter*. He was accused of employing "strong-arm" tactics, not only against certain recalcitrant downstate senators but against banker Abbot Mills who refused to exert what pressure he could on friends and associates serving in the legislature. Meier was rumored to have threatened to withdraw $600,000 from the Meier & Frank account at the First National Bank. As it was later revealed, he did withdraw $300,000 and deposited the funds with Olmstead's Northwestern National Bank. There is no record of whether or not Meier & Frank maintained a balance of that size through March of 1927, although the store did have funds on deposit when the Northwestern closed its doors. There can be little doubt, however, that Meier was instrumental in helping Emery Olmstead obtain Herbert Fleish-hacker's support in the fall of 1924 when Olmstead secured control of the Northwestern National Bank from the Pittock estate. Meier had worked closely with Olmstead during the reconstruction of the Liberty Temple and the proposed 1925 fair drew them even more closely together.

The exposition never came off, for a variety of reasons. The legislature, dominated by downstate interests, failed to enact the necessary tax referendum. The local Portland leadership, including Meier, was accused of dragging its feet. And the troubles at Ladd & Tilton together with the reluctance of Abbot Mills dampened the efforts of the private subscription drive. The ill-fated endeavor did, however, expose Julius Meier to the first of many close scrutinies that he was to receive over the next decade from Portland's more conservative newspapers and magazines.

According to editor Chapman of the *Oregon Voter*, "Mr. Meier used his financial power to bring financial pressure upon members of the legislature." To Chapman, a lesson was to be derived from "the whole affair":

"Money in the hands of a man of Mr. Meier's type can be and was used as a power to attempt to compel legislators to change their vote. The lesson gives a good deal to think about.

Meier & Frank Company in 1932 after completion of the southwest corner quarter block.

"Julius Meier's genius, resourcefulness and untiring energy have been the mainspring in making that great department store the huge and successful business it is today.... As against Mr. Meier, about the only thing that can be said is that he tries to boss people around.... Incidentally, Mr. Meier also has the reputation for dodging the doing of his share in public matters and in philanthropies. He is a headline hunter.... When the time comes to dig into his pocket and make a subscription proportionate to his means, it takes immense pressure to procure it from him."[35]

Despite the generally critical tone of the piece, Chapman concluded:

"We sincerely believe Mr. Meier has within him the qualities that make for leadership — qualities based upon his unusual ability and enterprise — but he must divest himself and his store of those practices which antagonize worthy manhood in other people or create distrust. He simply has some hard lessons to learn."[36]

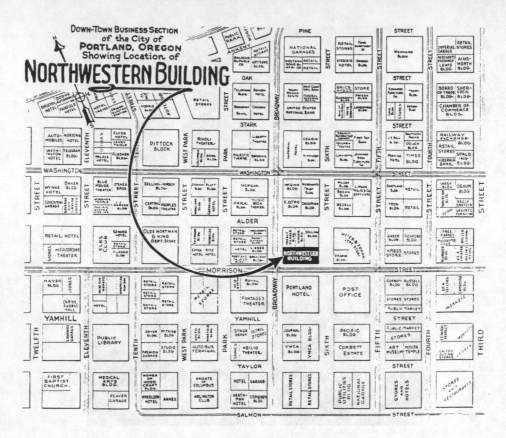

A 1927 map showing the Northwestern Building

Julius Meier's entrance into the banking profession provided him with some "hard lessons." He appeared at the wrong time.

Over the years, there has been general agreement by Meier's supporters and critics that George Joseph was the one who encouraged Meier to become a banker. C. C. Chapman was probably correct when he called Joseph the "prime minister of Meier & Frank." And yet, Julius Meier obviously did not need too much persuasion. For years he had yearned for Meier & Frank to own its own bank. The experience with Abbot Mills and the First National Bank in 1921 had revealed such feelings.

Meier had not been comfortable in his relationships with Mills and Ainsworth. Whether he detected feelings of anti-Semitism would be hard to document, but it would not have been surprising. Joseph knew that he and Meier could do an honorable and efficient job. They would never allow themselves to become entangled in the kind of web that had caught Emery Olmstead. Herbert Fleishhacker apparently agreed with them. He supplied some of the funds that allowed Joseph and Meier to buy the Pacific Bancorporation in September 1929

— one month before the Wall Street stock market crash. The funds for Meier's controlling shares were borrowed from the Meier & Frank Company, with Meier putting up company stock as collateral. This was normal procedure fifty years ago for investors who owned their own businesses. After all, Meier & Frank Company was in many respects like a bank. Not only did it cash thousands of checks for its customers, but it was the most profitable locally-owned business in Portland with large cash reserves and assets.

Pacific Bancorporation, a holding company of ten small banks from around the state, was organized in July 1928 by Marshfield utility executive Charles Hall. George Joseph handled the legal work and became secretary of the corporation. Hall had been a prominent Republican politician and had accepted Ku Klux Klan support in 1922 when he tried to secure the Republican gubernatorial nomination from Governor Ben Olcott. One of his close political associates at the time was Robert F. Smith, president of Portland's Lumberman's Trust Company. During the liquidation of the Northwestern National Bank, Smith played a prominent role in forming a syndicate to buy the building and property for $2.7 million. In the summer of 1927, Smith moved the Lumberman's Trust Co. into the southeast corner of the building and arranged for the organization of a new bank in the quarters of the old Northwestern which opened upon Morrison Street. Thus was born to a brief life the American Exchange Bank. In March of 1929, the American Exchange merged with the Portland National Bank to form the American National Bank which in turn was acquired by Pacific Bancorporation. In all of these dealings, George Joseph handled the legal transactions.

Six months later, the Portland financial community was surprised to learn that Pacific Bancorporation had been bought out by the Julius Meier interests. Meier became chairman of the board and Joseph continued on as secretary. Named as president was G. Spencer Hinsdale, chief executive of the American National Bank, the central jewel in the PacBancorp crown. PacBancorp in turn was reincorporated as the American National Corporation with total resources of $12 million.

The reaction of the *Oregon Voter* revealed some latent anti-Semitic racial attitudes embedded in Portland's financial and business establishment even though people like editor C. C. Chapman would have denied ever holding such feelings. To quote excerpts from the September 21st issue:

> "Important, also, is Meier's position as the third but by no means the least conspicuous member of Portland's Jewry to be engaged in the banking business. . . . Meier . . . has a position of leadership among his people that may enable him to attract huge deposits to the bank in which he now has an active . . . interest. Portland has been unusual in respect to the absence of Jews as factors in its banking institutions. . . . American National officials state that Herbert Fleishhacker's personal visit to that bank last Tuesday . . . was not an indication that this Jewish banker, public utility, wallboard, pulp-paper, etc., magnate, is in any manner interested in this Pacific Bancorporation ownership readjustment."[37]

Example of newspaper optimism

The Oregon Journal spoke for a number of Portland's more enlightened citizens when it congratulated Julius Meier as "a progressive spirit. . . . Portland needs him. . . . [He has] supreme confidence in the future of this territory and the institutions which reflect its growth."[38] Meier was going to need all of the confidence he could muster over the next four years, a period that saw depression destroy one-third of the nation's banking system.

The Crash and Its Aftermath

In the months leading up to the stock market crash of October 1929, most of Oregon's bankers, business leaders and newspaper editors revealed no apprehensions, at least publicly. As John Ainsworth wrote to a friend some years later:

"I guess we all thought that the good times would continue indefinitely and that if we were thrifty and applied ourselves to the job at hand, we would all be sitting pretty some fine day; — we took so much for granted, didn't we?"[39]

One of the few "bears" in Portland was E. B. MacNaughton who became a vice president of the First National Bank in 1928 following the accession of C. F. Adams to the presidency upon the death of Abbot L. Mills. MacNaughton was taken to task by News editor Fred L. Boalt for being too pessimistic. "Too much 'naught' in MacNaughton!" was the heading of a front page editorial in November 1928.

> "E. B. MacNaughton is a dignified gentleman who, having harnessed up a competency for himself, can afford to indulge his passion for gloomy epigrams of his own manufacture. . . . MacNaughton went before the Portland Realty Board the other day and made a speech so lachrymose that it left most of the hard-boiled realtors in tears. . . . He warned them of the dangers of trying to 'over-sell' Portland. . . . 'We are not an industrial city and might as well quit trying to be.' This came as a shock!"

Referring to the banker's former role in property management as a partner in the Strong & MacNaughton Trust Company, Boalt commented: "I fear that MacNaughton has been so occupied raising rents that he is out of touch with the actual industrial situation."[40] Of course, considering MacNaughton's recent

E. B. MacNaughton
(1880-1960)

391

experience with the Ladd & Tilton Bank, one might have expected him to be cautious. He was still involved in the final liquidation proceedings in 1928.

Another Portland "bear" was J. F. Bergesch, the assistant manager of the U. S. National Bank investment department. Bergesch was a bond specialist who had kept accurate records of bond yields and discount rates for over thirty years. He feared what he saw developing in 1929 and published a report in September warning that a "recession is due to begin in the near future." He concluded that the absolute peak had been reached in interest rates. The *Oregon Voter* did not agree. It quoted the perenially optimistic Andrew Mellon, the multi-millionaire Secretary of the Treasury, that "now is the time to buy bonds." Mellon had declared that "for many years bonds probably cannot be bought at materially lower prices than now."[41] Like most of his peers, Mellon was to be proved disastrously wrong.

On the morning of October 24, 1929, "the towering structure of American prosperity cracked wide open."[42] Before the day was through, the stock market values had declined over $5 billion. No one could hold back the tide, not even J. P. Morgan who tried to duplicate his efforts of 1907. Confidence had evaporated and the worst was yet to come. Five days later 16 million shares were sold and October 29, 1929, went down in history as the beginning of the Great Depression. Over the next three years, prices would move up but mostly down until market hit bottom on July 11, 1932, in the midst of the Hoover-Roosevelt presidential campaign.

Being three hours behind New York, anxious Portland investors heard the bad news while heading off to work on the 29th. Crowds inundated the local brokerage houses which reported "standing room only." Brokers became hoarse from answering phone calls and switchboard operators scarcely had time to unwrap fresh pieces of gum. One broker, when asked what stock he would recommend to buy, replied laconically "livestock." Another broker told a reporter about a woman who had come in the office three days earlier to buy some stock as a surprise for her husband. "What a surprise he's going to get now," the broker added.[43]

In company with investors all over America, Portlanders sustained severe losses. One trader saw $45,000 evaporate in less than a week. Particularly hard hit were the utility stocks, RCA and General Electric. Transamerica took one of the worst beatings, dropping in two weeks from $166 to $36 a share. Those who sold short — a distinct minority — stood to make fortunes. One Portlander cleared $100,000 in three days.

In the course of a few months, more than $30 billion in paper values vanished into thin air. By the spring of 1930, conditions began to worsen not only for stockholders, but for the American labor force. The volume of business dropped off drastically, registering a 20 percent decline in Oregon through December 1930. By the end of 1932, business volume was to decline another 23 percent and over 12 million Americans were to find themselves unemployed, including 24,000 family heads in Portland. Twenty percent of the Portland work force was

The Decline in Per-Share Value of a
Selected List of Stocks

Stock	9/3/29	11/13/29	7/11/32
			(lowest point)
American Can	182	86	30
American Tel. & Tel.	304	197	70
General Electric	396	168	9
General Motors	73	36	8
(reached 212 in '28)			
RCA	101	28	3
Amer. Power & Light	175	64	3
(parent co. of PP&L)			
U. S. Steel	262	150	21
Transamerica	166	36	*(bottomed at 2½ on 11/10/30)*

Trend of Bull Market and Bear Market for Nine Years

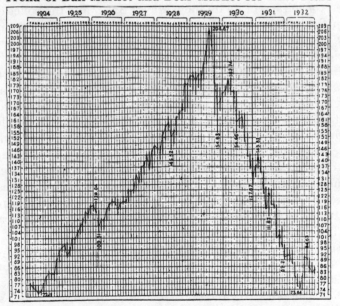

The above chart traces the course of the stock market, as reflected by the New York Herald Tribune's composite average of 100 representative stocks, for the nine years from 1924 to 1932.

393

affected. In Oregon as a whole, 866 plants closed their doors with logging employment dropping by 48 percent.

Even Portland's exclusive private clubs felt the pinch, with the Arlington, Waverley Country and University clubs down to less than 125 members apiece. Prominent names associated with the Kerr, Macleay, Collins and Ainsworth families, all large stockholders in the U. S. National Bank, were to see their fortunes shrink as the per share value of U. S. National Bank stock declined from a high of $405 in 1927 to a low of $30 in 1935. The Corbetts, Failings and Lewises encountered a similar fate with their First National Bank investments. And yet both banks weathered the depression in strong operational condition. Compared to those states where the speculative fever had run rampant, Oregon suffered far less because of its traditional conservatism. To old-time Oregonians, indebtedness was a cardinal sin.

The crash and the subsequent depression sharply lowered the prestige of businessmen, bankers and brokers. In fact, the entire American capitalistic system was to receive a probing and critical examination from all quarters. Reactions from the Left became more extreme, both nationally and locally. Portland's small but dedicated Communist Party increased its attempts to organize the mass of unemployed workers in the city. The city's press gave them no encouragement, in fact *The Oregonian* exhorted the city to stamp out the communist conspiracy in its infancy. Mayor Baker and the police department decided in the late summer of 1930 to place a spy in the Communist Party hierarchy. Chosen was M. R. Bacon, an auto mechanic and former bootlegger with an eighth grade education.

Early in September, the police began to round up and arrest as many communist organizers as they could find. Over 20 were jailed temporarily and by the end of the year, 16 had been indicted. Most of the cases were never tried, but the Boloff case achieved wide prominence. Russian-born Ben Boloff was an illiterate and itinerant sewer worker who had resided in the Portland area for 19 years. Accused of violating the state's syndicalism law, Boloff was tried and convicted during the winter of 1931, with much of the prosecution's case resting on informer Bacon's testimony. Boloff was sentenced to ten years in jail. Following two futile appeals to the state supreme court and increasing criticism by the state's press, Boloff was released from jail after 15 months because he had contracted tuberculosis. He died three months later.[44]

Despite the increased radical activity, life in Portland remained quiet during the early years of the depression. Business activity dropped way off and new construction ground to a halt after Meier & Frank opened its new wing in October 1930. The assessed valuations of downtown properties took a nose dive, particularly those located near to the waterfront, from S. W. Ash to Salmon Streets. The only commercial properties in the city to maintain stable values were those being acquired by Ralph B. Lloyd on the East Side near Holladay Park. The wealthy California oilman-investor was in a distinct minority in his exuberance for Portland's future.

City services were forced to operate with barely minimal resources. The city council was told in June 1930 that Portland's emergency fund was "right down to bed rock." The water bureau was forecasting annual deficits if rates were not increased. But the taxpayers were in no mood to suffer any further loss of income despite the announcement that Portland's per capita tax rate ranked near the bottom for cities in its class. Portland's rate was $1.71 as opposed to Seattle's $2.44. Only Kansas City and Columbus were lower, and by just five cents.[45]

Early in June 1930, the *Oregon Voter* seemed to capture the city's spirit when it printed a long article on Portland's quiet night life.

> "By 'night life' we refer to the kind that is wholesome — innocent merriment and amusement available to people who seek recreation after the theater. . . . Our visitors . . . notice this lack in Portland, and they talk about it. They have noted it for many years, and have talked about it for many years. The result is that Portland is known as a place where it is dull at night. . . . As a class, Portland people are home lovers. It is hard enough to drag them out of their delightful homes in the evening, to say nothing of late at night."[46]

A restrained civic style — moderation bordering on dullness — had characterized Portland city life as a whole for over 50 years. Portland "the spinster" was still an appropriate image. It prevented Portland from frittering away many qualities of life that prideful citizens yearned to preserve. Portland was still a privately oriented, home centered city. Almost 50 years later, Seattle writer Ivan Doig would encounter the same spirit. "It's a great place to live but would you want to visit?" he asked, in entitling his article for *The New York Times*.[47] The scale of building heights in downtown Portland reflected the restraint that long characterized the city's growth. Doig commented that "those who would build big . . . have a different set of scales, and they have recently made their mark in Portland. The 40-story tower of the First National Bank of Oregon is huge and sleek and featureless . . . "[48]

The First National Takes Off

In June 1930 when it was announced that Giannini's Bancamerica was coming "into Oregon through purchase of First National of Portland," the local financial community attached "immense significance . . . to the move." Was a new epoch about to be launched, embodying "new methods and new attitudes?" For sixty years, the First National was regarded as "typifying the extreme conservatism for which Portland has been celebrated for half a century."[49] The reasons for its sale confirmed that evaluation.

The string of events that led to the sale of the First National Bank began in mid-1928 when Elliott R. Corbett asked E. B. MacNaughton if the Strong & MacNaughton Trust Company would be interested in merging with the Security Savings & Trust Company that was owned by the First National.[50] The Corbett family had long been the major stockholders in the First National and Elliott

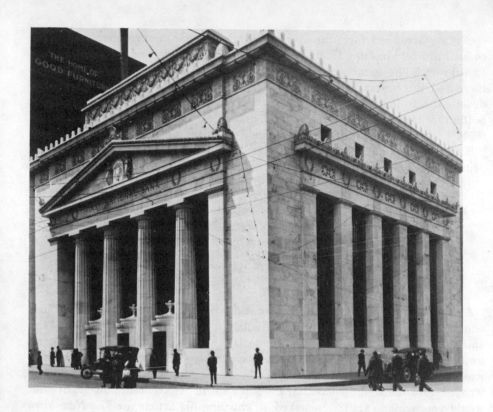

The headquarters of the First National Bank from 1916 to 1972, at S.W. Fifth and Stark. Dubbed the "marble temple," the bank's design bred confidence — a symbol of security. The First National was sold to Transamerica in June 1930. In 1972, the headquarters were moved to the new 40-story tower and adjacent administrative services building next to City Hall.

The "marble temple" was saved from destruction and given an historical landmark designation. It is now the home of the Oregon Pioneer Savings & Loan Association.

Abbot L. Mills was president from 1903 to 1927; C.F. Adams, from 1927 to 1932; and E.B. MacNaughton from 1932 to 1947.

Corbett served both as a vice president and a director of the bank. The oldest brother, Henry L., also a director, left the management of the bank and of the Corbett estate to his brother Elliott. Henry L. dedicated most of his time to state politics, to the Port of Portland Commission and to a myriad of other corporate and civic affiliations. Elliott Corbett wanted to groom a successor for C. F. Adams who was close to 70 and expecting to retire from the presidency of the bank in the near future. MacNaughton was offered a post as bank vice president while his partner, Robert H. Strong, was offered the presidency of the Security Savings and Trust Company.

The Strong & MacNaughton Trust Company, organized in 1911, specialized in commercial real estate transactions, mortgage loans, property titles and property management. For years it had managed the properties of the Corbett estate and Elliott Corbett had supreme confidence in both MacNaughton's ability and his working knowledge of the securities market. Corbett was worried about the future of the securities market as it might affect the bank and he wanted an experienced person at the helm. MacNaughton accepted Corbett's offer but Strong rejected it, preferring instead to remain with his own trust business which included managing the Corbett estate. This decision, like MacNaughton's, was to launch a similar series of events, in this instance leading to the formation of Commonwealth, Inc., in late 1929.

MacNaughton bought 1000 shares of First National Bank stock for more than $300 per share and moved into the bank as the senior vice president. Early in 1930, he became concerned about the bank's future — a future in which he now had a sizeable personal stake. What made him particularly uneasy was the merger of the West Coast Bancorp into the U. S. National Bank in March. As a long-time proponent of branch banking, he clearly sensed that the bank's future health depended on consolidation and expansion. A year earlier he had organized the First National Corporation, following by three months a similar action taken by the U. S. Bank. But the First National Corporation controlled only three banks while the U. S. National Corporation could boast of 17.

MacNaughton knew that the Corbett, Failing and Lewis families — the controlling stockholders of the First National — were overly cautious and conservative. They were worried about the decline in value of their large bank stockholdings. Led by Elliott Corbett, the major stockholders were clamoring for more liquidity and the sale of the First National seemed to offer the best solution. The last thing they wanted to do was to invest more funds in the bank and incur a sizeable debt in order to compete with the U. S. National. They were opposed to issuing more stock, an action that could only dilute their control. In May of 1930, therefore, MacNaughton was instructed to begin negotiations to sell the First National, and Giannini's Transamerica (including the Bank of America and Bancitaly) appeared to offer the best deal.

Transamerica agreed to exchange 666 shares of its stock for 100 shares of First National. With First National worth $310 a share, the value of a Transamerica share equated to $47. At the time the deal was struck, two weeks before it was formally approved by the Transamerica board of directors, Giannini agreed verbally that Transamerica would be willing to "take back" by purchase three-fourths of its own stock that was to be issued to the First National stockholders. It was assumed by Elliott Corbett and E. B. MacNaughton that the purchase price would be $47 per share. Transamerica had rebounded from $36 a share in November 1929 and Giannini expected it to stabilize at close to the $47 figure.

Unfortunately for the First National Bank stockholders, by June 12th, Transamerica had dropped to $31 a share. Elliott Corbett and the other major stockholders wanted to increase the number of Transamerica shares that were to be exchanged for each share of First National stock from 6.6 to 9, but the agreement had been ratified and publicized at the original ratio.[51] Corbett then wanted Giannini to take back by purchase for $47 a share only those Transamerica shares to be issued to the major stockholders. The minor stockholders were to be excluded and would have to accept the $31 per share price if they wished to sell. According to E. B. MacNaughton's account, he strongly opposed this tactic. He held out for the $31 figure for all stockholders "as the only businesslike thing to do."[52] MacNaughton also felt that in fairness to Transamerica, the $31 figure had to be accepted. By assuming this posture, of course, MacNaughton gained the respect of Giannini. What the San Francisco banker did not know at the time, however, was that MacNaughton and the Corbetts had transacted a short sale of most of their recently acquired Transamerica stock. By late July, when the stock declined to $10 a share and MacNaughton and the Corbetts executed their purchase agreements, considerable profits were realized — in MacNaughton's case nearly $150,000. This windfall precipitated a bitter disagreement between Elliott Corbett and E. B. MacNaughton who felt that the short sellers should split their profits with the other major stockholders.

MacNaughton prevailed and the Lewis and Failing estates benefited accordingly. Most of the other former First National Bank stockholders who kept varying portions of their Transamerica shares watched in horror as the stock hit an all time low of $2.50 per share the following November. Predictably, the local stockholders were incensed. The resultant uproar was heightened by the realization that Transamerica had dispatched salesmen to Portland during the summer and early fall to sell "with confidence" the company's stock to local buyers who were encouraged to invest in the future of "their" First National Bank. Needless to say, the bank's image plummeted along with the stock. As one observer wryly noted: "What else could be expected? The First National had sold out to some shrewd California vegetable peddlers."[53]

Giannini's shrewdness was implied in a letter to John Ainsworth from Wells Fargo president F. L. Lipman: "How these people [at Transamerica] have managed to sell the idea [of a stock exchange] to the First National group . . . passes my understanding. . . . I have little reason to believe that they [Transamerica shares] are worth anything like even the present market price of around $29. Holding these views, the recent action of the First National group seems to me almost incredible."[54] Of course, neither Lipman nor Ainsworth was aware of the short sale transaction.

E. B. MacNaughton would not have appreciated hearing these comments. He was convinced that the Transamerica deal had been most successful, certainly for the major stockholders anyway. As for himself, it assured him a long and secure future with the First National Bank. Initially, Giannini had expected to replace the top command. For some reason, he changed his mind. He obviously respected MacNaughton's toughness and integrity. MacNaughton was asked to stay on as executive vice president until C. F. Adams retired in 1932 at which time MacNaughton could be expected to receive the presidency. Adams' primary role for two years was to protect the interests of the minority stockholders, to assure them that the bank, through Transamerica, was a sound investment. MacNaughton noted that in his first two years with the bank he had discovered "much bank held corporate paper under water." The bank's assets had been inflated accordingly. He had several nasty encounters with debtor local businesses when he told them "to pay up and get out."[55] He met his match one day when he directed his fire at New Yorker Harry Schwartz, a wealthy investor whose National Department Store chain had bought out Lipman, Wolfe Co. in 1925. "What I want to know is when are we going to get paid." Schwartz calmly replied: "If you are not patient, Never!"[56] Patience was not one of MacNaughton's virtues.

MacNaughton's former partner, Robert H. Strong, began searching for a merger that he could effect which would consolidate the trust company and mortgage banking business of Portland. He found just the right people in Harry Hawkins, president of the City Mortgage Company and G. F. Peek, president of the Union Abstract Company. Together they formed the Commonwealth Trust & Title Company, with assets of over $1 million. At the time the merger was announced in November 1929, Strong made it clear that Commonwealth would not engage in any form of real estate brokerage. The company would perform all the duties of a trust company except in the matter of taking bank deposits.[57]

Commonwealth's board of directors was as high powered a group of Portland businessmen as has ever been assembled in one company in the city's history. Included in it were lumberman E. S. Collins, Henry L. Corbett, Kenneth Dawson of States Steamship, insurance executive Horace Mecklem, investor Drake C. O'Reilly, E. C. Sammons, Amedee M. Smith, Cameron Squires, Simeon R. Winch and Aubrey Watzek, a wealthy lumberman who was to play an important role in Portland's civic and business life for 40 years. In 1931, Commonwealth became a holding company for three divisions: The trust and title company, a securities corporation and the Equitable Savings and Loan Association, an institution organized originally in 1890 with over 20,000 depositors in 1931. The Commonwealth Securities corporate division brought in William Hemphill whose family had enjoyed a distinguished record in Portland's financial history. The merger also attracted to the board of directors two prominent lawyers: Ralph H. Cake, whose family had long been involved in state and national Republican Party affairs, and Alfred A. Hampson, a partner in the firm of Dey, Hampson and Nelson, the attorneys for the Southern Pacific Railroad in Oregon.

Under Strong's direction, Commonwealth appeared to move off to a healthy start. The company bought a half block on S. W. Sixth and prepared plans to construct a 27-story headquarters building. But at the beginning of 1932, with the depression growing more severe by the month, some internal dissension

The Equitable Building (now the Commonwealth Building) was Portland's first skyscraper in 20 years. It was the first of its type to be built anywhere in the world and brought international recognition to Portland architect Pietro Belluschi, who later became the MIT Dean of Architecture. Equitable Savings & Loan was to be totally divorced from Commonwealth Inc., which was later sold three times. Equitable moved to a new, larger center in 1965. The U. S. National Bank, on the right, presents an interesting contrast — 30 years of architectural change.

developed and Robert H. Strong was forced to resign. Apparently Elliott Corbett had not been too happy with Strong's management of the Corbett estate properties that Strong had taken with him to Commonwealth. Two junior Commonwealth executives, A. D. Norris and George Beggs, left Commonwealth to open their own realty firm and took the Corbett business with them. Without the Corbett estate, Robert H. Strong was of no value to Commonwealth. He was replaced by Harry Hawkins who was to direct the company's affairs for many years. Norris and Beggs soon joined forces with David B. Simpson, and together the three young entrepreneurs began to build Portland's foremost realty and property management firm. In subsequent decades, Simpson was to play a preeminent role in Portland's physical development.

After Strong's departure, Commonwealth sold its trust business to the Portland Trust & Savings Bank, one of Henry L. Pittock's early establishments. In 1932 it was headed by Dean Vincent, a name that was to become prominent in commercial real estate sales. Commonwealth proceeded to organize a highly successful property management and sales department headed by Chester A. Moores. The company became involved in a variety of prosperous real estate developments that included Charles F. Swigert's Sun Dial Ranch near Troutdale, Maywood Park and Cedar Hills near Beaverton. Equitable Savings and Loan, meanwhile, grew even faster and was soon to operate independently of its parent holding company. In fact, it was Equitable that finally built on the Commonwealth Sixth Avenue property, over 25 years later, providing Portland with its first post-World War II modern glass office structure, designed by the noted Pietro Belluschi.

More Bank Problems: Hibernia and American National

In the fall of 1930 while Transamerica's stock was declining precipitously, The Hibernia Commercial & Savings Bank, one of Portland's old and most honored banks, found itself short of "quick assets." The city's sixth largest bank, with assets of over $8 million, was reported offered for sale to the First National Bank. The transaction never materialized and for the next 14 months Hibernia's condition became steadily more precarious. Public confidence in banks was degenerating and John C. Ainsworth was mystified. The price of U. S. National Bank stock continued to drop, by almost $10 a month. In November 1930, it reached $85 — a shocking retreat from its high of $405 three years earlier. As Ainsworth wrote to Jack Blodgett in Michigan, "The condition of this Bank was never so good in its history. . . . Our earnings will approximate $930,000 for the calendar year, not including the earnings of the ten banks which we now operate." Ainsworth was predicting that the U. S. Bank stock would rebound "after the turn of the year."[58] By December 18th it fell to $70 a share. By May of 1931, public confidence had diminished to the point that the U. S. National Bank found itself unable to loan more than 25 percent of its deposits in Portland.

401

As Ainsworth commented to bank director Roderick Macleay, Portland had always been a poor loaning market. "In the past 32 years we have never been able to loan a third of our deposits in Portland."[59]

The closest that the U. S. National Bank came to experiencing a run on its deposits occurred on Saturday morning, December 19, 1931, and the following Monday. The Hibernia Bank had closed its doors on the 19th following a mild panic. Hibernia's deposits had dropped to $5.8 million, declining $700,000 in the two days prior to closure. As Ainsworth described the disturbing reaction to Wells Fargo's F. L. Lipman:

> "The so called Reds made this an excuse to work one of those telephone call campaigns, and some of the detectives estimated there were as many as 10,000 telephone calls all over the city, asking people to withdraw their money from our bank and from the First National, across the street, at the earliest possible date, if they wanted to save it. That was all there was to the message, and the next number called. . . . We do not expect them to get far, as they were quite unsuccessful when a similar thing was worked in Seattle some two years ago. . . . The jam continued all day Monday and up to 11 o'clock Tuesday."[60]

On Tuesday, December 22, 1931, the U. S. National and First National ran full page ads in all the daily newspapers, notifying bank depositors that legal notice to the banks would be required before the banks would permit savings deposit withdrawals. Ainsworth was not too happy about taking the action. To Lipman he implied that MacNaughton had forced his hand. "Out of some 59,000 savings accounts, only between 450 and 500 signed the withdrawal notices. We intend to remove the withdrawal requirements at the earliest possible legal date."[61]

Lipman responded to Ainsworth the next day, complimenting the U. S. National Bank for "steering the ship wisely."

> "It is no surprise to us . . . to find out how enormously liquid you have been running. The figures that you give of your immediate cash resources are so fine . . .
> Conditions of today remind me of a statement I had occasion to make a few years ago to the effect that whatever the public might expect of business men they did not want their bankers to be enterprising so much as safe and strong."[62]

The rules by which Lipman and Ainsworth operated their respective banks could be summarized briefly as follows:

1. A bank should have quick assets — cash, government securities, commercial paper — of at least one-half the total of its deposits.

2. A bank should not accept deposits of more than 17 times the amount of its capital, surplus and undivided profits.

3. The ratio of deposits to loans should be one and one-half to one.

The banks that found themselves in trouble had violated these rules.

In March of 1932, three months after the Hibernia had closed, Julius Meier's American National Bank ran into some difficulty. In May of the previous year, the American National had acquired the small Columbia National Bank headed by county commissioner Frank Shull. It thus achieved the ranking of Portland's fourth largest bank following the Hibernia's removal from the scene. Although Meier harbored great expectations for his fledgling institution across the street from his store, the American National found itself in a familiar strait jacket during the early months of 1932. It had insufficient liquid assets and its ratio of loans, many of which had turned sour, was too high for its level of deposits.

Meier was now the Governor of Oregon and he was really too busy to give the bank the attention it deserved, although many contemporaries would argue that

Julius Meier, Aaron Frank and L. H. Hoffman on the site of the new wing being built for Meier & Frank Company in 1929-1930. Hoffman was the general contractor.

403

Meier's presence in itself would have made little difference. George Joseph's death in 1930 created a void in the bank's management that was never filled. Intelligent legal counsel was a necessity for assuring sound bank management. And even though Meier and his nephew, Aaron Frank, who assumed responsibility for the store's operation when Meier went to Salem, were both lawyers, neither of them had the experience to provide proper legal supervision. By temperament, Julius Meier was not a banker. He was too impatient and emotional. He was a first rate merchandiser and promoter but the banking profession required other qualities.

As the depression deepened during 1932, Meier was forced to borrow increasingly larger sums from the store, putting up his Meier & Frank stock as collateral. Just how much he invested in the bank is not known. But when he settled his accounts with the store in 1934, he owed the company over $750,000 — some of this indebtedness resulting from his unprofitable hotel investments of the previous decade. The person who came to Meier's rescue was his nephew Aaron Frank. Against his better instincts, Frank had been helping his uncle for several years. He had bitterly opposed Meier's running for governor, and yet he loaned him over $40,000 for the campaign — a sum that was never repaid.[63]

Like his Uncle Julius, Aaron Frank was trained as a lawyer. He had practiced with Joseph and Haney until he entered the store in the mid-1920s. Despite some serious differences of opinion, Frank had an enduring feeling of respect and affection for Meier. He joined the bank board and became increasingly involved with its affairs. Early in 1933, upon the death of his mother, Julius' older sister, Aaron Frank inherited enough Meier & Frank stock to give him control of the company. In addition to his own shares, he also voted the shares of his brother Lloyd who had left the store in disgrace, divorced his wife and established a trust to be administered by Aaron for 30 years. Early in 1933, Aaron advanced the bank sufficient money to keep the doors open long enough to negotiate a suitable sale to either the U. S. National or the First National. He replaced Meier as chairman of the bank's board. By the time of the American National's sale to the First National Bank in June 1933, the bank's deposits had dropped over $2 million to $4.3 million.

In later years, E. B. MacNaughton was to praise Aaron Frank for doing the people of Portland "a great service."[64] He had prevented what could have become a severe bank disaster that might have adversely affected Portland's remaining banks. The crucial months were in the winter of 1933 when banks all over the country were closing. One of President Roosevelt's first acts was to declare a week-long national bank holiday on March 6, 1933. By June, relative stability was to be achieved, particularly after the passage of the Glass-Steagall Act that permitted national banks to open branches. The American National Bank became the Sixth and Morrison Branch of the First National Bank, located in the American Bank Building where it resides today.

Aaron Frank did more than save the American National Bank. He also saved Julius Meier's reputation. This fact accounts for the bitterness that developed 32 years later when Frank accused the Meier family, together with Lloyd Frank's children, of betraying him when the company was sold to the May Department Store chain. This complicated story will be related in a future book. Suffice it to say, Aaron Frank went to his death in 1968 believing that his efforts in behalf of his uncle had not been appreciated by the surviving Meiers and Franks, excluding his own children who strongly supported their father. He "had bailed Julius out," but in the competitive business world of 1965, his earlier generosity had been all but forgotten.

Meier for Governor

The depression not only had a severely disruptive effect on banks and business generally, but it also had a shattering impact on the state's political structure. Traditional party loyalties became strained. Neither of the major parties was providing the requisite leadership to deal with the serious problems that were emerging. As the Washington County *News-Times* noted:

> "The public business of the state of Oregon just now needs a fearless and able executive. . . . This state has been drifting along for a good many years, directed by a little oligarchy of moneyed men in Portland. . . . Under the leadership of these financial 'big wigs' of Portland, we have had a string of nice pleasant old lady governors of Oregon, who were personally honest and did their feeble best, but against the 'big wigs' they were about as effective as a consumptive policeman sent out to arrest a Kansas cyclone. This year big business mergers, franchises, water power sites, cheap electrical power so necessary to Oregon's development, are up for consideration."[65]

On the same day, *The Woodburn Independent* declared that the "most prominent issue in this campaign [the May 1930 gubernatorial primary] is whether the people shall control public affairs or that they should be in the grasp of what is virtually Wall Street."[66] Both papers gave voice to a rising tide of protest that was reminiscent of the Populist and Progressive eras. And the political leadership that began to emerge from this reaction was lodged in the progressive wing of the Republican Party — a faction that had been closed out of state and local party influence for many years. The leaders were men like Col. A. E. Clark, Rufus Holman, U. S. District Attorney George Neuner and George Joseph. And the primary issue that gave focus to their efforts was the public development of hydroelectric energy.

The incumbent governor in May 1930 was Republican A. W. Norblad of Astoria. As president of the state senate, Norblad had succeeded to the governorship upon the death of Governor I. W. Patterson in December 1929. Although an honorable and energetic official, Norblad was considered a political enigma. He was not personally dynamic and he enjoyed no particular political power base. Among the party's traditional "big wigs" in Portland his support was minimal.

In searching for a new face, a man whom they could trust to be opposed to public power and still present an image of some enlightenment, the "old guard" party leaders chose Henry L. Corbett, one of the most popular state senators in Multnomah County's history. A former president of the Portland Chamber of Commerce and a six year veteran of the Port of Portland Commission, the grandson of pioneer banker Henry W. Corbett seemed to embody just the leadership qualities needed by both the Republican Party and the State of Oregon. What more could be asked from a man whose campaign slogan in three previous legislative elections had been: "Service to Oregon. Honesty in Government. Economy in Administration." Even among his political opponents, Corbett was considered "a fine gentleman, a highly respected person whose word was always good." But to the progressives, Corbett had three political liabilities: His inherited wealth, his sympathy with the private utilities and his lack of personal charisma.

The factors that led George Joseph to seek the Republican nomination have already been mentioned. But the major force behind his campaign was former county commissioner Rufus Holman who had nearly beaten George L. Baker in the 1924 mayoralty campaign. Holman was a tireless worker in his role as president of the Joseph for Governor Club. In most of his own speeches in Joseph's behalf, he concentrated on the public power issue, reminding the voters that Joseph had fought for years for the right of the people to control and develop their own hydroelectric power system. He lashed out at the "power trust," which he accused of incompetence, willfulness and an inability "to economically serve the public demands for power." This failure, declared Holman,

> " . . . is detrimental to the public welfare in that it [has] embarrassed the growth of Oregon industry, with its consequent deleterious effects, which ramify the commercial, social and political life of our state."[67]

In gaining the Republican nomination Joseph showed impressive statewide strength. He successfully identified his candidacy with the interests of the common people, the consumers. But his victory struck terror in the hearts of the "old guard." In fact, the conservatives of both parties feared him. They mistrusted him. He was viewed "as a tyrant and a terrorist." Many conservatives were reluctant to oppose him publicly out of fear that their business interests would "suffer severely . . . when he is in a position of power. The leaders in those lines of business," reported the *Oregon Voter*, are not anxious to stir him up. Aroused, he might be far worse than if let alone."[68]

After Joseph's sudden death in mid-June, the responsibility to select a replacement candidate fell to the Republican State Central Committee headed by Phil Metschan, Jr., the Imperial Hotel owner who had long been identified with the party's conservative wing. Prior to Joseph's nomination, Metschan had strongly opposed the public power plank in the Joseph platform. He had also opposed Joseph's advocacy of abolishing the state public service commission of three members, to be replaced by one public service commissioner to be appointed by the governor. With *The Oregonian*'s backing, Metschan began to round up support for a candidate who would repudiate the Joseph platform.

Julius Meier became involved in the preliminary negotiations when he asked Henry Hanzen, the political editor of the *Telegram*, to search for a strong, aggressive candidate who would carry Joseph's banner. He offered to finance such an effort to the amount of $50,000. Hanzen and Holman soon came to the realization that "Julius L. Meier was the one man to pick up the Joseph torch and carry on triumphantly for the cause."[69] When the Republican state convention convened to consider the recommendations of the state committee, Hanzen and Meier were surprised by the number of old line party conservatives who had swung behind Meier as the one candidate who could assure victory in November. But such revelations of support were too late. The machine had made its decision: Phil Metschan, Jr., was to be the Republican candidate and the Joseph platform had been scrapped. Without too much urging, and with strong

A Travelling Show is on the Road

support from his family, Meier announced a few days later that he would run as an Independent. The convention that nominated Meier was as wildly enthusiastic as any in the state's history. Meier endorsed the Joseph platform, literally word for word, and promptly received the influential backing of the State Federation of Labor and the Oregon Grange.[70]

The Democratic Party was nearly as fragmented as the Republican Party in the spring of 1930. The conservative wing was led by former governor Oswald West who opposed Joseph's stand on public power. In fact, West had been a paid lobbyist for the Pacific Power & Light Company for over a decade. The liberal wing was headed by former governor Walter Pierce who favored the essentials of the Joseph power plank. West's candidate, State Senator Ed Bailey of Eugene, barely won the nomination but he dodged the public power question. Later in the campaign, he assumed a position similar to Metschan's, i.e., that he would support federal, but not state, hydroelectric development. At issue was a statewide initiative measure on the November ballot, providing for the creation of People's Utility Districts by majority vote of the people residing in such districts. The private power companies launched a well financed campaign to defeat the measure and knock off Julius Meier at the same time.

While "Big Ed" Bailey, the congenial lawyer from Eugene, ran a quietly dignified campaign, Metschan and Meier took off the gloves and battled each other for nearly three months. Metschan delivered a series of radio talks in which he attacked Meier's local press support — the "three monkeys" as he called them: The *Telegram*, *News* and *Oregon Journal*. Disregarding the *News* which he considered socialistic, and the *Journal* which was traditionally Democratic, he singled out the *Telegram* for his abuse, citing the paradox that Herbert Fleishhacker, the paper's major owner, was "the recognized head of the power trust in California."[71] He disputed Rufus Holman's contention that public power rates in Seattle and Tacoma were cheaper than Portland's private power rates and he cited other comparisons to bolster his case. As far as one can tell, both sides were able to produce copies of power bills from the same cities, each designed to prove that one or the other was cheaper.

The debate that began with the election of 1930 was to rage unabated to the present day. Despite the generally unreliable rate comparisons, the arguments in the early days, at least, were largely based on philosophy: Free market vs. control by "the people." It was essentially a political and ideological argument as opposed to the debates of more recent days which have been narrowed to two basic economic questions: Who can provide the lowest rate and what are the capital costs involved?[72]

Apart from the public power issue, the 1930 campaign focused on the personal differences of the two major candidates. Metschan emphasized his early pioneer life with slogans like: "Native son of the old west." Here was a candidate who sold vegetables as a boy to earn his spending money. Later in his mid-twenties when he bought a small hotel in Heppner, he received the guests, made beds, cooked and doubled for the bell boy and the porter. "He made his

A New Recruit in the Band of Hope

hotel a success. . . . He has worked hard all of his life."[73] Meier, on the other hand, was depicted as a wealthy "big businessman whose sinful greed is anathema to the liberal-minded."[74] Meier was criticized for his business ethics and for the low scale of wages he paid to Meier & Frank employees. His alcoholic habits also came under attack. Said the *Oregon Voter*: "When Julius entertained that distinguished dry, Dr. Clarence True Wilson, at his home, did he take him downstairs and show his elegant bar? Or was it already boarded up for the campaign?"[75]

Despite such attacks, Meier gained the support of most of the larger non-Portland papers, including *The Medford Mail Tribune* and *The Salem Capitol Journal*. He started the campaign with wide name familiarity. Anyone who had ever been to Portland had visited Meier & Frank at least once. His being a Jew did not seem to hurt his candidacy in spite of the fact that eight years earlier the Ku Klux Klan had attacked Jews along with Catholics as agents of an international conspiracy. In fact, the *Oregon Voter*, in a backhanded way, admonished its readers by declaring: "It is a disgrace to Oregon that among our citizens are a number who oppose Julius Meier for governor solely because he is a Jew." The *Voter* went on to point out: "As we well know, many of Oregon's

409

leading Jews were distressed at the prospect of Julius Meier running for governor, so doubtful were they as to his qualifications."[76]

The election results were conclusive. The voters wanted a new face in politics and they favored the Joseph platform. Meier polled 134,396 votes to Ed Bailey's 62,121. Metschan trailed badly with 46,797. As to the PUD initiative, Oregon voters gave the measure a 33,000 vote affirmative margin. In fact, Oregon's PUD enabling act proved to be more popular than Washington's which only passed by 22,000 votes.

The two state measures were different in one important respect, however. The Washington voters passed a single stage law that not only permitted the formation of PUDs, but enabled PUDs to issue revenue bonds without a subsequent public vote. Oregon's law required two separate votes: One to approve a PUD and another to approve the issuance of general obligation or revenue bonds. This difference was to prove a major obstacle in subsequent efforts to establish public power districts in Oregon. The Oregon law made it easier for the private utilities to defeat public power efforts because they had two chances for every attempt. If the district formations were not defeated, the bonding proposals usually were.

Despite Julius Meier's overwhelming victory, Oregon's private utilities were to be successful in blocking most subsequent efforts to establish People's Utility Districts. Large sums of money were to be spent on media advertising and lobbying activities. After nearly 50 years, the record speaks for itself. Eighty percent of Oregon's residents are today served by private power companies; in Washington the figures are reversed, with only 20 percent being served by the private utilities.

Attached to Her Bill

Chapter 14

The Private Utilities and
Public Power

By 1932, over 90 percent of the electricity marketed in the United States was sold for private profit, and 75 percent of the private power output was controlled by 16 giant holding companies. Portland's electric and gas utilities were integral parts of the interstate holding company networks. The utilities' officers and directors were front men, or puppets, whose decisions and actions were ordered from above — from the financial centers of New York and Chicago.

The Private Utility Networks

The public utility holding company was born in the years before World War I. Its inventor was Samuel Insull, the former secretary to Thomas A. Edison, the inventor of the electric incandescent lamp. Insull realized early in his career that the most important single fact about marketing electric power was that it could not be stored. In order to service an expanding market, huge amounts of capital would be required to build the necessary generating and transmission facilities. To gross one dollar was going to take an investment of five or six dollars. Following the example set by John D. Rockefeller in the oil industry, Insull devised the electric power monopoly. Funding would come primarily from large individual investors and banks, and later from bank controlled investment trusts. In less than 30 years, Insull was to build the third largest utility empire in America by outright acquisitions, mergers and the purchase of stock through holding companies that he had organized. Before he went bankrupt in 1932 and was indicted for fraud, Insull had become president of eleven power companies, chairman of 65 and the director of 85.[1]

In the summer of 1924, *The Byllesby Bulletin* extolled the virtues of public utility holding companies for investment purposes. The H. M. Byllesby Company of New York was one of the giants that controlled a myriad of electrical, gas, water and telephone companies scattered all over America. Reported the *Bulletin*, as reprinted in the *Oregon Voter*:

"Public utility holding companies not only have been financial successes, but they have made their way steadily in the face of discouraging circumstances and a lack of knowledge of the vital part they have played in the development of electric, gas, telephone and traction properties throughout the United States. . . . By consolidating the requirements of a chain of diversely

411

located properties, the holding companies have been able to bring financing, legal, operating and engineering ability of the highest class to work out problems which isolated properties could not hope to overcome."[2]

This statement is a classic rationale for corporate mergers even today. According to Byllesby, acceptable investments in small independent companies were difficult to promote without "the holding companies back of them. . . . By the character of their management, the holding companies . . . established credit ability and reputations of the utmost value to the operated properties."[3]

As all utility executives have known for years — and today even more painfully so — utilities have never been able to earn enough to save up for their own expansion. They have had to borrow new money every year, and often several times a year, in order to meet future as well as current needs. And to attract the new money, the utilities have had to rely increasingly on the issuance of bonds and stocks which appear to offer a high rate of return to the investor. In June 1925, PEPCO President Franklin T. Griffith wrote an article in Portland's *Spectator* praising the capitalistic system and the Portland investors for their loyal support of the local utilities. By buying so much stock and "investing so heavily," local investors were "a great help to the utilities in meeting their capital requirements."[4] Although Griffith was a lawyer by training, after ten years in the job he had become — like most utility executives — a finance man. Increasingly, utility executives found themselves thinking in terms of credit, not in terms of sales. And since most of the large banks and investment houses were in New York, Wall Street became the physical and psychological headquarters of the utility industry.

Reporting on a study of Wall Street utility holding companies, *Fortune* commented:

> "If the first layer of holding companies began life pure in heart and with honest intentions, they were soon surrounded with temptations more dangerous to their virtue than to their efficiency."[5]

Companies like American Power & Light and its parent, Electric Bond & Share, were free of even the minimum state regulation that governed their underlying operating companies like Pacific Power & Light and Portland Gas & Coke. Their books were closed to the public eye. They were at liberty to make the most of their opportunities to profit by a greater margin than the six to eight percent return that was usually allowed by most state public service commissions.

The first step down "the ladder of shame" was the invention of devices to increase the capitalization of the holding company's subsidiaries without a large cash outlay on its part. This was done by restating upwards the values of the operating companies. One method was to buy up local companies for excessively high prices, incorporate them into existing holding companies, and then unload the holding companies' securities at advanced prices. This was one technique for "watering" the stock — inflating its value way beyond its true worth. Numerous other devices were employed to the same end, to the point that by 1932, more than 20 percent of the total fixed capital of operating companies like Pacific Power & Light was water.

In addition to increasing the values of their own securities, the holding companies exerted every effort to increase the capitalization of their subsidiaries; the higher the capitalization, the higher the dividend pay-out. The holding companies continually forced the operating subsidiaries to borrow to pay off debts to the holding companies — obligations that had been previously foisted upon them by the holding companies. Consumer utility rates were adversely

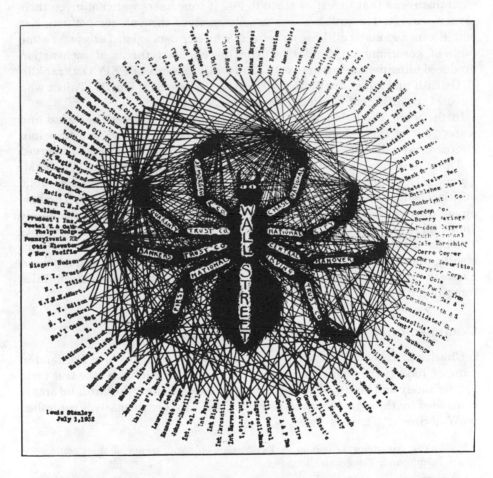

The famous "Spider Web of Wall Street" was published in a simplified form by the New Leader, *a Socialist Party paper, in 1928. It received national attention by Senator George W. Norris, who exhibited a six foot high enlargment of it during the early days of the 1933 congressional session.*

413

affected by such procedures because the operating companies were guaranteed by law a "fair return" on their total capitalization which included the market values of their securities and their funded debt. Inflated capitalization meant higher cash dividends that required higher utility rates to pay for them. Both the small investors and the consumers were being exploited.

Capitalism was in deep trouble but few of Portland's business and financial leaders were either able or willing to recognize the crisis. And *The Oregonian* followed along blindly, praising the private utilities and excoriating those like George Joseph for daring to suggest that public ownership might be more equitable for all concerned. Historically, one of the fundamental tenets of capitalism was that investors stood to lose if consumers were not given their money's worth. The problem was usually resolved through competition. But with the monopolistic utilities, no corrective mechanism existed except for some form of governmental regulation. And the slightest threat of such action produced bitter denunciations by the local utility executives, PEPCO's Franklin T. Griffith and American Power & Light's vice president Guy W. Talbot who directed the affairs of the Pacific Power & Light group.

In the main, the public power advocates wished to squeeze the "wind and water" out of the inflated utility securities market. They wanted to reduce electrical rates to the level that would provide a fair return to those who deserved it. The man who led the movement in Oregon, beginning in 1931, was Charles M. Thomas, Governor Julius Meier's appointee as Oregon's first single public utilities commissioner. The legislative enactment that produced Thomas' appointment also provided that the commissioner should obtain for the people "just and reasonable rates and service." The intent of the act, in Commissioner Thomas' words, was to place "the responsiblity . . . upon one man to obtain results, and the method used is left to his judgment."[6] For some years, Oregon has been unique among the states of the country with its single public utilities commissioner.

Commissioner Thomas and Electric Bond & Share

Charles M. Thomas[7] delivered a major address to the people of Portland in June of 1933 at the Civic Auditorium. He wanted to publicize "the true facts . . . definitely and bluntly." To begin with, he declared that "the Portland area is controlled by three great corporations which in turn are themselves controlled by Wall Street." Thomas cited:

1. The American Telephone & Telegraph Company, owner of the Pacific Telephone & Telegraph Company.

2. The Central Public Service Company (CPS) of Chicago, owner of PEPCO. (Thomas failed to mention that as of March 1933, the control of PEPCO had reverted to Portland after the CPS Company was in receivership. However, PEPCO had been milked by CPS and would find itself in receivership a year later.)

414

3. The Electric Bond & Share group, American Power & Light, with Inland Power & Light Company (indirect), Pacific Power & Light Company, Portland Gas & Coke Company and Northwestern Electric Company as subsidiaries.

In commenting upon utility company practices generally, Thomas cited a letter written by John Colton of the American Electric Railway Association — an indictment of the utility system by one of its own members:

"The thing about the utility industry that disgusts me is the lying, trimming, faking and downright evasion of trust, or violation of trust that marks the progress toward enormous wealth of some of the so-called big men in the industry. When I see some of these fellows waving the flag, I am filled with not only disgust but rage, for they are anything but patriots."[8]

MAMMA POWER TRUST WITH HER BABIES.

Telephone Trust

National Economy League

P.E.P. Co.

Multnomah Tax Economy League

Gust Franklin T. Griffith Anderson

East Side Taxpayer's League

Oregonian, Power Trust Paramour

Milo B. Mack, Oregonian's Hack

THIS CARTOON IS FROM THE FRONT PAGE OF TOM BURNS'S HARPOON. A PAPER TO BE SOLD FOR THE UNEMPLOYED. ON THE STREET SATURDAY, NOV. 5, 1932. HOT STUFF. PRICE 5 cents. WATCH THIS WINDOW.

Tom Burns was known for many years as the Mayor of Burnside Street. In 1932, at the age of 56, he considered himself a veteran of a 40 year struggle in behalf of the oppressed. He hated communists and had forsaken socialism after World War I, although he had been a member of the IWW. He strongly supported union strike efforts for higher wages. He operated a clock shop on West Burnside Street, stuffed full of books, and described by a friend as "a veritable Valhalla of odds and ends."[9] Over the years, he printed and distributed various sheets to which he gave a variety of names. The "Harpoon" was aimed at the "power trust."

415

Passing over the first two corporations, Thomas decided to focus his analysis and comments on the Electric Bond & Share group (EBASCO). He displayed his chart of the holding company structure and pointed out that the financial control was in the Morgan Bank of New York. "The contest before Oregon," declared Thomas, "is not with the local utilities. It is with the guiding, controlling, dominating head, — the Morgan Bank."[10]

Much of Thomas' information came from the files of the Federal Trade Commission which had launched an investigation of Electric Bond & Share in October 1928. Although the company refused to testify initially, deploying tactics of "legal evasion, brazen defiance" and contempt, the federal court ordered it to produce its records in April 1930. The revelations were interesting. The Federal Trade Commission found $926 million of watered stock, including $68.5 million ascribed to the American Power & Light group. It was little wonder, therefore, that when such information became known, EBASCO was to suffer the largest loss ever recorded by any United States corporation in one year. During 1931, its capital surplus declined $469 million. By July of 1932, American Power & Light stock was to hit bottom at less than $3 per share, wiping out the investments of thousands of local stockholders including Guy W. Talbot, the president of the Pacific Power & Light group and a vice president of American Power & Light.

Talbot, one of Portland's two or three most powerful business leaders, had been an outspoken opponent of the 1930 PUD election. His three companies had spent over $85,000 to defeat the measure, and he had mailed out thousands of printed letters over his signature in October 1930 citing the dangers of publicly-

416

owned power districts, warning of the waste of "taxpayers' money" for the "promotion of freak political schemes." No mention was made of any conceivable danger to stockholders' money if the private utilities were allowed to continue their existing financial practices.

Commissioner Thomas told his Portland audience that he had served Talbot's Northwestern Electric Company with four orders, beginning in September 1928, to provide him with an inventory of the utility's properties. He never received them. However, Thomas did discover, through the offices of the Federal Trade Commission, that the Northwestern Electric Company had over $10 million of watered stock.[11] He also discovered a damning telegram sent to Guy Talbot in November 1930 from American Power & Light headquarters in New York. Labeled by Thomas "a species of treachery and deceit," the wire was sent in code but Pacific Power & Light attorney John A. Laing refused to decode it for the commissioner. Laing, it should be noted, was also a director of the three Pacific Power & Light related companies, a member of the city planning commission and a close colleague of banker John Ainsworth, a 20 year director of Pacific Power & Light. When Thomas had the wire decoded by an outside expert, he discovered that Laing was deeply involved in the "treachery and deceit."

The wire related to the construction of "transmission lines crossing the Columbia River and to the construction of a new substation within or near Portland City limits." Because EBASCO owned both Northwestern and Pacific Power & Light, it made no difference to New York which company was to be used for "financing puposes. . . . But we suggest," said New York, "that you discuss with Laing . . . the following points: first if substation is built within city and by Northwestern and city upon recapture is bound to purchase substation would the additional burden upon the city be helpful to us . . . ?"[12]

To Commissioner Thomas, the wire's implication was clear. Talbot and Laing were to use "that particular company and build in the way that will put the greatest possible burden on the people of Portland if they decide to take over the Northwestern." The Northwestern franchise contained a provision whereby the city could acquire the property with voter approval. To protect themselves against such an eventuality, Talbot and Laing were instructed to load up Northwestern with any new construction that might also be used by Pacific Power & Light, thus increasing the value of Northwestern's properties and making the voters less willing to accept the added costs of municipal ownership were the issue to arise at some future date.

Where was the "economy and public service" that "should always be first consideration" in any utility construction? asked Thomas. There was "no such thought" from two of Portland's most "public-spirited" citizens. Other examples of "devious and duplicit" behavior were cited by Commissioner Thomas, all previously denied by the utility executives. One related to the financial affairs of Guy Talbot's Portland Gas & Coke Company, the only Portland utility with a perpetual franchise.

"Let us look at the record," said Thomas. From 1922 to 1925 inclusive,

Portland Gas & Coke Company plant at Linnton

Portland Gas & Coke obtained funds from ten different American Power & Light operating utilities around the country. "The borrowings were as high as $4 million." In the same period of time, Electric Bond & Share borrowed $587,000 from Portland Gas & Coke. In late 1927, when American Power & Light decided to reorganize its subsidiaries and issue new higher valued stock in exchange for the shares of its local operating companies — coincident with the move of the Pacific Power & Light group into the new Public Service Building — American Power & Light required its subsidiaries to repay their borrowed funds. Portland Gas & Coke owed $3.8 million. But of course it did not have the funds available, so it borrowed the $3.8 million from the Banker's Trust Company in New York. Inland Power & Light Company, another subsidiary, was also required to repay "borrowed" funds. Portland's U. S. National and First National banks came up with $850,000 of the needed amount on December 30, 1929. The presidents of both banks, J. C. Ainsworth and C. F. Adams, were on the Pacific Power & Light Company board of directors. The local "money was sent back to New York and used for purposes unknown." The main beneficiaries of these transactions were the banks; the losers were the rate payers who in effect were subsidizing the interest charges for the contrived indebtedness that had been incurred primarily for reasons of stock speculation and secondarily for meeting plant expansion costs.[13]

Commissioner Thomas' revelations showed the importance of bank-utility ties through interrelated boards of directors. As power company directors they approved actions that required bank funding, and as bank directors they approved loans to the power companies. The system was unbeatable as long as the market continued to climb and speculative stock could be foisted upon a ravenous, unsuspecting public. Behind all such transactions, however, was the guiding hand and domination of the holding company, situated in New York, ordering its "puppets" to follow its directions. The local companies, of course, justified all of the reorganization and refinancing schemes as necessary to increase their capital for expansion purposes. But it was borrowed capital that carried high risk and service charges because much of the borrowing was

The Utility Banker-Underwriter

419

contrived, that is, manufactured to inflate capitalization. The system was far more complicated than it needed to be. It was also a wasteful system from which little good came except to the highly paid corporate attorneys who devised the schemes in the first place.

Charles Thomas described to his audience one final series of transactions involving Pacific Power & Light. In August 1931, American Power & Light loaned Pacific Power $9.4 million at six percent. On the same day, this amount was loaned by Pacific to Inland Power & Light on an unsecured note. Then Inland Power & Light paid over to American Power & Light the amount of $7.9 million that was owed on a previous loan and kept $1.5 million for its own purposes. The whole transaction was performed in New York. The result of all this was that American Power & Light profited from the interest charges, gave up no actual funds of its own and stuck Pacific Power & Light with guaranteeing the remainder: The $1.5 million kept by Inland Power & Light. The local officials contended that by such transactions they were constantly exercising "their best independent judgment in conducting the business of the companies they [were] supposed to serve."

For such services, American Power & Light and its parent, Electric Bond & Share, charged the subsidiary operational companies a high fee that was accounted a justifiable business expense, and ultimately paid for by the consumer. From 1910 to 1932 inclusive, service fees paid by the three local utilities to American Power & Light totalled $3.2 million. For the year 1930 alone, service fees amounted to $200,000. Thomas considered such charges unjustified. For the year 1930, he also found $150,000 of excess costs charged off to new business and $380,000 of unjustified general expense including excessive executive salaries and benefits. Cited as examples were the 103 memberships in the Portland Chamber of Commerce paid for by the three utilities. All of the executives' club and associational memberships were paid by one or more of the companies. One executive belonged to nine clubs including three local country clubs. Another executive even charged his membership in the Chicago Opera Association. And Guy Talbot received credit for a $3000 gift to the Portland Art Museum.

Concluding his comments, Commissioner Thomas charged the three local American Power & Light affiliates with $17 million of watered stock. He also asserted that "conservative business management would reduce expenses of the local Electric Bond & Share, without affecting the employees, by approximately $920,000 a year." Thomas did not see any chance for improvement.

"The Electric Bond & Share group has made its record and from it there is no hope of fair treatment in the future. A leopard does not change its spots. It is the system and the system will therefore contest to the end. The Northwestern franchise expires in 1937. It is my recommendation that it not be renewed. No franchise should be granted hereafter by Portland unless, (1) The applicant is incorporated under the laws of Oregon; (2) No holding company contracts or fees permitted; (3) The capitalization is free from water; and (4) Lower rates."

Endorsing public ownership, Thomas declared that "power districts are proper and essential instrumentalities through which the public can procure the relief to which it is entitled."[14]

Some Local Consequences

Thomas was not alone in encouraging Portland residents to municipalize their electric power system. Commissioner Ralph C. Clyde had been proposing such action for over two years. In January 1931, Clyde introduced a resolution calling for "The City of Portland to declare itself in favor of a municipally owned and operated power and light system for the City of Portland."[15] Clyde told his council colleagues that the city was eligible to receive a $25,000 appropriation from Commissioner Thomas' office to contract for both a study and a plan that would be submitted to the council within the year. Mayor George Baker opposed the resolution on the grounds that Governor Meier was expected to propose state power legislation and Congress was considering legislation to develop a power project at the Umatilla Rapids on the Columbia River. Portland should not undertake "independent action," he said. The city would be "throwing a monkey-wrench into the machinery." The $25,000 "would be wasted." Baker called Clyde's plan "an intangible dream — a gesture far remote from accomplishment."[16] After a month of intermittent debate, Clyde's resolution was passed 3-2, with Clyde, Barbur and Mann favoring the action. Baker and Pier were opposed.

The firm of Carey and Harlan of Tacoma was engaged to undertake the study. During the ensuing months, progress reports were submitted to the council. Carey and Harlan discovered many of the same facts that Thomas was to relate in his 1933 Portland speech: Northwestern Electric had over $10 million of inflated stock on its books and it had been paying a 10½ percent return in dividends whereas 8 percent was the legal limit. In June 1931, Carey and Harlan told the council that "the city is entitled to lower rates for residential and commercial power."[17]

Apparently the Hooker Chemical Company of Niagara Falls, New York, had felt the same way when it rejected Portland in favor of Tacoma, Washington, in 1929. In the winter of 1928, U. S. Bank director Roderick Macleay had written John C. Ainsworth that President E. L. Hooker was planning a large factory in the Northwest toward which he was prepared to expend up to $3 million. "Hooker is a very rich man. . . . I think he can be landed for Portland," Macleay noted. The company needed cheap power. It was "using 15,000 horsepower" at its Niagara Falls plant. Macleay asked Ainsworth to "get the chamber of commerce busy." He also suggested that Ainsworth arrange a "golf game for him at Waverley and drive him on the Columbia River Highway on a good clear day." Ainsworth was also advised to discuss "the power situation with Franklin T. Griffith and Guy Talbot."[18]

In his reply to Macleay, Ainsworth said he would do what he could to help but that Tacoma was "underbidding Portland for power." Like much of Seattle, Tacoma had a municipal power system. To the dismay of the private utility companies, it also enjoyed the lowest rates on the Pacific Coast, nearly 30 percent below those in Portland. The chamber of commerce prepared a 50 page report,[19] custom tailored to the Hooker Company, but the effort proved fruitless.

In the light of recent disclosures about Hooker Chemical's waste disposal practices, one is left with the feeling that Portland may have gained far more than it lost when Hooker chose Tacoma. Some of Portland's numerous gullies might have achieved the notoriety of Niagara Falls' Love Canal — a local disaster of tragic proportions.[20]

In July 1932, Carey and Harlan formally presented three plans to the city council:[21]

1. The city could finance a municipal light and power project through a Reconstruction Finance Corporation loan of $25 million. Included would be the acquisition of the Northwestern Electric transmission and power facilities within the city and the construction of a 50,000 horsepower capacity hydroelectric plant at Beaver Creek Dam.

2. The city could acquire the Northwestern Electric distribution system and steam generating plant within the city limits for $15 million.

3. The city could acquire the transmission and generating facilities within the city limits of both PEPCO (PGE) and Northwestern Electric and build the Beaver Creek Dam plant, all for $50 million.

The utilities would obviously have contested Carey and Harlan's appraised values had the city attempted to purchase the properties. But in retrospect, the appraisals were reasonably close to the properties' real worth regardless of what valuation method was used. Today, it seems almost ludicrous to imagine that Portland might have been able to develop a municipally-owned electric power system for just over $50 million, or that it might have been able to purchase the power facilities of Portland General Electric for approximately $25 million. The city council had the opportunity at least to place the issue before the voters, but it failed to do so for several reasons.

To begin with, the private power lobby was just as keen-witted and ruthless as it was at the state and national levels. Mayor Baker, it should be remembered, was personally indebted to Franklin T. Griffith of PEPCO for the burning of his home mortgage. Baker continually received "advice" from Griffith, Ainsworth and Laing, and he was not about to risk destroying his future opportunities as he contemplated retiring from office in 1933. Commissioner S. C. Pier, a veteran insurance man, had never favored public power, and he was not expected to change his ground in 1932 despite all of the revelations about the power trust.

The key vote belonged to the commission position occupied by John Mann who had supported commissioners Barbur and Clyde on earlier motions. Unfortunately for the public power advocates, John Mann was indicted for larceny in January 1932 and subsequently recalled from office. In the spring of 1932, the council appointed A. G. Johnson to replace Mann. Johnson was a Harvard educated engineer who had worked previously for the city engineer's office and before that for the Strong & MacNaughton Trust Company. No doubt existed in anyone's mind that both Messrs. Strong and MacNaughton were strongly opposed to public power in the City of Portland. But there was more to their opposition than that. MacNaughton and Strong were influential in securing the city's receipt of a $2 million Reconstruction Finance Corporation (RFC) loan for a new public market that was being built on the waterfront. They had personal and business reasons for promoting this obligation. And since only so much RFC money was available, they did not want to jeopardize the market's financial future by encouraging RFC funding for a public power project. Including the public market loan that had just been approved, the city council already had before it eight possible projects, totalling $24 million.

When Commissioner Clyde introduced his public power ordinance in September 1932 he knew he faced a difficult task. He reluctantly ruled out of consideration a loan application to the Reconstruction Finance Corporation. Instead, he proposed a $15 million bond issue to purchase the Northwestern Electric system. He would have preferred to sell utility certificates but the money market was too low. He assured his colleagues that user revenues would more than carry both bond interest and payments, similar to the procedure long followed by the city in financing its municipal Bull Run water system. Clyde reminded his fellow commissioners that the city was paying $400,000 to the utilities just for its own electric needs. "Over 2000 towns and cities in the United States have municipal ownership," Clyde declared. Portland should join them. But on the first vote, the motion was defeated 3-2, as Clyde had feared might happen.[22]

Commissioner Thomas was obviously disappointed by the outcome of the city council vote. He faced a similar problem of his own after the legislature convened in January 1933. He drafted and presented Senate Bill No. 19, designed to give the public utilities commissioner the necessary authority and funding to compel fair treatment for the consumer. Despite a strong message of endorsement from Governor Meier, the House of Representatives so weakened the bill by amendment that "destruction was complete." As Thomas told a Klamath Falls audience in April 1933, "about the only recognizable feature remaining . . . are the words of the title."[23] The Senate, by a 14-14 vote, refused to alter the House amendments. Henry L. Corbett sided with the private utilities as Joseph had predicted would happen before the 1930 gubernatorial primary. Governor Julius Meier refused to sign the bill. He could have vetoed the measure, but he realized that a weakened bill was better than no bill at all.[24]

In his hard hitting public addresses, Commissioner Thomas repeated one basic theme: "If the people of Oregon mean business, they should investigate the members [of the legislature] and their records. . . . They will find the charge that the utilities are in the business of politics, controlling legislation, is true." The

Guy W. Talbot
(1873-1961)

utilities, declared Thomas, "are the most powerful lobby the State has ever had."[25]

No one knew this any better than Guy W. Talbot who had presided over the affairs of Portland's American Power & Light subsidiaries for 23 years. Along with PEPCO's Franklin T. Griffith, Talbot had become a master of the art of influencing politicians and newspaper editors. In early 1933, however, Talbot's health was suffering along with his finances. He resigned as president of the Pacific Power & Light group and went to England to recuperate. A month before Thomas gave his Portland speech, Talbot wrote John Ainsworth that he could not afford to repay a loan to the U. S. National Bank that Ainsworth had personally guaranteed. "I have lost everything," he said, "but I expect to make money again. . . . It's hard to make $1 million; harder to make $1 million and keep it; harder still to make, lose it and not complain."[26] Talbot would return to Portland and be given a $7000 annual retainer fee by Pacific Power & Light which he would continue to serve as a director for 16 years.

Talbot maintained his faith in the utility system to which he had dedicated his working career. Although he had never earned over $34,000 a year, his stockholdings had made him a millionaire, if only briefly. He would continue supporting the lobbying efforts of the private utilities as they faced the awesome legislative attacks of President Roosevelt's New Deal. The growth of public power, embodied in such federal projects as the Tennessee Valley Authority and the Bonneville Power Administration, was to consume much of his interest. It also became a primary concern of his successor, Paul B. McKee.

A San Franciscan by birth, the 41 year old McKee was elected president of the Pacific Power & Light group following Talbot's resignation in February 1933. An electrical engineer graduate of Stanford, McKee had achieved an impressive administrative record with two Electric Bond & Share Company subsidiaries: The California Oregon Power Company and the Brazilian Electric Company from which post he came to Portland carrying Sidney Z. Mitchell's highest recommendation. McKee was more than to fulfill Mitchell's fondest hopes in his 32 years with Pacific Power & Light. He was to prove to be an exceptionally able administrator and a tough and relentless defender of private utility interests. More than any other single person, McKee was to be responsible for checking the further growth of Oregon's public power development. Supporting him strongly in these efforts was Franklin T. Griffith, the 20 year veteran president of the Portland Electric Power Company (formerly Portland Railway Light & Power Company).

Some Difficult Years for PEPCO

From the time that Franklin T. Griffith assumed the presidency of the former Portland Railway Light & Power Company in 1913 until the sale of the giant utility in September 1929, the firm was controlled by the E. W. Clark interests of Philadelphia.[27] Although Griffith ran the company with proprietorial independence and tenacity, he was essentially a manager who was ultimately responsible to absentee owners residing 3000 miles away. His immediate superiors were the company's directors of which he was one. Three members of the Clark family sat on the board although they rarely attended meetings. The board of directors of an operating utility company, owned by an absentee group or investment trust, was a kind of legal fiction. Its formal approval was required before the company could incur any major financial obligations such as floating stocks and bonds and borrowing from banks. But in most cases, affirmative board actions merely rubber-stamped the decisions of the majority owners. The local directors were usually company officers, large minority stockholders and bank presidents who were useful when any local financing was needed. Besides Griffith and the three Clarks, the 1928 PEPCO board included Charles F. Swigert and bankers John C. Ainsworth and E. B. MacNaughton. Former New York Congressman Ogden L. Mills, in 1928 the Assistant Secretary of the Treasury, was also a board member by virtue of his grandfather's large holdings in the old Portland Railway Company.

During the decade following the war, the company had a generally successful record. Its bonds were quoted at par or better and its preferred stocks were close to par. Like most utilities, the company had a somewhat complicated capital structure. It had its regular common stock and four or five issues of preferred stock, some voting and some non-voting. The common stock and a substantial portion of the voting preferred stocks were held by the Clarks and their clientele. The Clarks were investment bankers, and through their banking connections placed a large amount of the common and preferred stocks among their clients. They kept enough for themselves to maintain control of the company.

The bulk of the company's net profits came from its electric power sales. Although the traction operations were not losing money despite a drastic reduction in the number of revenue passengers carried, from 66 million in 1921 to 55 million in 1929, Griffith was constantly complaining to his owners that the net income was insufficient to pay a fair return on the capital invested in the traction properties. In 1922, he had secured approval of an eight-cent fare for the urban streetcar system. But by 1928 expenses were fast overtaking revenues. In the majority of cities comparable to Portland in size and service, the streetcar fare was already ten cents. Griffith realized that a fare increase was inevitable, but he was not looking forward to the struggle involved. Comparative studies indicated a lean operation. In fact, Portland's cost per unit was under both Seattle's and San Francisco's. One reason was that Portland paid the lowest trainman compensation on the Pacific Coast.[28] The average hourly wage was 64 cents in 1929. The bright side of the traction operation was the rapid growth in freight revenues. From 1925 to 1929, freight carriage increased from 8.6 million ton miles to 21.13 million ton miles.

Early in 1928, a series of events unfolded that was to have unanticipated and far reaching consequences for both Franklin Griffith and the City of Portland.[29] Griffith knew that the Clarks were considering the sale of the company, and he came up with a scheme that looked promising. After considerable discussion with Guy Talbot and John Ainsworth who was a director of both PEPCO and Pacific Power & Light, an agreement was reached, with the Clarks' support, to form a merger between PEPCO and the Northwestern Electric Company.[30] Under the terms of the proposed consolidation, PEPCO was to acquire all of the physical properties of Northwestern in exchange for PEPCO stock. Once the deal was consummated, the merged properties were to be sold to the American Power & Light Company. Some thought was given, but no decision reached, to selling off the traction properties whose future did not look too promising.

One major hurdle remained, however. The merger required the consent of the Portland voters because of the terms of the Northwestern franchise approved by popular vote in 1912. As an inducement to the voters, Griffith and Talbot pledged their word that electrical rates would be reduced $400,000 a year for a period of at least five years. Considerable savings would accrue to both companies, so it was claimed, by eliminating duplication of transmission lines and by more efficient use of existing generating facilities. The utility executives also promised that the merger would not throw men out of work. And finally, both companies agreed to pay the $40,000 cost of a special election to be held on April 9, 1928.

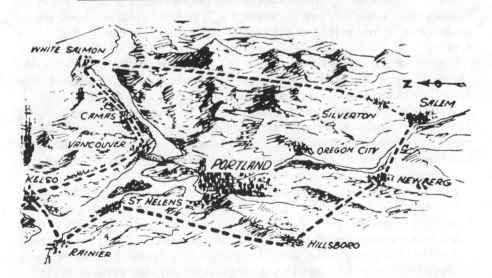

Map showing the service area of the PEPCO-Northwestern operations. PEPCO had expanded as far south as Newberg and Salem, while Northwestern was concentrated in the northern and eastern portions of Portland and southwestern Washington.

The announcement caught Portlanders by surprise and it immediately aroused suspicion among the public power advocates led by George Joseph. As the *Nation*'s correspondent, Julia N. Budlong, commented: "Such magnanimity on the part of the companies gave rise to the anti-merger slogan . . . 'There's a nigger in the woodpile, or a monkey up a tree — perhaps both.' "[31] Although the companies did not spell out their future course of action if the merger vote were positive, George Joseph rightly concluded that it made no sense for PEPCO, the larger but more heavily indebted company, to expect to take over the newer and more profitable Northwestern. American Power & Light would never let it go. Obviously, the properties would end up with American Power & Light, but they would operate henceforth under PEPCO's "perpetual"[32] franchise. No longer would the people be able to vote on future utility franchise renewals. Northwestern's would expire in 1937, and Joseph hoped that this occasion would provide Portland with the opportunity to municipalize Northwestern's Portland operations. Joseph further feared the effects of creating a monopoly. Without Northwestern, the voters would lose their leverage on at least one-third of the city's consumer market.

Joseph and Griffith engaged in a number of heated debates before groups like the Realty Board. Joseph accused the power companies of "insolence" by attempting to "rush through" the merger with an early vote. Griffith countered that it would be "an economic crime" to force the utilities "to continue to operate as under the existing system." Declared Griffith: "There is no Ethiopian hidden in the merger woodpile." Griffith asked "the people to believe us. We are in the business and know whereof we speak. . . . It is not fair to condemn such a proposition, or any other, simply because of failure to understand all of the details."[33]

Despite strong support from the City Club, and from *The Oregonian*, the *Oregon Voter* and *The Oregon Journal*,[34] which was normally supportive of Joseph's electric power views, the proposal was soundly defeated 30,000 to 14,500. Only 47 percent of the registered voters had bothered to go to the polls. The measure carried in the more affluent precincts of Portland and Willamette Heights, Westover, Nob and King's Hill, Eastmoreland, Irvington, Alameda and Piedmont. The election marked the first use of voting machines, but they were confined to the West Side.[35]

With the merger defeat and the growing stock market boom, the Clarks began to look earnestly for a potential purchaser. Finally in the fall of 1929, the Public Utilities Holding (PUH) Corporation of New York made an offer for the stock at prices which were unusually attractive. The Clarks required that any sale must be a public offer to all stockholders. The sale was consummated on September 29, 1929, and went into effect on October 19th, just ten days before the stock market crash. The Clarks had anticipated disposing of all their own holdings, but being the gentlemen that they were, they gave preference to their customers. When the transaction was closed they were still left with a substantial block of PEPCO preferred stock. The PUH Corporation paid $18.5 million for the stocks they

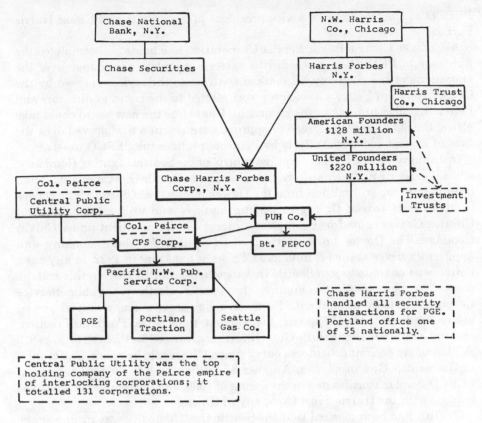

```
┌─────────────────┐                      ┌─────────────────┐
│ Chase National  │                      │  N.W. Harris    │
│  Bank, N.Y.     │                      │ Co., Chicago    │
└─────────────────┘                      └─────────────────┘

  ┌─────────────────┐              ┌─────────────────┐
  │ Chase Securities│              │  Harris Forbes  │
  └─────────────────┘              │      N.Y.       │
                                   └─────────────────┘
                                                    ┌─────────────────┐
                                                    │  Harris Trust   │
                                                    │ Co., Chicago    │
                                                    └─────────────────┘
                                   ┌─────────────────┐
                                   │American Founders│
                                   │  $128 million   │
                                   │      N.Y.       │
                                   └─────────────────┘
                                   ┌─────────────────┐
                                   │ United Founders │
                                   │  $220 million   │
  ┌─────────────────┐              │      N.Y.       │
  │   Col. Peirce   │  ┌─────────────────┐
  ├─────────────────┤  │Chase Harris Forbes│         ┌─ ─ ─ ─ ─ ─┐
  │ Central Public  │  │  Corp., N.Y.    │           │Investment │
  │  Utility Corp.  │  └─────────────────┘           │  Trusts   │
  └─────────────────┘                                └─ ─ ─ ─ ─ ─┘
          ┌─────────────────┐        ┌───────────┐
          │   Col. Peirce   │        │  PUH Co.  │
          ├─────────────────┤        └───────────┘
          │    CPS Corp.    │    ┌───────────┐
          └─────────────────┘    │ Bt. PEPCO │
                                 └───────────┘
          ┌─────────────────┐
          │ Pacific N.W. Pub.│
          │  Service Corp.  │          ┌─ ─ ─ ─ ─ ─ ─ ─ ─ ─ ─ ─ ─┐
          └─────────────────┘          │ Chase Harris Forbes      │
                                       │ handled all security     │
  ┌─────┐  ┌──────────┐ ┌──────────┐   │ transactions for PGE.    │
  │ PGE │  │ Portland │ │ Seattle  │   │ Portland office one      │
  └─────┘  │ Traction │ │ Gas Co.  │   │ of 55 nationally.        │
           └──────────┘ └──────────┘   └─ ─ ─ ─ ─ ─ ─ ─ ─ ─ ─ ─ ─┘

  ┌─ ─ ─ ─ ─ ─ ─ ─ ─ ─ ─ ─ ─ ─ ─ ─ ─ ─┐
  │ Central Public Utility was the top │
  │ holding company of the Peirce empire│
  │ of interlocking corporations; it    │
  │ totalled 131 corporations.          │
  └─ ─ ─ ─ ─ ─ ─ ─ ─ ─ ─ ─ ─ ─ ─ ─ ─ ─┘
```

Utilities Control Chart[36]

acquired. PUH's only interest was to keep a minority position in PEPCO and then peddle the company to an aggressive empire builder who would add it to his expanding pyramid of operating utilities.

Just such a buyer was found in the person of Col. Albert E. Peirce of Chicago, the president of the Central Public Service Corporation (CPS). When Peirce bought PEPCO on February 18, 1930, the purchase price was approximately $21 million, giving PUH a paper profit of over $2 million in the transaction. Peirce had required that PUH sell all of its stock; he wanted total control. The stock market crash had only slightly affected utility transactions of this sort. In fact, stock values of acquired utility companies would continue to remain inflated for several more months. Of the $21 million, only $7 million was in cash; the balance was in Central Public Service Corporation stock.[37] In effect, PUH acquired a substantial interest in the Central Public Service Corporation, a factor that would play an important role in PEPCO's future. PUH was the creature of the Chase Harris Forbes Corporation, one of the nation's most aggressive underwriters of utility stock promotion schemes. The key person in the sale of

PEPCO to Col. Peirce was a vice president of both PUH and Chase Harris Forbes.

As soon as Central Public Service Corporation had made and completed the purchase of PEPCO, it proceeded to exercise complete dominance over the operations of the company, in marked contrast to the style employed by the Clarks. Seven of Peirce's associates were elected to the board of directors and Peirce installed himself as the chairman. But before the new board could take office, the old board was forced to approve a transaction that proved to be the first of several successful efforts by Peirce to plunder the PEPCO assets.[38]

In January 1930, CPS had acquired control of the Seattle Lighting Company, whose corporate name was afterwards changed to Seattle Gas Company. It had been bought for $6.7 million from the Dawes interests of Chicago. The Dawes brothers were two of Chicago's leading bankers and utility financiers and Charles G. Dawes had just completed a term as vice president under Calvin Coolidge. The Dawes brothers received CPS stock for their company and apparently never cashed it in before CPS went bankrupt in 1932. In any case, Peirce was anxious to join Seattle Gas together with PEPCO. To this end, he created a new holding company, the Pacific Northwest Public Service Corporation, to be an umbrella for three major groups: The electrical power, under Portland General Electric; the traction, to be called Portland Traction; and the gas, to be called Seattle Gas. He further arranged for PEPCO to issue $16 million of six percent debentures out of which CPS would be repaid $7.2 million for its Seattle Gas properties. Another $7 million was to be used to pay off PEPCO bond maturities due in the spring of 1930, and the remainder was to be banked with the Harris Trust Company in Chicago.

Griffith had been assured that the Seattle Gas Company was in fine shape even though one audited statement had raised some serious questions in his mind. But there was little that he or his local PEPCO directors could do. Their hands were tied. Furthermore, funds needed to be raised to meet the bond maturities coming due in four months. On February 18, 1930, the same day that the PEPCO board ratified the sale of the company to Peirce's CPS, it also ratified the new $16 million debenture issue and the purchase of the Seattle Gas Company. Finally, it ratified the creation of the Pacific Northwest Public Service Corporation (PNPSC) as the holding company for the PEPCO assets. Within six months, the Portland General Electric and Portland Traction divisions would be incorporated as separate operating companies. But also within six months, Griffith would begin to suspect that PEPCO may have been plundered.

The Seattle Gas Company properties ultimately turned out to be worthless. CPS and Col. Peirce had lifted $7.2 million out of PEPCO's treasury and used the money to repay themselves for their previous error. In short order, Griffith found himself holding a doubtful utility and a $16 million debenture obligation. The Seattle Gas episode was to be the basis of a successful lawsuit that would be filed years later against the Chase National Bank, from which PGE would ultimately receive $4 million. Because the Chase Bank and Harris Forbes & Company were linked together — Chase Harris Forbes handled the $16 million issue — Chase was to be held legally liable for Peirce's misuse of the proceeds.

During the first 18 months of CPS control, matters went from bad to worse. A series of refinancing transactions occurred that increased the indebtedness of the Pacific Northwest Public Service Corporation by $17 million. But only about $6 million of this amount actually went for new capital expansion and operational needs. In fact, the company continually found itself short of capital fund requirements while its funded debt was increasing rapidly. The following episode provides a clear example of what Griffith had to endure.

PGE needed approximately $3.5 million for new construction. CPS advanced the money on its own account. Then to obtain repayment for the advances, it directed PGE to float $7.5 million in gold notes, with Harris Forbes & Company underwriting the issue. As in all of these transactions, the underwriters and banks received their generous commissions at PGE's expense. Beyond that, CPS tacked on a management fee of three percent of gross earnings. When the notes were sold in PGE's name, the proceeds were endorsed through PGE to CPS and the money was banked in Chicago. In October 1931, when Griffith was east, he became concerned about CPS' financial condition. Its stock had declined precipitously and he wondered if CPS would have sufficient funds to pay the next dividends on its preferred stock. Many Portlanders, including himself, owned thousands of shares of CPS preferred stock which had been exchanged for PEPCO or PNPSC stock. He tried to get possession of the balance of the $7.5 million gold note proceeds in order to place them in a special trust account to be reserved for the preferred stock dividends, but he discovered that they had disappeared. It was only after threats of legal action that Griffith was able to persuade Peirce to give PGE 127,000 shares of preferred stock of another CPS subsidiary, Central Gas & Electric Company, in partial satisfaction of PGE's claim.

Like many of his employees, Griffith had voluntarily exchanged PEPCO and Pacific Northwest Public Service Corporation stock for Central Public Service Corporation preferred stock. But Col. Albert Peirce was not content with the number of earlier exchanges that were purely spontaneous expressions of good faith in PEPCO's new owner. During the summer of 1930, Peirce's personal brokerage firm came to Portland and set up its own sales organization. It compelled Griffith's companies to cooperate by using departmental employees to assist in the sales promotion. According to a 1932 investigation by Commissioner Thomas, over $11 million of CPS preferred stock was sold in Portland during the following year. One of the promotion circulars used by the salesmen read as follows: "Do not be like an old muzzle-loading rifle of pioneer days, that shot once and was then out of ammunition. . . . Be like a Browning machine gun, so that if one bullet misses the mark, you have another to bring him down to earth."[39] Peirce's "Prosperity Special" was so persistent, that one holder of PEPCO shares was approached by 22 different salesmen.

Widows were a vulnerable mark for the Peirce gang. Commissioner Thomas' investigation produced a letter from Peirce's Chicago office to a Portland salesman:

"We have been informed by the insurance department that death claims have been paid as follows, with a recommendation that an effort be made to sell corporation stock to the beneficiaries: Mrs. _____, Pacific Northwest Public Service Company, $2000; and Mrs. _____, Pacific Northwest Public Service Company, $2000. Will you be kind enough to see that a report is made as to the outcome of this suggestion."[40]

Three weeks later, the salesman replied to Chicago:

"You wrote me recently, regarding two widows, Mrs. ____ and Mrs. ____, who had recently received insurance premiums from the company. Mrs. ____ has invested all her money in four-dollar Central Public Service stock and some additional, and we are still working on the other."[41]

Franklin T. Griffith had encouraged the stock exchange campaign in its early days. Like most everyone else in the utility business, he believed that the depression would soon end and prosperity would resume its inevitable course. Dividends were being paid regularly during 1930 and the first half of 1931. When Griffith went east in October 1931, however, he realized that it would be impossible for CPS to maintain its dividend record and if such were to happen, he, President Griffith, would be placed in a most unenviable position *vis-a-vis* his employees and the stockholders whom he had encouraged to purchase or convert to CPS stock. Griffith's company was at least paying its dividends from its own net income, but CPS had been dipping into former surpluses and subsidiary accounts, such as PGE's balance from the gold note proceeds that Griffith attempted to find and rescue. Despite his protests, Peirce greedily continued the sales campaign until December 1931 when CPS was nearly bankrupt. In 15 months time, over 174,000 shares were either sold or exchanged. In the words of attorney B. A. Green who was hired to protect employee

The Electric Building
S. W. Broadway and Alder

433

stockholder interests, the employees who had purchased thousands of these shares on a company sponsored installment plan "stood to lose all they had put in . . . because they had traded their good [PEPCO stock] for the phony stock of the grafters of Chicago, which stock was worthless."[42] Until the demise of CPS, the chief "grafter," Albert E. Peirce, continued to draw his $268,000 salary that included $5000 from the coffers of the Pacific Northwest Public Service Corporation.

During the first six months of 1932 as the depression worsened and CPS ceased paying any dividends, a number of lawsuits were brought against CPS, Albert Peirce & Company and Pacific Northwest Public Service Corporation. Individual officers of the several corporations, including Griffith, also faced legal action. In Griffith's words, "The suits constituted a menace to the whole corporate structure in Portland."[43] Griffith came to realize that the only hope for resolving the threatened litigation was "to remove the control of the PNPS Corporation from the Chicago group."

Attorney Green's account of what happened is both informative and amusing, but not entirely accurate:

> "I had many conversations with Franklin T. Griffith and Cass Peck [Griffith's law partner]. I made no progress until I definitely told Griffith and Peck and the directors of these companies that I was going to sue them for fraud. Griffith asked me to wait for about ten days [in late October 1932] so he might get an answer from Chicago. I had signed up about 250 employees.
>
> One day, Franklin T. Griffith called me and said he was the happiest man in the world, that the Chicago grafters, through the Chase National Bank, were going to pay all the money that had been invested by the employees. This amounted to about $300,000. Later on Griffith told me that the only way he had been able to make the Chicago grafters and the Chase National Bank pay any money was by telling them that he, Griffith, knew as soon as he returned to Oregon he would be indicted, and that he was going to do his part in securing indictments of some of the Chicago grafters and ended his remark by saying to them, 'I like to play bridge, and there will be enough of you fellows with me at Salem to always make a foursome.' "[44]

There was much more to the story than Green related. Commissioner Charles Thomas' public inquiry during the fall of 1932 prepared the groundwork for Griffith's actions. Apart from securing reimbursement for the employees, Griffith also had to seek just recompense for the stockholders. Furthermore, he had to reclaim more than $2 million of unaccounted funds. And finally, he had to convince the Chase Bank in New York to refinance the $7.5 million gold note with a new, collateralized, note, secured by a mortgage covering the company's properties.

Griffith actually made two trips east. In late October he forced Peirce and the CPS Corporation in Chicago to transfer all of its common stock and all of the preferred stock of the old PEP Company to Portland in exchange for the remainder of the gold note proceeds that had vanished. The stock was placed in the hands of three trustees who were Griffith, E. B. MacNaughton and J. C. Ainsworth. A voting trust was formed, thereby removing control of the company from CPS and reinstating it in the control of the Oregon stockholders. Griffith also secured the reversal of the exchange of stock certificates, thereby reinvesting the stockholders with their original PEPCO preferred stock. Control was officially transferred to Portland in March 1933, but it was to take two more years to complete the reversal of stock certificates.

The trip to New York occurred in early December 1932, and it was on this occasion that Griffith, after some delay, secured his audience with Chase Bank's president by sending in word that "if they were too busy to see him, he would be glad to see them when they all got in jail together."[45]

By Christmas of 1932, a lot of corporate smoke and rubble had been cleared away. Franklin T. Griffith had performed an almost insurmountable task. He had saved "his company" which retook the PEPCO name. But there were still some serious problems that would arise in the spring of 1934, financial and legal matters that would not be fully resolved until 1948, after the company had experienced two bankruptcy reorganizations. The first reorganization was to result from the company's inability to pay interest on the $16 million debenture issue which Peirce had forced PEPCO to float in February 1930. Because allegations of fraud were to be brought against the Chase Harris Forbes Company — the $16 million had been partially used to purchase the worthless Seattle Gas Company — the federal court decreed a refinancing of the note by the issuance of $16.6 million of collateral trust income bonds. At the most, the company was to be given five years to pay 30 percent of the bond's principal, some $5 million. The company's inability to meet this obligation in the spring of 1939 was to force its second entrance into bankruptcy proceedings that would last nine years.

The briefs that were filed in the earlier proceedings gave due credit to Public Utility Commissioner Charles M. Thomas. The commissioner was the first governmental official to publicize the fraudulent treatment accorded PEPCO and its stockholders. His findings actually strengthened Franklin Griffith's bargaining position in his negotiations with both Chicago and New York. It was ironic, however, that Thomas, the strong public power advocate, should have played such an important role, albeit indirect, in the restoration of PEPCO control to Portland.

Thomas' remarks to his Portland audience in June 1933 accurately summarized the impact of the PEPCO-CPS imbroglio:

"The Central Public Service group activities and practices are all familiar. These pillagers on the high seas of frenzied finance, under the guise of honest men, entered this community, armed with every conceivable instrument of modern, immoral, financial method including depraved and poisonous tongue, pursued their activities and practices with a brutality and heartlessness that would have shamed a buccaneer of former days, and left in their wake, thousands of honest and trusting investors in poverty and distress, a saddened and broken-hearted group of employees, and an operating company crippled and bathing its near-mortal wounds over the loss of sixteen and one-half millions of dollars."[46]

When Franklin Griffith read this speech he must have had mixed emotions. Everything that Thomas said was true. He must have reflected on the defeat of the 1928 merger proposal, and on Joseph's argument for preserving the city's control over the Northwestern franchise. Had the merger been accepted by the voters, not only would his life have been spared the agony so poignantly described by Thomas but the lives of thousands of his stockholders and employees would have been spared as well. George Joseph did not live to see the totally unexpected consequences of his efforts. The consumers he was trying to protect became the victims of the speculative boom. Neither he nor Griffith foresaw that PEPCO would be sold to "pillagers" such as Col. Albert E. Peirce.

During the merger debates, Griffith had charged that Joseph's Northwestern franchise statements were specious. With the voters' assent, he declared, the city could take over PEPCO or Northwestern "tomorrow by condemnation if it saw fit."[47] Of course, Griffith would have fought such attempts by every conceivable tactic, just as he was to oppose the efforts of the Bonneville Power Administration in the late 1930s when it encouraged the formation of non-profit PUDs as competitive marketers of cheap federally generated power. The building of Bonneville Dam was to launch a new era for Oregon's hydroelectric power industry. And Griffith's initial reaction to the dam was favorable. He considered it "a magnificent gift . . . because taxpayers from all over the United States are paying for it."[48] The achievement of this noble goal had not been easy.

Bonneville Dam

The power potentialities of the Columbia River had been investigated as early as 1913 when the Oregon Legislature appointed a special committee to explore the possibilities. In the same year, the Portland Railway Light & Power Company undertook some borings at the river's edge near Warrendale, 35 miles east of Portland. The company's new president, Franklin T. Griffith, had been anxious to investigate possible dam footings. Nothing materialized from these efforts because the "private power interests . . . felt the problem too heavy for their approach alone."[49] This was the reason, according to Oregon's senior U. S. Senator, Charles L. McNary, that the federal government had to assume the initiative for "at least one big development on the Columbia River on the same basis as the Boulder Dam program, . . . giving the opportunity for the power to be offered to private consumers."[50]

McNary expressed these thoughts in a long letter to Henry Ford in December 1929. He knew of Ford's interest in the World War I Muscle Shoals project on the Tennessee River. The construction of the Wilson Dam and some nitrate plants at Muscle Shoals had initiated the first major nationwide controversy over the question of public or private ownership and operation of power facilities. McNary was soliciting Ford's active support for future developments on the Columbia River, "particularly in the use of hydroelectric energy that may be generated at one or more dams which will ultimately be built." As McNary reported to the automobile magnate:

> "We have very great power resources in the Columbia and its tributaries. We have striven for many years to get started on a development program. . . . A few years ago the Electric Bond & Share of New York bought the Priest Rapids site, with adjacent land for irrigation. . . . More recently, Stone and Webster of Boston applied for and secured a permit for a smaller development at Rock Island above Priest Rapids."[51]

McNary described his previous legislative efforts in behalf of power development, irrigation and improved navigation at Umatilla Rapids, 200 miles above Portland. Appropriations were made for a thorough study. "Reports revealed that about 420,000 horsepower of energy could be generated at the site." Columbia River developments such as the one at Umatilla Rapids would offer "the cheapest power" available in the United States.

McNary was largely responsible for securing federal funding of a $600,000 engineering study undertaken by the U. S. Army Corps of Engineers in 1927. The report's release in November 1931 left no doubt in the Oregon senator's mind that power development had to be promoted by federal resources. A summary statement from the report declared:

> "The Columbia River offers the greatest opportunities in the United States for the development of hydroelectric power. . . . The enormous power potentialities when fully realized would change the economic aspect of the whole Pacific Northwest."[52]

One of the eight dam sites recommended in the "master plan" was between the post office site of Warrendale and a small railroad stop at Bonneville, 40 miles from Portland where the river hurtled through a slot in the Cascade Mountains. Named after the French-born, West Point graduate, explorer, Captain Benjamin Louis E. de Bonneville, the area was a popular picnic grounds for people living along the river between Portland and The Dalles.

The Army Engineers report received wide publicity in 1932 and it assumed increased importance after Franklin D. Roosevelt's nomination for the presidency. As Governor of New York, Roosevelt had already endured numerous battles with private power companies. When he made his campaign swing through the Pacific Northwest in September 1932 he gave special attention to the potential for hydroelectric development of the Columbia River and to the role that should be played by the federal government. Apart from building dams and generating supplies of cheap power, the federal government should encourage the formation of publicly-owned utility districts. In words not to be forgotten, Roosevelt declared:

"Where a community — a city or county or a district — is not satisfied with the service rendered or the rates charged by the private utility, it has the undeniable basic right, as one of its functions of Government, one of its functions of home rule, to set up, after a fair referendum of its voters has been had, its own governmentally owned and operated service. . . . the very fact that a community can, by vote of the electorate, create a yardstick of its own, will, in most cases, guarantee good service and low rates to its population."[53]

Roosevelt felt that the main obstacle to effective public control of privately-owned utilities was the refusal by the companies to accept a fair and easily applied standard for valuation of their properties for rate-making purposes. In urging the adoption of the rule that efficiently operated utilities were entitled to receive a fair rate of return on money prudently invested, Roosevelt was enunciating a principle that would safeguard both investors and consumers. The "yardstick principle" was to be inserted in the 1937 act that established the Bonneville Power Administration.

Roosevelt's strong endorsement of federal power and water resource development, coupled with his fervent espousal of consumer interests, did much to ensure his overwhelming endorsement by Oregon's voters in November 1932.[54] It also acted to unify the state Democratic party that had been badly fragmented by the 1930 gubernatorial election. Although voters re-elected a Republican senator (Frederick Steiwer), and a Republican replacement for the First Congressional District (James W. Mott), Roosevelt's popularity undoubtedly helped to assure Democratic victories for Representatives Walter Pierce of the Second District and Gen. Charles H. Martin of Portland's Third District.

It would be eleven long months before the construction of Bonneville Dam was formally approved by President Roosevelt on September 26, 1933. The person who shared the major credit with Senator McNary for securing the $36 million appropriation (the dam ultimately cost $43.9 million) was Representative Charles H. Martin, a retired Major General of the U. S. Army and only the fourth Major General ever to be elected to Congress. A native of Illinois, Martin had graduated from West Point in 1887 and had been ordered to Ft. Vancouver, Washington, for his first duty. He married the daughter of one of Portland's most prominent business leaders, Ellis Hughes, and from that date on considered Portland his home base. He saw active duty in the Philippines, Mexico and France during World War I before being assigned to the Canal Zone as assistant chief of staff. At the time of his retirement in 1927, Martin was commandant of the Canal Zone. He returned to Portland to manage the properties of the Hughes estate that were centered in the Irvington district. As a Democrat, he was drafted to run for Congress in 1930, in the same election that provided victory to Julius L. Meier. Martin's views on public power development were more akin to those of his friend Oswald West than to those of Meier, but he was strongly in favor of building a dam as close as possible to Portland. The cheap generation of power would benefit both consumers and the private power companies who counted Martin as a sympathetic friend.

The negotiations that led to the authorization for the construction of the Bonneville Dam were fully recounted in a memorandum[55] drafted by Martin shortly after the fact. Because of the dam's importance to Portland's subsequent development, portions of the document merit reproduction. It reveals how close Oregon came to not getting the dam authorization in 1933 and it also sheds some light on the character of Franklin D. Roosevelt.

Shortly after President Roosevelt's election, Congress enacted appropriations totalling $3.9 billion for emergency public works projects designed "to take the country out of the depression." Inasmuch as Representative Martin and Senator McNary had established a cordial working relationship and both men felt strongly the need for a Columbia River dam, they jointly decided to approach the President to urge his taking action in the matter. "He seemed sympathetic," and directed that all of the requisite documentation be placed aboard the presidential yacht for his perusal in the course of one of his Sunday cruises on the Potomac River.

Two weeks later, when the Oregon solons revisited the President, Mr. Roosevelt expressed surprise at the bulk of material to be examined. He could not possibly find the time to review all of it but he had learned that there were some problems. The Corps of Engineers was concerned about the apparent lack of rock foundation at Warrendale. There was also some latent opposition within the government to the heavy expense that such a massive project would entail. He told McNary and Martin:

> " . . . if we could find a rock foundation . . . in the vicinity of Warrendale he thought he might be willing to give us possibly as much as twenty-five million to build the dam."[56]

With this assurance, Martin secured an appropriation of $25,000 from the House Rivers and Harbors Committee of which he was a member and directed that a geological survey be conducted along the Columbia River between Bonneville and Warrendale. To the Oregonian's delight, on July 18, 1933, the Corps announced "that a rock foundation had been found at Bonneville where the swift current . . . had washed out . . . all the sand and gravel." With Congress about to adjourn for the summer and wishing to convey their good news to the President, Martin and McNary again called upon Mr. Roosevelt to urge his approval of the project. As Martin related the exchange that followed:

> "Senator McNary expressed the opinion that [Interior] Secretary [Harold] Ickes would oppose the construction holding that the authorization which the President had made for the Grand Coulee Dam of sixty-two million dollars was all the Northwest could urge. The President replied: 'You Gentlemen go on home on your vacation, and I will take care of brother Ickes.' "[57]

By the end of August, with no further word from Washington, both Martin and McNary became alarmed. They had read about the vast number of projects that had already been approved during the summer but no mention was made of the Bonneville Dam. They decided that Martin had better return to Washington as McNary was still recuperating from a serious illness. Upon his arrival in the capital, Martin called upon the President and was "shocked" to find that his interest in Bonneville had apparently waned. Mr. Roosevelt asked for more time to examine the matter and told Martin to "come back within a few days." According to Martin:

> "I was unwilling to let the matter rest there, but went down to the Office of the Chief of Engineers. The Engineers would build the dam if authorized. The Chief . . . was an old friend of mine. . . . When I went into his office his introduction was: 'Well Martin, you have lost your Bonneville Dam. There is a crowd around here that have succeeded in what they say is pulling the President out of a hole. He promised you and McNary too much. . . . '
> A few evenings afterward, I noticed an item in the *Evening Star* authorizing the expenditure of Two Hundred Fifty Thousand Dollars to uncover a site for a dam on the Columbia River near Bonneville. I realized at once that this was a kiss-off, to let us down easily."[58]

Martin phoned McNary long distance and told him in no uncertain terms that he had to return to Washington so that they could make a joint personal appeal to the President. Although not feeling completely recovered, McNary caught the first train east and Martin went to the White House to arrange an appointment. The secretary told Martin that the President could not see either him or McNary as he was much too busy and was heading off the following week to Hyde Park to seclude himself with some important work. "The matter was closed," he told Martin.

After McNary's arrival, the two undaunted Oregonians decided upon some desperate strategy. They would go to the White House early Monday morning and sit down in the secretary's office and remain there until they received some attention. According to Martin's account:

> "On Monday morning we took our seats as suggested, where we found the Secretary's office filled with people who wished to see the President. Another Secretary, our old friend McIntyre, came over to us and greeted us very cordially. He had always been our good friend. [Marvin McIntyre came from Salem, Oregon.] He left the room. In a short while he returned to tell us that the President would see us at 11:15. At the appointed hour we were ushered into the President's private office and greeted in the most charming manner, for which he was noted, to be told that he had authorized the expenditures of money to get a foundation for our dam."[59]

Mr. Roosevelt then informed his visitors that he had requested from the Corps of Engineers a memorandum that would detail the specifications and costs for three possible dams, varying in height from 36 to 72 feet and containing up to a maximum of ten power units. As soon as he received the Chief of Engineers' recommendation he would inform Messrs. Martin and McNary of his decision.

440

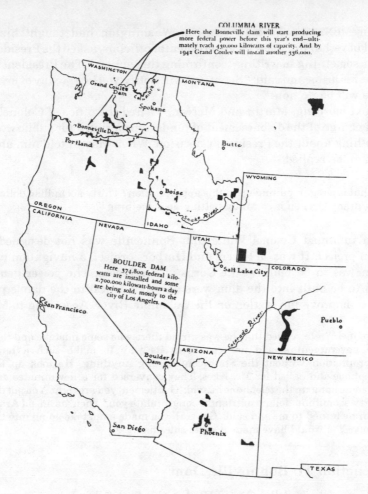

COLUMBIA RIVER
Here the Bonneville dam will start producing more federal power before this year's end—ultimately reach 430,000 kilowatts of capacity. And by 1942 Grand Coulee will install another 336,000.

BOULDER DAM
Here 374,800 federal kilowatts are installed and some 2,700,000 kilowatt-hours a day are being sold, mostly to the city of Los Angeles.

At this point, Representative Martin took from his pocket a copy of the memorandum that the Chief had given him but which the President had not yet seen. The accompanying recommendation called for a $36 million project. When he had finished reading the report to the President, Mr. Roosevelt asked no questions. He looked squarely, first at Senator McNary and then at Martin, and at last raised his arms and said: " 'Gentlemen, I can go for thirty-six million dollars.' I was so surprised," Martin noted, "that I walked around his desk and took his hand and said:

> 'Mr. President, you are following in the footsteps of . . . Thomas Jefferson, and by this act you are sending out a new Lewis and Clark Expedition to rediscover the Pacific Northwest. The country has been held back by a lack of power, so essential in our modern civilization. We have no oil, and little coal, and that of inferior grade, but by this act, you are harnessing the Columbia River and giving us an unlimited supply of the cheapest power in the country. You will rebuild the Northwest.' "[60]

441

Senator McNary, whose 15 years in Washington had taught him to be skeptical of verbal promises by governmental officials, asked the President if he could put something in writing "confirming this action." The President turned, threw out his arms and said: "Senator, I will notify you later today of my action, but there will be no note."

The next morning, Martin and McNary visited the office of Colonel Waite, who had charge of the disbursement of funds appropriated for public works. He knew nothing about the President's decision. When Martin told him about the $36 million, he replied:

> "What is Oregon putting up in this appropriation? Thirty-six million dollars is a grant. Oregon is certainly putting up something."

Martin informed Colonel Waite that Bonneville was not designed as an irrigation project. It was "a Rivers and Harbors project, a navigation project." The dam was to be built by the Corps of Engineers. The power generation facilities to be built into the dam were only incidental to the dam's primary purpose to improve navigation on the Columbia River. According to Martin:

> "Colonel Waite replied that he was afraid there was some mistake and that the government should not go out of its way to make such a large appropriation without the State contributing anything. He took up the telephone and called for Mr. Ickes. They conversed for a few minutes and when he hung up the telephone he said: 'Gentlemen, you are right. You got the thirty-six million dollars outright. I congratulate you.' Then, as an old Army man he turned to me and said: 'General, you made a mistake going into the Army. You would have made a super-salesman.' "[61]

The Reaction To Bonneville Dam

The Bonneville and the Grand Coulee, the first federal dams on the main stream of the Columbia River, became the cornerstones for the world's largest hydroelectric power system, which today includes 29 major federal dams and 124 other federal and non-federal hydroelectric projects. Of the nation's total hydroelectric potential, the Pacific Northwest today possesses more than 40 percent.[62]

During the early months of 1934, few people in either Washington, D. C., or the Northwest foresaw the possibilities of such expansive growth. As one observer has noted, "No river in history has undergone so complete a metamorphosis in such a short period of time."[63] Both Bonneville and Grand Coulee were "crash programs" undertaken in the early days of the New Deal to provide jobs to the unemployed and in the process to help stimulate the nation's sagging economy. As General Martin's memorandum indicated, improvement of navigation was the primary function to be served by Bonneville Dam. Power generation was strictly a secondary consideration. But regardless of how the dam's purposes

were perceived, few could argue with *The Oregon Journal*'s comment that "for better or for worse, Portland is embarked on a great new adventure."[64] Some of the local realtors felt the same way. One firm, by the name of Keasey, Hurley and Keady, began buying up large chunks of land adjacent to the dam site. Between October 1933 and March 1934, property values increased from $30 an acre to between $250 and $500 an acre. The federal government was forced to move in quickly and to condemn much of the land on both sides of the dam site. The boom subsided as quickly as it had arisen.

Apart from giving Oregonians a psychological uplift, the proposed construction of Bonneville Dam had statewide political implications. It sharpened the debate between the private and public power forces and created severe fragmentation within both the Republican and Democratic parties as the 1934 gubernatorial primaries approached. More than any other issue, strong differences of opinion over public power prevented the Democratic Party from creating the type of coalition that would have allowed it to challenge effectively

443

the Republican Party's traditional dominance of the state legislature. During the New Deal years, Oregon remained essentially a Republican state despite the fact that Roosevelt carried the state twice and despite the anomalous elections of Independent Julius L. Meier and Democrat Charles H. Martin as governors. Martin was to be elected in November 1934 after a free-for-all campaign that left national political observers scratching their heads in disbelief.

When Julius Meier announced that he would not seek re-election, "Republican Party politics became a tangled skein."[65] Five candidates entered the Republican primary, including State Treasurer Rufus Holman, a long-time public power advocate. Representative Martin was induced to announce his Democratic candidacy by both Oswald West and President Roosevelt who apparently did not realize Martin's real views on public power. But even if he had, there was little he could do about the matter. Roosevelt was forced to work through the existing state party organization that was largely controlled by West who was the Democratic National Committeeman. As a paid lobbyist for Pacific Power & Light, West was obviously not sympathetic to public power development.

Martin, in fact, was already on record as opposed to FDR's "yardstick principle." In the fall of 1933, after the Bonneville Dam was authorized, Martin had told the Portland Realty Board: "The power which the government will develop at Bonneville is not intended to force down the rates of existing power companies. This power is intended for the great chemical and metallurgical reduction plants whose first consideration is cheap power and an inexhaustible supply."[66] This was the position, essentially, that both the Portland Chamber of Commerce and the private utilities were to maintain until after the passage of the Bonneville Power Administration Act in 1937.

Martin's position on the future distribution of federal power split the ranks of the Democratic Party. The public power faction in turn became divided over personality issues so that Martin was able to secure the nomination with 58 percent of the vote. The Republicans were equally fragmented over public power and personality questions. As a result, the most conservative of the candidates, Joe Dunne, won the nomination with only 30 percent of the vote. With neither of the major gubernatorial candidates favoring public power development, a third candidate emerged to secure nomination as an Independent. He was state senator Peter Zimmerman from Yamhill County, an old-time progressive Republican of the George Joseph-Julius Meier faction who was often accused of being a socialist.

The election results were hardly conclusive as a measure of public power's popularity. Martin won with only 39 percent of the vote cast. Zimmerman came in second with 32 percent and Dunne wound up third with 29 percent. Martin had the obvious advantage of name familiarity. Both he and Dunne had opposed an Oregon Grange initiative calling for the creation of an elective state commission to finance, transmit and distribute power. The initiative lost by only 14,765 votes and major credit was given to the expensive campaign waged against the measure by the private utilities. Paul McKee's presence at Pacific Power & Light was already being felt. This was to be the first of many successful campaigns that he was to fight against the "initiative" of the public power advocates.

A brief mention of Oswald West's activities is in order at this point. To the historian who fondly remembers West as the crusading, progressive, consumer-oriented governor of Oregon from 1911 to 1915, West's subsequent career between the two world wars has overtones of sadness and disappointment. He was not a man of any inherited means or marketable professional skills by which he could support his family. When he was offered the position as a paid lobbyist for the private utilities, he was at least assured a liveable income. From the utilities' vantage point, the hiring of West was a smart move. As a prominent Democrat and national committeeman, West would obviously prove useful. And indeed he did, but with the consequence that his political tactics helped to destroy the Democratic Party in Oregon. Increasingly, he opposed all liberal and progressive measures that were associated with the New Deal. And when Martin failed to win renomination in 1938, West offered little help to the party's more liberal candidate. In fact, Republican Charles Sprague, who became governor in 1938, was to prove far more sympathetic to Roosevelt's public power program than either Martin or West had ever been.

Bonneville Dam on the date of its dedication
September 28, 1937

President Roosevelt's visit to Portland, August 4, 1934. Governor Meier and Mayor Joseph K. Carson, in front of him, are seated between the President and Mrs. Roosevelt.

When President Roosevelt steamed into Portland's harbor aboard the *U. S. S. Houston* on August 4, 1934, he must have been aware that he was entering a political hornet's nest. However, he exhibited no visible concern for either the intraparty feud or candidate Martin's negative views on public power. The city was just recovering from the worst waterfront strike in its history (to be discussed in the following chapter) and most everyone the President met seemed to be both exhausted and relieved.

After a short parade through downtown Portland, the President and his motorcade proceeded to Bonneville by way of the Columbia River Scenic Highway. A special train transported over 1200 people to join the thousands who had arrived earlier by car. In company with outgoing Governor Meier and candidate Martin, Mr. Roosevelt dedicated the site for the new Bonneville Dam. In his brief remarks, the President emphasized what the dam would do for Western Oregon and particularly Portland. It was certain to lead to a "vastly increased population." Portland was the only large city on the main stem of the Columbia. It could grow so large that it might become "unhealthy" and such growth would be at "the expense of smaller communities." Declared Mr. Roosevelt, Portland "could become a huge manufacturing center close to the source of power, a vast city of whirling machinery." Or it might become a center for decentralized regional growth. It was obvious that the President favored the latter development.[67]

446

President Roosevelt was deeply committed to the concept of regional planning. Earlier in the year, he had encouraged the formation of the Pacific Northwest Regional Planning Commission as an offshoot of the National Resources Committee. A local office had already been established with Marshall Dana as the commission chairman and Roy F. Bessey as the staff director. Also included on the commission were prominent Spokane attorney Benjamin Kizer and City Commissioner Ormand R. Bean. The group's primary purpose was to examine some methods by which existing governmental bodies might cooperate more closely around common interests. The future use and distribution of Columbia River power drew much of their attention. The need to consider regional solutions was already in the minds of many officials of the Roosevelt administration as well as in the thoughts of a few political leaders like Idaho's Senator James Pope. Four months after Mr. Roosevelt's visit, Senator Pope was to introduce the first proposal for a Columbia Valley Authority (CVA), patterned upon the Tennessee Valley Authority (TVA) established by Congress in March 1933. The TVA was, in the President's words, "a corporation clothed with the power of government, but possessed with the flexibility and initiative of a private enterprise."[68] Its aim was the unified development of the Tennessee River system by a single, all-purpose program.

The notion of a CVA type development for the Pacific Northwest was anathema not only to the private utilities but to Oregon's congressional delegation, with the exception of Walter Pierce. For many Portland business and utility leaders, Mr. Roosevelt's mentioning of Portland as a future "huge manufacturing center" was ominous enough. But the thought of a government corporation assuming control over the marketing of federally generated power was nothing short of socialism. The CVA concept was to reappear on and off for 20 years but nothing ever came of it. Oregonians could not conceive of the kinds of power demands and shortages that were to occur 40 years later, creating crises that would require a regionally unified program of power distribution and marketing. In fact, the early critics of the dam construction program referred to Bonneville as "a dam of doubt." Where would this vast amount of hydroelectricity ever be sold, it was asked. "Generators surely would rust, spillways would crumble, wires never would be energized. The dams even were compared in obsolescence with the Pyramids of Egypt."[69] The Portland opponents of the BPA act in 1937 were to charge that the Northwest was already "choked up with power now." Why add turbines which would be useless? Naturally, the private utilities egged on these warnings that the government had erected costly tombstones across the surging Columbia[70]

The Evolution of the BPA

Despite fragmented opposition to the dam's erection and some apprehension it created in the minds of a few staid Portlanders who were concerned about its impact on the natural environment, the building activity that picked up momentum early in 1935 drew wide support from Oregonians generally. Particularly appealing was the fact that the dam was employing over 5000 workers in all of the interrelated efforts that went into its construction and equipage. One news release noted that the project was expected to provide 130,777 man-months of employment.[71]

Following these developments closely was the Portland Chamber of Commerce. The chamber leadership appointed a blue ribbon Bonneville Committee composed of: Amedee Smith, former county commissioner and associate of C. F. Swigert in the Willamette Iron and Steel Company, as chairman; R. B. Wilcox of the Wilcox Investment Company and Ladd & Tilton fame, as vice chairman; Henry F. Cabell, grandson of Henry Failing and large investor in PGE; Franklin T. Griffith; Philip L. Jackson, publisher of *The Oregon Journal*; William F. Woodward, prominent Portland businessman and the only member to favor public power; and C. C. Chapman, editor of the *Oregon Voter*. The chamber's primary interest in early 1935 was to search out and identify specific plots of public land which might be available for industrial sites that could take advantage of the future supply of Bonneville power. Named to head the investigation was local attorney George L. Rauch.

Rauch was a prominent member of the Portland business community. He was known for his energy, civic work and integrity. His report that was issued in October 1935 must have surprised some of his chamber colleagues. In the light of recent history, the document was prophetic to say the least. After reviewing various options available to the city, Rauch noted that:

> " . . . the City has, as now constituted, the right and power, . . . by eminent domain or otherwise, to secure electrical power to sell to manufacturing institutions. Perhaps with the same expenditures, the City of Portland could purchase the power facilities of Bonneville, to be distributed directly to industries upon terms sufficiently favorable to secure their location at Portland."[72]

In essence, Rauch told his chamber friends that the city and the chamber should be more concerned with purchasing power rights than with purchasing industrial sites. Certainly either the dock commission or the Port of Portland could acquire property on which to locate future industries that would require the use of Bonneville power. But for the same kind of investment the city could probably purchase a portion of either the facilities or the power output on a long-term contract. In other words, future power supply was more important than land. The implications of Rauch's recommendation did not sit well with the chamber's Bonneville Committee. Such an action, on the city's part, would have put Portland in the municipal power business, if only initially for industrial distribution purposes. Franklin Griffith could well imagine the long-term consequences of such a step. In the fall of 1935, the city council was already debating the desirability of acquiring the Northwestern Electric Company upon the expiration of its franchise in 1937.

448

In one respect, Rauch was way ahead of his time. Few people among the Portland business community in 1937 could imagine the day when a shortage of power and its high cost would threaten the industrial development of the Portland metropolitan region. In another respect, however, Rauch was no more far-sighted than his chamber colleagues. His recommendations were strictly local in nature. Even Rauch did not understand the need for long-term planning on a regional basis as advocated by the Pacific Northwest Regional Planning Commission.[73] But then, of course, in 1935, little support existed anywhere in the Pacific Northwest for a regional electric power grid system.[74]

A month before attorney Rauch delivered his report to the chamber, Commissioner Ralph C. Clyde presented his proposal to the city council to submit to the voters "the question of the acquisition of the Northwestern Electric Company's system." In his covering letter, Clyde wrote:

> "While we are all rejoicing in the fact that the Bonneville Power development has become a reality, in fact is nearing completion, it is the desire of your Commissioner of Public Utilities to again call to the attention of the Council that if the City of Portland is to reap any real benefit from this development, it must immediately take the necessary steps to provide the means of transmitting this electrical energy to the homes, merchants and manufacturers of our city."

Clyde restated many of the same arguments that he had made in January 1931, that is: (1) Over 2000 other American cities were successfully generating and/or distributing their own electric energy; (2) Eugene and Tacoma had the lowest light and power rates in the Northwest; and (3), once the bonds on a municipally-owned system are paid off, the rates are greatly reduced.

> "On the other hand, it is the policy of all private power companies never to reduce their bonded indebtedness and they must therefore charge rates sufficiently high to not only meet their expenses of operation but to pay interest on their bonds, dividends on their preferred and common stock as well. This calls for a higher rate structure on the privately-owned system than on the municipally-owned one."

Clyde questioned why the federal government would spend $40 million to build a federal power project for the benefit of the private power companies. "If the people of Portland are to benefit directly from this development then it is absolutely necessary that a publicly-owned distribution system be provided." With the franchise of the Northwestern Electric Company due to expire on October 22, 1937, Clyde wanted the voters to be given their rightful opportunity "to determine whether they desire the City to exercise its option to acquire the facilities." Clyde recommended that the issue be submitted at the May 1936 primary.[75]

During the first week of December 1935, the city council debated the merits of Clyde's proposal. The chamber of commerce submitted a lengthy statement to

Mayor Joseph K. Carson. It requested "full and public discussion" of the issue; the total cost of the acquisition and the amount of rate reduction to offset loss or disturbance of taxes. "The City Council must exert every effort to have the true facts of our [the chamber's] position presented and the false and misleading statements that are made at this time by the advocates of a move to put the city in the municipal power business discounted." The chamber concluded that a public hearing should "avoid creating the impression . . . that Portland is at a disadvantage when compared with other cities."[76]

Mayor Carson was not a supporter of Clyde's proposal. He was a close associate of Oswald West's and had won election as mayor in 1933 while he was secretary of the State Democratic Committee. Like his friend, Governor Martin, Carson had wanted Bonneville Dam primarily as a source of power for new industry. He was not in sympathy with any move to municipalize a private power company. After a lengthy hearing on December 6, 1935, at which Tom Burns of Burnside Street talked for over an hour, the council agreed to a compromise motion: To refer a $50,000 tax levy to the voters to pay for a survey and an appraisal of the Northwestern properties. If the voters approved the expenditure, a special election would be scheduled for February 1937. The levy was placed on the ballot for the January 31st municipal election that would also present the voters with the new Portland Traction Company franchise and a $300,000 airport bond issue.

Over the next six weeks, the tax levy took a backseat to the other two measures. Mayor Carson provided no leadership either way, while the private utilities conducted an extensive campaign in the newspapers and on the radio. The City Club surprised a number of tax levy proponents by voting against the measure. It was a waste of money, the club declared. The valuations had already been supplied by Public Utility Commissioner Thomas and the Tacoma consulting firm of Harlan & Carey. Commissioner Clyde agreed, but realized that without compromising on the tax levy approach, the council would have proceeded no further. Clyde probably suspected that he was caught in a no-win predicament. It was even conceivable that the utilities had secretly promoted the compromise while overtly opposing it, assuming that the more liberally inclined voters would agree with the City Club position and oppose it.

The debates between the forces of private and public power usually narrowed down to the question of which system provided lower rates to residential consumers. Each side presented its own set of figures. Few would disagree, however, that Portland's private power rates were low as compared with eastern or midwestern cities. The comparisons were always made, as they are today, with municipal operations in Seattle, Tacoma and Eugene. Despite the chamber of commerce figures, the preponderance of data indicated that the municipal operations were indeed cheaper, but not by much. As the consumption rate increased, however, the differential also increased. There were many methods of classifying rates depending upon the nature of the service. Only rarely did either side define the specific bases for its rate computations. A 1977 study by the TVA

450

Portland Traction Company's (PGE) "Rubber-Tire Transit" — 1931

showed Portland residential rates for 500 Kwh to be 95 percent higher than Seattle's. New York's were 600 percent higher.[77] In the light of history — considering the historical consequences of past decisions — the recent rate comparisons are far more significant. But 40 years ago, the differences did not appear sufficiently great to enough voters to warrant changing the system.

During the debates of the 1930s and 1940s the utilities always added a tax component to their comparative electrical costs. They maintained that taxes were higher in those cities with municipal power systems. But the tax rates that they quoted were not necessarily comparable. Furthermore, the tax question was a phony issue in the first place. The taxes paid by the private utilities were accounted expenses to be included in the rate base and charged to the rate payers. In essence, all rate payers were also taxpayers. In Portland, the consumer was paying his taxes through his utility bill while in Tacoma he was paying his taxes directly. The utilities also argued that for a city to convert to municipal power would reduce needed tax revenues. What was not indicated, however, was that the projected revenue loss nearly equalled the electric charges that the city owed to the private power companies for providing municipal services such as street lighting — charges that would be saved were the city to own its own distribution system.

Regardless of the arguments, the voters soundly defeated the $50,000 tax levy to fund an appraisal of the Northwestern Electric properties. They did approve the $300,000 bond issue for airport land acquisition and they gave Franklin T. Griffith's Portland Traction Company a new 20 year franchise. The following November, while they were joyfully re-electing Franklin D. Roosevelt, the great advocate of public power, Oregon's voters rejected two state Grange initiatives: One to establish a state hydroelectric board; the other to enable the state to enter into the power transmission business with particular attention to rural areas where the private power rates were higher.

In Retrospect

The day after President Roosevelt was overwhelmingly re-elected in November 1936, Governor Charles H. Martin wired him his hearty congratulations. An action of this sort is difficult to appraise historically without seeming cruel. Governor Martin had fought the New Deal's power policies for three years. He had opposed a CVA. He had vetoed the Grange sponsored legislation, forcing the Grange to submit the ill-fated initiative measures to the voters. As Public Utility Commissioner Charles M. Thomas had written to Representative Walter Pierce: " . . . politics are certainly funny. . . . Here I am supporting Roosevelt's power program and am opposed by a man [Martin] who was elected on a program to support the President and then [I was] ordered . . . to fight the President on Bonneville."[78] Needless to say, Thomas soon resigned.

Without strong leadership from the governor or the mayor, little chance existed for either the state or the city to enter the power distribution business. The utilities and their lobbyists were simply too strong and well financed. Furthermore, in Oregon, as opposed to Washington, the Grange and the American Federation of Labor were weak. Outside of Walter Pierce, Ralph Clyde and the newly organized Oregon Commonwealth Federation, a "non-partisan league of progressives" including socialists, there were increasingly fewer voices to warn Oregonians of the future consequences of their actions.

Commissioner Ralph Clyde urged Portlanders to terminate the Northwestern Electric franchise before it was too late. Clyde clearly saw — and most Portlanders today are experiencing — that cheap Bonneville power would be "hard to get at low cost unless the city owns its own system."[79] Neither the city council nor the voters heeded his advice as the franchise was renewed in August 1937. When the Bonneville Power Act was passed by Congress in the same month, the so-called "preference clause" was inserted: "[BPA] shall at all times in disposing of electric energy generated at said project, give preference and priority to public bodies and cooperatives."[80] Supported by court decisions, the "preference clause" has assumed an aura of sacredness, not to be tampered with.

Recent attempts by Oregon political leaders and news commentators[81] to play down the state's missed opportunities do not withstand historical scrutiny. The record indicates clearly, that with strong political leadership, Oregon could have joined Washington in the ranks of public power development. It might also be added that strong support from *The Oregonian* 42 years ago could have made a significant difference. In retrospect, one is forced to agree with Ivan Bloch, one of the most experienced electrical engineers in the country and one of the original members of the Bonneville Power Administration staff: "Oregon [and Portland] had its chance 40 years ago and blew it!"[82]

Chapter 15

Violence at the Port:
The Depression Years

Portland economic life was in a state of trauma during much of 1933. Lumber, Oregon's largest industry, was "dead."[1] Portland's three largest mills were shut down during the winter months. Wheat prices were far below cost of production, and a cold spell in early February froze out all the winter seeding. The consequences of such disasters were revealed in the unemployment figures.

A State of Mind

It was reported in early March that 24,000 unemployed family heads were registered at the Portland Public Employment Bureau, while 9100 families were receiving minimal welfare payments. At an average of four and one-half persons per family, the welfare rolls exceeded 40,000 people. As Franklin D. Roosevelt had declared during the course of his campaign: "Only a foolish optimist can deny the dark realities of the moment."[2]

Portland had its share of "foolish" people, optimists as well as pessimists, who occupied positions of high responsibility in both business and government. When the First National Bank's President C. F. Adams was asked by *The Oregonian* in 1932 to compare the current depression with those of the past that he had experienced, the crusty banker replied: "People today don't know what hard times are." As an example, he cited the fact that he saw people standing to get free meals who were smoking cigars and cigarettes. "There was nothing like that in the old days."[3]

At the governmental level, few could surpass the chairman of the Oregon State Highway Commission, Leslie M. Scott, in both foolishness and blindness. As one of Governor Meier's less notable appointees, Scott was in a crucially important position during the worst of the depression years. His agency had received $6 million of federal relief funds to provide jobs for the unemployed in various state highway related public works projects. As a *summa cum laude* graduate of the University of Oregon, Scott was far from stupid. But like his father, Harvey W. Scott, the late editor of *The Oregonian*, Leslie was insensitive to the changing social and economic needs of American society as it faced its most serious crisis in 70 years.

Being one-third owner and vice president of the Oregonian Publishing Company, Leslie Scott could normally count on the paper to publicize his activities. However, one distasteful encounter that he had in August 1933 was not fully reported in *The Oregonian*. On August 23rd, he was visited in his Yeon Building office by nine men and three women representing the Unemployed Citizens League. The group requested the meeting for the purpose of learning "the real situation of the unemployed relief and soliciting his aid as a private citizen."[4]

Scott welcomed the group and proceeded to describe the workings of the commission and how the federal money had been spent. Quoting from the deposition:

> "Scott said that at the end of September most of the highway construction work would be ended. He explained that he wasn't interested in unemployment, but only to keep the State from going into a deficit."[5]

When asked what he would recommend for immediate relief, he said that the only solution was a sales tax. Two months earlier, Oregon's voters had rejected a sales tax.

> "Then we asked him, 'What shall we do?' He shrugged his shoulders and replied, 'If you turn down the second proposed sales tax, you will have to starve.' "[6]

Various members of the group described specific cases of undernourished children whose fathers were unemployed. Again Scott shrugged his shoulders and replied: "I am not interested in that. No man has any right to have children that he can't provide for." When one of the delegation remarked that Portland's civic emergency funds had been used up, so that there was no money to take proper care of the children of the unemployed, Scott retorted, assuming that they were referring to themselves:

> "What did you do with your money anyway when you were making big wages? You just squandered it. You are right where you deserve to be. You wouldn't have sense enough to keep it if you did have it."[7]

Keeping its reserve in the face of such astonishing arrogance, the delegation asked what he had meant the past winter when he had recommended that minimum wages be cut to $1.50 a day. He replied that such a move would spread available funds to more people. He boasted how he had "worked hard for many a day for $1.50 himself." He did not say that he could have afforded to because his father had left an estate worth at least a half-million dollars. Then Scott added haughtily: "The unemployed wouldn't work anyway. The farmers couldn't even get help to harvest their crops." The delegation denied such assertions, stating that hundreds of unemployed had helped with harvesting crops. One member of the group asked Scott if the state would loan them the use of some trucks when not in actual service. They would furnish drivers who were currently unemployed state truck drivers. "The request was refused with the statement that 'it couldn't be done.' "

454

The delegation next raised an issue that made Leslie Scott explode. Scott was asked to support a statewide move to issue scrip.

> "He flew into a rage and said that scrip would never work, had never worked, and never would work in this world. That he would never accept a dollar of it. . . . The present system is the only way, he stated, and then he eulogized the monetary system. . . . He said, of course, **WE** couldn't understand the monetary system and that we hadn't any business ability or experience or we wouldn't be advocating scrip as a solution."[8]

Scott was reacting negatively to the City of Portland's issuance of scrip the previous spring. The program was in difficulty in August 1933 although the legislature would later resolve the matter. In his general defense of the traditional monetary system, however, Scott chose to overlook the machinations of the National City and Chase National banks of New York, the fraudulent practices of Albert Peirce and Samuel Insull, and the disastrous failures of over 9000 banks in America since 1930. If given the chance, Scott would have rejected the call for "something better" advanced two months earlier by the editors of *Fortune*, America's most respected business journal:

> "The only certainty is that neither the philosophy of the early 1900s nor the technique of the late 1920s will ever again receive a general political or social indorsement. We are sure that the industrial organization of the first thirty years of the present century was not good enough. The last three years convinced us. The 'something better' which will supersede it is something which it is for the next ten or twenty or thirty years to define and to establish."[9]

Leslie Scott was not concerned about finding new solutions to old problems. The thought of change in any form disturbed him no less than the threat of socialism, communism or bolshevism. The *status quo* was sacred. For a man who was at the time serving as the editor of the *Oregon Historical Quarterly*, Scott showed an abysmal ignorance of the lessons to be learned from recent history. Businesses and governmental agencies were dismissing people in droves. Even the U. S. National Bank, the largest and healthiest financial institution west of Minneapolis and north of San Francisco, had fired 20 percent of its staff by February of 1933.

During the winter of 1932, the city council had recognized that local government had a duty to help shoulder some responsibility for the city's growing number of unemployed. Although Portland already had an accumulated operational deficit of over $1.7 million which had been borrowed from the local banks — the loan was necessitated by tax delinquencies — the council approved a special bond election for May. The voters authorized the issuance of bonds in an amount not to exceed $1 million, the proceeds to be used for emergency relief in furnishing work to the unemployed on needed public

THE COMING WINTER

EMPLOYMENT

NOTHING TODAY

HOWARD FISHER

projects. By the early winter of 1933, however, it became apparent that the relief funds would soon be exhausted. Only $845,000 of the bonds had been sold.

Moving with haste, the city council, in conjunction with the county commission, approved a plan in late March 1933 to issue self-liquidating scrip to be used for the relief of unemployment. When the plan went into operation in April, over 18,000 unemployed men registered for work. The scrip was to be liquidated by the sale of stamps redeemable at the county treasurer's office. A strong effort was made by both governing bodies to secure general acceptance of the scrip. Over 2500 merchants agreed to take it, but considerable opposition arose from the banks, public utilities and the larger merchants. After the passage of the federal unemployment relief measures, however, the scrip plan was doomed and the scrip redemption fund proved insufficient to redeem the outstanding scrip. It was this condition that provoked Leslie Scott's ire at the August meeting. As it later turned out, a special session of the state legislature authorized Portland to issue $45,000 of the heretofore unsold relief employment bonds, the proceeds to be used for scrip redemption.[10]

Although the use of scrip was considered highly unorthodox by the likes of Leslie Scott, the plan did work. Thousands received employment, needed public works were undertaken, the merchants were fully reimbursed, and the bonds were repaid on schedule with the city's bond and general credit rating unimpaired.

Failing to interest Scott in a statewide scrip program, the delegation from the Unemployed Citizens League explained how they themselves had become victims of the mass lay-offs by banks, schools and local governments. Scott showed little sympathy for their plight. "What you people don't seem to realize," he declared contemptuously, "is that there is no demand for your labor any more. . . . We don't need any more roads. The taxpayer has no use for your labor." The delegation's deposition concluded as follows:

> "Looking over the group, he informed us that we looked capable of doing pick and shovel work, but to show his inability in judging people, he was talking to an aviator and former Captain in the United States Army under Major General Charles H. Martin, a contractor, a doctor, merchant, school teacher,

Leslie M. Scott
(1878-1968)

Henry L. Corbett
(1881-1957)

real estate salesman, and clerical workers. We informed him that we did not want charity, but an opportunity to work, even if it was with a pick and shovel."[12]

Scott was certainly not alone in holding such insensitive attitudes about the plight of the unemployed poor. The Republican leadership of the Oregon Senate had revealed similar sentiments when it encouraged the passage of a sales tax during the 1933 session. Under the prodding of local luminaries like Henry L. Corbett, the senate took the position that the sales tax "was the only way out" — meaning that it was only by means of the sales tax that the state deficit could be met.

In one of its more enlightened editorials, *The Oregon Journal* wondered whether the people could be induced

" . . . to vote upon themselves a tax that all know is a plan to fasten more and more of the cost of government upon those least able to pay. . . . The beginning of the state deficit came along when the very gentlemen who are now clamoring for a sales tax [i.e., Scott and Corbett] contributed more than $50,000 to repeal the Pierce income tax which was yielding a revenue of nearly $3 million a year. And it was revenue that was collected from those who were best able to pay."[13]

It is one of the paradoxes of Oregon history that the voters could repeatedly reject the sales tax and still elect political leaders with the convictions of State Senator Henry L. Corbett and Leslie M. Scott, who was to serve as the Oregon state treasurer from 1941 to 1948.

Corbett had deeper social concerns and was certainly more perceptive about human needs than Scott, but he was never able to make the transition from being a respected, passive conservative to becoming a forthright leader in quest of "the something better," to use *Fortune*'s phrase. Corbett was to be president of the Port of Portland Commission for 15 years, beginning in 1935. Like most of his peers, he was a prisoner of both his past and his present station in life. He was either incapable of perceiving the nature of the serious economic and social problems facing Portland during the depression, or he was unable to muster the strength to assume a more positive and enlightened stance. During the 1933 legislative session, senator Corbett's record was reactionary: He voted to weaken the Thomas public utility bill; he supported the sales tax; and he opposed any basic amendments to the 1921 anti-radical syndicalism law.

Even Governor Charles H. Martin recognized the basic problem: "Poverty — poverty in one of the God-blessed areas of the United States." Martin was particularly disturbed by the plight of the Willamette Valley farmers. As he wrote Raymond B. Wilcox in Portland:

"Formerly, as you know, the Willamette Valley was the stronghold of the Republican party but these farmers have marched right through the Democratic party and . . . have become little short of revolutionists."[14]

The Depression brought a "Hooverville" settlement to Sullivan's Gulch, from N. E. Grand Avenue to N. E. 21st Avenue.

It is doubtful that such concerns had much impact on Raymond B. Wilcox, who, nevertheless, did devote considerable volunteer time to his position as state administrator of federal emergency relief funds.

During the depression years, at least one Portlander did recognize the nature of the economic and social problems facing American society: The outspoken and prominent attorney, B. A. Green. As with his strong reproval of Mayor George Baker's heavy-handed treatment of radicals during the 1920s, Green was to challenge the policies and actions of both the chamber of commerce and the Port commission during the wave of strikes that began in 1934. Speaking before the Rotary Club in 1933, Green cited the major historical breakdowns in the American economic system.

> "During these periods the present order has failed to feed, clothe and house the people and furnish opportunities for work which human beings must have."[15]

Green blamed the system of production and distribution associated with capitalism: "The profit system, . . . more correctly . . . termed the acquisitive system of society." Green saw the root of the problem "in the doctrine of private property — to have and to hold and to use property for one purpose, profit to the owner. Or, as Justice Brandeis said, 'To endow property with a militancy and power over human beings.' " Green went on to point out that the benefits of "the profit motive" had not been universal.

> "To know how the benefits of this system have been allotted among the many component parts of the social order — if we were to divide the wealth of the country into one hundred parts and limit the individuals in the country to one hundred individuals and have the same distribution that we have at the present time, we would find that one person would have fifty-nine units; one person, nine units; twenty-two would have one and twenty-two hundredths units; and seventy-six would have less than seven hundredths of a unit. If you were raising a bunch of hogs and you permitted one hog to consume 59% of the food; one, 9% of the food; twenty-two, 1.22% of the food; and seventy-six less than seven hundredths of 1% of the food, you would soon go out of the hog business."[16]

Portland Society Hard Hit

The upper echelons of Portland society obviously did not concern themselves with the hog business unless they relied on farm income to maintain their life style. Although private club memberships dropped off precipitously during the

The "On To Oregon Committee": From right to left, John A. Zehntbauer of Jantzen Inc., Raymond B. Wilcox, Otto Mielke, John A. Laing of PP&L, and E. C. Sammons of Iron Fireman Inc. Appointed by the governor, this group of Portland business leaders dedicated their efforts to advertising the state as a place of residence and business. Headed by Wilcox, this activity was a business community response to the depression. To Wilcox's way of thinking, attraction of new business was the solution to the depression which was predicted to be of short duration — a mere aberration in the functioning of the traditional free enterprise system.

460

depression years, for those who remained on board, activities followed traditional patterns. The society pages in 1933 reported large dinner parties at the University Club for 150 guests, with old family names well represented. The president of the Waverley Golf Club in 1930-31 was Frank M. Warren whose role on the Port of Portland Commission was to face increasing criticism as the decade unfolded. The Arlington Club board of directors in the same years sported such names as lumber financier Henry F. Chaney, Guy W. Talbot, L. H. Hoffman, Cameron Squires and Hunt Lewis, all identified with Portland's old guard.

Two of the most prestigious social-civic organizations in town were the Portland Symphony Society and the Community Chest. The board of the symphony included wealthy lumberman Aubrey R. Watzek, banker John C. Ainsworth, utility executive John A. Laing, attorney Roscoe C. Nelson and investor Henry Failing Cabell. Such families as the Cookinghams, Corbetts, Honeymans, Kerrs, Ladds and Wilcoxes were also actively involved with the symphony. When the depression nearly closed its doors on the 1931-32 season, an appeal went out on mimeographed paper late in November 1931 requesting each symphony society member to enroll one new subscription, whether for $10 or $1000. "Are we, the members of the Symphony Society, going to allow the orchestra to disband because of our inertia?" asked Miss Isabella Gauld, one of the grand dames of Portland's traditional establishment. The campaign was successful.

With the exception of the Portland Art Museum, which received $100,000 from Miss Henrietta Failing in 1931, most Portland institutions that relied on private donations were suffering along with many of the wealthy who had traditionally supported them. The fortunes of the Ainsworth family, with 10,000 shares of U. S. National Bank stock, declined sharply when the price of the bank's stock tumbled from over $400 in 1928 to $30 in 1932. Roderick Macleay, whose father had founded the bank, was so hard up in 1934 that he had to borrow $750 to buy a new Ford car on the installment plan. Macleay, along with many other bank stockholders, wrote numerous letters to Ainsworth, complaining about the bank's low dividend rate. Several writers were so irate that they threatened legal proceedings. Andrew Porter, a bank director and resident of the Irvington district, had to resign from the board because he was being sued by a Detroit bank for payment on an overdue $400,000 note, the proceeds of which had been used to purchase extensive timber holdings. Kenneth Hauser, of the Multnomah Hotel family which had given Reed College its library, owed Porter $70,000 and refused to pay, claiming he had no money.

One of the more intriguing episodes relating to the depression occurred on the night of December 28, 1932. Lee Schlesinger, general manager of the Olds & King department store, left his comfortable N. W. Westover Terrace home after having dined with his family and promptly disappeared. He had driven away in his expensive yellow Lincoln phaeton which was found two days later on the bottom of the Columbia River off a Vancouver, Washington dock. The papers

461

reported that Schlesinger had obviously experienced an accident and drowned, although the Sheriff of Clark County was skeptical. No body was ever found. It so happened that Schlesinger was carrying a $250,000 life insurance policy which the insurance company refused to honor until it had investigated the disappearance.

Schlesinger, a graduate of Stanford, had come from a wealthy department store family which owned the Emporium and City of Paris stores in San Francisco, two of the Bay area's finest. His father had bought Olds & King in 1925 and Lee had been installed as manager. Lee was an avid polo player, in fact he was captain of the Portland Polo Club team. He was also an active member of the University Club. In late 1930, reports had begun to circulate that the store was in some kind of trouble and perhaps facing bankruptcy. Charges had been made that the management had attempted to conceal its assets.

Nothing further was printed in the Portland papers until the insurance investigators discovered Schlesinger two years later, alive and well, living in Los Angeles. Apparently the family had known of his whereabouts for over a year and had told no one. When queried by the press, Schlesinger declared that he had wanted a new life, "on his own terms." He subsequently divorced his wife, to whom he had supposedly been happily married, moved to Rio de Janeiro, changed his name and was married and divorced twice thereafter.

Troubles at the Port

An episode that was no less bizarre than the Schlesinger affair, but certainly more grisly, was the murder of Frank Akin on November 20, 1933. An experienced professional auditor, Akin had been appointed by Governor Julius Meier in December 1932 to investigate the management of the Port of Portland. Filing his report with the governor three months later, Akin charged the Port's general manager, James H. Polhemus, with mismanagement. Veteran Port chairman Frank M. Warren was also singled out for criticism. In June 1933, a special Port of Portland investigating committee launched four months of hearings that ended just one month before Akin's death. The timing and mysteriousness of the murder, which was never solved, generated numerous conspiracy theories to which the local press gave maximum coverage.

Public criticism of the Port of Portland management had become widespread during the fall of 1932 when the commission experienced its first membership election by public vote. The leading candidate was prominent Democrat Bert Haney, a long-time intimate and former law partner of Governor Julius L. Meier. Haney's major targets were veteran Port president Frank M. Warren, fellow commissioner Phil Metschan, Jr., and Port general manager James H. Polhemus. Scripps' *News-Telegram* gave maximum publicity to Haney's campaign with lead articles headed, "Charge Graft in Fight for Port Offices," and "Bert Haney leads campaign to end reign of Warren; Mismanagement cited."[17]

462

James H. Polhemus
General Manager of the Port of Portland
1923-1936

The background for the charges against Warren and Polhemus was detailed in Chapter 9. After Haney's election in November 1932 and the appointment of investigator Frank Akin in December, further accusations were to be levelled, particularly when Akin was called to testify before the legislature in February 1933. Apart from conflict of interest charges directed at both Polhemus and Warren, the Port management was accused of giving the States Steamship Company preferred treatment by reducing the dry dock rates as much as 40 percent. States vice president Kenneth D. Dawson had been a powerful and influential member of the commission since 1927.

The senate sub-committee found insufficient evidence to warrant further investigation. *The Oregonian* reached a similar conclusion when it editorialized that the charges were "trivial and unfounded," tending to "discourage patriotic public service."[18] Nonetheless, the verbal fireworks continued unabated throughout the winter and spring of 1933. *The Oregon Journal*, a supporter of Bert Haney's, called for a thorough public investigation.[19] In May, following the Port commission's decision to conduct its own investigation, the *News-Telegram* demanded that Governor Meier remove the entire commission and institute court proceedings against its members. In late May, prominent attorney Rogers MacVeagh, son-in-law of the late banker Abbot L. Mills and former partner of Joseph N. Teal, launched a series of radio addresses entitled "The Truth About The Port of Portland."

At the Port commission's annual meeting in early June, newly elected commissioner Bert Haney was installed as president, replacing Frank M. Warren who stepped down after 13 years at the helm. State Senator Henry L. Corbett, the commission's vice president, praised Warren for his long and dedicated service. Toward the end of the meeting, Haney appointed a sub-committee of himself, newly elected commissioner Paul Bates and Warren to conduct the Port's official investigation, scheduled to be launched on June 14th.

Frank Akin was the lead-off witness called by the Haney committee. He charged that the Port had unnecessarily lost revenues totalling $8.5 million during the previous 11 years. Not only had the States Steamship Company received preferred treatment, but dredges and other equipment had been sold at great loss due to excessively heavy depreciation. He implied that James Polhemus was guilty of conflict of interest, but because he was denied access to Polhemus' records, the charge could not be proven. Portland attorney Robert T. Maguire, hired by Polhemus to defend his administration, challenged much of Akin's testimony. He also attacked Akin's integrity and business acumen as an auditor. Maguire noted that the McCormick Steamship Company had supposedly received similar reduced dry dock rates and that Hillman Lueddemann, McCormick's general manager, also sat on the Port commission. Why, asked Maguire, had Akin excluded McCormick from the scope of his investigation?

Akin, in fact, had included the McCormick Steamship Company in his initial report but he was forced to remove the reference when he discovered that he had made a mistake. Hillman Lueddemann personally owned a large old freighter called the *Ernestine Meyer* that he leased to his employer, McCormick Steamship. When it was destroyed by fire, he bought a smaller ship and gave it the same name. When Akin was examining the dry dock records and noted a lower rate charged for what he thought was the same ship, he erroneously concluded that Lueddemann had received preferential treatment. As Lueddemann recalls the episode, he never asked for nor knowingly received any reduced rates for either his own ships or the 40 ship fleet that he managed for McCormick and its parent company, Pope & Talbot. But Lueddemann was so upset by the experience that he resigned from the Port commission in 1934.[20]

Although several Port employees admitted that varying the dry dock charges was traditional policy, and that States Steamship was the major beneficiary, Polhemus defended the practice. Lower rates were justified, he said, in order to get the business, especially over weekends when the dock was usually empty. Polhemus and Warren both went on record with the statement that the Port was not in business to make money, a paradoxical notion to say the least. Had the dry dock been operated by private enterprise, a practice advocated by many Portland business leaders, the shipping companies would have paid the higher regular rates. But as long as the dry dock was publicly operated at the taxpayers'

464

expense, sound business practice dictated preferred treatment to private shippers!

The Port investigating committee published its findings on November 4, 1933. By a vote of 2-1, the majority found the Port's administration guilty of mismanagement in a number of areas: Loss of rightfully due revenues, unwise sale of equipment, conflict of interest, negligence, carelessness, inefficiency and favored treatment to private shippers. Speaking for himself and commissioner Bates, Bert Haney accused the Port of "operation by cronyism." The public interest had been sacrificed to "the businessman knows best" doctrine. There was need for stricter standards of performance, public accountability, better judgment and greater objectivity. After citing a number of specific operational recommendations, the majority called for the resignations of James Polhemus, his assistant J. P. Doyle and the dry dock superintendent.

In defense of Polhemus and his own term of office, Frank M. Warren submitted a 31 page minority report. A brilliantly organized brief, prepared by attorney Robert T. Maguire, repudiated the charges one by one, concluding with a strong endorsement of Polhemus' performance.[21] *The Oregonian* commended Warren's statement and suggested that the Port should be judged on how well it served commerce, not on whether it "might have made a little more money" had it followed a different business policy.[22] *The Oregon Journal* did not feel that the major charges of wrongdoing were sustained by the recorded testimony of the hearings. On the other hand, the *Journal* implied that some serious mistakes had been made in policy formulation and judgment. If such were the case, the fault lay with the commissioners, not with their agents or employees.[23]

On November 19th, *The Oregonian* printed a strongly worded editorial declaring that the "whole Port investigation from the first has smelled of dirty politics."[24] Political it was, but whether it was "dirty" depended on "whose ox was getting gored." Hillman Lueddemann recalls that when Julius Meier appointed him to the Port commission he told him "to go up there and clean it out. There are too many crooks on the commission." Governor Meier apparently believed all that he read in the *News-Telegram*. Furthermore, he had little regard for Phil Metschan, Jr., his recent opponent in the 1930 election. Lueddemann found no crooks, at least on the commission, but he did sense some possible conflicts of interest, especially on James Polhemus' part. He supported the *Journal*'s position that the faults lay with the commission of which he was a member rather than with the employed staff.[25]

In retrospect, one would have to say that personal animosities were allowed to dominate the investigation. Frank Akin had been recommended to Governor Meier by Walter Smith of the Smith & Valley Iron Works. Smith had engaged in a long-standing feud with both the Port management and State Steamship's Kenneth Dawson. There can be little doubt that Akin was told to do a hatchet job on the entire Port of Portland operation.

The day following *The Oregonian*'s "dirty politics" charge, Frank Akin was found shot to death in his apartment and the *News-Telegram* exploited the event with gusto. Was it possible that Akin had been eliminated because he knew too much? Had some fearful soul hired a professional gunman? The police were baffled. A week before Christmas, the police department brought to Portland one of the nation's top criminologists, Professor E. O. Heinrich of the University of California, but even he was unable to unearth any leads. Stories began to circulate that Frank Akin had been a notorious "women's man" even though he was supposedly happily married. *The Oregonian* printed a story to the effect that Akin had had "many business and personal affairs with numerous women."[26] In February 1936, two unknown and unlikely characters were indicted by the grand jury, but they escaped conviction. The evidence was strictly circumstantial.

On December 15, 1933, the Port commissioners voted 6 to 3 to reject the majority report and approve the Warren-Maguire brief. Joining Warren and Metschan were commissioners Dawson, Duncan, Corbett and Lueddemann, with Lueddemann expressing some reservations. Although James H. Polhemus was exonerated, he knew that his future as Port general manager was limited. Within three years he would be appointed a vice president of Portland General Electric.

An unfortunate aspect of the whole investigation, topped off by Frank Akin's murder, was that the role of the Port and its future direction was never examined. The City Club had addressed these issues in a lengthy report published in August 1932. Among its recommendations were: (1) That the U. S. Army Corps of Engineers should assume responsibility for dredging and maintaining the channel from the inner harbor to the sea; (2) that the Port of Portland should turn over all of its dredging equipment to the federal government; (3) that the Port should seek federal reimbursement of excess funds spent for main channel dredging; (4) that once the federal government assumed the additional dredging responsibilities, legislation should be enacted to limit the taxing and bonding powers of the Port; and (5), that the legislature and city council should take immediate steps to effect a consolidation of the Port and dock commissions.[27]

Additional concerns were expressed that the Port had not given enough attention to the needs of the upper Columbia River and the Columbia River Basin. As the Columbia River Association had formally charged in November 1929, "Portland is a sleeping beauty. . . . Portland is over conservative. There are too many old timers down there who hold the money bags." This particular barb was directed out of Pendleton. Portlanders were warned to wake up. "The Port of Portland and dock commissions should look up the river, not down."[28]

The ludicrous nature of the Port investigation was characterized by Port commission president Bert Haney's repudiation of his own report in September 1935. Haney had just been appointed a judge of the U. S. District Court of Appeals. Upon resigning from the commission — to be succeeded as president by Henry L. Corbett — Haney publicly disavowed his own recommendations made in November 1933. "I was wrong," he declared. "I did a grave injustice to each of those men."[29] This metamorphosis has never been adequately explained. Hillman Lueddemann feels that Haney was pressured by his close friend Governor Meier to produce the majority report as published. On more than one occasion, Haney had told Lueddemann that he had found nothing seriously wrong with the Port's operation. Perhaps Haney was clearing his conscience before he climbed to the rarified heights of the federal bench.

If nothing else, Haney's recantation clearly revealed the political nature of the Port of Portland Commission. It had always been embroiled in politics; it is still embroiled in politics. The power of selection was restored to the governor by the legislature in 1935. The unpaid job of Port commissioner remains one of the choicest rewards that a governor can bestow upon his close friends and largest financial backers. The very nature of this kind of an appointive process is fraught with potential conflicts of interest. At least this seems to be the consensus of thoughtful and respected business statesmen like Hillman Lueddemann and the late Captain Homer Shaver.[30]

Waterfront Strike of 1934: The Cause

Two days after Bert Haney launched the Port of Portland investigation in June 1933, Congress passed the National Industrial Recovery Act which established the National Recovery Administration (NRA). Section 7a of the act gave workers the "right to organize and bargain collectively through representatives of their own choosing," and prohibited the employers from any "interference, restraint or coercion" on the process. The act also established a National Labor Board, chaired initially by Senator Robert F. Wagner of New York. Early in 1934, the board was authorized to hold elections of employees to determine their bargaining representatives.

The consequences of this piece of New Deal legislation were to be felt nationwide, particularly on the Pacific Coast among dock workers and longshoremen. For the first time in American history, unions received official recognition, sanctioned by federal law, and the right to strike became one of America's basic freedoms. For the employers, in Portland's case the ship owners, the implications were horrendous. A social and economic revolution was sweeping the country, a series of traumatic events that were viewed by the likes of Leslie Scott as part of a gigantic Marxist plot. There was no alternative but to resist and fight back, in defense of the traditional rights of private property and private ownership. The scene was set for a bitter struggle.

The roots of the 1934 strike led back to 1922 when the International Longshoremen's Association (ILA) shut down all of the major ports on the West Coast. The strike was broken by the shipping companies which employed an army of over 1500 strikebreakers who were moved from port to port, the entire operation being financed by the large New York banks whose shipping investments were threatened. From 1922 until mid-1933 there was no *bona fide* organization among longshoremen in Portland. The depression rekindled the fires of unionism: Competition among the shipping companies became severe and labor costs were slashed. The workers were pushed harder, shifts of over 36 hours became common and the hourly wage rates were reduced drastically. The majority of men were receiving from $40 to $60 per month. If they protested, they were fired. As one worker described the conditions:

> "They [the companies] would hire their gangs and you would be on the dock at seven o'clock Tuesday morning. And maybe that ship would get in at nine o'clock Tuesday night. But you didn't dare leave. You were hired but you weren't getting paid. . . . One time we worked eight hours between eating. . . . It got so bad . . . they didn't care whether you went to eat or not."[31]

After the passage of the NRA, the ILA was reorganized along the entire Pacific Coast as one union, Local 38. Membership in Portland grew rapidly to over 1100 men. Beginning in November 1933, the union branches in the various coastal ports asked the employers for conferences to discuss wages, hours and working conditions. The shipping companies refused to meet with the representatives of the union, in spite of the provisions of the NRA. In March 1934 the union voted to call a strike to enforce conferences as well as to enforce their demands. However, upon request of President Roosevelt and Senator Wagner, the union postponed calling the strike. A regional mediation board was established and the various union branches were requested to hold elections to determine whether the ILA actually represented the majority of workers in each port. Elections held in San Pedro (Los Angeles) and Seattle gave the union an overwhelming mandate. The Portland election was scheduled for May 11, 1934.

Following the first two elections, the employers announced that they would contest the procedure and carry the matter to the U. S. Supreme Court if necessary; they would not abide by the results of any election. Thereupon the union said, "There is no use in further delay." It would have taken at least two and a half years to secure a U. S. Supreme Court ruling.

The executive committee of Local 38 called a coastwide strike for May 9th, an action that created the most devastating work stoppage in Oregon's history. The 82 day strike was to wreak havoc upon Portland's economy. Maritime commerce ground to a halt. Over 3000 waterfront workers were affected and at least 50,000 other workers in Oregon were thrown out of employment, including 12,000 to 15,000 in Portland. Practically all of the lumber mills ceased export production and the export grain business all but dried up. Unaccountable millions of dollars of business were lost before the strike ended on July 31st.

To describe fully the entire episode would require a book in itself. The following account is confined largely to the interplay of business and political forces that tried to control and then break the strike. In both efforts, only frustration and failure resulted.

The Strike: Issues and Actors

"Our chief demand," declared local ILA leader C. G. Peabody, "is full recognition of our union and the right to bargain collectively with employers. It is our contention that the employers are violating the spirit of NRA in that they have refused to meet with us."[32] The basic issue was union control of the hiring process, to eliminate, in the ILA's words, "the blackball system" and "the slave driver tactics" used by the company foremen on the job. The Waterfront Employers' Association and the Portland Chamber of Commerce took the position that the "unqualified union control of hiring men and establishing rules and regulations" could not work. The system would be inefficient and costly to the ship owners.[33]

The speciousness of that argument was revealed by Portland attorney B. A. Green when he cited the experience of Tacoma, Washington, the home port of Jack Bjorklund who was the veteran secretary of ILA Local 38. "In Tacoma for 17 years, the very employers who in Portland, Seattle, San Francisco and San Pedro have refused to meet and deal with their workmen, have dealt continuously with the same union," under Bjorklund's leadership. In conferences with the employers, Green encountered at least five who told him that Tacoma had the most efficient group of longshoremen on the Pacific Coast. The union contended that the question of furnishing capable and competent men was "primarily a question for the union." Inefficient men could always be returned to the hiring hall, and some were. To the union, however, the problem did not relate to efficiency as such, but to the corruption of the hiring process administered by the ship owners.

No one in Portland was more closely involved with all sides of the strike than attorney B. A. Green. His sympathies were obviously with the strikers but he was not blind to the problems of the ship owners. In fact, he was the only person who continually met with all factions, trying to resolve the issue before too much damage resulted. He was instrumental in calling together Governor Meier, Mayor Carson and the police and sheriff's departments in an attempt to maintain order and peace. He would later be instrumental in bringing Senator Robert F. Wagner to Portland for a personal observation of the whole affair. During the month of July, he was to deliver several radio addresses in an attempt to explain the background of the union cause which received mostly adverse coverage in the local press. It was Green's unqualified conclusion that the precipitation of the strike rested "directly with the employers . . . as manifested by their contemptuous attitude."[34]

Before the strike ever began, the record indicates that the ship owners actually welcomed a strike because they believed that they could break the union as they had done back in 1922. The Waterfront Employers' Association in conjunction with the chamber of commerce clearly expected to defeat the union if sufficient support was received from the governmental authorities. The operator of the chamber of commerce cafe reported that "plans for the carrying out of the Water

Attorney Burl A. Green addressing an audience during the strike.

Front Strike . . . were formulated in the rooms of the Portland Chamber of Commerce. Those carrying forward these plans met with other organizations under assumed names and received the free use of the Chamber headquarters, lights, rooms etc."[35]

The day the strike was announced, the various steamship lines stated "they would carry on as usual. . . . Hiring would go on as usual through the longshoremen's halls." Declared the district manager of the American-Hawaiian Lines: "Little trouble will be experienced if the workers get adequate protection. Some of the men may be intimidated, but if they walk out we can get plenty of others."[36] But the events were to prove otherwise. On May 11, Arthur J. Farmer of the chamber staff noted that the strike was turning out to be more successful in Portland than anywhere else on the coast. According to Farmer, the police protection of strikebreakers was

" . . . not as effective as it could and should be. At the bottom of the strike is recognition of the ILA. Portland has probably been the outstanding open-shop operation on the coast. It would appear strikers' efforts are, therefore, most strenuous in Portland. . . . It is apparent shipping here will remain at a standstill until and unless protection is given the strike breakers."[37]

Three days later, Farmer wrote chamber executive W. D. B. Dodson in Washington, D. C., that "the strike is no longer a longshoremen's strike but a siege on Portland industry." Farmer described how Gray Line buses transporting strike breakers to the docks "were rendered useless when fundamental running parts were removed and tires deflated." One police lieutenant received a black eye and many strikebreakers were "manhandled." Passenger cars "containing breakers and company employees were overturned and damaged" and the police just stood by, offering "no fight to the strikers and no assistance to strike breakers."[38]

Portland's business leadership was particularly incensed by a raid on the McCormick Dock which was berthing the *Admiral Evans*, an old passenger ship being used as a hotel for strikebreakers and special police hired by the employers. According to Pilcher's account, between 75 and 100 men were involved in the raid. They assaulted a wooden fence surrounding the dock and a number of nails were left protruding from the boards. A regular Portland

Picket squad on duty during 1934 strike.

471

policeman who was guarding the gate was reported to have warned the attackers to be careful not to step on the nails.[39] As Farmer bemoaned to Dodson, "The regular policemen standing by offered no fight."[40] The special policemen on board the *Evans* were beaten back by broom handles and one was thrown in the river. The *Evans* was cut adrift and floated downstream to become wedged against the Broadway Bridge.

The reference to police inaction revealed an interesting feature characterizing the early days of the strike. The union had based its strategy on neutralizing the regular police force, keeping the police from intervening directly in strike activities. The employers, on the other hand, attempted to maneuver the police into protecting the strikebreakers. Both sides knew that police behavior would play a critical role in the outcome of the strike.[41] The union had instructed its members not to provoke the regular police, many of whom expressed sympathy with the longshoremen's demand for collective bargaining and higher wages. Through the first six weeks of the strike, the union strategy paid off, much to the distaste and frustration of the employers. As chamber manager Walter W. R. May wrote to Dodson, "Our police protection has been inadequate, disorganized and unwilling to fight the rioters." The strikers were now being called "rioters";[42] they would shortly be labelled "reds" and "bolsheviks."

As the level of employer frustration increased, the ship owners and their chamber friends attempted "to draw the red herring across the trail," to use B. A. Green's words. A memorandum from Arthur Farmer, reporting on a federally sponsored mediation conference, made reference to the labor representatives as "red." Farmer noted that toward the end of the session, "a Mr. Harry Bridges, an Austrian [he should have said Australian] reputed to be "red," was elected by the men to be present at all of the hearings. They [the employers] could get nowhere with him."[43]

The career of Harry Bridges has proven to be one of the ironies of American history. During the early 1940s, the government was to attempt numerous deportation proceedings against Bridges, an "undesirable alien and accused Communist." But the U. S. Supreme Court upheld Bridges' rights on each occasion, most notably in *Bridges v. Wixon* in 1945.[44] In 1978, Bridges was to be invited to address a distinguished audience at the National Portrait Gallery by virtue of his position as the most distinguished elder statesman of the American labor movement. Commenting upon the 1934 waterfront strike, Bridges said: "We wasn't fancy. We'd take money from anywhere we could get it, including Communists. . . . But one thing I didn't do, I didn't happen to be affiliated with the Communist Party."[45]

Few denied that there was not some communist influence exerted on the organization and direction of the strike. But calling the strike "communist inspired" and "communist led" merely obfuscated the real issues. Even though many of the strikers were former members of the IWW, the great bulk of the longshoremen were not radicals. The Wobblies did not exercise official control of the local when the strike began. The elective leadership was drawn from the

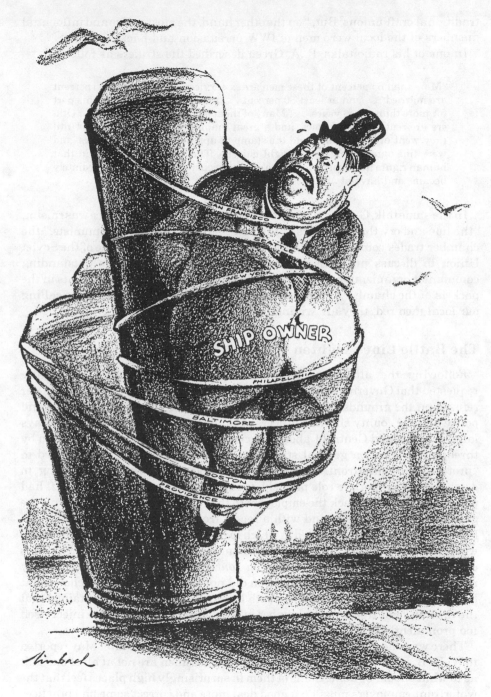

Tied up!

473

traditional craft unions. But, "on the other hand, the most active and influential members of the local were men of IWW persuasion and background."[46]

In one of his radio talks, B. A. Green described the strikers as follows:

"More than 65 percent of these men are ex-servicemen. More than 95 percent are married . . . and at least 80 percent . . . have been employed in this port for more than seven years. . . . Many of them own their own homes. . . . Others are renting their homes, and a great majority have children. . . . Until they went on strike, they had the stamp of approval of the employers, and were fine outstanding and upright citizens. The minute they . . . said that human rights henceforth should be prior to property rights, they immediately became and have at all times since been reds."[47]

In the same talk, Green noted that while the chamber of commerce was raising "the hue and cry that members of the ILA . . . were reds and communists," the chamber trades committee was sitting down with a representative of the Soviet Union to discuss problems of trade. "When trading with the outstanding communist organization . . . in the world today means dollars and cents in the pockets of the chamber of commerce committee of ship owners who are calling our local men red, they are willing to trade."[48]

The Battle Lines Tighten

Following the attack on the *Admiral Evans*, Mayor Carson formally requested that Governor Julius Meier call out the Oregon National Guard. Meier refused on the grounds that the Guard could only be activated if the Portland police and the county sheriff's officers could not maintain the peace. Five days later, the Portland Central Labor Council reinforced the governor's decision by threatening to call a general strike in Portland if the Guard were called to "protect" the waterfront. The chamber of commerce which was trying to downplay its supportive role publicly, found itself in a quandary. The staff had pledged privately to back the employers to the fullest extent. But faced with the governor's refusal to act, and with a report from U. S. Army Intelligence that Portland was "the worst hot bed in which to release troops" at the time, its hands were tied, or so the staff felt in late May. Chamber president Phillip Jackson was on the spot. As publisher of *The Oregon Journal* which had taken a cautiously restrained stand on the strike, Jackson did not have the freedom of choice that he might have desired personally. Both he and Simeon Winch maintained that the time was not ripe for the chamber by resolution or otherwise to inject itself too prominently into the picture.

There was another element that had to be considered. As Walter May reported to W. D. B. Dodson in Washington, "Our businessmen are not at all of one unit as to what should be done. Some of them in surprisingly high places feel that the waterfront employers must do a good deal more and correct some bad practices and bad conditions."[49] May was referring in particular to the management of the Doernbecher Manufacturing Company, Portland's leading furniture factory and one of the largest water transportation users in the city. President Harry Green had informed May that he and his men were inclined to take sides with the strikers because they believed that some of their demands were just.

Pressures of this sort compelled the Waterfront Employers' Association to agree to consider a new proposal for ending the strike. Called the "Portland Plan," the proposal was drafted by Governor Meier, PGE president Franklin T. Griffith, banker H. V. Alvard and attorney B. A. Green. But as with previous proposals, the strikers rejected the terms. Two days later, war was declared. The chamber executive committee resolved publicly that it would "utilize its entire resources in cooperation with the constituted authorities and other groups of citizens and business interests to open the port." Public opinion had been challenged by the strikers and the public interest had been defied.[50]

Mayor Carson and Sheriff Pratt agreed to provide waterfront protection to the ship owners in their attempt to open the port. Police Chief Lawson requested from the city council that 500 additional special police be recruited to help keep peace on the waterfront, but commissioners Bennett, Clyde and Riley opposed the action. After considerable debate, Riley switched his vote and a compromise was reached to hire only 200 extra law officers. Carson convinced the dock commission to turn over the facilities of Terminal No. 4 as the command headquarters for the special police, and the *Admiral Evans* was moved to a new and more secure berth. This action led to the first major confrontation of the strike.

As B. A. Green described the event, a supply train was prepared to move out to St. Johns' Terminal No. 4. The engine was preceded by a flatcar carrying a large number of policemen.

"There was a force of 100 police and deputy sheriffs at first. This force cleared the pickets off the track. Seventy-five police officers were sent to the terminal to reinforce the 40 already stationed there. There were 300 special police and 25 regular police on the train. As a result of delays the train crew found 100 pickets sitting on the track. Reinforcements were called for another 100 officers with tear gas bombs. Following a conference between the head policemen, the Chief of Police directed that 150 special police be called into duty. Some of these men were armed with shotguns. Pickets swarmed on the track several hundred strong with more pouring in from the hillsides. One shortrange tear gas gun used by Police Officer Boskovitch and a longrange gun used by Police Officer Nelson started firing. Four of the strikers were shot by the police. By this time there were fully 400 pickets at the scene. After dispersing the pickets, it was impossible to move the train which was on an upgrade because the pickets had greased the tracks with lard, soap and axle-grease. The train had to return to its regular terminal at Albina yards and did not unload."[51]

The loss of the "railroad battle" led to the formation of the Citizens' Emergency Committee, comprising 100 top leaders of Portland's business and financial community. Under the general direction of insurance executive

Horace Mecklem and industrialist Amedee Smith, the CEC was organized for two purposes: (1) To show the public, and the strikers, that the business community stood 100 percent behind the ship owners' attempt to open the port; and (2), to raise money to supplement public funds for paying the extra police. The chamber of commerce offices were designated as headquarters and all privately subscribed funds were collected and laundered by the chamber staff. On numerous subsequent occasions, the chamber staff had to deny publicly that any of **its** funds were being used for special police costs. But nothing was said about the $300,000 that was additionally raised to pay the salaries of the 620 special officers. Assuming a leadership role, the U. S. National Bank directors unanimously approved a donation of $2500.

All publicity releases were handled by prominent advertising executive Joseph R. Gerber, who wanted it understood that the Citizens' Emergency Committee was **not** a strike breaking organization but rather a group of dedicated businessmen who had only the public interest at heart. In Gerber's words, the committee was to be viewed publicly as a device "to fill the breach caused by the failure of the city council to abide by their oath of office" in disapproving the needed quota of special police officers.[52]

Under Gerber's guidance, the chamber of commerce began to crank out a variety of news releases and speakers manual outlines. One bulletin carried a radio address by Pacific Power & Light Company executive John Deardorf in which he stated that "Portland longshoremen and Portland business are suffering not so much because of unsolvable problems here [in Portland], but because an admitted Communist leader in San Francisco stands out for recognition of every demand." Another bulletin detailed the inner workings of the Communist Party, and a third release placed all of the blame on "a handful of men led by the Communistic Harry Bridges."

The early days of July 1934 were busy for both sides of the strike. The celebration of the Independence Day Anniversary was an appropriate time to organize a patriotic group of Minute Men known as the Citizens Emergency League. Claiming to represent only citizens and the public, the league declared that it was "not concerned with the merits of the strike" and was not taking sides on the issue. It was to become a permanent law and order group, to be called upon "by the constituted authorities in case of emergency." Although the group disavowed any direct concern with the strike, and although assistant chamber manager Lynn P. Sabin disclaimed any official tie to the chamber, the leaders of the Citizens Emergency League had played and were playing an active role in chamber efforts to crush the strike. The league's executive committee was composed of advertiser Joseph R. Gerber; E. C. Sammons, former and future U. S. National Bank executive and the then current vice president and general manager of the Iron Fireman Company; Robert L. Sabin, Jr., a prominent attorney; and Henry F. Cabell, wealthy investor, public official and manager of the Failing estate. The executive officer was Colonel William A. Aird, a former commander of a machine gun battalion in World War I.[53]

476

APPLICATION
CITIZENS EMERGENCY LEAGUE

A voluntary association of able-bodied, patriotic American Citizens, joined together to more effectively discharge our recognized duty as citizens; and to offer our services to a recognized Governmental authority to be used in cases of extreme emergency to maintain law and order; and for the protection of lives and property.

As this league is purely voluntary, connected with no other organization, and self supporting, I subscribe $............ to cover the cost of organization.

I hereby subscribe to the principles of this League and request to be enrolled as a member.

Signed..

QUESTIONNAIRE

1. NAME..
   Last   First   Middle

2. ADDRESS..Bet. what Sts..

3. Phone: { Res..
   { Bus..
   { Emergency..
   Married or single..
   Naturalized..

4. Birth place..Citizen............Nat. Born............

5. Parents both living..Where..

6. Where born..Citizens..
   Of what country

7. Number of dependents............Relationship..

8. How long have you lived in Oregon..

9. Do you own a home............Radio............Automobile............
   No. of passengers............Any other property..
   Where..

10. Educational qualifications..

11. Speak any language other than English..

12. To what organizations do you belong..

13. Do you own any firearms............If so, what kind..

14. List your military experience..

15. Have you had any experience with gas bombs..

16. Are you employed............Name of employer..

17. All applicants must give three references. **OCCUPATION**
    1..Address............
    2..Address............
    3..Address............

17. Accepted............Assigned............

18. Rejected............Rank............

As described by Lynn Sabin, the Citizens Emergency League was "purely a volunteer organization, self-sustaining, and headed by a strong executive group of men active in the affairs of Portland." In retrospect, they also appear to have been a group of frightened men who needed the trappings of a military organization to bolster their faith in America by giving them sufficient courage to face a national crisis, the true dimensions of which escaped their comprehension. The organization did not have a constitution or by-laws. But it did require the completion of a formal application blank that requested pertinent information relative to such matters as ownership of firearms, previous military service and experience with gas bombs. It issued to each of its reported 3000 members a medallion to be used as a pocket piece on which the member's number was stamped. Also distributed were red, white and blue arm bands on which were inscribed the letters "C. E. L." These distinguished bits of attire were to be worn by the members whenever they should be called out to serve as law enforcement officers. In structuring their organization, the members divided the city into 20 zones with each district headed by a zone commander who had the responsibility to form one to two companies of men who were classified according to military requirement. Only one week after its founding — after disclaiming any direct concern with the merits of the strike — Colonel Aird delivered a ringing radio address urging the ship owners to stand firm and speak out to the public "with their side of the strike issues."[54]

While the Minute Men were organizing, the strikers were also on the move. Thursday, July 5, 1934, came to be dubbed "Bloody Thursday." On that day began a series of violent clashes in all of the major West Coast ports as the employers initiated their drive to break the strike. Because several longshoremen were killed — none in Portland, however — the day on which the violent confrontation began became widely known as "Bloody Thursday." Large scale memorial demonstrations for those killed were held in all the ports being struck. In subsequent years, Portland's annual memorial "Bloody Thursday" parade ceremony became the largest and most impressive on the Pacific Coast.[55]

Portland's "Bloody Thursday" confrontation occurred in Linnton where 12 picketers were arrested for failure to disperse on order of a deputy sheriff. There was no obstruction of traffic, no violence nor interference from the pickets; they simply refused to move pursuant to attorney B. A. Green's instructions. Without any provocation, one of the deputies tossed a tear gas bomb into their midst and a general brawl resulted. Mayor Carson admitted to Green that he had no legal right to limit the pickets, but the matter was out of his hands. All strike breaking supervision and special police coordination had been given to one General Ulysses G. McAlexander whose salary was being paid by the Citizens' Emergency Committee. It was ironic, noted Green, that most of the men who were arrested were ex-service men, some of whom had served under General McAlexander during World War I. "When they were under his command and fighting for his country, they were wonderful citizens."[56]

Perhaps the most interesting incident provoked by the strike occurred on July 18, 1934, after the arrival in Portland of New York Senator Robert F. Wagner. Dispatched by President Roosevelt as his special emissary, Wagner hoped to effect a settlement. The President was due to visit in early August, to dedicate the Bonneville Dam site, and he hardly wanted to steam into Portland's harbor on the *U. S. S. Houston* and find himself embroiled in a bitter waterfront strike.

After meeting with the employers and strike committee, Senator Wagner accepted the committee's invitation to view the strike area along the river. As

Wagner's local host, attorney B. A. Green accompanied him on the venture and his account is worth quoting in full.

"All arrangements were made. I drove my car accompanied by Senator Wagner, Matt Meehan of the longshoresmen, C. L. Vines of the sailors, and Max Stern, a reporter for the Scripps-Howard newspapers, who had come to Portland with Senator Wagner from Washington, D. C. Fred Ross drove his car behind mine with Ernest Marsh, a federal conciliator, Roscoe Craycraft, and D. E. Nickerson. Permission was granted by the official in charge of the guards for Senator Wagner and his party, as named above, to inspect Terminal No. 4 and see what was going on. A guard was placed on the running board of each car. As we came away from Terminal No. 4, my car was in front and Fred Ross was following very closely behind. When I came up to the head guard, I slowed my car and the guard jumped off and waved his hand with a hearty goodbye. I looked through my rearview mirror and saw that Fred Ross was slowing down also. He was only a short distance behind me. We had proceeded probably three or four blocks when we heard bullets shizzing [sic] over the car. Senator Wagner said, "This can't be true." We drove on to the top of the hill where many pickets were stationed, and there found that Fred Ross' car had been shot through the trunk. Capt. Bill Browne and another officer came up immediately, and went down to arrest two of the guards who were behind sandbags. They were taken to the police station and about 11 o'clock that night were released. I was told that Fred Ross was going to be arrested for attempting to kidnap the guard riding on the running board of his car. This was never done, and the incident was closed.

"However, Mayor Carson went on the radio that evening and stated that everybody should be calm, as there had been no shooting. This was false. Mrs. Green listened to his broadcast and immediately called him on the phone at the radio station and told him that as Mayor of Portland she thought he should tell the people what actually happened. He was insulting and said he knew what he was talking about. She said, "This is **Mrs.** B. A. Green. Mr. Green just called me to tell me about the shooting and to say neither he nor Senator Wagner had been hit." He immediately became apologetic, and muttered, "Yes, Mrs. Green, etc., etc." She answered. 'It is your duty to tell the **truth** to the people,' and hung up the phone.

"Due apologies were made the next day by Mayor Carson to me for his insult to my wife. He said he had found out that there had been a shooting and he hadn't known it was Mrs. Green calling, and he was sorry he had insulted her and he was sorry he had made the statement over the radio. With this the incident was closed, except that no person, state policeman or guards behind sandbags were ever arrested other than as stated above. Most of the men who were behind sandbags armed with high-powered rifles were from Hill Military Academy, and a few young fellows who should be classed as scabs."[57]

The day following the shooting disturbance, Governor Julius Meier called out the National Guard and stationed it at Camp Wythecomb, southeast of Portland in Clackamas County. Perceiving this action as a signal to break the strike, the employers' spirits were momentarily heightened. This was the opportunity they had long awaited to expand their efforts to open the port. Portland's commercial life was paralyzed and over $30 million worth of business had been lost in the previous ten weeks. In the hope of involving the Guard to protect their aggressive actions, the employers made several unsuccessful attempts to move cargo from the shut down docks. The strikers were careful not to provoke any violence, or even to react to any threatened violence on the part of the strikebreakers. The National Guard remained in camp and the stranglehold on the port remained intact.

The chamber of commerce records are unclear as to exactly what happened next, but late in the day of July 20th, the Waterfront Employers' Association apparently agreed to submit all of the strike issues to arbitration, the very tactic that they had rejected on May 14th. They were licked and they knew it. Sensing the realities of the case, Port of Portland vice president Henry L. Corbett, who had kept his institution quietly in the background throughout the developing controversy, called a secret meeting of the top business command at the Arlington Club. Within two hours, a general agreement had been reached. Corbett knew that the strike had to be settled prior to President Roosevelt's visit two weeks hence. The future of Bonneville Dam was on the line and Portland's commercial life had already suffered too much.

Over the ensuing ten days, the procedures for establishing a mediation board were worked out between the union and the employers. On July 27th, Governor Meier announced that he would open all the docks on Monday morning, July 30th. The men were to report back to work at 6 a.m. on July 31, 1934.

Fears for the Future

Although the waterfront strike officially ended on July 31, 1934, Portland's labor problems were far from settled. In fact, the pace of labor unrest was to increase for the next four years. Not only would there be future waterfront disturbances, but a series of turbulent strikes against the lumber industry and numerous violent confrontations with the Teamsters Union. As the *Lumber News* reported in June 1935:

> "From the very beginning, the process of putting the Recovery Act into effect was accomplished by labor unrest. From June 1933, through the year 1934, and to date, the country has been swept by a series of strike waves. . . . The typical strike has not been for higher wages, shorter hours, or other improved working conditions. It has been a strike for 'union recognition' and against 'company unionism.' "[58]

Union recognition and the employment of non-union longshoremen were the issues that continued to plague subsequent waterfront negotiations. Four days after the strike terminated, the chamber's Arthur Farmer noted that:

> "Yesterday, the vicinity of the hiring hall in Portland was the scene of a pitched battle between 36 registered non-Union men and five to ten times as many ILA men, when the non-Union men approached the hiring hall in a

body for work. . . . Today, the hiring hall opened again, but no non-Union men would approach it; therefore, all men available were dispatched and they, of course, were all ILA members."[59]

It was in reaction to conditions of this sort — and the fears generated by the leadership of people like Harry Bridges — that propelled Portland's business establishment to seek a permanent organization that would carry on the work of both the Citizens Emergency Committee and the Citizens Emergency League. On the very day that the port was reopened, the chamber of commerce executive committee recommended the formation of a Civic Protection Committee. A partial list of the proposed members is worth noting:

> **Directors in Charge:**
> R. B. Bain, of Closset and Devers, spice and tea importers
> Amedee M. Smith, Realty Associates
>
> **Members:**
> C. C. Chapman, *Oregon Voter*
> General Creed Hammond, Retired
> Henry F. Cabell, Failing estate
> Frank McCaslin, Oregon Portland Cement Company
> Phil Metschan, Jr., Imperial Hotel
> E. C. Sammons, Iron Fireman Company
> Robert L. Sabin, Jr., attorney
> Horace Mecklem, New England Mutual Life Insurance agent
> Donald Bates, Oregon Transfer Company
> Lamar Tooze, attorney
> Hall S. Lusk, attorney and circuit court judge

In the words of the chamber's assistant manager Lynn P. Sabin, the Civic Protection Committee "is in effect our Americanization Institutions Committee, . . . appointed particularly to investigate and study communist activities here in the city and vicinity."[60]

At a meeting of the Citizens Emergency Committee, held in the Portland Hotel on August 20, 1934, and presided over by Amedee M. Smith, additional names were added to the roster of the Civic Protection Committee:

> Thomas Autzen, Portland Manufacturing Company
> L. C. Newlands, Oregon Portland Cement Company
> Henry W. Collins, Pacific Continental Grain Company
> Raymond B. Wilcox, Wilcox Investment Company
> Kenneth B. Hauser, Multnomah Hotel
> Ross McIntyre, Columbia Food Company
> Milton Markowitz, printer
> L. L. Campbell, Standard Oil of California
> Kenneth Dawson, States Steamship Company
> Paul B. McKee, Pacific Power & Light Company

Other prominent businessmen and bankers at the Portland Hotel session included: Charles E. Dant, L. H. Hoffman, E. S. Collins, Lloyd J. Wentworth, John H. Burgard, Franklin T. Griffith, Mason Ehrman, E. B. MacNaughton, Roy Bishop, and *Oregon Journal* editor Donald J. Sterling. As president of the Portland Chamber of Commerce, *Journal* publisher Phillip Jackson played a key role in forming the new organization. But the man who was increasingly to dominate the activity of the Civic Protection Committee was utility executive Paul B. McKee, a recent arrival on the Portland scene.

The fears underlying the formation of this "patriotic" group were implicit in a report presented by States Steamship executive Kenneth D. Dawson. As cited in the minutes, Dawson described the plight of the non-union men who were working at the Luckenbach Steamship Company Terminal:

> "Today, one Union gang dispatched to Luckenbach refused to work with non-Union men. A number of Union men approached the non-Union hiring hall at 14th and Alberta, discharged shots into the window, killed one man and seriously injured another."

Dawson depicted this incident as "gangsterism applied to labor organization." He recommended that "the permanent organization be ready immediately to forestall plans of the gangster element to complete unionization of all industry in the city."[61] Dawson correctly noted that the National Labor Board policy permitted the working of union and non-union men in separate gangs. But in doing so, he equated "complete unionization" — or the closed shop movement — with "gangsterism" and "unAmericanism." That this view was generally endorsed by the Civic Protection Committee membership was revealed in the motion authorizing its selection:

> "That a committee be appointed by President Jackson and authorized and instructed to study and inform the Portland Chamber of Commerce as to movements underway throughout this city and district which may be deemed to be of a communistic nature and to study and recommend as to proposed changes in court procedure, the efficiency of law enforcement agencies and other conditions vital to the welfare and growth of this city . . . "[62]

The chamber official who directed the staff work for the Civic Protection Committee was assistant manager Lynn P. Sabin. There was no question where he stood on the need to protect society from the "criminal communistic elements." Sabin composed the resolution, approved by the chamber's board of directors, urging the Multnomah County legislative delegation to the 1935 session "not to repeal and work against repeal of Oregon's Criminal Syndicalism Law . . . which is needed as a safeguard to the peace and welfare of this commonwealth."[63]

The DeJonge Case

What a blow it must have been to Sabin and his chamber associates two years later when U. S. Supreme Court Chief Justice Charles Evans Hughes challenged the enforcement of the Oregon syndicalism law in the case of Dirk DeJonge. Among the approximate 260 members of the Communist Party in Portland during the waterfront strike of 1934, young Dirk DeJonge had been one of the more obscure. He was a dedicated socialist who joined the Communist Party to protest against the actions of the ship owners whom he considered "tools of capitalism" and the "enemies of the working classes." Three days before the strike ended DeJonge and three other speakers were arrested at a protest meeting on S. W. Alder Street. The gathering had been well publicized and it carried the endorsement of the Communist Party. According to one of DeJonge's defense attorneys, Harry Gross, the police raid was planned and directed by the Citizens Emergency League.[65]

None of the speakers, including DeJonge, advocated violence. They were simply protesting the "brutal practices" of General McAlexander's special police force. Electing to be tried separately, DeJonge experienced judicial treatment tantamount to a kangaroo court. Judge Jacob Kanzler was a much decorated veteran officer of World War I, an active member of both the American Legion and the Veterans of Foreign Wars, a loyal Republican and a member of Portland's Americanization Committee. The special prosecutor, Stanley Doyle, was a former national official of the American Legion. The star witness, a police undercover officer named M. R. Bacon, was a former bootlegger and a member of both the Citizens Emergency League and the police department's "Red Squad." According to prosecutor Doyle, it was only necessary to show that DeJonge was a communist and had been present at the public meeting to prove his guilt under Oregon's syndicalism law. In the course of the trial, Doyle even admitted that he had tried to persuade a witness to change his testimony in support of the state's case.

The jury initially came in with a 6-6 tie vote. Under pressure, and given the assurance that DeJonge would be given leniency, four jurors changed their minds and DeJonge was found guilty. Instead of giving him the maximum of ten years, Judge Kanzler showed mercy and sentenced him to only seven years in the state penitentiary. Upon announcement of the sentence, a mild uproar resulted. Both *The Oregonian* and the *Oregon Voter* strongly criticized not only the conviction but also the law itself. *The Oregonian* correctly foresaw that DeJonge would not only become a hero but a tool of communist propaganda. Declared the *Oregon Voter*, the whole episode was "stupid."[66]

DeJonge's lawyers, with the support of the American Civil Liberties Union and the International Labor Defense Fund, carried the case on appeal to the Oregon State Supreme Court which affirmed the lower court's conviction in November 1935. With the aid of the ACLU and the ILD, defense attorneys Irving Goodman, Harry Gross and Gus Solomon[67] succeeded in petitioning the

483

U. S. Supreme Court to grant a hearing. On January 4, 1937, the Hughes Court unanimously reversed DeJonge's conviction but it did not invalidate the Oregon statute *per se*. Hughes' opinion drew a distinct line between criminal activity and membership in the Communist Party. "The right of peaceable assembly," declared Hughes, "is a right cognate to those of free speech and free press, and is equally fundamental."[68] Guilt by association was not a valid ground for conviction. In contrast to Lynn Sabin's defense of the Oregon law as the "safeguard to the peace and welfare of the commonwealth," Hughes emphasized the more imperative need "to preserve inviolate the constitutional rights of free speech, free press and free assembly. . . . Therein," declared Hughes, "lies the security of the republic, the very foundation of constitutional government."[69]

The Chamber and the Police vs. the Communists

In the thirty month period between DeJonge's arrest and Hughes' stirring decision, Portland's business leadership became increasingly frightened of potential communist activity. In August, Lynn Sabin wrote an in-house memorandum to the chamber's Arthur Farmer: "It is apparent to the Civic Protection Committee that the Communist situation on the Pacific Coast is serious and must be met and coped with in a very definite way."[70] The chamber's strategy was to involve the Portland Police Department and the Oregon State Police in undercover intelligence work. The chamber raised the funds to send Police Chief Harry Niles to a meeting in Washington, D. C., to educate him on the procedures for establishing a more effective anti-subversive unit within the department. Civic Protection Committee members Horace Mecklem and L. C. Newlands were the key chamber business executives in promoting and directing the new "Police Cooperative System," as it was called.

Anti-union and anti-radical feelings underlay much of the political unrest that plagued Portland during the fall of 1934. They most certainly influenced the election of conservative Democratic Governor Charles H. Martin. As a former army general, Martin had earned a reputation for being a "strict law and order man." Later in his term of office, he was to reveal his true feelings when he wrote Walter Pearson that union organizers were "pestiferous peewees."[71] According to Richard L. Neuberger, he reportedly advised law enforcement officers in the state to "beat hell out of 'em."[72] The appellation "old iron pants" was well bestowed. When he lost his party's renomination in 1938 to a liberal Democrat, Martin was to comment that he had been defeated by "Communists, Bolsheviks and Socialists."[73]

The equation of "law and order" with anti-radicalism and patriotism came easily to the chamber of commerce leadership. Three days after Christmas in 1934, the chamber sponsored a city-wide luncheon meeting of "all patriotic and civic organizations" to be held in the Chamber of Commerce building. The ostensible purpose of the gathering was to protest the city's renting of the Civic Auditorium to Scott Nearing who represented "the Friends of the Soviet Union."

484

On hand to address the group was police patrolman Walter B. Odale, Portland's local authority on communistic subversive activities.[74]

Along with officers M. R. Bacon, Bill Brown and J. J. Keegan, Odale formed the Portland Police Department's "Red Squad." For over 20 years, the "Red Squad" was to play a not insignificant role in the political life of Portland. During the last phase of its existence, it came under the command of Captain Bill Brown. During the mid-1930s, Odale used to boast that he had 10,000 names on file in his office. Included were some of the most prominent professionals in the state including future U. S. Senator Richard L. Neuberger and future U. S. District Court Judge Gus J. Solomon.[75]

Major General Charles H. Martin, who, as Governor of Oregon from 1935 to 1939, upheld law and order against "labor goons." During the strike laden years of 1937 and 1938, Martin received a "Weekly Report of Communist Activities" from Officer Odale of the Portland Bureau of Police. Martin also received weekly reports from the state police and had them sent to Odale. When such actions were publicly criticized by young Richard L. Neuberger, Martin called Neuberger "Oregon's No. 1 young radical."[76]

In 1935, Odale was to write and publish a pamphlet entitled "Does America Want Communism?" It was freely circulated by the chamber of commerce and its Civic Protection Committee. One of the many unsubstantiated charges made by Odale related to the ACLU. Obviously influenced by Dirk DeJonge's defense support, Odale cited the prestigious national organization and its local office as "the protector of the Communists."[77] Although Odale did not make the charge directly, implied in his writings was the notion that communism, the depression, unionization and excessive taxation were all part of an evil plot. Walter May, manager of the chamber, did however circulate a pamphlet published by the Industrial Association of San Francisco that actually printed such charges.

In Retrospect

The Waterfront Strike of 1934 produced one of the least civil and ugliest periods of Portland's history.[78] It also laid the foundation for the hysteria of the McCarthy Era in the early 1950s. Indirectly, it was to exert an influence on such issues as the private-public power controversy of the same period. Many of the public power advocates of the 1950s were the same individuals who had defended the longshoremen and the persecuted radicals like Dirk DeJonge. And the fact that a sprinkling of liberal Jewish professionals of largely foreign birth had previously been identified with such "radical" causes merely heightened the subsequent feelings of anti-Semitism held by many of Portland's business and professional leadership. One prominent Portland attorney should be singled out as an exception to this generalization: David Lloyd Davies, the senior partner of Portland's largest law firm. Davies not only supported the defense efforts of Dirk DeJonge, but he personally endorsed the nomination of Gus J. Solomon to the U. S. District Court in 1949, an appointment that received wide criticism from within the local business and political establishment.

Chapter 16

The Depression Years:
Some Federal Projects and Pitfalls

At the bottom of the depression in 1932, over 12 million Americans were unemployed — an astounding total that comprised 25 percent of the civilian work force. President Herbert Hoover's approach to unemployment relief was traditional Republican orthodoxy: Local government initiatives and private charities. When the more progressive members of Congress demanded federal spending for public works and direct relief, Hoover adamantly refused to alter his position.

Local and state governments were required to raise their own relief funds and develop their own work projects, most of which were related to highway construction and all of which were totally inadequate to meet the growing needs of the unemployed.[1] In the entire United States for the year 1932, only $25 million of **direct** federal funding was available for highways. In April 1932, Oregon State Highway Commission Chairman Leslie Scott announced that he had scraped together the magnificent sum of $1.6 million, 75 percent of which was designated for four thoroughfares: Fourth Avenue (S. W. Barbur Boulevard), S. E. 82nd Avenue, S. E. McLoughlin and Division Street east from 82nd. The extra federal funding was allocated because 82nd and McLoughlin were to be designated as segments of the U. S. highway network.

Like most orthodox Republicans, Leslie Scott strongly supported President Hoover's policies. He opposed the spending of tax dollars for the primary purpose of providing employment — especially federal tax dollars over which Oregonians exercised no direct control. As for the expenditure of state highway funds, 95 percent of which came from state and local sources, Scott distributed the money geographically, with little consideration given to where the largest number of unemployed were located. There were over 30,000 unemployed in Multnomah County alone, one third of the state's total jobless, most of whom needed some form of relief. Although the 1931 legislative session enacted a bill to allow the expenditure of state highway funds for city streets, Multnomah County's allotment in 1931 was less than ten percent of the total paid by county residents in gas taxes and license fees. Needless to say, the state highway commission was not popular in Portland.

In January 1932, Congress established the Reconstruction Finance Corporation (RFC) to lend funds primarily to banks, railroads and savings and loan associations. The Republicans viewed this action as a psychological weapon, although bailing out shaky banks was the primary purpose. Five months later, when Congress attempted to expand RFC authority to lend money to states and municipalities for self-liquidating public works and relief, Hoover angrily vetoed the measure. The proposal, he said, violated "every sound principle of public finance and government."[2] But with the election drawing nearer, and with it the need to broaden his public appeal, Hoover relaxed his principles and signed a revised Garner-Wagner Act in July 1932. He then departed on a western campaign tour, bypassing all of Oregon except for a five day fishing trip on the Rogue River.

Apart from the infusion of much needed relief funds, the RFC amendment provided Portland with ample resources to undertake one of the biggest boondoggles in the city's history: The construction of America's largest public market building, between Front Street and the seawall, an ungainly edifice that in later times became known as the Journal Building. It is unlikely that either future Vice President John Nance Garner or New York's Senator Robert F. Wagner ever contemplated that their prized bill would facilitate the execution of such a monstrous project. But as Arthur M. Schlesinger, Jr., was to comment, the RFC created an "enduring stronghold of government-business cooperation."[3]

The Public Market Fiasco

The Portland Public Market that operated along S. W. Yamhill Street was a thriving enterprise during the 1920s. But few could dispute its congestion: Street access was limited and parking was tight. As one planning commission report later described the market, "It gives the impression of a country village, indifferent to appearances."[4] By 1932, the planning commission was to conclude that the market did not offer sufficient "convenience and accommodation of the public."[5] This point was to be challenged with ferocity.

The seeds of a new, enlarged market facility were firmly planted in city engineer Olaf Laurgaard's 1923 waterfront plan. The architectural model provided for a five block monolith, running along the seawall, from the Morrison Bridge to the Hawthorne Bridge. Laurgaard's plan also allowed for an adjacent transportation terminal, with railroad and interurban tracks bunched together and buried below grade level back from the seawall. As later testimony was to reveal, the property owners supposedly agreed to pay their assessments for the seawall and sewer construction with the understanding that a new market would be built in the general area between Front Street and the river. In 1923, the possibility of a new market building was viewed by some Front Street property owners as an instrument for improving declining values that afflicted the entire waterfront. By 1931, however, the project was to be viewed as justifiable compensation to those particular property owners on whose land the future market would be built. Nothing was said about the other Front Street property owners, but it was assumed that their property values would be indirectly improved by such a massive investment of new capital.

Planning for the new market began to take shape as early as October 1926. In a letter to E. C. Sammons, banker John C. Ainsworth, who was also chairman of the city planning commission, commented upon a meeting that he had attended in John Yeon's office. Also present were future governor and department store executive Julius L. Meier, investor and legislator Henry L. Corbett, *Oregon Journal* publisher Phillip Jackson, and several others including Yeon and Frederick H. Strong, the veteran manager of the Ladd and Mead estates. The discussion focused upon a Seattle developer who had just built the Terminal Sales Building on land owned by the Mead estate. The developer was in the process of forming a corporation to construct a public market on the waterfront and he had optioned the five blocks on Front Street between the two bridges. The land would cost $650,000 and the market building approximately $1.5 million. In Ainsworth's opinion, "The whole project seems carefully planned and has a good deal of merit."[6]

By June of 1927, plans for the new building were ready for public announcement. The Portland Public Market Company had reduced the scope of the project, deciding to purchase just blocks 74, 75 and the south half of 76. The building was to be located on the waterfront, from Salmon Street to halfway between Morrison and Yamhill Streets. Nearly half of the property was owned by the Mead estate. (Stephen Mead of New London, Connecticut, was William S. Ladd's uncle.) As the former manager and recent co-purchaser of most of the undeveloped Ladd estate properties, Frederick H. Strong was also manager of the Mead estate. The other major property owners included Julius Meier and the Corbett estate, which was managed by Frederick Strong's brother, Robert H. Strong, in partnership with E. B. MacNaughton.

The financing of the project was to be achieved through the sale of stock and the issuance of bonds to the total amount of $1.5 million. The early stockholders were reported to be First National Bank president Abbot L. Mills, the three Corbett brothers who also controlled the First National, Meier & Frank Company, the Failing estate headed by Henry F. Cabell, Frederick H. Strong and U. S. National Bank president John C. Ainsworth, who personally invested $2500.[7] The corporate attorney was prominent Democrat Bert Haney who represented the Meier interests and was Julius Meier's former law partner. To put the expression in simple terms, the front-end leadership of the Portland Public Market Company had clout!

The record of events over the next four years is unclear as to exactly what happened to force a change in the financing procedures. In March 1928, John Ainsworth noted that stock subscriptions had exceeded the project's requirements by $50,000. He also noted that the city council and dock commission had approved the vacating of the ends of Yamhill and Taylor Streets at no direct cost to the Public Market Co. The council action confirmed the recommendation of the planning commission over which Ainsworth presided. In June 1928, a series of written exchanges between Haney and the Seattle National Bank which was handling the bond issue indicated that the bank wanted to withdraw from the project on the grounds that the company had made "misrepresentations" as to "the purchase price of the land, the cost of the building and the amount of cash which stockholders were investing." The bank requested payment of $10,000 for services rendered.[8]

Community opinion was strongly divided over the merits of placing a new market on the waterfront. Most of the existing market and stall operators were opposed to the move, largely on the grounds that the Front Street location was too far away from the retail core. Even the *Oregon Voter* indicated that there might be some justification for this concern:

> "No one knows exactly what will happen. Experience of some cities seems to indicate that a successful public market cannot be operated so far from the business center as the waterfront markets will be when completed. In that case the Yamhill Street institution [the existing market] may continue to yield sufficient rental income to prevent that street becoming another general retail area. 'Convenience' shoppers rather than 'price' shoppers may justify continuance of present uses of Fifth and Yamhill streets in the vicinity of the present federal block [the Pioneer Post Office and Courthouse]."[9]

The *Spectator* took a different position in strongly endorsing the waterfront location. It wondered why the project had stalled and it blamed the "politicians" in city hall who wanted a municipally-owned market without having the money to pay for it. The vacating of street-ends at no direct cost to the company was considered a political ploy because the company was required to set the building back far enough to allow for the future widening of Front Street. But more than this, by not making payment for the vacated streets, the company put itself in debt to the city if at some future time the city wanted to acquire the property.

Lawyer Dan J. Malarkey who represented the company before the city council was later to charge that the procedure vacating the street-ends created doubts in the minds of potential bond purchasers as to the future disposition of the whole enterprise. In an attempt to move the project along, Frederick H. Strong even offered to finance the undertaking privately and then turn it over to the city "on an operating basis."[10] The council did not accept the offer for two primary reasons: (1) Councilman Ralph Clyde's arguments against the waterfront site were persuasive enough to instill some doubts in other councilmen's minds; and (2), there was growing public pressure to keep the markets under city control within the 5th and Yamhill district.

Nothing further materialized until February 1931 when the chamber of commerce board of directors unanimously endorsed the Front Street location for the market building. At this stage of the negotiations, the city council was presented with a new set of conditions. The private financing schemes had collapsed along with the national stock and bond markets; a large number of subscriptions had simply been cancelled. If the city wanted a new public market it would be forced to issue over $1 million in utility certificates which would then be converted to bonds and sold on the financial market to private investors. Part of the proceeds would be used to purchase the property which the Public Market Company had agreed to buy but had not yet paid for, and the remainder would finance the building. Once completed, the company would transfer the building and the property to the city which would agree to pay the company certain commissions to be negotiated later.

This was an ingenious stratagem designed to bail out the original property owners and those stockholders who had already invested in the company. The chamber of commerce expressed no qualms in giving the entire arrangement its unqualified blessing. As chamber manager W. D. B. Dodson wrote Mayor George Baker:

> "While it is accepted that the City as a whole incurs no legal obligation to pay bonds that may be issued under the utility certificate plan pursued, there would probably develop a moral obligation on the part of the City for such payment in the event the enterprise failed to earn a fair return upon the investment; and in order to safeguard the City from the embarrassment of such a possibility the Chamber feels impelled to urge the Council very strongly to accept this site which may be developed at the lowest cost."[11]

Dodson was referring to the fact that two other sites in the existing old market district were also available for development but the land costs were considerably higher.

Dodson continued his letter to Baker with the statement that it seemed only fair and proper to purchase the waterfront site inasmuch as the property owners had willingly paid their sewer assessments on the assumption that the market would be built there. Apparently Dodson did not know the truth. The property owners of blocks 74, 75 and 76 owed the city a total of $73,500 in unpaid sewer charges and the city held a lien against the properties for that amount. The sewer lien would be added to the property cost.[12]

Dodson's concluding statement contained some classic implications *vis-a-vis* business and government. He declared that the chamber would have preferred

> " ... that the project be financed and handled by private capital, ... but in view of the fact that the municipal movement had driven away the private capital ready for the work, we feel that the final selection should now be made on the grounds indicated here."

What he was really saying was that as long as there were undue risks involved, the public taxpayers should assume the obligation. If risks had been minimized to the point that private profits could have been reasonably assured, then of course private capital and ownership would have been the preferred option. It did not seem to concern the chamber leadership that private purchasers of city issued bonds might be left holding the bag. To blame the evaporation of private capital on the possibility of a municipal takeover was ludicrous. This was a potential risk inherent in every private utility venture from traction companies to electric power companies. When Ralph Clyde had attempted to persuade the city council to purchase the Northwestern Electric Company through issuance of a similar type of utility certificates, he was denounced as a socialist by Portland's business leadership.

One month before the chamber issued its endorsement, the planning commission had glowingly accepted a 450 page report from Harland Bartholomew and Associates, the noted St. Louis city planning firm. Among its numerous recommendations was one that urged the city to develop a park along the entire west waterfront, approximately 200 feet in width between Front Street and the river wall. This feature of the plan was totally ignored by both the city council and the planning commission despite the fact that the report cost the city and county $24,000, including personal donations from John Ainsworth and John Laing of $1000 apiece. The Bartholomew Plan, which will be discussed later in this chapter, embodied a number of the same proposals that had been incorporated in the earlier Olmsted and Bennett Plans. And like its predecessors, it was to be largely disregarded. In fact, the only major physical development in Portland in 1933, the construction of the Public Market Building, was in direct opposition to the Bartholomew Plan.

When the public market proposal came before the city planning commission, according to one inside report, the commissioners "kept a terrible and awesome silence."[13] The planning commission minutes contain no record of any formal commission action on the public market proposal. However, the December 1932 "Plan-It," which had to be approved for publication by the commission members themselves, contained a statement of direct endorsement: "The planning commission believes that the construction of this market will provide Portland with an excellent and much needed public utility." The commission, however, did go on record as favoring in principle Bartholomew's recommendation that the city acquire the waterfront strip for park purposes.

The previously cited "inside report" asked an embarrassing question: "Why this silence?" from the commission members about the market project. "Could it be that powerful interests were lined up in back of that particular location for the market?" The historical record provides only one simple answer: "Yes."

Both Chairman Ainsworth and commission member Ellis Lawrence were clearly enmeshed in likely conflicts of interest. Not only had Ainsworth been an early investor in the market enterprise, but Lawrence was scheduled to be selected as the project architect — an action that was confirmed several months later. Lawrence had long been associated with Frederick H. Strong and the Ladd estate interests. He had designed several Laurelhurst homes and had been the late William M. Ladd's personal architect.

The city council began hearing formal testimony in early March of 1931. In response to pleas from attorneys representing over 200 farmers that the market remain close to the retail center, preferably on Yamhill Street, Public Market Company attorney, the colorful and dynamic Dan J. Malarkey, began to wave "the big stick." He reminded the council that the use of Yamhill Street for a market was illegal and could be stopped "any day a property owner makes an objection." Malarkey was referring to the placement of stalls down the center of a public street. He strongly intimated that the farmers would be ejected from their present stalls unless they "piped down" in their attacks on Front Street. Malarkey also reiterated the argument that the Front Street land was cheaper than property along Fourth or Fifth. If the city were to purchase the more expensive properties, the taxpayers would lose on two counts: The greater cost of the land and the greater loss of property tax revenues.[14]

Assuming a different tack, the Civic Emergency Committee headed by E. C. Sammons and R. B. Wilcox endorsed the Front Street project as an unemployment relief measure. They noted that the advance planning already completed would permit construction work to begin sooner than if a totally new site were to be chosen. Although some members of the council expressed doubts that the city could sell enough bonds to buy the Front Street property and then build the market, they voted on April 3, 1931, for the city to assume ultimate ownership of the total project and to issue utility certificates to finance it. Commissioner Ralph Clyde predicted that the market building would become a "White Elephant" and he was supported in this stance by both *The Portland News* and *The Daily Journal of Commerce.*

Nearly six more months of time were consumed in the drafting of an ordinance that detailed the procedures by which the city would purchase the completed market building and pay the Public Market Company specified commissions for services rendered. Commissioner Ralph Clyde, whose department had responsibility for public utility matters, was out of town attending a national meeting in October 1931 when the city council passed the ordinance, accepting the contract with the Public Market Company. Upon his return to Portland, Clyde was outraged that the council would take such an action in his absence. By attaching an emergency clause, the ordinance would go into effect within one month, thus precluding the possibility of a popular referendum. Clyde questioned his colleagues' rights to ignore so flagrantly the petitions of some 18,000 market customers who protested the moving of the market to Front Street. Similar petitions were received from 246 farmers. Clyde charged that the public was being betrayed for the gain of a few large property owners. He concluded his remarks with the prediction that the market operation would prove disastrous.[15]

After the council officially approved the transfer procedures, the market building still had to contend with several financial and legal roadblocks. It would be almost a year before the project would qualify for a RFC loan, but in the meantime, the company faced some litigation. In February 1932, local merchant Mike Rogoway was indicted for offering Mayor Baker a $10,000 bribe to vote against the Front Street site and in favor of the Fifth Avenue markets. In April another investigation indicted Baker and Commissioner Riley for accepting a bribe to vote for the Front Street location. Also indicted was prominent attorney Alfred A. Hampson who was accused of negotiating the bribe in behalf of the Public Market Company. In both cases, the indictments were quickly dismissed by the court on the grounds of insufficient evidence to merit a trial.

One of the charges stemming from the court hearings stated that the city offered $200,000 too much for the market site. While the realty board appraisers had valued the land at $480,000, it was worth no more than $280,000 according to Bartholomew's figures. The city's base offer was $280,000, but the purchase price was listed as $353,000 to include the $73,000 worth of sewer liens which were considered uncollectable. Thus the city forgave funds that it should rightly have collected itself and the utility certificate bondholders picked up the tab as part of the total land cost. Although the city finally received its sewer lien funds, the bondholders paid the bill, not the property owners. This was merely one more example of how the city fathers were overly generous with the public's resources when powerful private interests were involved.

The final act of generosity occurred in October 1932 when the city council accepted a $775,000 loan from the RFC, the proceeds to be used for the market's construction. The Garner-Wagner bill authorized such loans as long as they were judged to be self-liquidating. In exchange for the federal funds, the RFC was given a first mortgage lien on the property. As he had done previously, Ralph Clyde voted against the measure. He was not convinced that the loan could be self-liquidating.[16] Clyde also felt that there were many other types of relief projects in need of federal support that were far more important to the city's future health than a large public market building which neither the consumers nor the farmers wanted. With available RFC funds strictly limited, the market building loan removed most other applications from consideration.

The market did not begin construction until June of 1933. By superhuman efforts, it was later reported, the massive concrete structure was finished in five months and ready for opening ten days before Christmas of 1933. Over 200 men were employed full time accumulating a payroll of over $500,000. The haste of construction was one matter, but the cost accounting was another. Newly elected commissioner Ormond Bean discovered numerous examples of what he called "loose operations." The Public Market Company did not make the required submissions to the council for extra expenses. Bean was visibly disturbed by the lack of adequate cost controls.[17] Other commissioners expressed similar reservations about one or more aspects of the entire project. In fact, within one month of the market's opening, the city council was in no mood to accept either the building or the land. Recent elections had replaced the mayor and two commissioners. Only Earl Riley remained from the previous majority. Ralph Clyde's opposition was now joined by Mayor Joseph Carson and commissioners Ormond Bean and Jake Bennett.

On January 3, 1934, commissioner Bennett initiated the city council action that led to the city's refusal to accept the market. He charged that the old city council had exceeded its authority by obligating the city to purchase the market without prior voter approval. Beyond that, instead of costing the city $1.24 million, the added construction expenses together with the bond and loan interest had pushed the cost over $1.4 million. Finally, Bennett charged that the contract was faulty in the first place and that the company had not even

The pumping station, adjacent to the Burnside Bridge, part of the sewer interceptor system, the costs of which were assessed to the waterfront property owners.

The Public Market Building under construction in June, 1933

complied with its terms. The city was not required to accept the market until it was "a going public utility."

From its opening days, the tenant quota was never full. When the city closed the Yamhill Public Market stalls, expecting the farmers to move east four blocks, a minor rebellion occurred. Some 200 produce merchants and farmers formed a cooperative market in another building on Yamhill Street, between Third and Fourth, and refused to patronize the Front Street Market. Former Mayor George L. Baker had done his best to stimulate interest in the new market by personally leasing space for a wholesale florist business that he planned to operate in partnership with Tommy Luke, who later became Portland's most colorful floristic entrepreneur. But such efforts were of little avail. By January of 1936, the market was in serious trouble and the city attorney put the property up for sale for non-payment of liens and assessments totalling $111,000.

Between 1934 and July 1946 when *The Oregon Journal* purchased the market building and property for $750,000 borrowed from the U. S. National Bank, the Public Market Company found itself in constant litigation, either suing the city or being sued by the city and various taxpayer groups. Although the Oregon State Supreme Court finally ruled in June 1946 that the city was **not** the owner of the property, both the city and the company were liable for damages for failure to carry out the mutual obligations of the original contract. During the war years, matters had simmered quietly while the U. S. Navy leased the building, providing just enough revenue to meet current obligations. Finally, in the spring of 1968, the building was sold to the city for $1.3 million, with most of the funds being provided by the U. S. Bureau of Outdoor Recreation and the Oregon State Highway Department which planned to remove both the building and Harbor Drive, completed in 1943, in order to create the long sought riverfront park. The cost of demolition was $155,000.

At the time of its final sale, the Public Market-Journal Building was the subject of numerous articles and letters to the editor in the local press. One, by H. A. Herzog, is worthy of note:

> "We had a public market on Yamhill Street [that] . . . became known . . . all over the country. . . . It was unique, being in the core area. I never heard a good reason why it was abolished, except perhaps to aid the promotion of a new public market. . . . The gossip in town prior to its construction was that it was simply a real estate deal and that our city officials had been 'taken.' . . . I was present when the ground breaking ceremony was held. I said to those around me then that as sure as you see the spade going into the ground that a market in that location would never succeed. It was doomed to failure because people would not cross a race track [Front Street] to shop."[18]

Outside of the original property owners who got paid for their land and relieved of their sewer assessments, it is doubtful that any of the other major participants made much if anything from the whole fiasco, excluding, of course, the architects and builders. But their actions had an indelibly destructive effect

497

The main floor of the market shortly after its opening. The retail area contained 298 farm stalls. Deer meat sold for 16¢ a pound, C&H sugar, 10 pounds for 49¢, and Coast's High Grade coffee at 2 pounds for 43¢. Free parking for 650 cars was also provided.

The Market Building on Front Street. Note the number of automobiles parked on the roof and along the seawall, especially north of the Morrison Bridge ramp.

on Portland's future. Almost 40 years were to pass and endless tax dollars spent before the goals of the Bartholomew Plan could be at least partially achieved. Excluding the adverse impact on the riverfront itself, the market building fiasco together with the consequent destruction of the old Yamhill Portland Public Market launched a series of events that led to the gradual demise of public markets generally. The surviving privately-owned or -operated public markets — or farmers markets as they were often called — faded away one by one as the property owners replaced most of them with parking lots. The Public Market-Journal Building left painful memories in people's minds and Portland has never fully recovered from the experience. Today, Portland is one of the few major cities in the United States without a thriving, consolidated public market district within reasonable proximity to the retail center of the city.

The Bartholomew Plan

Harland Bartholomew and Associates of St. Louis were engaged to study the blighted areas along the waterfront (the original business section of Portland) and to prepare a report and recommendations leading to their rehabilitation. Their contract also provided for a study and revision of Portland's major street plan as drafted in 1927. The plan was presented to the city on January 20, 1932,[19] at which time Harland Bartholomew himself addressed a large public meeting at the Benson High School Auditorium. Some of his comments are worth repeating:

"There is a marked difference between eastern cities and middle western and coast cities in the matter of area occupied. The eastern cities, as a rule, tend toward congestion while middle western and coast cities of a size comparable with Portland usually have a radius of 15 miles or more. In cities of this type, the problem is not one of congestion but rather one of how much can we afford to spread out."[20]

Speaking to the city council and county commissioners the previous day, Bartholomew expanded his comments on city "over-spread." Portland, he declared, had spread so thin and maintained such a high development in its sewers, water mains and pavement, that it was questionable whether the city could do more than just support this expansion. In his opinion, Portland's development per capita was the largest in the country. "The science of city planning is now entering upon a new stage, the economic aspect — the relationship of public utilities and service to the density of population and the ability of the people to pay for them."[21]

In both of his speeches, Bartholomew traced the history of waterfront developments, from Louisville to St. Louis to Portland. He cited examples, showing how interest in particular improvements was usually a measure of cultural growth, when the value of "good appearances" began to be appreciated. He recounted the historical economic waste of "hit or miss" public improvements and quoted a leading life insurance company executive with years of experience in the mortgage market. "In normal times this country wastes around one billion dollars per year through unwise development." Had he made this speech two years later, he could have cited the Public Market Building as an example. It was Bartholomew's conviction that "a well worked out, safe and wise city plan will result in tax cost savings."[22]

Speaking specifically to the two major areas of his report, Bartholomew complimented Portland on the economies and costs of its street widening program which he cited as one of the most ambitious in the country. He compared Portland's low cost average of $300,000 per mile with St. Louis' cost of $1 million per mile. Chicago's, he said, was even greater. But he cautioned city and county authorities about the dangers of allowing the automobile to force ever wider expansion of residential and business developments to the point that mass transit and other public services could not adequately or economically meet the people's needs.

> "People have moved farther out toward the country and have demanded pavements, sewers, water mains, gas lines, electric service and other improvements. Cities have complied with that demand, and now as a consequence we find that great areas of vacant land or vacant lots have been hurdled in this movement and the cost of these improvements is far too heavy."[23]

As to the blighted areas along the waterfront, Bartholomew cited the general decrease in property values that had occurred since 1913. From 1913 to 1920, the decrease was only nine percent, but between 1920 and 1930, values had declined 130 percent, totalling $11 million. Rehabilitation of the area and the restoration of the property at something like its former value was held to be of prime importance. Only then could the exodus of business be expected to cease. The waterfront, Bartholomew declared, was "Portland's front door." It was a natural development for the area to be repossessed and rehabilitated, following the example of Chicago's lake shore.

Bartholomew traced the impact of the Broadway Bridge opening in 1913. This was the prime reason, he said, for the diversion of traffic and commerce away from the area between Fifth and the river. The extension of the new Burnside Bridge ramps in 1926 exercised a similar effect. He recommended the widening of Front Street and the replacement of both the Hawthorne and Morrison Bridges with widths of at least six lanes. He also supported the then current effort to build the Fremont Bridge. He concluded his remarks in both of his major addresses with the observation that he had found the traffic congestion into and out of Portland to be nearly twice as great as that in other cities of similar size.[24]

As was stated previously, the Bartholomew Plan was not taken seriously by either the public or the city and county authorities who were disinclined to tie Portland's future development too closely to any definite plan. For one thing, the real estate pressures were simply too strong. Another contributing factor to the

plan's unenthusiastic reception, in the mind of future city commissioner William A. Bowes, was the report itself. It "was so long and cumbersome, and so full of detailed data that the average busy businessman was discouraged from making any attempt to read it."[25]

Projects in Search of Federal Aid

If nothing else, the Bartholomew Plan did focus attention on the West Side waterfront section of Portland. It also stimulated a number of individuals and organizations to demand some action. There was no clear-cut blueprint which could command more than partial consensus, but most interested participants did seem to agree on the need to widen Front Street. The only problem was a financial one; federal aid was a necessity.

The chief promoter of total waterfront development was the veteran city engineer Olaf Laurgaard. After ten years, he was still pushing his 1923 plan, several features of which had already been realized by the early months of 1933. He could, and did, point with pride to the construction of the Front Street sewer interceptor and pumping plant, the seawall, the new Burnside Bridge, and the agreement to proceed with the new Public Market Building. His immediate goals — next on his list of priorities — included the widening of Front Street, a common user belt line railroad tunnel buried below grade along the riverfront, a unified interurban railroad station and a new municipally-owned bus terminal close to the waterfront, an esplanade along the seawall, and a vehicular tunnel for Front Street to pass under N. W. Glisan Street, to open up access to the N. W. terminal and industrial district. Laurgaard had other plans that did not relate to the waterfront. He wanted to complete Barbur Boulevard now that the Southern Pacific had abandoned its railroad tracks; he expressed interest in a 1.7 mile tunnel that would pass under a portion of Portland Heights, connecting S. W. Broadway with Bertha; and he favored the construction of a central parking garage to replace the Pioneer Post Office Building.[26]

In an attempt to pull together the thinking of the community as to how Portland might best achieve some of these goals, a general meeting was called at city hall on March 16, 1933. The event was colorfully described by young staff writer Robert C. Notson of *The Oregonian* (Notson later became both editor and publisher of *The Oregonian*):

"Aggressive and immediate action designed to start new life blood in the form of substantial loans from the Reconstruction Finance corporation coursing through the anemic frame of the building industries of Portland and Multnomah county was programmed yesterday at a conference between public and semi-public agencies."[27]

The group considered a number of issues:

(1) Unemployment relief funds were nearly exhausted.

(2) Although $2 billion of RFC funds had been appropriated and California had already received $200 million, Oregon had "yet to receive its first dollar from this relief reservoir." (The Public Market Building loan had been approved, but the funds had not been received.)

(3) There were a variety of projects in the greater Portland area capable of meeting the RFC requirements carrying a total price tag of $67 million.

The immediate need was to create a city-county fund of $10,000 to employ a technical staff to assemble the required data which would "convince the Reconstruction Finance Corporation of the deserving character of the proposed projects." The plan, as devised by the assembled group, contemplated

" . . . that as rapidly as these can be whipped into shape they will be forwarded through Governor Meier to the authorities at the national capital. . . . The fact that Oregon has not been able to 'crash through' and

A Ford Tri-motor passenger plane parked in front of the Portland Airport Terminal on Swan Island in the early 1930s. Opened in 1928, the airport was judged inadequate by the state in January 1936. In the same month, Portland voters approved a $300,000 bond issue to acquire land for a new airport site on Multnomah Drainage District No. 1 property along the Columbia River. The site was selected by the Port of Portland under Henry L. Corbett's general direction. A federal W.P.A. grant of $1.3 million was also secured. Over four million cubic yards of fill were placed on the site by the Port's hydraulic dredges, and the airport was finally opened in 1941.

obtain any portion of the waiting cash was ascribed to lack of proper preparations. Only by the employment of experts to perform this necessary task can loans be obtained and men put to work, it was pointed out."[28]

The priority items that totalled $67 million included projects all the way from The Dalles to Astoria, Laurgaard's complete wish list and the addition of a much desired new Portland municipal airport. An item that was high on everyone's list was the need for a new Portland sewage system and treatment plant. But due to the complicated nature of this project, and the fact that it involved two contradictory voter referendums, the subject will be covered separately in the next chapter.

At its April 3rd meeting, the city council decided to direct its efforts toward obtaining a RFC loan of $4 million for the "Front Street project." It declined to include the railroad tunnel because the railroads strongly opposed it. It also decided to give up the idea of constructing a public parking garage on the post office site. Finally, it endorsed the Tualatin tunnel project but did not include its funding in the RFC loan application. Twelve engineers and draftsmen were authorized to work out the plans for the approved projects.[29]

Almost two months were consumed in preparing the RFC application which carried a request for $3.75 million. During the interim, the council received some criticism for dragging its feet. Said a *Daily News* editorial on May 10th: "Portland has not yet received its just share of the government funds . . . be-

New Portland Airport — 1941

cause it has not worked out plans for which the RFC could, and would, advance money to finance."

It was at this point in the proceedings that Ralph B. Lloyd journeyed back to Portland to unveil his ambitious plans for an extensive East Side development that included a newly designed hotel. As he told *The Oregonian*, he sincerely hoped that his projects would win some federal funding. But he was too late to get into the action. Although his proposals won wide praise from many business and political leaders, they were too extensive and costly to be plugged into the federal pipeline in May of 1933.

On June 1, 1933, the city council approved the submission of a $3.75 million loan application to the RFC for Front Street and general waterfront improvements. Later in the month five more self-liquidating projects totalling $11.7 million were approved for application preparation. The city was finally getting its act together but the chances of gaining favorable consideration in Washington did not look too bright.

By early August, the city received word that its $3.75 million RFC loan application was in trouble. In behalf of the city council, Portland Commissioner of Finance Earl Riley wrote Interior Secretary Harold Ickes a long and detailed letter requesting that the application be transferred to the Federal Emergency Administration of Public Works, for a PWA loan.[30] Representative Charles H. Martin indicated that he would fully support the application in Washington. But there was one major hitch that the city council could not have foreseen. By the late summer of 1933, both Martin and Senator Charles L. McNary were committed to securing a PWA grant to build Bonneville Dam, a project that Ickes did not favor. President Roosevelt, in fact, overruled Ickes in awarding the $36 million Bonneville grant to Oregon. As far as Secretary Ickes was concerned, the Portland area had received more than its fair share of federal public works money, excluding matching grants for highway construction. Although the Bonneville Dam funds came out of a Rivers and Harbors allocation, it was still a public works project and fell under Ickes' general administration.

Portland was going to have to wait until 1940 before any work would begin on Front Street, or until the voters approved a $1.25 million bond issue to match federal and state funds that were distributed through the Oregon State Highway Department. Every public works project subsequent to Bonneville Dam, including major highway construction and a new airport, was in fact initiated only upon voter approval of a particular bond issue, the proceeds of which had to match whatever federal funds were available in whatever proportion the government set for the project. If Oregon, unlike the State of Washington, had been represented by at least one Democratic Senator who was close to either Ickes or Roosevelt, greater federal largesse might have resulted. Although Representative Charles H. Martin, the future governor, was a Democrat, he was not in sympathy with the New Deal and Ickes was well aware of the fact.

The final act in Portland's dramatic failure to achieve federal funding and loans for its various public works projects was the city council's decision on October 7, 1933, to fire Olaf Laurgaard, the 17 year veteran city engineer. Criticism of Laurgaard's policies and temperament had been increasing for some time, especially among members of the planning commission. City commissioners Clyde, Bean and Riley felt that he had outlived his usefulness and had become arrogant in his personal relationships. It was time for a change.

What to Do With the Post Office? Again!

City engineer Laurgaard's proposal in March 1933 to tear down the Pioneer Post Office and erect a central parking garage on the site reopened a controversy that was referred to in an earlier chapter. From an examination of John C. Ainsworth's correspondence during this period, one gains the impression that the much respected banker and veteran city planning commission member embraced no strong convictions on the subject. This factor in itself is revealing as to the perceptions and values held by some of Portland's leading citizens as the city struggled to create a new self image during the depression.

In a letter to Representative Charles H. Martin in Washington, Ainsworth presented a scheme that seemed to have some appeal, at least momentarily. He suggested that Martin approach President Roosevelt to see if the federal government would consider donating the building and property to the city. After all, it only cost $15,000 in 1873. Once in possession of the ancient structure, Portland would raise private funds to recondition the building for use by the Oregon Historical Society and the Colonial Dames. A small auditorium might also be added. He informed Martin that local architects had already agreed to furnish their services for nothing. Concluding with the statement that this was only a suggestion, Ainsworth wrote: "I feel confident in my own mind that you and Senator McNary by contacting the President at the opportune moment could put this over."[31]

Martin's response was rapid, diplomatic and clearly negative. "Have you no mercy upon my soul?" he asked. "Yours of the 13th puts us against the muzzle of a very big gun, heavily loaded." The former army general enjoyed using military metaphors, but he did not enjoy the prospect of seeing President Roosevelt over a matter of this sort. The President, he said, was concerned about broad national affairs. "An appeal like this just now . . . would seem to me like an imposition. We have just asked much of him [referring to the Bonneville Dam appropriation] and he has been kind to us." Such a request at this point might jeopardize future projects of greater need. Furthermore, asserted Martin, the Treasury Department would block such an action as illegal.[32] By law, the federal government could not donate a post office to a city.

Five days later, Ainsworth again wrote Martin, requesting that he disregard his letter of the 13th. He was now enamored of a new scheme, suggested by his fellow planning commissioner, architect Ellis Lawrence: To buy the old Post Office, demolish it and construct an eight-story office building which could still house the Oregon Historical Association in addition to such institutions as the Pioneer Association, the Boy Scouts, a museum and a small civic theater on the upper floors. The financing would be worked out by a complicated arrangement in which the NRA would accept a note to be repaid with interest from the building's revenues over a 30 year period. Ainsworth was quick to assert that in essence, the old building was not worth saving anyway because it was not fireproof.[33]

Once the word of this horrendous possibility leaked out, the local architectural

Aerial photo of downtown Portland in the early 1940s. The Post Office is tucked in between Meier & Frank and the Pacific Building. To its west are the Portland Hotel and the Jackson Tower. The Arlington Club can be seen at the head of the Park Blocks, and the Pacific Power & Light Building, right center, sporting a "Power Heat" neon sign.

fraternity erupted in smoke. Leading the opposition troops was the prominent A. E. Doyle firm which corralled the support of the Portland chapter of the American Institute of Architects. And right behind the A. I. A. were the loyal forces of the Colonial Dames who wanted to preserve the old Post Office at all costs. As Ainsworth's secretary wrote his boss: "This would block the improvement, plans for which were made by Lawrence & Holford."[34] Representative Martin also joined the opposition. With great delicacy, he informed his old friend Ainsworth that he "would prefer that the building be retained for historical and sentimental reasons."[35]

The matter simmered over the next 18 months until the powerful and prestigious Metropolitan Association under the leadership of the venerable William F. Woodward published a strong endorsement of preserving and restoring the pioneer structure. In support of Woodward were leading businessmen such as John W. Blodgett, Jr., Hamilton Corbett, Joseph Minott and T. B. Wilcox, Jr. *The Oregon Journal* blasted the suggestion of destroying the ancient shrine. "Sell the old post office block, and make it a parking station for automobiles? Sell it, and convert it into a block of skyscraping business buildings?"[36]

Not much further happened as the depression decade ran its course, but John Ainsworth did not give up his new found cause. The fact that the building was not fireproof seemed to concern him the most. "I am very much opposed to remodelling the present building," he wrote the chamber of commerce in July 1936. He had been informed by a government official that $900,000 was available in federal funds for a new combination office building and central post office. The government would give the city the top floor in an eight- or nine-story building for a civic theater and a home for the Oregon Historical Society. But Ainsworth had to admit one major obstacle to this grand plan. The government would not agree to such an arrangement if there was any strong local criticism "from our own citizens as to the destruction of the old Post Office Building."[37] And strong criticism there was. The historic structure was saved again.

The Highway Program

The Front Street and Barbur Boulevard projects consumed more public time and attention throughout the decade of the 1930s than other highway projects because neither was a designated part of either the state or federal highway networks. Both projects were going to require local bond proceeds to prime the federal pump. The recipient of the largest single award of federal and state funds was the connection between S. E. Union Avenue and the Oregon City highway, U. S. 99E. Planned as a "super-highway extension," and running alongside the Ross Island Sand & Gravel Company truck depot, McLoughlin Boulevard received a grand total of $1.45 million. S. E. 82nd, a designated state highway, received over $401,000. So rapidly did S. E. 82nd develop as a major north-south arterial that city council voted in August of 1937 to rezone the entire avenue for

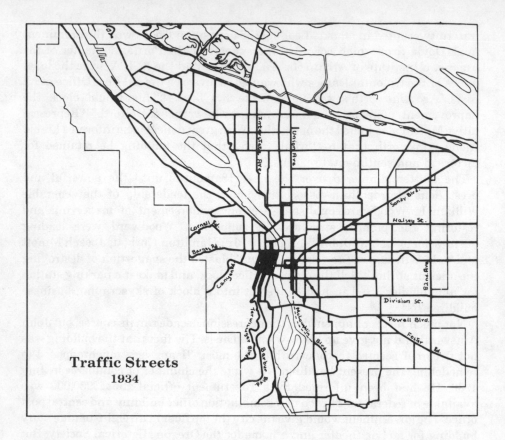

Traffic Streets
1934

commercial and industrial purposes, thus dooming the future of Montavilla as a residential neighborhood.

The rapidity of growth to the east and southeast worried downtown business and retail groups such as The Metropolitan Association. As the *Downtown Review* noted in April 1933:

> "Many west side property owners ... have become convinced that the development of a considerable population on and over the hills to the west is the only means of salvaging property values and preventing a 'slippage' of a considerable part of the retail section to the east side of the river."[38]

At the time, approximately 80 percent of the city's population resided on the East Side. "As population increases," noted the *Review*, "and extends farther and farther eastward, the traffic congestion at bridge heads and throughout the west side business district will become an increasingly greater handicap." The downtown business community believed that a "balancing of population" was a "prime necessity to the retention of the commercial supremacy of the west side."[39]

N. E. 82nd Avenue, looking south, in October 1932. The Halsey Street intersection is at the top of the rise.

The same view in May 1978, with Halsey Street overpass prominently in sight.

It was concerns of this sort that promoted a number of "improvements" designed to create access to west hills and west slope property. As the *Review* commented, "There are thousands and thousands of acres of the most desirable home-sites within many miles of this city, at ridiculously low prices."[40] Tunnels for N. W. Barnes and Cornell Roads were proposed to eliminate sections that were "too steep and tortuous for heavy traffic." Both were to be built ultimately, in the early 1940s, when the wartime related highway appropriations were sizeably increased by the federal government.

One project that never made it to completion, at least in the location earlier proposed, was a 7750 foot long tunnel from Marquam Gulch to the Bertha-Beaverton Highway. When originally publicized in January 1931, the Tualatin Tunnel, as it was called, stimulated much excitement and enthusiasm except for the East Side commercial and taxpayer groups who did not relish paying for a project that they felt could only cost them heavily. The internationally famous bridge engineer, Ralph Modjeski who had designed the Broadway Bridge, came to Portland and issued an optimistic report about the tunnel's feasibility. Modjeski estimated that 3.1 million motor vehicles would use the tunnel during the first year of its operation. To counter taxpayer objections, he proposed a 10-cent toll that would amortize 20 year construction bonds.[41] There was only one problem: Tolls could not be levied by the state highway commission without legislative approval. Several heroic efforts to gain such approval failed in the face of East Side opposition.

The Tualatin Tunnel proposal did stimulate other schemes, the most ambitious of which was a plan put together by local merchant Max Loeb and architect Ellis Lawrence. As envisaged, a memorial park would be built on the west hills above S. W. Broadway Drive, using the city-owned and undeveloped

Cornell Road Tunnel

510

A MEMORIAL PARK AND CIVIC CENTER
DEVELOPMENT AS PROPOSED BY MR. MAX LOEB
FOR THE HILL SOUTH OF THE PARK BLOCKS IN PORTLAND
MODEL MADE AND PRESENTED BY LAWRENCE·HOLFORD·ALLYN AND BEAN·ARCHITECTS
SCALE ONE INCH EQUALS ONE HUNDRED FEET   MODEL COMPLETED IN DECEMBER, 1938

Loeb Plan

Max Loeb and Ellis Lawrence conceived the notion of a memorial park to be built on the west hills above S. W. Broadway Drive in conjunction with the proposed Tualatin Tunnel. Neither the Tualatin Tunnel nor the memorial park came to pass.

Governor's Park as the nucleus. The Tualatin Tunnel was to be built in two sections, one running from the S. W. Park Blocks, near their current intersection with I-405, to the bottom of Marquam Gulch where it would surface and intersect with Sam Jackson Park Road before heading under the hills again for its terminus beyond Bertha. An elaborate stone and concrete bridge was proposed to connect the memorial park to Marquam Hill below the Medical School. The Marquam Ravine area, a portion of which has recently been purchased by the city and state park systems, was to be interlaced with roadways and walking paths. City council never took the plan seriously. It was too grandiose for Portland. And furthermore, the Portland Heights residents and real estate interests strongly opposed such an invasion by public facilities within their defended neighborhood. Such a large public development would also have removed some of the more expensive potentially developable real estate from the Portland tax rolls.

511

A related project that was taken far more seriously by business and governmental leaders was a proposed foothills diagonal boulevard that would have taken off from the southern extension of Front Avenue (Front Street was changed to Front Avenue in 1935), headed northwest in a curved pattern, and then north, bypassing closely the Multnomah Athletic Club stadium as it wound its way through the Northwest district to Linnton Road. During the course of several stormy city council sessions that ranged over five months, the bulk of the public testimony was strongly negative. Attorney R. R. Bullivant warned the council that Portland taxpayers were in revolt "against any further exactions, the largest part of which is paid by real estate." Attorney John F. Logan declared that the city was "cursed with taxes." He also contended that Portland did not need any more "booze boulevards for reckless drivers."[42] William F. Woodward, representing the Metropolitan Association, defended both the Foothills and Front Avenue projects, for the council was considering a new Front Avenue widening and extension proposal at the same time. Woodward noted that if Portland would assume the $3 million of right-of-way costs for both projects, $3.6 million would be released by the state highway department and the W. P. A. "Many men would go to work and much relief could be given while the city would get a real improvement."[43] Disregarding this argument, the council killed both projects on December 17, 1935.

One reason why the taxpayers were in a negative mood in 1935 was the growing feeling that the city had already breached a reasonable limit in its bonded indebtedness which the taxpayers were forced to amortize. The last successful highway bond election in November 1932 had added another $195,000 to the city's obligations and the taxpayers were beginning to feel the financial pinch. The fact that the Barbur Boulevard bond proceeds generated over $900,000 in state and federal funds, $800,000 of which were derived from emergency relief allocations, did not seem to assuage many feelings.

A quaint Dutch type "village" on Terwilliger Boulevard near Bertha, the kind of country atmosphere that many residents hoped to preserve before Barbur Boulevard was opened.

Sketch of an "ideal development," at the intersection of Barbur and Terwilliger Boulevards, prepared by the Pacific Northwest Regional Planning Commission in 1934. Barbur runs east-west. The downzoning began at the eastern edge of the intersection. Future developments bore no resemblance to the plan.

The Barbur Boulevard project created some additional foes of further highway development when the city planning commission voted on October 24, 1934, to downzone 635 acres along the right-of-way from the Terwilliger crossing to S. W. Hamilton Street. Not only was the area rezoned from business to residential use, but billboards were also to be excluded. Many of the property owners vigorously protested. They claimed that they had been looking forward to selling their holdings for future business sites at increased commercial prices. After the city council upheld the planning commission action, supporting commission president professor Charles McKinley of Reed College, several disgruntled property owners filed suit in the county circuit court. In a landmark decision (the case of *Corbett v. Carson*), Judge Hall Lusk ruled in favor of the city. "In its best sense," Lusk declared, "zoning looks backward to protect and forward to compatible developments in accordance with a comprehensive plan, . . . having as its basis the welfare of the city as a whole."[44]

Front Avenue Revisited

Between the summer of 1935 and May of 1940 when Portland voters finally passed a bond issue to improve Front Avenue and the adjacent waterfront, official thinking and planning ranged back and forth over one central problem:

513

Downtown Portland — 1936 — Note the Public Market Building

How best to accommodate both the need for park facilities and the need for traffic facilities in one narrow strip of land, 280 feet in width, from the seawall to the west curb of Front Avenue.

In August of 1935, the planning commission's streets committee approved the plan that was ultimately chosen: To build a trafficway along the harbor wall with underpasses at all bridges, but only on the condition that all property between Front Avenue and the river, from Glisan to Columbia, with the exception of the Public Market property, be acquired by the city. Gradually, the commission and the state highway department came to accept the notion that Front Avenue, although needing to be widened by at least 20 feet, should serve only as a feeder or a service street. Harbor Drive, as the new trafficway would be called, would provide a six-lane express highway with connections to Barbur Boulevard, and to the Ross Island, Hawthorne, Morrison and Steel Bridges, all of which would receive new ramps on the West Side. A narrow strip of park land would be developed between Front Avenue and Harbor Drive and an esplanade would be built along the top of the seawall.

By May of 1940, when the bond measure was being prepared, the total cost of the project was estimated at $4.05 million, of which $2.8 million was to be provided by the state highway commission. The Portland voters were being asked to pay the balance, $1.25 million.[45] The Metropolitan Association, which strongly supported the proposal, noted a marked change in the posture of the highway commission toward Portland's needs. When the Metropolitan Association had met with the Front Avenue property owners in August of 1938, William F. Woodward had revealed that in the 20 years of its existence, the highway commission had received over $70 million from Multnomah County

514

Downtown Portland in 1971. Note the Foothills Freeway (I-405) and the Harbor Drive crossover. Also note that 20 percent of the land area was in parking. Far more than Front Avenue had been "cleaned up."

residents in license fees and gasoline taxes, whereas it had only spent $14 million within the city. He credited state highway engineer R. H. Baldock and commission chairman Henry F. Cabell for the change in state attitude that portended well for the future of the Front Avenue project. What was not generally known, however, was that the Failing estate had been one of the original investors in the Public Market Building and Henry F. Cabell managed the estate of his grandfather. Cabell had a personal interest in the future welfare of Front Avenue.

Despite some criticism of the Harbor Drive installation as both an impediment to waterfront access and an unfortunate restriction of park space, the City Club and most other civic groups endorsed the whole project. The voters overwhelmingly registered their approval, 65,000 to 35,000. Times had changed. The local economy was on the mend and the future was viewed more optimistically. Furthermore, all of the advocates, including the top leadership of business and government, had done their homework. Of course, no one could imagine in 1940 that Harbor Drive would be removed 30 years later, after the completion of the Marquam Bridge and both the Foothills and East Bank Freeways which provided readier access to the downtown.

After the bond issue passed, several months of delay were encountered due to the refusal of the SP&S Railroad to remove its United Railways track from Front Avenue. As the Metropolitan Association's Executive Secretary U. L. Upson informed *The Oregon Journal*, "The United Railways (SP&S) is endeavoring to put selfish interests ahead of the public welfare." Mayor Harry Lane had predicted 33 years earlier that the railroad might act in this fashion when faced

S. W. Front Avenue, looking south from the Burnside Bridge ramp, with the United Railways tracks running down the middle. The prominent Dodd block (1888), left center, was demolished in 1942. (1940)

S. W. Front Avenue, between Morrison and Alder Streets. December 27, 1941.

The Barnhart and Miles Building (1857) on Front Avenue, corner of Pine St. A parking lot today. The ornate corner on the left belonged to the Starr block (1882), one of Portland's most famous pioneer buildings, demolished in 1942.

North waterfront in the 1930s, the future site of Harbor Drive. Front Avenue on the right. The large central building was the famous Allen and Lewis block (1892), demolished in 1942.

517

by changing public needs. His veto of the original United Railways franchise had been overridden by the city council. As Upson noted:

> "For a great number of years they have occupied Front Avenue with their tracks, purely on sufferance. Now they are endeavoring to make such use, by sufferance, a vested right. . . . It would seem that, in view of the favors and concessions which the railroads have received and are receiving from the city, they should be willing, in the public interest, to work out a perfectly simple solution of this problem. If not willing, they should be made to do so."[46]

And they **were** made to do so!

By the summer of 1942, most of the project was completed between S. W. Sheridan and Ankeny Streets. By the end of June, the last of the old buildings on Front Avenue had been removed, including many of the familiar landmarks of pioneer Portland.[47] A total of 79 buildings and houses were razed to make room just for Harbor Drive.[48] On November 20, 1942, a colorful parade was held on Front Avenue and Harbor Drive was dedicated with a ceremony at the site of the historic battleship *U. S. S. Oregon*. Attended by the governor, mayor and county commissioners, the dedication was also a memorial to two recently departed members of the Metropolitan Association who had worked for years bringing the project to fruition: William F. Woodward and U. L. Upson.

1944

Chapter 17

Urban Attitudes and the Quality of Life in the 1930s

Ever since the Lewis and Clark Exposition of 1905, Portland's business and community leaders had been engaged in an ancient controversy — one that in fact hearkened back to the days of Aristotle — over whether the city should grow rapidly or slowly. Although the slow-growth, cautious approach usually prevailed in Portland, the American economic system became increasingly geared to a concept of progress through growth that was premised on an expanding population and an unlimited energy supply. The debates generally confined themselves to the question of growth rate and the kinds of control, if any, that should be exercised over such developments.

How to Grow?

Almost from the time of its founding, Portland, like the nation as a whole, had planned its future on the assumption that physical growth would continue to be the major consideration in determining the city's quality of life. Writing in *The Portland Bulletin* in January 1931, attorney L. M. Lepper predicted that Portland would become one of America's greatest cities. It ranked sixth as a shipping port and 18th as a commercial city. It stood first in lumber, wheat, wool and apples and fourth in flour exports among all the ports of the United States.

> "Do you see what I see? The Greater City or the Greater Portland? Can we not now vision the time 30 or 40 years from now, when the Greater Portland will be a thickly settled Greater City, like New York, Detroit or Los Angeles. Settled solidly from Oregon City and South, up the Clackamas to Sandy and down the Sandy River to Troutdale, and up the Columbia River Highway to . . . Corbett. When we will have not one, but a number of Tunnels through the West Side crests or foothills into the rich Tualatin . . . valley."[1]

Loren Lepper was representative of an important segment in American society — the doers or boosters as they were often called. A Hoosier by birth, Lepper had taken his law degree at the University of Michigan and had worked in construction supervisory jobs with the Great Northern Railway. He came to Portland in 1910 to practice law, a pursuit that brought him wide success. A strong Republican, he was active in various community organizations of which he usually became president: The Multnomah County Federation of Community Clubs, the East Side Commercial Club and the Presidents Council. Although

519

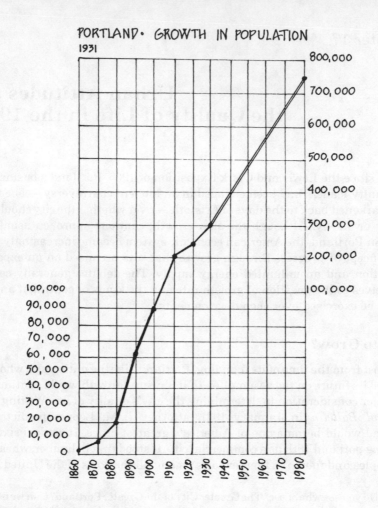

PORTLAND· GROWTH IN POPULATION

1931

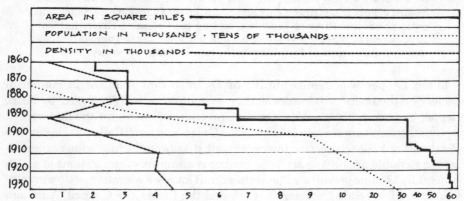

PORTLAND· GROWTH IN AREA ·1931·

AREA IN SQUARE MILES

POPULATION IN THOUSANDS · TENS OF THOUSANDS

DENSITY IN THOUSANDS

Lepper's assertions about Portland's glorious future may seem far-fetched today, he was expressing both a feeling and a faith that were widely held in the West throughout much of its history, even by entrepreneurs in sleepy Portland. As Lepper stated the basic assumptions of the case:

"The Almighty has made the climate, the resources, the water-grade haul, the mountains, with a thousand lakes, and with a hundred rivers, with 28 percent of the unharnessed water power of the nation, rushing seaward, on two of the earth's finest rivers, passing our very doors to the world's markets. What has not God given to us? We are in the favored spot of earth — Just in the making. The Almighty and nature have surely done their part. It is now up to man — it is up to us to take advantage of it and wake up! and do the rest, and make of Portland and vicinity the greatest city and metropolitan area on earth! Question — Will we measure up to the job?"[2]

The Portland Chamber of Commerce was posing similar questions in 1935 when it created a Committee on Urban Land Utilization. A relatively new element was injected into the chamber's thinking, however, and that was the need for a master plan to guide the potential growth. The United States Chamber of Commerce had officially sanctioned a revived interest in city planning at a meeting in August of 1934. Planning was now becoming an accepted profession, but one that needed guidance and direction from the business community.

In a report issued in September 1935, the chamber's urban land committee framed four indictments:

(1) "From a lack of proper planning, especially of her transportation facilities, Portland has lost 412,000 population, in comparison with the growth of competing Pacific ports.

(2) "From lack of proper planning, Portland, to meet demands of land speculators, has over-improved and expanded at a heavy cost to taxpayers and utility companies.

(3) "From lack of proper planning, Portland, by loss of business and improper zoning regulations, is steadily being undermined in her tax structure.

(4) "From lack of proper planning, Portland has allowed blighted areas to develop which depreciate property values, lower civic pride, and become menaces to health and safety."[3]

Implicit in these charges were some of the same conclusions reached in the Bartholomew Report. Portland was vastly over-improved, not with structures, but with streets, sewers, water and other utilities. The cost to the taxpayers had been exorbitant. In terms of size, Portland **could** accommodate a three or fourfold increase in population. Since 1914, by allowing overspread into the city's outer reaches, a condition that furthered the development of blight in the older districts along the river, Portland had lost $47 million in reduced land valuation. On the West Side waterfront alone, Bartholomew had figured that blighted conditions were costing $275,000 a year in decreased tax revenues.

Taking an implied swipe at the real estate interests which had encouraged overspread, the committee did not, however, conclude that Portland was "a dying organism."

> "We believe Portland, while very sick, has inherent vitality to weather the attack of what is called by some — the Willamette Hook-worm. It is a question of whether or no the people of Portland will take a proper course of medicine. . . . An excellent tonic . . . would be the joining together in common cause of preparing worthily for the God-given advantages of our city and Bonneville."[4]

Ralph B. Lloyd had evinced similar feelings when he declared to *The Oregonian* in May 1933: "If Portland does not succeed, then there is no hope for the rest of the country." Over the next four years, Lloyd was to express similar thoughts. He never could fathom an attitude of mind that he encountered in Portland. He ascribed this phenomenon to a sense of inferiority or a feeling of insecurity.

The chamber committee was concerned that nothing had happened since the Bartholomew Report was published. Sewage and water pollution problems were critical, to cite one example. Another related to the placement of industrial sites. The southwest industrial area along the river should be moved to Guild's Lake and Mock's Bottom, or to the lowlands north of St. Johns. Immediate action by the city council was mandatory. "Uncontrolled and unplanned development sooner or later spells financial ruin to any city."[5]

Prominent residential architect Jamieson Parker wrote chamber manager Walter W. R. May in the spring of 1935 that Portland needed to sell itself by starting "an advanced merchandising policy." But first the product needed to be redesigned. "Our present efforts to 'sell' Portland are handicapped in much the same way as an attempt to sell a fine 1935 automobile chassis equipped with 1895 conveniences." As Parker stated his case:

> "Portland has an attractive location, but it is an ugly city. Anybody questioning this should state his standards. . . . [It] has a frightfully serious handicap in its plan of small blocks, and alleys in place of streets. The full magnitude of these unpleasant facts must be realized before systematic progress can begin."[6]

The most astute analysis of the state of urban planning in Portland came from the pen of David Eccles, editor of the *Business Survey*, published by Commonwealth, Inc., in May 1936. Excerpts from this perceptive article are worth quoting:

> "The city of Portland is a graphic illustration of the 19th century's myopic vision, a myopia which has extended to the present day. It proves, if nothing else, that irrational civic enthusiasm is more greatly to be feared than healthy skepticism."[7]

Existing Land Uses — Portland, Oregon — Year 1933

Land Use	Area in Acres	Percent of Total City Area	Percent of Developed Area*
Streets	9,275	21.3	37.1
Parks	1,177	2.7	4.7
Public	913	2.1	3.7
Semi-Public	721	1.6	2.9
1-Family Dwellings	8,879	20.4	35.5
2-Family Dwellings	218	0.5	0.9
Multiple Dwellings (Apartments)	311	0.7	1.3
Commercial (Retail)	844	2.0	3.4
Light Industrial	434	1.0	1.7
Heavy Industrial	978	2.3	3.9
Railroad Property	1,226	2.8	4.9
Total Developed Area	24,976	57.4	100%
Vacant Land	16,164	37.1	
Water Area	2,383	5.5	
Total Corporate Area	43,523	100%	

The blanket zoning of 50 percent of the city for apartment use penalized home owners in many cases. It jeopardized the issuance of FHA home mortgages and it encouraged the deterioration of older homes and mixed neighborhoods in general.

Analysis of the existing zoning ordinance revealed that only 14.2% of the total area of the city was reserved for 1-family dwellings, whereas over 20% of the city was being used for that purpose. The ordinance also permitted apartments to be built in 35.5% of the area of the city, whereas less than 1% of the city's land was being used for that purpose.

Population Migration Data[8]

For the years 1929-1940: Net immigration to the four Northwest states amounted to 500,000, of which Washington received 200,000 and Oregon 175,000.

> **1935-1937**
> Period of heaviest
> migration to Oregon

Areas of origin:

North Great Plains:	34%	
South Great Plains:	19%	**25% farmers**
North Central U. S.	14%	**10% farm laborers**
California:	14%	
Utah, Ariz., Nev.:	5%	
The rest:	9%	

Not wishing to belittle the spirits of people like Lepper, Lloyd or even Parker, Eccles focused on the heart of the problem. Obviously Portland must grow and more space will be needed, Eccles declared, but attention should be directed primarily at the vacant lots and undeveloped areas within the city limits that comprised 37 percent of the total area.

> "For many years, the trend has been toward outer fringes and suburban satellites. Meanwhile land is left vacant nearer the axis and older developed areas are allowed to deteriorate while the periphery expands and develops."[9]

In a statement that is even more relevant today than it was in 1936, Eccles asserted:

> "The problem for city planners, property owners and real estate developers today is that of determining the sort of city we are to have in the future, readjusting their attitude toward real estate accordingly. This certainly will lead them to abandon the notion that urban real estate need only be purchased and held against the day when values will increase through sheer force of population growth."[10]

Eccles warned his readers not to expect Oregon's population to grow at the rate predicted by people like Lepper. He acknowledged the optimists' claim that Portland "is a young vigorous city, about to get cheap power, possessing a fine climate and tremendous natural advantages."[11] But Oregon also had one of the lowest birth rates in the nation. To grow, Portland was going to have to depend on immigration from other parts of the country. To provide jobs, new industries would need to be built. And this eventuality sounded a warning to Eccles: New industries were showing a preference for suburbs over metropolitan centers.

"In any case," asked Eccles, "is bigness the vital consideration? It often has been in the past. Cities have placed emphasis on size rather than on standards of living or culture."[12] Assuming that the level of past growth could not continue,

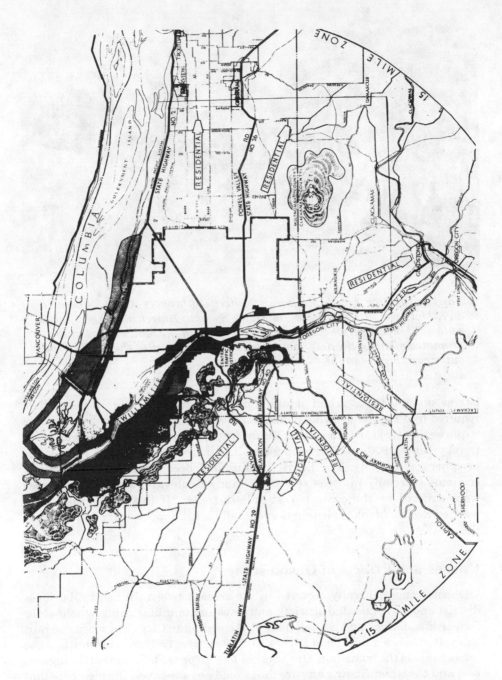

Projected residential growth patterns
1936

Thirty of realtor Frank McGuire's 90 licensed brokers. Open 24 hours a day, McGuire advertised his "McGuire System: America's largest home sellers."[13] McGuire, who was elected president of the realty board in 1925, promoted many of the new home sales in the periphery of the city. Spread-out meant profits to the "McGuire System."

Eccles suggested that urban planning must turn from "coping with essentials required by a rapidly growing population to problems of living standards. This requires that we know more about the future population . . . "[14] and its mobility trends. Since 1920, new developments had increasingly tended to seek the periphery of the city. The heaviest gains had been made in the northeast sections, especially in areas served by Sandy Boulevard. The greatest losses were suffered by the central West Side districts. "If this trend continues," warned Eccles, "deplorable things eventually must happen to land throughout the city."[15]

Causes and Effects of Obsolescence

Obsolescence generally occurred in the areas between the central business district and the residential districts, and between a manufacturing, wholesale or forwarding district and a retail district. According to City Commissioner Earl Riley, Portland's mayor from 1941 to 1949, there were two forces at work in these areas to effect the transition. One was holding up prices to a plane of the highest use, and the other, finding any use that would pay the taxes. Obsolescence that usually led to blight in commercial districts and to slums in residential districts followed the introduction of incompatible uses. It chief cause, according to

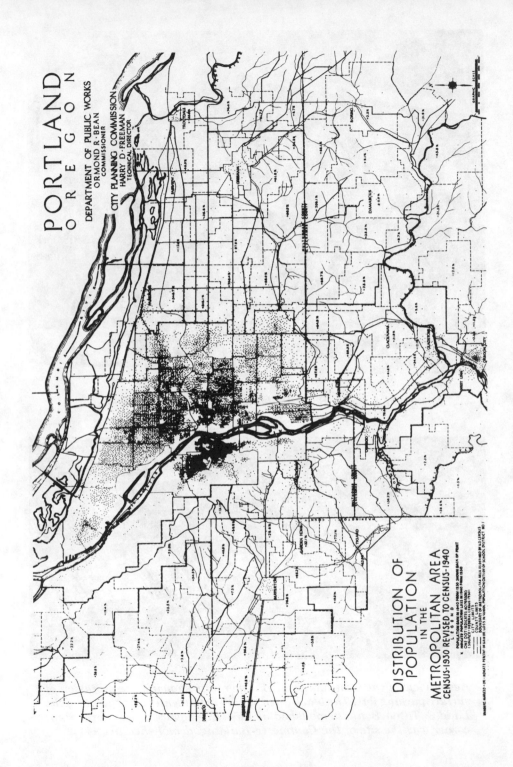

PORTLAND
O R E G O N

DEPARTMENT OF PUBLIC WORKS
ORMOND R. BEAN
COMMISSIONER

CITY PLANNING COMMISSION
HARRY D. FREEMAN
TECHNICAL DIRECTOR

DISTRIBUTION OF
POPULATION
IN THE
METROPOLITAN AREA
CENSUS-1930 REVISED TO CENSUS-1940

Ladd & Tilton Bank Building (1868) in the late 1930s.

Aerial view of the west Morrison Bridge ramp, showing the profusion of surface parking lots. The black lined square in the center was the site of the Ladd & Tilton Bank, demolished in 1954. The square in the upper right corner was the site of the Commerce Building, demolished in 1934.

Fortune, was "unregulated urban expansion,"[16] or as Riley called it, "the running-down and building-out process."[17] Riley put much of the blame on the tax system — the overreliance on property taxes, a traditional practice that was an outgrowth of an agrarian society. In a district of declining values, a downward adjustment in taxes always lagged several years behind. In the interim, the property owners' revenues declined and the building became unprofitable to operate. Poor maintenance, bordering on neglect, merely hastened the process of obsolescence. There were no tax incentives to restore old buildings.

In a 30 block district, from Fourth to Front, and Burnside to Taylor, where the access to the automobile was limited and congestion was tight, many of the well known pioneer buildings were in a state of near or actual abandonment, most of them having been converted to warehouses. What was the solution? According to realtor Chester A. Moores: "If older buildings that are losing money were torn down and new ground areas made available for parking space, the remaining office buildings would reap . . . advantage."[18] It was purely a matter of economics. And in commissioner Riley's case, it was also a matter of fire prevention. Over 1900 old buildings had been demolished since 1933. In the 20 year period from 1934 to 1954, two-thirds of the buildings in the 30 block section of the pioneer business district were torn down and replaced by either surface parking lots or parking garages. The Front Avenue-Harbor Drive project of the early 1940s and the new Morrison Bridge construction of the early 1950s forced and encouraged the removal of the largest percentage of these structures.

The first, and possibly the finest, of the 19th century buildings to face the wrecking ball was the Commerce Building. When it had been opened by George Markle in 1893 as The Chamber of Commerce Building, it had been advertised as the outstanding office structure in the Pacific Northwest. Over the years, it suffered a number of financial vicissitudes and ended up in the possession of the SP&S Railroad which made its headquarters there until 1933 before moving its local office to the American Bank Building. Located on S. W. Stark, between Third and Fourth Avenues, the Commerce Building was considered "a white elephant" by the SP&S. As one of its officials reported: "The interior is so old-fashioned it will not even maintain the taxes and upkeep. To make the building usable, we should literally have to gut it. That is entirely too expensive a program. We have no choice but to remove it." Following a course of action to be advocated five years later by Chester Moores, the building was demolished in January 1934 and replaced by an ugly surface parking lot which still survives. The absentee-owned railroad that refused to remove its Front Avenue tracks showed little reluctance to remove an historical landmark. Again, it was a matter of economics. *The Oregon Journal* raised one of the few public outcries against the fatal action:

> "The forward course of progress pays no heed to values of a sentimental nature. The fact the building is rich in history is of no consequence. That the

529

building has tenanted a great many of our state leaders who have gained national prominence is of no import. Nor are we concerned with the almost human personality of the building. Were it standing in a European city, it would probably be kept and used for 50 or 100 more years; but to impatient America, it is merely a symbol of a former era and is standing in the path of the juggernaut, Progress."[19]

The attitudes and thinking that encouraged "the juggernaut, Progress" continued unabated until the mid-1950s. New York city planner Robert Moses gave it further momentum in 1943 when his famous, and expensive, report even recommended the destruction of the Union Station as an obsolete facility. Moses was the father of the wide, sweeping bridge ramps that were designed to funnel thousands of automobiles into central business districts. Old buildings were deemed impediments to the realization of such dreams, a prime example being the Ladd & Tilton Bank on the southwest corner of First and Stark.

In the words of William J. Hawkins III, an authority on cast-iron architecture, "Few buildings more fully captured the essence of the cast-iron era in Portland than the richly decorated Ladd & Tilton Bank, built in 1868."[20] Long abandoned by the famous bank, in the late 1930s it had become the outlet for the Oregon Leather Company. In 1954, when extra parking spaces were deemed necessary to accommodate the flood of cars that would use the new Morrison Bridge, the building was condemned and destroyed, although many of the cast-iron fixtures were removed and saved. Today, the site is still an ugly surface parking lot providing cheap all day rates for early bird commuters.

Housing Blight

As *Fortune* magazine clearly documented the national case as early as June of 1932, the most severe "problem of the Blighted Area is ... squarely ... a problem of housing."[21] But its solution did not lie solely with private enterprise or private capital as long as the causes of the disease were not eradicated. Urban expansion, inadequate zoning, lax housing codes and generally faulty planning were primarily public matters requiring governmental action.

In addition to these factors, however, was a far more basic question that every city faced: Did government have a responsibility to see that the poorest classes of society were provided minimally decent housing at affordable rates? For over 20 years, the Portland answer had been negative. Portland's community leaders traditionally felt that individual initiative and private enterprise should be able to meet the city's housing needs without government "interference," which in their thinking implied a form of competition that was threatening to the private market. The Portland realty and apartment interests not only opposed municipal housing authorities as "socialistic" but denied that subhuman living conditions and slums even existed.

A Portland real property inventory made by the U. S. Department of Commerce in 1934 revealed that there were 6000 people living in 1372 dwellings which were unfit for human habitation. The inventory also showed that nearly 40 percent of Portland families in 1934 were paying $15 or less per month for rent, with many of the places unfit for human use. As city commissioner Ralph Clyde commented: "It may be argued that Portland is a city of low rents, but the true measure of the situation is 'What kind of housing is obtained by some of our low income families for the rent they pay?' "[22] In 1936, nearly 30 percent of Portland's reported annual incomes were below $1000.

The housing authority issue surfaced in 1938 because Oregon had been the first West Coast state to adopt enabling legislation to take advantage of the United States Housing Act of 1937. The 1937 Oregon law stated that there was a need for public support of housing for low income groups; that a substantial shortage of adequate dwellings for low income workers existed; that public funds should be made available for clearance and replanning of unsanitary and unsafe housing conditions; and that poor housing conditions constituted a menace to the health, safety and morals of the residents of Oregon.[23]

Throughout the early months of 1938, the city council debated what action it should take. Under the terms of both the federal and state laws, the council was empowered to create a housing authority with its members to be named by the mayor. Once the authority was established, it was to have full power to plan, finance, construct and operate municipal housing units. Congress initially

S. W. Slum Housing
Note the two-story outhouse.

531

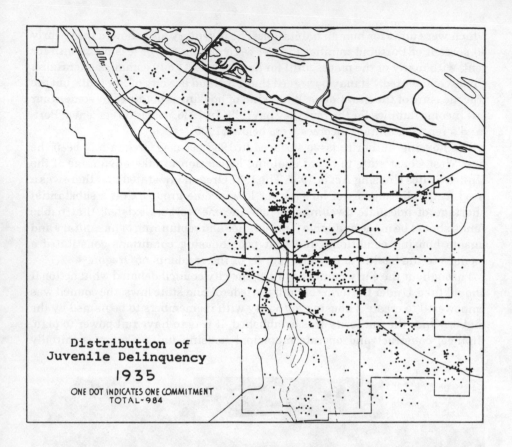

Distribution of Juvenile Delinquency 1935

ONE DOT INDICATES ONE COMMITMENT
TOTAL-984

appropriated $500 million for low rent housing and added an additional $300 million in 1938. The money was available in Washington, awaiting the city's decision. By June of 1938, Oakland, Los Angeles and San Francisco had already created housing authorities and been granted a total of $25 million for low rent housing programs on a 90-10 matching basis.

Under heavy pressure from realty and apartment interests, Portland's city council shied away from accepting its legal responsibility and voted, instead, to refer the decision to the people in the November 1938 election. Commissioners Clyde and Bean who strongly favored a housing authority were outvoted by Mayor Carson and Commissioners Riley and Bennett, the latter calling the proposal "communistic." The stage was thus set for a bitter and costly public debate, in which rational analysis gave way to emotional slogans.

Commissioner Ormond Bean, who no one of right mind could label a socialist, admitted publicly that his position had radically changed since he had personally visited substandard housing sites in the city. Not only were such structures of subhuman quality, but they were expensive for the city to service with fire protection. In fact, many of them were in such bad shape that they were deemed too risky to insure.[24] The costs of police protection were also exorbitant,

N. W. 19th Avenue and Thurman Street

Tenements in South Portland served by unpaved alleys

Garbage in the hallway of an apartment on S. E. Grand Avenue

with crime and juvenile delinquency rife in such areas. The 1935 map, showing the distribution of juvenile delinquency, revealed a higher than average correlation of commitment density with those districts containing the most units of substandard housing: Albina, close-in Southeast Portland and South Portland.

Reed College's professor Jesse Short joined commissioners Clyde and Bean in strongly advocating public approval of the housing authority ordinance. Miss Short conducted tours of the worst areas for those who were interested in first hand observation. At one location on S. W. 11th, she pointed out four apartments half-way below ground level, with no visible windows. Although constructed illegally and ordered to close, they had been occupied for some time because the city's one inspector was too busy to enforce the order. With 3000 units to supervise, most of his time was spent on complaints, very little on inspection tours. Miss Short noted that the owner of the four illegal apartments was the first man to announce at a city hall hearing that the apartment owners would oppose the measure "because a housing project would ruin their business."

As Miss Short was to comment, conditions had not improved since she first started such tours 20 years earlier. And the fact that the city had demolished 4000 residential units since 1928, under pressure from the fire marshal, merely tightened up the remaining supply of cheap housing. It was unprofitable for the private market to build new housing, or even to convert old housing, for the lowest income families. The city owned hundreds of vacant lots acquired through tax delinquencies. Many of them could well be used as sites for new low cost housing projects.

At a meeting of the city council on September 11, 1938, Jesse Short challenged one of Portland's leading realtors, Allison Dean. Citing a recent *Oregonian* ad, Dean had told the council that there was an abundant supply of low rental housing in Portland: 82 dwelling units were listed for rentals of $15 or less. Investigating each of the listings, Miss Short found nearly half of the units priced above $15, and at least one-fourth of them located in the most undesirable and blighted sections of the city, with unsanitary accommodations even to animals.[25]

Miss Short, who was not alone in being cited by the police department's Red Squad in 1938 as "a communist and dangerous radical," was one of a small but growing number of knowledgeable people who raised the basic question: "Why must we have blighted areas?" In a written report delivered at a public gathering she declared:

"At this time we are forced to recognize that many of the old theories about individualism and liberty to do what one likes with one's own, are unsound. Liberty may be an evil as well as a good thing, and it is an evil thing when it results in social injustice. If the liberty I have, to do with my own what I like, injures my neighbor and interferes with his liberty, then the city and the state should come in to prevent me from carrying out what is an unsocial or unjust operation. In the past we have placed too much emphasis on the sacredness of property and too little emphasis on the sacredness of life.... Planning commissions ... have been so occupied with street widening and traffic problems that housing has received little attention."[26]

Such plaints were dismissed by Portland's conservative establishment as the wails of "sociological-minded folk." Included in this group by the *Oregon Voter* were "some women's organizations, ... property-less New Dealers, ... and persons ... of socialistic slant." Against the housing authority measure, the *Voter* proudly listed "a great majority of realtors, mortgage men, apartment house and flat owners, worried owners of modest houses and a preponderance of business men."[27] Needless to say, the measure was soundly defeated. Only after the declaration of war in December 1941, when public war housing was required by the federal government for any city desiring lucrative war shipyard contracts, did Portland voters approve the establishment of a Portland Housing Authority. And its second chairman, ironically, was former Realty Board president Chester A. Moores, one of the leading opponents of the 1938 housing measure.

As a footnote to the 1938 defeat, a blunder for which Mayor Carson and his two commissioner colleagues only had themselves to blame, an article in *The Oregon Journal* of February 1939 carried the heading: "Slum Squalor Shocks

"Temporary" housing under N. E. Grand Avenue
Sullivan's Gulch — 1930s

535

Council." Apparently commissioner Bean had taken Carson and commissioner Riley on a tour of some severely blighted housing. They were shown rooms with little if any ventilation, kitchens with woodstoves but no water, buildings with 30 or more residents using one toilet, families living in 20 foot square confinement, and garbage piled high on fire escapes.[28] These units were cheap enough, ranging in rate from $4 to $12 a month and all of the residents were on relief. Such conditions of course were figments of the imagination to the *Oregon Voter*; they simply did not exist. As the *Voter* had concluded in October 1938: "Craving advances toward Utopia equally with our most revered idealists, [we] recommend voting against creation of the housing authority."[29]

Quality of Life for Minorities

During the 1930s in Portland, the quality of life for minorities, particularly Negroes, was even worse than it was for poor whites. If one happened to be both black and poor, little hope for improvement could be expected in the face of myriad legal, social and economic obstacles.

Historically, in Oregon and most other states, non-white minorities had been treated as second class citizens. The small size of their resident populations was an important factor in establishing a tradition that simply excluded them from the mainstream of employment opportunities. As one former longshoreman noted, it was possible to live in Portland prior to 1941 and be unaware of the existence of Negroes[30] who comprised only 0.6 percent of the population in 1940. The majority of Negroes worked for the railroads, with the remainder in positions of janitors, mail clerks, porters, waiters and household help. None worked on the waterfront, a condition that was as much the fault of management as of organized labor. In fact, Portland was the only major port on the Pacific Coast that had no Negro longshoremen.

In 1937, Kathryn Bogle wrote an article for *The Oregonian* in which she described her early experience in search of a job upon graduation from high school.

> "I started out buoyant and fresh with the dream of finding an employer without prejudice. I opened each new door with a hope that was loath to leave me. I visited large and small stores of all descriptions. I visited the telephone company; both light and power companies. I tried to become an elevator operator in an office building. I answered ads for inexperienced office help. In all these places where vacancies occurred, I was told there was nothing about me in my disfavor — except the color of my skin."[31]

Mrs. Bogle then described how several employers who refused her jobs in downtown Portland offered her employment as a domestic in their homes where her color would not be an embarrassment. "My employer [would] not be criticized if I were employed in his home in contact with his nearest and dearest!"[32]

Considering nursing as a career, Mrs. Bogle discovered that no Portland hospital would accept the application of a Negro woman for nurse's training. She also learned that there were no Negroes holding state jobs and only one with the city in a clerical capacity. She finally accepted a position as a domestic helper. After three weeks of working non-stop from 6:30 a.m. to 10:30 p.m. she quit in a state of exhaustion. She ultimately received a job in the dispensary of one of the larger department stores.

Experiences of this sort led her to wonder about the opportunities for American-born Negroes as opposed to foreign-born whites, of which Portland had a goodly number. "Anyone coming here from foreign shores can exercise all his rights as an American citizen as soon as he is naturalized."[33] But a Negro whose family may have lived in America for 150 years was barred from enjoying these same rights by virtue of her black skin.

In March of 1938, past chamber president Hamilton Corbett, the younger brother of State Senator Henry L. Corbett, received a thoughtful letter from Juanita Johnson, a black Portland resident. She informed Corbett that it would be to the advantage of both the city and the chamber if his organization would employ a Negro "to make surveys, gather data and keep it accurate concerning the Negro Community in Portland. It is unfair and almost impossible to expect a member of another race to really keep a finger on the civic pulse of another race for any length of time."[34]

What prompted Miss Johnson's action was an investigation that she had initiated after phoning the chamber's travel and advertising office in quest of current information on hotels serving Negroes. She was given the name of the Medley Hotel and of some "Japanese hotels along Burnside." This response sparked her curiosity.

"Having been a resident of Portland for more than ten years, I do not believe Burnside Street would attract a very fine class of people. The Medley Hotel is often filled. Besides we do not like to feel there is only one decent hotel accommodating Negroes. Upon inquiry, I found several better grade hotels that may be added to the list we might offer to Negro guests of Portland."

Miss Johnson cited the cases of several prospective residents "from the better class Negroes" who had cut short their vacations in Portland "because of embarrassment and inconvenience caused by lack of up-to-date and complete information regarding hotels, restaurants, beauty parlors, etc., available for Negro patrons." Miss Johnson also cited the fact that the chamber had given her the name of the Negro newspaper, *The Advocate*, and of its editor Mrs. Cannady Franklin. The chamber was unaware that *The Advocate* had ceased publication in 1935 and that Mrs. Franklin had moved to Los Angeles.

The chamber's reply, by assistant manager Arthur J. Farmer, was polite, diplomatic but negative. Having recently reduced its staff by several people, the chamber was in no position to offer Miss Johnson a job despite the "meritorious" nature of her proposal. If she desired to discuss the matter further, Farmer in-

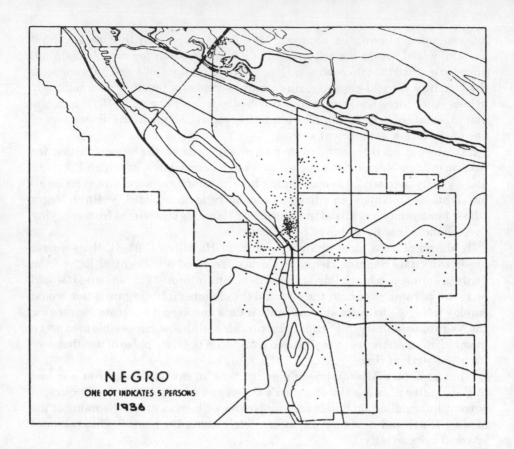

NEGRO
ONE DOT INDICATES 5 PERSONS
1936

dicated that he would be glad to have her call upon him at her convenience.[35]

The fact that Negroes, and other non-white minorities, felt obliged to inquire in advance about what public accommodations would serve them was humanly degrading to say the least. Implied in such a "system" was a deeply held conviction, rooted in American history, that non-Caucasians were inferior people. Attitudes of this kind were revealed each time the Oregon State Legislature was faced with a public accommodations bill that would outlaw discrimination because of race, creed or color. At least one such bill was introduced at every session from 1933 to 1953, and on each occasion except the last, the measure was either buried in committee or defeated on the floor. The major opponents were in the Oregon Hotel Association and the Association of Oregon Apartment House Owners. Mixing races, they told the legislators, was "bad business."[36] Irrational fears and mercenary considerations prevailed.

Apart from ingrained racial prejudices, economic factors also dominated the minority housing market. Although many of the prestigious residential developments had racial exclusion clauses written into their original sales contracts, the Realty Board's professional ethics canon pretty much determined

538

minority housing practices in later years. Realty Board members knew that they could be expelled if they willingly encouraged a minority family to assume residence in a Caucasian neighborhood or apartment complex. The maps indicating foreign-born and racial occupancy clearly revealed the established patterns. It was obvious that foreign-born whites encountered little difficulty in seeking homes of their choice; they were spread pretty evenly throughout the city except for the more densely populated districts west of the river.

The Realty Board did not publicize its racial exclusion policy until 1945. But a copy of a text manual, used by realtors in an evening extension course for apprentice brokers, quoted a statement made in 1939 by Portland realtor Chester A. Moores, a vice president of Commonwealth, Inc. Said Moores:

"We were discussing at the Realty Board recently the advisability of setting up certain districts for Negroes and orientals. We talked about the possibility

Dr. DeNorval Unthank
Oregon's "Doctor of the Year"
1958

of creating desirable districts which would actually cater to those groups and make life more pleasant for them. After all, they have to live too, the same as youngsters."[37]

The transcribed dialogue, printed in the text manual, noted that several brokers responded to Moores' suggestion by singling out Albina for Negroes and Ladd's Addition for Orientals. The majority of Portland's Negroes already lived in Albina by 1939. Ladd's Addition was in a state of transition from an upper to middle income residential mix that included a number of Italian families and a few Chinese. Chester Moores' comments obviously reflected the thinking of Portland's real estate and mortgage banking establishment. This was the same individual who was to be appointed the second chairman of the Portland Housing Authority which operated segregated wartime housing projects at both Guild's Lake and Vanport.

Few of Portland's citizens had the courage of the city's only black physician, Dr. DeNorval Unthank, when he moved his family to Ladd's Addition in 1930. He encountered every type of opposition from signed petitions and protest visits to property vandalism. The family had experienced similar reactions in Westmoreland. The Unthanks were required to move four times before they could find peace and security. Such uncivilized treatment, accorded one of the most kindly and humane citizens in Portland's history, was to leave an indelible stain on the city's image for many years. But being the forgiving Christian gentleman that he was, Dr. Unthank never expressed any resentment. He understood what was happening to American society. In fact, he felt sorry for the frightened property owners whose major concern was a feared loss of real estate values were blacks to move into a previously white neighborhood. Toward the end of his life in the early 1970s, in recognition of his unselfish services to Portland, the city dedicated a new park in his honor, located among the people who loved him the most — in Albina.[38]

Quality of Life on the River

Commercial activity on the Willamette River was quieter during the depression years of the mid-thirties than it had been a decade earlier. Captain Homer Shaver recalled that he was able to stay in business "but it was quite a rough show." Shaver Transportation was gradually shifting over to serving the towboat needs of the steamship companies. Previously, most of its business was in log towing, especially for the smaller lumber companies. As Shaver recalled the period some years later: "I could see that the timber from the lower river was gradually being cut off and Portland mills were still going but it was only a matter of time until the mills had to go to the timber."[39]

Within the shipbuilding industry, activities were limited in 1935. Only four plants were operating, performing mostly repair work: The Portland Shipbuilding Company in South Portland; the Commercial Iron Works in Linnton; the

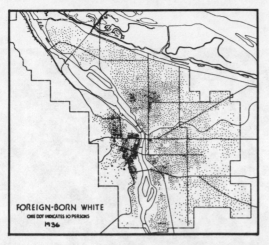

FOREIGN-BORN WHITE
ONE DOT INDICATES 10 PERSONS
1936

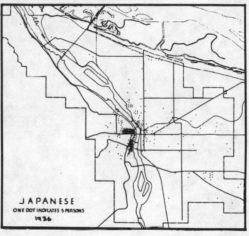

JAPANESE
ONE DOT INDICATES 5 PERSONS
1936

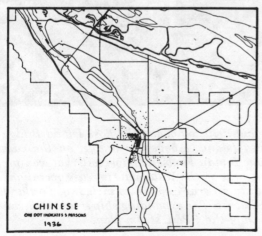

CHINESE
ONE DOT INDICATES 5 PERSONS
1936

541

The Willamette River in the mid-1940s, showing the Ross Island Bridge and the northern tip of Ross Island. Above the bridge, on the east riverbank, can be seen the huge Inman-Poulsen lumber mill that was one of the last of the eight original mills on the Willamette to cease operations (1954). The property was sold to several companies including Portland General Electric and Georgia-Pacific. The expanding ship scrapyards can be seen on the westbank, south of the PP&L steam plant.

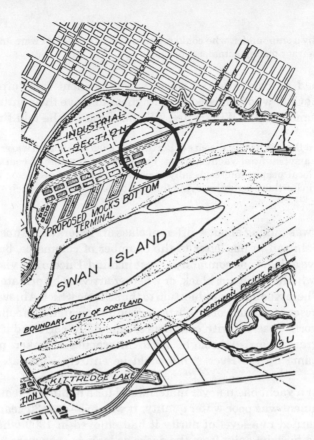

John Ainsworth's proposed yacht basin
1934

Albina Engine and Machine Works; and the Albina Marine Iron Works. The Commercial Iron Works was building the only ship under construction on the Pacific Coast in 1935, a Coast Guard Lighthouse tender, but it was using space in the Willamette Iron and Steel plant.

In the summer of 1934, banker John C. Ainsworth developed an idea that he thought had great promise — one that would instill some new life on the river. He wanted to build a yacht harbor east of Swan Island in the vicinity of Mock's Bottom. He had talked with Port chairman Bert Haney and Port general manager James Polhemus but they had not committed themselves as the long-range Port plan anticipated some commercial uses for the area.

He wrote to Aaron Frank trying to solicit his support:

"The problem would be to dredge a small circle from Mock's Bottom to the East of Swan Island to the depth of ten feet of water; move the logs that are in storage at this point east of the Island, and to build a small house which could

543

be used by a shipbuilder, who could maintain any yachts that were anchored in that harbor during summer months."

Ainsworth had already received warm encouragement from officers of the Oregon Yacht Club who indicated a willingness to move their entire operation from the Columbia to the Willamette. "We have found," he told Frank,

" . . . that there is no city the size of Portland or even smaller, on water, which has not a substantial yacht harbor. The purpose of same, of course, is to interest local people, and especially visitors, and to hold people as long as possible in Portland before hurrying through to Puget Sound for their summer vacation."[40]

Ainsworth was talking about a different class of visitors than those referred to by Juanita Johnson in her letter to the chamber of commerce, but they both seemed to have at least one common purpose in mind: Encourage visitors to stay in Portland, whether white or black, or whether arriving by private yacht or by private car. There was only one objection to the scheme which Ainsworth did not feel should present too much of an obstacle: The dirty water. The condition of the water, Ainsworth asserted with confidence, "should be corrected if our sewage disposal program is carried through." As to the practice of tankers pumping out oil as they came up the river, "this could be entirely eliminated by a city ordinance."[41]

The plan for a yacht basin never materialized for a number of reasons, but the major impediment was poor water quality. It was to be over 30 years before the river was returned to a level of purity it had enjoyed in 1900 when Portland residents used to swim daily from the docks as long as they were fully covered from neck to knees. And it was to be nearly six years before an operating sludge treatment plant and new sewer disposal system were installed.

The sanitary condition of the Willamette River in 1934 was appalling. Samples of the water examined by the Charlton Laboratory indicated practically no dissolved oxygen content between the foot of Jefferson Street and Swan Island. Between the Sellwood and Ross Island Bridges, where city sewage was observed to be backed up during high tides, the bacterial count "was surprisingly high." Quoting from the Charlton Report:

"From the standpoint of fish life, there is an absolute barrier of denuded water about three miles long where oxygen loving forms of life cannot exist. . . . From an esthetic standpoint, there is a large amount of floating debris and sewage which is a very unsightly welcome to incoming marine transportation. The Willamette River water has a very dirty brown color. . . . There seem to be sludge banks forming at the outfalls of some of the larger sewers because there are continual bubbles rising to the surface and large pieces of decaying matter churned to the surface. . . . A number of dead fish, principally carp and suckers, were noted floating on the surface."[42]

Over the next three years, during the period of time that John Ainsworth had hoped to see his yacht basin in operation, the water quality showed no improvement. In September 1937 State Treasurer Rufus Holman personally led an investigating team out on the river to test the water's oxygen count. At one spot, across the Willamette from the east end of the Ross Island Bridge where a gigantic open sewer released its contents, a score of salmon fingerlings and some mature trout lasted less than seven minutes after being dumped into a wire crate that had been lowered into the water. The group next went to mid-stream, near the battleship *Oregon* which was moored temporarily by the Public Market Building. Ten fighting trout were lowered into the submerged cage. Nine minutes later, they were all floating bellies up, either dead or dying. As one of Holman's party noted, "The fish would live longer in a frying pan or on dry land."[43]

Six months previously, the legislature had passed the drastically amended Carney bill which prohibited water pollution in Oregon by municipalities, but not by industry. As originally introduced, the measure had been all-inclusive. But industry lobbyists met privately with key legislators and worked out a "compromise" that excluded industrial and chemical wastes. Led by Irving T. Rau for the St. Helens Pulp & Paper Company, the lobbyists also succeeded in removing a provision to establish a state sanitary board. Municipalities like

The veteran battleship Oregon, *minus its engines, lying at temporary berth by the Public Market Building in 1938, prior to being moved to the southwest end of the Hawthorne Bridge. This was the approximate location of Rufus Holman's water purity test. The* Oregon *was sold by the U. S. Navy in 1942 and towed to Kalama, Washington, where its superstructure was slowly dismantled.*[44]

Portland were unhappy with the final bill because it discriminated against the cities in favor of industry. Portland was facing anti-pollution measures that would cost the city more than $5 million. But despite the legislation's inadequacies, Governor Charles H. Martin signed the measure as a first, but shaky, step in a process that would consume over 30 years.

As required by the Carney Bill, Portland was forced to take immediate action to construct a sewage disposal system that included a treatment plant. A charter amendment, empowering the city council to take the requisite action, was placed on the November 1938 ballot. By all rights, the system should already have been built, as John Ainsworth had assumed would happen in 1934. In July of 1933, the voters had approved a $6 million bond issue for the project. But design and legal difficulties prevented the bond sale. A revised project was presented to the voters and defeated in both 1934 and 1936. The new system was to be funded by user charges and an anticipated W. P. A. grant of approximately $2 million. However, in five years, the total cost had increased from $6 million to over $10 million.

In approving the proposal, the Portland City Club report noted:

"At the present time, 44 outlets empty Portland sewage into the Willamette River; 11 empty into Columbia Slough. The entire sewage of the city is poured into these waters. Because of ocean tides varying from 18 to 36 inches, the current of the Willamette is very small for four months of the year during late summer and early fall. When the water is high in the Columbia River, water backs up into the Willamette, retarding the current. During low-water, Columbia Slough is practically motionless.

"Water is deemed to be unpolluted when there is present ten parts of dissolved oxygen to one million parts of water. Tests made from mid-July until the fall rains began, in 1929 and in 1934, disclosed the following percentages of the required proportion of dissolved oxygen in the Willamette at the cities named:

Cottage Grove	85%
Eugene	93%
Corvallis	93%
Albany	93%
Independence	93%
Salem	89%
Newberg	76%
Oregon City	54%
Sellwood Bridge	43%
Ross Island Bridge	28%
Portland Flouring Mills	0%
St. Johns Bridge	0%
Linnton	28%

"As indicated by the foregoing table, the Willamette is not seriously polluted south of Newberg. The pollution occurring north of that point is mainly caused by sulphite wastes from paper mills situated at Newberg and Oregon City."[45]

As if further justification needed to be provided, the City Club committee reminded its members that the human sewage found in the Portland area was far more deleterious to human health than the paper mill sulfate wastes. Examples of ship propellers churning up quantities of decomposed matter were cited, as was the fact that swimming in the river within the city limits was prohibited by law. As a final bit of color, the report noted that "rats in large numbers thrive on river filth and there is good reason to believe that they carry germs to human food supplies stored in buildings on the river front."[46] The word got through. The voters really had little choice and the measure won approval.

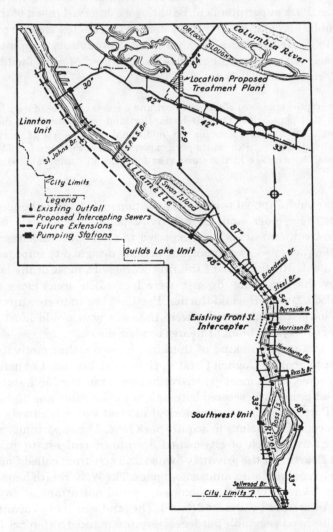

Map of the proposed sewage disposal system — 1938

Quality of Life on the Land: The Parks

The year 1936 marked a crucial turning point in Portland's public park development. Under the general direction of City Commissioner Ormond R. Bean, an architect by profession with wide experience in land use planning, the city planning commission made an exhaustive study of urban recreation areas and needs. Its published report won wide recognition throughout the United States for unusual foresight in park and recreational planning that was tied closely to neighborhood schools. The report was to be largely responsible for the voters' approval in 1938 of a ten year park program, involving the levying of a 4/10 mill tax. Park superintendent Paul Keyser deserved much of the credit for ultimate public acceptance after the voters twice rejected similar proposals in 1936 and 1937. He created a number of citizen advisory committees which worked closely with the neighborhoods most in need of such facilities.

As the Portland City Club noted in 1937:

> "The accepted standard of cities of Portland's size is one acre of park land to each 100 of population. On this basis, Portland is sub-standard about 50 percent.... There is room for an additional 1500 acres of park and playground area.... Per capita park expenditures in Portland in 1935 were 77 cents; the average in the same year for cities of comparable size, was $1.90."[47]

Of particular public appeal was the designation of districts to be served by new acquisitions: The older and more heavily populated sections of the city. Increased recreational areas were expected to arrest obsolescence and reduce juvenile delinquency — two important actions designed to improve the city's quality of life. Until the time of the first world war, most of the larger parks acquired by the city, some by gift, were located in areas close to wealthy neighborhoods. But by the mid-thirties, Portland began to recognize the social truth that lower income families were the ones who would most benefit by having the countryside brought nearer to their doors.

It was not exactly this kind of thinking, however, that motivated the city government to acquire Council Crest Park in 1936, because Council Crest was adjacent to some of the most expensive homesites in Portland. But the notion that the Crest property possessed both unique public value, the highest point in Southwest Portland, and great historical interest was a relatively new ingredient in city council decisions to acquire park land. The opportunity was offered to trade a quarter block of city-owned downtown real estate, just north of Yamhill on Fourth, for the privately-owned 22.8 acre tract called Council Crest, the site of a long abandoned amusement park. The W. K. Smith heirs, operating through the Ukase Investment Company, could not afford to pay the taxes which were in arrears by almost $15,000. The land was lying vacant except for some neighborhood vegetable gardens. Despite a marked difference in assessed valuation, the average of five different appraisals indicated both properties to be

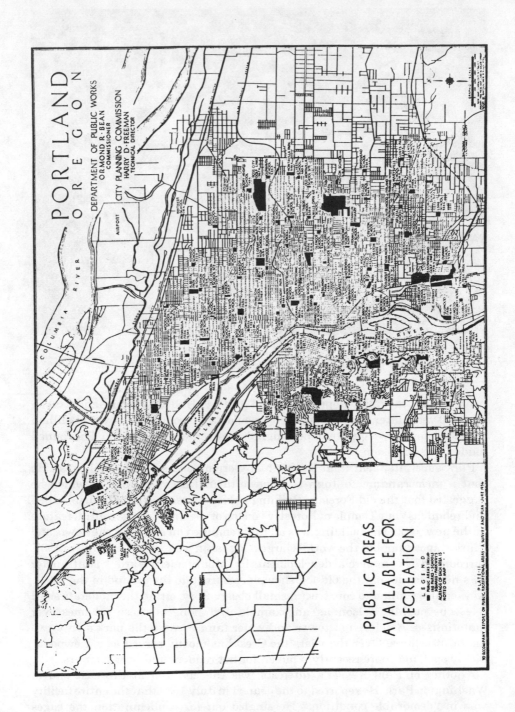

PORTLAND
OREGON

DEPARTMENT OF PUBLIC WORKS
ORMOND R· BEAN
COMMISSIONER

CITY PLANNING COMMISSION
HARRY D· FREEMAN
TECHNICAL DIRECTOR

**PUBLIC AREAS
AVAILABLE FOR
RECREATION**

LEGEND

■ PUBLIC AREAS
▦ PRIVATELY CONTROLLED
PARKS · SCHOOLS
SQUARES · PARKWAYS
ACREAGE OF AREAS
NOTED ON MAP

PLATE·II

TO ACCOMPANY REPORT ON PUBLIC RECREATIONAL AREAS - A SURVEY AND PLAN · JUNE 1936

549

The Portland Zoo, renamed The Washington Park Zoo

nearly equal in value, approximately $70,000.[48] Had this transaction taken place 40 years later, the Crest property would have brought well over $1 million while the downtown quarter block might have been worth $350,000. The council made a wise decision.

Park superintendent Paul Keyser had glorious plans for Council Crest. He sent a memorandum to John C. Ainsworth in December 1937 in which he suggested that the old Forestry Building in Northwest Portland be dismantled and rebuilt as "our Temple of Forestry" on top of the Crest, as the central feature of the new park. The building was all that remained on site from the Lewis and Clark Exposition, but the world's largest log cabin was "going to ruin" in 1937, surrounded by commercial developments like Montgomery Ward.[49] The transfer was never made and the old log showplace burned to the ground in the 1960s. Keyser also wanted to construct a small observatory, citing the moderate sized telescope on Mt. Wilson as an example. But none of these schemes ever materialized. A television tower and water tank became the park's only two major structures. Over the years the Crest has mostly served as a viewpoint, picnic spot and more recently a haven for hot-rodders and beer guzzlers.

Another of Paul Keyser's interests was the city zoo at the east end of Washington Park. He reported to the council in July 1937 that the entire facility was in "deplorable condition." He singled out for condemnation the cages holding the lions, wild hogs, vultures, prairie dogs and native deer. He doubted that the deer could survive their restrictive confinement. "Portland has never had a zoo in the true sense of the term," Keyser told the council. "All we have had . . . is a menagerie — a managed exhibit." He reviewed some past history, how Mayor Harry Lane had been opposed to caging animals, and how "the real-estaters beat" the city to some adjacent land that had been available for purchase in 1919 following the passage of a bond issue. In seeking a larger site, Keyser suggested either Ross Island or the West Hills Golf Course area[50] which was connected to Washington Park on the west. Twenty years later, the nine-hole golf course property was converted into an expanded, modern zoo that has continued to grow in size and popularity.

Lewis Mumford in Portland

Lewis Mumford, who has achieved recognition as one of the leading urban philosophers, planners, critics and writers of the 20th century, came to Oregon in July 1938 at the invitation of the Council of Education, Planning and Public Administration. He spent a few days exploring the natural beauty of the state before visiting Portland where he devoted time to the Northwest Regional Council, an offshoot of the National Resources Planning Commission.

On July 15th, Mumford was invited to address the Portland City Club, and he pulled no punches. After revealing how overwhelmed he was by Oregon's scenery, he told his listeners that Oregonians had been "asleep" in terms of protecting their natural resources.

> "The Columbia [River] land that needed to be controlled most vigorously has already been grabbed up. Certain persons are licking their chops and counting their gold,"

he declared, pointing to landowners who were "busy making eyes at industrial leaders." For future industrial sites, Mumford suggested the acquisition of lands not immediately on the river, to be developed into industrial parks. "Neglect of this [action] is nothing short of a public disgrace." Looking his audience square in the face, he asserted: "You have an opportunity for setting an example to the rest of the world," by designing new areas for industrial development before all of the available land should disappear.[51]

In January of 1939, Mumford published a memorandum containing some general impressions of his Oregon visit. There is no historical evidence that any of his observations or recommendations had any perceptible effect on either the thinking or subsequent actions of the Portland business-political establishment. But some of his printed words are worth noting in the light of what has transpired over the past four decades. As urban historian Carl Abbott has noted: "Lewis Mumford was a generation early in his visit to Portland."[52] Beginning with the governorship of Tom McCall in 1967, many of Mumford's ideas on

*An example of incompatible land use wherein dirty industry was located
adjacent to residential neighborhoods — the "congestion-for-profit school"
— in Southeast Portland.*

urban growth management, regional land use planning and resource conservation began to win acceptance. Today, some of them are firmly embedded in state and local law.

His major point, directed at Portland, related to what he called "the continued-congestion-for-profit school." Such people "would utilize [cheap] electric power to concentrate population in points where it is already congested and badly housed: Thus continue the dream of indefinite urban expansion." This school of thought, he noted, was popular in Portland, a city that had "already overpassed the limits of effective and orderly growth."[53]

Mumford's general points were his most controversial:

"(1) Historically, Portland had concentrated too much attention on its own growth and not enough on the regional areas of the hinterland. "The apparent financial prospects of . . . port cities undermined the base of the sounder development that could well have taken place in other parts of the region, on strictly modern lines.

(2) "The development and settlement of the Northwest involves transforming the metropolises themselves into regional centers and taking positive measures to build up cities with a strong industrial and cultural base in other parts of the country.

(3) "The problem, in the present state of American society, has nothing whatever to do with population: It is a matter of complicated economic readjustment, involving among other things the socialization of natural monopolies, the collective control of quasi-monopolies, the wiping out of inflexible price structures that have no close relation to the costs of production or market demand, and the raising of real wages through trade union pressure on one hand and through the expansion of vital public works, financed by current taxation, on the other. . . .

"At no point can the problem of regional planning be separated from that of ultimately controlling and directing, in the interests of the common welfare, the entire economic system. The wastes, the disorder and the foul building of our cities are associated with an essentially disorderly economic life, based upon purely individual efforts at wealth, security, or aggrandizement. The Northwest has paid for these defects in duplicated railroad systems, in abandoned logging towns and dead mining camps, in overbuilt boomtowns, and even in farms whose speculative prices placed an unbearable burden upon the cultivator."

Toward the end of his statement, Mumford inserted a plea for a Columbia River Valley Authority (CVA) modeled on the Tennessee Valley Authority (TVA). "Unless such an authority is called into existence, and put immediately to work, it is doubtful if the best development of the Columbia River Valley can take place."[54] In the light of current electric power shortage projections, Mumford's advice of 40 years ago might profitably have been followed. But in 1939, such words were received with unabashed horror by the private utilities which could not wait to market the plentifully cheap Bonneville power for their own private profit. Pacific Power & Light Company president Paul B. McKee must have viewed the likes of Lewis Mumford as a wide-eyed socialist. The mere mention of a CVA sent both McKee and PGE's Franklin T. Griffith into orbit.

By pure coincidence, Mumford's "socialistic preaching" bore close resemblance to a provocative editorial published by *Fortune* magazine in June 1938, one month before Mumford's visit to Portland. Would McKee and Griffith have dared to call *Fortune* a mouthpiece for socialism? In the words of *Fortune*'s editor:

"The fact is that in operating the capitalist economy American Business has consistently misappropriated the principles of democracy. American Business had made use of those principles to its own enormous profit but it has failed entirely to grasp the social implications of its profit making. . . . "

"**What failed was the doctrine of laissez-faire**, which made the fundamental assumption, that the economic system was not the concern of Government."

"What American Business faces is . . . a more socialized state. Possibly it will be necessary for Government to take certain industries — the railroads, for instance, or the utilities — out of the competitive system entirely and set them up as completely regulated monopolies, or even as state-owned monopolies, or even as state-owned enterprises. These, however, should be the exceptions."[55]

Which Way Portland?

The second world war that was beginning in Europe, and which would increasingly require America's industrial support especially after the United States itself joined the "Crusade For Democracy," detoured any further efforts to improve the region's human life style. The war demanded an acceleration of the very forces that Mumford and others had challenged. Portland became even more congested and segregated as thousands of new workers, many of whom were black, flooded into the city and its environs to fill wartime shipyard jobs.

After nearly two years of war, Portland's most noted contemporary architect, Italian-born Pietro Belluschi, composed some thoughts on Portland and its future. "The City of Portland is now at a turning point in its history," declared Belluschi.

"It is obvious that a city is more than a place where ships may dock or where products are manufactured. The city is primarily a community of individuals, and the individual has a soul, so the city must have a soul.

"Nature has been very generous with the City of Roses. The hills, the river, the green forests, and the climate all contribute to make it a pleasant place in which to live. What man has been contributing to those elements has not been very flattering to his foresight.

"It is not possible to achieve . . . a beautiful city without arousing everyone's interest and understanding in its program, without a tremendous amount of education as to the worth of planning for our future and knowing that the results are worthy of everyone's interest and effort."[56]

The quality life advocated by David Eccles, DeNorval Unthank, Jesse Short, Lewis Mumford and Pietro Belluschi was not going to be achieved, even partially, for more than two decades.

Chapter 18

Hydroelectric Power and the Growth of Portland, 1938-1948

Early in January 1950, *The Oregonian*[1] asked a number of Portland's prominent businessmen, bankers and civic leaders to cite the factors that in their opinion had most influenced the growth of the Portland community since the turn of the century. Although harbor and river improvement received more first place votes, the development of hydroelectric power was given honorable mention by more respondents as one of the most important determinants, especially since 1930.

From 1940 to 1946, Portland's population leaped an astonishing 35 percent — a figure that would decline and stabilize at 20 percent by 1950. World War II was, of course, largely responsible for the increase. Some of this growth resulted from a 50 percent expansion in the number of local manufacturing establishments, most of which derived their electric energy directly or indirectly from Bonneville Dam. Had there not been so plentiful a supply of cheap Bonneville power, it is doubtful that the three wartime Kaiser shipyards, employing 94,000 workers, would have located in the Portland-Vancouver area, a region far removed from the sources of raw materials.

Following World War II, although the Kaiser yards were to be dismantled and shipbuilding employment reduced to less than 3000, the Portland area did not experience severe retrenchment. On the contrary, over 600 new industrial firms and branch establishments (mostly of small and medium size) were to be located in the metropolitan area during the period from 1947 to 1953, many of them associated in one form or another with the electro-chemical and electro-metallurgical fields, all using Bonneville power. In fact, by the early 1950s, the metal industry was to replace the lumber industry as the leading employer in the Portland region.[2] Such companies as ALCOA, Reynolds Aluminum, Oregon Steel Mills, Pacific Carbide and PennSalt were to become familiar fixtures within the lower Columbia-Willamette basin.

Business Response to Bonneville

As Bonneville Dam neared completion in mid-1937, the Portland Chamber of Commerce exerted every effort within its resources to ensure that private power companies would receive maximum benefits from the electricity that was soon to be generated by the first two of the projected ten power units. Executive vice president W. D. B. Dodson spent nearly six months in Washington on the

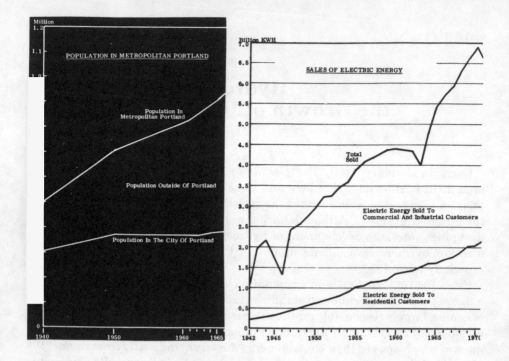

chamber's payroll acting as chief lobbyist for the private utility interests. The major thrust of the chamber's efforts was to invest the U. S. Army Corps of Engineers with the overall responsibility not only for operating the dam but more importantly for administering the power generation and transmission facilities. In the wrong hands, such authority could threaten the entire private utility network in the Pacific Northwest. The most feared consequence was a drastic reduction in wholesale rates, an action that would force would-be private purchasers of Bonneville power to lower their resale rates proportionately.

Historically, the Corps of Engineers and the private power companies had enjoyed a friendly professional and social relationship. Colonel Thomas M. Robbins of the Northwest District Office, a frequent Arlington Club guest[3] of both Franklin Griffith and Paul McKee, was on record to the effect that if the U. S. Army Engineers administered the marketing of Bonneville power, it would go where it was most in demand and by the most economically feasible routes. He would abide "no political power lines."[4] The words "political" and "politics" were employed by both the Corps and power companies as terms of derision, implying the injection of "socialistic New Deal" schemes into what they believed should be strictly economic transactions based upon the traditional precepts of private enterprise. Local newspaper editorials warned that Bonneville should keep out of "politics. . . . Bonneville ought to represent electric power, not political power."[5] Above all, Bonneville should not become just "another bureau to be run from Washington."

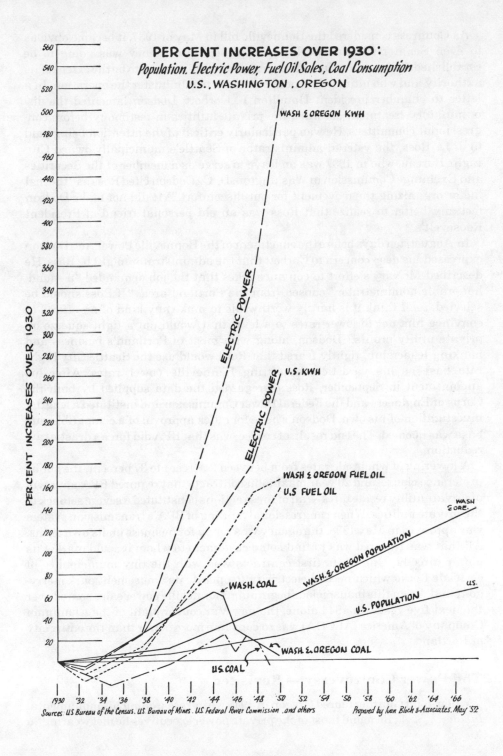

PER CENT INCREASES OVER 1930:
Population, Electric Power, Fuel Oil Sales, Coal Consumption
U.S., WASHINGTON, OREGON

PER CENT INCREASES OVER 1930

WASH & OREGON KWH

ELECTRIC POWER

U.S. KWH

ELECTRIC POWER

WASH & OREGON FUEL OIL

U.S FUEL OIL

WASH
& ORE.

WASH & OREGON POPULATION

U.S.

WASH. COAL

U.S. POPULATION

WASH & OREGON COAL

U.S. COAL

560 540 520 500 480 460 440 420 400 380 360 340 320 300 280 260 240 220 200 180 160 140 120 100 80 60 40 20

1930 '32 '34 '36 '38 '40 '42 '44 '46 '48 '50 '52 '54 '56 '58 '60 '62 '64 '66

Sources: U.S. Bureau of the Census, U.S. Bureau of Mines, U.S. Federal Power Commission, and others   Prepared by Ivan Bloch & Associates, May '52

As Congress considered the Bonneville bill in May of 1937, it became obvious to even Senator Charles McNary that a separate agency was going to be established. The major points of concern, therefore, seemed to be the extent of its authority and who ultimately would be chosen to administer the operation. In a letter to chamber president Hamilton F. Corbett, Dodson lamented the discriminatory treatment accorded the private utilities in testimony before congressional committees. He was particularly critical of the attention being paid to J. D. Ross, the veteran administrator of Seattle's municipally-owned City Light Bureau, who in 1937 was on leave to serve as a member of the Securities and Exchange Commission in Washington, D. C. Dodson cited Ross as "the real factor organizing the movement for our discomfort."[6] It did not make Dodson feel any better to realize that Ross was an old personal friend of President Roosevelt's.

In August, ten days before the enactment of the Bonneville Power Act, Dodson expressed his deep concern to Corbett that the administrator might be Ross. He described McNary's effort to convince Ickes that the job demanded "a sound, honorable administrator" chosen from the Portland area. "If Ross should be selected, . . . I think it is hardly worthwhile to make any kind of an effort" to convince him not to lower rates to a level that would put a tight squeeze on private utility profits.[7] Dodson, along with most of Portland's business and banking leadership, rightly feared that Ross would use the Seattle City Light rate base as his yardstick for setting Bonneville power rates. After his appointment in September, Ross disregarded the data supplied by both the Corps of Engineers and the Federal Power Commission and instituted a lengthy investigation of his own. Dodson's hope for quick approval of a compatible rate base was doomed. The end result, of course, was that BPA did force a drastic rate reduction.

A lowering of wholesale rates from between 2 percent to 37 percent, the public preference clause, and 20 year maximum contracts that required BPA approval of private utility resale rates — all of these actions constituted a severe setback to the private utilities. When congressional funding of BPA's transmission system was approved in May 1938, the agency was ready for business on its own terms. All that was required was to find some customers to whom it could market its power directly. One of its first contracts was with the tiny municipality of Cascade Locks which needed electricity to operate its amusement park merry-go-round. From this inauspicious beginning, Bonneville power sales soared over the next five years. In 1944 alone, the new Vancouver plant of the Aluminum Company of America (ALCOA) was to consume more power than the entire city of Portland.

The Power Controversy — Revisited

When John Gunther toured Oregon in 1945 while researching his monumental *Inside U. S. A.*, he found most of the private power executives he met wearing "a somewhat apologetic mood, and . . . inclined to be on the defensive."[8] They were obviously pleased by Bonneville's record output of hydroelectric power as a stimulant to generating new industrial growth in Oregon. But they were deeply worried that Bonneville's very success might threaten their own future operations and profits. As BPA official Robert W. Beck told a Reed Institute audience in 1939: "Private power is in existence for one primary reason, and that primary reason is profit. Public power is in existence for one primary reason, and that primary reason is service."[9] Not to discount the general truth of Beck's statement, the power manager of BPA was himself not immune to the enticements of making personal profits out of power — public power. He was fired by Interior Secretary Harold Ickes in 1939 for conflict of interest: Receiving a percentage of acquisition costs when BPA bought out a private utility. He was in cahoots with Seattle banker Guy Meyers, who was the principal financial organizer in assisting PUDs to get started. As one former BPA administrator was to comment: "Not all the rascals were in Portland."[10]

J. D. Ross — First Administrator of BPA

PGE's Franklin T. Griffith heatedly contested statements such as Beck's. It was a point of absolute conviction with Griffith that the private utilities were best able to serve the public needs. In a speech delivered to the Salem Chamber of Commerce in 1938, entitled "Cooperation in Public Service," Griffith asserted that private operations provided "a greater expression of initiative genius and human ingenuity," far exceeding "any such effort put forth by the public owned enterprises." There was "no miracle in public ownership."[11]

Gunther was somewhat amused by the private power rhetoric. "What really lies at the heart of the public-private power controversy," he wrote, "is the major question: What kind of society is to be built in the United States?"

> "Private power, say the public power adherents, serves to confirm or resurrect trends toward monopoly, exploitation and abuses of the system of free enterprise. Public power, say the private power adherents, means a trend toward socialization, bureaucracy and planned economy."[12]

Gunther summed up one side of the issue succinctly when he declared: "Private power hates public power for two overriding reasons: (1) Greed. . . . (2) Fear of government."[13]

In May 1937, in an article discussing Wendell L. Willkie, the enlightened Republican utility lawyer who was to oppose Franklin D. Roosevelt in 1940, *Fortune* magazine wrote:

> "Find a public-utility official who is a political liberal and you will have something almost as rare as a purple cow. . . . There has indeed been an oversupply not of conservatives but of arch-Tories in this business, men of so simple and realistic a sense of power that they preferred to indoctrinate the people against public ownership by influencing the schools and universities rather than by the roundabout method of low rates and progressive selling. It has been an industry run almost exclusively by two types of minds: The financier's and the engineer's. As a result its engineering technique has been . . . the best in the world, its finances both the stablest and fanciest, and its public relations the worst."[14]

Forty years later, a study of PGE's management by the Arthur D. Little Company reached a similar conclusion. With the exception of Griffith, most of PGE's top managers have been engineers, as was Paul B. McKee of PP&L. Although trained as a lawyer, Griffith became an astute financier. In fact, it was the unusual combination of his financial wizardry and his legal talents that kept PGE afloat through a series of financial reorganizations and threatened bankruptcies from 1933 until 1948. Although of different generations, experiences and temperaments, Griffith and McKee had much in common. But neither man had anything in common with Bonneville Power's first administrator, J. D. Ross — the personification of public power. According to one who knew and worked with both Ross and the private utility presidents, McKee "hated Ross' guts."[15]

Ross was a unique individual. In over 30 years as the popular manager of the

Seattle Power system he was reputed by his supporters to have made City Light one of the most successful utility businesses in the country. As the first great pioneer of the public power idea in the United States, he was, paradoxically, a Republican as well as a good Presbyterian. He was also a self-taught mathematician, an instinctively sharp businessman and "an old-style western evangelist all in one." Like most unusual men, according to John Gunther, Ross was full of quirks and oddities.

> "Not only did he build a dam and a power plant at Skagit, a hundred miles north of Seattle, as a source of energy for his precious City Light; he made it a municipal camping ground on a non-profit basis. Not only did he build parks and ornamental gardens; he installed hidden loudspeakers in the woods to play bird songs, in case the birds themselves didn't feel like singing."[16]

Ross is fondly remembered by Ivan Bloch who was an early member of the Bonneville staff in 1938. But memories of Ross also recall in Bloch's mind the great frustrations encountered by those who had to work with him. Not only did he give the impression of being disorganized, "he **was** disorganized in the usual business sense. He relied on his associates from his early Seattle days." He kept no written records; everything was stored in his head. When he died suddenly in March of 1939, much valuable information unfortunately passed away with him.[17]

Unlike his private utility counterparts in Portland, Ross cared little for material refinements. Although he had managed a $70 million Seattle business, "by the seat of his pants," one observer noted, he had never drawn more than $7500 a year in salary. Ownership of an expensive home and membership in exclusive clubs were of no interest to J. D. Ross, whose life style was dedicated to other concerns. As someone commented after his death, Ross' "love for mankind expressed itself in kilowatts," cheap kilowatts!

To his credit, Ross held a vision about the role of public power. Whether or not he could have implemented it with specific programs had he lived longer is open to speculation. In any case no one could deny that J. D. Ross was the father of the regional grid transmission system. He also established the policy of equal rates for all users, public and private. He was not, however, able to launch a program of power development. Upon his death, deep concern was expressed in both Washington and Portland about Bonneville's future. There was a growing need to generate income through sales but neither Ickes nor BPA wanted to be placed in bondage to the private utility companies.[18]

Shortly after Ross died, Oregon's first Congresswoman, Nan Wood Honeyman, daughter of C. E. S. Wood, wrote her good friend Franklin Roosevelt about Ross' successor: "What we must have," she asserted, "is a man with the public ownership policy not only in mind but in heart and to come as near as possible to Mr. Ross' vision." Mrs. Honeyman exhibited discouragement with her own state. "Oregon does not deserve much benefit from Bonneville,"[19] she told the President, as she described the way in which the private utilities had dominated the 1939 legislative session. For over 40 years, stories have been circulated by former PGE employees about how the local utility companies bought the services of many Oregon legislators in 1939 by actually placing them on the corporate payroll.

Following an interim appointment of Frank Banks who had been the chief construction engineer for Grand Coulee and who was a totally non-public power technocrat, the President appointed Dr. Paul Jerome Raver to be the new Bonneville Power administrator in August 1939. As a former professor of electrical engineering at Northwestern University and the incumbent chairman of the Illinois Public Service Commission, Raver was widely recognized as a highly knowledgeable and dedicated public power professional. He proved to be a far more efficient administrator than Ross and more thoroughly versed in the political realities of the day. He accepted Bonneville's political role and in time moved vigorously to make BPA the dominant force in the future economic development of the Pacific Northwest.

Before he arrived in Portland, however, Raver did not really have any concept of BPA's economic role. But after reviewing Ivan Bloch's development plan which neither Ross nor Banks had wanted to authorize, Raver decided to move promptly: The marketing of large blocks of cheap power to industry became his primary task. Bloch, to whom Raver gave the title of Chief of Industrial and Resources Development, was shortly approached by representatives of the Aluminum Company of America (ALCOA) to investigate the possibility of building a reduction plant in the Portland area.

A memorandum from the chamber's Dodson in December 1939, noted that applications for a million horsepower of energy had already been made by industrial operators. "I think," wrote Dodson, "this is probably the strongest industrial prospect facing us over many years and will be realized if the administrator is permitted to make a fair form of contract."[20] On the very day that Dodson reported these facts, ALCOA announced it would build a reduction plant just west of Vancouver on the Columbia River. To cost over $4 million, the plant was expected to employ 300 men. Dodson was not too happy with the news because the chamber had itself been negotiating with ALCOA to purchase a site in Portland. The chamber wanted to blame the loss on Oregon's higher taxes although ALCOA disclaimed this factor. The company reported that the site was simply the best one for its needs. The SP&S Railroad sold the 215 acres for $54,000 and ALCOA paid another $75,000 to fill the land.

ALCOA's signing of a contract for 32,500 kilowatts of power in January 1940 constituted BPA's first industrial sale. Within a few months after the first contract was written, ALCOA asked Raver for more power. Bloch informed Raver that additional sales to the same company might be in conflict with the anti-monopoly clause of the Bonneville Power Act. Raver was not happy with this prospect because sales were lagging and the temptation to take on more ALCOA business was overwhelming. Bloch recalls what happened at that point:

"I suggested we provide a *quid pro quo* to ALCOA: BPA would sell more power provided **ALCOA** would put in fabricating units . . . thus providing labor rather than power intensive outlets. . . . Raver took me to Washington to sit in the negotiations with Arthur Vining Davis [ALCOA's board chairman]. . . . I sat next to Davis. When I suggested the *quid pro quo*, Davis turned to me and in choleric tones which I vividly recall, stated 'Young man, that's socialism!' "[21]

Subsequently, an off the record agreement to construct a fabricating unit was apparently reached, at which point Raver agreed to ALCOA's purchase of additional power totalling 162,500 kws.[22] In the same way that Henry Kaiser was to save PGE, ALCOA saved BPA even though many members of the BPA staff were not overjoyed by such a realization. BPA's power capacity was gradually being reached. The first aluminum ingots that came off the line in September 1940 sold for 17 cents a pound, a price that increased only slightly during the first 20 years of the plant's operation. Dropping to 14 cents during the war, it returned to 17 cents in 1949. The relatively cheap cost of aluminum ingots was the major reason for the enormous expansion of aluminum use in the postwar domestic economy. And the Bonneville Power Administration had played a major role in this development.

When queried about the significance of the ALCOA power contracts in 1940, Ivan Bloch noted that this step was only the beginning. "The industrial east has had its iron and steel age," declared Bloch. "Now the far west, due to its possession of a large share of the aircraft manufacturing industry . . . , is sure to have a thriving and very important light-weight metals age." Bloch cited four probable basic industrial activities using aluminum and various Northwest raw materials that might be established in the region: (1) Magnesium plants; (2) aluminum-magnesium alloy manufacturing plants; (3) rolling mill and extrusion plants; and (4), casting plants. The future looked bright indeed.[23]

The basic concern that Bloch had, a fear shared by both Representative Walter M. Pierce and future Senator Richard L. Neuberger, related to the unlimited sale of increasingly large blocks of cheap power to one company, or even to an industry that employed so few people in proportion to the amount of power being consumed. With such thoughts in mind, Bloch and his BPA staff associate, economist Samuel Moment, worked hard to introduce competition to the aluminum industry which was under heavy wartime pressure from the government to increase production. But being well established, with both a monopoly on aluminum production and powerful friends in Washington, D. C., ALCOA succeeded in maintaining its dominant position. Furthermore, it received a government license to build three additional Northwest plants to meet the wartime emergency. Bloch and Moment, through BPA with Ickes' support, were at least able to force ALCOA to disperse construction of the plants into three widely separated locations: One in Troutdale, Oregon, one in Spokane and one near Tacoma.

Concurrent with these developments, the Reynolds Corporation requested permission to build an aluminum plant in Longview, Washington, an action that received BPA's warm endorsement. Not until after the war and after ALCOA's conviction for anti-trust violations did Moment succeed, with Ickes' support, in breaking ALCOA's regional monopoly. With the reluctant assistance of the U. S. Surplus Property Board directed by future Senator Stuart Symington, Moment and Raver convinced the government to sell the Troutdale plant to Reynolds and the Spokane plant to Henry J. Kaiser.[24] The Portland Chamber of Commerce viewed such developments with mixed emotions. It was glad to see the government get out of the aluminum business but it was distressed by the regional dispersal of all the plants. As Ivan Bloch recalls: "The Portland business community felt we rascals at BPA were spoiling its game to locate everything in Portland."[25] After the war, many Portland business leaders would have been happy to see some of the wartime regional aluminum operations dismantled — none was in Portland. Furthermore, with nearly 60 percent of BPA's output allocated to aluminum, a power shortage was predicted for 1947, a condition that threatened the postwar prosperity of the private utilities.

The policy of contracting with a small number of non-labor intensive companies for such a high percentage of electric power — an energy supply that in recent years has become both limited and expensive — has raised one major question retrospectively: Should BPA and the Portland Chamber of Commerce have made greater efforts to attract other kinds of large industries with more jobs per kilowatt hour?[26] Nearly 40 years later, Ivan Bloch answers with a definite "Yes." Although the chamber was to generate a lot of motion, Bloch feels that "no really concerted effort" was made to introduce to Portland larger, more labor intensive industries that would compete with existing firms. The crucial influence in the formulation of such policies was exerted by the U. S. National and First National Banks which tried to protect their existing customers from threatened competition.[27]

The second major task facing Paul Raver led to a head-on collision between BPA and the region's private utilities. Not long after assuming office, Raver suggested publicly that the private power companies should seriously consider selling out to Bonneville Power. Raver was clearly rejecting any notion of a partnership between private and public power, the very program that was to be heartily endorsed by the Eisenhower administration 13 years later. When the Portland City Council took Raver's cue and placed a PUD enabling measure on the May 1940 primary ballot, Raver encouraged members of his staff to take an active role in securing public support. State senator Harry Kenin, a former Port commissioner and a BPA official, became chairman of the Bonneville For Portland Committee. To Pacific Power & Light's Paul B. McKee, such an action was tantamount to a declaration of war and McKee was more than eager to take up arms.

Kenin started the action in February 1940 when the council was first considering the issue. In a public speech, he declared that "no business in the

United States, other than a privately-owned electric utility, charges its customers 17½ times as much as the service or product costs." Kenin accused the power companies of buying their BPA power at the rate of 10 cents for 50 kws. and then retailing it for $1.75.[28]

A previous report issued by the BPA staff asserted that a PUD was "feasible" for Portland. The book value of the Portland properties owned by PGE and Northwestern Electric was stated at $31.1 million. Assuming an interest rate of four percent and the use of power supplied by BPA, both systems could be amortized in 30 years, resulting in a substantial rate reduction for Portland consumers.[29]

Franklin T. Griffith quickly responded that the report did not take into consideration any severance damages, the value of the hydroelectric plants outside of the city, nor the values of the PEPCO building and Northwestern's steam plant on S. W. Lincoln Street. Over the next four months, Griffith made nearly 50 speeches and he increasingly emphasized the loss of tax revenues that the city would suffer were the private utilities to cease business. He was joined by Paul B. McKee, who took a more ideological stance. In a talk at Reed College one week before the election, McKee declared in resounding tones: "The preservation of private enterprise in America is essential to the preservation of free government in these United States." Public power people, McKee charged, are "bent on destroying a legitimate private industry through tax-free, government subsidized competition." He warned his audience that the same thing could happen to other industries.[30]

The City Club majority report also opposed the creation of a PUD. In essence it agreed with an *Oregon Journal* editorial charging that municipal ownership would create "an unnecessary, unnatural governmental agency." The *Journal* figured that it would take at least $50 million in bonds to purchase both private systems and it concluded that such an action would not lower rates. A PUD, said the *Journal*, would be "neither good business nor good judgment."[31] During the week before the election, the *Journal* and *The Oregonian* ran full page ads signed by hundreds of prominent citizens voicing their opposition to a PUD. Needless to say, the measure was badly defeated by a majority of nearly 3-1.

Three months after the election, the city power plan was back before the council. A proposal was submitted to place the issue before the voters again at the November 1940 presidential election. The public power advocates hoped that President Roosevelt's re-election campaign, which they assumed would be successful, might carry the measure to victory. When the council discussed the matter, Henry L. Corbett and E. C. Sammons led the opposition. The council gave the matter short shrift and voted 3-2 against resubmitting it to the voters, with Mayor Carson being joined by commissioners Bowes and Riley. The PUD issue was killed in Portland and would remain dead indefinitely.

The private power forces had not won their victory cheaply. In February 1941, the Federal Power Commission was to charge both Northwestern Electric and PGE with excessive spending for political campaigns and company expense

Paul B. McKee, President of Pacific Power & Light, who spent much of his 25 years in office defending the private utilities from statements such as the one printed by the Oregon Commonwealth Federation in 1940.

BONNEVILLE POWER IS READY FOR US!

Bonneville Dam is a reality — two to five times as much electricity for our money. Electric cooking, refrigeration, hot water: all are within reach. Tacoma's Public Ownership rates would save Portland and Salem residents $1.67 to $2.87 a month. Eugene's public system will sell Bonneville power to stores for $13.53 yet PEPCO now charges $30.75 for the same amount. . . . *No wonder the power trust wants to abolish our May primary and keep Oregon from sending pro-Roosevelt, pro-public power men to the national convention!*

accounts. Cited was a total expenditure by PGE of $222,000 during the previous eight years.[32] From 1931 to 1939, furthermore, PGE spent $63,170 just to finance its battles against public power.[33] For a company that entered into bankruptcy proceedings in 1939 because it lacked the funds to meet interest payments on its bonded debt, such expenditures were indeed questionable. Of course, both Griffith and McKee justified the costs. They said they had to defend their companies against "the incessant blitzkrieg attacks by Mr. Ickes' BPA." Ickes was spending the taxpayers' money to promote BPA which was nothing more than "socialized power."[34] According to one in-house PP&L report,[35] BPA printed 50,000 copies of an article entitled "Bonneville Power — Are You Getting Your Share?"

The companies certainly had a right to defend themselves, but the Federal Power Commission questioned the propriety of charging over one-half of the costs of such activities to operating expenses. The ratepayers were apparently expected to contribute their share to the defense of a system that most likely was costing them too much in the first place and over which they had even less control than the taxpayers could exercise over the Bonneville Power Administration.

PGE in Deep Trouble Again

On March 1, 1939, the Portland Electric Power Company (PEPCO) defaulted on accumulated unpaid interest due on income bonds that had been issued in March 1934 at the time of the company's first reorganization. It was unable to raise the $5 million which was both the amount of the unpaid interest and 30 percent of the face value of the income bonds. When the bonds had been issued, the stocks of PEPCO's two main subsidiaries, PGE and the Portland Traction Company (PTC), were pledged as collateral and New York's Guaranty Trust Company was appointed the indenture trustee for the bondholders.

On April 3, 1939, PEPCO filed a petition for reorganization in federal district court under Chapter X of the Federal Bankruptcy Act. One month later, U. S. District Judge James Alger Fee appointed two independent trustees to administer the financial affairs of the company until reorganization was completed and approved by both the court and the Securities and Exchange Commission. The judge also appointed legal counsel for the trustees.[36] By these actions, the court set in motion one of the most prolonged and complicated series of legal proceedings in Portland's history. At stake was the future of Portland's largest private utility.

After the petition was filed, PEPCO President Franklin T. Griffith, who was also head of the subsidiary companies, indicated that PGE, the major property, could be saved only if the following actions were taken:

(1) Defeat all efforts to create a PUD in Portland. Were a PUD to be approved by the voters, PGE stock would lose value and the collateral of the income bonds would be jeopardized.

567

(2) Sign a long term contract for BPA power with rates sufficiently high enough to produce revenues needed to meet bond interest, bank obligations and stock dividend requirements.

(3) Divest PEPCO of the Portland Traction properties. PTC was losing over $5000 a month.

(4) Secure compensation from New York's Chase National Bank for unethical injury inflicted upon the utility in 1930, at the time that the company was controlled by the Albert E. Peirce interests.[37]

The leading actors in the nine year drama, in addition to Griffith and his board of directors, were: (1) The court, represented by Judge Fee; (2) the Guaranty Trust Company as the indenture trustee; (3) the Chase National Bank; (4) various groups of PGE stockholders; and (5), the independent trustees and their counsel. Trustees Thomas W. Delzell and R. L. Clark and their counsel Ralph H. King played the key roles, and they were to be involved in the major conflicts that arose, with both the company management and the New York financial institutions as contestants.[38]

Thomas W. Delzell was the helmsman of the reorganization effort. An

Thomas W. Delzell

568

engineering graduate of Oregon State University, former assistant public utilities commissioner and an executive of the California-Oregon Power Company, Delzell logged over 19,000 hours on the job and spent over 450 days on the road, travelling to California, New York and Washington, D. C. A man of colorful language and occasional rough manner, Delzell proved a dogged investigator who, in his dealings with the various parties concerned, showed "firmness, consummate tact and bold ingenuity," to cite the words of federal bankruptcy referee Judge Estes Snedecor.[39] Delzell spent most of his time on PGE affairs while R. L. Clark, the president of BoDine & Clark, a livestock commission house, concentrated on the problems of the Portland Traction Company which was separated from PEPCO in September 1939 and administered by the trustees. Griffith resigned from the PTC board and Clark appointed veteran railroad freight expert E. E. Vanderahe as the general manager. Within one year, PTC was showing a profit of $21,400.

Trustee counsel Ralph H. King played a crucial role in PEPCO's reorganization. A Yale Law School graduate from Idaho with 20 years experience in Portland and a past president of the Oregon State Bar Association, King logged 11,000 hours of work personally. Adding in the time of his partners and associates, the King firm expended over 20,000 hours in professional service.[40] King proved instrumental in gaining the multi-million dollar judgment against the Chase Bank. From his first days on the job he had detected bank fraud and it became necessary for him to take certain actions which the PGE directors fought bitterly, not realizing that King's strategy would ultimately benefit both the company and its stockholders.[41] Feelings became so acrimonious that one director, Paul B. Wallace of Salem, accused King of being "bulbous and bumtious [sic],[42] epithets that bounced off King's tough hide with no apparent effect.

PGE's Problems with BPA and the PUC

PEPCO might well have escaped the agony of its second reorganization were it not for J. D. Ross' untimely death — one of those quirks of history that often produce unforeseen consequences of significant import. As the major source of PEPCO's revenues, PGE needed a firm long-term power contract with BPA that would guarantee the utility at least 50 percent of its generating capacity. Meeting with J. D. Ross in Washington toward the end of January 1939, Griffith realized that without such a contract in force, PEPCO could not hope to finance the bond interest due on March 1st. After several work sessions, Griffith and Ross apparently agreed upon the outline of a contract that would provide for a beginning of 20,000 kws. of firm power, gradually increasing to 80,000 kws. They also discussed a possible dump power (excess power) commitment to the company of 300,000 kws. annually. Ross told Griffith that he would execute a formal contract upon his return to Portland. Unfortunately for all parties concerned, Ross became ill and never returned to his office.[43]

When Paul Raver arrived on the scene in September 1939, he told Griffith that he was unwilling to be bound by the tentative agreement with Ross but that he would sign a short-term contract. At the time, Raver did not inform Griffith about a requirement that subsequently became the major stumbling block in future negotiations. Any long-term contract between BPA and PGE would have to include an option for BPA to purchase the PGE properties, not at a price arrived at through the usual condemnation procedures, but at a "fair price" to be determined by the BPA administrator. For over four years, Griffith was to protest this "ultimatum," presented to him in January 1941, as an unlawful extension of BPA authority. Thus, no long-term contract was to be signed until after the end of World War II. From 1942 until 1945, PGE bought BPA power on a short-term war duration contract.

Griffith knew what he was up against. When he met with Interior Secretary Harold Ickes in January 1941, Ickes told him about the Columbia Valley Authority act (CVA) that was pending before congress. If passed, the bill would have granted BPA the specific authority to acquire privately-owned public utility systems in the Pacific Northwest. Ickes fervently believed the passage of such a measure to be in the public interest. With three-fourths of the area of the state of Washington already on record as favoring public ownership, and with the federal developments at Bonneville and Grand Coulee that would undoubtedly dominate the supply of raw power in the area, public ownership was inevitable, Ickes declared.[44] The Secretary therefore opposed the issuance of long-term contracts that might impair the future operation of a CVA. Luckily for Griffith, and unhappily for Ickes, the approach of the war and its formal declaration on December 7, 1941, spelled doom for the CVA. Congress had more pressing matters on its collective mind.

The war aided PGE's survival and recovery in more ways than sinking the ominous Columbia Valley Authority. It produced an increase in revenues of nearly 100 percent. Between 1939 and 1946, PEPCO's net assets grew from $19 million to over $41 million, a total that included $8 million in cash received from the sale of the Portland Traction properties in August 1946. Despite Franklin T. Griffith's protests to the contrary, the short-term purchase of cheap BPA power beginning in the fall of 1939 put the private utility well into the black by the end of 1941, at which time it reported a net operating income of $1.5 million.

Griffith liked to boast that not only had PGE become a profitable enterprise again but that the utility had also reduced its rates in the two year period by $1.7 million. What he did not publicize was the fact that these reductions had been forced upon PGE by Oregon's Public Utilities Commissioner Ormond R. Bean. Appointed to office in 1939 by Republican Governor Charles Sprague, the former Portland city commissioner proved to be a sharp watchdog. As PGE's profits began to rise, Bean continually fought to secure lower consumer rates. And in the process he incurred the wrath of the Republican Party's big donors, especially PP&L and PGE. According to commissioner Bean, "Where the company gets its power is its business. What it charges is his business."[45]

In the May 1942 primary, conservative Earl Snell defeated liberal incumbent Charles Sprague for the Republican gubernatorial nomination — an action that was tantamount to election in Oregon. If the record of past political contributions by the private utilities was any indicator, it could be assumed that Griffith and McKee funneled considerable funds into Snell's campaign. In their minds, Governor Sprague had not turned out to be a true friend. And in Ormond Bean's mind, he knew that his days as public utilities commissioner were numbered. He did not expect to be reappointed, as in fact he was not.

As a parting testament to his dedicated work in behalf of Oregon's consumers, Bean filed a formal complaint against PGE on March 31, 1943. In a letter to *Oregon Journal* associate editor Marshall Dana, Bean indicated that he felt the new state administration would probably not pursue the complaint. The consumers themselves would have to initiate action. "The case," he wrote, "might well end in the Supreme Court."[46]

Bean's complaint was the result of two weeks of study by two of Oregon's most eminent attorneys with wide experience in regulatory rate matters: William C. McCulloch of the Joseph N. Teal firm, and McDannell Brown, who had represented a number of PUD supporters in previous PUC hearings. Among the numerous questions raised, two dealt with PGE's excess earnings since 1941. Not only did the document ask for a reduction in domestic and general service rates in Multnomah and six surrounding counties, but it sought a recapture of excess earnings achieved during 1942. It recommended that such earnings be turned over to the PUC for disbursal. The complaint concluded that net profits to PGE in the Portland area were "larger than reasonable." Bean in fact charged at a subsequent press conference that the Portland rates were "oppressive," in contrast, for example, to those in Salem.[47]

Fortunately or not, depending upon one's point of view, World War II saved the Portland General Electric Company and its parent holding company, PEPCO. The 30 percent growth in population, the building of Vanport as America's largest new city, and the entrance of many new industries into the Portland area, all of these developments produced enormous demands on Portland's largest private utility. And the catalyst of this growth was the decision by Henry J. Kaiser to locate three shipyards along the Columbia and Willamette Rivers.

Henry J. Kaiser Enters Portland

On January 12, 1941, announcement was made in the Portland press that Kaiser, his son Edgar and some local industrialists had acquired 87 acres immediately north of Terminal 4 in the St. Johns district.[48] This was to be the site of the Oregon Shipbuilding Corporation which contemplated erecting an eight-way yard in which to build an original order of 31 cargo ships for the British government. Extensive negotiations had preceded this announcement and Portland's chamber of commerce was intimately involved in all of them.[49]

As early as June of 1940, the chamber's industrial promotion department was in correspondence with the U. S. Navy about the area's potential for accepting national defense construction projects. The Kaisers moved into prominence in early November when the chamber's Arthur Farmer noted that Edgar Kaiser was preceding a British mission on its trip west to inspect possible shipbuilding sites. Apparently, Kaiser would take a plane ahead of the mission and arrive at the next city where it was to stop. His purpose, he admitted, was to keep the mission from talking with anyone except those to whom he wished to steer them. In Portland, the Britishers visited only the Willamette Iron and Steel Company (WISCO) which had enjoyed a close relationship with Henry Kaiser for some years. In the same month, WISCO was awarded the first World War II shipbuilding contract in Oregon, for construction of two Navy amphibious landing craft at a total cost of $14 million.

Migrating to Spokane, Washington, from the East Coast while he was in his early twenties, Henry Kaiser had entered the sand and gravel business by 1914. Soon he was to organize the Kaiser Paving Company and successfully bid on a series of large highway construction projects in western Canada. By 1930, he had become a big enough operator to be invited to join with five other major western construction firms to form the syndicate that built the Boulder (Hoover) Dam. As the elected chairman of the group in 1931, he became friendly with Portland contractor Charles F. Shea and Pacific Construction Company's Charles F. Swigert who were both members of "The Six" (as the syndicate was called). Swigert, who was also board chairman of WISCO in the early thirties, had handpicked Austin Flegel, the firm's president who was responsible for securing Portland's first defense shipbuilding contract. WISCO, however, was not large enough to meet the needs of Henry Kaiser. During the war, WISCO was to build over 70 vessels of various types, but they were of much smaller dimensions than those that Kaiser was called upon to produce.

Early in his spectacular career, Kaiser established a reputation for being able to tackle a project of nearly any size, do a thorough job and finish the work well ahead of schedule. Hoover Dam was completed in half the allotted time. This accomplishment allowed him to bid successfully on the construction of Grand Coulee Dam which was going to serve his home region of Spokane. In the midst of this gigantic undertaking, Kaiser also sought and secured the major Bonneville general contract.

When the Allies found themselves in desperate need of ships in 1940, the British sought out the Kaisers whose skill at marshalling men and materials efficiently was well known to them. After Henry Kaiser signed several large contracts with the British Mission in New York in late November 1940, he quickly had to find a site on which to build the 31 cargo ships, and Portland was one of two then under consideration. The chamber of commerce staff was following events closely. On November 26th, manager Walter W. R. May wired Franklin T. Griffith who was staying at the Ambassador Hotel in New York City:

"Henry J. Kaiser now at Waldorf [next door]. Plans shipyard at Oakland or Portland . . . but feels Portland lukewarm in interest. Could you and Mr. Polhemus [James H. Polhemus was president of PGE in 1940] see him and impress community's interest, available labor and other advantages Willamette River. Dick [U. S. Bank president Paul Dick] and others wiring. All feel your call important in getting decision for Portland."[50]

Franklin Griffith obviously did not need much encouragement to undertake this assignment. He knew only too well that the future salvation of PEPCO would depend on Portland's ability to woo large enterprises like a Kaiser shipyard. He must have been convincing, for within ten days, negotiations were underway to locate a suitable site in Portland. The dock commission owned 80 acres just north of Terminal 4. Adding these to an 11 acre tract owned by the Mark P. Miller estate, the Portland Shipbuilding Company was organized with Charles F. Shea as president and Edgar Kaiser as vice president. The firm's title was later changed to the Oregon Shipbuilding Corporation and the site was expanded to over 300 acres.

Besides Griffith, several other local business and civic leaders played a role in convincing Kaiser to choose Portland. Portland Chamber of Commerce President Ross McIntyre, a retail chainstore executive, was the brother of President Roosevelt's closest aide, appointments secretary Marvin H. McIntyre. Although Ross was a Republican, he not only had obvious White House connections but he was also an old friend of Henry Kaiser's, as was *Oregonian* editor E. Palmer Hoyt. U. S. Bank President Paul Dick, the chairman of the chamber's industrial committee, and his son Harvey Dick, owner of the Hotel Hoyt, both added their efforts to soliciting Kaiser's business. Harvey Dick's machinery plant had previously subcontracted some jobs for Henry Kaiser. Harvey was to profit greatly from the subsequent growth of both the shipbuilding and scrap iron industries. In 1942, he convinced the U. S. Defense Plant Corporation to build the Columbia Steel Casting plant in Sullivan's Gulch, on the old Pacific Car Foundry site adjacent to Rose City Park. Columbia Steel Casting was destined to turn out hundreds of propellers and stern frames for Kaiser's ships.

With the launching on May 19, 1941, of the *Star of Oregon*, Portland's first Liberty ship, Kaiser was off and running. He managed to develop an inside track with both the U. S. Maritime Commission and the U. S. Navy, connections that paid off handsomely. In January 1942, he opened his 400 acre Vancouver yard which was to turn out over 50 baby aircraft escort carriers, and in March 1942 Swan Island started production of 147 T-2 tankers. Portland became the Liberty and Victory ship capital of the country. In the fall of 1942, the *Joseph N. Teal* was built in a record ten days and President Roosevelt slipped secretly into town to watch his daughter, Anna Boettiger, christen the vessel.

Of the 455 ships delivered to the U. S. Maritime Commission from the Oregon Shipbuilding yards, 20 were sent to Russia under the lend-lease program. They were launched with familiar names, but departed with Russian names, crews and flags. The *Henry L. Pittock* became the *Ashkold*; the *Elijah P. Lovejoy*, the *Alexander Suvorer*; the *Henry L. Corbett*, the *Alexander Minsky*; and the *Willis P. Hawley*, the *Stalinobad*.[51] So much cargo was being shipped out to Russia by 1945 that Portland's harbor ranked third in the nation for exports — behind only New York and Philadelphia.

Describing the city's Russian encounters during the late war years, Richard L. Neuberger wrote:

The Hotel Hoyt, at N. W. Hoyt Street and Sixth Avenue. Built in the early years of the century, the Hoyt was acquired by Harvey Dick before the war. It was demolished in 1977 to provide space for a new city bus depot, a project that was subsequently cancelled by the bus companies. A gigantic boondoggle, the transaction cost the city and county nearly $1 million. In its heyday, the old Hoyt enjoyed an illustrious, even boisterous, life as one of the more colorful hostelries in Portland. During the war years, Harvey Dick cleverly used it as a gathering place for out-of-state workers disembarking from trains at the nearby Union Station. He offered temporary lodging in the hotel and free beer in his saloon. After selecting out the workers he wanted for his Columbia Steel Casting plant, he would send the rest over to Kaiser or Willamette Iron and Steel. Across Sixth from the Hoyt was the "ramshackle Rainier Hotel, a bordello of sorts" that provided additional services to the arriving war workers.[52]

"This was a stern blow to Portland's anchorites, and to the police department's vigilant Red squad. Soviet sea captains were free to roam Portland streets and drink pure Mount Hood water from . . . [Simon Benson's] bronze . . . fountains. . . . Some of the Russian skippers were women with ample bosoms and sturdy legs, and old-line Portlanders peered in awe from behind their brocaded curtains as the seafaring amazons trudged in and out of the brownstone mansion the Soviet purchasing mission had taken over."[53]

Neuberger was referring to the old Theodore B. Wilcox home at the corner of S. W. Park and King Streets, across from the garden of the exclusive women's Town Club.

Kaiser's Impact on the Portland Community

Housing was Portland's most serious problem during the first years of the war. Over 72,000 migrant workers swarmed into the city by every known means of transportation. Kaiser actively recruited workers in the East and South and ran special transcontinental trains directly to Portland. Overnight, Portland became a high pressure defense city. In addition to the Kaiser yards and Harvey Dick's Columbia Steel Casting Plant, four long established Portland companies sharply increased their employee ranks: The Commercial Iron Works, Willamette Iron & Steel, Albina Engine and Machine Works and Gunderson Brothers. Allied to these larger firms were another 700 subsidiary industries which were required to add to their personnel rosters. The existing housing stock, almost entirely private, was totally unequal to the demands. The lack of proper shelter became a far more serious threat to the war effort than a feared attack on the Oregon Coast by the Japanese Navy.

In fact, it took the Japanese attack on Pearl Harbor to force the city council to take an action it should have taken four years earlier: The creation of a public housing authority. Portland was the only major city on the West Coast without such an agency and yet it was faced with the most severe housing crisis on the entire coast. Moving with unusual dispatch, the city fathers created the Housing Authority of Portland (HAP) on December 11, 1941, and the action was none too early. Mayor Earl Riley appointed the initial five members, including prominent realtor Chester A. Moores who had vociferously opposed the creation of just such an agency during peacetime. Although Moores was not named chairman until September 1944, his presence dominated the HAP for four years. In fact, the agency itself was dominated by the real estate, apartment and mortgage banking interests throughout much of its early history.

Because federal wartime housing funds were not available until late in 1942, the Kaiser Corporation became the prime contractor for the major projects such as Vanport and Guild's Lake. Subcontractors were chosen to carry out the actual construction work at each project. The need for haste and the old game of power politics created innumerable cases of conflict of interest. One involved Charles

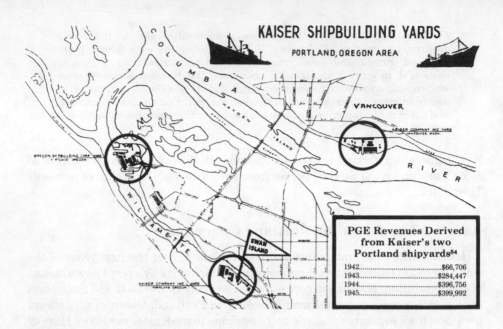

KAISER SHIPBUILDING YARDS
PORTLAND, OREGON AREA

PGE Revenues Derived from Kaiser's two Portland shipyards[54]	
1942	$66,706
1943	$284,447
1944	$396,756
1945	$399,992

The Oregon Shipbuilding yards in St. Johns

Mrs. Iona Murphy, a welder at the Oregon Shipbuilding yards

B. Wegman who was appointed to HAP in April 1942 while Vanport was in its preliminary design stages. Wegman resigned from HAP when ground was broken in September 1942. His firm was one of the two chosen by HAP and Kaiser to build the "miracle city." Before his work was completed — and very shoddily at that — he had erected 349 apartment buildings, and all of the special public and service buildings.

The other Vanport subcontractor was the George H. Buckler Company which constructed 371 apartment buildings and that portion of the ring dike which was to collapse on May 31, 1948, the day after the first breach to the west under the SP&S railroad tracks. On that day a 12 foot wall of water swept in and covered the entire Vanport development.

Together, Wegman and Buckler built nearly 10,000 dwelling units, five times as many as the second largest contract for the University Homes site in St. Johns. Local builder Ross B. Hammond won that plum, along with one of the eight Guild's Lake contracts. Previously Hammond had achieved some notoriety as the contractor for the Portland Public Market Building.

Portland's 25 wartime HAP projects gave employment to nearly every architectural firm in the region, but the largest slice of the business went to the firm of Wolff & Phillips which was chosen to design Vanport. As the predecessor firm of the current Portland giant, the Zimmer Gunsul Frasca Partnership, Wolff & Phillips inaugurated a long professional relationship with Henry and Edgar Kaiser which has continued to the present day. Wolff & Phillips, however, could not be blamed for the collapse of the dike. That stigma unfortunately belonged to the SP&S Railroad, and to the Kaiser Company and the Oregon State Highway Commission, both of which approved the construction of an underpass below Denver Avenue, weakening the eastern defenses of Vanport.

When Vanport was completed in record time, in September 1943, it won nationwide acclaim, that is until a congressional subcommittee reported it had found grave problems during the course of a five day visit. Many of the housing units were discovered to be shoddily constructed. The city was overcrowded, the roads were deteriorating and public services were inadequate. More than one critic was later to conclude that Vanport was "one of the world's worst examples of city planning."[55] Built on an inadequately filled swamp between two major rivers, "Vanport was never more than a huge collection of 'crackerbox houses strung together fast and cheap,' according to one of its former residents."[56]

This opinion even seemed to be shared by at least two members of the housing authority itself, realtor Chester A. Moores and apartment owner Herbert J. Dahlke, both of whom were on the executive committee of the Oregon Apartment House Association. In a letter of September 1944, the association expressed its position on the quality and future of wartime housing:

"After the war emergency, all such housing should be sold to wreckers and demolished. The locations and construction of such housing would only

Ten Local Housing Authorities with Largest Number of Dwelling Units under Management or Construction by Type of Accommodation

As of February 29, 1944

	Total	Family Dwelling	Dormitory	Stop-gap
Portland, Oregon	18,504	18,394	110	——
New York, New York	13,173	13,173	——	——
Vallejo, California	12,702	8,750	3,942	——
Vancouver, Washington	12,389	12,389	——	——
Los Angeles (City), California	10,703	7,578	3,000	125
Mobile, Alabama	10,608	8,353	1,754	501
Baltimore, Maryland	9,849	8,754	595	500
Philadelphia, Pennsylvania	7,878	7,878	——	——
Richmond, California	7,754	6,754	1,000	——
Seattle, Washington	7,289	6,328	961	——

VANPORT CITY
aerial map of the world's largest war housing city

1. Road to Oregon Shipyard.	17. Nursery No. 6.	32. Administration building.
2. Storage yard.	18. Play area.	33. Island Avenue.
3. Nursery No. 3.	19. Lake Avenue.	34. Cottonwood Avenue.
4. Theater.	20. Central fire & police station.	35. Athletic field.
5. Dyke.	21. Hospital.	36. Victory Boulevard.
6. School group No. 2.	22. Social center No. 3.	37. Broad Acres Avenue.
7. Main drainage pump.	23. Social building No. 1.	38. Park.
8. Swift Boulevard.	24. Play area.	39. Nursery No. 5.
9. Nursery No. 4.	25. Nursery No. 2.	40. Denver Court.
10. Shopping center No. 2.	26. Cafeteria.	41. Denver Ave. (Portland to Vancouver).
11. Bus stop.	27. Road to Vancouver.	
12. Fire station No. 3.	28. Schools.	42. Nursery No. 1.
13. Social building No. 4.	29. Force Avenue.	43. Typical sewage pump sta.
14. Dyke.	30. Shopping center No. 1.	44. Fire station No. 2.
15. Railroad fill.	31. Post office.	45. Access to Denver Avenue.
16. Recreation building No. 2.		46. New East Vanport.

promote slums. All such housing are labor inflated shacks with about as much value as the powder shot out of a cannon. Unheard of high wages were paid to inexperienced, unskilled labor and the building materials used have very little value. . . . The locations would make much better industrial sites than homes. . . . Keep all housing in the hands of private ownership. In the United States of America there is no place for government ownership of any kind of business."[57]

Besides shoddy construction, both Vanport and Guild's Lake were plagued by another even more serious problem, especially in terms of future consequences. This was a racial one. In Vanport, over 6000 blacks resided in segregated inelegance. Nearly 5000 at Guild's Lake lived under similar conditions. Both projects had the makings of a postwar ghetto unless, of course, they should happen to be demolished and replaced by new industry. And in both cases, racial residential patterns were dictated by housing authority policy. A June 1945 in-house memorandum from HAP staff member K. E. Eckert to executive director Harry D. Freeman defined the policy in clear terms:

"It has always been our impression that the Commissioners' desire in the matter of housing Negroes was to segregate them, and this policy has been followed by the staff from the beginning. . . . It was brought out by the Commission three years ago that the Housing Authority should not set the pattern for the community and house Negroes in areas where there were few, if any, living at that time . . . and where there was no precedent and no home-owner who might feel that the influx of Negroes had lowered his property value."[58]

After the war was over, a strong case could be made for demolishing the "crackerbox" houses in both Vanport and Guild's Lake. But no one in authority, including the leaders of Portland's business-political establishment, could figure out what to do with 11,000 blacks who comprised over 50 percent of Portland's war-inflated black population. As Eckert told Freeman: "The housing of the in-migrant Negroes during . . . the post war period . . . is a

Guild's Lake "crackerbox" housing, similar to Vanport's

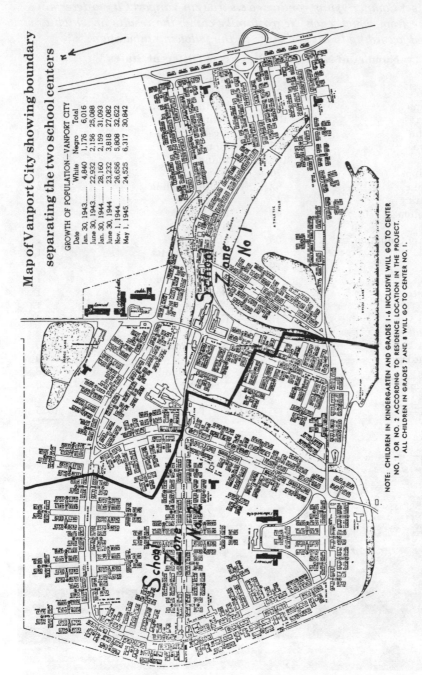

Map of Vanport City showing boundary separating the two school centers

GROWTH OF POPULATION—VANPORT CITY

Date	White	Negro	Total
Jan. 30, 1943	4,840	1,176	6,016
June 30, 1943	22,932	2,156	25,088
Jan. 30, 1944	28,160	2,159	31,093
June 30, 1944	23,232	3,818	27,082
Nov. 1, 1944	26,656	5,808	32,622
May 1, 1945	24,525	6,317	30,842

School Zone No. 1

School Zone No. 2

ATHLETIC FIELD

NOTE: CHILDREN IN KINDERGARTEN AND GRADES 1-6 INCLUSIVE WILL GO TO CENTER
NO. 1 OR NO. 2 ACCORDING TO RESIDENCE LOCATION IN THE PROJECT.
ALL CHILDREN IN GRADES 7 AND 8 WILL GO TO CENTER NO. 1.

(*Author's note: The black population resided in School Zone No. 2. This was the area that was flooded first, on May 30, 1948. By requiring elementary school attendance according to residence location, grades 1-6 in Zone No. 1 were kept "pure white."*)

581

The Kaiser Company, Inc., conducted a survey in Vanport City to determine the state from which each Negro family came, the results of which are arranged according to rank of state in the following tabulation:

Number of Negro Families From Different States[59]

Texas	242	Minnesota	6
Arkansas	231	Utah	6
Oklahoma	129	North Carolina	5
Missouri	108	Pennsylvania	5
Louisiana	104	West Virginia	5
Alabama	103	Montana	4
Illinois	101	Idaho	3
Mississippi	70	Wisconsin	3
California	62	South Carolina	2
New York	47	Virginia	2
Washington	45	Florida	1
Nevada	40	Kentucky	1
District of Columbia	35	Maryland	1
Colorado	20	Massachusetts	1
Oregon	19	New Jersey	1
Kansas	18	North Dakota	1
Tennessee	17	South Dakota	1
Iowa	15	Wyoming	1
Arizona	13	Connecticut	0
Nebraska	13	Delaware	0
Georgia	11	New Hampshire	0
New Mexico	9	Maine	0
Indiana	8	Rhode Island	0
Michigan	7	Vermont	0
Ohio	7		
		Total	1525

The Bess Kaiser Hospital

serious problem of which I am sure the Commission is fully aware."[60] The Vanport flood was to resolve part of the problem for HAP but it would only make it worse for those black victims who were forced to flee to Albina.

The Kaisers, who were responsible for the actual hiring of nearly 70 percent of Portland's total war labor force, were opposed to segregated housing and racial discrimination in employment. But their social convictions had little impact on the Housing Authority of Portland. After the war, Edgar Kaiser was to advocate that Vanport be improved and made into a permanent residential community. The Vanport flood eliminated that possibility.

In matters of employment, the Kaiser efforts achieved more success only after President Roosevelt himself threatened federal action. An Executive Order of May 27, 1943, mandated that "there shall be no discrimination in the employment of any person in war industries . . . by reason of race, creed, color, or national origin."[61] But the unions, particularly the Boilermakers and Shipbuilders which controlled 65 percent of the shipyard work force, delayed in their compliance for as long as possible. They finally established black auxiliary locals, membership in which carried none of the traditional union benefits. With no job security or seniority, over one-third of the black wartime labor force were to find themselves unemployed by the winter of 1947, only eighteen months after the war was over.

Conditions became so bad that a National Urban League official depicted Portland as "just like any Southern town . . . the most prejudiced [city] in the west."[62] After the Portland Urban League's first executive director, Edwin C. (Bill) Berry, arrived in town, he sensed immediately that many members of the Portland establishment hoped that most blacks would return to the south or wheresoever they had come from. Mayor Earl Riley was not alone in holding feelings that the war had created a bad racial situation. The city could not absorb more than a certain number of blacks, but during wartime, patriotism compelled the community to "forget some of [its] previous ideals."[63] Berry told a group of businessmen that he had yet to unpack his bags; that if they wanted

---

Results of a Kaiser Survey, 1944

Nearly 52 percent of Kaiser's 91,000 workers wanted to remain in the Portland area after the war. Less than one-quarter of the group classified itself as skilled labor in their prewar occupations. In their response to the question: "What living condition in the Portland area causes you the most inconvenience, if any?", over half cited no criticism. Transportation was cited by 21 percent, housing by 9.5 percent and shopping by 8.8 percent. Of the 3,461 Negroes interviewed, 14.4 percent definitely intended to stay, while 33.3 percent would stay if jobs were available. Only 163 of the Negroes interviewed had lived in Portland longer than three years.[64]

583

him to direct a black exodus he was prepared to take the next train back to Chicago.[65]

Apart from housing and employment, Kaiser's long-term impact on the Portland community was probably most felt through the establishment of a wartime medical care program. Henry Kaiser's mother had died in his arms when he was 16 years old for what he considered to be inadequate medical care. With this memory in mind, he established the non-profit Kaiser Foundation medical care program by opening a rambling ranch-type hospital and outpatient clinic near Vancouver to serve the needs of his shipyard employees and other residents also in need of care.

From this modest beginning, Kaiser built the world's largest private initiative system of hospitals, clinics and prepaid medical care — a successful enterprise that was fought by the American Medical Association no less strenuously than private power fought public power. In 1958, the foundation built the Bess Kaiser Hospital on North Greeley Avenue in memory of Henry Kaiser's first wife. Today, the Kaiser-Permanente medical care program is possibly the most complete and extensive one in the Portland-Vancouver metropolitan area, with two large medical centers and several clinics serving over 250,000 people (nearly one person in five residing in the Portland-Vancouver region).[66]

Preparing for the War's End

World War II was less than a year old when Portland City Commissioner William A. Bowes spoke of the need for the city to "plan now" for the postwar period. Bowes was concerned by a number of matters all stemming from the vast increase in the metropolitan population. He was concerned about jobs. Portland had never been an industrial city. In 1940, less than one-sixth of the labor pool was industrially employed. By the war's end, the amount would rise to 50 percent. Could Portland accommodate such a large number without attracting new industries to replace the expected decline in shipbuilding contracts? Bowes was also concerned about permanent housing for the war workers who elected to remain in the area. Finally, and most importantly to the commissioner, was the problem of adequate arterials and highways to handle the expected increase in automobile use that could only worsen the existing congestion.[67] Like most of his colleagues in city government, however, he showed little concern for minority problems: How was Portland prepared to house an eight-fold increase in the Negro population in a city that not only permitted but defended residential segregation?

In the spring of 1943, Mayor Earl Riley directed Bowes to appoint the Portland Area Postwar Development Committee (PAPDC). Bowes put together about as varied and eminent a group of local leaders as could be drafted out of the greater Portland community with two notable omissions: No women and no Negroes. Chosen as chairman was Portland's leading commercial realtor, David B. Simpson of the firm Norris, Beggs and Simpson. As vice chairman, Bowes

584

Realtor David B. Simpson
(1898-1976)

Aaron Frank
(1891-1968)

selected L. T. Merwin, president of the Northwestern Electric Company and a vice president of its parent firm, Pacific Power & Light. The committee was to function for the better part of five years and there were few issues of local importance during that period that escaped its attention. The chief power and influence resided in six people: Simpson, Merwin, E. C. Sammons, Harry Banfield, Chester A. Moores and Aaron Frank. These men literally ran the city of Portland — if not all of the commissioners then at least the mayor's office. Mayor Earl Riley seldom made a move without consulting Meier & Frank president Aaron Frank. When Frank would return to the city from a business trip, he would call Riley's office and inform the secretary, "I'm back in town."[68]

The PAPDC was dominated by the private utilities and the banks, especially the U. S. National — a not unusual phenomenon in Portland's history. Its two most powerful and influential voices were those of Simpson and Banfield. Simpson was to be elected president of the Portland Chamber of Commerce in 1944, the same year that he joined the U. S. Bank board. In 1940 he had been selected by Franklin T. Griffith to become a director of the Portland Traction Company. Banfield, the president of Iron Fireman, was a director of both the U. S. Bank and PP&L's Portland Gas & Coke Company. He was also a 13 year veteran of the dock commission and was to be appointed chairman of the state highway commission in 1944. Although there were at least three representatives of the Bonneville Power Administration on the PAPDC at various stages of its existence, they exercised only a minor influence on its major decisions. Ivan Bloch recalls that Simpson could be brutal in his attitude toward the public power agency. According to Bloch, "Simpson kept control in the old guard hands."[69]

Arthur D. McVoy, who was employed as the secretary-director of PAPDC, wrote a lengthy article in 1945 on the history of Portland's city planning efforts. As published in the *Oregon Historical Quarterly*, McVoy's account depicted PAPDC as a group of "leading public-spirited citizens representing the principal interests of the city."[70] From an examination of the available records, it would not be uncharitable to conclude that "the principal interests" were to be given far more attention than the public spirit — or the public interest, to be more precise.

Through this committee went all of the planning for future public works, particularly those related to highways and arterials — information that was of utmost value to the placement of future industrial and shopping center sites. Merchant Fred G. Meyer carried on a continuous correspondence with Chester A. Moores and was kept fully informed about the plans of the Oregon State Highway Commission.[71] One letter that Moores wrote to Meyer on February 12, 1942, was illustrative of the relationship:

> "Late in December . . . I spent an hour in Mr. Baldock's office of the State Highway Commission in Salem and he enumerated a number of projects aggregating approximately thirty millions of dollars which they are getting ready for construction immediately after the war. Included in this program are the Fremont Street Bridge, Foothill Boulevard, Aurora-Wilsonville Highway and a number of other projects of particular interest to us here in Portland. . . . If at any time you know of any particular project which you think should be followed up closely I trust you will not hesitate to advise us."[72]

Realtors David B. Simpson and Chester A. Moores had front row seats on all postwar land use planning which could only benefit their existing and future clients. These businessmen did in fact devote many hours of their time to formal PAPDC deliberations, but such efforts could hardly be construed as personal sacrifices undertaken solely in the public interest. When the Fred Meyer shopping center chain began its explosive growth in the 1950s, David B. Simpson was the person who not only arranged many of the primary real estate transactions but also provided financing through national institutions like the New England Mutual Life Insurance Company with which Norris, Beggs and Simpson had long been associated.

The Moses Plan

Soon after its appointment, the PAPDC decided that it should address its first efforts to the programming of public works projects for the immediate postwar period. They chose to hire "America's number one public works planner,"[73] New York City Park Commissioner Robert Moses who in 1943 was at the peak of his powerful career.[74] Moses arrived with a working staff in September 1943, spent the better part of a week examining the city, departed for home and submitted his report in early November. To raise the $75,000 to pay Moses' fee, the PAPDC persuaded the city, county, school board, park commission and Port commission to underwrite the project.[75]

When Moses' "Portland Improvement Plan" was published in the press on November 10th, it received mixed reactions. Commissioner Bowes and the PAPDC seemed pleased. Were the plan to be fully implemented, said Bowes, it would "provide public employment on a scale unprecedented for Portland."[76] It called for $60 million of labor expenditures to employ 20,000 and $15 million for land purchases. His complete arterial street plan carried a price tag of $30 million. Expressing enthusiasm, Roi L. Morin of the local chapter of the American Institute of Architects exclaimed: "The facts are that all moneys expended in the last 75 years to guide the growth of this city have been insignificant and inadequate. . . . The city has just 'growed up like Topsy.' "[77] Here was an ambitious plan that could propel Portland to greater heights. Ever since the war had begun, city planning had become nearly defunct, and most of the city zoning, housing and building ordinances had been relaxed "for the duration" by city council action.

The extensive plan contained many constructive proposals. But its greatest weakness lay in the fact that it had been done too hastily. Moses had simply not spent enough time consulting with more Portlanders who knew the local problems, as well as the city's attachment to certain landmarks such as the Union Station which Moses advocated demolishing. Moses had two basic commitments: To new public facilities and to the automobile. He had no interest in renovation or restoration. And as a "rubber tire man," he believed that the automobile would continue to transform American society. Any new transportation system had to be designed to accommodate changing habits as basic and popular as increased automobile ownership and use.

Improvement of highway facilities was the key to the plan. Moses advocated a loop parkway system around the congested areas of the city, a new bridge, widened bridge ramps and a new depressed East Side highway, running between Seventh and Eighth Avenues. The Union Station area in Northwest Portland was designated for total reconstruction: An 11 block station and bus depot plaza "to modernize and beautify the traveller's first impression of the City of Roses."

Moses' other major recommendation called for a 20 block civic center along Front Avenue, between S. W. Salmon and Columbia Streets, running west as far as Sixth Avenue. Additional Moses proposals were directed at new schools and school recreational areas, improvement of the docks and airport, and the acquisition of potential park lands such as were to be included two years later in Forest Park. The plan advocated the immediate construction of a sewage disposal system to eliminate Willamette River pollution.

The more general recommendations related to city planning matters: The city's zoning code needed drastic amendment to reduce the space allocated to apartments. There was also need for a more orderly development of land on the city's fringes — "the future slums of the city." Too much land was zoned for commercial activity and billboards needed tighter regulation, especially adjacent to residential districts.[78] One recommendation that particularly pleased Chester A. Moores was the suggestion that "temporary and unneeded war housing be disposed of." On the other hand, Moses directed attention to the need to rehabilitate "obsolescent areas and neighborhoods." Consideration should be given "to the principles of neighborhood organization and integration inherent in modern urban planning and successfully demonstrated in actual housing and community developments and operations in recent years."[79]

When all was said and done, the Moses Plan seemed to gain fairly wide support within the community. Such organizations as the City Club and the Retail Trade Bureau, in addition to the PAPDC, granted their general endorsement. Commissioner Bowes felt that if nothing else, the plan

" . . . aroused great interest in the problems of planning . . . among the people of the Portland metropolitan area. It also gave Portland nationwide publicity for having attempted in a very bold manner to meet its immediate postwar needs."[80]

Such sentiments may have expressed the immediate reaction. But in the months that followed, certain specific criticisms began to surface. As Arthur McVoy noted, some of the routing of the plan's highway loop was not "studied out enough in detail, and much of it was contained in previous proposals."[81] Mel Scott, in his exhaustive study of American City Planning Since 1890, was later to comment:

"The Portland procedure of calling in a man with a big name to warm over plans and proposals with which community leaders were familiar necessarily lacked the dynamism of postwar planning programs generated by the people themselves."[82]

Although the city council did not officially approve the plan "in principle" until September 1944, it accepted the PAPDC's recommendation to place four bond measures on the May 1944 primary ballot. The council, like many members of Portland's business community, realized that a shortage of funds created the major obstacle to the plan's fulfillment.

As selected, the bond issues included: A sewage disposal plan ($12 million), dock improvements ($3 million), school board needs ($5 million), and county roads and bridges ($4 million). The voters approved the $24 million package on May 19th. Purposely deleted from these proposals was any funding for parkways and arterials. In a report issued the previous March, the PAPDC streets committee declared that the "Moses report on highway improvements" was not "a comprehensive plan for highway development in the Portland metropolitan area." Along with the City Club, the streets committee felt that most of the future industrial growth would be in "the northern end of the peninsula at the confluence of the Willamette and Columbia rivers"[83] — the current Rivergate district. The City Club emphasized that cheap power, a favorable labor market, easy access to resources and to the markets of the world — all of these factors encouraged development in North Portland. Because an improved transportation network was considered "the principal means of realizing these advantages," the problems were deemed too complex to be translated into bond issues in May 1944. They were going to have to be faced soon but they needed further study.

Since the publication of Robert Caro's biography of Robert Moses in 1974 (*The Power Broker*), several local commentators have tended to blame Moses for the excesses of Portland's subsequent freeway construction, particularly for the ill-fated Mt. Hood Freeway that was planned and then cancelled.[84] The record does not support such contentions. Although Caro credits Moses as being responsible for the overall interstate highway program that was heavily funded during the Eisenhower administration, all of the freeway routes that were to be constructed in Portland had been tentatively selected by the state highway commission prior to June 1943.

According to city traffic engineer Fred T. Fowler, in a report to Bowes, the only Moses recommendation that had not been previously considered was the East Side depressed freeway.[85] Ironically, in the light of history, this was probably one major Moses suggestion that should have been taken seriously. The east bank of the Willamette River might have been spared not only permanent disfigurement, but the placement of one of the most dangerous and congested traffic arterials in the state of Oregon. According to Bowes in 1946, the depressed highway was never given consideration due to cost.[86]

Bowes' 1946 plan called for a viaduct passing over East Water Avenue. This arrangement would also have provided for the creation of a riverbank park. In the early 1960s, in opposition to the efforts of Mayor Terry Schrunk and city commissioner Ormond R. Bean, the Oregon State Highway Commission chose the existing route along the riverbank and in the process created the dangerous curve on the east ramp of the Marquam Bridge. The reason was again cited as one of cost. It was cheaper to use filled land than to build a viaduct. In addition, the railroads opposed the viaduct that would have covered over their tracks.[87]

No one paid much attention in 1946 to planning expert Walter Blucher when he spoke in Portland on July 14th. In total disagreement with Robert Moses, the executive secretary of the American Society of Planning Officials warned city

Portland Freeway Loop — Dangerous curve (circled) of East Bank Freeway — 1975

taxpayers against the building of major highways through city centers. He also warned city officials against allowing the construction of large surface parking lots to accommodate the automobiles that would use the highways. Such a policy, declared Blucher, was "suicidal for cities." It would only encourage downtown workers to become commuters, to live and pay their taxes outside of the city.[88]

Moses' Civic Center Proposal

The civic center proposal was one of Robert Moses' more controversial offerings and it divided the leadership of the downtown community. The concept was far from new. At least five different proposals had been placed on the drawing boards since the time of Edward H. Bennett in 1912 and all had suffered defeat. The one common element in each plan was the general location, in the vicinity of the city hall and county courthouse with a sweep to the river. The Moses plan simply infused some warm blood into a cold corpse, and the AIA local chapter took up the challenge.

Working with city commissioner Bowes' blessing, the planning commission,

590

under the leadership of Banker Guy E. Jaques and colleagues Charles McKinley and Glenn Stanton with the assistance of AIA architect Ernest C. Tucker, drafted an ambitious scheme that was even larger than that proposed by Moses: Twenty-four blocks in all, including four already owned by the city. In presenting the plan to the city council, the planning commission called it the "greatest opportunity to become a great city of the future." Without acceptance of some such plan, the commission cautioned, "Portland is likely to fall back into a relative position of obscurity, with the accompanying indictment of a reputation for limited progress and the attendant problems of unemployment and economic depression."[89] Recommending that the center be built in three stages, the planning commission told the city council that the land could be purchased for under $5 million because the site contained the most depressed property values in downtown Portland.

As laid out by the planning commission, the voters would first be asked to approve an enabling act, allowing the city to create a special improvement district. The voters would also be asked to authorize the city to sell $2 million of general obligation bonds and to levy no more than a 2 mill tax that would raise a maximum of $3 million. The improvement district would be a type of holding corporation. Its general purpose would be to direct the elimination of blight in the downtown area, with the same kind of scope and authority that was to be given to the Portland Development Commission a decade later. The civic center project would be only the first, albeit the largest, of several attempts to clean up the whole area from Sixth Avenue to the waterfront. To be appointed by the mayor, the improvement district members would fix assessments and float the necessary bonds. By selling the improved property to the federal and state governments and to any other agencies that might locate within the center, the city could expect to recoup at least 50 percent of the land acquisition costs, or at least enough to pay off the bonds. Additional projects within the improvement district would be presented for voter approval at a later date. After a series of lengthy discussions, the council voted in March 1945 to place the package before the voters at a special June election.

The reaction of the business community was mixed. The PAPDC was only lukewarm in support, with many of its members openly opposed. The City Club and organized labor endorsed the plan, along with the League of Women Voters, the Retail Trade Bureau and most home and commercial building groups. The opposition was led by three prominent Portlanders: Lawyer Robert T. Mautz, and businessmen Kenneth Beebe and Selwyn Bingham. It was charged that the center would wipe out too many tax paying properties which, although old and in many cases dilapidated, still provided needed tax revenues to the city. A number of the buildings, furthermore, were of pioneer vintage and should be preserved, not destroyed. Perhaps the cleverest argument related to the Public Market Building. "Don't burden Portland with another White Elephant" was the theme. Posters and mailing cards were distributed all over Portland carrying this warning. Expensive publicity campaigns were waged by both sides. But the

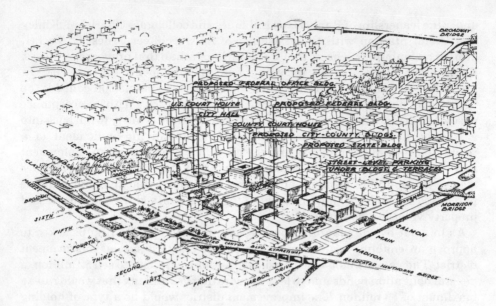

1946 Civic Center Plan

end result was probably predictable considering the degree of opposition that the plan engendered. It was rejected two to one.[90]

Undaunted by the defeat, the planning commission and city council, led by commissioner Bowes, approved another ballot measure for November 1946. The civic center plan was scaled down to 20 blocks, including six already owned by the city. But like its predecessors, it too suffered defeat.

In retrospect, one can observe that the city's waterfront would look radically different today had the civic center been built. Many of the current multi-million dollar construction projects such as the Marriott Hotel would not be located in their present sites. Gone would be the Benjamin Franklin and PGE's Willamette Centers. On the other hand, the city and county would not be arguing over where to place a new central jail facility, and those who have longed for a small music hall-theater would not be disappointed.

Regardless of the merits of the two plans, the city planning commission proved to be accurate in predicting the consequences of defeat. Downtown Portland did revert into "a relative position of obscurity." With the exceptions of the Equitable (now the Commonwealth), Oregonian and State Office buildings, no new construction on a grand scale, either public or private, was to occur for more than a decade. To architects like Pietro Belluschi who designed all three structures, the experience was discouraging. Some even elected to leave Portland to practice in more fruitful climates. In 1950, Belluschi took a position as dean of the School of Architecture at MIT in Cambridge, Massachusetts.

Industrial Sites vs. Housing

The subject of public housing and its future became a significant public issue in the fall of 1944 as both the PAPDC and the HAP began to wrestle with the future of Vanport. HAP chairman Chester A. Moores informed the *Journal* that the issue was "wide open"[91] when in fact it was not. Both agencies had made up their minds privately that wartime housing had to go, but they had not confirmed their decisions publicly. The *Journal* wrote an editorial requesting public input, but in the process it loaded one side of the issue by labeling those who favored continuance of public housing as "socialistic-minded schemers."[92] In response to the *Journal*, Portland citizen Ed Willison wrote:

> "I sincerely hope that the Housing Authority will not be influenced by those capitalistic interests which might wish to obtain possession of the units for speculative purposes, or that the units be wrecked in an effort to sustain either real estate rental or sales prices. There are thousands of people in the substandard wage brackets who have been and are still unable to buy the average modern home because of inability to make a substantial down payment and assume a mortgage. Why not give these thousands of the underprivileged a chance to purchase these units at a low figure and remove them to wherever they wish to live?"[93]

Chester A. Moores
HAP Chairman

593

Vanport's future as a permanent city had been strongly advocated three weeks earlier when Mrs. Samuel I. Rosenman, chairman of the national committee on housing, visited Portland to inspect the housing areas and talk with Edgar Kaiser. The wife of President Roosevelt's special counsel proposed the gradual rebuilding of Vanport into a permanent community of 12,500 homes. With the exception of Edgar Kaiser, however, few if any of Portland's business or labor leadership took such thoughts seriously. On September 30, 1944, the Oregon State Federation of Labor, whose vice president H. J. Detloff was a HAP commissioner, advocated that Vanport be demolished and converted into industrial sites.[94] Two weeks later, Mayor Earl Riley wired Edgar Kaiser that he had met with Aaron Frank, David Simpson and Chester A. Moores on October 12th and they had decided that "Vanport City should be cleared of present housing facilities immediately when its usage for war housing no longer exists. . . . The area should be made available for industrial development."[95] The final decision had been reached even though the HAP commission did not formally ratify the action until a week later and despite the well known fact that the Kaiser Company had already proposed the construction of several hundred permanent dwellings in the area.

The attitude of HAP was clear. Chester Moores and his friends did not view the

City Commissioner William A. Bowes

594

public housing authority as a social agency to help provide low cost housing to the poor. HAP was an agent of private enterprise whose sole function was to manage wartime housing projects and dispose of them as soon as practicable. As Moores wrote the regional director of the Federal Public Housing Authority on October 20th:

> "Suffice it to say we are firmly convinced that the distinct, almost unique, advantages and adaptability of Vanport City for comprehensive industrial development, inspire us with the challenging hope that we may convert what might have been a troublesome blighted area into a constructive community asset."[96]

The words "troublesome blighted area" referred primarily to the section of Vanport occupied by Negroes.

Over the following months, little happened as the HAP waited to see what Kaiser would decide to do and what the federal government's position would be on converting Vanport to industry. Moores determined to keep HAP's intentions secret, at least from the public. He wrote the chamber's W. D. B. Dodson in December that "it does not seem wise to press energetically just at this time, at least in any public manner, an effort to advance our plans to have the housing at Vanport eliminated. . . . We are working quietly to further that objective."[97] With Vanport housing full, and over 300 applications from Negroes on file, Moores and Mayor Riley were fully aware of the possible adverse political repercussions of publicly announcing such a policy. Moores chose instead to pursue the less direct, more circuitous approach of securing support from a variety of community and governmental sources in order to create a favorable climate of opinion.

Two weeks after he was elected to the U. S. Senate, Wayne Morse told W. D. B. Dodson and Moores that he would agree to make the Vanport issue one of his major efforts.[98] Moores also orchestrated a series of newspaper articles and editorials in support of HAP's unannounced policy. *The Wall Street Journal* published a lead story headed "Northwest Wonders What to Do With Huge U. S. Housing Projects."[9] *The Oregonian* cranked out a series of favorable editorials such as the one on April 29, 1945: "Industrialize Vanport." Moores also initiated negotiations with the Port of Portland through its chairman Henry L. Corbett to see if the agency would be willing to assume ownership of Vanport for the development of future industrial sites. In June he won the unqualified support of the Multnomah County commissioners when chairman Frank L. Shull wrote him about the value of the site with its highway connections and river access. "Of great importance," noted the Benjamin Franklin Savings & Loan executive who dedicated much of his time to county government, "is the matter of power. There are now transmission lines from Bonneville that will make available the lowest cost power that can be had anywhere. . . . The tract is large enough so that it can be platted in a manner that would make its advantages to every type of industry."[100]

Throughout all of these lengthy proceedings not one word was mentioned, at least for the record, about the future disposition of the black population at either Vanport or Guild's Lake. The city planning commission did hold a special meeting in February 1945 to discuss "Negro Housing," but the session failed to face the hard issue. Instead, the discussion focused on determining "the desirability of various types of housing to be restricted to Negro occupancy."[101]

During the spring of 1945, the newly organized Interracial Council of Vanport City conducted a campaign which, in the words of its president Ennie M. Whaley, was designed "to introduce a real democracy in regard to housing of the war workers in Vanport."[102] The group requested and secured a meeting with the HAP staff to discuss some of the problems. From the staff report it would appear that HAP was placed in an uncomfortably defensive position because the interracial council desired "complete integration of Negroes and whites in all projects."[103] HAP staff member K. E. Eckert reported that:

> "The Urban League, recently formed, seems to feel the same way about this situation but are also willing to take steps a little slower."[104]

The Housing Authority of Portland, led by realtor Chester A. Moores, was not prepared to do anything to help resolve the interracial problems in public housing projects. In fact, it was prepared to do just the opposite: To eliminate the problems by forcing the blacks to leave both Vanport and Guild's Lake. Where they would go was not HAP's concern. The strategy for this action was spelled out in a memorandum from the chamber of commerce's W. D. B. Dodson to Oregon Portland Cement Company president Frank E. McCaslin who was also president of the chamber in 1945.

Referring to a meeting that was held on June 23, 1945, between Chester Moores and some federal housing officials, Dodson wrote:

> "Everyone covering the meeting yesterday was deeply impressed that the negro [sic] problem was possibly the most serious aspect of our effort [to industrialize Vanport]. Vanport is now housing many of the colored people. They will undoubtedly want to cling to those residences until they can get something better. No section of the city has yet been designated as a colored area which might attract them from Vanport. The Government will not evict. . . . Should the property be transferred, the problem of Uncle Sam evicting would be removed. On the other hand, it would be difficult to force people out of Vanport until they have some other place where they can live. In brief, this colored situation is very important in connection with our efforts."[105]

There is much evidence to indicate that had the Vanport flood not occurred in May 1948, the transfer and eviction strategy would have been carried out. It was delayed for almost three years for two reasons: (1) Kaiser did not decide to pull up stakes and leave Portland until April 1947 and (2), the preliminary engineering study of Vanport's soil and drainage conditions was discouraging.

DISTRIBUTION OF NEGRO POPULATION IN PORTLAND

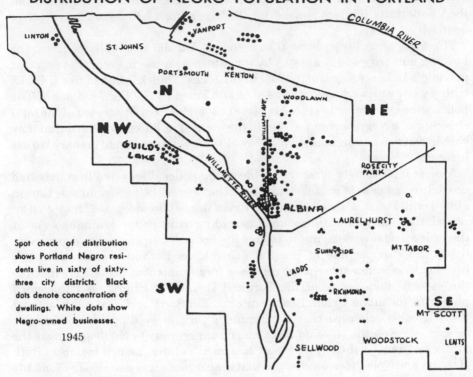

Spot check of distribution shows Portland Negro residents live in sixty of sixty-three city districts. Black dots denote concentration of dwellings. White dots show Negro-owned businesses.

1945

Portland's black population was already heavily concentrated in the Albina district before the Vanport flood forced an even greater density upon the area. Below, an Albina home — 1945.

The Port engineers indicated that for the secure placement of heavy industry on the Vanport site, it might be necessary to drive pilings into the soil to a depth of as much as 150 feet.

The kind of social problem that bothered, but did not really concern, the housing authority was dramatically illustrated by a tragic event that occurred at Guild's Lake on August 20, 1945. Ervin Jones, a black father of five children with a good war work record, was shot and killed by the Portland police. The police were attempting to enter his home in search of a man accused of the fatal shooting of a Negro woman earlier in the night. The officers claimed that they shot in self-defense because Jones, they alleged, was armed and prepared to use his gun.[106]

Almost immediately after the incident, the police discovered that they had erred. It was a case of mistaken identity. The "Jones" being sought was Earvin alias Irvin Jones, a former convict. Ervin Jones, the deceased, had a clean record. He simply made the mistake, according to the police, of aiming a gun at the officers who were trying to invade his home. Thus, the police department listed the case as one of justifiable homicide. Both a district attorney's investigation and a subsequent coroner's jury exonerated the officers much to the extreme displeasure of the Portland Council of Churches. The council plaintiffs, including Urban League director Bill Berry and civil rights activist Ruth Haefner, charged that the coroner's jury proceeding was unfair: No Negroes were on the jury and there was no opportunity to challenge any of the jurors selected. In their final report two months later, council members Ruth Haefner and Nels Peterson charged that the coroner's jury decision to exonerate the police "invited lawlessness," and would result in a serious threat to the future security of Portland's Negro population.[107]

Three weeks after the coroner's jury decision, the Port of Portland and the Housing Authority of Portland announced the sale of 28 acres of Guild's Lake property to three industries. The action was to require the razing of 252 public wartime housing units, approximately ten percent of the Guild's Lake housing stock. In contrast to Vanport where the federal government owned the land — having bought it from Kaiser after the project's construction was begun — at Guild's Lake the wartime public housing was built on land leased from either private owners or the Port of Portland. There were no legal obstacles to prevent HAP from liquidating its Guild's Lake housing stock, a process that was to continue with increasing rapidity over the next decade. Beginning with the first three industries — Standard Oil of California, Pacific Chain and Mt. Hood Soap — one industrial developer after another took the plunge, spurred on by the private power companies. Portland General Electric and Pacific Power & Light, assisted by BPA, even established industrial development departments to entice new industries. Over the years, the major purchaser was to be the company that had held the largest amount of Guild's Lake property before the war, the SP&S Railway which was controlled by the Great Northern and Northern Pacific Railroads.

Guild's Lake wartime housing was squeezed by industrial development in 1947.

A crucial meeting affecting the future of Guild's Lake and that of public housing generally was held in July 1947. Represented were the HAP commissioners, Mayor Riley, Urban League director Bill Berry and the chamber of commerce's Chester K. Sterrett who was the staff person in charge of the chamber's industries committee. Berry cited the need for low income housing. Nearly one-fifth of Portland's residents were inadequately housed. Berry also feared that residential discrimination would produce further acts of racial violence similar to the Jones homicide two years earlier. Mayor Riley was not sympathetic. He told Berry to work through the housing authority which had a number of vacant units. Yet the HAP staff admitted that it could not fill the vacancies with Negroes "without creating a mixed occupancy." And there was no official desire to modify that policy. Finally, as its major contribution to the discussion, Chester Sterrett demanded that HAP and the city "get public housing off the sites where industrial building is to take place."[108]

It was calloused attitudes of this kind, coupled with a general community unwillingness to face the human dimensions of inadequate housing, that produced a hard-hitting City Club report in June 1948. The committee on standard housing charged that "neither private enterprise nor the Portland Housing authority has met the permanent housing needs of low-income

Vanport City, the day after the dikes broke, May 31, 1948. The Columbia River is seen to the north.

groups."[109] The Vanport disaster had brought the issue to a head. As numerous survivors of the flood were to testify, Portland's business leadership showed a complete disregard for the human consequences of the tragedy. "When people talk or write about Vanport, they only talk about the flood," survivor Julia Ruuttila later declared.

> "They don't deal with the fact that thousands of us were left homeless or were forced to live in trailers or in barracks on Swan Island for months afterward. The housing authority did nothing to find replacement housing — we had to find it for ourselves, which was almost impossible because of housing shortages and the fact that most of us were financially wiped out by the flood."[110]

The consequences for Vanport's black residents were even worse. As one black survivor was later to relate:

"We in the NAACP used to chide [the] Mayor . . . about the segregated housing at Vanport. 'Get the people in town!' 'Where are you going to put them . . . there's no place for them . . . ' Well, bless my soul, May 30th, when that dike broke, they found a place for them. And what did they do? They congregated right down on Albina, in that area."[111]

Notwithstanding the fact that 5294 units of Vanport housing were destroyed, dislodging and stranding nearly 17,000 people, the housing authority and the chamber of commerce pushed stubbornly ahead to liquidate the remaining Guild's Lake units in favor of industrial development. The units could have been spared for at least a few more years. New industry could have been located in North Portland, above St. Johns, but the private interests that controlled Guild's Lake real estate were too entrenched, insensitive and greedy. Along with the railroads, utilities and oil companies, their considerable influence and power were destined to prevail. As an example, Mrs. L. H. Hoffman, a great-granddaughter of Captain Couch and the wife of Portland's leading contractor who was also a Port of Portland commissioner, dispatched a blistering letter to the housing authority in June 1950 demanding the return of her four leased acres which contained 62 units of public housing. She would do anything to get her land back and have the units removed. She had received many business propositions to sell the property, but of course was prevented from doing so as long as the units were inhabited.[112]

Barracks, on and adjacent to Swan Island, built in 1943 by Kaiser to house construction workers. Kaiser made the units available to house the flood victims, many of whom were forced to remain for over a year.

601

With the election of reform Mayor Dorothy McCullough Lee in 1948, public housing received its first strong support from the mayor's office. But progress was to be slow. In May of 1950, the voters rejected a housing ordinance presented by Mayor Lee's newly constituted housing authority. Introduced by commissioner Bowes, the measure would have authorized the city and HAP to construct 2000 badly needed low rent housing units. A 1949 survey had revealed that Portland contained 4242 families with gross annual incomes of $2100 or less.

The well financed opposition was as much ideological as anything else. A leading Portland homebuilder likened such programs to "Hitler's, Mussolini's and Stalin's pet projects." They amounted to pure "regimentation."[113] Many financial institutions opposed the measure because the program threatened their traditional policies and practices. They questioned the feasibility of amortizing the low-cost FHA built units over a 30 year period. They claimed that the construction would not be of good enough quality to justify 30 year financing.[114] Despite well reasoned arguments to the contrary by the City Club, churches and other enlightened civic groups, the measure went down to defeat.

Undaunted by this setback, and taking advantage of new federal legislation, the Portland City Council adopted a resolution six months later permitting HAP to purchase 4300 dwelling units from the federal government. The following month, another block of units, some on leased land, was approved for purchase. Thus, by the end of 1950, the housing authority owned 6500 units of temporary housing. The purchase price, under the federal law, was the original cost of the land, which was $466,614 for 435 acres. The improvements were acquired at no cost. With such an action, the Housing Authority of Portland, under new leadership, passed an important milestone in its history. It also voted to desegregate all public housing under its jurisdiction.[115]

PGE Comes Through

As was stated earlier, World War II saved the Portland General Electric Company and its parent holding company, PEPCO. From 1939 to 1948, power sales to customers increased almost 300 percent. Henry Kaiser's shipyards and the Vanport housing project had played key roles in the company's rejuvenation. Notwithstanding such factors, much credit was also due the independent trustees and their counsel who had administered the financial and legal affairs of the company throughout this period.

Judge James Alger Fee ruled on June 29, 1946, that the company's reorganization was completed. It was now time to award compensation to Messrs. Delzell, Clark and King. One month later, when federal bankruptcy referee Judge Estes Snedecor announced the amounts, a minor outcry was heard from some of the company's stockholders who had never accepted the trustees in the first place. The compensation was to be paid out of PEPCO's net revenues.

Thomas W. Delzell was awarded $180,000; R. L. Clark $49,500 and counsel Ralph H. King $285,000. *The Oregon Journal* reacted by publishing its July 26th

602

evening edition with the prominent headline, "Lawyer's Request 'Shocking' — PEPCO." When Ralph King saw this, he exploded. He immediately filed suit in the circuit court seeking $500,000 damages from the *Journal* for alleged defamation of character. In his complaint, King charged that the article was intended to "inflame and arouse approximately 12,000 stockholders of PEPCO against the plaintiff." The next day, King went to see *Journal* editor Donald J. Sterling to demand a retraction. After discussing the basis of the fee and the implications of the story, Sterling agreed to print the requested retraction in a prominent place on the front page, but only under one condition. Ralph King's name would never again be mentioned in *The Oregon Journal* as long as he, Sterling, was the editor. According to King, Sterling kept his word.[116]

With these matters concluded, others still remained to be resolved. The Guaranty Trust Company, the indenture trustee for the bondholders, refused to vote favorably the major blocks of PGE stock which it held as collateral. Without such support, the reorganization plan could not gain final approval. Much time was spent during 1947 in litigation with the Guaranty Trust Company and its lawyers. Judge Fee became angry and accused the bank of circulating misleading statements about the plan to both the major and minor stockholders. At one point he threatened the bank's vice president with contempt of court. Fee was forced to order the transfer of PGE's stock from the bank to the independent trustees whose work was obviously not completed. The company was ordered to distribute a healthy dividend directly to the stockholders, who promptly changed their minds and approved the plan. The reorganization proceedings were officially terminated on July 6, 1948.

Another important aspect of the reorganization plan involved the Portland Traction Company properties which had been administered directly by the trustees since 1940. Before recommending their sale in August 1946, Delzell and Clark reported to the court that the traction company had greatly improved its financial position during the war. Under the management of E. E. Vonderahe, costs had been cut, inefficiencies eliminated and passenger and freight revenues more than doubled. According to Delzell, several questionable practices had been discovered: (1) An unequal, and unjustifiable, allocation of costs between the urban and interurban divisions; (2) favoritism in the placement of insurance policies; and (3), irregularities in the sale of scrap (outworn wires, rails, etc.) to the Barde Steel Company.

After the PTC was sold for $7.9 million to a San Francisco holding company which took the name Portland Transit Company, E. E. Vonderahe brought the Barde matter to the attention of the new principal owner, C. C. Bowen. An investigation disclosed that PTC's purchasing agent, Merritt Simmonds, had for some time been selling scrap cheaply to Jack Barde, the wealthy and prominent owner of a series of scrap metal firms. Normal bidding procedures had not been followed. Barde, who specialized in liquidating war surplus equipment and who had been accused in 1921 of operating a similar scheme against the U. S. Government, had been cleaning up at PTC's expense. When

Trolley bus crossing the Burnside Bridge — 1948

Bowen became convinced of Simmond's complicity, he fired him. Shortly afterwards, Simmonds became an assistant city purchasing agent.[117] Jack Barde and Mayor Riley were old friends and Barde must have asked the mayor to give Simmonds a job. There is no record of what transpired subsequently — whether or not Barde worked a similar arrangement with the city — but by 1962, Simmonds was to become head city purchasing agent.

Under its new ownership, PTC elected to discontinue its streetcars and purchase no more trolley buses. Vice president and general manager Gordon Steele wanted to order only new gas driven vehicles. When BPA engineer T. M. C. Martin attempted to convince both the city council and Steele that a modernized electric transportation system would better meet the future needs of Portland, his words fell on deaf ears. Martin was an authority on rail electrification and had actually written a report on the subject which BPA published. As Martin related to Ivan Bloch, he discovered "that there had already been some 'deal' made with General Motors to buy gasoline-operated city buses."[118]

The East Side streetcars ended operation in August 1948 and the West Side's last route — the Council Crest — ceased operation in February 1950. The interurban properties, carrying mostly freight, were split up and sold to the major railroads in the early 1950s. In April 1948, future Senator Richard L. Neuberger commented upon the changing transit conditions. His conclusions were applicable to both urbans and interurbans.

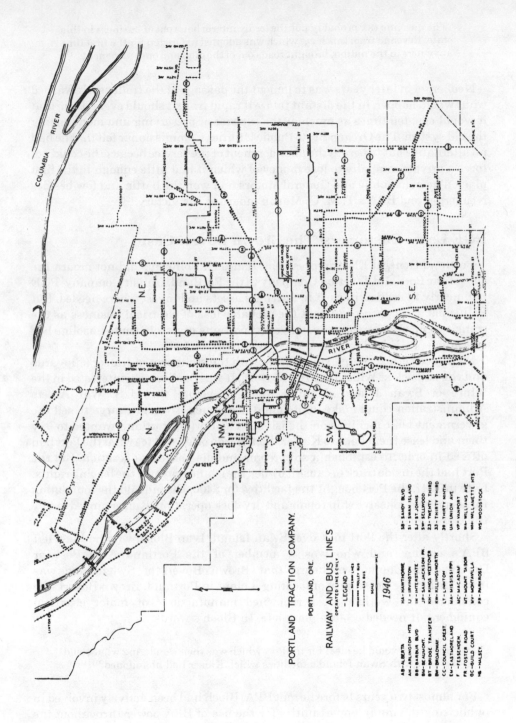

PORTLAND TRACTION COMPANY.
PORTLAND, ORE.

RAILWAY AND BUS LINES
OPERATED LINES ONLY

— LEGEND —
━━━ RAILWAY LINES
╌╌╌ TROLLEY BUS
· · · GAS BUS

SCALE   MILE

1946

AB—ALBERTA
AH—ARLINGTON HTS
BB—BARBUR BLVD
BM—BEAUMONT
BT—BRIDGE TRANSFER
BW—BROADWAY
CC—COUNCIL CREST
EM—EASTMORELAND
F—FESSENDEN
FR—FOSTER ROAD
GC—GUILD COURT
MS—HALSEY

HA—HAWTHORNE
IJ—IRVINGTON
IN—INTERSTATE
JP—SAW JACKSON PK
KH—KINGS WESTOVER
KW—KILLINGSWORTH
LT—LINNTON
MA—MISSISSIPPI
MC—MACADAM
MT—MOUNT TABOR
MV—MONTAVILLA
PR—PARKROSE

SB—SANDY BLVD
SI—SWAN ISLAND
SJ—ST JOHNS
SW—SELLWOOD
23—TWENTY THIRD
33—THIRTY THIRD
39—THIRTY NINTH
UA—UNION AVE
VP—VANPORT
WA—WILLIAMS AVE
WH—WILLAMETTE HTS
WS—WOODSTOCK

605

"The gasoline tax probably put the lordly interurbans out of business in this state. Revenue from this levy, which was adopted in Oregon for the first time anywhere in the nation, brought roads out of the mud and onto pavement."[119]

Neuberger in later years was to lament the passage of the trolleys. He warned what would happen in the distant future if rapid transit should ever return; that it would cost ten times as much as the expense of preserving and modernizing the old system. The Oregon State Public Utilities Commissioner felt that he had no alternative but to permit the abandonment of the service because he could not force a private company to lose money of which it had little enough in the first place. The automobile and General Motors had won the battle and few besides Neuberger and BPA's T. M. C. Martin mourned the victory.[120]

PGE Loses Customers: The Brown Boveri Case

Portland General Electric president James H. Polhemus did not mourn the sale of the Portland Traction Company to the Portland Transit Company. PGE had nearly $8 million in cash to fatten its assets and invest where needed. But Polhemus was concerned about the probable loss of electrical business as the transit company increasingly converted portions of its system to gasoline bus operations. PGE had predicted this eventuality in 1945.

PGE faced other energy sales losses with the shutdown of Kaiser shipyards and the cutback at Willamette Iron & Steel. It was particularly interested in the future of Swan Island. Months went by before the U. S. War Assets Administration could make up its mind how much it would charge to sell the government built facilities on the island. The Port of Portland wanted to buy them and lease them back to Kaiser. Jack Barde offered twice what the Port had offered in order to establish a ship repair and dismantling operation. But the Port had the inside track because it owned the island and held the leasing rights. Late in 1947, the Port bought the facilities for $400,000 and laid the foundation for its present massive ship repair and dry dock operation. Kaiser moved out by the end of 1947.

Shortly after the Port took over Swan Island, Ivan Bloch, who had just left BPA's employ and who was a member of the Portland Area Postwar Development Committee, heard that Brown Boveri of Switzerland was interested in the possibility of locating a plant in Portland. Brown Boveri was considered the world's most renowned manufacturer of major electrical equipment. It needed a large plant site. In Bloch's words:

"I felt this would be ideal for the Port which was then wondering what could be done with Swan Island's facilities which Kaiser had abandoned."[121]

For almost two years before he quit BPA, Bloch had been actively involved in publicizing the many opportunities for the use of BPA power throughout the

606

Northwest region for both industrial and agricultural development. He and his staff, with the guidance of Roy F. Bessey who had long been involved in BPA's regional resource planning, published a widely heralded "blue-print" entitled *Pacific Northwest Opportunities*. It was distributed world-wide and was most likely one of the factors that stimulated the Swiss firm to scout out Portland, Oregon. Its influence, in fact, was much greater outside of the Portland area. As the following episode well illustrates, within the Portland business and banking fraternity any report, or any enthusiasm whatsoever, emanating from BPA was immediately suspect, particularly by the banks and the private utilities.

Bloch took his Brown Boveri proposal to his friends on the Port commission. Both president Henry L. Corbett and vice president W. L. (Billy) Williams were enthusiastic. They could see that the potential employment was in the hundreds. Optimistically, they decided to invite Brown Boveri's president to Portland for a personal visit.

Acting as a consultant to the Port, Bloch hosted Brown Boveri's president Schindler on his tour of the Portland facilities. The fact that Bloch's father, the eminent composer Ernest Bloch, was a native of Switzerland helped to create a warm feeling between host and guest. After Dr. Schindler saw the Swan Island facilities, he expressed "**great** interest," so much so that Corbett and Williams thought it best to have a luncheon conference to give the Swiss executive a chance to meet some of Portland's leading businessmen and bankers. As Bloch tells the story:

> "I think, up to that point, I felt a deal could be clinched! The luncheon was held at the Arlington Club (of course). Hoffman [L. H.], Corbett, Williams, Sammons [E. C., U. S. Bank president], Bloch and a few others (Dave Simpson?) were invited. After a very delicious lunch (leave it to Harry Corbett, with the appropriate wines), either Billy or Harry reviewed very briefly the background of Brown Boveri, the potential of an operation in Portland, etc. They did it very well. Then Dr. Schindler said a few words and asked for questions. Sammons pursed his lips, got his banker's eye colder, and started cross-examining Schindler as though Schindler were applying for a loan at USNB. He was so rude that both Harry and Billy were palpably nervous. I was shocked at the rudeness. Schindler was also obviously non-plussed. He coolly answered some of the questions and then indicated he was, indeed, a very busy man and was on his way to Tacoma to look at facilities there! The message was clear: Either you want me or the heck with it. And that's what it was! A few days later Dr. Schindler called me. (He told me not to apologize as he said he understood.) He'd decided to start a small plant in Tacoma."[122]

Bloch's memory of the luncheon details is dim except for his recollection of "Sammons' direct cut at the jugular, the expressions of disbelief and anger of Billy, and utter amazement on Harry's face." Holding a post-mortem session after Dr. Schindler's departure, the three came to the conclusion that either General Electric or Westinghouse must have had local accounts at the U. S. National Bank. Sammons amassed a record of trying to kill projects which would competitively threaten the bank's existing customers. He was to exert efforts of this kind when the Harvey Aluminum Company decided to build a reduction plant in the The Dalles during the early 1950s and when the new Hilton Hotel was planned for downtown Portland a few years later. There might have been additional reasons: A former BPA official, with BPA's support, was promoting the scheme; and too much power was already committed by BPA to aluminum and associated power intensive industries at a time when the region was facing a power shortage.

The fact that Portland's most influential banker and perhaps most powerful business figure (on a par with Aaron Frank) showed such open hostility was usually enough to kill any project, let alone the Brown Boveri one. Portland's loss was also PGE's loss. According to Bloch, "The amount of direct BPA power would have been zero; this would have been a load for PGE."[123] In 1976, Brown Boveri recorded a world-wide sales total of $3.4 billion!

608

Chapter 19

Cronies, Culture and Crackers:
Some Episodes of the 1940s

The adminstrations of Joseph K. Carson, Jr. (1933-1941) and Earl Riley (1941-1949) were undistinguished in both accomplishment and spirit. The major concern of both mayors was to cut costs, balance budgets and maintain a cosmetic appearance of law and order sufficient to please the business establishment. Rarely expressed in the thoughts and actions of either man was the kind of public vision for the future that architect Pietro Belluschi enunciated in 1943.

"Business as usual" was the guiding theme of the mayor's office during the 1940s. Leadership was defined in narrowly selfish terms: Give the people — usually one's friends — what they want. The pursuit of such practices led to the creation of cozy arrangements between the mayor's office and some of the city's leading business figures — men who were both ambitious and greedy for private gain or power, or both. Within the general population, understandably, this type of "government by crony"[1] bred attitudes of cynicism and apathy which were clearly reflected in the operation of Portland's police department that was directly responsible to the mayor's office. Mediocrity and indifference at the top produced equally mediocre and indifferent enforcement of the law, particularly in matters related to vice. Like Siamese twins, greed and vice were inseparably linked. The double standard of public morality that selectively enforced the law infected the standards of private morality that governed business and financial affairs. Conditions had not changed much in fifty years, or since the time when the late editor of *The Oregonian*, Harvey W. Scott, admitted that the persons most concerned in the maintenance of such abuses were usually "the principal men of the city."[2]

Vice Conditions and the Police

In February 1948, the City Club published a stinging report on local gambling and prostitution activities which, it charged, had been "carried on openly and notoriously throughout the city for a period of several years past." It found that prostitution was not confined to any definite "red light" district, although it was apt to be found in "certain fairly well defined localities."[3] According to the City Club files,[4] the majority of houses were located north of Burnside Street, along N. W. Sixth. The Saranac and Atlas Rooms, for example, were owned by Joe Schnitzer, a prominent bail bondsman with close police connections, who had spent a year in the federal penitentiary after conviction for interstate trafficking in stolen jewelry. The famous Richelieu Rooms, between Burnside and Couch, were in the Richelieu Hotel owned by the Penn Mutual Life Insurance Company and managed by Norris, Beggs and Simpson, headed by Riley confidant David B. Simpson.

Before his death, prominent Portland jeweler Julius Zell, "the mayor of Morrison Street," made the comment to an interviewer:

> "Almost 80 percent of the prostitutes and madames were Jewish. There was not a rooming house from N. W. Second and Burnside to the depot, particularly along Fifth and Sixth, that was not run by a Jewish madame, employing Jewish pimps."[5]

In addition to eleven known houses of prostitution, the City Club files noted five horse bookie joints, five baseball pools, eight bootleggers, all on the West Side of Portland. Gambling action on the East Side was confined largely to the area around Burnside and Grand, and in the North, to St. Johns.

The City Club report did not pass judgment on the morality of these operations as such. But it clearly revealed how the existence of illegal activities, condoned by the police and higher authorities, corrupted the whole law enforcement process. It attracted "a considerable assortment of safe burglars, stick-up men, dope peddlers and other underworld characters."[6] Organized vice provided high profits to the operators, the property owners and their managers like Norris, Beggs and Simpson. To the police it produced approximately $60,000 a month in protection payments. And to the city it brought the dubious distinction of Portland's having "the second highest rate of incidence of venereal disease in the nation."[7]

An account of Portland vice activities drawn from a retired police informant noted that:

> "The town was wide open. . . . 'Jesus, there were hookers of every color, size and shape. Every game of chance you could think of. Lots of poor men's follies — one arm bandits and poker players. . . . Nobody gave a hoot until, Dorothy Lee showed up [Mayor Lee, elected in 1948]. . . . As housing for workers and servicemen were thrown together at Vanport, funny little prostitution rings would spring up overnight. Signals with shades in a certain position, the lights just so, became customary."[8]

In assessing the public's responsibility for the widespread existence of vice, the City Club report noted 95 major press releases over a span of 12 years, each referring to some aspect of the problem.

> "Public interest and apathy follow a regular pattern, like the peaks and valleys on a seismograph. Every manifestation of an aroused public opinion produces a violent reaction in the police department and a rash of publicity about raids and arrests. The excitement soon subsides and the underworld

settles back into its accustomed methods of operation until public opinion again awakens. Several police officers when interviewd, frankly stated that they found it difficult, if not impossible, to enforce laws which they felt the general public was not interested in having enforced."[9]

Judge Lamar L. Tooze agreed with the officers. In a letter to the City Club investigation committee, Tooze wrote:

"Vice is a condition that exists in every large city. We have good people and we have bad people, and sometimes I wonder if the sinners are not in the majority. It is a well-known fact that when a decided majority of the people want a particular condition eliminated, it will be eliminated. Law enforcement cannot rise above decided public demand and public cooperation."[10]

Not discounting the truth of such statements, however, had the police been more efficiently organized and furnished with honest and aggressive leadership from city hall some positive progress might have been achieved. Historically, one of the qualities of effective leadership has been the ability to generate public support for a program that the leader believes to be in the public interest.

The City Club committee further charged that the responsible police authorities had no established policy and no definite program for the control or

Mayor Joseph K. Carson
(1933-1941)

611

Mayor Earl Riley
(1941-1949)

suppression of gambling, prostitution and other forms of vice. Apart from the mayor, much of the blame had to rest with the chiefs of police. Carson appointed Harry M. Niles who was 60 when he assumed office. An old line traditionalist who did not like to cause trouble, Niles kept a low profile. He was a loyal American and a veteran Elks member who knew his place in the local power structure. Riley kept Niles on for seven years, until 1946, before the chief finally retired at age 72. Then Riley resurrected the spirits of the past by appointing former chief Lee V. Jenkins who was in his seventies. Obviously and purposely no drastic changes or surprises were to be expected from the man who had run George L. Baker's police department for 16 years.

By the summer of 1947, however, sufficient public criticism of police operations had been generated to persuade the city council to order an evaluation of Portland's police bureau. Mayor Riley, whose department of public safety was responsible for bureau operations, assented reluctantly to the inevitable. The resulting report, published one month before the City Club's in mid-January 1948, blasted the Portland Bureau of Police to its very roots. According to August Vollmer, the retired chief of police of Berkeley, California, for at least the previous seven years Portland's police bureau had been "overcostly, underproductive, poorly organized, inadequately supervised and

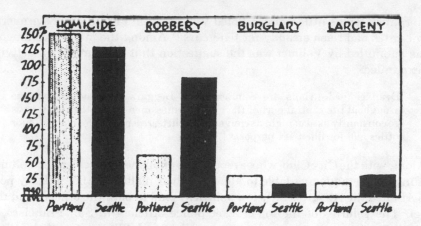

Homicides have increased in Portland 250 per cent since 1940, slightly above the same type of crime in Seattle. Portland robberies have increased only 60 per cent compared to Seattle's 178 per cent, however, according to a Vollmer survey.

(From The Oregonian, January 15, 1948)

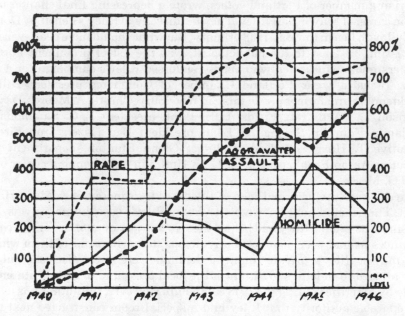

How rape, aggravated assault and homicide have increased in Portland since 1940 is shown in this sketch from the Vollmer report. Figures indicate percentage of increase over 1940. Auto theft also has mounted rapidly but burglary, larceny, robbery have increased by lesser percentages, Vollmer said.

underpaid." It was little wonder, noted Vollmer, that Portland's above average crime rates had risen steadily for ten years.[11] Among the many recommendations submitted by Vollmer was the suggestion that foot patrolmen activities be expanded:

> "Drunken pedestrians are commonplace. Beggars or moochers operate throughout the central part of the city. Businessmen report their doorways are constantly used at night as convenient toilets, receptacles for empty liquor bottles and for illicit sex purposes."[12]

Along with the City Club, whose report was published too soon after Vollmer's findings were made available to allow for their inclusion, the Berkeley police expert cited the "disgracefully low salaries" paid to both the officers and their chief. The salaries of the top-bracket police officials in San Francisco, for example, were practically double those of Portland. What astounded Vollmer, considering Portland's low pay scale, was that 55 percent of the police bureau was in the top intelligence bracket. The Los Angeles department, whose pay scale was even higher than San Francisco's, placed only ten percent in the top group.

The Vollmer and City Club reports, whose findings apparently shocked a surprising number of Portland voters, wrote a depressing final chapter to the public career of Mayor Earl Riley. They led directly to Riley's defeat by Dorothy McCullough Lee in the May 1948 primary. But what should have been even more depressing, at least to the public spirit, was the list of prominent Portland bankers and businessmen who openly endorsed Riley's campaign for a third term. Included were: Portland Chamber of Commerce president Hillman Lueddemann and former presidents Sid Woodbury, Chester A. Moores, David B. Simpson and Arthur L. Fields; U. S. Bank president E. C. Sammons and Benjamin Franklin Savings & Loan president Ben Hazen; Iron Fireman executive T. Harry Banfield, architect Glenn Stanton, department store executive Aaron Frank, contractor L. H. Hoffman and shopping center owner Fred G. Meyer.

These were "the principal men of the city," to requote the words of Harvey Scott. They should have known better, but in Riley's case the matter was one of "business as usual." Riley had helped them in one way or another, and in certain instances he had even conducted private business with some of them while he was mayor. Riley's private financial dealings were never disclosed publicly, only alluded to in letters to editors of the local press and in certain statements made by his critics during the 1948 campaign. However, the author has learned on reputable authority that Riley had a special room constructed next to his office in city hall on which was installed a bank vault combination lock. It was common knowledge among his closest aides that the room was the repository for city hall's percentage of the vice protection payments. According to one informant, "The mayor got the loaf and two other commissioners got the crumbs."[13]

Although U. S. National Bank president E. C. Sammons was later to admit that he had some doubts about Riley's honesty,[14] he still supported him and even presided at a Riley farewell banquet. The city, after all, had been a good customer of the U. S. National Bank. During the 1940s, when it was solvent, the city kept on deposit between two and three million dollars with both the U. S. National and First National Banks. In Portland's business-political relationships, business interests transcended ethical considerations. This type of behavior by some of Portland's leading citizens was common. It was the way "the game was played."

Business in Government

Another game that was played, with profit to the participants, also involved some "principal men of the city." Ever since the earliest days of the insurance business, the sale of insurance policies to public agencies had been a profitable enterprise and one that was also fraught with potential conflict of interest. An insurance policy register for the years 1938 to 1949, found buried in the city hall archives, produced some illuminating revelations. Neither the register nor the city council minutes indicated any competitive bidding on the city's insurance coverage, although the business was spread widely, divided between a number of agencies which had maintained close ties with city hall for years. Beginning in 1942, two prominent Portland insurance agents who happened to be close friends of Earl Riley secured some lucrative contracts covering a variety of city-owned properties. One was John H. Burgard, the veteran chairman of the city dock commission, and the other was Phil Grossmayer, the general agent for the Travellers Insurance Company, a director of Commonwealth and a founder of Portland's Rotary Club. In a four year period, Burgard wrote policies with premiums totalling $14,000 to provide liability coverage for city hall offices and a small dock commission boiler plant.

The largest contracts went to Phil Grossmayer. In eight years, he sold policies with total premiums of $111,115, mostly to cover the city's fleet of automobiles. Until 1948 he had split the premiums with other agents. Then in Riley's final months in office, Grossmayer became the exclusive agent for all of the city's automobiles, for which he issued Travellers policies with premiums totalling $45,600. When Grossmayer died at age 88 in 1968, he was to leave an estate worth nearly $1.5 million.

Not all of this wealth came from insurance premiums. Being a director of Commonwealth Inc., Grossmayer became involved in real estate investments in addition to servicing most of the company's extensive insurance needs. One of the deals that helped to bring him early wealth was reported in the *Oregon Voter*[15] in 1927. In the 1920s, Grossmayer was also general agent for the New Hampshire Fire Insurance Company which reinsured a Portland fire insurance company called Pacific States whose stock was widely held locally. Pacific States fell on hard times and its stock price plummeted. Early in 1926, New

615

John H. Burgard

Hampshire Fire Insurance offered to purchase Pacific States for $15 a share, about 50 percent more than its market value. It later turned out that Grossmayer, who was a director of Pacific States and privy to the plans of New Hampshire Fire Insurance, had been quietly buying up large blocks of Pacific States stock at depressed values of as low as $6 a share. It was also later revealed that he was in cahoots with the president of New Hampshire Fire Insurance who was doing the same thing. Needless to say, when the sale was consummated, Grossmayer and his colleague back in Manchester, New Hampshire, both made a killing. The local stockholders who had trustingly purchased the original offering in 1910 lost over 50 percent of their investment.

Phil Grossmayer typified the kind of crony with whom Mayor Earl Riley surrounded himself. Jack Barde, whose exploits were discussed previously, was another, and so was veteran dock commission chairman John H. Burgard.

The Art Museum Gets Cheated

Portland's city hall was not the only local institution to suffer "government by crony." The Portland Art Association was similarly afflicted. For years it had been run by a tightly knit board of directors comprising the leaders of Portland's upper crust society and a sprinkling of cultural luminaries. The male dominated leadership reflected the prevailing attitudes of Portland's business and banking community — people who knew each other socially and who unquestioningly accepted the financial judgment of their peers.

The "system" was to undergo severe strain in the postwar years when the association's board of directors found itself faced with two crises of enormous proportions: (1) A growing dissatisfaction with the museum's professional leadership that split the business and artist constituencies; and (2), a shocking realization that the museum's endowment had been fraudulently mismanaged. The museum's problems became public knowledge in October 1948 when the association filed suit in circuit court against the Eastern and Western Lumber Company, its officers and 30 others, all of whom were charged with committing an act of fraud involving the museum's endowment fund which had formerly contained a large block of the lumber company's stock. It was the sale of this stock in 1945, and the conditions under which it was sold, that produced the legal action three years later.

The basis of the charge was that the art museum's previous board of directors had been unwisely persuaded on grounds of misleading information to sell 1650 shares of Eastern and Western stock from its endowment to an unnamed group of purchasers who offered to pay the museum between $80 and $100 per share. Because the stock was not paying dividends and its price had varied little in recent years, the museum's board was advised by its finance committee to accept the offer as the future of the local lumber industry looked bleak. The museum's endowment fund, they reasoned, could only benefit from the sale because the proceeds could be invested in other securities which would promise a higher return.

Within six months of the deal's consummation, it was revealed that the purchasers of the stock were Eastern and Western's officers: President Frank H. Ransome, secretary-treasurer C. B. Duffy and vice president and general manager Kurt H. Koehler, all prominent in the Portland community. With majority control assured, the officers elected to close down the business, sell its dock and sawmill properties to the dock commission, and then later dispose of its vast timber holdings. When the assets of the company were finally liquidated, each share of stock proved to be worth approximately $450, over four times the value received by the art museum for its shares.

Once the facts became known, the Portland Art Association, owner of the museum, filed its suit, asking the court to cancel the stock sale and award the museum $500,000 in damages to be paid by the lumber firm's former key officers. Additional suits were filed by the Buehner family which previously owned the second largest block of stock and by an eastern relative of the Ayer family whose holdings had exercised effective control over the company until they were bequeathed to the museum. The brokers who had purchased the stock for the unnamed buyers were also sued on charges of deceptive practices.[16]

The Eastern and Western stock had been left to the museum's endowment fund by the company's founder, Winslow B. Ayer. Under the will filed in 1931, the museum was made the beneficial owner of the stock until the death of his widow, at which time the museum would become the legal owner — a transaction that was effected in early March of 1945.

During the war years the company had suffered along with most Portland area lumber operations as the source of timber moved farther away. Many of the mills had closed, including the large Clark-Wilson operation in Linnton. The officers of Eastern and Western could see that the future was not bright either for the company or for them. Being salaried employees with only minor holdings of the company's stock, they devised the scheme to make themselves the sole owners so that when the company was liquidated, they, and not absentee stockholders, would derive the benefits which they felt were owed them by virtue of their years of dedicated service.

Beginning in 1942, the company's annual statements failed to publish accurate figures of either business operations or of the value of the company's timber reserves which comprised 50,000 acres of land in Klickitat County, Washington. The purpose of this strategy, of course, was to decrease the published assets of the company to the point that a per share value of $80 or $100 would seem reasonably fair. As another tactic, dividend payments were eliminated in 1944 and 1945.

The original mastermind of the scheme has never been accurately identified. One of the plaintiffs in the case informed the author that president Paul Dick of the U. S. National Bank was the real culprit; that the bank held a large number of Eastern and Western shares in its investment portfolio and wanted to liquidate them for as high a value as possible. Another person, whose father worked with Dick, discounted this notion. But had the trials been held in federal court, as would have happened several years later following the enactment of a federal law that would have covered such abuses, the bank might well have been included as a defendant. As it was, in 1948 no state court judge would have entertained a suit against the U. S. National Bank.

Kurt Koehler was to deny any direct responsibility for the scheme. A Harvard graduate and son of Henry Villard's Portland representative (the German-born Richard Koehler who became a vice president of the Southern Pacific Railroad), Kurt Koehler was held in generally high esteem by Portland's social establishment. A member of all the important clubs, Koehler had been president of the Portland Symphony Society and had been considered generally supportive of the arts. In disclaiming guilt, Koehler had asserted that he only signed the necessary documents to facilitate the officers' purchases but that he himself had not been a party to the transactions. The discovery in the Abbot L. Mills, Jr., Papers of a memorandum relating to Koehler contradicts such statements. Early in April 1945, Koehler borrowed $73,900 from the U. S. National Bank to use in the purchase of 739 shares of Eastern and Western stock. As a bank vice president and director who approved the loan, it is hard to imagine that Abbot Mills did not have some inkling of what Koehler, Ransome and Duffy were really up to. Furthermore, Mills was also on the art museum board and a member of the finance committee that recommended the sale of the museum's stock.

As subsequent court hearings revealed, shortly after the art museum became the legal owner of its Eastern and Western stock in March 1945, the company's officers began buying up all of the outstanding shares through the local brokerage house of Butchart and Phillips. Nowhere in the sales pitch was there any mention of liquidating the company's properties, or even of closing down the Portland sawmill. The victims were encouraged to sell because the price was fair, dividends were minimal or non-existent and there was little hope for any future improvement.

The reaction of the art museum board and its finance committee was either unusually naive or stupid, although it is hard to believe that at least one of the directors — Abbot Mills — did not have an inkling of what was happening. The finance committee was headed by Cameron Squires, the museum's treasurer. Squires' past experiences, particularly with the ill-fated Ladd & Tilton Bank, would hardly seem to have qualified him to be treasurer of any institution. As one close observer of the episode told the author: "Squires was dumb! A remittance man! He had the money [albeit Wilcox money] to give his time to organizations like the art museum and do the work that other busy people could not or would not do. He was a man about town, smooth with the ladies etc."[17]

Other members of the finance committee included Abbot L. Mills, Jr., contractor L. H. Hoffman, historian Burt Brown Barker and lumberman Aubrey Watzek. When the committee recommended to the board that the museum accept the offer to purchase its Eastern and Western stock, only one person spoke in opposition, Mrs. Lawrence Wheeler, the sister-in-law of the late John E. Wheeler of Northwestern National Bank notoriety. Mrs. Wheeler thought that timber prices were going to rise after the war; in fact they were

The Ayer Wing of the Portland Art Museum, designed by Pietro Belluschi

619

Eastern & Western Lumber Company Dock on N. W. Front Street, sold to the dock commission in 1946 as an addition to Terminal No. 1

already increasing. As a member of a lumber family, she knew the value of timberlands. When she asked why the board did not examine the corporate records of Eastern and Western, she was told that such an action would have embarrassed Aubrey Watzek who was engaged in competing timber operations. This was a curious response. For one thing, Watzek should have agreed with Mrs. Wheeler. He knew the current timber values — particularly his own — which were rising rapidly in 1945. One of Watzek's corporate holdings was the Roaring River Logging Company whose assets were to have increased 14-fold in seven years by the date of its liquidation in 1949.[18]

In reflecting on the fateful meeting in March 1945, Mrs. Wheeler recalls that as the only woman present, she felt somewhat intimidated by the overwhelming presence of some of Portland's leading businessmen who were supposed to know the economic facts of life.[19] As it later turned out, Mrs. Wheeler had asked the crucial questions. That they were disregarded or unanswered was to cost the museum dearly.

The pre-trial proceedings revealed that one of the key issues was going to be the role of the dock commission headed by insurance man John H. Burgard. The duplicit intentions of the Eastern and Western officers were recorded in the record of conversations between the officers and the commission that began as early as October 1944[20] when the officers offered to sell the company's entire waterfront property to the dock commission. Eastern and Western owned nearly 1300 feet of dock space just north of Municipal Dock No. 1 which the dock commission wanted to enlarge. However, the commission at the time only wished to purchase 200 feet so the deal was put on the back burner. After nine months of further negotiations, an agreement was reached to sell the south 600 feet of the Eastern and Western property to the dock commission for $380,000. The company agreed to lease back the other 400 feet for no more than three years.

In all of the dealings with Eastern and Western, the dock commission was represented by T. Harry Banfield, one of the most influential directors of the U. S. National Bank and a close confidant and friend to E. C. Sammons, who was to return to the bank as president in 1945. It seems unbelievable that Banfield did not have some notion of what was behind the company's desire to liquidate its waterfront property. In fact, within four months, the dock commission was to change its mind, possibly under bank pressure, and agree to purchase the remainder of the Eastern and Western property, including the sawmill. By November of 1945, the officers already had possession of most of the company's stock and they were free to act in any way they saw fit. On December 15, 1945, the company announced that it would shortly shut down its Portland operations throwing 270 employees out of work.

At its January 8, 1946, meeting, Harry Banfield formally proposed that the dock commission buy the rest of the Eastern and Western property after reading into the minutes letters from the mayor, chamber of commerce and Port of Portland encouraging the commission to use the property for a municipal lumber terminal. On January 22, 1946, the action was approved. Fourteen acres were purchased for $440,000. Ten months later, the company filed a certificate of dissolution and almost two years later the Portland Art Association brought charges against the officers and their stockholders.

The case did not go to trial until August of 1950. By that point, the art association had already agreed to settle out of court for $254,000 rather than to press for the full compensation of $500,000. Many of the museum's board of directors were unhappy with the settlement. Several of them have informed the author that they are still convinced that the settlement was an accommodation to Kurt Koehler, his friends and some other leaders of the Portland business and financial community who might have been embarrassed by an open trial.

As it turned out, however, some dirty laundry was destined to be washed in public. The Buehner family elected not to settle but to press for full compensation. The Buehners had bitterly opposed selling their stock in the first place. They knew the potential value of the company's timber reserves. But once the officers had acquired a majority of the stock and with it a majority vote on the company's board of directors, the Buehners were forced to sell at the offered price. The Buehners ultimately won over $1 million in compensation and damages. The art museum might well have received more than its requested $500,000 had it not prematurely agreed to the terms negotiated by attorney Ralph H. King.

As for Kurt H. Koehler, his share of the company's liquidated assets was $394,958 on which he paid a capital gains tax of $79,487. Deducting what he owed the U. S. National Bank, the deal netted him $241,571. The court settlements forced him to give back $132,765.[21] He still wound up with a tidy net profit of $108,806. At the time of his death in 1954, following an accident at the beach home of his old friend John H. Burgard, litigation was still not concluded. In 1961, his attorney Prescott Cookingham was to bring suit against the Internal Revenue Service in behalf of Koehler's estate. He wanted a tax refund because the taxable gain on the Eastern and Western stock had been nearly cut in half by the amount that he had been forced to return.[22]

E. B. MacNaughton — A Refreshing Contrast

In August 1948, banker E. B. MacNaughton wrote a friend in Honolulu:

> "Right now I am busier than a lone clown in a three-ring Ringling circus what with my personal business, the bank's duties as Chairman of the Board, and President of the *Oregonian* and President of Reed College. I am having a good time with it all."[23]

It is doubtful that any other Portlander, Oregonian or even American for that matter, ever combined at one time three more diverse interests and roles of high responsibility than Ernest Boyd MacNaughton who was known throughout his long and colorful life as "E. B." The previous year he had retired as president of the First National Bank and moved up to become chairman of the board. Early in 1948, when Reed College's president Peter Odegard left abruptly for a post at the University of California, former trustee chairman MacNaughton was persuaded to assume the college's top administrative role until a permanent replacement could be found, a task that was to take nearly four years. His third major responsibility which he assumed in 1947, the presidency of the Oregonian Publishing Company, was probably the most challenging and certainly the most frustrating of the demanding duties that he was attempting to fulfill simultaneously. It was also the one that was to bring him the most criticism because it was the least understood by the public at large.

Criticism never seemed to bother the architect turned banker, at least publicly. Few Oregonians of his generation were less fearful of speaking out on so many issues and few men in Portland's history became as involved in so many varied activities. As one observer commented following MacNaughton's death in 1960 at age 79, his "was the career of a successful businessman with soul. Someone who cared primarily about people and their welfare."[24] On numerous occasions MacNaughton used to encourage his business and banking associates to think beyond profits. In a statement that Portland's current growth oriented bank executives might do well to heed, MacNaughton declared: "Business men must get their noses out of their account books and take a long look at human values."[25]

The many talented MacNaughton possessed a complex personality.[26] He could be a tough banker with an imperial air bordering on self-righteousness. He was often accused by his detractors of wanting to control everything to which he

622

became attached. But as one close friend explained, it was not a question of MacNaughton always searching out some new activity over which he could exercise his authority. "When someone was needed to help out on a good cause, he was always there."[27]

Lumberman Winslow B. Ayer had recognized this quality in 1925 when he had recommended MacNaughton to Frederick Pratt in New York as the one individual who might be able to salvage the Ladd & Tilton Bank. Frederick W. Leadbetter recognized the same quality in 1939 when he asked MacNaughton to join the board of directors of the Oregonian Publishing Company. He was not a newspaperman by any means. But he was an expert in financial management, a skill which the Oregonian Publishing Company desperately needed in the pre-war years. By coincidence he was also the father-in-law of one of Henry L. Pittock's granddaughters. Pittock, it should be recalled, had fired the young Boston educated architect 28 years earlier after the Marquam Building had collapsed while it was being reconstructed for Pittock's bank headquarters.

The much contested Pittock Trust terminated in 1939 and the newspaper passed into the control of the heirs of Pittock and his editor Harvey W. Scott. The Pittock family owned four-sevenths of the stock and the Scotts three-sevenths, the same proportions that had been set in 1876 when Pittock and Scott reassumed control of the paper from Henry W. Corbett. As chief administrator of the Pittock family interests, wealthy industrialist Fred Leadbetter was concerned about the status of *The Oregonian* in 1939. He told MacNaughton that a trust was incapable of operating a newspaper and as a result *The Oregonian* had been suffering for years. *The Oregon Journal* had moved ahead of its major rival in both circulation and advertising revenues. Being an evening paper before the days of televised evening news, the *Journal* held the advertising advantage of being able to promote the Thursday and Friday night retail store sales. It also had secured all of Fred Meyer's advertising ever since the day when *The Oregonian* had printed an article reporting "rats in the basement"[28] of one of Fred Meyer's stores. According to MacNaughton, in the early 1930s *The Oregonian* had become so lethargic that "if Christ had been speaking on the streetcorner at Fifth and Morrison, *The Oregonian* would not have known about it till two days later."[29]

That time had happily passed, however, particularly since the appointment of E. Palmer Hoyt as editor in 1935. Hoyt "pepped up the paper"[30] but it still had a number of financial and operational problems, most of which stemmed from a small outdated plant. Underlying the paper's difficulties, furthermore, was the long-standing and deep-seated bitter feud between the Scott and Pittock heirs. The enmity surfaced in 1939 and it was to plague the paper for 11 years. Until the day the paper was sold in December 1950, Leslie Scott continued to entertain a fervent desire to assume the editorship himself.

After MacNaughton's arrival on the board, the need for a new plant became increasingly obvious.[31] The requirements of modern publishing mandated production lines that moved horizontally. With the old Oregonian Building, the lines moved vertically by elevator and conveyor belts. MacNaughton suggested that *The Oregonian* get together with the *Journal*, whose old building (the current Jackson Tower) suffered from similar limitations, to buy or build a new plant to print both papers. But the Scotts vetoed the motion. They "hated the *Journal* as much as the Pittocks."[32]

After the war was over, *The Oregonian*'s board purchased the former block site of the William S. Ladd mansion that had been demolished 20 years earlier. According to Robert C. Notson, Leslie Scott "grumbled at the $100,000 price,"[33] although three years later, as state treasurer, he was to vote his approval to spend $300,000 for the state to buy a nearby block to house a new state office building. Both structures were to be designed by Portland's leading contemporary architect, Pietro Belluschi. The difference in price for two comparable blocks of downtown property reflected a short-lived postwar boom in Portland commercial real estate sales. Chester A. Moores noted in 1946: "There has never been so much activity in the entire 100 year history of the city as there has been in the past two or three years."[34] Moores may have been exaggerating slightly. His well known optimism often colored his evaluation of events. But it was a fact that 125 blocks on the West Side business area between the river and 19th Avenue, the Union Station and College Street, had been sold between 1943 and 1946.

State Office Building; Pietro Belluschi, architect

624

The new Oregonian Building (lower center) facing on S. W. Broadway, shortly after its opening in 1948. One block to the north can be seen the new Federal Courthouse and Post Office, built in the early 1930s. At the top is the American Bank Building. The Jackson Tower, home of The Oregon Journal *until 1946, can be seen in front of the American Bank Building, overlooking the YMCA that was demolished in 1977.*

The boom mentality undoubtedly influenced *The Oregonian*'s decision to build a grandiose structure that was destined to be far too large for its needs. Belluschi was instructed to provide space for the paper's KGW radio station and for a projected new television studio. Also contemplated was a "large, magnificent dining room."[35] Because of a shortage of materials and a soaring inflation, the management signed a cost-plus construction contract with L. H. Hoffman. Adding to the length and cost of the construction activity, architect Belluschi's plans were apparently "never ready," according to MacNaughton. The delays caused by the "day by day plans" plus the extravagance of design proved to be "ghastly" to quote MacNaughton's observation after he assumed the presidency of the publishing company in 1947.[36] For the first time since 1893, the paper was forced to borrow from the banks. After the First National Bank's loan limits were reached, MacNaughton had to secure additional financing from the Bank of America in San Francisco. Having personally assured the Bank of America that he would guarantee the loans, MacNaughton took out his red pencil and began eliminating an extra elevator, the dining room and the radio-television studios.

In spite of such drastic revisions, the building still cost nearly $4 million, twice the original estimate. The new million dollar presses also added to the toll. The cash flow became so severe that the paper's reserves evaporated. Shortly after the building opened in 1948, the management sold it to the Connecticut Mutual Life Insurance Company for $3.6 million with a contract to lease it back for 24 years. With the proceeds the Bank of America's loan was repaid but the paper still faced a heavy drain on its resources: Remaining bank loans had to be serviced, general operational costs were going up along with labor costs, and newsprint was in short supply, forcing the paper to pay premium prices in order to meet its daily requirements.

MacNaughton saw the proverbial handwriting on the wall. The paper's assets along with a portion of the Pittock family assets were in jeopardy unless a buyer for *The Oregonian* could be found. Every time the matter came up for discussion among the board of directors, however, Leslie Scott adamantly opposed any thought of such an action. He blamed the Pittocks for the paper's financial woes. "The Pittocks were all spenders while the Scotts were savers," Scott declared on more than one occasion.[37] Knowing such feelings, MacNaughton secretly put out the word that *The Oregonian* was available for sale at the right price. Sometime during the fall of 1949, Samuel I. Newhouse, owner of one of the largest eastern newspaper chains, made contact with MacNaughton and decided to fly west to appraise the properties. According to an article published subsequently, when Newhouse first saw *The Oregonian* plant he declared: "It's three times too big."[38] Such an observation undoubtedly stimulated some preliminary thinking in Newhouse's fertile mind that the building was probably large enough to accommodate two newspapers. In fact he was reported to have commented at the time of his first visit that he might be interested in also purchasing *The Oregon Journal*, a possibility that would become a reality 11 years later.

After some delicate negotiations that mostly involved one or two reluctant Pittock family stockholders, Samuel I. Newhouse offered to purchase 100 percent of *The Oregonian*'s stock for $8000 per share. With 700 outstanding shares, the sales price totalled $5.6 million, payable in cash. The building was excluded and KGW was picked up for an additional $600,000.[39] The Scotts had fought to the bitter end, but with all of the Pittock shares lined up against him, Leslie Scott was forced to accept the inevitable.

When *The Oregonian* published the news of the sale on December 11, 1950, shock waves reverberated through the community. Another Portland landmark institution had been sold to absentee owners. Newhouse announced that there would be no change in management but numerous fears were to persist. The new owner not only remained true to his word but he immediately put the paper on a strong financial footing. For nearly 30 years, *The Oregonian* has proved to be one of the more profitable in Newhouse's extensive publishing empire.

As for E. B. MacNaughton who had performed his fiduciary duties with meticulous dedication, some ill-founded criticism was to be expected. A senior vice president of the U. S. National Bank wrote a friend in Honolulu: "Guess Mr. MacNaughton is a real true to form liquidator, having sold Ladd & Tilton back in 1925; the First National Bank later, and now the Oregonian."[40] Such a reputation led to the coining of one of the many epithets that were to decorate MacNaughton's life before he finally retired from active service at death. He became known as "The Great Liquidator." This was an unfortunate appellation because it was not grounded in fact. Individual circumstances determined the necessary actions in each case. And had *The Oregonian* not been sold in 1950, its fortunes would have continued to suffer along with those of the Pittock and Scott heirs. If any blame could be attached, it should have been directed against Henry Pittock's will that had created the 20 year trust which nearly ruined the paper before it was terminated.

E. B. MacNaughton left other legacies that distinguished him from most of Portland's business-political leadership in the late 1940s. For one thing, he was an educated and cultured man who read widely, appreciated the arts and even dabbled in water colors. He used to tell a favorite joke about the pioneers who headed west over the plains and mountains until they reached a junction with an arrow pointing north marked "Oregon." Those who could read came on to Oregon, while the rest kept heading south to Nevada and California. Writing in *The Oregonian* one year before his death, MacNaughton expressed his feelings about Oregonians in the following words:

> "One of the best assets Oregon has is the people who live here and want to come here. For the most part, they are intelligent, practical, skilled and venturesome folk. They comprise an integrated racial group with principles grounded on American ideals."[41]

Racially integrated, legally perhaps, but not in fact. Yet, despite this somewhat exaggerated statement, MacNaughton did expend much energy during the last decade of his life in efforts to promote both inter-group harmony in housing and civil liberties in the treatment of minorities. He took the lead locally in welcoming back to their Oregon residences the Japanese-Americans who had been uprooted from their homes and interned in out-of-state prison encampments during the war. For these and similar efforts he was posthumously honored by the Oregon branch of the ACLU which named an annual award in his memory, to be given to an individual who had made an outstanding contribution in the field of civil liberties. Several years before his death, in recognition of his national leadership among liberal churchmen, he was elected the national lay moderator of the Unitarian Church. Never able to break totally with his New England family background, he used to define himself as "a Republican with a move on." He loved life. He enjoyed almost everything that he

627

did. And he continually gave more of himself than he ever expected to receive in return, either in money[42] or in gratitude. A man of simple tastes, he used to walk to work from his modest house on King's Hill because the experience allowed him to see more of what was actually going on in his beloved hometown.

Fred G. Meyer — Another Contrast

A man of even simpler personal tastes than E. B. MacNaughton was merchant Fred G. Meyer who was six years younger than the banker whom he knew for over 40 years but with whom he had little in common. Each in his own way made a lasting contribution to Portland's history. If one were to draw a simple distinction, it might be said that MacNaughton's contribution was more spiritual than material while Meyer's was almost entirely material. When Meyer died in his 92nd year, the firm that he had founded in his early thirties, and maintained control over until his death in 1978, was ranked 45th by sales among *Fortune*'s 50 largest retailing companies. To do justice to the remarkable Meyer career would require a book in itself.[43] Apart from briefly describing the man and his accomplishments, this section will deal with only two separate events: The building of a warehouse along Sullivan's Gulch and the opening of the 16th store on S. W. Barbur Boulevard in 1950.

The secret of Meyer's success lay in his imagination, extraordinary self-discipline, directed concentration, uninterrupted work and his longevity. He had few if any interests besides his business and his wife Eva, who was his co-

Fred Meyer's first shopping center on N. E. Sandy Boulevard in the Hollywood district — 1931

Fred Meyer

partner for 40 years until her death in 1960. Starting with literally no capital and no formal education, he built an empire that should exceed $1 billion in sales during 1979. He left an estate of more than $60 million with nearly the entire amount bequeathed to a charitable trust, the income to be used for "religious, charitable, scientific, literary or educational purposes." Such were the bottom line accomplishments of the man who opened Portland's original cash and carry food store; the man who was the first to use coupons and the first to offer discounts. All items were packaged and priced to allow for self-selection and self-service. At the time that he opened Portland's first shopping center in 1931 at the south end of the Hollywood section of Rose City Park, Meyer had already coined several of the slogans or aphorisms that were to become his trademarks:

> "Keep learning, keep earning."

> "Business is always good for merchants — adopt, adapt, adjust — try to do business the way the customer wants it done."

> "Eliminate, combine, rearrange, supply."

> "Buy Oregon products."

Although he lived austerely by current middle class standards, often in small apartments near one of the stores, and rarely owned an automobile, he did not refrain from paying himself and his wife a reasonably healthy stipend in the early years. During the depression in 1934, for example, Meyer and his wife together earned more than any other salaried banker or business executive in Portland: $60,000.[44] But as he grew older, with extensive personal holdings, he kept his salary well below that paid to others of similar rank in companies of similar size: $126,000. Regardless of what he was paid, however, he spent very little on personal tastes. He had no recreational interests besides walking, no cultural interests besides the opera, and practically no social life outside of the business. He went to headquarters six days a week and sometimes on Sunday, maintaining the same schedule as long as his health would permit. The day after his 92nd birthday in his office, the author found him alert in mind although halting in speech and fragile in appearance. The following summary of the interview should provide a certain perspective for understanding the significance of the two episodes that will be discussed.

Meyer tended to downplay his own role — the personal element — in the growth of the Fred Meyer company. He firmly believed that the firm's great progress was entirely due to the "economic system." There was "no room for emotion in business management." Let the system function, he said, and "the business will flourish." Implied in such statements was the notion that government exists to serve the private economic system. Meyer felt no responsibility to the public in deciding where to locate stores or warehouses. It was a matter solely of the most economical location, a site that would generate the most business for the least investment. The implication of course was that if Fred Meyer, Inc., thrived, the city would also thrive.

Meyer opposed public planning by the government. There was "no need for zoning." He admired the Houston plan. "It works," he declared. As to the automobile, he showed little concern. He believed that people should be able to do what they wanted with their cars. "Give them what they want," he stated more than once. Clearly implied in such declarations was the notion that future generations could deal with the consequences. The attempt to weigh the historical consequences of an action as far as the public was concerned, held no value for him. For that matter, neither did the writing and reading of history. Self-interest was the primary motive in society. "Let the system work by itself," he said. People will act in their own best interests and society will benefit accordingly.[45]

The Warehouse on Sullivan's Gulch

At the time of his 90th birthday, Fred Meyer was quoted as saying that "Portland waits for its opportunities while Seattle goes after them." An examination of Meyer's Portland career reveals a different pattern of behavior. He rarely if ever waited for his opportunities to develop. From his earliest days in

630

business he created his opportunities by accurately predicting and even influencing where the commercial activity would be centered 10 or 20 years later. He had a good fix on future highway routes and he acquired hundreds of cheap, "far out" acres of property on which to locate future shopping centers. Multnomah County was a particularly fruitful area for creating development opportunities because the county had no zoning codes in the unincorporated areas to restrict his long-term plans.

Even within the city of Portland, which was zoned, he was to encounter few defeats when he sought zone changes to allow the construction of shopping centers in districts previously zoned residential. He suffered his first defeat in 1938 when he attempted to build a shopping center adjacent to Eastmoreland. He ran head-on into the strong opposition of Portland's two leading business-men-bankers: E. C. Sammons and E. B. MacNaughton, who was living near Reed College at the time. Perhaps this was one reason why he entrusted his local funds to the Bank of California. He was to try a similar ploy in 1951 and suffer a similar fate. When the Eastmoreland Association tried to buy the property at the junction of McLoughlin and Bybee Boulevards, Meyer refused the offer. "Not for sale," he declared. The association wanted to donate the land to the city park system. "There is already too much park land in Oregon," he asserted. In a rare moment of public anger, Meyer warned the neighborhood group: "We'll see what the future holds!"[46]

To counter such opposition, Meyer hired the most prominent attorneys he could find. For many years his litigation was handled by Dan J. Malarkey and his younger partner Robert L. Sabin, Jr. It was Sabin who carried the Fred Meyer banner to city hall in December 1945 when the council chamber was packed with Laurelhurst residents who were protesting the construction of a large warehouse on Sullivan's Gulch, between S. E. 44th and 47th Avenues in the Providence Hospital district. S. E. 44th was the eastern boundary of Laurelhurst and the last thing the residents wanted was a noisy, truck-laden commercial enterprise to upset the peace and calm of their neighborhood.

Unfortunately for the affected residents, the land east of 44th Avenue was zoned for industrial and commercial use. Sabin informed the council that they had bought and built at their own risk. Meyer planned to invest $660,000 in the structure of which amount $85,000 had already been spent preparing the site.[47] The citizens continued to protest. They wanted the city to condemn the land and make it into a park. Over $12,000 had already been pledged privately to help buy the land. Fearing a law suit and under the usual Meyer pressure, the council turned down the protest and gave Meyer its blessing.

The council, under Mayor Riley's leadership, had only itself to blame for the problem. Two months earlier, the state highway commission, with support from the planning commission, had requested that the council upzone the area from III to II, to prevent the very kind of costly investment undertaken by the Fred Meyer Company. It wanted to keep the south side of Sullivan's Gulch clear of any industrial development because the gulch was tentatively designated as the

January 1946

*Fred Meyer, Inc.
Warehouse under
construction*

1948

*Before the Banfield
Freeway*

1978

*Remains of the ware-
house on the Ban-
field Freeway*

route for a new postwar expressway. The council had taken no action and the city had granted Meyer a building permit. Sabin maintained that the city had no legal right to change the zoning considering his client's rather sizeable vested rights.

In late January, as Meyer was rushing his warehouse to completion as fast as he could, the state highway commission's attorney went before the city council to protest that the warehouse was smack in the middle of the highway right-of-way. But such objections were overruled. The project was too far along to cancel. And furthermore, such an action would prove costly to the city's taxpayers.

Within five years, the Fred Meyer warehouse was to prove mighty costly to the state's taxpayers. The state highway commission was forced to condemn the facility and pay Meyer $750,000 for the entire warehouse. It cut off the northern portion needed for the freeway and sold the remainder to the Bemis Bag Company for $250,000.[48] In later years, the facility was taken over by the Friedman Bag Company and Royal Crown Cola. Meyer moved his warehouse to some filled land near Swan Island where the Kaiser Corporation had recently abandoned its wartime housing.

It was ironic that Fred Meyer, who continually criticized government officials for wasting taxpayer dollars, should himself have been responsible for the loss of $500,000 of taxpayer's money because of his own obstinately narrow self-interest. When the author raised this issue with him in 1978, he refused to admit that the highway commission had issued such a protest. He replied that "there was no highway program till Eisenhower's administration." Meyer had forgotten that he had been privy to the 1943 PAPDC highway plan which clearly

The Fred Meyer warehouse center — early 1950s

showed that an expressway was designated for Sullivan's Gulch. It is no wonder that Fred G. Meyer had little use for history.

The Barbur Boulevard Store

The Barbur Boulevard shopping center was a symbol of progress to the Fred Meyer organization. It represented the company's first penetration of the Tualatin Valley on the West Side of Portland. As an *Oregonian* headline noted, "New Center Indicative of West Hills Growth." The paper accurately predicted that the new store, which opened in August 1950, would bring increased business expansion to the area following "the history of other business districts where Meyer has built shopping centers."[49]

Fred Meyer's 16th store was several years in the making. In 1946, while the warehouse was under construction, Meyer secured a zone change from I to II to permit him to build on the corner of S. W. Terwilliger and Barbur Boulevards. He had owned the land for several years. In fact this was one of the sites that he had discussed with Chester A. Moores at the time that Moores was keeping him informed on the deliberations of the state highway commission in 1943. Meyer had been especially interested in the postwar improvement and extension of Terwilliger Boulevard which was formerly called the Hillside Parkway.

CONVENIENTLY LOCATED
To Serve the
SOUTHWEST AREA
THE FOCAL POINT OF S. W.
PORTLAND AND NEIGHBORING CITIES

14 Minutes from BEAVERTON
2 Minutes from CAPITOL HILL
4 Minutes from HILLSDALE
5 Minutes from MULTNOMAH
14 Minutes from OSWEGO
25 Minutes from OREGON CITY
7 Minutes from GARDEN HOME
35 Minutes from FOREST GROVE
25 Minutes from HILLSBORO
45 Minutes from McMINNVILLE
13 Minutes from METZGER
12 Minutes from PROGRESS
6 Minutes from RALEIGH HILLS
10 Minutes from PORTLAND HTS.
7 Minutes from TIGARD

HURRY HURRY

Thrilling
FAIR
★ Giant Ferris Wheel
★ Carnival Attractions
★ Demonstrations
★ Free Samples
★ Exciting Exhibits
DAILY 2 to 10 P. M.
IT'S ALL FREE!

Part of Oregonian *ad promoting the opening of Barbur Boulevard store, Aug. 2, 1950*

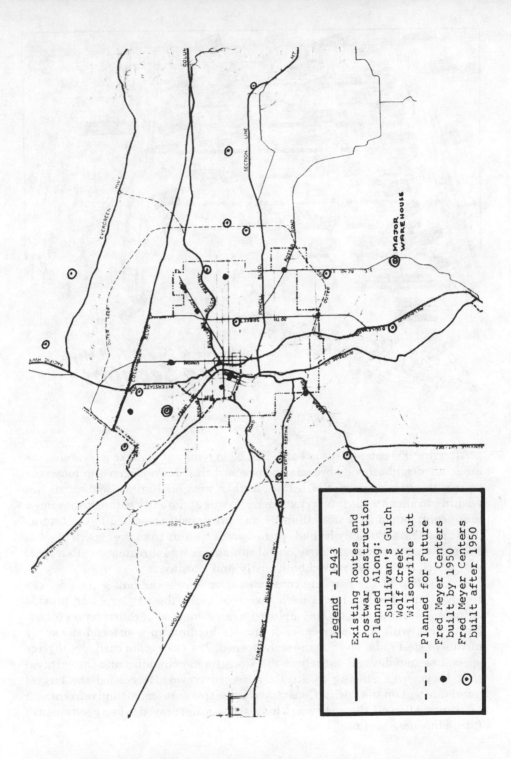

Legend – 1943

Existing Routes and
Postwar construction

Planned Along:
Sullivan's Gulch
Wolf Creek
Wilsonville Cut

Planned for Future

● Fred Meyer Centers
built by 1950

⊙ Fred Meyer Centers
built after 1950

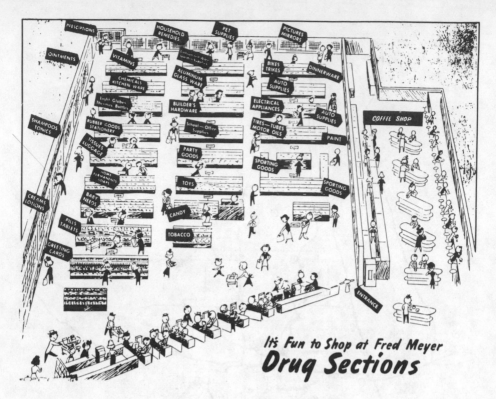

It's Fun to Shop at Fred Meyer
Drug Sections

August 3, 1950 Oregonian *ad*

After 160,000 cubic yards of earth had been removed to make a level site, the adjacent neighborhoods became so incensed that Meyer agreed to move the store's location a quarter of a mile farther west on Barbur Boulevard. Not wishing to alienate his future customers, he was apparently willing to assume a more compromising posture than he had previously presented to the Laurelhurst residents. Possibly he had learned some lessons from the experience, but the real reason was most likely one of timing. He was threatened with a court suit which could have proved both costly and lengthy.

Preparation of the new site consumed over a year, as half a hillside was removed and dumped into a deep ravine to make the site level and provide sufficient parking spaces. He employed a novel method of construction for the Northwest, with five large concrete trusses holding up a suspended roof by means of steel rods. The day the store opened, *The Oregonian* carried a 13 page special section devoted entirely to the store, its merchandise and the carnival that Meyer was staging to attract a record crowd. He erected the largest available tent on the Pacific Coast to cover the free amusement and refreshment offerings. All in all, the event was a huge success and proved to be a good omen of future business profits.

The Barbur Boulevard (Burlingame) Fred Meyer store being prepared for opening in the summer of 1950. Note the two levelled sites above, at the intersection of Terwilliger and Barbur Boulevards.

An early 1960s aerial photograph showing the population growth north of the store and the construction of the Salem (Baldock) Freeway.

One of the consequences that did not set happily with city commissioner William A. Bowes who had originally supported the development was the amount of rebuilding that Barbur Boulevard was forced to undergo at public expense. It had to be widened and new access roads had to be constructed. It was the memory of this event more than anything else that led Bowes to oppose Fred Meyer's second attempt to build his Eastmoreland center in 1951. Bowes and his council colleagues were slowly learning a painful lesson: The public costs of private developments that were not an integral part of a comprehensive public plan could exceed the increased tax revenues derived from such developments. The subsequent population explosion in the region led to eight separate annexations to the city and forced the council to rezone large portions of the areas along the major arterials including Barbur Boulevard from single family residential to apartment use.

The westward growth toward suburban Washington County had begun. The Bertha-Beaverton Highway to Raleigh Hills was soon to be widened and rezoned for apartment and commercial use and Fred Meyer would locate a store at the center of the action. As the development pressures increased toward Beaverton, Meyer was to add still another store a few miles down the Bertha-Beaverton Highway. By the early 1960s, Washington County was to become the fastest growing region of metropolitan Portland. In 1979, the Fred Meyer Company will open its largest single shopping center at the junction of three major highways on the eastern edge of Beaverton, a $6 million concrete testament to 30 years of steady progress.

Fred Meyer in Retrospect — The Impact of the Supermarket

In 1960, Fred Meyer president Earl Chiles, stepson of the founder and chairman of the board, wrote an article for a management handbook in which he cited a number of changes in American society that were directly related to the growth of suburban shopping centers. In the light of Fred Meyer's experience, some of his points are worth noting.

"It is hard to understand why the great growth of retailing followed so far behind that of manufacturing industries. In method, until the thirties, most retailing was in the Caleb Cabot stage of development. Of course, the great population shift to the suburbs, the improvement of marketing and distribution techniques, and many other factors played a role in bringing about change. When markets were concentrated in the center of cities and transportation was slow and uneven, there was hardly the necessity for the great markets of today.

But I am inclined to believe that the greatest single factor forcing the growth of supermarkets was the immense social change which took place during and immediately following the depression years. Greater wealth, spread over a greater population, demanded more convenience and all the rest of the things which have paralleled retailing growth.

Today we have hundreds of gleaming supermarkets for food. But this is

Sullivan's Gulch highway route through the East Side — 1948

only the bare beginning. The supermarkets are already branching out into many lines other than food. Our own chain, which only recently became a two-city organization, has just as much space devoted to the marketing and selling of apparel as to food. We have another division, just as large, which sells drugs, medicines, and all variety items that might be found in any first-rate drugstore. And we have complete coffee shops (cafeterias) in many of our stores.

Other chains are doing this, too. Only space and real-estate requirements in the larger metropolitan areas are preventing faster growth. But the trend is on its way. The day of the one-stop supermarket is already here."[50]

NABISCO's New Cracker Factory

Early in March 1946, as Fred Meyer was putting the finishing touches on his much disputed warehouse, the National Biscuit Company management in New York City decided that it wanted to consolidate its small Portland and Seattle plants into one large regional location, in either Portland or Seattle. Railroad siding access was important, so the local railroad development people in conjunction with the Portland Chamber of Commerce's Industries Department played an active role in showing the company a number of possible sites. Quoting from a letter by the manager of the chamber's Industries Department, Chester Sterrett: "The only area that appealed to them [NABISCO] was on the Union Pacific on the north side of Sullivan's Gulch, west of 74th Street. . . . This property runs up to the Rose City Golf Links."[51]

As Sterrett explained the reasons for the preference:

"They like the setting very much. They would not even consider any location in the Guild's Lake district. They want to be away from any heavy industrial plants."[52]

In a memorandum to PP&L's Paul B. McKee four months later, Sterrett commented that NABISCO "would like to get into a semi-residential neighborhood where they can put up a modern, nice-looking structure."[53] Sterrett had noted somewhat prophetically in an earlier communication:

639

"Of course, we may have some trouble in delivering this site as most of it is now zone 2 and we would have to get the city fathers to change this zone. However, they are very cooperative and unless some opposition would develop, from nearby residential districts, I do not think we would have any trouble."[54]

Sterrett apprised McKee of another possible site lying between the Union Pacific Railroad and North Columbia Boulevard. The property was outside of the city limits and therefore not subject to zoning restrictions. But, as Sterrett informed McKee, this location did not carry the appeal of the Rose City site.

Over the next three months, the chamber busily laid the groundwork for its choice industrial prospect. A letter from Sterrett in October illustrates how the business organization directed its tactics:

"Our Industries Executive Committee had an off the record session with the members of the City Council about a week ago and I feel sure that after this meeting, I can go to the City Council and get them to approve such a program. However, there is always the possibility that some residential property owners in that area might raise an objection."[55]

Negotiations continued on into January 1947 and the chamber's Sterrett kept the NABISCO management in New York fully abreast of the strategy. Talks had been held with the state highway commission which approved the industrial zoning for the golf course site that abutted Sullivan's Gulch. Further "off-the-record" meetings were held with the mayor, city commissioners and members of the planning commission, all of whom seemed supportive. The pressure that the business-political leadership could exert was evident in planning commission chairman Glenn Stanton's reversal of a position that he had taken one year earlier. In April 1946, architect Stanton had written a memorandum to commissioner William A. Bowes which stated that:

"The planning commission is determined to adhere to their conceptions of good planning. While we need space for industrial expansion, it should be done in an orderly manner and in harmony with the many other component parts of a well composed community. Residential areas cannot be sacrificed for industry because of the chance location of a rail line."[56]

NABISCO finally decided on the Rose City site. It wanted to acquire 24 acres, including four unplatted blocks owned by investor Harry Mittleman and nine blocks in the Santa Rosa Park Addition containing few residences. In April, the company made its formal offer to the chamber of commerce which was designated the agent for putting together the whole package. The chamber, or its nominee, had three months to obtain permanent industrial zoning and necessary easements, arrange for the vacation of all streets and removal of all structures, arrange for title conveyances and for removal of all sub-surface facilities. For doing this, NABISCO agreed to pay $10,000 to the city for street conveyance and $225,000 for the properties. It also agreed to abide by city

640

restrictions relative to the siting of the facility. The buildings were to be limited to three stories in height, except that on ten percent of the 24 acres, they could rise to a maximum of 125 feet.

Needless to say, Chester Sterrett had assumed a gargantuan task. The company was prepared to invest between $5 and $6 million in a plant that would employ 1000 workers, ten times the number then employed in the small factory on N. W. Davis Street. The importance of the new biscuit factory to Portland's postwar needs seemed to justify almost any amount of effort required to achieve success.

President George Coppers, writing from NABISCO headquarters in New York, was almost ecstatic over the prospects. The plant would be designed by the best architects and built by local labor. The result would be "the ultimate in modern streamlined bakery." The men and women would work under ideal conditions and because the plant would be located in a residential district, he hoped that they would live nearby. Extensive health and recreational facilities would be made available and beautifully landscaped grounds would cover the 14 acres not used for the plant itself. President Coppers concluded: "We have faith in the future growth of the Portland market."[57]

It was well, indeed, that he did, because it would be a frustrating 18 months more before ground could be broken, but not next to the Rose City Golf Course; rather, up on North Columbia Boulevard between Union and Vancouver Avenues, next to the Union Pacific's main North Portland tracks. What happened makes an interesting tale. To begin with, on April 24, 1947, the same day that President Coppers wrote his eulogy of Portland, the chamber's Sterrett and Harry Mittleman executed an amazing document. This was an option agreement in which Mittleman consented to sell his unplatted property for $125,000 provided that the City Council would enact two ordinances, changing from residential to apartment zoning, two parcels of land owned by Mittleman: One on N. E. 33rd adjacent to Laurelhurst and one along S. E. 60th next to Mt. Tabor. If Mittleman could not erect apartments on N. E. Tillamook, he wanted absolute assurance that he could build them in two other residentially attractive areas not zoned for multi-family development.

Not only was Sterrett over his head in work to be done, but he, the agent of a private organization, had committed a public governmental body to take an action before the fact, before any ordinances had even been introduced, let alone read and discussed publicly as required by law. Sterrett then made an agreement with L. C. (Jack) Binford, a local attorney, and one of the two major property owners on N. E. Tillamook Street, to seek options on the rest of the Santa Rosa tract. Binford agreed to a sale price of $100,000 for most of nine blocks, or a bit more than $6000 per acre. Mittleman was charging about $14,000 an acre for four unplatted blocks. Considering Mittleman's other requirements, it would appear that he knew how to pursue a good deal when he saw one. Ten days after the option agreement was signed, the chamber issued the first of many press releases designed to create public support for the venture. Harry Mittleman was complimented for his "civic spirit in helping pave the way for this project." He was credited with being willing to postpone a garden court apartment project of his own, pending the outcome of the National Biscuit Company negotiations.[58] No word was mentioned about the required deal with the city and the two favorable ordinances that would need to be passed first. By the avid pursuit of such self interest, Harry Mittleman subsequently became one of Portland's largest property owners, including the Bank of California Building and the land under most of the U. S. National Bank branches.

Once the publicity was released, the feared opposition to the development began to be heard within surrounding neighborhoods. As might be expected, Fred Meyer dispatched a note of support to Chester Sterrett.

To Chester K Sterrett C/C

Am sending attached as I thought you may find it interesting and useful.

hope this deal goes thru without too much grief.

Fred Meyer
Portland, Oregon

we gave National Biscuit first real boost in this area, and believe we had much to do with them achieving a volume market in this area. And it is volume that often helps make location decisions.

So we are especially interested in their success. Keep in mind that retailers can aide greatly in getting industries here, by volume of business they contribute. We have had many cases thereon.

So get retailers to co-operate wherever they can aide *Fred Meyer*

Sterrett replied as follows:

"Dear Mr. Meyer:

I wish to thank you very much for your note with respect to the National Biscuit Company. As you have probably seen in the papers, some of the residents in the vicinity of this project are complaining bitterly about it.

The Planning Commission has approved the necessary zone changes and this whole matter will come up for a public hearing before Council on Thursday afternoon, May 22nd, at 2:00 p.m. I am pretty sure that the Council will go along with us on this matter, but it would help materially if certain of our leading retailers would appear at this meeting to emphasize the importance of new jobs to the community as a whole."[59]

As the newspaper coverage increased along with the neighborhood protests, all kinds of other problems were beginning to confront the beleaguered Sterrett: Certain owners of small parcels were reluctant to sell; it was to take five weeks to approve the street vacation petitions; the planning commission got tangled up on the industrial zone change, even though Chairman Glenn Stanton and most of its members were in support of the action. The commission was thus prevented from acting upon Mittleman's two zone change requests. Finally, some of the options began to run out, including Mittleman's.

Local industry and business generally came out in strong support, led by the chamber. On personal request from Chester Sterrett, both *The Oregonian* and the *Journal* wrote strong editorials of endorsement. Declared the *Journal*:

> "The city zoning ordinance is not a static thing. In its very nature it must be flexible if the city is to progress and if the best and highest use of land is maintained. Zoning of 1924 does not necessarily make sense today. Admittedly sentiment is on the side of the embattled home owners who threaten to tie up the whole deal by taking it to the supreme court — if the city council approves the zone change. But the realities are still on the other side — on the side of a $2 million payroll, on the side of 1000 new jobs, on the side of the progress of Portland. These things cannot be denied."[60]

The property owners adjacent to the Rose City golf course took exception to such statements and their implications. In reply to a similar *Oregonian* editorial which had downgraded the area for residential construction, four aroused residents wrote as follows:

> "Apparently the only people who aren't deliriously happy over the move are property owners in the peaceful residential neighborhood which would be invaded by the industrial development. These are dismissed by The Oregonian as 'residents not of the optioned site but of nearby streets who fear that property values will be lowered.'
>
> All property values in Portland are lowered by the cynicism evidenced by the city commission, planning commission, Chamber of Commerce and newspapers in this case. No property in Portland is safe, none has protection against undesirable neighbors, as long as a residential zone may be changed suddenly and arbitrarily to an industrial zone. This is precisely what zoning is designed to prevent. Zoning is valueless where, as in Portland, city officials apparently lack the intestinal fortitude to abide even by their own rules. And where those faithless to the public trust are abetted and applauded by a commercial organization and the press.
>
> The facts in the biscuit factory case are that the property for which the zone change is requested has not, as The Oregonian implies, been unattractive to home builders, but has been held off the market for years, apparently for speculative purposes, which will be served handsomely if the factory deal goes through; that several other sites exist in Portland which would meet the requirements of the company without necessitating zone changes and without destroying residential neighborhoods; that the requirements of the company from a raw materials supply and products distribution standpoint assure erection of its plant in Portland rather than in Seattle; that millions of dollars of high-class residential property would suffer losses of an estimated

30 per cent in value if the zone change is made; that the utility of Rose City municipal park, which the proposed plant would directly adjoin for a distance of five and one-half blocks (factory buildings 50 feet from the edge), would be greatly lessened by the development; that hundreds of property owners in the vicinity are organized to defend our homes.

Happily the choice in this case need not be one between industry or homes. There is room here for both. It is not necessary to jumble them in a hodge-podge and to build factories in the middle of residential neighborhoods.

If the editors of The Oregonian really believe that in this case 'the planning has been all in the direction of making the plant a neighborhood and community attraction,' the embattled home owners of this section will gladly let you have this cracker factory for your own front yard."[61]

The city council voted 3-1 on June 5, 1947, to approve the zone change, with commissioner William A. Bowes leading the affirmative forces and Dorothy McCullough Lee in the minority. The owners of five lots in the Santa Rosa Park Addition immediately filed suit in circuit court. By June 26th, the options had nearly expired and the National Biscuit Company formally abandoned the site. The chamber's Sterrett was undaunted. Aided by the Union Pacific Railroad and realtors Ritter & Lowe, a new site at N. E. Union Avenue and Columbia Boulevard was assembled in November 1947.

In an action that constituted direct conflict of interest, planning commission chairman Glenn Stanton was hired by NABISCO to be the local consultant to the New York architectural firm of Ford, Bacon & Davis. The construction contract was awarded to L. H. Hoffman in September 1948. The plant opened in

NABISCO

The Binford Apartments in Rose City Park

August 1950 and a large formal celebration was held at the Multnomah Hotel in January 1951. In all, almost $10 million had been invested in the project.

The outcome of this frenzied endeavor must, ironically enough, be considered a happy one for most of the parties concerned. Certainly for investor Binford, the results have been extremely gratifying, although 30 years ago the project's cancellation left him financially embarrassed. Binford borrowed $2 million in federal housing funds and built one of the most attractive patio apartment developments in the Pacific Northwest. Overlooking the golf course and park, the design of the complex was based on some ideas that Binford picked up in California and Mexico. Containing nearly 1000 dwellers, the Binford Apartments were full from the day they opened. Recently the loan was paid off and the complex sold to American Condominium Homes. The sprawling 15.6 acre parcel of land and the 274 apartment units are expected to yield the new owners over $10 million in sales.

Despite the fact that L. C. Binford was appreciative of the chamber's efforts of 30 years ago, for as he told the author, "Had they not requested me to acquire the land, the development would never have happend,"[62] the process that permitted it to happen was of doubtful merit. Like many of the historical episodes treated in this book, the NABISCO story was a tale of social insensitivity and environmental blindness wherein narrowly selfish private interests determined the formulation of public policies.

The break in the railroad dike at Vanport, May 30, 1948

In Conclusion

Portland at Mid-Century

Dorothy McCullough Lee's election in the May 1948 primary was viewed by many voters as the beginning of a new era in Portland's political history. She overwhelmingly defeated incumbent Mayor Earl Riley but she would have to wait nearly eight months before assuming office. During the interim, city government would continue to stagnate in the face of enormous social problems that had been increasing with severity throughout the immediate postwar era. The Vanport flood, striking ten days after the election, merely intensified the state of paralysis in which the Riley administration had been suspended for some time. Few periods in Portland's history have witnessed as corrupt, morally insensitive and generally impotent a mayorship as Earl Riley's, and the business community had to bear some of the blame. By supporting, let alone condoning, such leadership in city hall, Portland business and banking executives revealed a high degree of ethical myopia.

Reaction and Reform?

Dorothy Lee did not consider herself a reformer. Her major campaign promise was "to enforce the law." But she realized that certain reforms would have to be effected if the law was to be strictly applied — reforms primarily in police operations. To this day, Mrs. Lee ascribes her reluctant candidacy to a murder that was committed on January 14, 1947, a grisly event that shook a number of Portlanders out of their accustomed lethargy.[1]

On the evening of the ill-fated day, Captain Frank B. Tatum, skipper of the ship *Edwin Abbey*, went ashore for a night on the town. He was well dressed, wore his prized platinum watch as well as his cameo ring and carried almost $700 in cash. Within sight of Portland's two major banks and the Salvation Army mission, Tatum entered a small boardinghouse-type club that was known to serve liquor by the drink, an unlawful practice in Oregon at the time. Other delights were also known to be available for those willing to pay the price. The Cecil Club, on S. W. Sixth between Pine and Oak Streets, had been raided several times by State of Oregon Liquor Control Commission officers but had never been bothered by the vice squad even though it was located within shooting distance of police headquarters.

The next morning when Captain Tatum failed to return to his ship prior to its scheduled departure time, a missing persons report was filed with both the police department and the U. S. Maritime Commission office. One week later, his body was discovered at the foot of a 50 foot cliff on Santanita Terrace in Northwest

Portland. Missing were his wallet, watch and ring. The cause of death was a broken neck.[2] A subsequent investigation implicated the club and three of its employees who were tried, convicted and packed off to the state penitentiary. The owner, an ex-convict, received a life sentence while his two accomplices got by with 15 years.

The incident provided Portlanders with a vivid illustration of the close ties between vice and violent crime. Public indignation was immediate. *The Oregonian*, in a blazing editorial headed "Stench Behind the Roses," noted that the dive had operated for years without apparent interference from the Portland Police Department. The concluding sentence asserted bluntly:

> "The chain of callous murder and robbery which started in the Cecil Rooms is merely an exaggeration, because of the death of the victim, of such vicious, almost nightly occurrences behind the placid front of the City of Roses."[3]

On the day that Captain Tatum's body was found, Mayor Earl Riley left town on a five week business-vacation trip.

Throughout the next 12 months, Portland Commissioner of Public Utilities Dorothy Lee was approached by numerous citizens at social events and speaking engagements, all of whom suggested that she run for mayor in 1948. Following the publication of the Vollmer and City Club reports on police corruption, the pressure on Mrs. Lee increased. Until she finally made the fateful decision in March 1948, she politely rejected all overtures on the grounds that she was too busy to consider such a matter. According to her husband, one of the City Club investigators went to her privately and told her about conditions that were excluded from the club's report because they could not be completely verified.

> "He was so incensed . . . that he became almost a zealot in his enthusiasm to make things better. . . . These people who came to her were not reformers . . . or crackpots but sincere decent citizens who were appalled at the extent to which this cancer had eaten into the nerve centers of respectable democratic government in their city."

One such "decent" citizen was Herbert A. Templeton, a successful lumberman and future benefactor of Lewis and Clark College, who was the only prominent Portland business leader to actively support Mrs. Lee's candidacy. Templeton's involvement was to cost him a lot of money,[4] but the staunch Presbyterian was true to his convictions. In contrast to many of his business peers, Templeton was not afraid to put his money where his mouth was.

Dorothy McCullough Lee possessed a distinguished background in both family antecedents and professional experiences. Her maternal grandfather, Thomas Hill, was a prominent painter of western scenes whose "Driving the Last Spike" now hangs in the California State Capitol Building in Sacramento. Her father, Dr. Frank McCullough, was the Fleet Surgeon of the U. S. Navy before World War I. When she settled in Portland in 1924 as a bride of 23 with a recent law degree from the University of California, the native San Franciscan was Oregon's youngest woman lawyer. Her husband, an industrial engineer with the Standard Oil Company of California, had been assigned to the Portland office.

Not long after her arrival, she was encouraged by some women acquaintances to run for the state legislature in 1926. Failing in her first bid, she ran again in 1928 and was elected to the first of three terms in the House of Representatives. She was elected to the Oregon State Senate in 1939 and appointed to the Portland City Council in 1943 to succeed the late Ralph B. Clyde. Although a registered Republican, party affiliation was of secondary importance to the serious lawyer-legislator-commissioner. She was fascinated by the challenges of the job and rarely let politics influence her decisions. This unusual quality in American political life helped her to win the mayorship in 1948 but it also hindered her chances for re-election in 1952, as a later volume of this history will record.

The Lee Administration

Dorothy Lee's years in office were to prove trying. The fact that she was a woman — Portland's first and only popularly elected woman mayor to date — plagued her from the beginning. The newspapers gave her only lukewarm support although *The Oregon Journal* became slightly more enthusiastic as the election date approached. "Dorothy Lee will be no petticoat administrator," declared the *Journal* after her election. "The brain behind Mrs. Lee's very feminine appearance operates with an analytical clarity and vigor worthy of any masculine standard." The *Journal*, like most male dominated institutions in America, expressed the traditional stereotyped perception of a woman's societal role.

Mrs. Lee is convinced that her womanliness was the major reason for the business community's rejection of her leadership, although the historical record points to another factor: The business community could not control her as it had her predecessors. Possessing a strong and independent spirit, Mrs. Lee was committed to doing what she felt was right rather than what might prove expedient politically.

During the months before her inauguration, Mayor-elect Lee exhaustively researched the whole subject of slot machines and their impact on city life throughout America. She concluded that the existing law should be executed uniformly and impartially. Although the machines had long been outlawed by city ordinance, the police had only selectively enforced the ban on those operators who would not pay protection money to city hall.

Early in January 1949, she issued a strong statement outlining her intentions and the reaction was instantaneous. Howls erupted not only from the slot machine operators and their gambling cohorts, but from certain segments of the

The first outdoor art exhibition in Oregon, held in the Park Blocks during Mayor Lee's administration, on July 24, 1949. It was presented with the city's support by the Oregon Society of Artists.

business community which feared the economic consequences of eliminating a lucrative commercial enterprise. One former "First Citizen" of Portland dubbed Mayor Lee "Mrs. Airwick."[5] The private clubs were particularly incensed when the mayor also included them within the coverage of the law.

Some years later, a North Burnside observer of the Lee era who was a retired police informant told writer Joe Uris:

> "The first thing she closed was the Chinese gambling joints. Around the station and even in the newspapers, everyone took to calling her No Sin Lee."[6]

According to Uris, Mayor Lee did not change the scene for long. "She dampened things down, closed most of the after hours joints and put a lot of working girls on the streets for awhile. Eventually she even drove them out, but in the county, outside her jurisdiction, it was business as usual."[7] Another veteran of Skid Road told Uris:

> "Dorothy McCullough Lee was a wonderful person, a real lady. Issa [sic] shame she got into politics. But, I'll tell you this, when she started to clean up, she appointed a man from the Oregon State police, not some Berkeley psycho, as her chief of police."[8]

650

The mention of the Oregon State Police officer referred to Charles P. Pray, the first superintendent of the state police force established by the legislature in 1931. Before Mrs. Lee took office, she visited Pray who had retired to Eastmoreland to raise roses. She convinced him that she needed someone she could trust to assume command of the police force and sort out the good eggs from the bad. She wanted to identify those officers who would be qualified to assume future leadership within the department. Donald McNamara, who was to serve as Mayor Terry Schrunk's police chief, was one of those selected by Mayor Lee for top bureau responsibility.

The combined efforts of Lee and Pray led to a sniping and whispering campaign that was launched with increasing ferocity in the early spring of 1949. The effort was designed to make Mayor Lee look ridiculous. According to her husband's recollection:

> "We had information to the effect that a large sum of money came into Portland from sources in Chicago for the purpose of propagating material of this nature."[9]

The newspapers made little effort to distinguish fact from fiction when they reported some of the rumors as news items. One of the most widespread of tales related to Mayor Lee's supposed delicate state of health. It was pure fantasy but it unsettled a number of citizens, including even many of the mayor's friends

Sporting one of her famous hats, Mayor Dorothy McCullough Lee was photographed chatting with Father Thomas Tobin, one of her appointees to the Housing Authority of Portland and Philip Murray, president of the CIO.

651

who believed such to be true. Thirty years later, at the age of 78, Mrs. Lee is still actively pursuing the practice of law!

Scott Lee blamed the press for many of his wife's difficulties:

> "Portland's metropolitan dailies did not distinguish themselves by militant support of vigorous and impartial law enforcement. . . . It does seem reasonable to suppose that responsible newspapers, with considerable property investments in the community and whose continued prosperity depends upon the adequate protection of those property rights as well as adequate protection of the entire community from lawlessness, would militantly support officials making a determined effort to bring about impartial law enforcement."[10]

One series of attacks on the mayor was labelled by her husband as "the famous battle of the hats." It all started with a letter to the editor of *The Oregonian* in June 1949:

> "If we have to be inflicted with all those numerous pictures of our dear Dorothy Lee, would it be too much to ask that she refrain from wearing those audacious 'blobs' of felt or straw which always seem to be on the verge of falling down over her honor's eyes."[11]

This plaint was followed by a deluge of letters to the press, some praising and other criticizing "Dorothy's hats." The whole affair became so ridiculous that *The Oregonian*'s associate editor, Ben Hur Lampman, could not resist the temptation to produce one of his more entertaining pieces:

> "The [editorial] page is agreeable to concede that there are few women who could wear the hats Mayor Lee wears, without most woeful result to the ensemble but that's precisely the point. The point is that fair Dorothy can and does. That piquant photogenic pulchritude of hers is more than a match for any hat, nor do we mean maybe. . . . All that we know is that Mayor Lee can give any hat odds, long odds, and beat it to the punch with that calm yet provocative face of hers, that serene regality. She can, we say, and she does."[12]

The end result of all this foolishness was the initiation of a recall effort that began in September 1949. It failed for lack of enough signatures but it was indicative of the temper of the times. It was also indicative of the kind of indiscriminate behavior that has plagued democratic government throughout history. The bogus attempt to recall Mayor Lee was inaugurated simultaneously with a justified and successful effort to recall Multnomah County Sheriff Mike Elliott who had been fraudulently elected in November 1948. Two more different people could not have entered office in Portland on January 1, 1949, than Dorothy McCullough Lee and Marion Leroy (Mike) Elliott.

Elliott had been a deputy sheriff for two years when he challenged the 16 year incumbent Martin T. Pratt, one of the few officials who was to receive high praise for his rescue efforts during the Vanport flood. He put on a well financed campaign calling for a reduced budget, smaller county automobiles, a five day work week and no discrimination. He billed himself as a college graduate who had spent six meritorious years in the U. S. Marine Corps before and during World War II.

Odd as it may seem, no one bothered to check Elliott's record before the election. It was not until after he had fired some key administrators and turned the sheriff's office into a circus that the truth was revealed. Not only had he not attended the University of Michigan and played varsity football, but he had never gone beyond the tenth grade where he amassed a record of C's, D's and E's. He did enter the marine corps in 1939 but received a bad conduct discharge before the war ever began on grounds of excess absence and drunkenness. During the war he had apparently worked at Swan Island as a guard and then received an appointment in 1946 as a county jailer.

Elliott was an appealing demogogue — a 200 pound extrovert. He became the favorite of the Democratic Central Committee that was eagerly searching for a charismatic figure who could defeat veteran Republican Martin Pratt. It was later revealed that much of Elliott's financial support came from the slot machine interests which rightly feared that Dorothy Lee would force them out of the city and into the county. Under the circumstances, it was imperative that the sheriff be a friend. Although Pratt was not known as a strict law enforcer, the gamblers and their Chicago bosses could ill afford to take any risks. Elliott became their man and for eight months in office a very good friend.

The results of the recall election in October 1949 were not as conclusive as one might have expected given the appalling revelations of Elliott's true past. He was expelled from office by a plurality of only 14,000 votes out of a total of nearly 104,000 cast. The county commissioners then appointed Portland Fire Department Captain Terry D. Schrunk to fill Elliott's vacancy. Schrunk was thereby launched on his exceptional political career that would see him elected sheriff in 1952 and mayor in 1956. But that is a story in itself which awaits future telling.

Downtown Portland in 1950

The Year 1950

Portland was in the doldrums during 1950. It was a period in the city's history that was marked by political and cultural dullness, by municipal insolvency and by social discrimination. Politically, Mayor Lee was having a difficult time even though she had successfully survived a minor recall effort. Although not a colorful person, Mrs. Lee was probably more qualified by experience and training to serve her office than anyone in Portland's previous history. But she lacked the degree of enlightened support from the leadership ranks of either business or the general community that could have provided her administration with a vital forward thrust. Political idealism and enthusiasm gained small favor from a population that was both apathetic and cynical.

The business leadership, as represented by the Portland Chamber of Commerce, was tired, well beyond middle age in vigor and outlook. The city's leading business executives and bankers tended to float with the prevailing current, excluding E. B. MacNaughton who charted his own independent course that rarely involved anything directly political. The typical Portland business executive of 1950 was a practical man who had the unfortunate habit of repeating the mistakes of his predecessors. He tended to be so practical that he generally ignored the basic economic, social and political forces that surrounded him. Low taxes were still considered the prime requisite of a healthy society. Naturally, Earl Riley had been popular because he had opposed increasing municipal revenues through higher taxes. Instead, he simply depleted the city's reserve funds derived from delinquent tax property sales. When Dorothy Lee took office, she found the city broke. Within nine months, the city went $1.3 million into the red and was forced to borrow operating funds from the U. S. National Bank.[13]

As for the realtors like Chester A. Moores and David B. Simpson, an explosive increase in Portland's population was still being predicted.[14] Portland business executives continued to measure society's progress solely in terms of growth — primarily economic growth as reflected in the bottom line profits. Throughout the period covered by this book, few major business leaders besides John C. Ainsworth, Ben Selling and E. B. MacNaughton ever showed any real concern for society's broader social problems.

Fundamental Convictions Threatened by Change

Like its counterparts in other major American cities during the first half of the 20th century, Portland's business-political establishment possessed certain deeply rooted personal convictions and perceptions that shaped its general behavioral pattern. As might be expected, the same fundamental beliefs were held by the population at large:

> Portlanders considered the rights of private property to be sacred.
>
> Portlanders were rurally oriented.
>
> Portlanders had a deep-seated Anglo-Saxon bias.
>
> Portlanders viewed their city as a center of problems: Crime, rising taxes, minorities and welfare recipients.
>
> Portlanders wanted above all else to keep their neighborhoods familiar and unchanging.
>
> Portlanders wanted to improve their lives by moving on.

The desire for the familiar, mixed with the preference for smaller places, lower densities and richer environmental amenities made Americans the most mobile people in the world by 1950, and Portlanders were no exception. The trend which started early in the century, aided and abetted by the automobile and rising family income levels, has continued to the point that nearly 50 percent of metropolitan Portlanders moved their residences during the five year period from 1965-1970. This factor helps to explain what Brian Berry has called "the emergence of a new urban form, of which commuting shifts are dramatic indicators."[15] During the five year period from 1972-1977, Portland suffered a net loss to the suburbs of families with children approximating seven percent.[16]

Henry Ford, the man who helped to launch the exodus to the suburbs with his invention and mass production of the Model T, predicted the trend in 1924 when he said:

> "The modern city has done its work and a change is coming. The city has taught us much, but the overhead expense of living in such places is becoming unbearable. The cost of maintaining interest on debts, of keeping up water supply, sewage and sanitary problems, the cost of traffic control and of policing great masses of the city. Industry of the future will be organized on a big scale, but competition will force it to parts of the country where labor is steady and overhead costs are low. Instead of making the man come to the city, we will take the work to him in the country."[17]

Add Alexander Graham Bell's telephone to Henry Ford's Model T and the suburb became a reality.

The Impact of Technology

As the history of the period from 1915 to 1950 has revealed, the automotive revolution caught Portland and most American cities unaware. Portland was platted and developed as a small town. It matured under the economy of the nineteenth century. By 1950, the city had become wholly unsuited to the efficient use of the motor car and truck. As a consequence, Portland began to experience distress, losing population and suffering a decrease in property values within the older districts. Concurrent with this development was the gradual decline of one of the nation's most complete mass transit systems to the point that by 1950, the last electric streetcar faded into history.

Few of Portland's leaders could foresee the effect on mass transit of the five day work week. That change alone accounted for a one-sixth decline in revenue riders. The automobile captured not only the working commuter but the weekend and holiday traveller. The growth of the federal highway system merely hastened the process. Another factor furthered the demise of mass transit: The unwillingness of the taxpayer and his political leaders to acknowledge that mass transit was a needed public service incapable of profitable, let alone self-supporting, operation. Such perceptions were grounded in the same deeply held convictions that shaped land use decisions: The sacredness of private enterprise and its twin brother, private property.

Technology in company with the acquisitive drive of the real estate trade promoted the decentralization of metropolitan Portland. Suburban towns became self-sustaining cities, offering full commercial and professional services. The accompanying chart (opposite) well illustrates the trend that moved with increasing rapidity from 1940 to 1950.

In 1915, Portland's urban area (see map opposite) was only four percent larger in population than its central city. By 1950, the urban area was nearly 200 percent larger than Portland. During this 35 year period of growth, most of the

Trends of Growth of Selected Economic Functions in the Outlying Districts and the Downtown* Core Area of Portland

Economic Function	1940 No.	1940 %	1950 No.	1950 %	1955 No.	1955 %	Increase 1940 to 1955 Per Cent
Attorneys							
Downtown	659	96.9	789	96.1	849	89.3	+ 28.8
Outside	21	3.1	32	3.9	102	10.7	+ 385.7
Total	680		821		951		+ 39.9
Accountants							
Downtown	74	87.1	194	73.8	210	65.0	+ 183.8
Outside	11	12.9	69	26.2	113	35.0	+ 927.3
Total	85		263		323		+ 280.0
Architects							
Downtown	44	84.6	59	66.3	65	49.6	+ 47.7
Outside	8	15.4	30	33.7	66	50.4	+ 725.0
Total	52		89		131		+ 151.9
Dentists							
Downtown	282	70.5	286	61.0	243	49.4	− 13.8
Outside	118	29.5	183	39.0	249	50.6	+ 111.0
Total	400		469		492		+ 23.0
Physicians							
Downtown	412	81.3	474	64.5	380	48.3	− 7.8
Outside	95	18.7	261	35.5	406	51.7	+ 327.4
Total	507		735		786		+ 55.0
Insurance							
Downtown	207	92.8	261	91.3	246	89.1	+ 18.8
Outside	16	7.2	25	8.7	30	10.9	+ 87.5
Total	223		286		276		+ 23.8
Lumber							
Downtown	15	55.6	44	54.3	36	44.4	+ 140.0
Outside	12	44.4	37	45.7	45	55.6	+ 275.0
Total	27		81		81		+ 200.0
Mfg. agents							
Downtown	31	68.9	49	45.8	29	25.2	− 6.5
Outside	14	31.1	58	54.2	86	74.8	+ 514.3
Total	45		107		115		+ 155.6
Variety stores							
Downtown	3	42.9	3	4.8	3	4.3	----
Outside	4	57.1	60	95.2	67	95.7	+1,575.0
Total	7		63		70		+ 900.0

Source: Telephone directories; data on insurance companies from city directories.
All telephone numbers were counted, even though there may be some duplication.
* Downtown core area, the region bounded by Burnside and Jefferson, Front and Fourteenth.

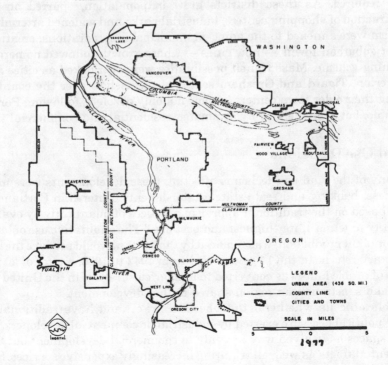

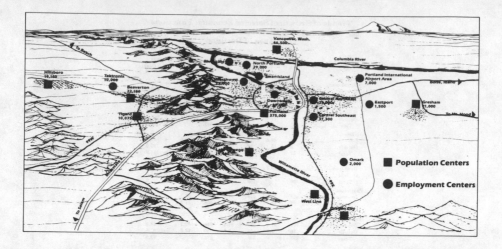

Population Centers
Employment Centers

suburban expansion occurred outside of the incorporated suburban towns, and for one particular reason. Following World War I, the state legislature enacted a series of laws that permitted the establishment of special rural service districts: Drainage (1915), water (1917) and fire (1929).

These units of government, with their own taxing powers, either created their own services or contracted with nearby incorporations for those services that were required. As these districts grew in population, spurred on by the construction of shopping centers, industrial parks and widened arterials, some of them were annexed to the adjacent municipal incorporations, creating ever larger suburban towns — now cities — whose growth followed no perceptible planning scheme. Mass transit possibilities were overlooked as cities such as Beaverton, Tigard and Gresham scattered themselves over the countryside, letting their older town centers become not only obsolete, following Portland's example, but overwhelmed by commuter, residential and commercial traffic.

Land Use Decisions

Many of the land use decisions affecting these developments were made by business, banking and real estate establishments centered in Portland. They were based on the traditional appraisal practices of quantitatively evaluating property in terms of its "highest and best use." The qualitative use of land, i.e., food or plant production, was replaced by the use that would produce the highest monetary return. In the 14 year period from 1942 to 1956, a total of 20 million acres of arable land was converted to nonagricultural use in the United States. Portland's metropolitan region shared in that development.

Public officials, whether in the suburbs or in Portland, have traditionally bent to the political pressure exerted by industrial or commercial developers. Urban open spaces have given way not only to commercial development but to large residential tracts as well, all requiring increasingly expensive services. Several years ago, eastern developer James W. Rouse criticized the large unplanned tracts that were replacing urban farm land and other types of open spaces:

> "At first one point and then another, zoning crumbles under pressure, and each break in the zoning wall leads to further breaks. Commercial uses bite at the edges of highways and waterways and spread their ugly unplanned clutter."[18]

The process is still going on in Portland's three metropolitan counties as the local authorities struggle to develop a comprehensive land use plan that will set future urban boundaries. The Rose City Park neighborhoods defeated NABIS-CO's efforts to despoil their environmental balance but this type of victory was rare in Portland's history until recently. In the suburbs and surrounding unincorporated areas, where neighborhood strength is weak or nonexistent, narrowly selfish private interests, many of them funded by Portland financial institutions, continue to determine the formulation of public land use policies.

One of the themes that appears to have run throughout Portland's business-political history — and that of most other cities — is that an owner should be permitted to do what he wishes with his property no matter how it was acquired, provided of course that he can establish a vested interest. If the property is later sold, especially to a public body, the owner is justified in reaping a maximum windfall profit, regardless of whether the value increase is due to a public decision favorably affecting the property's future use.

Needed: A Vision and a Commitment

During the 35 year period covered by this book, few members of the Portland business-political establishment entertained any public vision about the metropolitan region's future development. Few held any notion of a public interest that was greater than a combination of immediate private interests. Few questioned the traditional view that private development was synonymous with human progress and welfare. Few were either able or willing to deal with questions of basic economic or social policy which could serve to give fundamental direction to changing economic and social forces.

What was lacking in 1950, and may still be lacking in 1979, was a basic commitment to quality — politically, culturally and socially. Quality requires financial support; it also requires personal sacrifice and dedication. Traditionally in Portland's history, many projects were conceived and even started but few were completed. Portland investors preferred their private lives to the public experience; they preferred to clip their coupons or cash in their profits and put them in the bank.

Without some conceptual framework of human values to guide them, one that transcended traditional perceptions, Portland's leaders were doomed to making self-defeating decisions with dire consequences. No better example is offered than the city's historic treatment of its minority population. In 1950, over half of

Portland's 9500 Negroes were housed in census tracts #22 and #23 in the Williams Avenue-Albina district.[19] The Eliot and Boise elementary schools became predominantly black. Thirty years later, Portland is being forced by federal judicial mandate to desegregate its schools and the consequences have proved unsettling to the white community — to say the least! Threatened with a black boycott, the Portland establishment finds itself caught in a desperate quandary. The consequences of post-World War II decisions made by Portland's business-political leadership are proving increasingly costly in 1979.

The noted developer of Columbia, Maryland, and Boston's Quincy Market, James W. Rouse — in 1957 a governor of the Mortgage Bankers Association — singled out the crucial issue that American cities faced 22 years ago and still face today. He declared:

> "We will never make our cities what they ought to be simply by clearing slums and eliminating blight. There is a lot more wrong with our cities than the physical condition of the buildings, the streets and the alleys. A gigantic and fully effective physical cleanup program would simply restore the physical condition of our cities to the beginning point of the deterioration pipeline, but it would have little effect upon the forces for deterioration which dragged them down in the first place.
>
> It is not merely the physical condition of our cities which is out of kilter. Even the well-maintained, unblighted areas of most of our cities fall far short of the hopes and aspirations of our families and far short, too, of our knowledge of and technical capacity for better living.
>
> The fact is that the city is out of scale with the human being. It is beyond his scope and capacity. It is unmanageable. It is only in an abstract way that the human individual can feel a part of his city.
>
> We must make the city consist of communities which are in human scale — communities of which the individual can feel a part and for the life of which he can feel a sense of participation and responsibility."[20]

Apart from population growth, the major force that has diminished the human scale of our cities — and of American life generally — has been the unrelenting expansion of American corporate and financial enterprises. The merger movement that began at the turn of the century has continued unabated and metropolitan Portland has suffered its share of the consequences. Highly centralized economic interests, many of which are headquartered outside of Oregon — and increasingly, outside of the United States — exert a dominant influence over local business, financial and political decisions. Examples are numerous, particularly in matters related to the use of landed property. Although political and economic conditions have changed radically over the past 70 years, the basic issue is still the one that Theodore Roosevelt addressed at Osawatomie, Kansas, in August 1910. In advocating the primacy of human welfare over property rights, Roosevelt declared that "Every man [and he included banks and corporations in this category] holds his property subject to the general right of the community to regulate its use to whatever degree the public welfare may require it."[21]

Statue of Theodore Roosevelt in the S. W. Park Blocks, one of four similar gifts in the early 1920s by Portland benefactor Dr. Henry Waldo Coe, a prominent physician and personal friend of T. R.'s. The First Congregational Church Tower is in the background.

Acknowledgments

I. Published and Manuscript Materials

The author wishes to acknowledge permission to publish materials from the Manuscript Collections of the Oregon Historical Society, the Oregon Jewish Oral History and Archives Project, and Reed College, and from the Special Collections Library of the University of Oregon, the Archives of the Port of Portland, and the Files of the Portland City Club and Portland Bureau of Planning. He also acknowledges permission to publish excerpts from letters contained in these and other collections as granted by the heirs of the writers. Finally he acknowledges permission to reprint from the following published works:

The Crisis of the Old Order, by Arthur M. Schlesinger, Jr., © 1957 by Arthur M. Schlesinger, Jr. Used with permission of Houghton Mifflin.

The Coming of the New Deal, by Arthur M. Schlesinger, Jr., © 1959 by Arthur M. Schlesinger, Jr. Used with permission of Houghton Mifflin.

Autobiography of Will Rogers, by Will Rogers, © 1949 by Houghton Mifflin.

Romantic Revolutionary: A Biography of John Reed, by Robert A. Rosenstone, © 1975 by Alfred A. Knopf.

The Search for a Usable Past, by Henry Steele Commager, © 1967 by Henry Steele Commager. Used with permission of Alfred A. Knopf.

The Harding Era, by Robert K. Murray, © 1969 by the University of Minnesota Press.

The City in History, by Lewis Mumford, © 1961 by Lewis Mumford and Harcourt, Brace & World.

Top Management Handbook, ed. by H. B. Maynard, © 1960 by McGraw-Hill. Used with permission of McGraw-Hill Book Company.

Wye Island, by Boyd Gibbons, © 1977 by Resources For the Future. Used with permission of The Johns Hopkins University Press.

American Diplomacy, by George F. Kennan, © 1951 by the University of Chicago Press.

Crisis on the Columbia, by Oral Bullard, © 1968 by Oral Bullard. Used with permission of The Touchstone Press.

The Conscience of a City, by Ellis Lucia, © 1966 by The City Club of Portland.

The Urban West at the End of the Frontier, by Lawrence H. Larsen, © 1978 by The Regents Press of Kansas.

Frederick Law Olmsted and the American Environmental Tradition, by Albert Fein, © Albert Fein. Used with permission of George Braziller.

663

The Constitution and What It Means Today, by Edward S. Corwin, © 1954 by the Princeton University Press.

The Grand Era of Cast-Iron Architecture in Portland, by William John Hawkins III, © 1976 by Binford & Mort.

An Oregon Crusader, by George S. Turnbull, © 1955 by George S. Turnbull. Used with permission of Binford & Mort, Publishers.

Making the Day Begin, by Robert C. Notson, © 1976 by Robert C. Notson and Oregonian Publishing Company.

The Portland Longshoremen, A Dispersed Urban Community, by William W. Pilcher, © 1972 by Holt, Rinehart and Winston.

Edwin Vincent O'Hara, American Prelate, by J. G. Shaw, © 1957 by Farrar, Straus & Giroux.

Democrats of Oregon: A Pattern of Minority Politics, by Robert Earl Burton, © 1970 by the University of Oregon.

The Ties Between, by Julius J. Nodel, © 1959 by Rabbi Julius J. Nodel. Used with permission of Temple Beth Israel, Portland.

Brandeis, A Free Man's Life, by Alpheus Thomas Mason, © 1946 by Alpheus Thomas Mason. Used with permission of The Viking Press.

Bridges, The Spans of North America, by David Plowden, © 1974 by David Plowden. Used with permission of The Viking Press.

Inside U. S. A., by John Gunther, © 1947 by John Gunther and the Curtis Publishing Company. Used with permission of Harper & Row.

Damned Old Crank, A Self-Portrait of E. W. Scripps, ed. by Charles R. McCabe, © 1951 by Harper & Brothers. Used with permission of Harper & Row.

Only Yesterday, by Frederick Lewis Allen, © 1931 by Frederick Lewis Allen. Used with permission of Harper & Row.

The Big Change, by Frederick Lewis Allen, © 1952 by Frederick Lewis Allen. Used with permission of Harper & Row.

The Changing Shape of Metropolitan America, by Brian J. L. Berry and Quentin Gillard, © 1977 by Ballinger Books.

"The Politics of Reform in Municipal Government in the Progressive Era," by Samuel P. Hayes, *Pacific Northwest Quarterly* 55 (October 1964) 157-169, © 1964 by the *Pacific Northwest Quarterly*.

"A Conscientious Objector: Oregon 1918," by Annette M. Bartholomae, *Oregon Historical Quarterly* 71 (September 1970) 213-239, © 1970 by the Oregon Historical Society.

"A. R. Wetjen: British Seaman in the Western Sunrise," by Howard McKinley Corning, *Oregon Historical Quarterly* 74 (June 1973), © 1973 by the Oregon Historical Society.

II. Reproductions (cited by page number)

Photographs

Oregon Historical Society Photographic Library: xiv, 2, 9, 13, 16, 23, 25, 33, 36, 40, 43, 44, 48, 49, 51, 53, 56, 57, 58, 59, 63, 67, 71, 72, 75, 86, 88, 101, 108, 113, 114, 115, 117, 139, 141, 146, 148, 150, 164, 166, 169, 171, 181, 186, 188, 203, 204, 231, 233, 236, 242, 248, 253, 262, 270, 272, 275, 278, 282, 285, 287, 308, 311, 314, 318, 319, 320, 323, 324, 329, 330, 331, 336, 342, 346, 348, 349, 351, 369, 370, 373, 376, 383, 391, 396, 400, 403, 424, 433, 445, 446, 451, 457, 459, 460, 463, 485, 495, 498, 502, 503, 509, 511, 512, 516, 517, 526, 531, 533, 535, 539, 545, 552, 566, 568, 574, 576, 577, 580, 585, 593, 594, 597, 601, 611, 612, 616, 628, 637, 650, 651, 661

Randy Wood: Back cover

Barbara Gundel, *Willamette Week*: 629

Photo Art Studios: 4, 27, 37, 61, 72, 75 (left), 82, 91, 185, 193, 200, 246, 250, 345, 352, 359, 396, 506, 518, 528, 542, 583, 590, 599, 600, 604, 624, 625, 632, 637, 646, 654

Oregon Voter: 156

Portland Chamber of Commerce: 192, 619

University of Oregon Library, Special Collections (General File): 2, 18, 19, 78, 79, 148, 191, 267, 280, 311; (Angellus Collection): 9, 217, 529, 620; (Ellis Lawrence Papers): 63, 71, 85, 86, 175, 299, 359, 497; (Olaf Laurgaard Papers): 90, 93, 107, 317, 318

Portland Development Commission: 317

Author's Collection: 13, 68, 75, 93, 311, 349, 429, 509, 632, 644, 645

Gerry Frank: 585

Portland City Planning Commission: 306, 306

Fred DeWolf: 550

Eileen Tong: 351

W. W. Pilcher: 471

B. A. Green Family: 470

Maps

Laurgaard Collection: 318

Fortune Magazine: 441

Portland City Planning Commission (Bureau of Planning): 64, 89, 96, 104, 111, 300, 306, 327, 354, 388, 427, 508, 523, 525, 527, 532, 538, 543

Kaiser Corporation: 576

Housing Authority of Portland: 579, 581

Portland City Club Bulletin: 239, 258, 294, 295, 547, 597

Elizabeth Rocchia renditions: 45, 55, 81, 131

Portland Commission of Public Docks: 216, 245, 541

Portland Chamber of Commerce: 212, 214, 220, 261, 500, 592, 635, 657

Portland Development Commission: 121

Mayor's Message and Annual Report (1921): 243

Charts

Ads, Cartoons, Sketches

Comments on Sources Used

I have not included a separate bibliography as I did with *The Shaping of a City*. The sources used are included in the Notes. Published materials from which I have quoted are cited under Acknowledgements. I have also omitted a lengthy historiographical commentary for the reason primarily that there are few works in print covering the specific subjects of this book. The author is fully aware of, and has read most of, the major works by urban historians and geographers which deal with the broader aspects of urban history. Such have not been cited except where they make a direct contribution to this study. For students new to the subject, I recommend consulting the five volumes (to date) of the *Journal of Urban History*, published by Sage Publications.

Two works of general value which have long been recognized for their worth are: *Empire of the Columbia: A History of the Pacific Northwest* by Dorothy O. Johansen and Charles Gates; *The Pacific Slope: A History of California, Oregon, Washington, Idaho, Utah and Nevada* by Earl S. Pomeroy. More recent works of some value to this study are: *Space, Style and Structure: Building in Northwest America* by Thomas Vaughan and Virginia Guest Ferriday (Portland: Oregon Historical Society, 1974); *The Western Shore: Oregon Country Essays Honoring the American Revolution* edited by Thomas Vaughan (Portland: Oregon Historical Society, 1975); and *Oregon, A History* by Gordon B. Dodds (New York: W. W. Norton, 1977).

Of the most useful sources consulted, I cite the following collections from the University of Oregon, Special Collections Library: The Portland Chamber of Commerce Papers, John C. Ainsworth Papers, Burl A. Green Papers, Ellis Lawrence Papers, Olaf Laurgaard Papers and the Portland General Electric Records. From the Oregon Historical Society Manuscript Collection, I have found of particular value: The Housing Authority of Portland Files, Franklin T. Griffith Scrapbooks, Ormond R. Bean Papers, Earl Riley Papers, Ladd & Tilton Corporate Papers and the William A. Bowes Papers. From the Reed College archives, the E. B. MacNaughton Tapes proved to be highly significant. And from the possession of Mrs. Wayne Rogers, the Chester A. Moores Papers provided extensive data.

Anyone working in this field must, of course, consult the official records of such public bodies as the Portland City Council, Portland Bureau of Planning (Portland City Planning Commission), the Port of Portland (including the former Portland Commission of Public Docks), Multnomah County Assessor and Probate Offices; also the official publications of the various departments of city government. The *Oregon Voter* and the Portland daily press (*The*

Oregonian, The Oregon Journal, News and *Telegram*) are uneven but important sources. For city and state government topics, the files, reports and bulletins of the City Club of Portland are absolutely essential.

For ethnic history, three recent brief works are exceptional: *Portland's Chinatown: The History of an Urban Ethnic District* by Nelson Chia-Chi Ho (Portland: Bureau of Planning, 1978); *Burnside: A Community* by Kathleen Ryan (Portland: Coast to Coast Books, 1979); and *Blacks in Oregon, A Statistical and Historical Report* edited by W. A. Little and J. E. Weiss (Portland: Portland State University Black Studies Center and the Center for Population Research, 1978). For Jewish history, the Oregon Jewish Oral History and Archives Project at the Mittleman Jewish Community Center contains a wealth of material.

Notes

Introduction

1. As quoted in *Oregon Apartments*, 2 (April 1932) 1.
2. Charles H. Chapman, "Oregon: A Slighted Beauty," *The Nation*, 116 (February 7, 1923) 142.
3. Lewis Mumford, *The City in History* (New York: Harcourt Brace Jovanovich, 1961) 426.
4. E. B. MacNaughton, Tapes (Portland: Reed College Library Archives) Reel 1, June 1960.
5. *Arlington Club and The Men Who Built It* (Portland: Arlington Club, 1967) 1.
6. Transcribed interview with Gus Solomon, February 14, 1976, (Portland: The Oregon Jewish Oral History and Archives Project.
7. Interview with Edwin C. (Bill) Berry, *The Oregonian*, January 1, 1956. Berry later became director of the Chicago Urban League.
8. Chapman, *op. cit.*, 142.
9. Lawrence H. Larsen, *The Urban West At The End Of The Frontier* (Lawrence: Regents Press of Kansas, 1978) 19.
10. *New York Times*, January 6, 1937.
11. *Oregon Voter*, July 12, 1919.
12. John Leader, *Oregon Through Alien Eyes* (Portland: publisher unknown, 1922) 85.
13. John Gunther, *Inside U.S.A.* (New York: Harper and Row, 1947) 88.
14. As quoted in Alpheus T. Mason, *Brandeis: A Free Man's Life* (New York: Viking, 1946) 252. Between the time of his argument and the court's decision, Brandeis was appointed to the supreme bench and had to disqualify himself from voting.
15. J. G. Shaw, *Edwin Vincent O'Hara, American Prelate* (New York: Farrar, Straus & Giroux, 1957) 47.
16. Leader, *op. cit.*, 100.
17. *Oregon Voter*, July 12, 1919.
18. Leader, *op. cit.*, 97.
19. C. E. S. Wood to Harry Lane, letter of July 23, 1913, Richard L. Neuberger Papers "Lane File" (Eugene: University of Oregon, Special Collections Library).
20. Wood to Lane, *op. cit.*, March 31, 1914.
21. According to attorney Joseph N. Teal who gave $100 along with banker Emery Olmstead, Joseph N. Teal Papers (Portland: Oregon Historical Society).
22. Wood to Lane, *op. cit.*, June 1, 1914.
23. *Ibid.*, June 1, 1914.
24. *The Oregonian*, July 3, 1914.
25. Wood to Lane, *op. cit.*, June 1, 1914.
26. *Ibid.*
27. Samuel P. Hayes, "The Politics of Reform in Municipal Government in the Progressive Era," *Pacific Northwest Quarterly*, 55 (October 1964) 167. See also, Bradley R. Rice, *Progressive Cities, The Commission Government Movement in America, 1901-1920* (Austin: University of Texas Press, 1977).

Chapter 1

1. Wilbur Hall, "Portland the Spinster," *Collier's Weekly,* 58 (May 19, 1917) 30.
2. Article by Charles Olaf Olsen, *The Oregonian,* July 23, 1925.
3. "Autobiographical Notes of Lee V. Jenkins," Portland Chamber of Commerce Papers, Box 36 (Eugene: University of Oregon, Special Collections Library).
4. Doug Baker, "The Way Portland Was," *The Oregon Journal,* May 9, 1975.
5. Hall, *op. cit.,* 30.
6. *Ibid.,* 31.
7. Robert A. Rosenstone, *The Romantic Revolutionary, A Biography of John Reed* (New York: Alfred A. Knopf, 1975) 182.
8. Roderick Macleay Scrapbook, in the possession of his daughter, Mrs. Richard Phillippi. Macleay was vice president of the Arlington Club in 1915.
9. Rosenstone, *op. cit.,* 242.
10. Letter of July 11, 1916, box labelled "Morality" (Portland: City Archives).
11. *The Oregon Journal,* June 30, July 1, 1916.
12. *Ibid.,* July 7, 1916.
13. William F. Ogburn, "The 1914 Elections in Oregon," *Political Science Quarterly,* 34 (Spring 1919) 413-433.
14. Hall, *op. cit.,* 36.
15. City arrests were reduced 40 percent in 1916; charges of drunkenness declined by 65 percent, from 6600 to 2300. In 1917, the arrest record dropped another 20 percent and drunkenness another 50 percent. See *Mayor's Message and Annual Report,* 1915, 1916, 1917 (Portland: Oregon Historical Society).
16. As quoted by Helen Barney, "Sporting Women," *Metropolis,* March 1973.
17. "Autobiography of Joseph N. Teal," 61, Joseph N. Teal Papers, (Portland: Oregon Historical Society).
18. Member of the law firm of Teal, Minor and Winfree, predecessor of the present day firm of Rankin, McMurry, Osburn, Gallagher and VavRosky.
19. "Autobiography of Joseph N. Teal," *op. cit.*
20. Joseph N. Teal Papers, Box 3, Folder 6, *op. cit.*
21. See Fred Lockley, *The Oregon Journal,* December 3, 4, 1919; also Stewart Holbrook, "Simon Benson, the All-Steam Bunyan," *The Oregonian,* May 12, 1935; also the Simon Benson vertical file (Portland: Oregon Historical Society).
22. Lockley, *op. cit.,* December 3, 1919.
23. The State Highway Commission was first established in 1913 with the three state officers as members and with the governor as chairman, similar in structure to the State Land Board. In 1918, Benson appointed his friend, ex-Governor Jay Bowerman, as the State "Right-of-Way" Agent.
24. See C. Lester Horn, "Oregon's Columbia River Highway," *Oregon Historical Quarterly* 66 (September 1965) 249-271; Ronald J. Fahl, "S. C. Lancaster and the Columbia River Highway: Engineer as Conservationist," *Oregon Historical Quarterly,* 74 (June 1973) 101-144.
25. *The Oregon Journal,* November 21, 1920.
26. Hall, *op. cit.,* 36.
27. See *Oregon Voter,* November 27, 1920. Yeon died in 1928 at age 63.
28. See Percy Maddux, *City on the Willamette* (Portland: Binford & Mort, 1952) 156.
29. The Galveston Plan called for the replacement of part time councilmen with four full time commissioners, each assigned a major department of city government by the full time mayor who also administered at least one department, usually the police. The commissioners and the mayor held equal votes in legislative matters; the veto was abolished. District or ward representation was also abolished, with each commissioner

elected city wide by following a system of preferential voting. City elections were no longer conducted on a partisan basis. With the Galveston Plan, the mayor and the commissioners assumed both legislative and administrative responsibilities. All citizen boards were abolished except for civil service.

30. *Portland City Club Bulletin*, October 13, 1933.

31. Ellis Lucia, "Portland's Modern Vigilantes," *The Oregoni*

32. The club's 50th Anniversary history, written by Ellis Lucia was entitled *The Conscience of a City* (Portland: The City Club of Portland, 1966).

33. See E. Kimbark MacColl, *The Shaping of a City, Business and Politics in Portland, Oregon 1885-1915* (Portland: The Georgian Press, 1976) ch. 13.

34. Lucia, "Vigilantes," *op. cit.*

35. *The Oregonian*, April 22, May 4, 1920. The U.S. Attorney General buried the indictment.

36. Interview with E. C. Sammons, April 3, 1975.

37. *Commission of Public Docks — Second Annual Report* (Portland, 1912) 5.

38. Interview with C. P. Keyser, *Metropolis*, January 1972.

39. *Mayor's Message and Annual Report, op. cit.*, 1915, 1917.

40. *The Oregon Journal*, April 18, 1917.

41. Hayes, *op. cit.*, 168.

42. *The Oregonian*, December 15, 1916.

43. *Ibid.*

44. *Ibid.*

45. Henry E. Reed Papers, folder marked "Notes on the 1913 Campaign," (Portland: Oregon Historical Society).

Chapter 2

1. James G. Woodworth to John C. Ainsworth, letter of November 4, 1913, J. C. Ainsworth Papers, "Woodworth File," (Eugene: University of Oregon, Special Collections Library).

2. *Ibid.*

3. E. B. MacNaughton, "Tapes" (Portland: Reed College Library Archives), Reels 1 and 2.

4. Wilbur Hall, "Portland the Spinster," *Collier's Weekly*, 58 (May 19, 1917) 31.

5. *Ibid.*, 36.

6. E. Kimbark MacColl, *The Shaping of a City, Business and Politics in Portland, Oregon 1885-1915* (Portland: The Georgian Press, 1976) ch. 14.

7. Funds were provided from the following sources: City, $57,441; state, $62,254; county, $186,536; *The Oregon Journal*, November 24, 1916.

8. Data contained in the *Oregon Voter*, July 12, 1919; later annual economic reviews in the *Voter* up to 1930; also, "Pacific Telephone and Telegraph Survey of 1916," *The Oregonian*, April 20, 1917.

9. *The Oregonian*, April 20, 1917, "Pacific Telephone and Telegraph Survey," *op. cit.*

10. "Zoning and City Planning," Report of the Portland City Planning Commission, Bulletin #1, June 1919, Portland Bureau of Planning Library.

11. *Oregon Voter*, July 12, 1919.

12. James J. Sawyer, "Portland's Reasons for Adopting a City Zoning Plan," *The Architect and Engineer* (March 1919) 85.

13. "Pacific Telephone and Telegraph Survey," *op. cit.*

14. Hall, *op. cit.*, 36.

15. *The Oregon Journal*, May 19, 1917.

16. *The Oregonian*, July 5, 1918.
17. Bess C. Owen, "Fighting Unemployment and Destitution in Portland," *The Survey*, (April 10, 1915) 52.
18. "Portland Housing Authority Papers, 1918-1940," Jesse Short File, Box 2 (Portland: Oregon Historical Society).
19. *Oregon Voter*, March 23, 1918.
20. *The Oregonian*, July 5, 1918.
21. For a discussion of this problem, see George M. Smerk, "The Streetcar: Shaper of American Cities," *Traffic Quarterly*, 21 (October 1967) 574-577.
22. See MacColl, *op. cit.*, 126-137.
23. *Neighborhood Profiles of the City of Portland 1960-1970* (Portland: Office of Planning and Development, July 1978).
24. J. G. Shaw, *Edwin Vincent O'Hara, American Prelate* (New York: Farrar, Strauss & Giroux, 1957) 35.
25. See Charles S. Rosenbloom, "Housing and Housing Reform in Portland, 1900-1934," (undergraduate thesis, Reed College, Portland, 1972), Oregon Historical Society. This is an excellent treatment within a solid conceptual framework.

Chapter 3

1. Julius J. Nodel, *The Ties Between* (Portland: Congregation Beth Israel, 1959) 71.
2. E. Kimbark MacColl, *The Shaping of a City, Business and Politics in Portland, Oregon 1885-1915* (Portland: The Georgian Press, 1976) ch. 4, 8, 9.
3. Nodel, *op. cit.*, 48.
4. *Ibid.*, 49.
5. *The Oregonian*, January 13, 1931.
6. Nodel, *op. cit.*, 49.
7. Transcript of an interview with Mrs. Laurence Selling, The Oregon Jewish Oral History and Archives Project.
8. *Rahles v. Selling*, before the Supreme Court of Oregon, 1932. Nelson's lower court argument is presumed similar to his brief filed with the supreme court. A copy was made available to the author by his son, Roscoe C. Nelson, Jr.
9. Information derived from several interviews with Isaac's son, Harry Gevurtz, during 1977-1978.
10. Nodel, *op. cit.*, 69.
11. *Ibid.*, 51.
12. Much of the material for this section has been excerpted from E. Kimbark MacColl, Jr., "The Growth of Citizen Involvement in Urban Renewal: A Selective Case Study of Portland, Oregon, 1945-72," (unpublished senior thesis in history, Princeton University, 1972) 108-116.
13. *The Oregon Journal*, January 17, 1935.
14. *Neighborhood Profiles of the City of Portland 1960-1970* (Portland: Office of Planning and Development, July 1978).

Chapter 4

1. *The Oregon Journal*, February 4, 1917.
2. *Ibid.*

3. See E. Kimbark MacColl, *The Shaping of a City, Business and Politics in Portland, Oregon 1885-1915* (Portland: The Georgian Press, 1976) ch. 14.

4. *The Oregon Journal*, February 4, 1917.

5. *The Oregonian*, October 3, 1915.

6. Letter of Leo Friede to Joseph N. Teal, November 14, 1918, Joseph N. Teal Papers (Portland: Oregon Historical Society).

7. *Pacific Northwest Real Estate Bulletin*, 4 (August 1926) 2.

8. *The Oregonian Souvenir, 1892.*

9. Alfred Staehli, *Preservation Options For Portland Neighborhoods* (Portland, 1975) 53. See also, *The Oregon Journal*, August 23, 1976.

10. See Staehli, *op. cit.*, 39, 40, for an account of how the Ladds acquired the property.

11. Michael Ryan, "Laurelhurst," (undergraduate report for History 410P, Portland State University, Spring 1978).

12. *The Oregonian*, October 2, 1921; also, *The Oregon Journal*, September 13, 1976.

13. *Neighborhood Profiles of the City of Portland 1960-1970* (Portland: Office of Planning and Development, July 1978).

14. *Ibid.*

15. Ryan, *op. cit.*

16. Dorothy Palmer, "Eastmoreland," (undergraduate report for History 410P, Portland State University, Spring 1978).

17. Ratio of owner occupied to renter occupied homes was 12-1 as opposed to Laurelhurst's 6-1.

18. *The Oregonian*, December 3, 1911.

19. *Ibid.*

20. Minutes of the Proceedings of the City Council, 24:693(Portland: City Archives).

21. *Neighborhood Profiles of the City of Portland 1960-1970, op. cit.* Although the median housing value in 1970 was $38,000, the range of values has been the most extreme one in all of Portland since 1900, from million dollar mansions to $5000 cottages. For a high income area (the 1970 median family income was $20,000) Portland Heights has an unusually low ratio of owner to renter occupied homes, 3.8-1, with practically no Negroes in residence.

22. Ellis Lawrence to H. E. Raymond, December 28, 1914, Ellis Lawrence Papers (Eugene: University of Oregon, Special Collections Library).

23. Several of these homes have recently sold for over $100,000. In the Arlington Heights section to the southwest, the median housing value in 1970 was the same as Portland Heights, $38,000 with a low ratio of owner to renter occupancy of 3-1. See *Neighborhood Profiles of the City of Portland 1960-1970, op. cit.*

24. *Neighborhood Profiles of the City of Portland 1960-1970, op. cit.* 41.

25. Lewis Mumford, "Suburbia: The End of a Dream," *Horizon*, July 1961. See also, *The City in History* (New York: Harcourt Brace Jovanovich, 1961) ch. 16.

26. *Ibid.*

27. *The Oregonian*, April 29, 1917.

28. Letter of Hildegarde Plummer, quoted in Kenneth Hawkins, "Villa Eichenhoff, The Home of Col. Henry Dosch (undergraduate report for History 410P, Portland State University, Spring 1978).

29. For the information on the Wilcox estate, the author is indebted to James Wood, a student in History 410P, Portland State University, Spring 1978.

30. *The Oregonian*, April 22, 1918.

31. For the information on Dunthorpe, the author is indebted to Harold Lee, a student in History 410P, Portland State University, Shring 1978.

32. Letter of John C. Olmsted to Peter Kerr, January 1, 1910, Ellis Lawrence Papers, *op. cit.*

33. Albert Fein, *Frederick Law Olmsted and the American Environmental Tradition* (New York: George Braziller, 1972) 68.

34. Olmsted to Kerr, August 11, 1910, Ellis Lawrence Papers, *op. cit.*
35. *The Oregon Journal*, October 28, 1954.
36. The appellations "African" and "Mongolian" were used extensively in public statements during the 1850s and '60s. One *Oregonian* article on March 3, 1865, declared that "Africans" and "Mongolians" were "not fit to govern."
37. A copy of the deed, in the William M. Ladd file, Ellis Lawrence Papers, *op. cit.*
38. W. F. Burrell, E. L. Thompson and J. L. Hartman, the latter two being prominent private bankers. Wilcox assumed the original mortgage.
39. For a general account of Rose City's history, see *Rose City Park History: 1907-1977* (Portland, 1977); also, article by Rod Paulson, *The Community Press*, July 16, 1975; also, *The Oregon Journal*, November 1, 1976.
40. *The Oregon Journal*, November 1, 1976.
41. Poole & McGonigle and Columbia Steel Casting.
42. "Franchise file, Historical Documents," "OR&N" folder, January 1911 (Portland: City Archives).
43. Olaf Laurgaard, "Grade Crossing Elimination in Portland, Ore.," *The American City* (May 1919) 464-465. Laurgaard was the city engineer in charge of the project.
44. *The Oregon Journal*, November 1, 1976.
45. *Neighborhood Profiles of the City of Portland 1960-1970, op. cit.*
46. James G. Sawyer, "Portland's Reasons for Adopting a City Zoning Plan," *The Architect and Engineer* (March 1919) 85.

Chapter 5

1. E. Kimbark MacColl, *The Shaping of a City, Business and Politics in Portland, Oregon 1885-1915* (Portland: The Georgian Press, 1976) 254-256.
2. James B. Kerr Papers (Portland: Oregon Historical Society).
3. *Ibid.*
4. *Ibid.*
5. Alpheus T. Mason, *Brandeis, A Free Man's Life* (New York: Viking Press, 1964) 531.
6. Kerr, *op. cit.*
7. *The Oregonian*, June 2, 1913.
8. The sales were contested in federal court, July 23, 1909, according to the U. S. Attorney Files, Box 6, Oregon Historical Society.
9. See MacColl, *op. cit.*, ch. 10.
10. 1978 payments to Multnomah County were $940,558; to Washington County, $543,625; to Clackamas County, $4,789,080. The largest payment went to Douglas County in Southern Oregon, $21.615,578.
11. The most comprehensive account of the interurbans is still Harold L. Throckmorton's, "The Interurbans of Portland, Oregon, A Historical Geography" (Master's thesis in geography, University of Oregon, 1962, Eugene: University of Oregon, Special Collections Library). See also Dick Pintarich, "Rise and Fall of the Oregon Electrics," *Oregon Times* (March 1978) 38-48; also, Randall V. Mills, "Early Electric Interurbans in Oregon," *Oregon Historical Quarterly*, (March, December 1943) 82-104, 386-410.
12. *The Oregonian*, January 1, 1895.
13. *Neighborhood Profiles of the City of Portland 1960-1970* (Portland: Office of Planning and Development, July 1978).
14. *The Oregon Journal*, June 8, 1924.
15. *Ibid.*, December 20, 1976.
16. *Neighborhood Profiles of the City of Portland 1960-1970, op. cit.*

17. See Mills, *op. cit.*, 101-103.

18. The largest population growth from 1910 to 1920 was within the Portland city limits. Gresham more than doubled in size, from 540 to 1103; Milwaukie only increased by 312 to 1172; Oregon City picked up 1400 to 5686; and Troutdale went from 309 to 648. See Throckmorton, *op. cit.*, 146.

19. The Oaks Park was sold in 1940 to the Bollinger family which had managed the property for PGE (PRL&P). Its primary offerings today are roller skating and carnival rides.

20. See Throckmorton, *op. cit.*, 150-153.

21. Of January 18, 1913, as quoted in Throckmorton, *op. cit.*, 91.

22. From 1910 to 1920, West Side suburban population growth was as follows: Beaverton, from 386 to 580; Hillsboro, from 2016 to 2468; and Forest Grove, from 1772 to 1915 (Throckmorton, *op. cit.*, 146). From 1910 to 1920, Oswego grew from 1107 to 1818. In May 1922, The Oregon Iron & Steel Company began an aggressive campaign to sell residential building lots around Lake Oswego, and its ads emphasized the Red Electric service.

23. The early history of United's bitter negotiations with Mayor Lane's administration was thoroughly covered in MacColl, *op. cit.*, ch. 11.

24. Article by Tom Hallman, *The Oregonian*, July 27, 1976.

25. *Ibid.*

26. Paul Shoup, "Coordination of Other Forms of Transportation with the Electric Railway," (no date) J. C. Ainsworth Papers (Eugene: University of Oregon, Special Collections Library).

27. *Ibid.*

Chapter 6

1. Franklin T. Griffith Papers, Scrapbook No. 1 (1913-1917) 6-7 (Portland: Oregon Historical Society).

2. See "Public Utility" folder, 1915, Council Papers (Portland: City Archives).

3. Edward S. Corwin, *The Constitution and What It Means Today* (Princeton: Princeton University Press, 1954) 33.

4. Most of the data on the public service commission came from the Claude R. Lester Papers (Eugene: University of Oregon, Special Collections Library). There are three boxes entitled "Investigations of Public Utilities." They are not well organized or titled, often devoid of proper identification.

5. Franklin T. Griffith Papers, Scrapbook No. 1, *op. cit.*

6. *The Oregon Journal*, October 5, 1917.

7. Franklin T. Griffith Papers, Scrapbook No. 1, *op. cit.*

8. Joseph N. Teal Papers, 1918 file, (Portland: Oregon Historical Society).

9. Claude R. Lester Papers, "PSC Report," *op. cit.*

10. Franklin T. Griffith Papers, Scrapbook No. 1, *op. cit.*

11. *The Oregonian* editorial, June 1, 1913.

12. Scrapbook No. 75 (Portland: Oregon Historical Society).

13. See E. Kimbark MacColl, *The Shaping of a City, Business and Politics in Portland, Oregon 1885-1915* (Portland: The Georgian Press, 1976) 238.

14. *The Oregon Journal*, January 24, 1918.

15. Franklin T. Griffith Papers, Scrapbook No. 1, *op. cit.*

16. *Ibid.*

17. Scrapbook No. 71: 116 (Portland: Oregon Historical Society).

18. Franklin T. Griffith Papers, Scrapbook No. 1, *op. cit.*

19. Firm of Griffith, Peck and Coke; now Phillips, Coughlin, Buell, and Black.
   Director, Hawley Pulp & Paper Co.
   President, Title & Trust Co.
   Chairman of the Board, Griffith Rubber Mills
   Chairman of the Board, Donald M. Drake Co.
   President, Firtex Insulating Board Co.
   Partner, Heath Shipbuilding Co. (WW I period)
   Director, Ross Island Sand & Gravel Co. (mid-twenties)
   Partner, Investors Co. of Oregon
   Partner, Realty Associates of Oregon
   Principal investor, Wilhoit Hydro Health Resort Co.
20. James B. Kerr Papers (Portland: Oregon Historical Society).
21. Minutes of the Proceedings of the City Council, 60:284, 304, April 12, 16, 1918 (Portland: City Archives).
22. Franklin T. Griffith Papers, Scrapbook No. 2, *op. cit.* This evaluation was made by E. A. West, an engineer with the Passenger Transportation and Housing Division of the U. S. Emergency Fleet Corporation.
23. Claude R. Lester Papers, *op. cit.*, order no. 581, June 10, 1920.
24. *Ibid.*
25. *Ibid.*
26. See Michael J. Doucet, "Mass Transit and the Failure of Private Ownership: The Case of Toronto in the Early Twentieth Century," *Urban History Review* (#3-77) 3-33.
27. See Robert M. Fogelson, *The Fragmented Metropolis, Los Angeles 1850-1930* (Cambridge: Harvard University Press, 1967) 172-175.
28. See Donald F. Davis, "Mass Transit and Private Ownership: An Alternative Perspective on the Case of Toronto," *Urban History Review* (#3-78) 62-98. Davis has challenged some of Doucet's conclusions.

Chapter 7

1. Letter of March 23, 1917, writer unknown, "Lane File," Richard L. Neuberger Papers (Eugene: University of Oregon, Special Collections Library).
2. "Lane File," *op. cit.*, quoted in a 1938 article written by Neuberger, most likely notes for a speech.
3. *Ibid.*
4. *Ibid.*
5. See George F. Kennan, *American Diplomacy, 1900-1950* (Chicago: University of Chicago Press, 1951) ch. 4. Kennan, a Russian history expert, is one of America's most distinguished former diplomats. Winston Churchill also held the same opinion.
6. "Lane File," *op. cit.*
7. *Ibid.*
8. *Ibid.*
9. *Ibid.*
10. *Ibid.*
11. See Malcolm Clark, Jr., "The Bigot Disclosed: 90 Years of Nativism," *Oregon Historical Quarterly*, 75 (June 1974) 109-182.
12. Franklin T. Griffith Papers, Scrapbook No. 7 (Portland: Oregon Historical Society).
13. Frank Sterrett in *The Oregonian*, "Northwest Magazine," (May 15, 1966) 24.
14. *Ibid.*
15. *Ibid.*

16. *Ibid.*

17. Ellis Lucia, "Portland's Modern Vigilantes," *The Oregonian*, October 16, 1966.

18. "Autobiographical Notes of Lee V. Jenkins," Portland Chamber of Commerce Papers (Eugene: University of Oregon, Special Collections Library).

19. U. S. Attorney Files (Portland: Oregon Historical Society). The files are not well indexed but they are chronological.

20. For these and other stories, see Charles F. Gould, "The Germans," *The Oregonian*, "Northwest Magazine," November 24, 1974; also, Stewart Holbrook, "Northwest Hysterias," *The Oregonian*, "Northwest Magazine," April 4, 1937; also, Portland *Telegram*, July 27, 1921; also, Scrapbook files (Portland: Oregon Historical Society).

21. Jeff Johnson, "The Heyday of Oregon's Socialists," *The Oregonian*, "Northwest Magazine," December 19, 1976.

22. Holbrook, *op. cit.*

23. *Ibid.*

24. Letter of January 8, 1918, U. S. Attorney Files, *op. cit.*, Box 7.

25. *The Oregonian*, June 30, 1918.

26. *The Oregonian*, April 19, 1918.

27. Named after John Francis Carroll, editor of the *Evening Telegram*, who had initiated the effort to establish the market in the spring of 1914.

28. *The Oregon Journal*, May 19, 1917. Not long after the first drive opened in May 1917, *The Oregon Journal* headlined a front page article: "Colored man buys $800 of Liberty Loan Bonds this morning."

29. *Ibid.*, March 10, 1918.

30. *Ibid.*

31. *The Oregonian*, March 11, 1918.

32. See Annette M. Bartholomae, "A Conscientious Objector: Oregon, 1918," *Oregon Historical Quarterly*, 71 (September 1970) 220.

33. *Ibid.*, 226.

34. *Ibid.*, 229.

35. *Ibid.*, 230.

36. *Ibid.*, 231.

37. *Ibid.*

38. *Ibid.*

39. *Ibid.*, 234.

40. *Ibid.*

41. Kennan, *op. cit.*, 65-66.

42. Bartholomae, *op. cit.*, 239.

43. *Ibid.*

44. *Outlook*, 127 (March 16, 1921) 410-411.

45. *The Oregon Journal*, May 15, 16, 1918.

46. See Janet W. Bryant, "The Ku Klux Klan and the Compulsory School Bill of 1922," (Master of Arts seminar paper, Reed College, no date) 30-33 (Portland: Oregon Historical Society).

47. *Oregon Voter*, July 19, 1919.

48. *The Oregonian*, December 21, 1918. For an excellent study of Oregon's anti-radical legislation, the author is indebted to M. Paul Holsinger of Illinois State University, who presented the paper, "Patriotism and the Curbing of Oregon's Radicals, 1919-1937," at the 17th Annual Conference of the Western History Association, Portland, Oregon, October 14, 1977.

49. *The Oregonian*, December 21, 1918.

50. *The Oregon Journal*, January 15, 16, 1919.

51. *Ibid.*, January 16, 1919.

52. *The Oregonian*, January 30, 1919.
53. *The Oregonian*, February 10, 1919.
54. Holsinger, *op. cit.*, 2.
55. Burl A. Green, "Autobiographical Sketch," 6 (Eugene: University of Oregon, Special Collections Library).
56. Frederick Lewis Allen, *Only Yesterday* (New York: Harper and Row, 1931) 49.
57. *The Oregonian*, September 16, 1919.
58. *Ibid.*, September 14, 1919.
59. *Oregon Voter*, January 24, 1920.
60. *Ibid.*
61. *Ibid.*, February 14, 1920.
62. *Ibid.*
63. *Ibid.*
64. *Ibid.*, January 24, 1920.
65. Holsinger, *op. cit.*, 3.
66. *Portland Evening Telegram*, February 3, 1921.
67. *Ibid.*, February 8, 1921.
68. Green, *op cit.*, 5.
69. As quoted in Allen, *op. cit.*, 67.
70. For the growth and activities of the Klan in Oregon see Eckard V. Toy, "The Ku Klux Klan in Oregon: Its Character and Programs," (Master's thesis, University of Oregon, 1959); also, David N. Chalmers, *Hooded Americanism: The First Century of the Ku Klux Klan 1865-1965* (Garden City: Doubleday and Company, 1965) 85-91; also, Kenneth T. Jackson, *The Ku Klux Klan in the City, 1915-1930* (New York: Oxford University Press, 1967) 196-214; also, M. Paul Holsinger, "The Oregon School Bill Controversy, 1922-1925," *Pacific Historical Review*, 37 (August 1968) 327-341; also, George S. Turnbull, *An Oregon Crusader* (Portland: Binford & Mort, 1955), the life of George Putnam, editor and publisher of the Salem *Capital Journal*; also, Bryant, *op. cit.*; and Clark, *op. cit.*
71. *Portland Telegram*, June 17, 1921.
72. *Ibid.*, July 1, 1921.
73. As told to the author by Walter H. Evans, Jr., son of the Multnomah County District Attorney in 1921.
74. *Portland Telegram*, August 1, 1921.
75. *Ibid.*
76. *Ibid.*, August 2, 1921.
77. *Ibid.*
78. Turnbull, *op. cit.*, 65.
79. *Ibid.*, 68.
80. Lem Dever, *The Confessions of an Imperial Klansman*, (Portland, 1924) 40.
81. *Ibid.*
82. *Oregon Voter*, October 4, 1919.
83. *Catholic Sentinel*, May 11, 1922.
84. Turnbull, *op. cit.*, 92-93.
85. *Ibid.*, 136. As quoted by Putnam.
86. *Ibid.*
87. B. A. Green, "Portland's Mayor-Made Revolution," *The Nation*, 115 (December 6, 1922) 605.
88. Burl A. Green, "Autobiographical Sketch," 5 (Eugene: University of Oregon, Special Collections Library).
89. B. A. Green, *The Nation, op. cit.*
90. Waldo Roberts, "The Ku-Kluxing of Oregon," *Outlook*, 133 (March 14, 1923) 491.
91. *Ibid.*, 490.

Chapter 8

1. Robert K. Murray, *The Harding Era* (Minneapolis: University of Minnesota Press, 1969) 445.

2. Frederick Lewis Allen, *Only Yesterday* (New York: Harper and Row, 1931) 160.

3. Interview with Harold E. (Mike) Sanford, October 23, 1978. As the former veteran manager of the Continental Grain Company's Northwest and Pacific Coast operations (a French company), Sanford entered the local grain business in 1919. He has observed its fortunes closely for 60 years.

4. *The Oregonian*, July 5, 1923.

5. *Ibid.*

6. Allen, *op. cit.*, 136.

7. Abbot L. Mills, "The Business Man's Interest in Government," *Oregon Voter*, May 3, 1924.

8. *Ibid.*

9. *Ibid.*

10. In a speech to the Society of American Newspaper Editors, January 17, 1925.

11. As quoted in Allen, *op. cit.*, 180.

12. *Ibid.*

13. As quoted in Scripp's unpublished "Self-Portrait," edited and revised by Charles R. McCabe who married Scripps' granddaughter. See Charles R. McCabe (ed.), *Damned Old Crank* (New York: Harper and Row, 1951) xi.

14. *Ibid.*, 145.

15. *Ibid.*, 143-144.

16. As quoted by Richard L. Neuberger in *The Saturday Evening Post* (March 1, 1947) 23.

17. John Leader, *Oregon Through Alien Eyes* (Portland: publisher unknown, 1922) 86.

18. As quoted in "A Conversation with David C. McClelland and T. George Harris," *Psychology Today* (January 1971) 36. See also McClelland's pioneering work, *The Achieving Society* (New York: The Free Press, 1961). McCelland has spent 30 years of his professional life researching and documenting the dimensions of this relationship across the span of recorded history.

19. As discussed by Brian J. L. Berry, *Growth Centers in the American Urban System* (Cambridge: Ballinger, 1973) 1:36.

20. *Oregon Voter*, May 3, 1919.

21. *Ibid.*

22. Interview with Harold E. (Mike) Sanford, *op. cit.* Sanford also came originally from Pomeroy and his family had known the Housers for years.

23. *Oregon Voter*, November 15, 1924.

24. From information contained in the Abbot L. Mills Papers (Eugene: University of Oregon, Special Collections Library).

25. Robert C. Notson, *Making the Day Begin, A Story of the Oregonian* (Portland: Oregonian Publishing Co., 1975) 8. Notson was for many years the editor and then publisher of *The Oregonian*.

26. McCabe, *op. cit.*, 225.

27. Notson, *op. cit.*, 7.

28. E. B. MacNaughton, "Tapes," Reel 2 (Portland: Reed College Library Archives).

29. McCabe, *op. cit.*, 225-226.

30. *The Oregonian*, July 27, 1921.

31. *Ibid.*

32. *Ibid.*

33. *Oregon Voter*, April 9, 1927.

34. Unpublished autobiographical notes of Homer Shaver, a copy of which was given to the author during an interview on March 17, 1977, a year before Shaver's death.

35. The material for C. F. Swigert's life came from a variety of published and unpublished sources and interviews with the family and various other people. Most of the financial data was found in a fragmentary collection of assorted papers on file at the Oregon Historical Society, Portland.

36. For data on the woolen industry, see *Oregon Voter*, August 24, 1923; November 12, 1927; April 30, 1929.

37. Information derived from Blyth & Co. records, Portland office, 1927-1931 (Portland: Oregon Historical Society); *Oregon Voter*, November 12, 1927; *Willamette Week*, "Garment Empire," October 12, 1977; Standard & Poor's Stock Summaries.

38. As related to the author by a member of the Bishop family.

39. Information derived from Blyth & Co. records, *op. cit.*; "Garment Empire," *op. cit.*; personal knowledge of the company's history by the author through family and relatives.

40. *Oregon Voter*, August 20, 1927.

41. The technical financial information on the company's early years was derived from a Blyth, Witter voting trust certificate offer, dated November 21, 1928, Blyth & Co. records, *op. cit.* See also *Oregon Voter*, December 14, 1929; also, *Fortune*, March 1930; also, author's interview with E. C. Sammons, April 3, 1975.

42. Portland *Evening Bulletin*, January 10, 1929.

43. See article by Gerry Pratt, *The Oregonian*, August 12, 1964.

44. For a thorough review of Ladd & Tilton operations in the early 1900s, see E. Kimbark MacColl, *The Shaping of a City, Business and Politics in Portland, Oregon 1885-1915* (Portland: The Georgian Press, 1976) 364-366.

45. Particilarly, O. K. Burrell, *Gold in the Woodpile — An Informal History of Banking in Oregon* (Eugene: University of Oregon Press, 1967) 90-91.

46. As reported in *The Oregon Journal*, August 23, 1960.

47. E. B. MacNaughton, "Tapes," *op. cit.*, Reel 3.

48. Fred Lockley, *History of the Columbia River Valley* (Chicago, 1928) ii:616.

49. E. B. MacNaughton, "Tapes," *op. cit.*, Reel 3. This and other Ladd & Tilton tales were confirmed by C. B. Stephenson in his unpublished autobiography, "The Way It Was," 1971, in the possession of his daughter Mrs. Ferris F. Boothe. Stephenson was president of the First National Bank from 1953-1960 and succeeded MacNaughton as chairman of the board. He worked for Ladd & Tilton, 1923-1925, and handled the bank's liquidation for MacNaughton 1925-1929.

50. E. B. MacNaughton, *op. cit.*, Reel 3.

51. See the Ladd & Tilton Papers, "Corporate Records" (Portland: Oregon Historical Society).

52. *Ibid.*, March 6, 1919.

53. Letter of E. C. Sammons to John C. Ainsworth, written from New York where Sammons had seen Eddy, October 6, 1926, J. C. Ainsworth Papers (Eugene: University of Oregon, Special Collections Library).

54. The entire *Governor's Report on Security Frauds* was published in the *Oregon Statesman* of Salem, August 20, 1924. The Portland papers only briefly summarized it.

55. *Ibid.*

56. See *Oregon Voter*, October 5, November 16, 1929.

57. *Portland Telegram*, January 29, March 12, 1926.

58. The account of this episode consumes Reels 3 and 4 of E. B. MacNaughton, "Tapes," *op. cit.* It is partially corroborated by the bank's "Corporate Records," *op. cit.*

59. Stephenson, *op. cit.*

Chapter 9

1. "The Port of Portland," *Portland City Club Bulletin*, August 26, 1932.
2. *Ibid.*
3. *The Oregon Journal*, September 6, 1912.
4. "Portland Shipping," *Portland City Club Bulletin*, October 15, 1926.
5. Henry L. Corbett to J. N. Teal, December 31, 1917, Joseph N. Teal Papers (Portland: Oregon Historical Society).
6. Lawrence Kaye Hodges, *Twenty Eventful Years* (New York, 1937) 506. A compendium of dated *Oregonian* editorials written by Hodges.
7. S. M. Mears to J. C. Ainsworth, December 19, 1927, J. C. Ainsworth Pahers (Eugene: University of Oregon, Special Collections Library).
8. *Ibid.*
9. *Ibid.*
10. As reported in the *Portland City Club Bulletin*, April 2, 1926.
11. *Ibid.*
12. Hodges, *op. cit.*, 389.
13. *Ibid.*, 392.
14. *Ibid.*, 508.
15. *Ibid.*, 413 (*The Oregonian*, February 18, 1928).
16. As described in a letter to Philip Buehner from John C. Ainsworth, February 3, 1930, J. C. Ainsworth Papers, *op. cit.*
17. The States Steamship Company, whose base operations moved to San Francisco in the mid-1950s under the ownership of Jack Dant, C. E. Dant's son, filed for bankruptcy in December 1978.
18. Undated, from the Richard Fagan Papers (Portland: Oregon Historical Society).
19. *Oregon Voter*, July 26, 1919.
20. *Ibid.*, June 9, 1918.
21. Minutes of the Port of Portland Commission, April 1921 meeting, Port of Portland Commission Library, Portland.
22. A copy of the subscription form and pledges received was found in the Joseph N. Teal Papers, *op. cit.*
23. Minutes of the Port of Portland Commission, *op. cit.*, March 19, 1920.
24. *The Oregon Journal*, June 5, 1920.
25. *Oregon Voter*, July 26, 1930.
26. In 1924, the holdings were valued at $196,000.
27. *Oregon Voter*, *op. cit.*
28. Minutes of the Port of Portland Commission, *op. cit.*, January 13, 1919.
29. Simeon G. Reed Papers, "Swan Island Realty Co. file," (Portland: Reed College Library). See also, Minutes of the Port of Portland Commission, *op. cit.*, December 8, 1921. See also, file of Deeds and Titles, Port of Portland Commission Library, Title No. 192, dated January 4, 1922.
30. *Biennial Report of the Port of Portland Commission* (1927-1928) Portland, 1929, 6-7.
31. Final Report of "The Committee of 15," Port of Portland Commission Library. The author has italicized some of the words for emphasis.
32. By the author.
33. There is a discrepancy between this figure as listed in the Port of Portland Commission, Deeds and Titles, *op. cit.*, and the figure of $121, 077 that is listed in the *Biennial Report* of the Port of Portland Commission (1921-1922) 15.
34. An editorial in the *Portland Telegram*, February 8, 1926, accused the Port of giving undue attention to Guild's Lake and not enough to the dredging of the west channel *per se*.

35. See *Portland City Club Bulletin*, April 22, 1921; also, Port of Portland Commission, *op. cit.*, December 8, 1921, April 13, 1922.

36. Port of Portland Commission, Deeds and Titles, *op. cit.*, Deed No. 106.

37. Minutes of the Port of Portland Commission, *op. cit.*, May 1, 1928.

38. As related to the author by James W. Cook's daughter, Mrs. Cornelia Cook Menefee, May 25, 1978.

39. Published by the Port of Portland Commission in 1920.

40. *The Oregonian*, October 5, 1926.

41. Blyth & Co. records, Portland office, "Oregon Terminals Company" (Portland: Oregon Historical Society).

42. *Ibid.*

43. The literature and documentation on reclamation and drainage districts is extensive. See *Land Development in Oregon, Through Flood Control, Drainage and Irrigation*, Oregon State Planning Board (Salem, July 1938); *Drainage District Laws of Oregon*, Oregon State Water Board (Salem, 1919); *Biennial Report of the State Reclamation Commission* (Salem, 1929, 1931, 1933, 1935); *Mayor's Message and Annual Reports* (including that of the City Engineer) City of Portland, 1921 (Portland: Oregon Historical Society).

44. *Portland Telegram*, August 3, 1921.

45. *Biennial Report of the State Reclamation Commission*, 1935, *op. cit.*

46. Port of Portland Commission, Deeds and Titles, *op. cit.*, Deed Nos. 284, 286, 301, 413, 469, 479, 536, 537, 549, 558.

47. *The Oregon Journal*, January 5, 1926.

48. *Portland City Club Bulletin*, October 3, 1924.

49. Commission of Public Docks, October 28, 1926.

50. *Ibid.*, February 11, 1937.

51. *The Oregonian*, September 7, 1977.

52. *The Oregon Journal*, September 1, 1927.

53. *Ibid.*, September 14, 1927.

54. Arthur M. Schlesinger, Jr., *The Crisis of the Old Order* (Boston: Houghton Mifflin Co., 1957) 76.

55. *The Oregonian*, October 6, 1929.

56. Port of Portland Commission, *op. cit.*, September 30, 1929.

57. The obituary of founder A. A. Riedel, Sr., reported 1928. *The Willamette-Western 1977 Annual Report* stated 1929.

58. *News-Telegram*, February 4, 1933. As of 1933, Polhemus was telling the truth. Twenty years later, the profit would prove to be considerable.

59. *News-Telegram*, May 5, 1933.

60. Probate Records, Multnomah County Clerk's Office, Fee Book No. 99938.

61. Large stockholdings included: $125,000 in Texaco; $50,000 in Standard Oil of California; $52,000 in Insurance Company of North America; $33,000 in Dupont. His PGE stock was worth $46,000.

62. *Oregon Voter*, November 29, 1924.

63. Port of Portland Commission, *op. cit.*, December 1, 1931.

64. Probate Records, *op. cit.*, Fee Book No. 57902.

Chapter 10

1. Raymond A. Mohl, "The Industrial City," *Environment* (June 1976) 38.

2. C. C. Ludwig, "Problems of Government Simplification in Portland, Oregon," *National Municipal Review* (January 1925) 36-41.

3. *Ibid.*, 39.

4. Letter to the Board of County Commissioners, April 1, 1924, "Exhibit I," C. F. Swigert Papers (Portland: Oregon Historical Society).

5. Report of the Oregon Technical Council, *Portland City Club Bulletin*, April 18, 1924.

6. *The Oregon Journal*, April 2, 1924.

7. *News*, April 4, 1924.

8. *Ibid.*, April 5, 1924.

9. Lem Dever, *The Confessions of an Imperial Klansman* (Portland, 1924) 40. His relationship to the Klan, and the degree of control that it exercised over him, was later described by former Klansman Lem Dever when he published his *Confessions of an Imperial Klansman*.

10. *News*, April 10, 1924.

11. *The Oregon Journal*, April 12, 1924.

12. Barbara Walker to the author, May 18, 1979.

13. *The Oregon Journal*, June 16, 1924.

14. *The Oregonian*, July 12, 1929; September 10, 1930.

15. See Hooker Chemical Company folder, Box 23, Portland Chamber of Commerce Papers (Eugene: University of Oregon, Special Collections Library).

16. Letter of W. B. Dodson to McNary, December 19, 1929, Ford Motor Company folder, *ibid.*

17. Hooker Report, *op. cit.*

18. 14th Census of the U. S.: 1920, *ibid.*

19. Roy W. Winton, "Portland and the Paradox," *The Playground*, 17 (June 1923) 168.

20. *The Oregon Journal*, March 6, 1919.

21. William W. Pilcher, *The Portland Longshoremen* (New York: Holt, Rinehart and Winston, 1972) 68.

22. *Ibid.*

23. *The Advocate* (Portland) September 19, 1927, quoting Beatrice Cannaday. The author wishes to acknowledge the assistance of the Oregon Black History Project and its director Elizabeth McLagan for spotlighting some of this material. A history of Oregon's blacks is in the process of being edited for publication at some future date. The main coverage will extend to the period of World War II. A CETA grant made this project possible.

24. John Leader, *Oregon Through Alien Eyes* (Portland: publisher unknown, 1922) 130-131.

25. Letter of July 16, 1930, to Harry H. Fair, J. C. Ainsworth Papers (Eugene: University of Oregon, Special Collections Library).

26. See Kit and Frederica Konolige, *The Power of Their Glory: America's Ruling Class: The Episcopalians* (New York: Wyden Books, 1978).

27. Rough draft of a biographical sketch, date circa 1928, J. C. Ainsworth Papers (Eugene: University of Oregon, Special Collections Library).

28. *The Oregonian*, October 5, 1921.

29. Frank Sterrett, "Portland's Kissing Mayor," *The Oregonian*, "Northwest Magazine," May 15, 1966.

30. *The Oregonian*, March 18, 1926.

31. *The American City* (July 1921) 50.

32. See Floyd R. Marsh, *20 Years A Soldier of Fortune* (Portland: Binford and Mort, 1976) 181-182. Marsh died in January 1979.

33. *The Oregon Journal*, November 16, 1926.

34. *Mayor's Message and Annual Report*, 1923 (Portland: Oregon Historical Society).

35. See Marsh, *op. cit.*, 187.

36. *Ibid.*, 186-189.

37. *The Oregon Journal*, June 18, 1924.

38. *Oregon Voter*, October 18, 1924.

39. Mabel L. Walker, "Rating Cities According to the Services Which Their Citizens Are Getting," *The American City* 41 (July 1929) 131.

40. "Autobiographical Notes of Lee V. Jenkins," Portland Chamber of Commerce Papers (Eugene: University of Oregon, Special Collections Library).

41. *Ibid.*

42. Portland *Evening Telegram*, January 7, 1921, editorial.

43. *The Oregon Journal*, April 8, 17, 21, 1924.

44. *News*, May 23, 1924.

45. *Oregon Voter*, October 25, 1924.

46. *Ibid.*

47. *Ibid.*, August 30, 1924.

48. As quoted in *The Oregon Journal*, October 3, 1929.

49. Quoted in the Portland *News*, February 26, 1924.

50. Howard McKinley Corning, "A. R. Wetjen: British Seaman in the Western Sunrise," *Oregon Historical Quarterly* 74 (June 1973) 161. See also, John M. Tess, *Uphill Downhill Yamhill* (Portland 1977).

51. *The Oregon Journal*, April 13, 1924.

52. The seven page report was found in the Jesse Short File, Box 2 (Portland: Oregon Historical Society). Miss Short was a Reed College biology professor, active in housing and consumer affairs. The approximate date is circa 1922.

53. Walker, *op. cit.* The Johns Hopkins University study was unable to secure adequate comparative data for these services.

54. *American City* 34 (June 1926) 645.

55. Report of Miss Alice Barrows, Federal Bureau of Education, Washington, D. C., to the City Club, *Portland City Club Bulletin*, May 7, 1926.

56. *Ibid.*

57. Rough draft of a speech by Mayor Baker, dated "1929", found in the Olaf Laurgaard Papers (Eugene: University of Oregon, Special Collections Library).

58. Minutes of the Proceedings of the City Council, 96:147(Portland: City Archives).

59. *The Oregonian*, March 7, 1931.

60. See "Report of Harland Bartholomew & Associates," (1931) 110, Portland Bureau of Planning Library.

61. Baker Speech, 1929, *op. cit.*

62. A. L. Barbur, "Cash Savings on Asphalt Streets," *The American City Magazine* (April 1923) 389-390.

63. "The Collection and Disposal of Municipal Wastes," *Portland City Club Bulletin*, November 24, 1922; also an article of the same title, condensing the City Club report in *The American City Magazine* (April 1923) 355-357.

64. *Evening Telegram*, December 19, 1929.

65. *The Oregonian*, December 12, 1894.

66. *Oregon Voter*, November 22, 1924.

67. *Ibid.*, March 22, 1924.

68. As reported in *ibid.*, November 22, 1924.

69. *The Oregon Journal*, July 2, 1926. See also, "Tax Limit Amendment," *Portland City Club Bulletin*, June 25, 1926.

70. *Oregon Voter*, August 2, 1930.

71. *Ibid.*, February 11, 1922.

72. E. Kimbark MacColl, *The Shaping of a City, Business and Politics in Portland, Oregon 1885-1915* (Portland: The Georgian Press, 1976) 162.

73. *Portland City Club Bulletin*, July 30, 1926.

Chapter 11

1. Lewis Mumford, "The Fourth Migration," *Survey 54* (May 1, 1925) 130-133.
2. Portland City Planning Commission, "The Plan-It," December 1927; also E. Kimbark MacColl, *The Shaping of a City, Business and Politics in Portland, Oregon 1885-1915* (Portland: The Georgian Press, 1976) 425-430.
3. Letter of Ormond Bean to F. M. Byam, July 1, 1935, Ormond Bean Papers (Portland: Oregon Historical Society). Bean was a MIT graduate in architecture.
4. Letter of E. B. MacNaughton to Donald J. Sterling, March 26, 1929, J. C. Ainsworth Papers (Eugene: University of Oregon, Special Collections Library).
5. "The Plan-It," December 1927, *op. cit.*
6. "City Plan of the West Side Flat of Portland," a special report of the City Club, October 1921, published in the *Portland City Club Bulletin*, appended to v. 8 (1927-1928).
7. Portland City Planning Commission, "The Plan-It," June 1927.
8. A. L. Barbur, "The Future of Portland and Planning For It," *The Architect and Engineer of California* 56 (March 1919) 81-83.
9. See the Minutes of the Portland City Planning Commission, vol. 1, Portland Bureau of Planning Library.
10. *Oregon Voter*, August 9, 1919.
11. *Ibid.*
12. City Planning Bulletin No. 1, June 1919, Portland Bureau of Planning Library; also, Charles E. Cheney, "Zoning in Practice," paper delivered at the National City Planning Conference at Buffalo, N. Y., May 29, 1919, Ellis Lawrence Papers (Eugene: University of Oregon, Special Collections Library).
13. Letter to the city council from the Zoning Committee of the Portland City Planning Commission, March 17, 1930, Minutes of the Proceedings of the City Council, 66:521 (Portland: City Archives).
14. *The Oregon Journal*, March 14, 1920.
15. From an account found in the papers of former commissioner William A. Bowes, ca 1945, William A. Bowes Papers (Portland: Oregon Historical Society).
16. *The Oregon Journal*, March 14, 1920.
17. *Ibid.*, March 21, 1920.
18. Quotes from the City Planning Commission's Secretary's notes in 1923, Portland Bureau of Planning Library.
19. Bowes, *op. cit.*
20. George H. Coffin, "Zoned into Oblivion," a speech contained in a report of the Portland City Planning Commission, September 17, 1934, found in the files of the Portland City Attorney (Portland: Oregon Historical Society).
21. "The Plan-It," *op. cit.*, December 1927.
22. As reported in *The Oregon Journal*, January 17, 1923.
23. Letter of Rabbi Jonah B. Wise to Jesse Short, November 8, 1928, Short File, Box 2 (Portland: Oregon Historical Society).
24. *The Oregonian*, February 17, 18, 21, 1931.
25. Portland Housing and Planning Association, *Bulletin*, June 1933, Henry E. Reed Papers, (Portland: Oregon Historical Society).
26. Portland City Planning Commission, "Buckman Neighborhood Rezoning," prepared in January 1977 and approved by the city council in April 1977. Much of the area was downzoned.
27. *Ibid.*
28. *Neighborhood Profiles of the City of Portland 1960-1970* (Portland: Office of Planning and Development, July 1978).

29. The information on these transactions came from newspaper files and a "confidential" office memorandum by John C. Ainsworth, dated September 8, 1930, J. C. Ainsworth Papers (Eugene: University of Oregon, Special Collections Library).

30. Letter of John C. Ainsworth to E. C. Sammons, March 8, 1928, J. C. Ainsworth Papers, *op. cit.*

31. For an account of the Hoffman Construction Company's history, see "The City The Hoffmans Built," *Portland Commerce Magazine*, February 2, 1973; also, "Building Oregon," *The Oregonian*, December 4, 1950.

32. *The Oregon Journal*, May 10, 1925.

33. *The Oregonian*, July 23, 1925.

34. Letter of John W. Blodgett to John C. Ainsworth, August 12, 1927, J. C. Ainsworth Papers, *op. cit.*

35. *Oregon Voter*, December 31, 1927.

36. *Ibid.*

37. *Ibid.*

38. *Ibid.*

39. Letter of C. N. McArthur to Philip V. W. Fry, March 28, 1921, J. C. Ainsworth Papers, *op. cit.*

40. Letter of Fred G. Meyer to Chester A. Moores, February 28, 1928, Chester A. Moores Papers, in the possession of Mrs. Wayne Rogers, Portland.

41. *Oregon Voter*, December 31, 1927.

42. *The Oregonian*, December 7, 1928.

43. There is much literature covering the Laurgaard Plan: Portland Bureau of Planning Library, *City Club Bulletins*, newspapers, and the Olaf Laurgaard and Ellis Lawrence Papers (Eugene: University of Oregon, Special Collections Library).

44. Memorandum by Ellis Lawrence, Ellis Lawrence Papers, *op. cit.*

45. *The Oregonian*, September 12, 1924, Lawrence Kaye Hodges, *Twenty Eventful Years* (New York, 1937) 519.

47. *Portland City Club Bulletin*, March 20, 1925.

48. Letter of John C. Ainsworth to Ellis Lawrence, February 16, 1921, J. C. Ainsworth Papers, *op. cit.*

49. *Portland City Club Bulletin*, March 20, 1925.

50. As reported in the *Oregon Voter*, November 19, 1927.

Chapter 12

1. In numerous letters referring to Lloyd's activities, banker John C. Ainsworth cited "the Irvington" area.

2. Letter of Charles H. Martin to Ritter & Lowe, May 20, 1920, Charles H. Martin Papers (Portland: Oregon Historical Society).

3. Letter of E. J. Lowe to C. H. Martin, December 18, 1920, C. H. Martin Papers, *op. cit.*

4. *Ibid.*, September 8, 1921.

5. *Ibid.*

6. *Ibid.*, May 26, 1922.

7. *Ibid.*

8. Most of the material on Ralph B. Lloyd was found in the John C. Ainsworth Papers (Eugene: University of Oregon, Special Collections Library); also the Chester A. Moores Papers, in the possession of Mrs. Wayne Rogers, Portland; also the files of *The Oregonian* and *The Oregon Journal*.

9. Letter of Ralph B. Lloyd to John C. Ainsworth, J. C. Ainsworth Papers, *op. cit.*

10. See *Neighborhood Profiles of the City of Portland 1960-1970* (Portland: Office of Planning and Development, July 1978) 17-27.

11. Letter of Ralph B. Lloyd to John C. Ainsworth, October 5, 1928, J. C. Ainsworth Papers, *op. cit.*

12. *Ibid.*, September 25, 1928.

13. *Ibid.*, June 7, 1930.

14. *The Oregonian*, August 17, 1930.

15. *Ibid.*, September 9, 1930.

16. Letter of Ralph B. Lloyd to John C. Ainsworth, September 25, 1930, J. C. Ainsworth Papers, *op. cit.*

17. Letter of W. H. Hemphill to John C. Ainsworth, October 16, 1930, *ibid.*

18. Letter of Robert H. Strong to Ainsworth, December 17, 1930, *ibid.*

19. Letter of John C. Ainsworth to E. B. Tanner, December 18, 1930, *ibid.*

20. Letter of John C. Ainsworth to Lloyd, December 29, 1930, *ibid.*

21. Letter of Ralph B. Lloyd to Ainsworth, January 17, 1931, *ibid.*

22. By Franz Drinker who worked for the Lloyd Corporation in 1931 as a young property manager. The author has long known Drinker and considers him absolutely reliable.

23. *The Oregonian*, February 26, 1931.

24. Letter of Ralph B. Lloyd to C. C. Hall, March 9, 1931, J. C. Ainsworth Papers, *op. cit.*

25. Letter of Ralph B. Lloyd to Ainsworth, June 24, 1931, *ibid.*

26. *Ibid.*, August 13, 1931.

27. *The Oregonian*, May 7, 1933.

28. *Ibid.*

29. *Ibid.*

30. *The Oregon Journal*, May 4, 1937.

31. *Ibid.*, October 12, 1926.

32. Blyth & Company records, Portland office, "Eastmoreland" issues, 1926, 1930 (Portland: Oregon Historical Society).

33. Letter of John C. Ainsworth to John A. Shepard, February 11, 1926, J. C. Ainsworth Papers, *op. cit.*

34. *The Oregon Journal*, May 10, 1925.

35. *Ibid.*, May 23, 1925.

36. *Ibid.*, September 26, 1921; also *The American City Magazine*, 26 (June 1922) 611.

37. *The Oregon Journal*, October 21, 1926.

38. *Ibid.*, October 16, 1932.

39. *The Community Press*, December 21, 1977.

40. See article by Jack Pement, "Freeway Blight Begins," *The Oregon Journal.* September 12, 1977. Also, "This Is Commonwealth, Incorporated," 1939 brochure highlighting company activities.

41. Letter of Sinclair A. Wilson to John C. Ainsworth, October 10, 1928, J. C. Ainsworth Papers, *op. cit.*

42. Letter of John C. Ainsworth to E. B. MacNaughton, March 27, 1929, *ibid.*

43. Letter of John C. Ainsworth to John Laing, September 19, 1929, *ibid.*

44. David Plowden, *Bridges, The Spans of North America* (New York: Viking Press, 1974) 290-291.

45. *Ibid.*, 291.

46. *Ibid.*

47. *American City* 21 (September 1929) 138.

48. *Ibid.*

49. Minutes of the Proceedings of the City Council, 112:499 (Portland: City Archives).

50. C. P. Keyser, message to Mayor George L. Baker, January 25, 1924, Mayor's Message and Annual Report, 1923 (Portland: Oregon Historical Society).

51. *Architectural Record*, 61:23.

52. See article on a federal demonstration grant of $562,000 to the Portland Parks Bureau for planning and redevelopment of five neighborhood parks and two new sites, *The Oregonian*, January 14, 1979.

53. The information for much of this episode comes from the Ellis Lawrence Papers (Eugene: University of Oregon, Special Collections Library), and the A. C. Dixon Papers, "Board of Regents" box (Eugene: University of Oregon, Special Collections Library). Dixon was president of the board of regents.

54. Letter of Ellis Lawrence to A. C. Dixon, December 4, 1915, Ellis Lawrence Papers, *op. cit.*

55. Letter of Ellis Lawrence to Dixon, *ibid.*

56. Letter of A. C. Dixon to Mrs. George Gerlinger, May 5, 1917, Dixon Papers, *op. cit.*

57. Letter of Ellis Lawrence to K. A. J. Mackenzie, July 3, 1917, Ellis Lawrence Papers, *op. cit.*

58. *The Oregonian*, December 25, 1924.

59. *Portland City Club Bulletin*, August 13, 1926.

60. *The Oregonian*, December 20, 1929.

61. *Ibid.*

62. "The Plan-It," *op. cit.*, August 1928.

63. Information derived from a letter issued by Cameron Squires in March 1929 relative to a 75,000 share stock offering, J. C. Ainsworth Papers, *op. cit.*

Chapter 13

1. Alpheus T. Mason, *Brandeis: A Free Man's Life* (New York: Viking, 1946).

2. *Will Rogers, The Autobiography of Will Rogers* (Boston: Houghton Mifflin, 1949) 373.

3. *Fortune*, February 1930.

4. *Ibid.*, March 1930.

5. Lawrence Kaye Hodges, *Twenty Eventful Years* (New York, 1937); *The Oregonian*, May 23, 1928.

6. See "Branch Banking: The First Step," *Fortune*, December 1932.

7. John W. Blodgett to John C. Ainsworth, letter of November 9, 1927, J. C. Ainsworth Papers (Eugene: University of Oregon, Special Collections Library).

8. Ainsworth to Blodgett, letter of November 16, 1927, *ibid.*

9. As quoted in the *Oregon Voter*, March 15, 1930.

10. Blyth & Co. records, November 1, 1926 (Portland: Oregon Historical Society).

11. John C. Ainsworth to E. C. Sammons, letter of October 13, 1926, J. C. Ainsworth Papers, *op. cit.*

12. See E. Kimbark MacColl, *The Shaping of a City, Business and Politics in Portland, Oregon 1885-1915* (Portland: The Georgian Press, 1976) ch. 5.

13. *Ibid.* ch. 10.

14. Background information on the Wheeler family was provided the author by Mrs. Lawrence Wheeler, widow of Jack Wheeler's youngest brother who ran the *Telegram*. Numerous conversations were held over a period of time with Mrs. Wheeler, whom the author has known for some years. Jack is *not* fondly remembered.

15. *Fortune*, December 1932.

16. See the extensive account of these proceedings in the *Oregon Voter*, April 9, 1927.

17. Memorandum of February 3, 1925, J. C. Ainsworth Papers, *op. cit.*

18. Frank Sterrett, "Portland's Kissing Mayor," *The Oregonian*, Northwest Magazine, May 15, 1966.

19. *The Oregon Journal*, March 30, 1927. Most of the material for this episode is contained in a large file dealing with the Northwestern Bank in the J. C. Ainsworth Papers, *op. cit.*

20. Robert C. Notson, *Making the Day Begin, A Story of the Oregonian* (Portland: Oregonian Publishing Co., 1975) 13.

21. John C. Ainsworth to John Blodgett, letter of April 27, 1927, J. C. Ainsworth Papers, *op. cit.*

22. John C. Ainsworth to J. G. Woodworth, letter of April 19, 1927, J. C. Ainsworth Papers, *op. cit.*

23. *Ibid.*

24. John C. Ainsworth to John Blodgett, letter of April 27, 1927, J. C. Ainsworth Papers, *op. cit.*

25. *The Oregon Journal*, January 24, 1928.

26. *Oregon Voter*, April 19, 1930.

27. Author's interview with E. C. Sammons, April 3, 1975.

28. *The Oregon Journal* carried lengthy accounts of the Cooke episode, beginning with January 31, 1928. The most significant dates were: February 2, February 4, February 28, March 19 and August 22, 1928.

29. *Oregon Voter*, November 26, 1927.

30. *The Oregon Journal*, February 4, 1917.

31. Anonymous source, by interview with the author.

32. "George Joseph File," Henry M. Hanzen Papers (Portland: Oregon Historical Society).

33. *Oregon Voter*, November 26, 1927. For material on the Wemme case, see *Oregon Voter*, January 12, 1924; also the Hanzen Papers, *op. cit.*

34. Ellis Lawrence Papers (Eugene: University of Oregon, Special Collections Library).

35. *Oregon Voter*, January 14, 1922.

36. *Oregon Voter*, January 21, 1922.

37. See the *Oregon Voter*, September 21, 1929, for a generally accurate account of Meier's entrance into the banking world. The Fleishhacker comment was incorrect. Much of the other information was derived from a variety of sources, including interviews by the author with members of both the Meier and Frank families who are well known to him.

38. *The Oregon Journal*, September 14, 1929.

39. Ainsworth to a friend, letter of April 9, 1937, J. C. Ainsworth Papers, *op. cit.*

40. Portland *News*, November 21, 1928.

41. As quoted in the *Oregon Voter*, October 5, 1929.

42. Frederick Lewis Allen, *The Big Change* (New York: Harper and Row, 1952) 145.

43. See *The Oregonian*, October 30, 1929, for numerous accounts of activities in the local brokerage houses the day before.

44. For a detailed account of the Boloff case, see M. Paul Holsinger, "The Oregon School Bill Controversy, 1922-1925," *Pacific Historical Review* 37 (August 1968) 327-341.

45. *The Oregon Journal*, March 5, 1930.

46. *Oregon Voter*, June 7, 1930.

47. *New York Times*, October 17, 1976.

48. *Ibid.*

49. *Oregon Voter*, June 14, 1930.

50. Much of the information for this sketch came from the E. B. MacNaughton, "Tapes" Reel 4. (Portland: Reed College Library Archives).

51. The transaction was fully described by John C. Ainsworth in a letter to Wells Fargo Bank president F. L. Lipman on June 19, 1930, J. C. Ainsworth Papers, *op. cit.* Ainsworth's account appears to be more accurate than MacNaughton's memory, as recorded 30 years later.

52. MacNaughton, "Tapes," Reel 4, *op. cit.*

53. *Ibid.*

54. F. L. Lipman to John C. Ainsworth, letter of June 21, 1930, J. C. Ainsworth Papers, *op. cit.*

55. MacNaughton, "Tapes," Reel 4, *op. cit.*

56. Harry Schwartz to the author, January 7, 1977.

57. *The Oregon Journal*, November 10, 1929.

58. John C. Ainsworth to J. W. Blodgett, Jr., letter of November 24, 1930, J. C. Ainsworth Papers, *op. cit.*

59. J. C. Ainsworth to R. L. Macleay, letter of May 23, 1931, *ibid.*

60. J. C. Ainsworth to R. L. Lipman, letter of December 23, 1931, *ibid.*

61. *Ibid.*

62. F. L. Lipman to Ainsworth, letter of December 24, 1931, *ibid.*

63. The author saw the signed notes which are in the possession of Aaron Frank's son, Gerald. Much of the information for this sketch came from discussions with members of the families who are well known to the author. The old Meier & Frank Company corporate ledgers were also examined. They are in possession of Jack Meier, Julius' son.

64. MacNaughton, "Tapes," Reel 4, *op. cit.*

65. O. H. Holmes, "This and That," Washington County *News-Times*, May 1, 1930.

66. *The Woodburn Independent*, May 1, 1930.

67. As quoted in the *Oregon Voter*, June 12, 1930.

68. *Oregon Voter*, May 31, 1930.

69. Henry M. Hanzen, "The Joseph-Meier Political Revolution," ch. 27-30, unpublished manuscript, Hanzen Papers, *op. cit.*

70. August 7, 1930.

71. Address of Phil Metschan, Jr., September 30, 1930, Metschan Papers (Portland: Oregon Historical Society).

72. For an enlightening inquiry into the whole question, see Alan S. Larsen, "Public vs. Private Power Revisited: An Oregon Power Authority Proposal," *Environmental Law* 7 (Winter 1977) 315-44.

73. Campaign literature, Metschan Papers, *op. cit.*

74. Salem *Statesman*, quoted in the *Oregon Voter*, August 23, 1930.

75. *Oregon Voter*, *ibid.*

76. *Oregon Voter*, August 16, 1930.

Chapter 14

1. See Sheldon Novick, "The Electric Power Industry," *Environment* 17 (November 1975) 11-13.

2. *Oregon Voter*, August 9, 1924.

3. *Ibid.*

4. *Spectator*, June 27, 1925.

5. *Fortune*, May 1935, pp. 167-168.

6. Charles M. Thomas, "Portland Address," June 13, 1933, Frank J. Lonergan Papers (Eugene: University of Oregon, Special Collections Library).

7. Charles M. Thomas was born in Iowa in 1877 and moved to Medford, Oregon, as a young lawyer. He served as a circuit court judge and state senator before accepting Governor Meier's appointment in February 1931 to be the Oregon Public Utility Commissioner. Upon leaving office in 1935, Thomas practiced law in Portland until his death in 1938 at 61 years of age.

8. Thomas, *op. cit.*

9. *The Oregonian*, October 18, 1931.

10. Thomas, *op. cit.*

11. John Dierdorf's authorized corporate history, *The Story of Pacific Power and Light* (Portland 1971) praises EBASCO's founder and chairman until 1933, Sidney Z. Mitchell. It states "how a holding a company could help the progress of the electric industry" (pp. 10-

11) by citing the organization of the American Power & Light Company. In a glowing account, no mention is made of any of the actions and problems cited by Commissioner Charles M. Thomas.

12. Frank Silliman, Jr., to Guy W. Talbot, wire of November 15, 1930, Thomas, *op. cit.*

13. For an "outsider's" account of the gas and power company refinancing, see *Oregon Voter*, December 31, 1927.

14. Thomas, *op. cit.*

15. Minutes of the Proceedings of the City Council 93:311, January 7, 1931 (Portland: City Archives).

16. *Ibid.*, 93:312.

17. Council Papers, *op. cit.*, "Public Utility Box."

18. Letter of R. Macleay to J. C. Ainsworth, n.d., J. C. Ainsworth Papers, Hooker Chemical Folder, Box 23 (Eugene: University of Oregon, Special Collections Library).

19. Portland Chamber of Commerce Papers (Eugene: University of Oregon, Special Collections Library).

20. The uncompleted 1888 canal bed that became a major repository for deadly chemical wastes that began surfacing in the mid-1970s. To date, $22 million has been spent on clean-up and $2.6 billion in claims and suits against the city and Hooker Chemical have been filed.

21. Minutes of the Proceedings of the City Council, *op. cit.*, "Public Utility Box."

22. *Ibid.*, 96:754.

23. Lem Dever, *Off With The Lid In The Name Of The Law* (Portland:1936) 18.

24. The bill was passed on March 9, 1933.

25. Quoted in Dever, *op. cit.*, 18.

26. Guy W. Talbot to John C. Ainsworth, letter of May 20, 1933, J. C. Ainsworth Papers, *op. cit.*

27. For the early history of the company and its predecessor companies, see E. Kimbark MacColl, *The Shaping of a City, Business and Politics in Portland, Oregon 1885-1915* (Portland: The Georgian Press, 1976).

28. In its January 18, 1930 issue, the *Oregon Voter* devoted ten pages to comparative streetcar costs.

29. Much of the information for this section of the chapter comes from ten boxes of "Portland General Electric Records Relating to the Reorganization of 1939-1948," taken from the Office Files of Tom W. Delzell (Eugene: University of Oregon, Special Collections Library), hereafter cited as PGE.

30. Ainsworth endorsed the merger in a letter to all newspapers, dated March 21, 1928.

31. "Portland Votes No," *The Nation* 126 (May 23, 1928) 587.

32. Although PEPCO operated under the authority of three franchises granted before 1900, their renewal was automatic. Only the payments and performance requirements could be revised by the city council. The voters had no say in the matter directly. In practice, the franchises were "perpetual."

33. *The Oregonian*, March 17, 1928.

34. *The Oregon Journal*, February 19, 1928.

35. *The Oregonian,* April 10, 1928.

36. The data for this chart come from the PGE Files and the records of the Oregon Public Utility Commissioner in the Claude R. Lester Papers (Eugene: Special Collections Library). For a detailed description of the investment trusts and Chase Harris Forbes, see *Fortune*, February 1934 and February 1938; also John C. Flynn, "Investment Trusts Gone Wrong," *The New Republic* (April 2, 1930) 181-184.

37. The details of this transaction are contained in the report of attorney Robert F. Maguire, to the U. S. District Court, August 9, 1939, PGE, *op. cit.*

38. These proceedings are thoroughly detailed by F. T. Griffith in a 28 page memorandum filed with the U. S. District Court in 1939, *ibid.*

39. As reported in *The Oregon Journal*, October 13, 1932.

40. *Ibid.*, May 18, 1932.

41. *Ibid.*

42. Burl A. Green, "Autobiographical Notes," (Eugene: University of Oregon, Special Collections Library).

43. Griffith, "Memorandum," *op. cit.*

44. Green, "Autobiographical Notes," *op. cit.*

45. Maguire, "Report," *op. cit.*

46. Thomas, *op. cit.*

47. As quoted in *The Oregonian*, March 17, 1928.

48. Oral Bullard, *Crisis on the Columbia* (Portland: Touchstone Press, 1968) 48.

49. Charles L. McNary to Henry Ford, letter of December 19, 1929, Portland Chamber of Commerce Papers, *op. cit.*, Box 23.

50. *Ibid.*

51. *Ibid.*

52. As reported in *The Oregon Journal*, November 22, 1931.

53. Douglas Scott and James Blomquist, "A Crossroads for Northwest Energy," *Sierra* (May 1978) 38.

54. 214,000 to 136,000 (61.7% of the registered voters voted).

55. A copy of the memorandum, undated, was given the author by General Martin's son, the late Samuel H. Martin. A copy may also be available in the Charles H. Martin Papers (Portland: Oregon Historical Society).

56. *Ibid.*

57. *Ibid.*

58. *Ibid.*

59. *Ibid.*

60. *Ibid.*

61. *Ibid.*

62. For a comprehensive study of the impact of Bonneville and the other Columbia River dams, see: *Region at the Crossroads — The Pacific Northwest Searches for New Sources of Electric Energy*, Report to the Congress of the United States by The Comptroller General, August 10, 1978.

63. Bullard, *op. cit.*; see also, "Bonneville Dam," a special section of *The Oregonian*, January 1, 1934.

64. As quoted by Richard Neuberger, "Portland, Oregon," *The Saturday Evening Post* (March 1, 1947) 25.

65. For a detailed analysis of Oregon party politics during the 1930s, see Robert Earl Burton, "A History of the Democratic Party in Oregon, 1900-1956," unpublished Ph.D. history dissertation (Eugene: University of Oregon, 1969) 139.

66. *The Oregon Journal*, October 15, 1933.

67. *The Oregonian*, August 5, 1934; also Neuberger, "Portland . . . ," *op. cit.*

68. Wayne Andrews, ed., *Concise Dictionary of American History* (New York: Scribners, 1962) 934.

69. Richard L. Neuberger, "Vendetta Against Aluminum," undated article from the Neuberger Papers, *op. cit.*

70. *Ibid.*

71. *The Oregon Journal*, January 10, 1935.

72. Report of George L. Rauch to the Portland Chamber of Commerce, October 18, 1935, Portland Chamber of Commerce Papers, *op. cit.*, Box 23.

73. The author discussed this matter with the commission's former director, Roy Bessey, on April 5, 1978. Long known by the author, Bessey at 88 has a clear memory of the events and issues of the 1930s.

74. See Charles McKinley, *Uncle Sam in the Pacific Northwest,* (Berkeley: University of California Press, 1952), chapt. 4.

75. Report of Ralph C. Clyde, September 21, 1935, Portland Chamber of Commerce Papers, *op. cit.,* Box 23.

76. Letter from Walter W. R. May, Manager of the Portland Chamber of Commerce to Mayor Joseph K. Carson, December 3, 1935, *ibid.*

77. *Region at the Crossroads, op. cit.,* 2, 5.

78. Letter of June 11, 1935, quoted by Robert Earl Burton, *Democrats of Oregon, A Pattern of Minority Politics, 1900-1956* (Eugene: University of Oregon, 1970) 83.

79. *The Oregonian,* August 19, 1937.

80. As quoted in Alan S. Larsen, *op. cit.,* p. 319.

81. See Robert C. Notson, "History supports attempts to change BPA power allocations," *The Oregonian,* June 21, 1978. The retired publisher of *The Oregonian* presents a specious argument.

82. Interview with Ivan Bloch, December 29, 1977. The author has known Bloch for many years and has discussed this and other matters with him on different occasions.

Chapter 15

1. Letter of J. C. Ainsworth to F. W. Sherman, February 14, 1933, J. C. Ainsworth Papers (Eugene: University of Oregon, Special Collections Library).

2. Quoted in *The Oregon Journal,* March 8, 1933.

3. *The Oregonian,* January 3, 1932.

4. Quoted from a copy of a sworn deposition filed with Multnomah County by the Unemployed Citizens League, Portland Chamber of Commerce Papers, Box 170 (Eugene: University of Oregon, Special Collections Library).

5. *Ibid.*

6. *Ibid.*

7. *Ibid.*

8. *Ibid.*

9. *Fortune,* June 1933, 104.

10. For coverage of the scrip bond issue, see the *Portland City Club Bulletin,* May 4, 1934.

11. Unemployed Citizens League, *op. cit.*

12. *Ibid.*

13. *The Oregon Journal* editorial, March 8, 1933.

14. C. H. Martin to R. B. Wilcox, letter of July 20, 1936, Portland Chamber of Commerce Papers, Economic Development file (Eugene: University of Oregon, Special Collections Library).

15. "Speech of B. A. Green before the Rotary Club," n.d., Burl A. Green, "Autobiographical Sketch," (Eugene: University of Oregon, Special Collections Library).

16. *Ibid.*

17. *News-Telegram,* October 28, 1932. The Port of Portland Archives contain an extensive file on the Port controversy during the years 1932 to 1934.

18. *The Oregonian,* February 17, 1933.

19. *The Oregon Journal,* February 20, 1933.

20. Hillman Lueddemann to the author, April 10, 1979.

21. Both the majority and minority reports are on file at the Port of Portland Archives, Port of Portland Commission Library.

22. *The Oregonian,* November 9, 1933.

23. *The Oregon Journal,* November 11, 1933.

24. *The Oregonian*, November 19, 1933.
25. Lueddemann, *op. cit.*
26. *The Oregonian*, November 21, 1933.
27. *Portland City Club Bulletin*, August 26, 1932.
28. As reported in *The Oregon Journal*, November 5, 1929.
29. *Ibid.*, September 9, 1935.
30. As expressed to the author personally by both Lueddemann and Shaver.
31. As quoted in William W. Pilcher, *The Portland Longshoremen* (New York: Holt, Rinehart and Winston, 1972) 42.
32. As quoted in *The Oregonian*, May 5, 1934.
33. W. D. B. Dodson, executive vice president of the Portland Chamber of Commerce, to the National Longshoremen's Board, letter of August 22, 1934, Portland Chamber of Commerce Papers, *op. cit.*
34. Radio address over KEX, July 5, 1934, Burl A. Green, *op. cit.*
35. As reported in a letter to chamber assistant manager Lynn Sabin from Alan Wilson, July 24, 1934, Portland Chamber of Commerce Papers, *op. cit.*
36. *The Oregonian*, May 8, 1934.
37. A. J. Farmer to L. P. Sabin, letter of May 11, 1934, Portland Chamber of Commerce Papers, *op. cit.*
38. A. J. Farmer to W. D. B. Dodson, May 14, 1934, *ibid.*
39. Pilcher, *op. cit.*, 44-46.
40. A. J. Farmer to L. P. Sabin, May 14, 1934, *op. cit.*
41. See R. B. Buchanan, "The History of the 1934 Waterfront Strike in Portland, Oregon" (Master's thesis, University of Oregon, 1964), ch. 4, "The Police and National Guard as Factors in the 1934 Strike," (Eugene: University of Oregon, Special Collections Library).
42. Walter W. R. May to W. D. B. Dodson, letter of May 29, 1934, Portland Chamber of Commerce Papers, *op. cit.*
43. Memorandum dated May 29, 1934, Portland Chamber of Commerce Papers, *op. cit.*
44. 326 U. S. 135.
45. As quoted in *The Oregonian*, January 18, 1978.
46. Pilcher, *op. cit.*, 42.
47. Green, Burl A. Green Papers, *op. cit.*, radio address, July 5, 1934.
48. *Ibid.*
49. Walter W. R. May to W. D. B. Dodson, letter of May 29, 1934, Portland Chamber of Commerce Papers, *op. cit.*
50. File copy of the Portland Chamber of Commerce resolution, dated June 17, 1934, *ibid.*
51. Green, B. A. Green Papers, *op. cit.*
52. The Portland Chamber of Commerce file has many items of correspondence as well as numerous memoranda detailing these points. None has been previously made public.
53. See *The Oregonian* and *The Oregon Journal* for July 4, 1934; also letter of Lynn P. Sabin to F. W. Mathias, September 5, 1934, Portland Chamber of Commerce Papers, *op. cit.*; also letter of Joseph R. Gerber to Walter R. May, July 5, 1934, Portland Chamber of Commerce Papers, *op. cit.*
54. *The Oregonian*, July 11, 1934.
55. According to Pilcher, *op. cit.*, 49.
56. B. A. Green, radio address over KEX, July 6, 1934.
57. Green, B. A. Green Papers, *op. cit.*
58. *The FOUR L Lumber News*, editorial, June 15, 1935.
59. Arthur J. Farmer to A. H. Lundin, letter of August 4, 1934, Portland Chamber of Commerce Papers, *op. cit.*
60. Sabin to Mathias, *ibid.*, September 5, 1934.
61. Minutes of the Citizens Emergency Committee, August 20, 1934, *ibid.*

62. Memorandum from Lynn P. Sabin to Arthur Farmer, August 21, 1934, *ibid.*

63. Memorandum of Lynn P. Sabin, dated December 21, 1934, Portland Chamber of Commerce Papers, "Communism Folder," *ibid.*

64. According to a chamber of commerce memorandum, dated January 3, 1935, *ibid.*, Box 19.

65. Harry L. Gross, "Vigilante Justice in Oregon," *The Nation* 139 (December 26, 1934) 742.

66. See *The Oregonian*, November 27, 28, 1934; also *Oregon Voter*, December 1, 1934.

67. The author discussed this case with Senior U. S. District Judge Gus J. Solomon whom he has long known. Judge Solomon related the problems the defense encountered from the Oregon Communist Party which did not trust the ACLU attorneys. The Communist Party leadership also questioned the ACLU strategy.

68. *DeJonge v. Oregon*, 299 U. S. at 364.

69. *DeJonge v. Oregon*, 299 U. S. at 365.

70. L. P. Sabin to A. J. Farmer, August 21, 1934, Portland Chamber of Commerce Papers, *op. cit.*

71. Letter of May 1, 1935, C. H. Martin Papers (Portland: Oregon Historical Society).

72. Richard L. Neuberger, *Our Promised Land* (New York: Macmillan, 1938) 315.

73. Green, B. A. Green Papers, *op. cit.*

74. Notice of meeting, Portland Chamber of Commerce Papers, Box 19, *op. cit.*

75. Green, *op. cit.*

76. Radio address by Governor Martin, May 17, 1938, Martin Papers, *op. cit.*

77. A copy of Odale's work was found in the Portland Chamber of Commerce Papers, Box 20, *op. cit.*

78. In 1938, the Oregon Chapter of the National Lawyer's Guild published a *Report of the Civil Liberties Committee* which detailed the activities of the Portland red squad from 1934-1937. Gus J. Solomon was both a member of the committee and a member of chapter's executive board.

Chapter 16

1. Data on highway expenditures, national as well as local, and unemployment figures, is to be found in *The Statistical History of the United States* (New York: Basic Books, 1976), Introduction and User's Guide by Ben J. Wattenberg.

2. Schlesinger, Arthur M., Jr., *The Coming of the New Deal* (Boston: Houghton Mifflin, 1959) 425.

3. *Ibid.*

4. "The Plan-It," December 1932, Portland City Planning Commission.

5. *Ibid.*

6. J. C. Ainsworth to E. C. Sammons, letter of October 13, 1926, J. C. Ainsworth Papers (Eugene: University of Oregon, Special Collections Library).

7. *The Oregon Journal*, June 26, 1927; also J. C. Ainsworth Papers, *op. cit.*

8. Letters and other information derived from the Portland Chamber of Commerce Papers, Box 37 (Eugene: University of Oregon, Special Collections Library); also J. C. Ainsworth Papers, *op. cit.*

9. Undated article from the *Oregon Voter* written in mid-1928 from J. C. Ainsworth Papers, *op. cit.*

10. Undated article from the *Spectator*, Oregon Historical Society vertical file on "Public Markets." The article appears to have been written in mid-1928.

11. W. D. B. Dodson to G. L. Baker, letter of February 14, 1931, Portland Chamber of

Commerce Papers, Box 37, *op. cit.*

12. Minutes of the Proceedings of the City Council (October 7, 1931) 728 (Portland: City Archives). The author is indebted for some of this information to Jerri Tess for her report on "The Public Market," Portland State University, History 410, Spring 1978.

13. An anonymous document, published by a planning commission staff member in 1933, exact date unknown, found in the J. C. Ainsworth Papers, *op. cit.*

14. Untitled and undated newspaper article from the "Public Market" vertical file, Oregon Historical Society. Malarkey spoke on the opening day, March 3, 1931.

15. Tess, *op. cit.*

16. Minutes of the Proceedings of the City Council (October 5, 1932) 814, *op. cit.*

17. Ormond Bean Papers, 1934 file (Portland: Oregon Historical Society).

18. *The Oregon Journal*, December 28, 1968.

19. Copies of the Bartholomew Plan are available at the Portland Public Library and the library of the Portland Planning Bureau.

20. From a partial transcript of the speech in the Portland Chamber of Commerce Papers, *op. cit.*, "City Planning" file.

21. As quoted in *The Oregonian*, January 20, 1932.

22. *Ibid.*

23. *Ibid.*, January 25, 1931.

24. For a general examination of the Bartholomew Report and other Portland planning efforts in the early 1930s, see Earl O. Mills, "Portland's Planning Perseverance Pays," *Western City* (May 1932) 13-16.

25. Speech of William A. Bowes, undated 1945, William A. Bowes Papers (Portland: Oregon Historical Society).

26. *The Oregon Journal*, March 15, 1933; see Portland Chamber of Commerce Papers, *op. cit.*, "City Planning" file for extensive correspondence between Laurgaard and various organizations, beginning in November 1931.

27. *The Oregonian*, March 16, 1933.

28. Ibid.

29. *Daily Journal of Commerce*, April 4, 1933.

30. Letter of Earl Riley to Harold Ickes, August 5, 1933, Portland Chamber of Commerce Papers, *op. cit.*, "City Planning" file.

31. J. C. Ainsworth to C. H. Martin, January 13, 1934, J. C. Ainsworth Papers, *op. cit.*

32. Martin to Ainsworth, January 18, 1934, *ibid.*

33. Ainsworth to Martin, January 23, 1934, *ibid.*

34. Letter of January 29, 1934, *ibid.*

35. Martin to Ainsworth, January 30, 1934, *ibid.*

36. *The Oregon Journal* editorial, August 16, 1935.

37. J. C. Ainsworth to the Portland Chamber of Commerce, letter of January 7, 1936, J. C. Ainsworth Papers, *op. cit.*

38. *Downtown Review*, April 7, 1933.

39. *Ibid.*

40. *Ibid.*

41. *The Oregonian*, January 18, 1931.

42. *The Oregonian*, December 3, 1935.

43. *The Oregon Journal*, December 17, 1935.

44. *The Oregonian*, August 22, 1935; also, Lloyd T. Keefe, "History of Zoning in Portland, 1918 to 1959," (prepared for the Portland Bureau of Planning, August 1975, Portland Bureau of Planning Library) 33-34.

45. See *The Portland City Club Bulletin*, May 3, 1940, for a detailed report on the "Front Avenue Bond Issue."

46. U. L. Upson to Marshall N. Dana, letter of August 21, 1940, Chester A. Moores Papers, in the possession of Mrs. Wayne Rogers, Portland.

47. For a brief history of Front Street and its pioneer days, see Henry E. Reed, *Cavalcade of Front Street* (Portland: 1941). The pamphlet is still in print.

48. Resumes of the construction costs can be found in the Bowes Papers, *op. cit.*

Chapter 17

1. Article by L. M. Lepper, Portland *Bulletin*, January 23, 1931.
2. *Ibid.*
3. "Master Plan For Portland," prepared by the Committee on Urban Land Utilization, Ellis Lawrence, chairman, September 6, 1935, Portland Chamber of Commerce Papers (Eugene: University of Oregon, Special Collections Library).
4. *Ibid.*
5. *Ibid.*
6. Letter of Jamieson Parker to Walter May, May 22, 1935, *ibid.*
7. Article by David C. Eccles, *Business Survey*, May 16, 1936.
8. "Planning News," June 1940, published by the Pacific Northwest Regional Planning Commission (Portland: Oregon Historical Society).
9. *Ibid.*
10. *Ibid.*
11. *Ibid.*
12. *Ibid.*
13. Portland *News* advertisement, February 26, 1924.
14. Eccles, *op. cit.*
15. *Ibid.*
16. *Fortune* (June 1932) 114.
17. Address by Earl Riley to the Portland Realty Board, April 29, 1938, Earl Riley Papers (Portland. Oregon Historical Society).
18. Chester A. Moores, Address to the National Association of Real Estate Boards, Los Angeles, October 27, 1939, Chester A. Moores Papers, in the possession of Mrs. Wayne Rogers, Portland.
19. *The Oregon Journal*, December 17, 1933.
20. William John Hawkins, III, *The Grand Era of Cast-Iron Architecture in Portland* (Portland: Binford & Mort, 1976) 44.
21. *Fortune* (June 1932) 114.
22. Ralph E. Clyde, memorandum to the council, June 17, 1938, Jesse Short File, Box 2 (Portland: Oregon Historical Society).
23. As paraphrased from the *Portland City Club Bulletin*, May 20, 1950.
24. Article by Ormond Bean, *The Oregon Journal*, October 23, 1938.
25. Report contained in the Short File, *op. cit.*
26. Undated report, mid-1930s, *ibid.*
27. *Oregon Voter*, October 8, 1938.
28. *The Oregon Journal*, February 3, 1939.
29. *Oregon Voter*, October 8, 1938.
30. William W. Pilcher, *The Portland Longshoremen* (New York: Holt, Rinehart and Winston, 1972) 68.
31. Kathryn Bogle, writing in *The Oregonian*, February 14, 1937. In later years, Mrs. Bogle's son, Richard, was to become one of Portland's leading TV newscasters on KATU, an ABC affiliate.
32. *Ibid.*
33. *Ibid.*
34. Juanita Johnson to Hamilton Corbett, letter of March 8, 1938, Portland Chamber of

Commerce Papers, "Minorities file," (Eugene: University of Oregon, Special Collections Library).

35. Arthur J. Farmer to Juanita Johnson, letter of March 10, 1938, *ibid.*

36. As reported in the *Oregon Voter*, March 18, 1939.

37. "Real Estate Appraisals, A Transcription of Lectures and Discussions Given at the Real Estate Classes of the General Education Division, Oregon State System of Higher Education, in Cooperation with the Portland Realty Board" (Portland, 1939) 144, Moores Papers, *op. cit.*

38. The author was privileged to know Dr. Unthank for some years, and to have worked with him on two Portland City Club research committees. He was indeed a strong, kindly man!

39. Unpublished autobiographical notes of Homer Shaver, a copy of which was given to the author during an interview on March 17, 1977, a year before Shaver's death.

40. J. C. Ainsworth to Aaron Frank, letter of August 15, 1934, J. C. Ainsworth Papers (Eugene: Universityof Oregon, Special Collections Library).

41. *Ibid.*

42. Charlton Food and Sanitary Laboratory, "Preliminary Report," October 5, 1934, Portland Chamber of Commerce Papers (Eugene: University of Oregon, Special Collections Library).

43. *The Oregonian*, September 22, 1937.

44. See Sanford Sternlicht, *McKinley's Bulldog, the Battleship Oregon* (Chicago: Nelson-Hall, 1977).

45. *Portland City Club Bulletin*, October 7, 1938.

46. *Ibid.*

47. *Portland City Club Bulletin*, October 23, 1937.

48. *Portland City Club Bulletin*, August 28, 1936.

49. C. P. Keyser, "A Scheme for Council Crest," December 15, 1937, J. C. Ainsworth Papers, *op. cit.*

50. Minutes of the Proceedings of the City Council, July 7, 1937, 112:499-501 (Portland: City Archives).

51. *The Oregon Journal*, July 15, 1938.

52. Carl Abbott, writing in *The Oregonian*, February 1, 1979.

53. Lewis Mumford, "Regional Planning in the Pacific Northwest: A Memorandum — General Impressions," January 3, 1939 (Amenia, N. Y.).

54. *Ibid.*

55. "Business-and-Government," *Fortune* (June 1938) 52.

56. Pietro Belluschi, memorandum dated September 30, 1943, published by the Portland Development Commission in "Portland Profile 3," n.d.

Chapter 18

1. *The Oregonian*, January 1, 1950.

2. "A Study of Industrial Land in the Portland Area," Portland Chamber of Commerce, November 1954, Portland Chamber of Commerce Papers (Eugene: University of Oregon, Special Collections Library).

3. Before Robbins was transferred to another station in April 1938, he was entertained at the Arlington Club by Griffith, McKee and Ainsworth, among others. After his retirement from the Corps, Robbins became a consultant to PGE along with two other retired officers of the Corps.

4. Oral Bullard, *Crisis on the Columbia* (Portland: Touchstone Press, 1968) 52.

5. *Ibid.*

6. W. D. B. Dodson to H. F. Corbett, letter of May 27, 1937, Portland Chamber of Commerce Papers, "Power File," *op. cit.*

7. *Ibid.*, letter of August 10, 1937.

8. John Gunther, *Inside U. S. A.* (New York: Harper and Row, 1947) 128.

9. Transcription of the Reed Institute of Northwest Affairs proceedings, July 11, 1939, filed in the Pacific Northwest Regional Planning Commission Papers (Portland: Oregon Historical Society).

10. Ivan Bloch to the author, letter of July 30, 1979.

11. Franklin T. Griffith, address of February 21, 1938, as printed in the *Oregon Magazine* 24 (February 28, 1938) 10.

12. Gunther, *op. cit.*, 129.

13. *Ibid.*, 128-129.

14. *Fortune* (May 1937) 89.

15. Bloch, letter of July 30, 1979, *op. cit.*

16. Gunther, *op. cit.*, 130.

17. Author's interviews with Ivan Bloch on several occasions since 1975.

18. Author's interview with Samuel Moment, August 1, 1979. A friend of many years, economist Moment was Chief of the Market Analysis Section of BPA from 1940-1948. Moment was to be responsible for drafting the U. S. government's policy for the Surplus Property Board to dispose of the government owned aluminum companies in the Pacific Northwest following World War II, a policy aimed at breaking up the ALCOA monopoly.

19. Nan Wood Honeyman to FDR, letter of March 19, 1939, Nan Wood Honeyman Letters, 1930-1952 (Eugene: University of Oregon, Special Collections Library). Nan Wood was married to David T. Honeyman of a prominent pioneer Portland family associated with the hardware business. She was in Congress from 1937 to 1939 and was U. S. Collector of Customs in Portland from 1942 to 1953.

20. Dodson memorandum to Frederick Greenwood of the Bank of California, December 20, 1939, "Power File," Portland Chamber of Commerce Papers, *op. cit.*

21. Bloch, letter of July 30, 1979, *op. cit.*

22. Information on the ALCOA project is contained in the "Industries File," Box 23, Portland Chamber of Commerce Papers, *op. cit.* See also, article by Herbert Lundy, *The Oregonian*, January 14, 1940.

23. As quoted in Lundy, *op. cit.* Other electro process industries involved the manufacturing of chlorine and caustic soda, and calcium and silicon carbide.

24. Moment interview, *op. cit.*

25. Bloch, letter of July 30, 1979, *op. cit.*

26. *The Oregon Journal* editorial, March 1, 1977. Although raising the question, the *Journal* supported the policies of the early 1940s.

27. Ivan Bloch to the author in various discussions, including June 30, 1979.

28. Date of news release, February 25, 1940, as contained in the Franklin T. Griffith Papers, Scrapbook 6 (Portland: Oregon Historical Society).

29. As reported in *The Oregon Journal*, January 24, 1940.

30. As quoted in the Franklin T. Griffith Scrapbook 6, *op. cit.*

31. *The Oregon Journal*, May 16, 1940.

32. Franklin T. Griffith Scrapbook 6, *op. cit.*

33. *Ibid.*, November 1940, date unspecified.

34. *Ibid.*

35. "Essay on Power" by Charles H. Heltzel, counsel for PP&L. Heltzel wrote the essay in 1960 for private consumption. He was the Oregon Public Utilities Commissioner from 1952-1957. The author was privileged to read the essay which is a traditional defense of the private power position during the years under review.

36. "Portland General Electric Records Relating to the Reorganization of 1939-1948," taken from the Office Files of Tom W. Delzell (Eugene: University of Oregon, Special

Collections Library), hereafter cited as PGE.

37. These points were later to be included in Franklin T. Griffith's testimony before a SEC hearing in Washington, in November 1939.

38. The author discussed many of these matters with the late Ralph H. King on July 22, 1977.

39. "Report of Estes Snedecor," relative to compensation and reimbursement of expenses, June 8, 1948, PGE, *op. cit.*

40. *Ibid.*

41. The Chase litigation extended over four years and involved 224 days in the taking of depositions, the examination of 80 witnesses, 14,362 pages of transcript, and 7714 exhibits.

42. Letter of Paul B. Wallace to Franklin T. Griffith, August 7, 1942, Franklin T. Griffith Papers, *op. cit.*

43. As reported in a speech by Franklin T. Griffith, March 11, 1943, contained in a PGE memo to stockholders, *ibid.*

44. F. T. Griffith speech, March 11, 1943, *ibid.*

45. As reported in *The Oregon Journal*, April 1, 1943.

46. O. R. Bean to Marshall Dana, letter of March 31, 1943, Ormond R. Bean Papers (Portland: Oregon Historical Society).

47. *The Oregon Journal*, April 1, 1943.

48. *The Oregonian* and *The Oregon Journal*, January 12, 1941.

49. Portland Chamber of Commerce Papers, Box 24, *op. cit.*

50. Walter W. R. May to F. T. Griffith, letter of November 30, 1940, *ibid.*

51. See article by Lawrence Barber, "Liberty Ships Fading Away," *The Oregonian*, January 15, 1978.

52. See article by Kerry Hoover, "The Heritage of the Hoyt Hotel," *Portland Today*, November 1977; also Doug Baker, "Memories of Hoyt's era," *The Oregon Journal*, May 26, 1977.

53. Richard L. Neuberger, "Portland, Oregon," *The Saturday Evening Post*, March 1, 1947.

54. Information contained in PGE 1st Mortgage 30-year bond prospectus (1945), Franklin T. Griffith Papers, *op. cit.*

55. See Michael McCusker, "Vanport: The Town Nobody Wanted," *Metropolis*, December 1973; also, Stanley Radhuber, "Vanport," *Portland Today*, April 1978.

56. Quoted by McCusker, *op. cit.*

57. W. A. Carpenter to C. A. Moores, letter of September 15, 1944, Chester A. Moores Papers, in the possession of Mrs. Wayne Rogers, Portland. This position was unanimously approved at a meeting of HAP, October 19, 1944; see "HAP Minutes," Chester A. Moores Papers.

58. K. G. Eckert to H. D. Freeman, letter of June 19, 1945, *ibid.*

59. As quoted in the *Portland City Club Bulletin*, July 20, 1945.

60. K. G. Eckert to H. D. Freeman, *op. cit.*

61. *Portland City Club Bulletin*, July 20, 1945.

62. *The Oregonian*, February 27, 1944.

63. *Ibid.*

64. *Ibid.*, October 4, 1942.

65. Story as told to the author by a friend of long standing, E. Shelton Hill, an Urban League staff member at the time and subsequently the executive director of the Portland League.

66. *The Oregon Journal*, August 25, 1967; *Portland Magazine*, September 1976.

67. As reported in the Forest Grove *News Times*, October 28, 1942, William A. Bowes Papers (Portland: Oregon Historical Society).

68. As told to the author by Mrs. Rogers MacVeagh, a long time friend who was a volunteer secretary in Riley's office in 1942.

69. Ivan Bloch to the author, conversation, December 29, 1977. The author has known Bloch for many years and has discussed this and other matters with him on different occasions.

70. A. D. McAvoy, "The History of City Planning in Portland," *Oregon Historical Quarterly*, 46:10.

71. Chester A. Moores Papers, in the possession of Mrs. Wayne Rogers, Portland.

72. C. A. Moores to Fred Meyer, February 12, 1942, Chester A. Moores Papers, *op. cit.*

73. Bowes' words, as contained in Bowes Papers, *op. cit.*

74. See Robert A. Caro, *The Power Broker, Robert Moses and the Fall of New York* (New York: Alfred Knopf, 1974).

75. Bowes, *op. cit.*

76. *Ibid.*

77. *Ibid.*

78. See *The Oregonian*, November 10, 1943; *The Oregon Journal*, November 11, 1943.

79. *Portland City Club Bulletin*, a special issue on "The Moses Plan" (January 28, 1944) 90.

80. Bowes, *op. cit.*

81. McVoy, *op. cit.*, 11.

82. Mel Scott, *American City Planning Since 1890* (Berkeley: University of California Press, 1969) 404.

83. Minutes of the PAPDC Streets Committee, March 16, 1944, Portland Chamber of Commerce Papers (Eugene: University of Oregon, Special Collections Library).

84. See Alan Webber, "The Influence of Robert Moses," *Old Portland Today*, February 1, 1975.

85. Report of Fred T. Fowler to Commissioner William A. Bowes, November 17, 1943, Bowes Papers, *op. cit.*

86. Bowes speech, January 28, 1946; also F. T. Fowler to Bowes, December 18, 1945, Bowes Papers, *op. cit.*

87. The Terry D. Schrunk and Bean Papers contain numerous references to such efforts, Oregon Historical Society. Also confirmed to the author in an interview with Oregon State Highway Commission Chairman, Glenn Jackson, March 26, 1975.

88. As reported in *The Oregon Journal*, July 14, 1946.

89. Portland City Planning Commission, "Pencil Points" (December 1944) 88.

90. Bowes, SB, *op. cit.*

91. *The Oregon Journal*, September 12, 1944.

92. *Ibid.*

93. *Ibid.*, September 15, 1944.

94. Letter of Executive Secretary J. T. Marr to Chester A. Moores, September 30, 1944, Chester A. Moores Papers, *op. cit.*

95. Earl Riley to Edgar Kaiser, wire of October 13, 1944, Chester A. Moores Papers, *op. cit.*

96. C. A. Moores to Frank M. Crutsinger, letter of October 20, 1944, Portland Chamber of Commerce Papers, *op. cit.*

97. C. A. Moores to W. D. B. Dodson, letter of December 19, 1944, *ibid.*

98. *The Oregonian*, November 20, 1944.

99. *Wall Street Journal*, April 16, 1945.

100. Frank L. Shull to C. A. Moores, letter of June 15, 1945, Portland Chamber of Commerce Papers, *op. cit.*

101. Portland City Planning Commission, "The Plan-It," February 9, 1945.

102. Letter of the Interracial Council of Vanport City to Chester A. Moores, June 13, 1945, Portland Chamber of Commerce Papers, *op. cit.*

103. Report of K. E. Eckert to Harry D. Freeman, Executive Director of HAP, June 19, 1945, *ibid.*

104. *Ibid.*

105. W. D. B. Dodson to F. E. Caslin, letter of June 23, 1945, *ibid.*

106. *The Oregon Journal*, August 21, 1945.

107. *Ibid.*, October 11, 1945.

108. *The Oregonian*, July 26, 27, 1947.

109. *Portland City Club Bulletin*, June 18, 1948.

110. McCusker, *op. cit.*

111. Quoted from the Oral History Collection of the Oregon Black History Project, by Elizabeth McLagan, director of the project and author of an unpublished manuscript detailing the history of blacks in Oregon, sponsored by the Oregon Black History Project.

112. A memorandum dated June 6, 1950, paraphrasing Mrs. Hoffman's letter was found in a HAP file in the City Hall Archives.

113. Although this statement was made in 1946, by C. W. Huntington, it was re-made in 1950 by several opponents.

114. *Portland City Club Bulletin*, May 20, 1950. The election was held on May 24, 1950.

115. See the "Annual Report of HAP," December 1950, HAP, *op. cit.*

116. As related to the author by Ralph H. King, *op. cit.*

117. This story was confirmed to the author by E. E. Vonderahe who was with Bowen when Bowen confronted Barde and Simmonds at Jake's Crawfish.

118. Bloch to the author, *op. cit.*

119. *The Oregonian*, April 11, 1948.

120. For an excellent account of the changes in urban transportation, see Mark Foster, "City Planners and Urban Transportation — The American Response, 1900-1940," *Journal of Urban History* 5 (May 1979) 365-396.

121. Ivan Bloch to the author, letter of April 7, 1977.

122. *Ibid.*

123. *Ibid.*

Chapter 19

1. Words used by Interior Secretary Harold Ickes at the time of his resignation in 1946.

2. As quoted in E. Kimbark MacColl, *The Shaping of a City, Business and Politics in Portland, Oregon 1885-1915* (Portland: The Georgian Press, 1976) 196.

3. *Portland City Club Bulletin*, February 20, 1948.

4. Working papers in the files of the City Club; see also Multnomah County Assessor's Office files.

5. Transcription of interview with Julius Zell, February 2, 1975, on file at the Oregon Jewish Oral History Archives.

6. *Portland City Club Bulletin*, February 20, 1948.

7. According to John Gunther, *Inside U. S. A.* (New York: Harper and Row, 1947) 91.

8. Joe Uris, "Vice in Portland," *Old Portland Today*, October 1975.

9. *Portland City Club Bulletin*, February 20, 1948.

10. Lamar L. Tooze to the City Club, letter of July 7, 1947.

11. *The Oregonian*, January 15, 1948.

12. *Ibid.*

13. Author's interview with Dorothy McCullough Lee, August 8, 1979.

14. In a conversation with the author.

15. *Oregon Voter*, October 27, 1927.

16. See articles in *The Oregon Journal*, October 6, 1948; *The Oregonian*, October 7, 1948. The facts of the case have been derived from many sources besides the press: Interview with attorney Ralph H. King; discussions with former members of the Art Museum board of directors and Henry Buehner; corporate files at the Oregon State Archives; Abbot L. Mills, Jr., Papers, *op. cit.*, Box 5.

17. Anonymous source.

18. Aubrey Watzek, selected papers, "The Roaring River Logging Company," (Portland: Oregon Historical Society).

19. From one of several discussions between the author and Mrs. Wheeler whom he has known for some years.

20. Minutes of the Portland Commission of Public Docks, 1944, 1945, Port of Portland Archives.

21. *The Oregon Journal*, October 5, 1961.

22. *Ibid.*

23. E. B. MacNaughton to John J. Winn, Jr., letter of August 12, 1948, John J. Winn Papers (Eugene: University of Oregon, Special Collections Library).

24. As quoted by Frank Dillow, "E. B. MacNaughton: Businessman with Soul," *The Oregonian*, April 4, 1971.

25. As quoted in *The Oregon Journal*, August 23, 1960.

26. As a young administrator-teacher at Reed College in the early 1950s, the author came to know the MacNaughtons, especially his second wife Cheryl MacNaughton who was the widow of Reed's second president, Richard F. Scholz. MacNaughton stories were legend all over the Reed campus.

27. Dillow, *op. cit.*

28. E. B. MacNaughton, Tapes, Reels 6 and 7, (Portland: Reed College Library Archives).

29. *Ibid.*

30. *Ibid.*

31. For a different slant on MacNaughton's *Oregonian* career, see Robert C. Notson, *Making the Day Begin, A Story of The Oregonian* (Portland: Oregonian Publishing Co., 1976) 42-45.

32. E. B. MacNaughton Tapes, *op. cit.*, Reel 7.

33. Notson, *op. cit.*, 42.

34. C. A. Moores to William A. Bowes, letter of April 17, 1946, William A. Bowes Papers, Box 2, (Portland: Oregon Historical Society).

35. E. B. MacNaughton Tapes, *op. cit.*, Reel 7.

36. *Ibid.*

37. *Ibid.*

38. According to Dick Fagan in *The Oregon Journal*, July 26, 1951.

39. E. B. MacNaughton Tapes, *op. cit.*, Reel 7.

40. Letter to John J. Winn, December 11, 1950, Winn Papers, *op. cit.*

41. Dillow, *op. cit.*

42. MacNaughton left an estate worth $600,000.

43. The most complete account of Fred Meyer, Inc., was published in three consecutive articles by the editors of *Willamette Week*, for the weeks ending March 28, April 4, April 11, 1977.

44. Drawn from figures published in March 1936, as contained in W. F. Woodward's scrapbooks, SB 206:33 (Portland: Oregon Historical Society).

45. Author's interview with Fred G. Meyer, February 22, 1978.

46. *The Oregonian*, January 10, 1951.

47. *The Oregonian*, December 8, 1945.

48. The facts of the case were compiled by Lloyd T. Keefe in his "History of Zoning in Portland, 1918-1959," prepared for the Portland Bureau of Planning in 1975.

49. *The Oregonian*, August 8, 1950.

50. Earl Chiles, "The Evolution of the Manager," *Top Management Handbook*, ed. by H. B. Maynard (New York: McGraw-Hill, 1960) 80-81. Fred G. Meyer also wrote a chapter for the handbook, entitled "Communicating."

51. Chester K. Sterrett to C. H. Spiering, letter of March 29, 1946, Portland Chamber of Commerce Papers, Boxes 6, 23 (Eugene: University of Oregon, Special Collections

Library).

52. *Ibid.*

53. Sterrett to McKee, July 18, 1946, *ibid.*

54. Sterrett to Spiering, March 29, 1946, *ibid.*

55. *Ibid.*

56. Glenn Stanton to W. A. Bowes, April 19, 1946, Bowes Papers, *op. cit.*

57. George Coppers to Sterrett, letter of April 24, 1947, Portland Chamber of Commerce Papers, *op. cit.*

58. Release of Sunday, May 4, 1947, *ibid.*

59. C. K. Sterrett to Fred Meyer, May 10, 1947, *ibid.*

60. *The Oregon Journal* editorial, May 31, 1947.

61. *The Oregonian,* May 21, 1947.

62. L. C. Binford to the author, one of several telephone conversations during the fall of 1977.

Conclusion

1. Interviews with Dorothy McCullough Lee, August 9, 10, 1979.

2. *The Oregon Journal,* January 21, 1947.

3. *The Oregonian,* January 24, 1947. For the account of this episode and its effect on Dorothy Lee's candidacy, the author is indebted to some biographical notes written in 1949 by Mrs. Lee's husband, the late W. Scott Lee, and made available to the author by Mrs. Lee.

4. According to his daughter, Mrs. James E. Bryson, a friend of the author's.

5. Lee, biographical notes, *op. cit.*

6. Joe Uris, "Vice in Portland," *Old Portland Today,* October 1975.

7. *Ibid.*

8. *Ibid.*

9. Lee, biographical notes, *op. cit.*

10. *Ibid.*

11. *Ibid.*

12. *Ibid.*

13. Dorothy Lee to the author, *op. cit.*

14. *The Oregonian,* February 11, 1948.

15. Brian J. L. Berry, Quentin Gillard, *The Changing Shape of Metropolitan America* (Cambridge: Ballinger Books, 1977) 109. See also, Berry, *Growth Centers of the American Urban System,* 2 vols. (Cambridge: Ballinger Books, 1973).

16. See *Residential Study For Portland,* April 1978, prepared for the Office of Planning and Development, City of Portland by the Center for Population Research and Census, Portland State University.

17. From the Strong & MacNaughton *Bulletin,* quoted in the *Oregon Voter,* November 15, 1924.

18. Boyd Gibbons, *Wye Island* (Baltimore: Johns Hopkins Press) 187.

19. According to 1950 census figures contained in a Portland City Club working paper, "A Study re effects of non-white purchases on market prices of residences in Portland, Oregon," n.d.

20. James W. Rouse, "The Highways and Urban Growth," Technical Bulletin 31, Urban Land Institute (Washington, D. C., 1957) 25.

Index

706

708

712

713

716